1,000,000 Books

are available to read at

Forgotten Books

www.ForgottenBooks.com

Read online
Download PDF
Purchase in print

ISBN 978-1-332-13910-1
PIBN 10289953

This book is a reproduction of an important historical work. Forgotten Books uses state-of-the-art technology to digitally reconstruct the work, preserving the original format whilst repairing imperfections present in the aged copy. In rare cases, an imperfection in the original, such as a blemish or missing page, may be replicated in our edition. We do, however, repair the vast majority of imperfections successfully; any imperfections that remain are intentionally left to preserve the state of such historical works.

Forgotten Books is a registered trademark of FB &c Ltd.
Copyright © 2018 FB &c Ltd.
FB &c Ltd, Dalton House, 60 Windsor Avenue, London, SW19 2RR.
Company number 08720141. Registered in England and Wales.

For support please visit www.forgottenbooks.com

1 MONTH OF FREE READING

at

www.ForgottenBooks.com

By purchasing this book you are eligible for one month membership to ForgottenBooks.com, giving you unlimited access to our entire collection of over 1,000,000 titles via our web site and mobile apps.

To claim your free month visit:
www.forgottenbooks.com/free289953

* Offer is valid for 45 days from date of purchase. Terms and conditions apply.

English
Français
Deutsche
Italiano
Español
Português

www.forgottenbooks.com

Mythology Photography **Fiction** Fishing Christianity **Art** Cooking Essays Buddhism Freemasonry Medicine **Biology** Music **Ancient Egypt** Evolution Carpentry Physics Dance Geology **Mathematics** Fitness Shakespeare **Folklore** Yoga Marketing **Confidence** Immortality Biographies Poetry **Psychology** Witchcraft Electronics Chemistry History **Law** Accounting **Philosophy** Anthropology Alchemy Drama Quantum Mechanics Atheism Sexual Health **Ancient History** **Entrepreneurship** Languages Sport Paleontology Needlework Islam **Metaphysics** Investment Archaeology Parenting Statistics Criminology **Motivational**

HISTORY

OF THE

JOHNSTONES

1191-1909

WITH DESCRIPTIONS OF BORDER LIFE

BY

C. L JOHNSTONE

AUTHOR OF "HISTORICAL FAMILIES OF DUMFRIESSHIRE"

W. & A. K. JOHNSTON LIMITED
EDINA WORKS, AND 2 SAINT ANDREW SQUARE, EDINBURGH
6 PATERNOSTER BUILDINGS, LONDON, E.C.

PREFACE.

THE eminent genealogist, Mr Fleming, Q.C., asserted in the House of Lords that no pedigree ever compiled was not capable of alteration or additions, and although many thousands of original documents in the Register House of Edinburgh, the Record Office in London, several private charter chests, the Hotel des Archives in Paris, and MSS. in the British Museum had been examined before this book was begun fresh information is constantly being produced. Many families have never troubled about their antecedents or kept any family letters or family Bibles; others have sent no reply to inquiries; and if nothing has brought any member of these families prominently before the public, it is a work of too much time and labour to find out anything but their names.

Twelve hundred registered documents were presented to the House of Lords concerning the Johnstone family by the claimants of the Annandale Peerages in 1876-81; but the main object of this book is to show that, besides the acknowledged heir through females — Mr Hope Johnstone of Annandale — the ancient Johnstoun chiefs are still represented in the male line.

By the insertion of family letters and domestic details in the seventeenth and eighteenth centuries it is hoped that a more agreeable impression of the civilisation of Scotland—at least in Dumfriesshire—may be suggested, than has been gathered from some of the descriptions which have appeared in modern times of the manners and customs of that period.

The different ways of spelling the name are of no consequence. In the sixteenth and seventeenth centuries phonetic spelling was in vogue. Brougham is spelt Brume; Tollemache, Talmash; Graham, Graeme; and Johnstone in thirteen different ways, but always with the *t*. Those families who left Dumfriesshire before 1715 generally spelt it without the *e*.

Several correspondents were under the impression that they descended directly from one of the Earls of Annandale, but the belief was founded on traditions handed down by their own near relatives; and since the Earldom was created sufficient proof is forthcoming to account for all the legitimate descendants in the male line of those later Johnstone chiefs.

Special thanks are due to Professor Christopher Johnston, of Baltimore, for copies of original documents; to J. Humphreys Johnston, Chevalier of the Legion of Honour, Venice, for the same; to Mr George Harvey Johnston for the use of his collection of charters, and for the addition of the Pedigrees and the copious index; to Colonel G. Hamilton Johnston of Kilmore for information about the Johnstons of Ireland; to Senator Joseph Forney Johnston for his MS. on the Johnstons of America; to Miss Frances Mary Johnstone for the use of her family pictures of the Johnstones of Alva, and to Mr C. C. Johnstone for photographing them; also to the Rev. John Anderson, Curator of the Historical and Antiquarian Department, Edinburgh.

C. L. J.

ANN FOORD'S HOUSE,
  WINDSOR.

November 1909.

LIST OF SUBSCRIBERS.

Aberdeen University Library.
E. G. Allen & Son, Ltd., 14 Grape Street, Shaftesbury Avenue, London, W.C. (2 copies).

Rev. Hubert Humphrey Middlemore Bartleet, M.A., Hallow Vicarage, Worcester.
A. Baxendine, Bookseller, Edinburgh.
Birmingham Corporation Libraries (Reference Department), per Cornish Bros., Ltd., Birmingham.
Colonel Hon. Robert Boyle, 95 Onslow Square, London, S.W.
Wm. Brown, Bookseller, Edinburgh (13 copies in all).

Richard Cameron, Bookseller, Edinburgh.
Miss L. M. Christie, Rayne, Braintree, Essex.

Right Hon. Lord Derwent, Hackness, Scalby.
Dumfries Book Club, Ewart Public Library, Dumfries, per Andrew Elliot, Edinburgh.
Ralph Dundas, C.S., per Richard Cameron, Edinburgh.

Right Hon. Lord Elphinstone, per Wm. Brown, Edinburgh.

W. & R. Holmes, 3 Dunlop St., Glasgow.
Rev. A. J. Hook, 16 Lambrook St., Glastonbury, Somerset.

Lieutenant-Colonel A. Bell Irving, per Wm. Brown, Edinburgh.
J. B. Irving, per Wm. Brown, Edinburgh.

Major Wm. Jardine, Craigdhu, Tamboers Kloof, Cape Town, per A. H. Lisett, London.
Alex. A. Johnston, South Lodge, Ealing Green, London, W.
A. V. Johnston, Halmstad, Sweden.
Alfred W. Johnston, F.S.A.Scot., 29 Ashburnham Mansions, Chelsea, London, S.W.
Alderman Charles Johnston, 17 Aldersgate St., London, E.C.

LIST OF SUBSCRIBERS

Christopher Johnston, John Hopkins University, Baltimore, Maryland, U.S.A.
David Johnston, 24 Huntly Gardens, Glasgow.
Colonel Sir Duncan A. Johnston, C.B., K.C.M.G., Branksome, Saffrons Road, Eastbourne.
Francis Alexander Johnston, 16 Draycott Place, London, S.W.
George Ben Johnston, M.D., 405 East Grace St., Richmond, Virginia, U.S.A.
Lieut.-Colonel George Hamilton Johnston, Kilmore, Richhill, Co. Armagh.
G. Harvey Johnston, 22 Garscube Terrace, Murrayfield, Edinburgh (2 copies).
Lieutenant-Colonel Horace James Johnston, Watch Hill House, Canonbie, Dumfriesshire.
James M. Johnston, 1628 Twenty-first Street, Washington City, D.C., U.S.A. (2 copies).
John Humphreys Johnston, Palazzo Contarini dal Zaffo, Venice.
J. R. Johnston, per Wm. Brown, Edinburgh.
John T. Johnston, Marchwood, Bathgate.
John W. Johnston, Priory Hill, Sunny Gardens, Hendon, N.W.
Joseph F. Johnston, Birmingham, Alabama, U.S.A.
Joseph G. Johnston, 2 Charleston Road, Rathmines, Dublin.
L. Campbell Johnston, Woodcote Grove, Coulsdon, Surrey.
Miss Mary H. Johnston, 1 rue Spontini (Ave. du Bois de Boulogne), Paris.
Max. von Johnston und Kroegeborn, Chamberlain of His Majesty the Emperor of Germany, Castle of Nieder-Rathen, County Glatz, Silesia, Germany.
Miles Johnston, High Lea, Bideford.
Mrs Johnston of Glynn, Co. Antrim.
Mrs Johnston, Northlands, Winchester (2 copies).
Mrs T. Johnston, 3 Kinnoull Place, Dowanhill, Glasgow, per J. Smith & Son, Ltd., Glasgow.
Mrs W. A. Johnston, Hazelwood, Wimbledon Hill.
Major R. A. Johnston, per Wm. Brown, Edinburgh.
Reginald E. Johnston, Terlings, Harlow, Essex.
Thomas J. Johnston, per Wm. Brown, Edinburgh.
Walter Johnston, Oakbank, Redhill, Surrey.
W. H. Johnston, 13 Kent Gardens, Ealing, W.
Sir Wm. Johnston, Buckhursthill.
Hon. Sir Alan Vanden-Bempde Johnstone, G.C.V.O., British Embassy, Copenhagen, Denmark (2 copies).
C. L. Johnstone, 5 Park Street, Windsor (11 copies).
Charles Hope Johnstone, 19 Bloomsbury Place, Brighton.
D. Johnstone, Bookseller, Edinburgh (2 copies).
Lieutenant-Colonel F. F. Johnstone, 47 Lansdowne Crescent, Leamington Spa, Warwickshire.
George J. St. P. Johnstone, 85 Park Mansions, Albert Gate, London, S.W.
Henry Johnstone, 25 Moorgate St., London, E.C.
Major Hope Johnstone, R.F.A., Selhurst, South Farnborough, Hants.

LIST OF SUBSCRIBERS

J. J. Johnstone, per Wm. Brown, Edinburgh.
James Johnstone, R.N., per Wm. Brown, Edinburgh.
Colonel M. Johnstone, D.S.O., per Wm. Brown, Edinburgh.
Miss Johnstone, 57 York St. Chambers, Bryanston Square, London, W.
Peter Johnstone, Harrison River, British Columbia, Canada.
Captain Somerset James Somerset Johnstone, R.N., 120 Westbourne Terrace, Hyde Park, London, W.
Thomas P. Johnstone, Shrewsbury.
T. W. Johnstone, La Retraite, South Road, Weston-super-Mare.
W. A. Johnstone, Deepdean, South Hampstead, per Hugh Rees, Ltd., London.
John Rylands Library, Manchester.
Jones & Evans, Ltd., Booksellers, 77 Queen St., London, E.C.
Mrs Helen Jones-Parry, Hill Cottage, Seaford, Sussex.

J. J. Keswick, Mabie, Dumfries, per J. Anderson & Son, Dumfries.
Wm. Thos. Knight, Canok Lodge, Walton Park, Clevedon, Somerset.

Library of Congress, Washington, D.C., U.S.A.
Miss Jemima Lixenden, Rosemount, Bralton, near Westbury, Wilts.

Miss M'Gilchrist Gilchrist, 4 Queen St., Edinburgh.
Macniven & Wallace, Booksellers, Edinburgh.

John Orr, Bookseller, Edinburgh.

Frank G. Penman, Invergarry, New Barnet, Herts.
Mrs Pitman, Cran Hill, Bath.
Major H. G. Purdon, Stramore, Gilford, Co. Down, Ireland.

Frederick Raimes, Hartburn Lodge, Stockton-on-Tees.
Royal Library, Berlin, per Asher & Co., London.
Royal University Library, Göttingen, per Asher & Co., London.

Wm. A. Shaw, 25 Duane St., New York City, U.S.A.
Signet Library, Edinburgh, per Wm. Brown, Edinburgh.
John Smith & Son, 19 Renfield St., Glasgow.
J. Wingrove Smith, 23A St. James St., London, S.W.
Mrs Stockdale, Baslow Hall, Derbyshire.

William Tait (Secretary, Proudfoot Institute), Church Place, Moffat.
J. Thin, Bookseller, Edinburgh.
Mrs H. M. Tyler, Dixton Cottage, Monmouth.

CONTENTS.

CHAPTER I.

                                                                                                             PAGE

THE EARLIEST JOHNSTOUNS—BRUCES—WALLACE—DOUGLAS . . . 1

CHAPTER II.

THE JOHNSTOUNS' SERVICES TO THE CROWN—JAMES IV. PRESIDES AT AN ASSIZE IN DUMFRIES 7

CHAPTER III.

THE JOHNSTOUNS OF ELPHINSTONE 12

CHAPTER IV.

THE JOHNSTOUNS OF WESTRAW—FRANCIS JOHNSTOUN—CASTLEHILL—TUNDERGARTH—HALLEATHS—COWHILL—AUSTRALIA—CLAUCHRIE AND DUCHRAE—AMERICA 18

CHAPTER V.

JOHNSTOUNS OF ELSIESHIELDS — KIRK — KIRKTON — WARRISTON — KELLOBANK—AUCHINSKEOCH—LAY ABBOTS OF SAULSIT—MILNBANK AND LOCKERBIE—BEIRHOLME—GUTTERBRAES—ANNAN 29

CHAPTER VI.

JOHNSTOUNS OF POLDEAN — SMALLGILLS — CRAIGABURN — MAXIMILIAN VON JOHNSTOUN UND KROEGEBORN—NEWTON, ETC.—EMIGRATION—JOHNSTONS OF HAZLEBANK 39

CHAPTER VII.

Various Johnstouns in the Fifteenth Century, and their Relationship to the Chief—Gretna or Graitney and Lochmabenstane—Early Marriages 45

CHAPTER VIII.

Maxwell Attacks the Crichtons—Johnstoun is Pledge for the Young Laird of Graitney and Others—War with England—Johnstoun's Settlement—The Battle of Solway Moss—Death of James V.—Capture of Annan and Conquest of Dumfriesshire—The Infant Queen—Peace—The Grahams 50

CHAPTER IX.

William, Laird of Graitney—The Barony of Newbie—Margaret Crichton—Wamfray—Queen Mary—Johnstoun—Civil War—The Queen—Death of John of Newbie—Johnstoun Wills—Feud between Maxwells and Johnstouns—Battle of Dryfe Sands—Third Baron of Newbie—The King Visits Newbie—Union of the Crowns—Clan System Repressed—Note on Scotland 66

CHAPTER X.

Younger Sons of Johnstoun after the Union—Clergy—Medicine—Merchants—Westraw—The Laird—Corrie—Wamfray—Newbie—In Edinburgh—Attack on Newbie Tower—The Estate Passes to the Laird of Johnstoun—His Murder—Barbara Johnstoun Tried for "Papistry"—Her Daughters—A Romantic Marriage—Robert of Raecleuch—The Earl of Wigton 93

CHAPTER XI.

John Murray—The Claimants to the Newbie Estate, and the Kindlie Tenants—Edward Johnstoun of Ryehill—The Sons of the House of Newbie—Death of Castlemilk and Marriage of his Widow to Ryehill—John of Mylnfield—Execution of Maxwell—Graitney Sold to Murray—Descendants of the Graitneys—Murray's Descendants—Ryehill's Letter to Primrose—The Grahams of Blaatwood—Ryehill's Death—Heriot's Executor 110

CHAPTER XII.

Johnstouns of Kirkton and Warrieston—Castlemilk and Pomfret . 127

CHAPTER XIII.

JOHNSTOUN OF GALABANK, "CALLIT OF MYLNFIELD"—THE FAREIS FAMILY—ACTIONS AGAINST GALABANK—YOUNG GALABANK—THE GRAHAMS—THE LAIRD OF JOHNSTOUN—JOHNSTOUN OF WARRIESTON—THE CIVIL WAR—CROMWELL—THE YOUNG EARL OF ANNANDALE—NEWBIE CASTLE BURNT . 133

CHAPTER XIV.

JOHNSTOUN OF GALABANK—WITCHES BURNT—CIVIL WAR—WESTRAW—ELSIESHIELDS—JOHNSTOUN—JANET KIRKPATRICK—FAMINE—EDWARD JOHNSTOUN—HIS MARRIAGE, DEATH, AND WILL—WESTRAW—LOCKERBIE AND HIS DESCENDANTS—CARLILES 145

CHAPTER XV.

GALABANK—LAWSUITS—MARRIAGE—CHILDREN—JAMES JOHNSTONE DIES IN LONDON—RISING OF 1715—POVERTY IN SCOTLAND—SECRETARY JOHNSTON—THE FIRST MARQUIS OF ANNANDALE—HIS BROTHER JOHN—HIS SECOND MARRIAGE—THE SECOND MARQUIS—JOHNSTONE OF WESTERHALL—COLONEL JOHN JOHNSTONE MARRIES THE MARCHIONESS 156

CHAPTER XVI.

YOUNG GALABANK—THE CHURCH OF SCOTLAND—THE THIRD MARQUIS OF ANNANDALE—HE PRESENTS TO MOFFAT—WILLIAM JOHNSTONE'S DEATH IN THE WEST INDIES—CARLILE OF ANTIGUA—SCOTTISH PHARMACY—THE RISING IN 1745—DUMFRIESSHIRE MEN WHO ASSISTED PRINCE CHARLES—THE CHEVALIER JOHNSTONE 167

CHAPTER XVII.

JOHNSTONES OF WESTERHALL—SIR WILLIAM—HIS SONS—SIR JAMES MEETS DR SAMUEL JOHNSON—SIR WILLIAM PULTENEY—GOVERNOR JOHNSTONE'S CAREER—JOHNSTONE OF ALVA—GIDEON JOHNSTONE AND MRS JORDAN—LADY OGILVIE—MISS JOHNSTONE 175

CHAPTER XVIII.

YOUNG GALABANK VISITS FRANCE—SETTLES IN WORCESTERSHIRE—LORD LYTTELTON—GALABANK'S WRITINGS—CORRESPONDENCE WITH HIS FAMILY—MANY DEATHS—THE MINISTER OF MOFFAT—LETTERS TO AND FROM THE WESTERHALLS—LORD JOHN JOHNSTONE—DEATH OF THE LAST MARQUIS—HIS AFFAIRS—GALABANK'S FAMILY 184

CHAPTER XIX.

JOHNSTONE OF GALABANK—WORCESTERSHIRE—YOUNG JAMES IN SCOTLAND—HIS LETTERS—EDINBURGH 213

CHAPTER XX.

JOHNSTONE'S BOOKS—DEATH OF LORD LYTTELTON—CORRESPONDENCE WITH MRS MONTAGU—THOMAS'S ILLNESS—JAMES'S LETTER—SETTLES IN WORCESTER—GALABANK'S LETTER AND DEATH—EDWARD'S ILLNESS—IN EDINBURGH—LETTERS FROM DRS CULLEN AND GREGORY—IN BIRMINGHAM—SAMUEL JOHNSON AND DR PRIESTLEY—VISIT TO THE LOCKHARTS—ASSEMBLIES AT SUTTON COLDFIELD—MRS MONTAGU'S LETTER—GORDON RIOTS—THE JAIL FEVER—DEATH OF YOUNG JAMES—HIS CHARACTER—HIS FATHER REMOVES TO WORCESTER—MEMBERS OF THE LITERARY SOCIETY—THE ASSIZE . 221

CHAPTER XXI.

VISIT OF GEORGE III. TO WORCESTER—THE KING'S ILLNESS—JOHN JOHNSTONE—DEATH OF THE SECOND LORD LYTTELTON—MRS MONTAGU'S LETTER—SIR WILLIAM PULTENEY AND THE ELECTION—GOVERNOR JOHNSTONE—HIS ILLNESS AND DEATH—THE ELECTION FOR DUMFRIES—WESTERHALL—DR PARR—MR ORTON—MISS PULTENEY—EDWARD JOHNSTONE—DR ASH . 234

CHAPTER XXII.

BIRMINGHAM—THE RIOTS—EDWARD JOHNSTONE—DR PARR'S LETTERS AND PAMPHLET—THE DISSENTERS—MRS WEBSTER OF PENNS—SUNDAY SCHOOLS—FAMINE—MARRIAGE—FORMER OWNERS OF FULFORD HALL—LOCKHART—GALABANK—DEATH OF MRS E. JOHNSTONE 246

CHAPTER XXIII.

THE AUFRERES—THE LOCKHART TRAGEDY—THOMAS JOHNSTONE—LETTERS—KING EDWARD'S SCHOOL, BIRMINGHAM—YOUNG JAMES—LITTLE HANNAH—JOHNSTONE OF WORCESTER—DEATH OF MRS JOHNSTONE, FOLLOWED BY THAT OF HER HUSBAND—MRS MURRAY 259

CONTENTS

CHAPTER XXIV.

Dr Carmichael Smyth, and John Johnstone's Defence of his Father—Wilberforce's Letter—John's Second Pamphlet—Sir W. Pulteney's Letter—House in Foregate Street—Belsham's Letter—Edward's Second Marriage—The Pearsons—Dr Withering—Visit to Portugal—Johnstones of Westerhall—John's Marriage—Edgbaston Hall—The Monument—Visitors—Edward Irving—Thomas Carlyle—The Children of Edgbaston Hall—Letters—The Adult School—The Rent Dinner—Eminent Artists 266

CHAPTER XXV.

Scarcity in 1816—Employment Found for Starving Workmen at Edgbaston—Dinner at Lord Hertford's—Colonel Henry Johnstone—Lockhart—The Peace of 1814—The Advocate-General of India—Death of Dr John and Dr Edward Johnstone—Their Heirs—Dr James Johnstone—Mrs Buckley (Westerhall)—General Sir James Johnstone—His Heirs and other Relatives 280

CHAPTER XXVI.

Johnstones of Westerhall—Alva—Derwent—Francis Johnston's Descendants 297

CHAPTER XXVII.

Johnstons of Elphinstone—Wishart and Knox—Younger Sons—Salton—Cousland—Johnstons of Newton—Edinburgh, etc. . . . 307

CHAPTER XXVIII.

Johnstons of Carnsalloch—Johnstones of Saughtrees—of Beatok—Roundstonefute, etc.—In Fife—Straiton—Wales—Prominent Members of the Clan—in Ayr—Ireland—America—New Zealand—Orkney . 318

CHAPTER XXIX.

The Johnstons of that Ilk and Caskieben—Arthur Johnston, the Poet—in Corstorphine—Perthshire 343

ARMORIAL BEARINGS 349

INDEX 355

PEDIGREES.

(In Pocket at End of Book).

THE JOHNSTOUNS OF THAT ILK AND ANNANDALE.
THE JOHNSTONS OF ELPHINSTONE.
THE JOHNSTONES OF WESTERHALL, ALVA, AND HACKNESS.
THE JOHNSTONES OF NEWBIE AND GRETNA.
THE JOHNSTONS OF ELSIESHIELDS, KELLOBANK, WARRISTON, SHEENS, HILTON, AND LOCKERBIE.
THE JOHNSTONS OF POLDEAN.
THE JOHNSTONS OF KILMORE.
JOHNSTON OF THAT ILK AND CASKIEBEN, ABERDEENSHIRE.

MAPS.

ANNANDALE (NORTH) . . . . *At End of Book*
ANNANDALE (SOUTH) . . . . ,, ,,

LIST OF ILLUSTRATIONS.

Frontispiece—WILLIAM, FIRST MARQUIS OF ANNANDALE
(*From Mezzotint by J. Smith, after Sir G. Kneller*)

Plate No.

I.	LOCHWOOD TOWER, DUMFRIES—LOCHHOUSE TOWER, DUMFRIES	*Facing page*	4
II.	LOCHMABEN STONE, DUMFRIES—LOCHMABEN CASTLE, DUMFRIES	,,	6
III.	STAPLETON TOWER, DUMFRIES—ELPHINSTONE TOWER, HADDINGTON	,,	14
IV.	THE TOWNE OF ANNAND, 1563-6—MAINS OF DUCHRAE	,,	26
V.	BEN JONSON, 1573 (?)-1637	,,	62
VI.	ELSIESHIELDS, DUMFRIES—NEWBIE CASTLE, ON THE SOLWAY, DUMFRIES—COTTAGE ON THE GALABANK, DUMFRIES	,,	84
VII.	ELIZABETH JOHNSTON OF BEVERLEY—W. H. JOHNSTON AS AN ETON BOY	,,	132
VIII.	ARCHIBALD JOHNSTON, LORD WARRISTON	,,	138
IX.	JOHN JOHNSTONE OF GALABANK, 1688-1774—JAMES JOHNSTONE OF GALABANK, 1690-1729	,,	158
X.	JOHN JOHNSTONE OF ALVA, 1734-95	,,	178
XI.	MARGARET JOHNSTONE, LADY OGILVIE	,,	182
XII.	JAMES JOHNSTONE OF WORCESTER, M.D., 1730-1802—HANNAH, WIFE OF JAMES JOHNSTONE OF WORCESTER	,,	192
XIII.	EDWARD JOHNSTONE, M.D., 1757-1851, AND HIS WIFE, ELIZABETH PEARSON	,,	270
XIV.	WESTERHALL, DUMFRIES—ALVA HOUSE, CLACKMANNAN	,,	296
XV.	JAMES RAYMOND JOHNSTONE OF ALVA—MARY CHOLMELEY, WIFE OF JAMES RAYMOND JOHNSTONE OF ALVA	,,	298
XVI.	THE SIXTEEN CHILDREN OF JAMES RAYMOND JOHNSTONE OF ALVA AND MARY ELIZABETH CHOLMELEY, HIS WIFE	,,	300

NOTES AND ERRATA.

Page 27, *line* 7. This name is written M'Cullock, then M'Guffog, and finally M'Guffock, when Hew of Rusco was chosen to represent the Barons of Kirkcudbright in the Scottish Parliament of 1700.

Page 29, *line* 23. The decision of the Ecclesiastical Court is not extant, but Gavin the younger could not have inherited if it had been unfavourable.

Page 42, *line* 6. Maximilian von Johnston und Kroegeborn wishes the statement that he is a Count to be contradicted.

Page 43, *line* 35. Symon was returned heir to his grandfather, Ninian.

Page 57, *line* 42. Buchanan says he was brother to the Laird of Roslin.

Page 63, *line* 37. In 1542 the Lord Treasurer's Account records a small payment to James Johnstoun of Cottis, "sent to England by his Grace to get advertisement of the Englishmen's purposes." Also to "the Laird of Graitney for a horse for his Grace, and for horses to move his Grace."

Page 69, *line* 13. The evidence submitted to the House of Lords in 1881 stated that John of Wamfray left no heir, but further research shows that John married Janet, daughter of Sir John Spens, she being endowed with the annual rent of a house in Dumfries. The couple left a son, John, who married Katherine Boyle, and died *s.p.*

Page 70, *line* 17. The date of Bombie's murder is given from an old "Scottish Peerage," but the remission to his eight assailants, granted Jan. 13, 1538-39, states that it occurred in 1527-28.

Page 132, *line* 6. Sir John Dillon was made a Baron of the Holy Roman Empire by the Emperor Joseph II. of Austria (eighteen years before he was made a Baronet), on account of his success as a member of the Irish House of Commons in obtaining permission for Roman Catholics to attend their own churches.

Page 139, *line* 32. A petition was presented to the Privy Council in 1661 from the wife, daughters, and remaining children of Archibald, late Lord Warrieston, praying that the execution may be suspended owing to his severe "illness, till he has recovered his memory and strength of mind." Lauderdale insisted on it being carried out at once.

Page 165, *line* 3. *For* "brother" *read* "nephew."

Page 182, *line* 16. Captain Gideon Johnstone died at Hawkbill, Edinburgh, May 12, 1788.

Page 316, *line* 29. Of the Johnstons of Eccles, Colonel George Johnston left four daughters, besides his son, George Arthur. Three brothers of the grandfather went to America —Patrick, Adam and William. An account of Dr George Johnston and his books is in the *Dict. Nat. Biog.*

Page 327, *line* 32. Buchanan says that when Buccleuch, Bothwell, Maxwell, and Mark Ker were released from Edinburgh Castle in 1530 "to gratify the King, one of the hostages, Walter Scott, killed Robert Johnston," a man of notorious violence, who seems to have been also a hostage. The Laird of Johnstoun is elsewhere mentioned as being put in ward with the above chiefs, and Robert may have replaced him; but they were probably nearly related, as the slaughter "bred a deadly feud between the Johnstouns and Scotts."

CHAPTER I.

THE EARLIEST JOHNESTOUNS—BRUCES—WALLACE—DOUGLAS.

SO late as the time of Sir Walter Scott, Dumfriesshire was still known as the Southern Highlands. Its Keltic inhabitants, aided by the Scoto-Irish immigrants were the most determined opponents of the Roman legions and of all who followed them, till they were subdued by the peaceful policy of David I.

This prince, the son of Malcolm III. and of Margaret, the sister of Edgar Atheling, accompanied his sister to England when she married Henry I. He was struck with the result of the superior education of the Normans, and the advantages of the feudal system in enabling the King to control a mixed community; and as the independent tribes of Dumfriesshire were a thorn in the side of England when she annexed Cumberland, peopled as it was by the same race, he followed the example of William Rufus, who had planted colonies free of taxes in Westmoreland and Cumberland, not only to defend the border but to repress the natives. David gave the lordship of Annandale to his old companion in arms, Robert de Brus, and encouraged settlers from Flanders to introduce a superior style of building. Sir Herbert Maxwell thinks it probable that the Houses of Douglas and Moray[1] were derived from a common Frisian or Flemish stock.

The Danes and Norsemen had already made settlements in Dumfriesshire, and probably found wives among the natives, who were undoubtedly mixed with the descendants of the Roman Legion formerly quartered in those parts.

The ancestors of de Brus, or Bruce, had an early connection with Orkney when they were Norwegian chiefs, and the family owned estates in Normandy and Yorkshire. In 1123 they were accompanied or preceded to Dumfriesshire by the seigneurs of Bailleul or Baliol (also from Yorkshire), Jardine and Comin, with others of the Anglo-Norman race.

Bruce and his son did not appreciate Annandale, because there was "no wheaten bread," and the elder lived chiefly in England, but the 500 followers of his descendant, and of Prince David of Scotland, who accompanied Richard I. to the Holy Land, included a large proportion of Dumfriesshire

[1] *House of Douglas.*

THE EARLIEST JOHNESTOUNS

men, "three-score Carvels (Carliles) from Cockpool," and a Corrie, Crichton, Kirkpatrick, Jardine, and Johnstoun, with retainers. These families still use the same shield as their chief, Bruce, with a saltire or St. Andrew's Cross to show their part in the Crusades, but with different augmentations.

David of Scotland had severe experiences. He was shipwrecked in Egypt, taken captive by the Turks, and bought by a Venetian, who carried him to Constantinople, then a Greek city. Here he was recognised and set at liberty by an English merchant. At last he arrived safely at Alectum, in Scotland, and gave it the name of Dei Donum, corrupted to Dundee, in gratitude for his return, but it is unlikely that the Scots who accompanied him were able to effect their escape.

Again a contingent from Annandale accompanied Robert Bruce, father of the king, to the Crusade, in which Edward I. and Louis IX. took part. Bruce was a more fortunate leader than Prince David. He even had the honour of lending £40 to Edward, so was probably able to bring his clansmen safely home.

The wars between two countries now happily united have little interest at the present day, except to show that if nations once so bitterly hostile could amalgamate, no hereditary enemies need be irreconcilable. It was the Border warriors who for centuries preserved Scotland's integrity, and bore the brunt of every invasion, and Camden, writing in the time of James VI., points out that among these the Johnstouns were the most noted. They owed their civilisation, superior in the Middle Ages to that prevailing in Galloway and the Northern Highlands, to the Norman blood pervading the chief families. The adaptable Normans intermarried with the natives of the districts where they received lands, and introduced law, order, and a rude justice.

A Scottish Border antiquary (d. 1851) was of opinion that the original Johnstoun,[1] like Bruce, Baliol, Gordon and Jardine, came from France with William I. He identified him with the Seigneur de Jeanville mentioned by the old chronicler, Guillaume de Tailleur, as assisting at the battle of Hastings, and the name appears again, half Saxonised into Janvil, on the roll of Battle Abbey.

Gulielmo de Joyneville signed a deed connected with a grant to the Carlile family in Dumfriesshire from William Bruce between 1191 and 1215, and Geoffrey, or Guibert, de Jeanville, for he is called both in different copies, an adherent of Baliol, came to France in 1299 with the English Commissioners, all nobles, knights or bishops, to sign a Treaty between Edward I. and the Scottish king, John, with Philip of France. The Scottish Commissioner, like his English colleagues, must have been a man of weight.

[1] The horrible incidents connected with the Wolf of Badenoch and that recorded in the *Legend of Montrose* in the sixteenth century show a different social standard to that of the Johnstoun chief who in 1598 wrote to the English Warden that he considered all his horses of less value than the life of one servant; or to the Laird of Newbie, who in his Will, 1576, directed his son to be good and friendly to the poor men of Annan, his tenants. The wills and documents with their own signatures of the Keltic families at that date are rare compared to those of men of Norman origin by marriage and descent. Lord Carlile in 1568 could not write his own name, and Johnstoun autographs are found throughout that century. The head of a Keltic clan in Dumfriesshire could not write in 1613.

THE EARLIEST JOHNESTOUNS

The Scottish form of the name appears first between 1194 and 1214, but at the earliest Court held by William Bruce as Lord of Annandale, about 1191, Dunegal, son of Udard, resigns to Bruce nearly one hundred acres of land in Wormanbie and fifty in Annan for the use of Gilbert, son of John. Among the vassals represented are Hoddam, Kirkpatrick, Jardine, Pennersax, Dinwoodie, Lockerbie, Herries, and Corrie, Kirkpatrick being only called Ivo. As Wormanbie was owned by Johnestoun in 1574, though feued by Carruthers, Gilbert, son of John, is apparently the same as Gilbert de Jonistun, who soon afterwards is a witness to a Charter from William Bruce to Ivo, now called Kirkpatrick. A little later Jonistun is one of seven cautioners that Bruce should fulfil a compact between Bruce and his mother, remarried to Patrick, Earl of Dunbar. He or his son is called Sir Gilbert de Jonestoune when he witnesses a grant of rights by Robert Bruce in the wood of Stapleton (near Graitney and Annan) before 1245. The same is witness to an agreement between Robert Bruce, the competitor, and one of his tenants at a court at Dryfesdale, in 1249, that Bruce and his heirs should for ever own the lands and advowson of Ecclefechan.

The next link seems to be Hugo de Johnestoune, as about 1285 his son, Sir John, confirmed a grant of lands in Haddington made by his father to the monastery of Soltray, or Salsit, and added the advowson of the church of Johnstoun as his own gift for the good of their souls. Salsit was particularly intended for the reception of pilgrims and strangers, and for many years the Abbot was always a Johnstoun. Sir John de Jonstone and his wife, Maria, daughter of Robert, Earl of Strathearn, also appear in the cartulary of the Abbey of Inchaffray, Perthshire, founded by her ancestor, Gilbert, in 1200.

Sir Johann de Jonestone, Chevalier del Comitat de Dumfries, his son, Gilbert, and Thomas, John, and Walter Jonestone signed in 1296 the Bond commonly known as the *Ragman's Roll*, which acknowledged Edward I. and his heirs for ever to be sovereigns of Scotland. Nearly all the gentlemen of Scotland did sign it, though each only on his own behalf, not on that of his family. It was forced from many of them (as was pleaded in a memorial to the Pope in 1320) "by the threats and horrid tortures" to which Edward I. had subjected all who opposed him. The attempt of Wallace to effect the emaneipation of Scotland from Edward I. occurred between 1296 and the flight of Bruce from England in 1305. In Dumfriesshire the Keltic population welcomed Wallace, for Edward's wars were wars of race.

In Blind Harry's *Life of Wallace* it is stated that when Wallace took the Castle of Lochmaben he sent for Johnestoun, "a man of good degree who had married the second daughter of Halliday, Wallace's dear nephew," and made him great Captain of Lochmaben. Halliday's elder daughter was married to Sir John the Graham (connected with Johnstoun, as his mother was daughter to an Earl of Strathearn), one of Wallace's warmest supporters. Another supporter was Kirkpatrick, related to Wallace's mother. She was a daughter of Sir Ronald Crawford, Sheriff of Ayr. While Johnstoun held Lochmaben, Kirkpatrick was sent with his men into Eskdale, where John Johnstoun,

THE EARLIEST JOHNESTOUNS

evidently the same man, had a tower and retainers. These, with Adam Corrie[1] and his men, reinforced Wallace on a subsequent occasion at Lochar Moss, when his own horses and followers were exhausted, "good Currie" providing the Chief with a fresh mount, so that they were able to chase Maxwell out of Carlaverock, put up there for the night, and the next morning ride on merrily to Dumfries.

It is a long step from the aristocracy of Europe—the progenitors of its kings—to plain John, a Keltic peasant without a surname, whom a modern author prefers to have been the founder of the family. Yet the first mention of the Tower of Johnstoun in a Charter is to be found in the Laird James's retour to his father's lands, which included Cavertholme and Dunskellie, near Graitney, in 1513. This was more than 230 years after Johnstouns had signed their names to Charters granted by the Bruces, and more than 200 years after the Chief in Eskdale had assisted Wallace. Sir W. Fraser thinks that the first Johnstoun "must have been a person of considerable importance" (1170-94). If so, he probably had a surname when he "obtained lands in the heart of Bruce's great lordship," for all but peasants had surnames. Even the Norman foot soldier was called after the town whence he came.

Anyway, at a time that the Norman nobility were more civilised than the natives, and when French and Latin was the speech of educated men, the Johnstouns held their own, and from the term "gentle" applied to them later on were accredited with long descent. Yet they owned very little in Annandale, and that little was scattered, compared to Carlile, Corrie, Carruthers, Charteris, and Crichton before the middle of the fifteenth century, and the name of Johnstoun on the old rent rolls and title-deeds is less common about Lochwood and the parish of Johnstone than farther south. Lands called Joinville are early found in Eskdale and Annandale.

The author of the *Bruces and Cummings* says that the Johnstouns intermarried with the Bruces, and in that way obtained lands in Annandale, but it is a question if they did not precede the first Bruce.

Gilbert, the son of Thomas de Jonestoune (probably the Thomas who signed the *Ragman's Roll*), had a grant of Redmyre and Whitriggs in Kincardine from David II., lands which later belonged to Irving of Drum. In 1334 a Charter of lands in Annandale from Edward Baliol, Rex, to Henry Percy is signed by Gilbert de Johnstoune of Brakenthwaite, an estate owned later by the Carliles, who at this very time possessed Lochwood, or Loughwood, the chief Johnstoun stronghold in the sixteenth century. A grant from Thomas Randolph, Earl of Moray (d. 1322), of Ruthwell and Comlongan to his nephew, William Murray, is signed by John de Johnestoune and his son, Gilbert, and in 1347 Gilbert de Johnestoune is cited by the English king, who owned Annandale while David II. was a prisoner in England, to preside over the jury which declared Carlile to be his uncle's heir.

John, the son of Gilbert, was Warden of the Borders, and knighted by

---

[1] The Corries held the Barony of Corrie, which included Newbie at that time. The Hallidays owned Hoddam and other estates in Dumfriesshire under the Bruces.

PLATE I.

LOCHWOOD TOWER, DUMFRIES.

LOCHHOUSE TOWER, DUMFRIES.

THE EARLIEST JOHNESTOUNS

King David Bruce. He is the Chief described by Andrew Wyntoun, the Prior of Lochleven,[1] in his *Original Chronicle*, circa 1405, which records the fame of Bruce and of the Scottish leaders, his contemporaries, for in 1370 this knight defeated the English army which invaded Scotland towards the end of the reign of Edward III.

Sir John de Johnestoun's son, John, is mentioned in a letter from Robert II. (1385), where the King thanks Charles VI. of France for the succour he has given him against the English, and for 40,000 livres which Charles sent to be divided among his faithful allies, the Scottish nobles. Johnestoun received 300 of them. He also fought under Douglas at Chevy Chase. He was one of the "scutiferi," or constables, appointed to keep order on the Borders, and in 1384 obtained a safe conduct to England.

In 1413 a safe conduct to England was given to Adam, Lord of Johnstoun, sent by the Earl of Douglas, superior of Annandale and Galloway, as one of the securities for a debt owed to Sir John Philip by the Princess Margaret Steuart, wife of Douglas. He was back in 1419, as he then witnessed a Charter at Lochmaben, and was a witness at Pennersax in 1432 and 1441. He was a conservator of the peace on the Scottish border (1449-53).

In 1421 James, William, John, and Walter Johnstoun were released with other Scottish prisoners of war from the Tower of London, and allowed to return to Scotland to bring their ransoms. After depositing the money they would be free to go home.

In 1464 a safe conduct was given to Adam of Johnstoun, Robert and John Johnstoun, Gilbert de Johnstoun, and Matthew de Johnstoun for a whole year in England, with ten Scotsmen in their company, also for two of them to trade at English ports with three boats of 15 tons burden, manned by competent masters and mariners. This seems to be the earliest effort in Dumfriesshire to create a mercantile marine, but it was soon stopped by the Albany rebellion. In 1485 Gilbert de Johnstoun and many other Borderers applied for a safe conduct to England.

Thomas de Johnestoun signs a Charter for the first Earl of Erroll, Constable of Scotland (1452-63).

In 1459 Andrew Ker of Cessford, John Johnstoun of that Ilk, who succeeded his father Adam, Charles Murray of Cockpool, William Carlile of Torthorald, among others, are bracketed as "scutiferi" or constables. Again

---

[1] "When att the wattyr of Solway
Schyr Jhon of Jhonystown on a day
Of Inglismen wencust a grete dele
He bore him at that time sa wele
That he and the Lord of Gordoune
Had a sowerane gude renowne
Of any that was of that degree
For full they war of grete bownte."

Buchanan wrote in 1572 of the same period, when the English were driven out of Annandale : "In the Western Borders John Johnstoun so managed it that he got both honour and booty; for he so exercised his neighbouring foes, with small, but frequent incursions, that he did them as much mischief as a great army could have done."

their names appear as "naval admirals" in the list of Border chiefs charged with the care of the Marches, James II. having made some effort to establish a navy.

One of the duties of the sheriffs and constables was to see that beacon fires were maintained along the frontier. At a conference with the freeholders, held by Douglas in 1448, ten places were appointed for that purpose—Gallowhill, Kinnelknock, Blois, Brownmuirhill, Barr (near Hoddam), Dryfesdale, Quhitwoollen, Cowdens, Trailtrow, and Lochmabenstane in Gretna. It was a necessary precaution, as Dumfries had been burnt twice in an English raid in thirty-three years.

Note.—Mr G. H. Johnston's book, *Heraldry of the Johnstons*, describes the crest and arms of the various branches of his family. The records of the Tower of London show that Johnstouns were imprisoned there, and tradition says that one of them warned Bruce to escape secretly to Scotland by sending a spur with a grouse wing attached. It was adopted as the family crest.

CHAPTER II.

The Johnestouns' Services to the Crown—James IV. Presides at an Assize in Dumfries.

THE annexation of Dumfriesshire by Edward I. proved that the south was Scotland's most vulnerable point. It was essential for her independence to have strong men of tried loyalty on the Borders, chiefs whose relatives and dependers formed an unpaid standing army "always ready," the Johnstone motto, to defend it.

Robert I. gave the lordship of Annandale and Galloway to his friend James Douglas, whose heir, also Lord of Nithsdale, was too powerful for the safety of the Sovereign, and excited the jealousy of other Border chiefs. He compelled the weak Robert III. to break his word to the Earl of March, late Warden of the Borders, who in revenge joined with England to annex Dumfriesshire in 1400.

Again the county was agitated throughout the Duke of Albany's Regency, after which Douglas increased in power, till his sudden death gave his rival, the Chancellor, Sir William Crichton, an opportunity of crushing it. He invited the young Earl and his brother, David, boys of fourteen and fifteen, to meet King James II. at Edinburgh. They came with a grand retinue and had supper with the Royal youth, when they were suddenly seized and executed in the courtyard. The previous year (1439) Norman de Johnestoun gave up Comlongan Castle to Douglas. It had been granted to Norman by James I. in 1430, being part of the escheated property of the Earl of March.

A grand-uncle succeeded young Douglas, so no immediate revenge was taken, and his son at eighteen was made Commander of the King's army, the Douglases were exalted to keep the Crichtons in their place. But James II. in a fit of passion stabbed his General after supper in the palace at Stirling (1452), and this brought on the great Douglas rebellion, which stirred up not only the south-west, but all Scotland, before it was suppressed. The rebel chief gave Comlongan Castle to Symon Carruthers of Mouswald, to attach a strong man to his cause.

A civil war on the Borders always brought an English army to assist the rebels, though Douglas pointed out how little advantage could be gained by a march into Scotland. "The houses of the gentlemen are small towers with thick walls which even fire will not destroy. As for the common people, they dwell in mere huts, and, if the English choose to burn them, a few trees from the wood is all that is required to rebuild them."

The murder of Douglas was the more impolitic as his brother had commanded the army which defeated 6000 Englishmen under Earl Percy and Sir John Pennyton in Oct. 1448. His colleagues were "Sir John Wallace, the Lord of Johnstoun, Lord Somerville's son, Steuart of Castlemilk, the Sheriff of Ayr, with other sundry gentles of the Westland. Their men were called 4000." So far the chronicler of Auchinleck; but Holinshed also mentions Maxwell. The battle was fought at Lochmabenstane, in Graitney, but Murray, who claimed both Comlongan and Graitney, is not mentioned. It was obvious that so important a post as Graitney could not be left unguarded or in doubtful hands, and five years afterwards Gilbert de Johnstoun de Gretno signs his name to a Maxwell retour at Dumfries, showing that one of Sir Adam de Johnstoun's relatives was in Graitney Tower. The Johnstouns had opposed the Welsh (or Galloway) men, the fiercest detachment of the enemy—a special service to the county where Galloway men were notorious for their barbarity.

The next time that the English with Douglas's followers entered Scotland they avoided Graitney and came by Langholm, where they were defeated by the Maxwells, Johnstouns, Scotts, and Carliles in 1455.

According to the Auchinleck chronicler the Lord of Johnstoun's two sons took the royal Castle of Lochmaben from the two sons of Carruthers of Mouswald, and they kept it for the King; and as Mouswald's Tower at Lochwood and one of Douglas's forts at Lochous came to Johnstoun at this time, it was probably in acknowledgment of these services. But the chief part of the Douglas and March estate was given by the King to his second son, Alexander, Duke of Albany, a child of three, who was made Lord of Annandale and Galloway. Before he was seven his father was killed by the bursting of a gun, and twenty-four years later he recalled Douglas from his long exile in England to assist him in driving his brother, James III., from the throne. Henry VII. sent an army to assist the wild crew which Albany had recruited in Galloway, but they were defeated at Lochmaben and on the Kirtle by Maxwell, Johnstoun, Murray of Cockpool, Crichton of Sanquhar, Carruthers of Holmains, and Charteris of Amisfield in 1484, and Albany's lands appropriated to the Crown and redistributed among the loyal chiefs.

The Crown had no power on the Borders except through the chiefs, and the recipients had to secure the confiscated lands as they best could, opposed by the armed dependents of the late owners, and as often by neighbours, who thought they had a prior claim. There were no maps, and the kings of Scotland were certainly not acquainted with the details of the estates they gave away. The Carliles had a grant "from Wamfray to Greistna grene inclusive," from William the Lion; and the Murray grant of 1320, of Comlongan, Ruvell, and Rampatrick (Gretna, Dornock, etc.), overlapped the Carlile boundaries. The Corries succeeded the Carliles, and the Barony of Corrie, confiscated for

LOCHMABEN STONE, DUMFRIES.

LOCHMABEN CASTLE, DUMFRIES.

THE JOHNESTOUNS' SERVICES TO THE CROWN

George Corrie's share in the rebellion of 1483, was given to Thomas Carruthers of Holmains, a loyalist, though his kinsman had joined Douglas.

The Corrie Barony included Newbie, and subsequent events point to this portion having been conferred on Johnstoun, who would otherwise have had nothing for his services in 1483. It was essential to him to possess it, for he was the pledge (*i.e.*, bound in a sum of money) that George Corrie should not return to his estates, while Corrie, being connected with Lord Herries of Hoddam and Cuthbert Murray of Cockpool, near neighbours to Newbie, had their support. Murray got a Charter for himself of the Barony of Corrie from Lord Maxwell, the Warden, Feb. 8, 1492. Two years later John Murray, as a descendant of the first grantee, was returned his father's heir in Cockpool, Ruthwell, and Rampatrick including Graitney, although for forty years or more Johnstoun had controlled Graitney, and a footing on the Solway was absolutely necessary for his duty as a constable of the Border. If the Murrays reclaimed Graitney, the owner of Newbie could block Johnstoun's only other passage to the Solway by the Annan. Probably his small ships assisted in war, hence the naval rank conferred upon him.

John of Johnstoun joined the expedition which the King led in person against Thrieve Castle, Douglas's stronghold in Galloway. On Nov. 20, 1469, "Domino de Johnston" was one of the nobles present in the Parliament at Edinburgh.

Johnstoun was assignee to the late Cockpool in spite of their differences —there had been a Murray and Johnstoun marriage—but in 1503 James, Master of Johnstone, was surety for his father, Adam, and his father was surety for him, that Murray should be safe from attacks either from themselves or their followers. That this arrangement included the cession of Graitney to Johnstoun and no further resistance to his claim on Corrie and Newbie[1] in exchange for Comlongan seems probable, as in 1511 Adam Johnstoun *de Newbie* was a baron of assize, and William Johnstoun in 1513 is called the young laird of Graitney.

In 1516, after long delay, James of Johnstoun (great-grandson of the "Admiral") received a Crown Charter of the Barony of Corrie, and his second son, Adam, married the heiress.[2] The same year Herbert Corrie sold his shadowy claim on Newbie to his cousin, Thomas Corrie of Kelwood, and a Crown Charter emphasised it.

Lords Maxwell and Crichton had greatly increased their property in the scramble of the fifteenth century, when Maxwell, Cuthbert Murray, and Johnstoun were by turns Warden of the Borders. On Oct. 26, 1476, Johnstoun was commissioned by James III. to adjust a Crichton dispute, which ended in his purchase of Wamfray.

The Chief of Johnstoun (Adam), who fought at Lochmabenstane in 1448,

---

[1] Robert Corrie of Corrie paid the taxes for Newbie, and therefore owned it in 1464. Murray's attacks on Newbie cost him 160 golden angels to Corrie, 1483, and in 1492, £1000. See *Reg. Decreets*.

[2] See Corrie's *Records of the Corrie Family:* London, 1899.

was married to Janet (widow of William, Lord Seton), a daughter of the rebel Earl, George, of March and Dunbar, and his eldest son's wife was the daughter of Lord Maxwell. As the next brother was named Gilbert, but had not yet married Agnes of Elphinstone, he is possibly the Gilbert de Johnestoun de Gretna who signed the retour of the young Lord Maxwell in 1453. He was knighted for his services against the English, and was a guarantor of the peace signed with England in 1483. When Sheriff of Edinburgh the next year, he deputed his nephew, Adam of Johnstoun, to summon Sir James Liddel to surrender on a charge of "ganging awa' into England with the Duke of Albany." His elder brother, John, was the Chief who, like himself, fought at Arkinholme in 1483. The citation is witnessed by Robert of Johnstoun and William Johnstoun, besides John of Carruthers, Sir John of Murray (the chaplain), and others.

Sir Gilbert of Elphinstone was Sheriff-Depute of Dumfries in 1472, when he received a gift of the lands of Drumgrey (Rahills, etc.) from the Crown. They were granted "for faithful service" in 1408 to his relative, William of Johnstoun,[1] but were now claimed by Robert Charteris of Amisfield (ancestor to Earl Wemyss). Charteris was ordered to show his writs of the time of Robert III. and James I., for which the Clerk of Registers in Edinburgh was also to search, and Sir Gilbert was summoned to appear there on his own behalf. Gilbert was sued in 1491 for non-payment for "certain merchandize from Ellen Halyburton, as was proved by the said Ellen's compt book." She gained her case, but agreed to delay the execution of letters of distress till Whit Sunday,—a judgment very creditable for that time. The debt was not paid till after Gilbert's death, when his son, Adam, was sued for it.

The rebellion of 1484 was hardly crushed when the new one broke out in Dumfriesshire under Archibald Douglas, Earl of Angus, in which James III. lost his life (1488). Maxwell was nominally on the side of the King, but contrived to gain the favour of his opponents, and was appointed with the rebel Angus to rule Dumfriesshire during the minority of the young James IV.

Adam of Johnstoun, nephew to Sir Gilbert, was on the side of the King. He was cousin to Maxwell, and married to Marion Scott of Buccleuch. A precept of sasine from the Earl of Bothwell in 1493 to our lovit Adam of Johnstoun of that Ilk and others charges them to infeft Walter Scott of Buccleuch in the lands of Roberthill, one of the earliest possessions of this family in Annandale.

In 1504 James IV. held an assize at Dumfries, when Adam of Johnstoun and his son, James, were pledges for each other, and both for several of the Murrays. James Johnstoun was returned heir to his father in 1513 in the Barony of Johnstoun, the advowson of its church, the mill and lands of Dunskellie or Cove, Cavertholme, and Brotis, within the parish of St. Patrick (Kirkpatrick Fleming, and Graitney) and Wamfray, all "sequestered at the King's instance for certain fines of Justice Courts, which now his Majesty freely discharges and dispones the land to him again."

This meant that no rents had been received by the Laird or his family for some years, and was perhaps connected with Adam of Johnstoun's attack on

[1] In William's Charter they are described as in the Barony of Amisfield.

THE JOHNESTOUNS' SERVICES TO THE CROWN

Glendining, in Eskdale, a fief claimed by the Armstrongs, a Keltic family, who were unruly as early as 1261, and allied to the Maxwells. Gavin Johnstoun of Elsieschellis assisted his Chief and the Laird of Dunwiddie. The case was tried before James IV. at Dumfries, when Kirkpatrick was pledged for Dunwiddie and Johnstoun himself for Gavin that they should pay compensation to Glendining, who was Sheriff of Eskdale.

It often happened when there was a specially active laird of Johnstoun that one of his rivals obtained the support of the Crown to put him into ward, and the family were increasing their estates considerably just then. Yet the possession of Newbie and Graitney enabled his clan to become the bulwark of Scotland on the south-west.

CHAPTER III.

THE JOHNSTOUNS OF ELPHINSTONE.

THE descendants of Sir Gilbert de Johnestoun and Agnes of Elphinstone took little part in the affairs of Dumfriesshire after 1587. In the comparative calm of East Lothian they prospered, and filled posts in the Government, and seem to have been able to give assistance to their Chief when the clan was hard pressed by foreign invasion and civil war.

Sir Gilbert died about 1501, and his son, Adam, in 1507. This Adam, described as son and heir of Sir Gilbert Johnestoun, brought an action before the Lords Auditors in 1484 against John, Laird of Johnestoun, apparently a result of the Laird's purchase of Broomehills in 1480. Gilbert, Adam's son, appears in 1507-8. John of Johnestoun was one of the conservators of the peace with England in 1457, a Warden of the Marches, and always acted, writes Douglas, "with vigour and intrepidity against the enemies of his country."

Sir Adam of Elphinstone (he was knighted) had a brother, George, who was possibly identical with George of Johnstoun, mentioned in 1463 with regard to South Dumfriesshire. Andrew Johnstoun in Stapleton (Tower) appears a little later, and his son, George, in 1504. Stapleton, where David I. signed the grant of Annandale to Bruce, is described as one of the strongest and most roomy towers on the Border, and, like Graitney Tower, required armed men to defend it. These posts were filled by the relatives of the landowners, and in times of peace, as well as in war, the garrisons so close to the English border more than once joined their lawless neighbours in the Debateable Land in a foray over the Solway to revenge old injuries, but it was returned with double interest. Stapleton was afterwards incorporated in the Barony of Newbie; but in earlier times, like Graitney, it was under the control of the Earls of March when Keepers of the Borders.

Sir Adam Johnstoun of Elphinstone was succeeded by his son, Gilbert, who was killed at Flodden in 1513. The next year Andrew Johnstoun was returned heir to Leuchie, part of the Elphinstone property; and in 1533 there is an action by "Dame Amabel (also called Agnes) Hog, relict of the late Sir Adam, against Andrew of Elphinstone, Superior of the lands of Nethermagask, concerning her liferent of the same." The case went on for some years. A daughter of Andrew of Elphinstone married Sir William Cranstoun, according to a writ in favour of this couple and their son, 30th May 1533.

The Johnstoun descent qualified a future Cranstoun for the Provostship of Annan in 1607, as it was essentially a Johnstoun preserve. Another daughter married Crichton of Drylaw.

In the cartulary of the Abbey of Inchaffray a lease is signed by Archibaldus Jonstone, and witnessed by Sir Maurice Johneston, chaplain, July 18, 1521. This Archibald probably belonged to the Elphinstone branch. The Sinclairs of Roslin, near neighbours to Elphinstone, were, like the Johnstouns, descendants of the founder of Inchaffray, Gilbert, Earl of Strathearn.

There is an action by Andrew Johnstoun of Elphinstone, on June 30, 1526, against George, Lord Seton, for damages relating to a "coal trench," showing that his family had already begun to make use of the coal in that neighbourhood. Andrew's ancestress, Agnes of Elphinstone, was only endowed with a portion of the estate, not enough to support younger sons. But Seton was killed at Pinkie, and on Sept. 15, 1549, the Crown gave to Andrew Johnstoun of Elphinstone, "his heirs and assignees, the ward and non-entry of the lands of Elphinstone and Tranent, Sheriffdom of Edinburgh and Constabulary of Haddington, in the Queen's hands by ward since the death of George, Lord Seton, last possessor thereof, and for all time till the lawful serving of the righteous heir." After this he was in difficulty about his son's marriage contract, as on Feb. 11, 1553, there is a "gift to Margaret Johnstoun, elder, Agnes Johnstoun, Margaret Johnstoun, younger, and Janet Johnstoun, daughters to Andro Johnstoun of Elphinstone, their heirs and assignees, of the goods of the said Andro, now in the Queen's hands by escheat, by decreet interponed to a contract between the deceast William, Lord Ruthven, and Margaret Ruthven, his daughter, on one side, and him and James Johnstoun, his son, on the other."

Andrew was married to Margaret Douglas of Corhead, and left four, if not more, sons—James, Robert, Adam, and John. In 1551 he was one of the twelve jurors who returned Alexander as heir to his father, George, Lord Home.

In 1561 a decreet, signed at Holyrood House, gives Andrew of Elphinstone "license to remain at home from all the Queen's armies and from all presence at assemblies, and from appearing and passing or serving of briefs, for all the days of his life." He was alive June 12, 1562, when his heir, James, signs an agreement with his brother, Robert.

This James, having acted as cautioner for Lord Ruthven in a money bond, incurred sequestration of his estate for the payment. But he was able to buy the ten pound land of Ballincrieff, confirmed to him by "Henry and Mary, King and Queen of Scots," in 1565, and the next year he was concerned with Lord Ruthven and others in the murder of David Rizzio in the presence of the King and Queen. He was respited for his share in this tragedy; and on July 18, 1566 another precept for remission is dated at Edinburgh to James Johnstoun of Elphinstone and John Crichton of Brunstoun for their treachery and participation with James, Earl of Morton, the deceased Patrick, Lord Ruthven, and Patrick, Lord Lindsay, in the detention of the persons of the

THE JOHNSTOUNS OF ELPHINSTONE

King and Queen within their palace of Holyrood House in the month of March last.

The Laird of Elphinstone was denounced in 1584 for supporting his Chief against Maxwell.

In 1587 there is an action by the youthful Laird of Johnstoun against the Earl of Angus, his uncle, Robert Johnstoun, parson of Lochmaben, and others, his curators, he being now over fourteen, for the purpose of continuing the tutorship during his minority, and adding James Johnstoun, Laird of Elphinstone, to the list.

During his father's lifetime Elphinstone had been granted the goods of Edward Duncan of Cousland, escheated by the Queen on account of Duncan having severely wounded Elphinstone's servant, George Wood. Duncan was probably a tenant, as there had been a dispute between Lord Ruthven and Laird Andrew in 1532 about the division of the lands of Cousland, near Elphinstone, which both claimed. There is a grant of them from William, Earl of Gowrie, Lord Ruthven, with consent of Dorothy Stewart, his spouse, to Elphinstone in 1583.

There is no proof but the fact that Cousland was part of the Elphinstone Barony to show any kinship with the occupants, but in 1620 there is a marriage contract between William Johnstoun, indweller in Cousland, and Christian Lindsay on behalf of Thomas Johnstoun, his eldest son, and Agnes, daughter of the said Christian, and her late husband, James Hopkirk. Edward Johnstoun is the witness. The Will of Edward Johnstoun of Cousland, in "Innerask parish, Sheriffdom of Edinburgh," is dated July 24, 1627, when he was too ill to write. His wife was Agnes Hunter, and his eldest son, William. His brother, Thomas Johnstoun; Thomas Johnstoun, the elder; Sir Jerome Lindsay; and James Wood sign it.

The value of the goods and money owed to the deceased was £2216, 10s.; his property, besides crops, included three staigs valued at £10 each, six horses and mares valued at £30 each, eleven oxen at 40 marks each, and sixteen sheep with eight lambs.

In 1588 James, the elder of Elphinstone, was one of the witnesses to the Laird of Johnstoun's retour. He died in 1594, having married, first, Margaret, daughter of William, Lord Ruthven (1549-50), and had James, Patrick, John, perhaps more; secondly, Janet, daughter of Sir James Melvill (1564), and had James, Robert, and John. Leuchie was settled on Robert in 1575. He died before 1620, as that year Archibald Douglas of Tofts proceeds against his widow, Susanna Hamilton, and their son, John, as well as against "Samuel Johnstone, oy and heir to the late James Johnstoun of Elphinstone, his guidsir, anent right to the non-entres of the Lands of Leuchie."

Among the registered obligations is one by the Rt. Hon. James Johnestoun of Elphinstone, Oct. 29, 1613. He died, as appears from the above, before 1620; and in 1625 Samuel Johnestoun, his heir, borrowed money from Sir John Hamilton of Preston, Kt. Perhaps it was to purchase the baronetcy of Nova Scotia, which he obtained in 1627. Samuel's father, Patrick, whose Will was proved in 1607, married Elizabeth Dundas, and left four younger children—

STAPLETON TOWER, DUMFRIES.

ELPHINSTONE TOWER, HADDINGTON.

Patrick, Barbara, Martha, and Mary. Samuel married Jean Douglas of Spott, and, besides John, the second Baronet, left five daughters—Jean, Elizabeth (who married, first, John Seton, and for her second husband the Earl of Hartfell), Helen, Mary, and Anna.

Samuel was an enterprising man, who, in conjunction with the Primroses, ancestors of the Earl of Rosebery, began to export the coal that his predecessors had worked in East Lothian, a business which eventually ruined the family. It was stopped by the Lords in Council for fear the supply should become exhausted. Elphinstone represented the loss he was incurring, and that, worked as he was doing it, the coal would last 100 years in spite of exportation. On April 23, 1623, an Act of the Privy Council decreed that "as Samuel Johnstoun of Elphinstone had already expended 20,000 marks upon his coal heughs, to his great hurt and apparent wreck, in supporting forty families of men, women, and children at their work, whose weekly charges exceeded 200 marks," he was allowed to export coal for seven more years. Miners were serfs by a law passed in 1606, but that he was a humane employer is shown by the average weekly gain of a collier's family being 5 marks, or 5s. 6d.

Elphinstone obtained a permit to visit England and the Continent in 1635. He died Feb. 18, 1637, leaving his only son and heir, John, his sole executor, his house at Elphinstone and his residuary legatee. To his unmarried daughter, Mariot, two parts of his goods; and to his youngest daughter, Anna, a third of all his goods and gear, apprised at £959, 6s. 8d., but he was owed £516, 12s. He also owed an arrear of teind duty of the lands of Elphinstone to James Johnstoun, Lord Bishop of Edinburgh, wages to one maid and four menservants, besides sums to three more, probably tradespeople or workmen. His brother, Patrick, left neither wife nor child, and his debts exceeded his assets. Sir David Home of Wedderburn and his son, George, were in his debt.

Sir John married Margaret Keith, and died in 1662. There is a discrepancy between his Will and the retour of the next heir, as the first distinctly states that Margaret, Jean, Elizabeth, and Anna, his daughters, were the only nearest of kin to him, "David Sinclair of Rysie being spouse to the said Elizabeth." Like his uncle, Patrick, he died in difficulties, as the inventory is only sworn at £180, and he left debts. John M'Cara, son to the Commissary Clerk at Inverness, is cautioner, and John Lightfoot, Writer in Edinburgh, his only executor. Elphinstone Tower appears to have been already alienated. But on May 5, 1666, "Dominus Jacobus Jonstoun de Elphinstoun miles baronettus" is returned as heir to his father, John, "militis baronnetti," and to his grandfather, Sir Samuel. On June 2, 1673, he was returned heir to his father in the lands of Leuchie. It may be assumed that James was not a lawful heir, but perhaps, as a suit was being carried on against Sir John's daughters, it was worth no one's while to prove it. He was buried, it is believed, in Greyfriars Churchyard, Edinburgh, where four boundary stones, erected in 1727, with just the name, marked the grave.

Things seem to have gone on prosperously with the Elphinstones till the export of coal from Haddington was finally stopped by the Lords in Council. As the home trade was overstocked, and the employers had to support their men, misfortune overtook them. James is said to have moved to Newmonkland, where he again farmed and mined for coal about 1693, but except his traditional grave nothing more is known of him; and in the eighteenth century it was believed by the Marquis of Annandale and the Johnstones of Westerhall that the descendants of the Baronets of Elphinstone were extinct.

But this is not easily proved of the collaterals, particularly of those who had mixed in the life of the neighbouring city. James Johnstoun of Elphinstone left younger sons, one of whom, John, was probably the John Johnston who, in Sept. 1567, received the clerkship of the Commissary of Edinburgh, "which was given by the King's mother to Sebastian Denellourt, Frenchman, but now taken from him because of his unfitness for the office, and because of his holding of the same is against the treaty made by the said King's mother, promising to give no such office to foreigners." In 1596 John Johnestoun, Writer[1] to the Signet, was appointed to the clerkship of the Commissariat of Edinburgh in succession to James Johnstoun (who was connected with Elphinstone). John resigned the next year, 1597, when his eldest son, another James Johnstoun, was appointed to the post.

In 1599 John Johnstoun of Elphinstone and others were "directed by the Town Council of Edinburgh to make a perfect inventory of all the town evidents (writs) being in the Charter House to put them in good order and to call in the writs that are given forth or missing." In 1602 he was made Commissioner " for taking order with all the town's affairs concerning the Kirk's livings within and without this burgh."

This John Johnstoun's Will, dated at Prestonpans, near Elphinstone, Oct. 31, 1607, is witnessed by Samuel Johnstoun of Elphinstone and John Ramsay. Among his many debtors was the tutor of Borthwick, Mr Mungo Rig of Carbery, Sir James Bannatyne of Brochtoun, Sir Robert Melvill, Bessie Borthwick, relict of Mr Adam Johnstoun, Provost of Crichton, and James Johnstoun, her son. Altogether he was owed £17,202, 3s. 8d., the amount being confirmed by David Home of Godscroft, and the inventory was only £696, 13s. 4d. He left no debts. His executors were his two sons-in-law —Mr John Ker, Minister at Prestonpans, and Sir Robert Hamilton—and his youngest daughter, Rachel. His son, John, is not mentioned except in a decreet in 1613 with his sisters, Barbara, called of Elphinstone in 1635 (the Rev. John Ker's wife), Janet, and Rachel.

John Johnstoun of Elphinstone, merchant in Edinburgh, appears in 1581. He seems to have been Andrew Johnstoun's younger son, John, described as "an indweller in Edinburgh," and father "of Jonathas" of Elphinstone, who was at Douay College in 1581, after being under a tutor at Seton.

[1] There had been many political changes between 1567-96, and, as the Johnstouns warmly embraced the cause of the Queen and fought at Langside, he was probably deprived of his post and reappointed in 1596.

In 1587 there was a gift to Mr James Johnstoun and Martha Johnstoun, their heirs, etc., of the escheat of the estate of James Johnstoun of Elphinstone, now belonging to the King on account of the said James being denounced a rebel since Nov. 28 for non-fulfilment of a contract with Robert Richardson. This is followed six months later by an escheat of William Bonar of Rossie being given to Robert Johnstoun, Elphinstone's son, for the non-fulfilment of an obligation. Such escheats seem to have been generally given to a creditor, or were purchased by relatives who restored the goods to the old owners for an equivalent, and Mr James Johnstoun was probably Elphinstone's eldest son. In 1591 Mr John Johnstoun, son lawful to James Johnstoun of Elphinstone, is given his father's escheat, and it appears that Elphinstone had been security to the deceased Lord Ruthven, who had made the contract.

John Johnstoun of Elphinstone, who is called brother to Patrick Johnstoun of Elphinstone, was cautioner for Sir G. Home of Wedderburn when he borrowed money from David Johnstone of Newbie, merchant of Edinburgh, in 1606. He had a brother-german, also called John.

Mr James Johnstoun [ante] burgess of Edinburgh, died there in August 1597. He is described in his Will as Clerk-deliverer of the Bills before the Lords of Session, and Clerk of the Commissariat of Edinburgh, but resigned in 1596, Michael Finlayson being one of the witnesses. He left £2043, 2s. 9d., and was owed £6448, 17s. 11d. His mother, Margaret Clerk, was among his creditors. His wife was Marion Laurie, a widow when he married her, as appears by his legacies of 1200 marks to her two unmarried daughters, Katrena and Helen Symsoun, and £200 each to his wife's grandchildren, Marion and Christian Marjoribanks. His sons, David and John, were minors, but he directs that John should "be trained by Joseph Marjoribanks in the trade of merchandise." He left his own brother, John, as well as John "callit of Elphinstone, to be overseers and helpers to his said spouse and bairns, his only executors." From several of the Home family, including the Chief, being among his creditors, with a Douglas, Lady Airlie, Sir Michael Balfour of Burlie and others, the testator appears to come off the House of Elphinstone, and possibly from one of the two younger sons of Andrew Johnstoun of Elphinstone.[1]

George Johnstoun, his wife, Isobel Leslie, and their son, John, appear in 1613, and in 1617-19, with regard to the ownership of the Abbey Mill of Haddington.

John Johnston of Polton was a baillie of Edinburgh in 1672, when the Earl of Annandale appointed him one of the guardians of his children. From this he would appear to have been a relative, and probably from the Elphinstone branch. He recorded arms in the Lyon Office, 1676, which are cut on the stone dial still at Polton House, and left an only daughter, Magdalen, who married Sir James Murray, fifth Baronet of Hilhead.

[1] The conjectural descendants of Elphinstone appear in Chapter XXVII.

CHAPTER IV.

THE JOHNSTOUNS OF WESTRAW—FRANCIS JOHNSTOUN—CASTLEHILL—TUNDERGARTH—
HALLEATHS—COWHILL—AUSTRALIA—CLAUCHRIE AND DUCHRAE—AMERICA.

THE parish of Peddinane, adjoining Carstairs in Clydesdale, is a picturesque spot among the hills in Lanark, and was the residence of Johnstoun of Westraw for 150 years. No evidence has been found to dispute the theory that it was given to the Chief of Johnstoun as a reward for the services of his clan in suppressing the Douglas rebellion, and by him bequeathed to one of his sons, though no official document exists to confirm it. But Matthew of Johnstoun, Armiger (Esq.), was granted a Charter in 1455 of "the lands and house of Andrew Clercson, commonly called Westraw," and, as was customary, summoned the tenants to confirm them in their occupation of the lands.

A MS. preserved at Auchinleck of uncertain date, describing the Douglas rebellion, states that "the laird of Johnstoun's two sons took the castle of Lochmaben from the laird of Mouswald called Carruthers and his two sons, and other two or three men, and all through treason of the porter and since then the King gave them the keeping of the house to his profit." One of these Johnstouns was Herbert, who received £40 as captain of the castle for the year 1455. That the other was Matthew, and that they were brothers, rests on conjecture, but it appears that a Matthew Johnstoun received payment for twenty lance staves (4s. 6d. each), besides gunpowder, and charcoal to make it, supplied to the castle for its defence by John of Dalrymple in Flanders, by order of the King, in 1456; and in the year ending July 1460 Matthew and Herbert Johnstoun were fined for not producing Andrew Halliday at the criminal court at Dumfries.

As to the tradition of the division of the £40 lands of Pettinane by the Crown between Lord Carlile and Johnstoun in 1455, Carlile claimed the whole as his heritage. There were several actions by the Carliles against the Johnstouns. One in 1476, before the Lords in Council, when John Johnstoun was fined £40, and again in 1498, Pettinane being "wrongously laboured by Adam of Johnstoun and others." A judgment against Symon Carruthers of Mouswald (married to Adam's aunt), Gavin of Johnstoun, grandson to the late Gavin of Esbie, and Adam of Johnstoun, grandson and heir of the late John of Johnstoun of that Ilk, has reference to this, as William, Lord Carlile, grandson and heir of the late John Carlile, claimed money due to his grandfather from Carruthers and from the late Lairds of Johnstoun and Esbie. In 1503, in the same record, John Johnstoun of Pettinane is mentioned, and in 1504 Adam of Johnstoun of that Ilk was pledge for Matthew Johnstoun, John Johnstoun, and Clement Johnstoun of Wamfray. Lord Carlile brought another action in 1517 against Herbert Johnstoun of Pettinane and William Johnstoun for occupying his land.

The Johnstouns of Westraw were far removed from the troubles which wrecked the fortunes of some branches of the clan. They do not appear to have taken part against the English in the numerous invasions which wasted Dumfriesshire in the sixteenth century and the last part of the fifteenth. On Jan. 5, 1545, a respite under the Great Seal is granted by Queen Mary "to Herbert Johnstoun of Westraw, his son Herbert and sundry other persons for their treasonable remaining at home from the Army convened by the late King (James V.) for resisting the Duke of Norfolk and the army of England." In 1548 Herbert of Westraw was one of the jury to return James Lockhart as the heir to Allen Lockhart of Lee.

Johnstoun of Westraw is not mentioned among those who were respited after the battle of Dryfe Sands, but when his Chief, through the aid of several courtiers, was expecting a respite to be granted to himself and his surviving followers for their part in that battle, Westraw accompanied him secretly within five miles of Edinburgh to await the result of the deliberations of the Privy Council. Lord Hamilton was sent to seize Johnstoun, but he had already been warned by Sir John Carmichael, who sent a page on one of the King's horses to advise him to escape, 1594.

A Charter was granted in 1560 to John, brother to James Johnstoun of Westraw. He was a merchant in Edinburgh, where his Will is proved in 1576, and in which he mentions another brother, named John. James Johnstoun of Westraw and James Johnstoun of Elphinstone were accused in 1565 of being concerned with Ruthven and Douglas, to whom both were related, in the murder of David Rizzio in Holyrood Palace.

The nearest connection between Westraw and Elphinstone was through the Homes and Douglases, with whom they intermarried, and both acted as pledge for William Johnstoun of Reidhall when the Regent Moray was encamped at Canonby in October 1569 after the battle of Langside.

Westraw reappears in Annandale affairs in 1588, when Patrick Porteus of Hawkshaw makes over his gift of the escheat of the liferent, goods, etc., of James of Westraw and of his mother, Florence Somerville, to the Laird of Johnstoun. The escheat was in consequence of the slaughter of Henry Williamson in Walterheid. The transfer is signed at Moffat, Dec. 10, and witnessed by Robert Johnstoun, lay parson of Lochmaben, his son, Robert, afterwards tutor of Johnstoun, and John Johnstoun of Graitney.

Before this date Westraw and Johnstoun had become connected on the maternal side—the mother of Florence Somerville's husband, who died in 1570, being sister to David Douglas, afterwards seventh Earl of Angus, the second husband of Margaret Hamilton, mother of the Laird John of Johnestoun who died in 1586, in fact, step first cousins.

Matthew de Johnstoun, the first of Westraw, was dead in 1491, having married Elizabeth Graham. Their son, John, who died in 1508, is believed to have married a daughter of Home of Wedderburn, and left two sons—Herbert, who lived till 1555, and John, married to Barbara Weir. David of Harthope, Matthew's younger son, made a bond of manrent with Simon Johnstoun of Powdene, and both with Lord Maxwell in 1520, one of the witnesses being Robert Johnstoun. David was able to write, but Simon signed with his hand at the pen.

David of Harthope died about 1523. In 1535 Herbert Johnstoun of Westraw made a protest against James Johnstoun, the Sheriff of Lanark, apparently his nephew, for refusing to return him as Harthope's heir. His eldest son, Herbert, who married a Douglas, died before him, but his grandson, James of Westraw, was returned heir to Harthope in 1569, and David is then described as brother to Westraw's great-grandfather. There had been serious disputes on the subject between the Chief and Westraw, so that the Chief bound himself to have "no communing with any Johnstoun of Westraw." But in 1604 Westraw obtained the Charter of the coveted land, and is at that time described by his connection, Lord Somerville, as "a stout asserter of his chief's interest, in whose just quarrels and his own defence he committed many slaughters, being one of the famousest Border Riders." Yet Westraw and Somerville had a noted quarrel, which ended in a fight in the street at Edinburgh, 1594.

The elder Herbert of Westraw had a younger son, John, whose son, Robert, only appears once in the records, but he left a son, James Johnstoun of Lanark. The younger Herbert, husband to Angus's sister, died in 1554. His son, James of Westraw, was given the escheat in 1588 of either his own brother's or uncle's goods, "Gavin, son to the deceased Herbert Johnstoun of Westraw, now in the Queen's hands, through putting of the said Gavin to the horn for not finding surety for art and part in the cruel slaughter of the deceased John Lindsay in Corsig."

James, Laird of Westraw, was killed after the siege of Draffan in 1570 by his connections, Claud and John Hamilton, sons of the Duke of Chatelherault and lay Abbots of Paisley and Arbroath. Letters of Slain were taken out by his widow and her children, but the matter was compromised by a payment of 2000 marks, which was generally done at that time when every life was of consequence to defend the country against "its auld inimys of Ingland." Florence signs the contract with her hand at the pen, being unable to write herself, a common difficulty with Scottish ladies in the sixteenth century. She was obliged to find sureties to obtain from her son the third part of the liferent of Westraw, her marriage settlement.[1]

---

[1] Morals were extremely low at that period. The only tutors and spiritual advisers, the priests and monks, were abolished by law, and the Reformation had not as yet sufficient ministers to supply their place. The abuse of laymen holding Church benefices prevailed before the Reformation, when the chief patronage was in the hands of the King and the landowners, and its continuance after the Reformation probably helped to wreck Episcopacy in Scotland.

The arrangement with the Hamiltons was possibly considered derogatory to the Johnstouns, for, in a letter to Walsingham from the English Ambassador, Nicolson writes: "As for the offers the Lord of Arbroath (Hamilton) make for the slaughter of one Westraw, the Regent does not think it good for his own surety and the King's service to have it taken up yet. The Lord of Arbroath presses the matter . . . and will demand leave to travel till it be ended, for that he dare not remain there for fear of the revenge of the dead man's friends, who be the Johnstouns and their kinsfolk and dependers of the Earl of Angus" (Sept. 19, 1574).

James of Westraw was under age when he inherited his father's property; but in 1583 he petitioned the Lords of Session to be infefted in the lands of Moit, to which he could "not obtain entry because of the deadly feud and enmity between his superior Maxwell and the laird of Johnstoun, to whom he was near friend and special depender." A year later he and his mother were still engaged in a suit against Lord Maxwell "regarding the decreet he had against them to remove from Moit, in the Sheriffdom of Lanark."

Westraw married Johnstoun's sister, Margaret, in 1594, and in a post-nuptial contract settled the ten pound land of Westraw, "with its fortress and pertinents in Lanark, on the said Margaret and their children, whom failing on his own children, whom failing on Sir James of Dunskellie and his male descendants, whom failing on William Johnstoun second lawful son to Mungo Johnstoun of Lockerbie and his heirs male, whom failing on Sir James's male heirs whatsoever, bearing the arms and surname of Johnstoun, conformable with another contract between the two parties, reserving the lady's life rent, in case of children therein named, a provision for the heirs female, and an obligation by Dunskellie to pay 1000 marks to Westraw as a dowry with his said sister" (Feb. 8, 1594). A third contract is more in the form of a tack of the Barony and Castle of Johnstoun and other estates to Westraw and his heirs male, whom failing, to return to Dunskellie and his heirs male bearing the surname and arms of Johnstoun, to be holden from him for 400 marks yearly, and doubling the feu-duty at the entry of every heir. This contract reserved the liferent to the granter and his wife, Sara Maxwell, and contained a clause for the redemption of the estates by payment of "a Scots thistle noble of gold valued at 11 marks Scots money" (Nov. 5, 1594).

Westraw was nominally at the horn at this very time, but on Dec. 4, 1599, he was respited by the Crown for burning the church of Lochmaben in July 1589, when his brother, Robert, was killed. The Chief of the clan was in dire straits for money, his estates were sequestered, and he had been put to the horn for the battle of Dryfe Sands. The respite to himself and his followers had cost him much, and he was just restored to the wardenship of the Borders, with the Castle of Lochmaben as a residence. Many of his dependents had got beyond his control at a time when, we are told, no man dared to take any of them into his house, and since the death of Lord Maxwell, with many followers, in that battle, the Maxwell relatives were waiting for revenge. To rid himself of the troubles of his estates, filled with ruined tenants, seemed a good idea.

His sister had been given an escheat by the Crown, so had a little of her own, and he was borrowing large sums from his relatives, the Edinburgh merchants.

Margaret died before June 6, 1599, as at that date Westraw's wife was Eufemia Oliphant, daughter to his neighbour in Lanark. The *Annandale Book* states that Margaret left children, but Westraw's heir was the son of the second wife.

In 1502 the Laird Adam of Johnstoun tried to obtain the lands of Glendining, in Eskdale, which his family had once owned, by force. Westraw bought this estate in 1605 and came to live there, apparently to escape the enmity of the Maxwells and their friends. His lands in Lanark had been escheated and given to Carmichael. In his petition about Moit in 1584 he stated that he was "cruelly left for dead in the county of Annandale" by certain of the Carliles, servants and dependers of Maxwell; and in 1607 he petitioned the Privy Council to protect him from Lord Herries, Edward Maxwell, his brother, John, Lord Maxwell, Sir Robert his brother, and others of less note.

The events which caused this enmity appear further on. The Maxwells had to find cautioners for over £2000, but the next year Dunskellie, as he was then called, or the Chief of Johnstoun, fell a victim to the hereditary feud, and Maxwell had to hide himself in the most remote part of the country, till he was brought to justice in 1613.

The purchase of Glendining, and also of Carlile's portion of Pettinane (1601), partly with money borrowed from Gilbert Johnstoun in Edinburgh, brought Westraw into difficulties. Robert Scott, reader at Thankerton Kirk, proceeded against him in 1619, when he was still "at the horn," for a previous debt of 3000 marks, for which Gilbert Johnstoun of Corhead was cautioner, and to pay it he sold his paternal estate. The writ, in which "James Johnstoun of Westraw, superior of the lands," makes over four oxgates of land in Pettinane parish to Mr John Lindsay, is dated Edinburgh, Nov. 26, 1624, and witnessed by James Johnstoun of that Ilk, Edward Johnestoun of Ryell (Newbie), John Johnstoun, Writer, and Mr James Hamilton of Lesmahago. A second writ is "in favour of James Carmichael, sewar to Prince Charles of Scotland and Wales, of the 20 mark land of Pettinane, sometime belonging to Elizabeth, Lady Carlile; also the lands of Pettinane, now called Westraw, sometime pertaining to Alexander, Master of Elphinstone, and assignation by James Johnstoun, elder of Westraw." A ferry boat on the Clyde is included.

On June 5, 1629, there is an action by James Johnestoun of that Ilk, heir to the late Sir James Johnestoun, against James Johnestoun, sometime of Westraw, for production of a decreet dated Feb. 9, 1605. Westraw brings a counter action against his Chief. He died in 1633, and his son, James, married to Isabel Scott, a relative of the Laird's grandmother, came to an agreement with the Laird, by which Westraw acknowledged him as his superior in Harthope and Over and Nether Dryfe, while the Laird, now raised to the peerage, set forth: "It being nowise the intention of the said noble lord to disquiet the said James Johnestoun of Westraw himself; regarding the weal always of the house of Westraw, which is descended from him, so he minds not to be hard with him or any flowing from the stock his lords (hip) is come off, and in testimony thereof the noble lord binds and obliges him and his heirs never to seek any benefit of the said lands so long as the said James Johnestoun and his heirs shall bruik the same undisposed nor to move any pursuit against them."

In 1600, when Westraw was considering the purchase of Glendining, his name appears among the chiefs charged with the care of the Borders. His family was called of Westraw long after he had parted with it, and before his great-grandson obtained the Crown Charter which incorporated Glendining, Daldurhame, and other lands into a barony of Westerhall.

In 1629 an Edinburgh tailor carries a decreet, obtained two years before against Westraw, to the Privy Council, for payment of £97, 2s. 8d. for clothes made for himself, his late wife, Eufemia, their son, James, their daughter, Elizabeth, and their manservant, possibly a poor relation, as he had the same name as his master. "Given for pursuer."

A MS. family history by Mrs Dewar, née Johnstone, of Westerhall, states that Westraw, who married Isabella, daughter of Walter Scott of Harden, Jan. 2, 1643, left a second son, Francis, who is said to have married an Edmonstone, and left a son, Francis, born 1669, died about 1712, having married Agnes Brown. The elder Francis is probably the same as Francis Johnstoun, merchant in Clydesdale, one of the twenty-one who on June 22, 1680, rode into Sanquhar and nailed to the Market Cross the famous " Declaration and Testimony of the True Presbyterian, Anti-Prelatic, Anti-Erastian persecuted party in Scotland," which disowned Charles II.'s authority, and brought death, exile, or a prison on all who supported it.

The merchant, Francis Johnstoun, was accompanied by Richard Cameron, who had been chaplain and tutor in the family of Scott of Harden, the maternal relative of James and Francis Johnstoun of Westerhall. Cameron was killed on the side of the Covenanters in one of the first battles.[1]

The Johnstouns of Tundergarth appear in 1483, when the Lords Auditors decree that John Johnstoun of Tundergarth, his son, Matthew, and John of Ayill (Isle) should restore twenty-one oxen, four horses, and twenty-one sheep

[1] Francis is not a common Johnstoun name, but in 1714 there is a sasine in favour of Francis Johnston, second lawful son to James Johnston of Castlehill, in the lands of Langshaw, and others, also in the lands of Castlehill in Tundergarth; and in 1728 John and Francis Johnston (brothers), were baillies of Dumfries. In 1741 there is a sasine in favour of Francis Johnston, merchant, one of the baillies of Dumfries, in lands in Holywood parish for a debt. His daughter Margaret, married to John Graham, inherited lands from him in Dumfries the next year. John Graham sues James Leslie Johnston of Knockhill, who was in pecuniary difficulties in 1744.

John, the elder son of James Johnston of Castlehill, was returned his father's heir in 1730, and is called the elder in Castlehill in 1746. His son, Mr John Johnston, minister, owned the lands of Torbeck Hill in 1749; Thomas in Castlehill acts as a witness in 1714, perhaps the same who, two years before, renounces his claim to Persbie and Pressbutts in favour of John Johnston of Persbiehall, and sets up at Brocketlea, in the parish of Canonby. Thomas Johnston in Castlehill is described as a merchant in 1749.

In 1712 there is a sasine in favour of Francis Johnston, son of Mungo Johnston in Ragiwhat, in the liferent of lands belonging to Robert Johnston of Wamfray. Agnes Johnston, wife of this Francis Johnston, seems to have been a Wamfray.

taken by them from the lands of Inglistoun of Drumgrey. Possibly this was the same Matthew Johnstoun who, with William of Johnstoun, was an executor to the late Thomas Johnstoun in 1479. From that time they seem to have been a well-behaved branch, as very little is heard of them; they are mentioned in 1504, 1569, 1585, 1618, and 1671, generally as loyal followers of the Chief. Andrew Johnstoun of Tundergarth appears in 1604, and in 1613 John Johnstoun is called gudeman of Tunnergarth. John and Andrew Johnstouns of Tundergarth alternate till 1739, when "John Johnstoun, late of Tundergarth, now in Comlongan," was receiving the annual rent of lands in Penlaw. There was a connection between the Johnstouns of Castlehill (in Tundergarth) with those of Penlaw.

The Johnstouns of Halleaths appear in the sixteenth century. In 1672 an heiress, Agnes Johnstoun, married to John Kennedy, owned Halleaths; after that the lands were mortgaged to a Johnstoun of Priestdykes. In 1715, during the Jacobite rising, Johnstone of Broadholm was one of the sheriff's deputes at Dumfries.

In 1721 Janet Forsyth, the widow of William Johnston, in conjunction with John Forsyth, brought an action against George Kennedy of Halleaths and obtained the liferent of Over Halleaths; and in 1739 John, Samuel, David, and Nicolas Johnston, children of the late George Johnston, drew the rents of the lands of Halleaths.

In 1740 William Johnston, surgeon in Dumfries, brought an action against Herbert Kennedy in Halleaths, and another the same year against Thomas Johnston of Clochrie, also against Archibald Douglas, younger of Dornock, in 1743.

The present owner of Halleaths, John Johnstone, was eldest son of Andrew Scott Johnstone, J.P. (died 1901), who married Margaret, daughter of James Mackie of Bargaly and Ernespie, Kirkcudbright. Mr Johnstone, like his father, was educated at Eton. He was born in 1881, and lives on his estate.

From their arms the Johnstons of Cowhill, mentioned in 1769 as new proprietors, appear to be cadets of Westerhall. George Johnston of Cowhill, previously of Conheath, born 1738, was at the drinking competition at Friar's Carse in 1789, immortalised by Burns in his poem "The Whistle." Sir Robert Laurie, M.P., Mr Riddell, an elder of the kirk, and Fergusson of Craigdarroch, competed for an heirloom in the same way in which it had been won some centuries before. When Sir Robert fell under the table Riddell withdrew from the "unholy contest," leaving Fergusson to win by finishing five bottles of claret, as was certified by M'Murdo, the judge, and witnessed by Patrick Millar and Cowhill. If such feats were at all common, it accounts for the reduced average of life and extinction of families in the male line which is rather noticeable in the eighteenth century.

Mr Johnston bought Cowhill from a Jacobite Maxwell in 1750, and pulled down the tower to replace it by a large modern house. He was cousin to Major George Johnston, who commanded a regiment in Australia during the Governorship of Admiral Bligh, the cause of the celebrated mutiny of the

Bounty. Bligh had an illness, which, in the tropical summer of New South Wales, made him violent, so, in 1805, Johnston arrested him on his own responsibility and sent him to England. The voyage cured him, and he brought a charge of mutiny against Johnston, with the result that the Major was cashiered and outlawed, and made his permanent home in Australia. His descendants are among its wealthiest inhabitants.

The late owner of Cowhill was William Johnston, Esq., J.P., formerly in the Civil Service in India. He was born in 1831, and the son of the late Admiral Charles Johnston of Cowhill and of Lilias M'Alpine, his wife. He married first, 1854, Elizabeth, daughter of the late Hon. J. Thomason, Lieutenant-Governor of the North-West Provinces of India; and secondly, Eleanora Jane, daughter of C. W. M'Killop, Esq., Bengal Civil Service, by whom he had a son, James Thomason, born 1860.

The Johnstons of Clouthrie, or Clauchrie, near Closeburn, are cadets of Westerhall. Walter, their ancestor, appears in Knokilshane, Co. Dumfries, early in the sixteenth century, and Roger, described as his son, bought lands in Auldgirth in 1561. The same Charter transfers to him the share of his late brother, George, bought of the same vendor, William of Dunduff.

A family of Johnstoun, who lived as feuars on the lands of Duchrae, in Galloway, seem to belong to the Clauchries, who were particularly associated with Dumfries and Glasgow in the sixteenth and seventeenth centuries. Thomas Johnston of Clouthrie and John, his brother, are the last two names on the respite to the Laird of Johnestoun and his followers (1594) after the battle of Dryfe Sands, and John Johnston, "called Clouthrie," was, among a Jardine and several Johnstouns, accused (March 2, 1619) by John Jardine of abstracting the tithe sheafs from the complainer's land at Apilgarth. This was a mild protest against the Reformation by those who had not yet accepted it. John of Clauchrie got into other difficulties, and fraternised with the more lawless members of the clan.

Archibald Johnston of Clauchrie married Bessie Williamson of Castle Robert, and was on the War Committee of Dumfries in 1644. He lent £885 to Roger Kirkpatrick of Wod and others in 1612, and probably, owing to losses in the Civil War, was obliged, with consent of his son, John, in 1653 to mortgage Clauchrie to Robert Neilson, sometime servitor to Sir Robert Grierson of Lag. The mortgage was paid off to Charles Neilson (Robert's nephew) by John Johnston, a merchant and magistrate in Glasgow, in 1663, with 9084 marks, including interest and sheriff's fee. His brother, James, witnessed it, also George Edgar, servant to their late father, Archibald.

The Charter of Clauchrie included the lands of Nether Clochrie, Knowhead, Auldgirth, and Dunduff. John of Clauchrie recorded arms in the *Lyon Office* in 1673. He married, 1633, Janet, daughter of John Craik, a merchant of Dumfries, and had a sister married to Robert Herries, and two brothers, George of Castle Robert (1649), and Alexander of Clochrie (1678).

In 1675 there is a sasine in favour of John, only son of Mr John Johnston, doctor of physic in Paisley, and Elizabeth Cunningham, daughter of the deceased Mr John Cunningham of Dargavell, *alias* Lochermore. If he is the same as the physician who died in 1714, he married twice, and his younger children, George, and Helen, who married Donald Gowan, belonged to his second wife, Helen Little.

In 1690 a Charter under the Great Seal settles Clochrie on John Johnston, M.D., and his direct heirs, whom failing, to his brother, George. He was the first Professor of Medicine appointed to the University of Glasgow, and probably, like most Scottish doctors at that time, educated at Padua or in Paris. His Will calls him "doctor of medicine of Paisley," while his wife's Will styles him "doctor of medicine in Glasgow," and his brother's, "Johnston of Clochrie." He died in 1714, his widow, Helen Little (from Gretna), living till 1728. Dr Johnston was the eldest son of the merchant, from whom he inherited Upper, Mid, and Nether Dargavell. His son, John, a baillie in Glasgow, appears to be the same as John Johnston in Glasgow, married to Janet Cumyng, and the father of two younger sons—John, who received £1000 legacy from his great-uncle, James, and James, who had £400 from the same uncle—besides his heir, Thomas, who married Janet, daughter of Edward Maxwell, and owned Over and Mid Clauchrie (March 8, 1733). Thomas left one child, Margaret, married to Hugh M'Cornoch, of Dumfries.

A Crown Charter of 1706 grants to Captain Robert Johnston of Kelton (born 1642, died 1715), late Provost of Dumfries, second brother to Clauchrie (*i.e.*, the M.D.), and to Robert, his son, the lands of Threive Grange on the Dee, and the hereditary keepership of the Castle of Threive. Kelton was buried at Dumfries, where his handsome monument is still seen. He married Grizel Craik, who died 1732. Their son, Robert, married Margaret, lawful daughter to Sir A. Hope of Kerse Bank. He carried on a suit against John Little, in Gretna, where his family had bought land. He died *s.p.* about 1730, his sisters, Ann and Mary Ann Johnston, being his heirs.

Of the direct descendants of Dr Johnston, the third grandson, James, married Barbara Maxwell of Barncleuch, and their son, who was a surgeon in Calcutta, on inheriting his uncle's lands took the name of Maxwell. Wellwood Johnston Maxwell married Catherine Maxwell, and had thirteen children; the eldest surviving son, J. H. Maxwell, died 1843, was a Writer to the Signet. He married his cousin, Clementine Herries Maxwell, and their son, Wellwood, born 1817, married Jane, the eldest daughter of Sir W. Jardine. The present representative, Mr William Jardine Herries Maxwell is at the Scottish Bar. He was born in 1852, and married Dora, second daughter of C. M. Kirwan of Dalgin Park, Co. Mayo. He was an M.P. for Dumfriesshire in 1892, and succeeded his father in Barncleuch and Munches in 1900. Three of his great-uncles, Wellwood, Alexander, and George, were merchants in Liverpool.

As Duchrae, now Hensol, near Dalry, was once owned by Charteris[1] of Amisfield, the superior of some lands held by Johnstouns of Powdene, and Elsieshields in Dumfriesshire, a scion of one of these branches possibly migrated

---

[1] A family of Charteris, or Charters, lived in Duchrae till recent times, and married with the Johnstouns.

PLATE IV.

The towne of Airmond
1583-6

MAINS OF DUCHRAE, KIRKCUDBRIGHT.

to Galloway—the distance would not be more than about twenty-five miles. But the Christian names and connections point to a probable relation with their nearer neighbours of Clauchrie, of whom the first who appears in those parts, Captain David Johnston, seems to have been a cadet. His Will describes him "in Orchardtoun" in 1685. His heir and executor is his eldest son, William, and the witness, Sir Godfrey M'Cullock of Myrton.

In 1685 Hew M'Cullock of Rusco disposes of a tack of Parks in Netherlaw, held of Sir George Maxwell of Orchardton to William Johnstoun, Patrick Vans being the witness. In 1706 William wrote from Ballywillwill, Ireland (Chapter XXVIII.), to Sir George Maxwell, speaking of his tack of Netherlaw, his brother's illness, and of money owed to him by Maxwell. About this time William appears as a feuar in Duchrae, which was bought by the Provost of Dumfries, William Craik of Arbigland, in 1681. The district must have been nearly deserted, for the struggle carried on between the Covenanters and the troops sent to coerce them, from 1661 till 1689, had begun there, and continued with pitiless energy till the accession of William III. William Johnstoun in Duchrae was married to a daughter of a cadet of Grierson of Lag, and his landlord, Craik, was brother to the wife of John Johnstoun of Clauchrie, married in 1633. Duchrae's wife's relatives had also transactions with the Clauchries, and were connected with Dumfries, where the notorious Sheriff-Depute of Galloway, Sir Robert Grierson of Lag (Scott's Sir Robert Redgauntlet) ended his long life in a house in the High Street in 1733.

William Johnstoun in Duchrae appears to have founded a branch in Ireland; but a younger son was Robert Johnstoun of Nether Barcaple in Tongland, who in 1713 married a second wife, Mary Wallace, a relation of the Craiks, and whose family lived in Clauchrie. Their younger son, William, born 1718, feued lands in Duchrae from another William, probably his uncle or grandfather, and married an Ayrshire girl, Janet M'Cready, born 1721.

His maternal grandmother was a Neilson, as he was heir to two aunts of that name owning lands in Duchrae, but which were sold years before their death,[1] and his eldest son, William, born 1745, settled in Carlisle. A young brother, Robert, was drowned in the Bay of Luce, presumably in the engagement with the French fleet under Thurot, when several local ships assisted the British squadron (1759). A sister married Laidlaw of Mossgrove. The youngest brother, John, born at Balmaghie, 1749, the seventh son of a seventh son, died 1841, married Dorothea Proudfoot, daughter of an old Covenanting family at Moffat, and on her death, leaving an only child (John), married again, and had a second family.

John, the younger, settled in New York in 1804 at the age of twenty-three, and married Margaret, daughter of John Taylor, of Glasgow, the widow of R. Howard. Among other family treasures, he carried to America books and a seal bearing the family crest. He kept up his connection with Scotland by visits to Edinburgh and Galloway, and by sending donations to the churches in

[1] The lands were sold, says family tradition, because the old ladies had no title-deeds. After their death two silk bonnets were found with the lost writs cut up inside the silk.

Kirkcudbrightshire—perhaps to follow the old Scottish custom of giving donations to the neighbouring churches on the occasion of a death. His son, John Taylor Johnston, married Miss Frances Colles, of New Orleans, and was one of the founders, and the first President of the Metropolitan Art Museum of New York (1820-93). They left a son, John Herbert, and three daughters.

The younger of the first generation born in New York, James Boorman Johnston (1822-87), married (1853) Mary, daughter of M. Humphreys, of Philadelphia, eldest son of Major R. Humphreys, and left two daughters and a son, born 1857. This son, John Humphreys Johnston, of New York, and of Pallazzo Contarini del Zaffo, Venice, was created a Chevalier of the Legion of Honour in 1901.

Mrs Bard, the only sister of Mr J. B. Johnston, died at Rome in 1875. She and her husband founded St. Stephen's College on their property, Annandale, on the Hudson. The estate was so called by its former owners—Johnstons—from the Southern States.

.Possibly John Johnstoun, the merchant, described as of Westoun, Peddinane, and brother to the late James Johnstoun of Westraw, and who died in 1576, was the ancestor of John Johnstoun, a physician in Edinburgh, who sailed for New Amsterdam (New York) in 1645. The ship, 100 feet long, contained Gordons, Irvings, and other Dumfriesshire names, and was three months on the road. Nearly all the passengers died of scurvy before it arrived, but Johnstoun was spared to settle on lands in New Jersey, and there some of his descendants remain. He brought over books and his coat of arms (those of Johnstoun without a difference),[1] which are carefully preserved. His family believe that he came off the Westerhall branch. They have always kept aloof from American political life.

There was another scion of Westerhall, James Johnstoun, brother's son to the Laird of Westraw, in 1619, and William Johnstoun, called of Westerhall, after the Civil War took shelter in the Debateable Land in 1648.

[1] The Douglas heart was not added to the Westerhall coat of arms till the eighteenth century.

CHAPTER V.

JOHNSTOUNS OF ELSIESHIELDS—KIRK—KIRKTON—WARRISTON—KELLOBANK—AUCHIN-SKEOCH—LAY ABBOTS OF SAULSIT—MILNBANK AND LOCKERBIE—BEIRHOLME—GUTTERBRAES—ANNAN.

THE English Warden of the Marches, writing in 1583, estimates the men of the name of Johnstoun able to respond to a summons in time of war as 300 in Annandale, besides those near the Esk and Sark, about twelve more. He points out that this unity of all of the same surname constituted the strength of their Chief. The small possessions of the family as it increased in number obliged many to settle as copyholders or tenants on the lands of other leaders—Murray, Herreis, Carruthers, Crichton, Charteris, Gordon, Kirkpatrick, Jardine, Maxwell, Irving, Stewart, Douglas, and Scott. Some of them were paying feus to rivals of their own clan, but joined under the Laird of Johnstoun's banner directly it was unfurled, which led to many difficulties with their landlords. It was only ties of blood that could have kept these unpaid armies together with ruin to individuals; and there is no doubt that Elsieshields was one of the early Johnstoun cadets.

This eminent branch divided into several families in the sixteenth and seventeenth centuries. The estate lay near the royal Castle of Lochmaben, in the centre of the invasions and civil wars which long afflicted Annandale. It grew a bold, strong race, who spread over Mid-Annandale into East and Mid-Lothian, into Berwickshire, Yorkshire, and other parts. Gavin Johnstoun of the Wood, who appears in 1419, married Mariota Scott, and lived till 1485; his son, Archibald, predeceased him in 1480. Archibald's property was disputed on the score of the illegitimacy of the claimant, Gavin of Esbie, whose tutor was William of Johnstoun; but another Gavin, probably the second son of the old man, was ready to take it if the decision of the Lords in Council was against Archibald's son. Whoever succeeded was born about 1465.

Thomas Johnstoun of Brackenhill, who, with his wife, Katherine, appears in 1496, was an Elsieshields.

Adam Johnstoun and his wife, Margaret Simpson, citizens of Edinburgh, the proprietors of Mossop, under the superiority of Lord Hereis, in the parish of Moffat, in 1511, probably belonged to the Elsieshields branch. The witnesses to the Charter are John Williamson, parson of Dornock, Mungo Hereis, James Johnstoun, Sir Matthew Simpson, chaplain, Thomas Hamilton, etc.

William, second son of the elder Gavin, inherited Marjoribanks, near Moffat, and was ancestor of the Johnstouns of Dryfesdale and Lockerbie. From Gavin, the younger, living in 1498, came, among others, the line of Esbie, Elsieshields, Kirkton, Middlegill, Reidhall, Beirholme, Hilton, Sheens, Warriston, and Kellobank. Gavin Johnstoun of Kirkton, with his brother Herbert, appear in 1526. The Laird of Elsieshields was one of the five Johnstoun Lairds in Dumfriesshire in 1597, the other four being Johnstoun, Newbie, Graitney, and Corhead.

Archibald, younger son of the younger Gavin, gave up Greskin and Malinshaw to his Chief.

William, the eldest son of the younger Gavin, married, first, Katherine Douglas (1521), by dispensation from Pope Clement VII.; secondly, Katherine, daughter of Sir Alexander Kirkpatrick, in 1528. He was sent to the Castle of Edinburgh in 1533 for hindering the Warden of the Marches in arresting rebels. He was dead in 1536, when Katherine Kirkpatrick and her son, John Johnstoun, had a gift of the ward and marriage of John Johnstoun of Elsieshields, and the mails and duties of the lands of Chapelton and Esbie, held by the said John of the Crown, and also of the marriage of any other heir, male or female, of the late Johnstoun who died in Elsieshields. She was remarried to Jardine of Apilgirth. Probably Gavin Johnstoun of Kirkton was younger brother to William, whose second son seems to have been William Johnstoun of Reidhall.

Among those outlawed by Act of Parliament in 1548 for a surrender to the English were Gavin Johnstoun of Kirkton and Cuthbert Johnstoun of Lockerbie.

Gavin of Elsieshields and Kirkton was dead in 1555; his son was James of Kirkton. His nephew, John of Elsieshields, was given the escheat of the Laird of Johnstoun's goods when he was imprisoned in 1563, having been one of his curators three years before.

John Johnstoun of Elsieshields died Dec. 1574, and left a Will (Dec. 10), witnessed by James Johnstoun in Brumhill, Archibald Johnstoun in Kirk, William Johnstoun in Toddelmuir, and others. He owed £289, 16s. 8d., including rent, to Lord Maxwell, Lord Herries, and James Johnstoun, burgess of Dumfries. This was more than the value of his estate, but Herbert Jardine owed him £133, 1s. 2d., being a legacy from Katherine Kirkpatrick, his father's spouse. He desired to be buried in Lochmaben Kirk, and leaves his wife, Elizabeth McMath, and William, his eldest son, generally called Wilkin, his executors.

Among those respited in 1594 after the battle of Dryfe Sands were William, Adam, and James, brothers to William Johnstoun of Elsieshields, and about twenty more related to the same house. A resignation by Archibald Johnstoun, lawful son to Gavin Johnstoun of Elsieshields, in 1577 is signed by Sir Stephen Jardine, parson of Apilgarth, William Johnstoun of Foulderis, Sir Edward Johnstoun (a priest), and Adam Johnstoun of Moffat.

In 1554 Queen Mary charged all of the name of Johnstoun to assist their

Chief in arresting thieves; the order is repeated in 1560 by King Francis and Queen Mary to "the lesser families of Johnstoun and Graham"—for Elsieshields, Wamfray, and Corrie had been very deficient in that respect.

In 1580 Andrew Johnstoun was given the escheat of his own father, Andrew Johnstoun of Marjoribanks. In 1584 he received or bought "the escheat of all goods, movable and immovable, etc., which belonged to Sir Henry Loch, late Prebendary of St. Giles's Kirk, in Edinburgh, and Margaret Crauford, his spouse, now in England, also of all rents of the heritages, by reason of the said Sir Henry and his spouse passing to and abiding in England without permission of the King (Holyrood, Nov. 6)."

Seven years later one of the causes frequently brought against the Elsieshields and Powdene Johnstouns is recorded. Adam and Robert, brothers to Elsieshields, David Johnstoun in Reidhall, James and William Johnstoun in Hesilbrae, Nicolas Johnstoun in Elsieshields, and others of the same group, are sued for their "wrong spoliation of the complainer's horses, cattle, corn, goods, and gear." The whole clan has suffered in reputation from these lawless followers. If an assassin were wanted, he could be obtained at short notice, and while England and Scotland were disunited they were too useful in war to be effectually checked.

An act of revenge on the part of Johnstoun of Reidhall, a cadet of Elsieshields, for the death of his Chief, as well as of some of his near relatives, might have been one of the causes which induced the King, a few years later, to reduce the power of the clan, if his Majesty had not connived at it(?). The victim (Maxwell of Newlaw) is said to have been a zealous Protestant. The King, after his mother's execution, came to Dumfries in 1587 nominally to arrest Lord Maxwell, also to allay the agitation which Mary's death had caused in that quarter. The Proclamation he signed at Dumfries, April 4, describes the outrage. "Forasmuch as the late John Maxwell of Newlaw (ex-Provost of Dumfries), brother german to our dearest cousin and councillor, William, Lord Herries, being a gentleman answerable in all good qualities to his birth, but specially remarkable for the zeal and affection he always bore to our service, being specially employed by us, accompanied with the lieutenant and others of our guard, was on his way beset and most unmercifully murdered by Irving of Gretna Hill, Johnstoun of Reidhall, and others, their adherents and accomplices, thieves of detestable and most unworthy memory, without respect or reasonable pretext. . . . Our will is that ye pass to the market crosses of Dumfries, Lochmaben, etc., denouncing them by fire and sword."

Reidhall or his father had cost his securities, Elphinstone and Westraw, 2000 marks already by an escape from justice, and he got off again. The Elsieshields lands were thickly peopled, and not easily attacked in the heart of the Johnstoun territory, but an extract from the Privy Council Records shows that it was avenged. "In Feb. 1602 Lord Maxwell, with twenty followers armed with jacks, swords, steel bonnets, lance staves, hagbuts, pistolets, and other forbidden weapons, having conceived a deadly feud, rancour, and malice against the late William Johnstoun, brother to Wilkin Johnstoun of Elsieshields, for divers bloods standing unreconciled between the names of Maxwell and Johnstoun, went to the town of Dalfibble, in the Sheriffdom of Dumfries, and there cruelly slew the said William, at the same time setting fire to his dwellinghouse and biggings therein." Another account says he was with a Johnstoun of Hesilbrae in the house of James Johnstoun of Briggs, who was ninety years old, and perished in the flames. Maxwell was outlawed. William Maxwell of Kirkhous, whose brother was created Earl of Dirleton, assisted at it.

In 1608 there is a complaint by Sir Robert M'Clellan of Bomby that David, son of Willie of Reidhall, and another Johnstoun, his brother, and George Johnstoun, his brother's son, who for these twenty-four years past have been outlawed for the murder of John Maxwell, Provost of Dumfries, the complainer's (wife's) uncle, have been frequently received by Gilbert Brown in Land, nephew to the Johnstouns of Newbie and to the ex-Abbot of Sweetheart, but the defendant declared on oath that the complaint was not true, and was acquitted.

The next Laird of Elsieshields, another William or Wilkin, was Provost of Lochmaben in 1616, when he had four sons—James, who predeceased him, Archibald, William, and Adam. His brother, Robert, and Robert's son, John, were also living at that time. William or Wilkin was dead in 1626, and, as his eldest grandson died the next year, Archibald, his son, was returned his heir in 1630 to Elsieshields and to Howes (copyhold), in Newbie. The third brother, William, owned Templand, and was probably dead when another brother, Adam, obtained the Charter of it in 1636. Archibald carried on a suit against Lord Herries for several years in defence of his claim to his estate.

The Will of John Johnstoun of Elsieshields, grandson of Wilkin or William, was proved Jan. 11, 1688. He was Provost of Lochmaben and M.P. for the Dumfries Burghs (Chapter XIV.) (1665-82). His son, Alexander, was M.P. for the same (1693-1702). The younger Elsieshields married, first, Marion Grierson in 1684, by whom he had a daughter, Marion. His second wife, Janet Carruthers, was the mother of his two sons, and after his death in 1703 she married James Maxwell of Barncleuch. Gavin Johnstoun was served heir to his father in the lands of Elsieshields and Esbie, and of Newton in Kirkcudbright, and in 1707 he and his infant half-brother, James of Barncleuch were served heirs to his mother, Janet. Gavin's brother and heir, Alexander died childless in 1738, when the lands of Esbie went to James Maxwell, and Elsieshields to the heir of his half-sister, Marion, who had married Robert Edgar, a Writer in Dumfries. Their son, Theodore, who married Esther Pearson, was returned heir to his grandfather, Alexander, in 1738, and died in 1784. His sister's daughter, Marion, married John Dickson, of London, and their daughter, Marion, married William Byrne, also of London.

. Their grandson, Theodore Edgar Dickson Byrne of Elsieshields, a J.P. for Dumfriesshire and Kirkcudbright (1833-82), was a medical officer in the Navy during the Crimean War, and eldest son of John William Byrne of Elsieshields and of Eleanor MacAlpine, his wife, who died in 1876. Mr Byrne died in 1882, leaving by his wife, Ellen Eykyn, the present representative of this branch, Theodore Edgar Dickson Byrne, born 1879, and other children.

Archibald Johnstoun in Kirk, mentioned in the Will of 1574, had two sons, James and Cuthbert. The last came to Newbie when it was sold to the Laird of Johnstoun in 1606, and married Bessie Fareis, widow of John Johnstoun of Mylnfield. Their grandson, John M'Millan, was returned heir to Cuthbert in 1669. James and Joan M'Millan, with John, their son, held the lands that Cuthbert owned in Dryfesdale and the M'Millan lands in Galloway, in 1688. In 1701 these were sold to Robert Johnston, Dean of Dumfries, and Jean Cannon, his wife, from whom they came to the family of Elsieshields.

James Fareis of Dalfibble, a relative to Bessie, was a witness before the Privy Council about the Maxwell outrage in 1602.

More than a century earlier two of the junior branches of Elsieshields had become more important than its head. In 1587 Gavin of Kirkton, who had a Government post in Edinburgh, carried private letters from the wife of Sir John Johnstoun to be delivered personally to the King. His sister-in-law is stated, on no good authority, to have given the *coup de grace* to Lord Maxwell at Dryfe Sands, when lying wounded on the field he saw her looking for her husband, and asked her to assist him. This battle outlawed the whole clan, but her husband, James of Kirkton, and his father before him were in business in Edinburgh, and he only returned to Dumfriesshire to assist his Chief. Their son, Archibald, married Rachel Arnot, the daughter of the Lord Provost, Sir John Arnot, and must have been one of the richest men of his time. He paid £10,500 to the Laird of Johnstoun for a mortgage of Newbie Castle and estate, and appears to have bought the escheat of Westraw from Carmichael (Chapter IV.), as James Johnstoun of Westraw obtained his consent and that of his son, James, before finally parting with his hereditary lands. Archibald died in 1619, two years after his son, James, and, as his eldest grandson, Archibald, afterwards Lord Warrieston, was not of age, and the grandfather, Thomas Craig, was his tutor, a family suit about the division of a previous marriage settlement was not brought into Court till Feb. 16, 1627, when Craig was dead.

The case is thus recorded. Archibald, eldest son to the late James Johnstoun, merchant burgess of Edinburgh, Mr Samuel Johnstoun of Sheens, advocate, and Mr Joseph Johnstoun, his brother (Archibald's uncles and tutors), against Elspeth Craig, relict of the said late James, regarding a contract of marriage made between the late Mr Thomas Craig, advocate, Helen Arnot, his spouse, and the late Archibald Johnstoun, merchant burgess of Edinburgh, Rachel Arnot, his spouse, and the said late James Johnstoun, their son, and Elspeth Craig. A month later the same plaintiffs carry on the suit against Archibald's mother, Elspeth Craig, and his sisters, Rachel, Margaret, and Beatrix, and against Mr Robert Burnet (afterwards Lord Crimond), spouse to the said Rachel (parents to Gilbert Burnet, Bishop of Salisbury, author of *A History of our own Times*). In 1636 Elspeth Craig lent money to Francis, Earl of Bothwell. Her daughter, Beatrix, was the witness.

Besides belonging to the same branch of Elsieshields, the Johnstouns of Kellobank were nearly connected with those of Kirkton through the Craig family, as the mother of Archibald Johnstoun (of Warriston) was niece to Margaret Craig, James Johnstoun of Kellobank's wife. They came off the family of Elsieshields early in the sixteenth century. A Charter of the lands of Kellobank was granted by Michael, Lord Carlile, to James Johnstoun, burgess of Edinburgh, and another portion resigned to the same by Andrew Kirkpatrick in 1552. James was the son of William Johnstoun of Elsieshields and Reidhall, whose son, William of Reidhall, was living in 1569. A second Charter of these lands is made out to John Johnstoun, son of the said James, in 1573.[1]

The burgess of Edinburgh and owner of Kellobank, who married the sister of the King's physician, Dr John Craig, a member of a highly educated family, was as unlike his brother William as Jacob was to Esau. He died in 1572, when his effects were proved by his widow, Margaret Craig, Robert Johnstoun, his brother's son, also a burgess of Edinburgh, and Archibald Johnstoun to amount to £6800, including sums owed to him by the Earls of Huntly and Sutherland, James Johnstoun of Middlegill, Robert Scott of Thirlestane, the Abbot of Salsit, the Regent, James, Earl of Morton, William Johnstoun, Oliver Sinclair, James Douglas, the Laird of Balfour, Robert Craig, Adam Moffat, and others. He left Sir Thomas Craig, advocate, and John Arnot tutors to John, his eldest son; and in trust to his nephew, Robert, his share of the ship *Greyhound* for Robert's daughter, Margaret. Among the witnesses are Gilbert Prymrois, chirurgeon (brother to Archibald, the Earl of Rosebery's direct ancestor), and William Johnstoun, son and heir of the late William Johnstoun, burgess of Edinburgh.

In 1572 John Johnstoun of Kellobank and Symon Johnstoun were pledges for John Johnstoun, Abbot of Salsit, who was convicted of celebrating mass according to the Roman use.

In 1573 there is a complaint by John Johnstoun of Kellobank against John Urwen, callit the Duke's John, respecting lands in Trailtrow. He also bought Dunwoodie, and eventually Castlemilk from the Laird of Johnstoun, having, as his grandson wrote, "a plentiful fortune left him by his father, James Johnstoun, of the family of Elsieshield." He was an advocate, and married Barbara, daughter of Nicol d ard, Lord Provost of Edinburgh. The King made him lay Abbot of Salsit, and afterwards of Holywood, and at the time of his death, in 1613, he was Sheriff-Depute of Annandale. Of his four sons, the eldest, Thomas,[2] after losing the large property which he inherited, took service as a captain under Gustavus Adolphus in 1625. He appears in several deeds as late as 1620, when his brothers, Alexander and John, were securities for his tailor's bill in Edinburgh, and he was summoned that year as his father's heir

---

[1] William, Gudeman of Kellobank, produced the above Charters in 1619, when there was an enquiry into the titles of those who held land in Dumfriesshire. Forged writs as well as forged money were not unknown at that time.

[2] "My grandmother's brother," wrote Thomas's nephew, Nathaniel Johnston, "gave my oldest uncle such an education in France, &c., and encouraged him in such a prodigal way of living that be involved him in great debts" (M.S., Brit Mus.)

on account of a trust, but, as his stepfather, Edward Johnstoun of Ryehill, and other connections acted for him, he had probably left Scotland (Chapter XI).

The Johnstouns in Auchinskeoch (near Drumlanrig) were connected with the Elsieshields branch. They were feuars, and appear no more after 1622, when a Lyndsay, on the Dumfries Assize, is described as of Auchinskeoch. George Johnstoun, who was outlawed in 1513 for the slaughter of Ivon Corrie, is the first recorded.

William Johnstoun in Auchinstock, probably George's grandson, died in 1576. His Will was proved by his widow, Katherine Cuthbert, and his son, William, his only executors, the witnesses being Patrick Johnstoun in Auchinleck and James Johnstoun in Auchinstock, the Vicar of Kirkpatrick, and others. He left £414, 6s. 8d., and owed nearly as much to the Abbot and Convent of Paisley, to the Castle of Dumbarton, to the Minister of Kirkpatrick, Thomas Robertson, and Janet Atkins. Patrick Johnstoun in Auchinstock was among those respited after Dryfe Sands.

John Johnstoun, an advocate, brother to this William, purchased from the Crown the dues and lands belonging to the secularised Abbey of Salsit in 1595, and his Chief was ordered to put the new Abbot in possession of Garwald and Couran, which were given by their ancestor for the support of the religious house. The Commendator, as he was now called, paid the Laird 900 marks and £28 to maintain and defend him in these lands, which the Laird undertook to do, and he was legally established there, "when, on Nov. 8, 1595, the said Sir James directed, and sent out the following: his domestic servants, Symon his brother natural, Adam and James Johnstoun in Hesliebray, and William his son, James, son to David Johnstoun in Nether Garwald, William Johnstoun in Moling, and Ninian Johnstoun in Rowantrieknow, and others their accomplices, all being fugitives from the laws for cruel murders and depredations. They came to Conran and Garwald and violently ejected the said Commendator and Symon his brother forth thereof, and cast forth of the same, Cuthbert Johnstoun, their brother, being an impotent and decrepit person of 92 years or thereby, and Andrew Johnstoun, their brother's son; and intrenched themselves therein."

This appeal to the Privy Council gives a list of the stock which the Laird's friends had seized: Forty bolls of oats, and also fodder; seven cows, worth £20 each; forty ewes, worth 1s. each; two horses, £20 each; and the furniture and stores in the house. None of the defendants appeared, and Sir James was often called without effect, so a sentence of outlawry was passed against him, only a year after he had received a pardon for Dryfe Sands.

The Commendator died in 1599, when John Johnstoun of Kellobank and Castlemilk was appointed Abbot of Salsit. Nineteen years later John Johnstoun in Auchinstock—son to the late William, brother to the late Symon, brother to the late John Johnstoun, Commendator of Salsit, and apparent heir to the said Symon—and Robert Johnstoun of Raecleuch proceed against Captain James Johnstoun of Lochous to compel him to produce his title to the lands of Drumgrey, which the late Symon held in feu of Sir Alexander

Kirkpatrick. John, the plaintiff, produced the Kirkpatrick writ, and another, showing that he had sold his own rights to Robert Johnstoun of Raecleuch in 1608. The case went on for some time, judgment being given in favour of the appellants.

The new lay Abbot of Salsit retired in 1601 in favour of William Adair, having just received the more valuable endowment of Holywood, which Sir James Johnstoun had been obliged to resign. Holywood included a seat in Parliament.

The Lockerbie Johnstouns descend from William Johnstoun of Marjoribanks, the second son of the elder Gavin Johnstoun of Elsieshields. Cuthbert Johnstoun in Lockerbie appears in 1559, and was followed by Robert, Mungo, and his sons Francis, Symon, and William, the last a close friend and servitor of the Chief who was killed by Maxwell in 1608. In 1602 Andrew Johnstoun of Milnbank and John, his son, are accused of cattle-lifting from lands of Craufurd, in Lanark; and, rather later, Christopher Johnstoun of Milnbank joins with other tenants and feuars in resisting the new taxation imposed by James VI. Milnbank was a younger son's appanage in the same parish as Lockerbie, and had a strong tower, shown in Bleau's map, in 1660.

In 1678 Mungo Johnstoun is returned to Lockerbie as lawful heir to his father, Andrew. His brothers were Alexander, a notary in 1675, Robert of Roberthill, and George, a writer in Edinburgh (described as of Gumenbie, and son to Andrew Johnstoun of Lockerbie), who bought the estate of Knockhill, in Hoddam, from John Irving in 1655. George married Isabel Weir, and died in 1672, leaving a son, Andrew, two years old, who married Janet Corrie of Annan. His grandson, James, and his great-grandson, Andrew, fought on the side of the Jacobites in 1715 and 1745.

Mungo Johnstoun of Lockerbie's sons were Andrew, a Commissioner of Supply for Dumfriesshire in 1689, James, and Mungo, who married Lilias Johnstoun, and was in money difficulties in 1701. Andrew Johnstoun, younger of Milnbank, witnessed a sasine for the elder Mungo in 1681. He was probably the son who was owner of Lockerbie in 1688.

In 1716 there is a Charter of the lands of Dryfesdale in favour of James Johnstoun in Lockerbie, great-grandchild and apparent heir of the deceased Andrew Johnstoun in Milnbank. For his descendants, the Johnstone Douglases, see Chapter XIV.

In 1739 David Johnstoun is called portioner of Lockerbie. He had two sons, George and Robert.

James, the elder brother of Archibald Johnstoun, the merchant, succeeded his father in Beirholme and Middlegill. His son, Thomas, feuar of Beirholme in 1618, had a suit with Adam Johnstoun of Marjoribanks. Another son, Andrew, married the daughter of Christopher Irving.[1] Thomas's sons, Andrew and John, were living at Beirholme in 1621.

[1] Christopher was the son of John Irving of Bonshaw, died 1593, and of Mary, his wife, daughter of John Johnstoun of Newbie. He settled in Ireland, and founded the Irish branch of Irving.

William Johnstoun, the son of Archibald Johnstoun, and great-grandson of James of Beirholme, was a Commissioner of Supply in 1685 and Collector of the Customs in Dumfries in 1699.

A letter to Lord Annandale from Kennedy of Halleaths in 1702 reminds him that Archibald Johnston of Beirholme's second son is idle, "which is ill-breeding for a young man, and is not his choice. Your lordship posted his brother in Dumfries, and I hope he shall do very well in it." The writer suggests that there is a vacancy among the macers of the King's Guard at Edinburgh. "If your lordship would get that for Archie it would be a means of subsistence, and put him in a better capacity to be a servant to your lordship and your family."[1]

In 1723 William Johnston of Beirholm appears in a suit against Gavin Johnstoun of Elsieshields, and the next year, when he renews the suit, he is a citizen and innkeeper in London. In 1726 he was still in London, and a merchant, and in 1729 he is in Annan. He married Sara Douglas, and was dead in 1750, when a sasine is granted in favour of "Marie Johnston, wife of the Rev. John Nimmo, minister at Johnston, Grizel Johnston, relict of William Hamilton of Eldershaw, Charlotte Johnston, daughter of the deceased William Johnston of Beirholm, and Sara Douglas, only daughter of the deceased Janet Johnston, also daughter of the said deceased William Johnston, and Captain Alexander Douglas, husband of the said Sara Douglas, all as heirs of the said William, father of the said Mary, Grizel, and Charlotte Johnston, and grandfather of the said Sara Douglas, in the lands of Newton and Pashgillfoot." William had a brother, Archibald, living in 1723.

Robert Johnstoun of Gotterby, who acted as witness for the Laird in Edinburgh about 1624, was probably a member of a Mid-Annandale branch, and followed his Chief when he settled at Newbie. Johnston of Gotterbraes appears in 1625, and later as a baillie of Annan, and John Johnston of Gutterbraes was Provost in 1745. He married the daughter of Mr Howie, minister at Annan (1703-54), and their youngest son, Dr Bryce Johnston, was born there March 2, 1747. After studying at Edinburgh, he was licensed as a preacher Oct. 4, 1769, and ordained two years later as assistant to Mr Hamilton, minister of the Church at Holywood, whom he succeeded, and he remained there till he died, 1805. He supplied the article on Holywood Parish in Sinclair's *Statistical Account of Scotland* (1794), a volume of sermons, and one or two essays.

The local belief is that the name came from a Gutter running down the hill close to the house of this family in the town of Annan, but Gotterby is a well-known place in Dryfesdale. Mr John Johnstone of Beech Hill, Annan, and Dr Thomas Johnstone of Annandale, Harrogate, are the modern representatives.

Dr John Johnston of Sunnybrae, Bolton, is also an Annan man of Mid-Annandale descent. His grandparents, John Johnston and Elizabeth Beattie, came from Stobohill, in Corrie, and from Kirkpatrick to Annan, where they

[1] *Annandale Book.*

died, but they are buried in Dryfesdale Churchyard among their relatives. Dr Johnston's father, William, was born at Annan in 1824. William and his father composed the firm of Johnston, Builders, in Annan, and, acting up to the reputation of the Johnstoun clan, "that ever are true and stout,"[1] no structural deficiency or jerry building was ever found in their work. The Commercial Bank and some of the most important modern erections in the district were built by this firm, and when business was slack William sailed from Waterfoot to Liverpool to help in the completion of St. George's Hall. Before the railway, steamers carried the mails from Waterfoot to Liverpool.

William Johnston married Helen Roxburgh. Their youngest son, William Joseph, is a lawyer in Annan and Treasurer of the burgh; the elder, John, who graduated M.D. at Edinburgh with honours in 1877, late Hon. Surgeon to the Bolton Infirmary, was born at Carlyle's place, Annan, and has written an interesting memoir of his worthy parents. Besides contributions to the medical journals, he is the author of *The Wastage of Child Life, Musa Medica, Hospital Heroes, Doctors and Patients, Facts and Fallacies about Alcohol, In the Land of the Moor, A Spanish Bull Fight, A Visit to the Land of Burns*, and about eight or nine other books.

[1] *i.e.*, brave (*Lay of the Last Minstrel*).

CHAPTER VI.

JOHNSTOUNS OF POLDEAN — SMALLGILLS — CRAIGABURN — COUNT MAXIMILIAN VON JOHNSTOUN UND KROEGEBORN — NEWTON, ETC. — EMIGRATION — JOHNSTONS OF HAZLEBANK.

THE Johnstouns of Powdene, or Poldean, were an early branch who held their little estate in Wamfray from Jardine of Apilgirth. The first recorded, Herbert of Johnstoun of Powdene, was dead in 1496, when his widow, married to Jardine of Apilgirth, disputed with Symon Johnstoun of Powdene for the possession of the estate.

Symon, with the Laird of Johnstoun, Gavin Johnstoun of Esbie, and John Johnstoun of Wamfray, was a witness in 1514 to the retour of Lord Herries. In 1520 Symon of Powdene and David Johnstoun of Harthope formed a bond of manrent with Lord Maxwell. In 1514 Symon had a Charter of Poldean and Milkymoss from Jardine, and a year later he received the gift of the ward of a 5 mark land in Wamfray, a 10s. land in Poldean, a ½ mark in Grethead, and other small properties which belonged to Haliday of Brumehills, being, through his death, in the King's hands till the entry of the lawful heir, "for good and thankful service to the King and the Duke of Albany, his tutor."

On Jan. 28, 1532, Symon resigned the lands of Smallgills, in Moffat, to his son, Thomas, who is confirmed the same day in these lands, "for great and gratuitous service" against the English, by James V. Later on the same Thomas possessed Craigaburn. Symon was occupied less creditably, and was sued for it by James Johnstoun, burgess of Edinburgh, in oppressing the plaintiff's lands (*i.e.*, tenants) at Chapel Hill.

This James was Sheriff of Lanark and lay parson of Lochmaben, in which capacity he sued Gordon of Lochinvar and other Chiefs for debt. He was also Sheriff of Ayr. His son, William, was made Procurator for the Crown and one of the commissioners for trying heretics at Dumfries, Aug. 25, 1534, when the Reformers were entering Scotland from Holland and Germany. Sheriff James came off the Westerhall branch, but Chapelhill a little later belonged to Craigaburn.

Craigaburn was more important than Powdene, but Thomas got into difficulties, and was deprived of Smallgills "in default of goods distrainable." The King restored it by Charter in Oct. 1541 to Thomas's son, John of Craigaburn, who surrendered to the English in 1547 with sixty-four men, and was outlawed by Act of Parliament the next year.

Besides Thomas, Herbert, Gilbert, and James are mentioned in 1545 as sons of the deceased Symon Johnstoun of Poldean.

John, the son of Thomas, appears to have died before 1565, when a full pardon was proclaimed. He was probably elder brother to Thomas of Craigaburn, Herbert of Powdene, Gilbert of Corhead, and William—all brothers. In 1550 Thomas Johnstoun of Craigaburn was a witness to the bond of manrent between the Chief and his brother, James Johnstoun of Wamfray, and was also one of the delegates sent by his Chief to Edinburgh in 1576 to adjust their differences with the Maxwell clan.

In 1563 there is a contract between honourable persons, Herbert Johnstoun of Powdene and Gilbert Johnstoun of Corhead. They are not described as brothers, although two other documents prove this. John, son of the said Herbert, consents to the document and signs it. Herbert died in 1576. John married Katherine Carruthers, and had a son, Gilbert.

The eldest son of Thomas Johnstoun of Craigaburn, John Johnstoun of Smallgills, also called "in Corhead,"[1] was dead in 1577, when his brother, Symon, took over Smallgills. In 1581 Symon was killed by the Armstrongs, several of whom offered compensation to the Chief, and to the children of Symon, and to James Johnstoun in Chapelhill, his brother. They proposed to come "to the church of Moffat or other convenient place in our linen clothes, kneeling on our knees with our swords drawn in our hands, and shall deliver them to you by the hilts, in token of repentance for that wicked and unprovoked slaughter." This was an ordinary way of obtaining pardon for murder, and avoiding hereditary feuds.

Thomas of Craigaburn died in July 1581. He left many descendants, and appears to have been the third largest landholder among the Johnstouns. A Charter from George Douglas of Corhead entails upon Thomas, his son, John, and his heirs male whatsoever of the name of Johnstoun, reserving the liferent to Katherine Johnstoun, his wife, the town and lands of Moffat, Granton, Newton, and Corhead, except an acre of land called the Douglas Acre lying at the end of the town of Moffat, with buildings, mills, woods, and fishing, to be held of James, Earl of Morton, the superior. As Corhead was not held of the Crown it was not a lairdship, but the next heir to Craigaburn, young Thomas, called himself "of Corhead," so Monypenny places it among the Lairds of the name of Johnstoun in 1587.

Thomas of Craigaburn's two Wills are dated at Craigaburn in June 1580 and July 1581. He begs his sons to rally round his eldest grandson, Thomas, as the head of their branch of the clan, under the leadership of the Laird of Johnstoun. His son, Symon, being also dead, he left Dryfhead to Symon's son, James, half the lands of Smallgills to his widow, and the other half to his own son, James, in trust for Symon's son, John, James to enjoy the profits, but to keep the said bairn in meat and clothes till he was sixteen, if his

[1] He drowned himself, and Symon received his estate as an escheat.

mother cannot hold him (*i.e.*, support him), and to be his tutor till he was twenty-one. To the said James he left Chapelhill, to be held of Lord Herries; Gavelhill, in Wamfray, and Langhope, in Tweeddale, to his grandsons, John and James (the last to be held of Michael, Lord Fleming), and to his sons, Thomas, William, and Gilbert, to divide among themselves without cavil. Other lands he shares between his heirs and his wife, to whom he gives all his "moveable goods quick or dead, house and corn, horses, cows, etc., to sustain herself thereby . . . with the advice of her sons, James, Thomas, and Gilbert, making account of the same twice in the year, and the profits to be employed for the sustenance of his children and grandchildren in necessity, unless they prove wilful and ignorant, and will not use advice." He makes his Will with the consent of all the family, and *obliges* his children to live in the fear of God, and to serve the Laird of Johnstoun well and truly, "even if he be unkind to you." He leaves a charge of £40 a year to his widowed daughter-in-law, Marion Mure; and exhorts his descendants to send their corn to be ground at the mill at Moffat,[1] as Thomas, his "oy," is the leader of their branch under the Laird. To James, his second son, he left Glenquotto and lands on Tallow Water in Tweeddale. To his wife, his kindlie right to Glenhutton. His horses, cattle, sheep, grain, etc., are valued at £331, 11s. 8d.; the money owed to him £412, 4s. 10d., the creditors being Robert Johnstoun of Newton, for violent occupation of the lands of Newton, Robert and Thomas Moffat, the heirs of James Johnstoun of Middlegill, and of John Johnstoun of Langwodend; and he owed £351. The Will is complicated in its details, but the distribution to the minors, John, James, Frances, George, and John, was entirely left to his sons. No lawyer was employed, the dwellers on the lands were to serve their new masters; the patriarch's desire was a command, and it was all carried out as he wished.

The widow died on Nov. 1, 1582. Her sons, "James in Chapelhill, Thomas in Moffat, William there, and Gilbert in Corhead," were her executors. Her husband's debts were paid, and her sons were her only creditors except one merchant, but none of her husband's debtors had paid their accounts.

Symon Johnstoun, a son of one of the Johns mentioned in Craigaburn's Will, migrated to Poland, where there was a large colony of Scottish Romanists. He married Anna Becker, and his son, John, an author and naturalist, was born at Sambter, in Posen, in 1603.

John, Symon's son, was educated at Thorn, but in 1622 entered the University of St. Andrews, where he gained distinction in Hebrew and natural science. He returned to Poland in 1625, but four years later came to Cambridge to study botany and medicine, and continued it in London, where he wrote the chief part of his most important work, *Thaumatographia Naturalis*, an ambitious production in ten parts, illustrated with copper plates. This book was much esteemed in the seventeenth century, and translated from Latin into German, Dutch, and English. It is dedicated to four Polish noblemen, with two of whose sons he revisited England after he had graduated M.D. at Leyden, to

[1] This was a usual clause. It appears in the Laird's tacks.

receive the same degree at Cambridge. He eventually settled at Leyden, where he married, and had a large practice, but refused the Chair of Medicine at the University as well as a similar offer from the Elector of Brandenburg, and retired in 1665 to his private estate near Leignitz, in Silesia. He died there in June 1675, leaving one daughter, but his father's male descendants are represented by Count Maximilian von Johnstoun und Kroegeborn, Chamberlain to the Emperor of Germany, who printed two histories of his family, in 1891 and 1895.

Young Thomas Johnstoun of Craigaburn and Corhead received a gift of the 40s. land of Hennaland and all profits since the death of a Moffat of Knok in 1584; but a few years later Corhead was owned by James Johnstoun of Lochous, a near relative of the Chief, from whom it went to a natural son. Craigaburn also belonged to the Laird of Johnstoun in 1633, partly owing to escheat, as the family seem to have been active among the objectors to the tithes and other taxes introduced after the Union of the Crowns. There were several of this branch at the battle of Dryfe Sands.

Herbert Johnstoun of Powdene, brother to Thomas of Craigaburn, mortgaged part of his lands to Thomas, and on the death of their brother, Gilbert of Corhead, Gilbert the younger parted with his share of this estate to his cousins of Craigaburn. Ninian Johnstoun, Herbert's grandson, was in the Edinburgh Tolbooth with James Johnstoun of Westraw and others (for slaying Sir John Maxwell of Pook), when he was returned heir by Westraw, Robert Johnstoun of Corhead, Gavin Johnstoun, James Johnstoun of Brakinside, and several more of his fellow prisoners, to his grandfather's (Herbert of Powdene) lands in Peebles, which had been in the hands of the superior, Lord Hay of Yester, since 1573. Powdene and Westraw seem to have been for many years on very friendly terms. In 1621 Ninian Johnstoun of Poldean, Gawyne Johnstoun of Carterton, and James Johnstoun of Wylleis (later outlawed for slaughter) were witnesses to the written statement by the Laird of Johnstone and his curators, James Johnstoun of Westraw and Edward Johnstoun of Ryhill, concerning the ejection of Robert Johnstoun of Raecleuch from Newbie Tower.

In 1605 Ninian Johnstoun signed the Bond of Peace which Gilbert Johnstoun of Wamfray promoted among his kin, and in return received pardon for all former crimes. Ten other Johnstouns signed it—Ninian's brother (James of Milkymoss, also called of Smallgills and Wylleis), Gavin Johnstoun of Annanholme, John Johnstoun of Howgill, John, William, and Robert of Kirkhill, Thomas Johnstoun of Fingland, Cuthbert, Nicholas, and John.

In Murray's information of the *Feuars of Annandale* (1611-5) he ridicules the pretence of Powdene to be a Laird, as his land was held of Apilgirth, not of the King. He shows that Ninian Johnstoun married his cousin, one of two sisters, Janet and Helen, who were co-heiresses of four generations of a branch of Powdene.

A precept, signed at Edinburgh March 15, 1553, pardons four brothers—James, William, James, and David Johnstoun in Brumehill—and William and John Johnstoun in Rigfoot for "their treachery with the old enemies of Eng-

THE JOHNSTOUNS OF BRUMEHILL, ETC.

land, and for the murder of John Harknes of Reidhall and the burning of his house." In 1603 two Johnstouns of Brumehill were hanged for theft; so it is pleasant to find that their brother, David, in 1611, "lawful son to the late Gilbert, brother-german to the late Herbert, who was son and heir to the late Symon Johnstoun of Powdene," was making an honest living as a tailor in Edinburgh when he parted with Brumehill to Symon Johnstoun in Woodheid and Gavin Johnstoun, burgess of Edinburgh.[1] He left three, if not more, sons, William, David, and John, and three daughters, Helen, and Grizel and Bessie, who were twins.

Christopher Johnston, another of the Powdenes, was a sailmaker in Edinburgh in 1618, a trade followed by sailors on shore.

The Powdene group—Milkymoss, Newton, Annandholme, Hesilbank, Rowantriebrae, etc.—were the "old gang of Wamfray" whom the Government regarded as most troublesome in 1569, and only distant cousins to the descendants of James Johnstoun, who obtained a Charter of Wamfray in 1545. The Laird's domestic retainers seem to have been selected from among them, for they lived near Lochwood and were poor, so they were mixed up in every disturbance in which the Chief or his sons or uncles were engaged. In 1557 a pardon was granted to Gavin Johnstoun of Newton, son of Robert Johnstoun in Newton, and to Robert and John Johnstoun, brothers of the said Gavin, for assent, art, and part in the murder of Robert Moffat (not a fortnight before) during service in the Church of Moffat. It was before the Reformation, and the victim was possibly a church brawler, as the Edinburgh Court evidently thought there were extenuating circumstances.

In 1567 a pardon is granted to Robert and John, sons of the Laird of Johnstoun, to Gilbert Johnstoun of Poldean, and Graham and Carruthers for the murder of James Johnstoun of Middlegill and the mutilation of Gilbert Johnstoun in Howcleuch on his left and right arms. This was possibly done in a skirmish with the formidable two-handed sword used in Mid-Annandale.

Ambrose Johnston was returned heir to his grandfather, Ninian, in Poldean, as it was then called, and was living in 1650, when some of the soldiers of Charles II. were quartered in the house. It appears to have been haunted by a ghost, which, besides helping the family in many ways,[2] probably kept away any more of these hungry visitors. Ambrose had a brother, John, and two sons, Symon, who died *s.p.*, and Ambrose. Their father in 1644 was one of the War Committee, and signed the Covenant.

On March 30, 1724, Marie Johnston, lawful daughter of the late Robert Johnston, son of the deceased Ambrose, younger of Poldean, succeeded to the lands of Poldean and Milkymoss.

James Johnston of Milkymoss, Ninian's brother, left descendants, known as of Stenris Hill, by his first wife, and those of his second wife, Janet Porteous, were called of Granton. Ambrose Johnston, the representative of Stenris Hill, was a Colonel in the Guards about 1738. Of the younger family, James John-

[1] Son to James Johnstoun of Brackenside.
[2] Paterson's *Wamphray*.

ston of Granton, married to Betty, a daughter of John Johnston, merchant in Moffat, was living about 1739.

Either from John, the brother of Ambrose (1650), or from Habe or Herbert Johnstoun in Hesilbank, it may be assumed that the later Johnstons of Hazlebank descend. This Habe, who seems identical with a son of Herbert of Powdene (1576), and his three brothers, who would be Thomas, Symon, and Gilbert, were in 1585 ordered to find security for their good conduct. Thomas Johnstoun of Fingland was their pledge. Hazlebank and Poldean are very near, and owned by the same superior. Hazlebank was the appanage of younger sons.

The decrease of the population in Annandale during more than 150 years was partly caused by the enormous emigration to America. Ships, more or less ill-provided for carrying human beings, went direct from Waterfoot, at the mouth of the Annan, and among those who came to Maryland from Moffat was Christopher Johnston, the son of John, a merchant at Moffat, and his wife, Janet Swan, and the grandson of Christopher Johnston in Hazlebank, Wamfray, and of Elizabeth Corrie, his wife.[1] Mutual connections and a similarity in Christian names add to the probability that they came off the Poldean family.

The elder Christopher, born 1664, died 1724. The younger Christopher, born 1750, married Susanna, daughter of Griffin Stith, and died at Baltimore in 1819, leaving, with other issue, a son, Christopher, born 1800, who married Eliza, daughter of Captain Lemuel Gates, U.S.A., and died 1835. Their son, Christopher, M.D., Professor of Surgery in the University of Maryland, Baltimore, was born 1822, married Sarah Lucretia Clay Smith, of Washington, and died 1891, leaving, with other children, Christopher, born 1856, Professor of Oriental History and Archæology in John Hopkins' University, Baltimore, married to Madeline Tasker Tilghman, and has a son, Christopher, and two daughters.

Dr Johnston practised medicine, 1880-88, but early devoted much time to the study of ancient and modern languages. He wrote *Epistolary Literature of the Assyrians and Babylonians*, and has contributed many articles to technical journals, chiefly on Assyrian and Egyptology.

Christopher, the elder of Hazlebank, presumably had other sons besides John, of Moffat, and a Christopher Johnston, married to Elizabeth Campbell, had a daughter, Mary, born in Glasgow in 1718.

[1] For Corrie of Corrie and Newbie, see *ante, et seq.*

CHAPTER VII.

Various Johnstouns in the Fifteenth Century, and their Relationship to the Chief—Gretna or Graitney and Lochmabenstane—Early Marriages.

ADAM of Johnstoun, the Laird who assisted at the great battle of Lochmabenstane in 1448, was married to Lady Janet Dunbar. "She bare to him many sons," says the historian. She was probably his second wife, though not young, for her father was a Commissioner of the Peace with England in 1380; her eldest sister had been betrothed to David, the eldest son of Robert III., an engagement broken off by the influence of Douglas in 1402; her eldest son was killed in battle in 1424; and her grandson, Sir John Seton, was Ambassador Extraordinary to the Court of England in 1448.

Adam's sons were John, who married the daughter of Lord Maxwell, Warden of the Marches, Gilbert,[1] possibly the Gilbert de Johnstoun de Gretno who witnessed the young Lord Maxwell's retour in 1453, but known later as of Elphinstone, Herbert, Archibald, William, Patrick, James, most probably Matthew of Westraw. Thomas de Johnstoun de Breckonside has generally been omitted in a list of Adam of Johnstoun's family, but in a Murray Charter, dated 1438, he is called son and heir[2] of Johnstoun of that Ilk. Laurence de Johnstoun, brother of the said Thomas, is also mentioned as a witness. The other names in this Charter are Charles Murray, Laird of Ruthwell, William Jardine of Apilgarth, John Carruthers of Mouswald, Andrew of Gask, rector of Rampatrick (Dornock, Graitney and Kirkpatrick Fleming), Thomas Dyndum, rector of Annan, and Cuthbert Macbriar, rector of Hutton.

The Laird Adam died before 1455. His heir, John, had a second wife, Janet Hereis, mother of John of Wamfray, an estate bought from the Crichtons by his father. John's eldest son, James, died before him. David Johnstoun is called the son of John of Johnstoun in a Charter of 1476. The Laird owned Brotis, near Dunskellie or Cove, in 1460-4, as he paid the taxes for it during those years, and it was conferred on him by Crown Charter in 1465. That of 1476 is a sale of the 40s. land of Daubate by Haleday to David, son of John of Johnstoun of Brotis. As Laird of Brotis,

---
[1] His mother's family had owned Gretna Tower.
[2] Long after this, the term heir is used for all legal sons.

David was a Judge of the Assize at Edinburgh in 1511, with Adam Johnstoun de Newbie, Roger Carruthers of Wormanbie, the Laird of Castlemilk, and other local names, when a Jardine of Apilgirth was tried. The non-entres and lands of Brotis were bestowed by the Crown on the Chief in 1546, till another heir should appear, showing that David's direct heirs were extinct.

In 1476 Lord Carlile brought an action against John of Johnstoun of that Ilk for "occupying the lands of Overdryfe for the last nine years, since 'decessum' of his brother William of Johnstoun"; and Carlile claimed them. The case was brought before the Lords Auditors in Edinburgh, and John was ordered to give up the lands and pay 40 marks. Two years later another case before the Lords in Council was brought by William of Johnstoun, probably nephew to the preceding one, and five witnesses proved that the Sheriff, Robert Weir (Vere), had seized a herd of swine which belonged to him, on account of money owed by Lord Hamilton. William gained his case, and paid 15s. to the witnesses.

The Laird John must have been very old when he died in 1493. His daughter married Archibald Carruthers of Mouswald, and Marion Scott, the widow of another Archibald Carruthers, married his grandson, Adam of Johnstoun (1488-1509), as his second wife. The first seems to have been a Murray. John had made over his estate to his grandson, John, when his eldest son, James, died about 1484. The younger John only survived about four years, and then the estates of Johnstoun, Kirkpatrick Fleming and Cavartholme were transferred to Adam, already shown to have fought on the side of his sovereign at Lochmaben in 1484, and who now saw the chief authority in Dumfriesshire given over to his rival, Maxwell, a change practically felt by all his dependents. Johnstoun had a hard struggle to prevent his family being altogether pushed aside. Probably his father and uncle had been killed in the battles of 1484 and 1488, as their deaths took place in those years.

In 1498 there is an action against Adam of Johnstoun, Gavin Johnstoun of Elsieshields, Symon of Johnstoun, and John of Johnstoun for occupying Carlile's property in Pettinane. The two last may have been the Laird's near relatives, as, though not an invariable rule, "of" before Johnestoun usually describes a son, uncle, or brother of the Laird. The same Symon of Johnstoun is proceeded against by William Jardine and his wife, Elspeth Carruthers, for keeping back the rents of Powdene, which were owned by the said Elizabeth or Elspeth, spouse to the late Herbert of Johnstoun of Powdene, who left two daughters. Symon's heirs owned it, or claimed it for several generations.

Sir Symon Carruthers left only daughters, Margaret, Elspeth, and Janet, but a younger Symon Carruthers, the son of the late Archibald, apparently Laird Adam's stepson, took part with his stepfather, Murray of Cockpool, and others in one of these cases. In another action before the Lords in Council, 1498, the Crown sues Adam of Johnstoun of that Ilk, Thomas Dunwedy, Gavin Johnstoun of Elsieshields, Symon of Johnstoun and John of Johnstoun. The case is heard again in 1500, when John of Johnstoun, younger, showed that the said Adam of Johnstoun was pledge and security for them all.

THE JOHNSTOUNS OF THE FIFTEENTH CENTURY

This John, the younger, was probably Adam's grandson. The other who is mentioned in 1496 as John Johnstoun of that Ilk (the security that John, Lord Carlile, should not molest William Carlile, his heir) may have been brother or son to Laird Adam. Patrick Johnstoun of that Ilk, mentioned in 1542, appears to have been another of Adam's sons. Robert Johnstoun of Over Howcleuch, who had a dispute with a neighbour about some cows, a horse and some swine, July 13, 1492, is called in two documents the son of Adam of Johnstoun of that Ilk; in another "of the late Adam of Johnstoun of Pensak," Pensak or Pennersax having been owned by Kirkpatrick, who sold it to George of Corrie. A MS. pedigree, 149 years old, makes Adam of Pensak son to the Laird Adam (1413-54). These chiefs and their relatives, like the patriarchs of old, returned to their flocks and herds when the country was at peace.

Adam of Johnstoun was ordered by the Lords Auditors to deliver to Marion Liddell, widow of Sir Patrick Brown, a sack of wool, of 23 stone weight, owed to the late Sir Patrick by the late John of Johnstoun, his brother. The Laird's goods were to be distrained by force, as he was often called, but did not appear. No patriotic sacrifices in those days excused a man from paying family debts.

George de Johnstoun appears in 1463, in conjunction with William Douglas of Drumlanrig, Oswald Lokert, Robert de Crichton, John Sinclair, David Herries, apparent of Terregles, and Carmichael. Possibly this George is the same as George Johnstoun of Elphinstone.

Adam Johnstoun of that Ilk was pledge with Steuart of Castlemilk for James Johnstoun of Castlemilk, Thomas Johnstoun of Graitney, George Corrie of Corrie, and John Jardine of Apilgirth, 1493. In 1502 Thomas Johnstoun of Graitney is pledge for Humphrey Johnstoun, Murray of Cockpool, John Carruthers of Holmends, Robert Graham of Thornik, and John, the son of Laurence Johnstoun, while Laurence Johnstoun of Woodhous is pledge for his brother, John. The Woodhous estate returned to the Laird in 1544 owing to the failure of heirs.

In 1506-7 Carruthers of Holmends, who feued Wormanbie, near Annan, disputed the fines he was called upon to pay by the Warden for depredations by feuars for whom he was responsible on the Borders; and to save his property from being seized, Thomas Johnstoun of Graitney (Tower?) was ordered to pay £41 for William Irving, "flee by the sky"; and Gavin Irving was amerced for "certain other sums." His Majesty's Treasurer also proceeded against Lord Maxwell, Adam of Johnstoun, and Murray to pay various sums on behalf of certain depredators whom they were pledged to bring up for justice.

Among witnesses to Charters between 1493 and 1504 we find John Johnstoun in Hoddam, Fergus Johnstoun in Woodcoker, John Johnstoun of Hayhill, and Michael Johnstoun in Graitney. These names all refer to the lords of the soil or their relatives. The peasantry would not have witnessed Charters, and in other causes they were dealt with by the barons without the trouble of appearing before a court of justice.

48   THE JOHNSTOUNS OF GRETNA AND LOCHMABENSTANE

Adam of Johnstoun was dead in Oct. 1508, though his son, James, was not returned his heir till 1513. Reference is made at this time to the late Laird having been pledge for Irving of Bonshaw, a fief of Corrie, which shows that his ownership of the Corrie Barony was a fact.

The records are too much broken to know if the Laird Adam and his kin had a right from escheats conferred by the previous King to lands which they persistently claimed. The "good old rule, the simple plan" was very much in force, but it was the policy of the Crown to preserve the balance of power among the nobles, and the Johnstouns must have been much impoverished by their losses in battle. The chance of a rich prisoner's ransom was all the payment that even a chief received unless he got a grant of land, and it often had to be divided among several captors.

James VI. was asserted to have given money with his own hand to the Chief of a clan of thieves on the Borders to resist the power of the King's Warden, and the same kind of secret influence was exercised a century before. That Maxwell was growing too powerful for safety was shown a few years later, when he chased the Sheriff out of Dumfries. He already held one gateway into England through his allies, the Armstrongs. The other—Gretna —was safer in the hands of a small, brave clan, Maxwell's rivals, than with the Murrays who had followed their rebel Chief, and formed a bond of manrent with Maxwell.[1]

Gretna Green[2] is still called Lochmabenstane, its old name, in a document which Murray of Cockpool drew up in 1615 to show his ancient claim to it and to criticise the alleged rights of most of his neighbours. Murray stated that it only came lately to the Johnstouns, since the death of the Earl of Dunbar. He gives the names of the generations who had owned Graitney—John, then living; George, his father; William, his grandfather; and another whose Christian name is a blank, but whom an uncertified document of 1542 calls William. There were many scions of the family named William. Besides those already mentioned, one is alluded to in a Charter by John Halliday, who mortgaged some land in Hoddam to John Carruthers of Mouswald, May 31, 1439, for £10, lent him in his great "myster"—*i.e.*, need—"it was some time Will of Johnstoune's." Another William was son of the Laird Adam (1488-1509). In a lease by John Lindsay of Covington he is described as brother to James Johnstoun of that Ilk[3] (1509-24), who had himself a son named William, probably the same who was ordered to qualify himself for the office of sheriff-depute in 1523. The age of this last William may be approximated by the

---

[1] Aug. 27, 1487, the Murrays signed a bond of manrent with Maxwell, witnessed by Adam of Johnstoun and Herbert of Johnstoun.

[2] "From an ancient inscription in the Churchyard of Graitney it appears that a near relation of Wallace is buried there, and the ashes of many of the Johnstones of Annandale are said to repose within the precincts of the ancient church. At Redkirk Point once stood the Church of Redpatrick (or Rampatrick); not a vestige now remains."—*New Statistical Account of Scotland*, 1845.

[3] The Laird made several arrangements with John Lindsay of Covington, who leased to him for nineteen years the land of Polmoody, in Moffat. The Murrays of Cockpool held a mortgage on Polmoody.

EARLY MARRIAGES

brother who came next above him being married to a Corrie in 1516, and in receipt of a pension from the Crown for his services in 1531.[1]

The eldest brother is presumably the John of Johnestoun, younger, mentioned in 1500, and who was fined 100 marks for shielding Carruthers when he attacked Newbie in 1508, and obtained a safe conduct to England the next year in company with Lord Maxwell. Life began early and lasted long in Dumfriesshire, when not ended accidentally. Boys and girls married at eleven, twelve, and thirteen. Robert Johnstoun of Raecleuch was eleven when he fought at the battle of Dryfe Sands, and was respited twelve months later, in 1594. He was six when he acted as a witness in a document concerning his Chief in 1588. There are other instances of these very young witnesses at a time when only lairds and their sons, the clergy, physicians, and notaries, were expected to be able to write.

Thomas John*son* in 1404 married Margaret Douglas, who received from her sister, the Countess of Mar, a grant of the Mains of Bonjedward. Thomas and Margaret were probably ancestors of the Douglases of Bonjedward.

[1] William Johnstoun in 1509 is among the signatories to a Charter for Edward Maxwell at Tynwald, and his mother, Margaret Douglas, wife of the late John Carlile. Another of that name, on Feb. 15, 1513, witnesses a Charter confirming lands to the Edinburgh churches "dedicated to S. John the Baptist and S. John the Evangelist by John Craufurd, Prebendary of the Collegiate Church of the Blessed Giles."

CHAPTER VIII.

MAXWELL ATTACKS THE CRICHTONS—JOHNSTOUN IS PLEDGE FOR THE YOUNG LAIRD OF GRAITNEY AND OTHERS—WAR WITH ENGLAND—JOHNSTOUN'S SETTLEMENT—THE BATTLE OF SOLWAY MOSS—DEATH OF JAMES V.—CAPTURE OF ANNAN AND CONQUEST OF DUMFRIESSHIRE—THE INFANT QUEEN—PEACE—THE GRAHAMS.

AS the kings of Scotland had to depend on the loyalty of the Dumfriesshire chiefs to repel invasions and control robbers, whose depredations might lead to difficulties with England, they naturally took the side of the strongest in disputes between the clans, and probably their information was generally one-sided. In the time of Bruce, who, as Lord of Annandale, had seen the difficulties of the situation, the district between the Esk, Sark, and Leven, 8 miles long and 4 wide, called the Debateable Land, was set apart as a refuge for outlaws. In course of time whole clans crowded on it, with nothing to keep them but fish, game, and robbery. For Scotland it was an unfortunate arrangement, as these refugees could be easily bought, and England was more able to buy them. They furnished the necessary spies, and brought over their relatives farther inland to the English cause. The Maxwells were born courtiers and diplomatists, and by these qualities more than by arms gradually took the leading part in Annandale as well as Nithsdale, where their East Border ancestor had obtained Carlaverock by marrying the heiress of Galloway. They supplanted the Crichtons in Nithsdale, making use of some of the more simple Johnstouns to effect it. Then they turned round on the Johnstouns and undermined their influence in Annandale, and in the quality of Sheriff or Steward of that district outlawed the Johnstoun chiefs for protecting their own men.

In 1509 Lord Crichton of Sanquhar, the Sheriff of Nithsdale, held a Court at Dumfries. He brought a large number of followers, who were posted on the lower sandbeds outside the town, when they were attacked by Lord Maxwell—who held the office of Warden of the Marches, Baillie of New Abbey and Holywood, and Sheriff of Annandale—and by Sir William Douglas of Drumlanrig, coming along the Annan road. The Crichtons were put to flight, and Robert Crichton of Kirkpatrick, the Lairds of Dalziel and Cranchlay, and many others were killed. It was not till Sept. 1512 that Douglas, with his ally, Fergusson of Craigdarroch, was tried at Edinburgh in presence of the King and an assize of twenty-five barons. They were acquitted on the ground that Robert Crichton was an outlaw.

Four barons were enough, in April 1513, to sit on those for whom the Deputy-Warden, the Laird of Johnstoun, was made responsible—George Johnstoun of Auchinsbork for the slaughter of Ivon Corrie; William Johnstoun of Fouleduris for slaughter; Robert Graham, John Carmichael (the son of Laird Carmichael), John Vere, John Lockhart, and Robert Bertoon for the slaughter of William, Laird of Dalziell. Of these, the two first and the last were put to the horn and their goods escheated. The same sentence was inflicted on Thomas Johnstoun de Gretna, with £100 fine for his non-appearance; William Johnstoun, the young Laird of Gretna, was accused of underlying the law, and 100 marks penalty for his non-appearance. David Johnstoun, brother of John Johnstoun in Bartycupen (near Lochwood), was put to the horn, and cost his Chief 100 marks for his non-appearance, as did Adam Scott of Tuschelaw, who was also put to the horn and his goods escheated. James Johnstoun of Skare had the same penalty. Johnstoun himself had not received back his estates since their sequestration, but they were restored immediately afterwards.[1]

John Johnstoun of Wamfray was fined £40 for himself, and Douglas and Maxwell were ordered to make compensation to Lord Crichton.[2] To support the junior members of his own family and of his own clan was the duty of a chieftain, but on this occasion Johnstoun, who was a peacemaker in other matters, agreed to pay half of Maxwell's costs. There was a marriage connection between the two, for either the Laird or his eldest son, John, had married Maxwell's daughter. The older Maxwell histories say it was John.

The judgment was given just before the battle of Flodden, and Maxwell,[3] who was going to join the King with all the forces he could muster, had neither time nor money to spare. He with four of his brothers shared their Sovereign's fate, and was left dead on the field, besides an Irving of Bonshaw, Lord Herries of Terregles with his brother Andrew, Gilbert Johnstoun of Elphinstone, and many other Dumfriesshire gentlemen.

The English Warden, Lord Dacre, followed up the victory by an inroad into Scotland through Eskdale. Writing in Oct. 1513, he describes the great devastation he had made, "continually burning from break of day till one in the afternoon, and bringing away 400 head of cattle, 300 sheep, some horses, and much furnishing."

[1] Pitcairn gives an abstract of this trial, pointing out the mistake that either the Justiciary Record or the old Peerages make in Dalziel's Christian name. "This entry," he says, "is very obscurely expressed. It does not appear from it which of these parties were struck and which of them slain, or whether they were all struck and slain."
[2] In the Lord High Treasurer's accounts for Aug. 1508 there is payment to a messenger for summoning the Lord Maxwell and the Laird of Johnstoun to ward (prison). In April 1513 there is the same for summoning Lord Maxwell and the Laird of Johnstoun to ward. In the MS. account of the Herries family it is stated that Maxwell was imprisoned for this fray, "and paid a great composition for himself and all those who were with him."
[3] John, Lord Maxwell, was in possession of his father's estate Feb. 14, 1477. He married Agnes, daughter of Sir Alexander Stewart of Garlies, who was Laird in 1477 and dead in 1501, when his son, Alexander, succeeded him. Robert Maxwell succeeded his father in 1513 and died 1546.

The Scots retaliated, and, to show it was not from too great leniency on his part, Dacre writes on May 17, 1514: "For one cattle taken by the Scots we have taken 100, and for one sheep certainly 200. I assure your lordships I have caused to be burnt and destroyed six times more towns and houses within the West and middle Marches of Scotland, in the same season, than is done to us, all waste now, no corn sown upon none of the said grounds. . . . Upon the West Marches I have burnt and destroyed the townships of Annan [with thirty-three others described], and destroyed 400 ploughs and above; no man dwelling in them to this day save only in the towers of Annan, Steppel [Stapleton], and Wauchope."

The English Warden had deprived the Scots of the means of living, so they made raids into England to recover their live property and to rob farms.[1] The late King's cousin, the Duke of Albany, was Regent for the infant James V., and Dacre was not at all pleased with the little trouble he took after peace was made to restrain his subjects, the Queen, sister to Henry VIII., during the short time she acted as Regent, "being more diligent in the matter."

The young Laird of Gretna, assisted by two of the Irvings and Peter Graham, made a raid, in which an Englishman and three traitor Scots were killed. Again, on Nov. 12, 1515, Dacre writes that "The Warden of the Scottish Borders, with Lord Carlile, Sir John Murray of Cockpool, the Laird of Johnstoun, Symon Carruthers of Mouswald, Sir Alexander Jardine (Comptroller of the Duke of Albany's house), Carruthers of Holmains, Charteris of Amisfield, William Johnstoun of Gretna, Dunwiddie, the Lairds of Knok, Castlemilk, Kirkconnel, Tynewald, and others, came to Solam Chapel in England," where the said Warden "sent forth in a scrymmage the Laird of Johnstoun, Captain of Lochmaben, and others to the number of 400 horsemen and more. They came to Arthuret (on the Esk), burnt a grange and a whole village to the number of 16 houses."

Returning to Scotland, the Warden sent forth "in another scrymmage Sir John Murray, Jardine, Charteris, Tynewald, the Provost of Dumfries, and others, in all 700 horsemen," who robbed Bowness and burnt eighteen houses, with much corn and hay, and, after assaulting the tower for half an hour, returned.

In the Lord High Treasurer's accounts in 1516 there is payment to a

---

[1] The reader of the old story, that a Borderer's wife put nothing but spurs under a dish-cover at breakfast as a hint to her sons that the larder was empty, does not always realise that wild deer and other game were plentiful among the hills round Annandale, and that salmon were speared from horseback, a process of catching them described by several travellers in the eighteenth century. It need not have meant that they were to steal their food from England; yet when the laws of Scotland allowed "spulzie" from a neighbour as justifiable if the neighbour was in debt to the spoiler, it would have taken many more raids into England than are recorded to repay the Borderers for the cruel and unprovoked wasting of their lands by English armies in the fifteenth and sixteenth centuries, and the constant robberies committed by Armstrongs, Trumbles, and others protected by England. The fasts enforced by law for economic reasons as late as 1649, during Lent and at other seasons, made a close time for game. Buchanan's surprise at the fasts not being kept in Spain shows that he was accustomed to see them observed.

messenger who carries seven letters from the Regent to the Lairds of Johnstoun, Mouswald, Newbie, Holmains, and Cockpool.

In 1523 the Laird of Johnstoun was "ordained keeper of the West Borders." He died the next year. Lord Maxwell succeeded him, and entered into an arrangement with the new English Warden to pacify the Debateable Land, which was chiefly occupied by the Armstrongs.

The Earl of Northumberland, writing to the King's Treasurer in 1582, estimated the Armstrongs with their adherents to be capable of mustering 3000 horsemen.[1] A Cumberland MS. of the sixteenth century says they were tolerated by England because at any time they could produce 300 or 400 men to oppose the Scots.

Just before the above agreement was signed, the Earl of Angus ravaged the Armstrong territory as if it had been an enemy's, burnt many houses, and drove off 600 cattle, 3000 sheep, 500 goats, and many horses. The Armstrongs retaliated on the English border. But Maxwell saw that they might help him to reduce the influence of the Johnstouns and drive them out of Newbie. He formed a bond of manrent with their Chief, the celebrated Johnnie, and feued to him the lands of Stablegorton and Langholm, for the Johnstoun family claimed and owned Glendining and Arkilton in that neighbourhood.

John Johnstoun[2] succeeded his father as laird in 1524. The Keltic blood inherited from Scotts, Maxwells, Carruthers, Carliles, and other maternal ancestors predominated over any other in his composition, and many years of his life were passed in prison, or "at the horn" (as an outlaw), besides sharing in any dispute which happened to be taking place. He had already appeared before a court for molesting the Corries in Newbie, and enlarged his mind by a visit to England with Lord Maxwell, who was killed at Flodden.

There is no doubt that he supported William Johnstoun of Graitney in his occupation of Newbie in 1524, the year that Laird James, having been Warden for a year, died, and while Thomas Corrie was "at the horn." The Barony of Corrie after long delay had been conferred by Crown Charter on Laird James in 1516, and the same year his second son, Adam, married the heiress of Sir Thomas de Corrie. This settled the question of the part of the Barony called Corrie, and Adam Johnstoun inherited it without opposition on the death of his father. No deed exists to show how Arkilton and Cavertholme came to William of Graitney. The last is included in Laird James's retour and in the retours of his ancestors, but appears in the possessions of William in 1536, and his descendant owned it till 1618.

[1] Ten times more than the estimate of the Johnstone Clan in 1583.
[2] Sir W. Fraser, with no authority but the special pleading of Mr Fleming, Q.C., says that John was born in 1507. Mr Fleming interpreted the ward of his estate to refer to minority, whereas the term was used at that time when the Crown had outlawed a laird and sequestered the rents, and it suited Mr Fleming's case to make him as young as possible. The evidence is against this date. Why are his tutors or his "tutory" not mentioned, and who else was the John of Johnstoun who went to England with Lord Maxwell, and for whom Adam of Johnstoun stood security? Sir W. Fraser once stated that his younger brother, Adam, was married in 1516, and the Crown gave this Adam a "pension" in 1531. John's daughter was married in 1531.

Since the Royal Proclamation charging George de Corrie with treachery and rebellion in 1484 and depriving him of his estates, Newbie, the southern half of his Barony, had been persistently attacked by the Johnstouns and Corrie's neighbours. Its strong tower, its excellent fishings, mills, and pasturage, added to the Tower of Stapleton, and its seaport, with its command of the mouth of the Annan, made it a special prize. First the Murrays attacked it; then John Lindsay of Wauchope, who also acted as security for Thomas Rae, who destroyed the mill, house, and property in Newbie in 1488. Lindsay on the first occasion was ordered to pay a grey horse to William of Corrie, six cows to James Corrie, and £100 to Thomas Corrie, but it was not till 1530 that he was called upon to pay £140 and 16 marks to Corrie on Rae's behalf. In 1494 Symon Carruthers, Johnstoun's stepson, attacked Newbie. Then a Johnstoun appears in the Tower of Stapleton, in the Newbie Barony, and, as Adam of Johnstoun is made responsible for him as well as for William Johnstoun of Graitney, he must have been his "depender." Then a Carruthers of Wormanbie attacks Newbie, in company with Andrew Johnstoun and some Armstrongs, and kills a labourer and a tenant, and for this Carruthers is condemned to be hanged, but as his friends and neighbours were his judges they possibly let him escape.

In 1511 Adam Johnstoun de Newbie is on the Assize,[1] in company with David Johnstoun de Brotis, Roger Carruthers of Wormanbie, John Herries, and others. Whether this Adam Johnstoun de Newbie was the same who became Adam de Corrie when he afterwards married the heiress, or some other relative, it shows that Newbie was recognised as a Johnstoun possession twelve years before William of Graitney made it his own.

It has been shown that the acquisition of Newbie and Corrie by the Johnstouns influenced Maxwell in his patronage of the Armstrongs. They bordered on both halves of the Barony, and could feed their hungry families with Johnstoun's corn and cattle without invading England; and could effectually weaken Johnstoun by keeping his followers always on the defence. Maxwell was half-hearted in his allegiance to his own King, who was not the character to command a strong man's respect, and he was accredited with the intention to make the office of Warden, a lucrative as well as influential post, hereditary in his own family.

The King desired peace with his uncle, Henry VIII., and the Armstrongs disturbed it. Apparently by his wish, if not by his direct command, Johnstoun chased them as far as Carlisle, just after they had burned Netherby in revenge for Lord Dacre having pursued them into the Debateable Land. Johnstoun's action was represented by his enemies as a raid on English territory. The King in Parliament declared himself to be entirely ignorant of it, and Maxwell

---

[1] Buchanan (1572) explains how these courts were constituted. A man of position and good repute was placed at the head as convener, and the judges (jury) consisted of twelve or more, if the services of so many men of the same class as the accused could be obtained. A little later the plaintiff chose a friend or man of good repute to be his pleader (actornate), and another might act as baillie (also a pleader) for the defendant, all being amateurs, not professionals.

in his official capacity proceeded against Johnstoun and his colleagues, John, Andrew, and Roland Bell, and William and Matthew Johnstoun, accusing them of "the cruel murder of Symon (nicknamed Mickle) Armstrong" (the incendiary). James Douglas of Drumlanrig was their cautioner, and as they failed to appear they were all denounced rebels, so, for the second time in twenty-seven years, Johnstoun's estates were sequestrated, while his rival triumphed.

As William Johnstoun was engaged with his Chief against the Armstrongs, the opportunity was taken to respite Thomas Corrie, who had been an outlaw for four years, and enable him to proceed against the present owner of Newbie. An interim decreet, dated March 1527, is "anent the summons made at the instance of Kelwood, against William Johnstoun of Greitknow, for the wrong and violent, and masterful occupation, labouring and manuring (*i.e.*, settling labourers on the land) by himself, his servants and his accomplices, &c., without licence of the said Thomas Corrie, of the two parts of all and whole his lands and lordship of Newbie." William was summoned, but did not appear, being engaged in defending his country. It was decreed that he should cease from his occupation of Newbie, and repay Corrie for the fishing, the use of the mill, and profits of timber, etc. An unfortunate moment for a dispute over a Border tower, when the English were threatening war on account of the moss troopers of Liddesdale, Corrie's allies.

Lord Dacre wrote to Cardinal Wolsey in 1528 that "the Debateable Land is now clear waste owing to the Johnstoun and Maxwell feuds." On April 2, 1529, "the Lord Maxwell caused the Armstrongs to make a raid upon the Lord of Johnstoun, his own sister's son, who is at deadly feud with them for the killing of Mickle Armstrong, where they killed three of his friends, and the Lord Maxwell himself lay in ambush purposely to have killed the said Lord of Johnstoun if he had pursued them."

The same year Johnstoun and Edward Maxwell took the head of a thief to Edinburgh, and received £100 from the King.

Wharton succeeded Dacre as Warden of the Borders, and wrote to Henry VIII. in 1542 that "Lochinvar (Gordon) and the Johnstouns are the greatest enemies Maxwell had," owing to their wish to supplant him in the offices he held on the East and West Borders—one in Annandale, the other in Galloway.

Perhaps the young King James became a little alarmed at the English attitude, for he summoned Bothwell of Liddesdale, Maxwell, Johnstoun, Home, who called himself Earl of Dunbar, and Walter Scott of Buccleuch to Edinburgh, and imprisoned them in the Castle; while he marched with 8000 men to the Borders, and summoned the chiefs to meet him on the Solway. He hanged Johnnie Armstrong with thirty-one well-horsed followers, caused Sandie Scott, "a prowd thief," to be burnt alive for burning a widow's house with some of her children, and, in short, asserted the Royal supremacy.[1]

[1] Johnstoun was pardoned in 1529 for (being in ward) not meeting the King on the Solway.

In 1536 the King went to look for a bride in France. He took Maxwell with him, but Johnstoun was imprisoned in the Castle of Doune, in Galloway, during his absence, and his lands sequestrated. At once an English raid crossed the frontier and attacked Lochmaben. William Johnstoun of Elsieshields appealed for help to Ninian Crichton of Sanquhar, who had been Johnstoun's ally in a tribal quarrel, but was told that it had never been Sanquhar's duty to protect the Border. This forced the King to release Johnstoun, whose brother, Adam of Corrie, acted as his pledge. At the same time he formed a bond of manrent with Maxwell, in whose domains he was imprisoned, as a condition of his release.

Henry VIII. was incensed by his nephew's refusal to marry the Princess Mary, and James declined to meet his uncle in York to discuss it. The English seized twenty-eight Scottish ships, and enlisted the services of the Earl of Angus, once Regent (James's stepfather), and of his brother, Sir George Douglas, who were both in exile.

The Border was crossed on the East and West Marches, and William of Graitney and Newbie was made a "hereditary baron for good, faithful, and gratuitous service," and his Barony entailed on heirs male, or, in default of heirs male, on heirs bearing the name and arms of Johnstoun, Jan. 2, 1542. On the East Marches the Earls of Huntley and Home defeated the English, and took the commander, Sir Robert Bowes, prisoner at Haddon Rig.

James vainly applied to Henry VIII. for an indemnity for these forays, and went to Dumfries to inspect the Border liegemen, who were mustering to defend their King. By possessing Newbie and Graitney the Johnstouns commanded the services of the brave Irvings, Romes, and Bells, some of whom, it is stated in a legal process of 1611, lived in the Barony of Newbie without paying any dues for their military service. Irving of Drum was a laird, and unofficially the Irvings of Bonshaw[1] and Robgill were often so called. In legal writs they are gudemen or copyholders.[1] But it entailed on Newbie the responsibility for their misdeeds, and the fines that were imposed on him for Irving and Graham lawlessness obliged his family eventually to part with the estate.

When Sir Thomas Wharton, the English Warden, heard that James V. was in Dumfries, he proposed to Henry VIII. that, as the King had but a small escort, he might be seized and brought across the Border—just as, 260 years later, the Spanish Princes were brought across the Pyrenees by Napoleon. Henry was much pleased with the idea, but when he submitted it to his Council they advised that Wharton should "let no creature know that it had ever been thought of, on account of the scandal and deadly feud which it might cause." They also pointed out the thick population between Dumfries and the

---

[1] See *Monypeny's Chronicle*. "Callit the Laird" is a term used in legal documents; "Dukes" of Hoddam seems to have been a nickname. Robgill was feued to an Irving by Thomas Corrie of Newbie, and was included in the Newbie estate when William of Graitney bought it; but his Chief claimed it later as a fief of Lochwood. The tack of Sarkbrig and Conheath, as well as Stapleton, given by William Johnstoun of Graitney to Irvings, is often alluded to in the family papers, and were copyhold.

THE BATTLE OF SOLWAY MOSS

English Border, which would require so large a force to oppose, when retreating with the captive, that it would be almost impossible for that force to reach Dumfries unobserved, or to bring away the King alive.

It is noticeable that William Johnstoun of Graitney was ennobled before his Chief, and it must have been one of the last honours that James V. conferred.

A year later the Laird of Johnstoun was released from prison at Dumbarton, and his estates restored to him by the Regent Arran, acting for the infant Queen, and they were erected into a barony in the same terms that were used in the patent of William of Newbie. His eldest son was at that moment a prisoner of war in England, and Lord Maxwell, also a prisoner, was intriguing to place Dumfriesshire, if not all Scotland, under Henry VIII., but the brave Chieftain found time only a month or two after his release to make an elaborate settlement of his lands. In case his direct male heirs were extinguished, he settled his estate first on his brother, Adam of Corrie, and his male heirs, then on his brother, William, and his male heirs, and in the usual order on the younger brothers, Symon and John, and their male heirs. Another brother, James of Wamfray, is not mentioned—they were not on good terms; but in 1550 Wamfray formed a bond of manrent with the Laird, who is described in it as his brother-german. Johnstoun had long been a free baron, with the power of life and death over his dependents, but this was the first hereditary honour bestowed on the direct ancestor of the Marquises of Annandale. At the same time he was made Warden, his rivals in that office having been captured at the unfortunate battle of Solway Moss.

The circumstances of this battle were extraordinary. James V. wished to lead his army after the victory of Haddon Rig to attack the Duke of Norfolk, who was advancing on the English side of the Border with reinforcements, and who, as Earl of Surrey, had defeated James IV. at Flodden. But the Border Chiefs, who were responsible for their followers and had to support the widows and children, were at the end of their resources. A famine was imminent unless some returned home to get in the harvest;[1] and by crossing the East Border into England they would leave Dumfriesshire open to a raid from the Cumberland "statesmen." The King was enraged at this opposition, but apparently consented to Lord Maxwell's offer to lead the Border clans direct on to Carlisle—Maxwell for personal reasons again obtaining Johnstoun's arrest.

The Borderers were crossing the Esk and Solway Moss when they encountered a body of Englishmen. Oliver Sinclair, a gentleman of the King's household, at once exhibited a Royal Commission appointing himself Commander-in-Chief over the Warden and everyone else. He mounted on the shoulders of two stalwart horsemen, so that all might see it, and, according to Holinshed (1577), the Earls and Lords there present "thought themselves too much debased to have such a mean gentleman advanced in authority above them, and refusing to fight under him, willingly suffered themselves to be over-

---

[1] In Patten's *History of the Rebellion in 1715* he speaks of the Highland custom of returning home after a battle.

come, so were taken by the English without slaughter of anyone person on either side."[1] Sir Thomas Wharton's report says that twenty Scots were slain and some drowned, with about 1000 taken prisoners, of whom nearly 200 were gentlemen. He thought there were not ten English even missing.

The objection to serve under a man of lower rank, which wrecked the cause of Wallace, was again fatal to Scotland. Perhaps Maxwell, discontented with the King's caprice, still resented the execution of his ally, Johnnie Armstrong, and had resolved to act like one of his ancestors, and exchange his Sovereign. He may have seen that, sooner or later, southern Scotland would be joined to England, and that such a ruler as James, matched against the astute English King and Cabinet, was likely unknowingly to bring it about.[2] He was also in favour of the Reformation, which was dividing Scotland, as it was dividing England, and was already a factor in her policy. Oliver Sinclair had been James's chief adviser in opposing it.

James's death followed less than three weeks after this battle, and the infant daughter born to him in the interval was the sole remaining heir of his house. Another Regency, under the Earl of Arran, was necessary, when Scotland had hardly recovered from the last. The traitors Angus and Douglas were at once recalled, and Maxwell's first act on being released on parole was to give his daughter in marriage to Angus, with a handsome dowry, although this son-in-law had so lately assisted the English against the Scots, and was the divorced husband of Queen Margaret Tudor, the late King James's mother.

Before Maxwell was released on parole he subscribed a bond, with many of his fellow captives, to acknowledge Henry VIII. as Lord Superior of the Kingdom of Scotland. They swore on their knightly honour to do their utmost to put the Scottish strongholds into his hands, and to have the newly born Princess Mary delivered to his care. Maxwell was allowed to go to Scotland to further this idea with the Regent; but the first suggestion of a future marriage between Mary and young Edward seemed to the Scottish Council quite impossible. The Scots would never tolerate an English king. "If you had the lass, and we the lad, we might do it," said a Privy Councillor; but the whole country would rise against an English king.

Maxwell saw that it would be useless to make the more serious proposals. The Regent tried to persuade him to break his parole, but he refused, and returned to England, where the threat that he was to be imprisoned in the dreaded Tower, instead of remaining at Hampton Court, made him beg to be sent to Carlisle, where the Master of Johnstoun was a prisoner, that he might practise "on his own son and his sister's son." He offered to give up any castle of his own that would be commodious to the English for entering Scot-

---

[1] Also *Sir Ralph Sadler's Memoirs*.
[2] The intrigues of Wolsey and his agent, Lord Dacre, "to hold Scotland in cumber and business"—*i.e*, in civil war—and the money paid by Henry to this end, are described in Maxwell's *House of Douglas*, 1902. In *Sadler's Memoirs* we find that some of the Scottish nobility were in English pay, and that Argyll, Murray, Glencairn, Drumlanrig, Somerville, and Cassillis were all aiding and abetting the English invasion.

land; but Henry insisted, in addition, on the royal Castle of Lochmaben, to enable his officers to control Dumfriesshire.

Maxwell's eldest son, rather than carry out his father's order, contrived to be taken prisoner; and the next son, John, afterwards Lord Herries, whose whole career was honourable, refused to listen to any treacherous scheme. The Armstrongs, under Maxwell's influence, gave up Langholm Tower to the English, and Wharton wrote to Lord Shrewsbury, on Feb. 14, 1545, that he had placed a body of foot and fifty horsemen in it, and had long used one of Johnstoun's followers as an emissary to create discord between Johnstoun and Maxwell. A feud had broken out between them, which the Scottish Privy Council could not allay. He had offered 300 crowns to Johnstoun for himself and 100 to his brother, the Abbot of Salsit, and 100 to Johnstoun's other followers, on condition that young Maxwell should be put into his power. Johnstoun had entered into the plot, but "he and his friends were all so false" that Wharton "knew not what to say." But he would be glad "to annoy and entrap the Master of Maxwell or the Laird of Johnstoun to the King's Majesty, and his own poor honesty."

Johnstoun's "falseness" kept him true to his sovereign; and when a raid of English soldiers captured Carlaverock, or as a Scottish diary records, Oct. 28, 1545, "The Lord Maxwell delivereth Carlaverock to the English, which was great discomfort to the country," Johnstoun, Douglas of Drumlanrig, and Gordon of Lochinvar surrounded it three days afterwards with their followers, and eventually recaptured it. Meanwhile Lochmaben and Thrieve had been treacherously surrendered, but were recovered on Nov. 21.

Maxwell had taken refuge in Thrieve. He wrote to the Regent that his conduct had only been actuated by fear of death, and that he would take an oath to the infant Queen. He was pardoned, and Lochmaben was restored to his keeping, with the Wardenship of the West Marches and the post of Justiciar of Annandale, Nithsdale, and Galloway, but he died within a month (July 1546), when Johnstoun succeeded to his offices, having already renewed their former bond of manrent with his heir.

This happened directly after Johnstoun was released from prison at Dumbarton. The bond is signed by Carlile of Bridekirk, Cockpool, and others, but Andrew Johnstoun of Elphinstone is the only signature of his own name, most of his relatives being either prisoners with the English or engaged in opposing them. He alludes to "chance and fortune" having caused Maxwell's captivity, but he would not take advantage of it, and wishes to combine with all the clans to save their country. The Queen-Regent, in recognition of his loyalty, gave him all the oxen (he had to seize them) belonging to those landowners in Dumfriesshire who had refused to give or lend them to draw the Royal Artillery. He was also given (Oct. 28, 1545) a Charter of the lands of Castlemilk, "which superiority pertained to Matthew, formerly Earl of Lennox, and is now in the Queen's hands by reason of escheat on account of forfeiture against the said Earl, to be held by the said John, his heirs, and assignees of the Queen and her successors for the usual services."

His brother, Adam, being dead, he also obtained the ward of Corrie in 1544; and as the Grahams of Thornik were assisting the English, Johnstoun's daughter, Margaret, married to Ninian Graham, received a gift of all the lands belonging to the deceased Robert Graham, her father-in-law.

Laurence Johnstoun, the son of William, the son of Laurence, who was a son of the Laird (1436), being dead, his Chief received his lands of Woodhous till another heir should appear, and the lands of Brotis, owned by his great-great-uncle, David, till a nearer relative should be found. The young heir of Corrie, James, was a prisoner in England, and as he was not ransomed was induced to join the English armies. He is the only near relative of the Johnstoun chiefs who is described as having actually fought on that side, and he was outlawed till 1565. Neither he nor his son appear to have been restored to his father's position. They could not control the Irvings, for whom they were responsible; and in 1585 George Johnstoun of Corrie was denounced for assisting his Chief, and took refuge in Mylnfield on the north side of Annan.

Early in 1547 a combined effort was made to free Dumfriesshire from the English. Johnstoun, Lochinvar, and the Master of Maxwell advanced into Cumberland, while the Regent Arran captured Langholm Tower. But all forces were needed to check an invasion on the eastern border, and there the Regent sustained the terrible defeat of Pinkie.[1] Lochinvar, among others, was left dead on the field. The absence of so many men from the county enabled Sir Thomas Carleton to lead an English force by way of Teviotdale and Canonbie across to Dumfries, where he issued a proclamation calling on all to take an oath to King Henry, who was a dying man. A few lairds came in, but not Johnstoun, whom he particularly wanted to secure, for the new Lord Maxwell being in captivity, and some of his adherents having taken the oath, there only remained a small part of the county unsubdued.

Johnstoun was conquered by a ruse. Wharton sent forty light horsemen to burn Wamfray, his brother's demesne, as the flames could be seen from Lochwood Tower, and then put 300 men in ambush, "thinking that the Lord Johnstoun," as he wrote to Somerset, "would come to view them, and so he did, and pursued them sharply to their ambush." After a hard fight the Scottish Warden was captured, with the Laird of Corrie and the Abbot of Salsit,[2] though not till three spears had been broken on him and he had been severely wounded in the thigh. "140 of his men were taken prisoners, eight were killed, and many hurt, but only four Englishmen were hurt, never one slain nor taken."

[1] In *Sadler's Memoirs* it is stated that many Scots regarding this as a Holy War (owing to James V. having been advised by Henry to fill his coffers with the spoils of churches and monasteries), a whole regiment of bishops, priests, and monks carrying sacred banners were cut down at Pinkie.

[2] James Johnstoun of Wamfray, brother to the Laird (1524-67) has been confused with the Abbot of Salsit; but there seems no doubt that the last was a priest, and the day he was captured with his Chief was Thursday before Easter, when the family chaplain would be in attendance. His name, James, may have been a mistake for John, or he may have died in England, for in 1552, 1565, and 1569 John Johnstoun was Abbot of Salsit, and he was a priest, as he was "convicted of celebrating Mass" according to the Roman use. Symon, the youngest brother, received the lands of Ernemynie in the Barony of Crossmichael (Kirkcudbright) from his father, but resigned them to Johnstoun in 1546.

The English contingent at once escorted their prisoners to England, and did not trouble about Lochwood; but Carleton wrote a little later that, as the Laird of Drumlanrig and Carlile of Bridekirk with his son would not come in, he tried to get hold of some castle where he might be nearer the enemy. "Sander Armstrong came and told me he had a man called John Lynton who was born in the head of Annandale near to the Loughwood, being the Laird Johnstoun's chief house, and the said Laird and his brother, the Abbot of Salsit, were taken prisoners not long before, and were remaining in England. It was a fair large tower, able to lodge all our company safely, with a barnekin, hall, kitchen, and stables, all within the barnekin, and was but kept with two or three fellows and as many wenches."

This garrison was easily overpowered, and the place found to be well stocked with salted beef, malt, butter, and cheese. Carleton put Armstrong in the tower to keep it, and went on to Moffat, where he ordered the people to swear fealty to Edward VI.

King Henry's death seems to have saved Scotland, for the Duke of Somerset rushed home to secure the Protectorship during his nephew's minority, but all the power of England was now concentrated on Dumfriesshire, aided by the traitors within it. The Armstrongs and Fergus Graham offered to show to Carleton the road into Lanarkshire, hitherto untrodden by the enemy, "for at Crawford and Lamington he would find much booty and many sheep." He burned "Lamington and James Douglas's castle, where the men and cattle were all devoured with smoke and fire," and then returned to Lochwood or Loughwood, an isolated tower standing on a hill in the midst of marshes, which could only be crossed by strangers with a guide. From this fortress of the Chief, who, languishing in an English dungeon, still declined to take the oath to Edward VI., Carleton wrote: "We remained here very quietly, as if we had been at home in our own houses." Fergus Graham was made Captain of Castlemilk with a guard of English soldiers for its defence.

Writing to the Duke of Somerset (Protector), Wharton states that he has bribed the Earl of Lennox, and that those Scots he has spoken with "say they will serve King Edward in any part of the world. . . . They are more conformable from the little ministrations of justice I use among them, and they hope to live in peace and quiet under his Highness's laws. . . . It is the noblemen (*i.e.*, the lairds) that is the only let to this Godly purpose."

Johnstoun petitioned the Scottish Parliament for a loan to pay his ransom, and described his cruel imprisonment, first in Carlisle, then Lowther, Pontefract, Wharton Hall, and Hartley. "They laid irons and fetters upon me," he wrote, "and troubled me therewith in such manner that I behoved to lie on my back with all my clothes on my body as well by day as night. Intending to have gotten me secretly destroyed they gave me evil and unwholesome meats and drinks, and through eating and drinking thereof, I took heavy sickness, and lay therein by the space of six weeks in peril of my life." Yet he would not listen to "the mischievous purpose proposed to him by Wharton towards the hurt and destruction of this realm." So the Scottish chief had to stay where he was, while the other leaders of his clan, having no assistance from the Regent, were making the only terms they could with the enemy.

The south of Annandale still resisted Wharton's lieutenant in the north; but on Sept. 8, 1547, Lord Lennox and Wharton crossed the Esk, and halted at Graitney. The next day they marched to Castlemilk, which they reported to have walls 14 feet thick, and captured it. On Sept. 20 they encamped near Annan, and summoned Lyon, the captain of the castle, who defended it with 100 Scots, to surrender. The castle was built by Robert Bruce, and the chapel adjoining it was the only church in Annan. It stood in the midst of the old graveyard, where all that remained of the fortress in 1870 was a small heap of stones, now swept away. "The English," wrote Holinshed, "brought their artillery to bear against the walls, and undermined them, so that the roof of the church was shaken down, and many of those within crushed to death. At last the captain, moved by the Earl of Lennox, to whom he was related, gave himself up with the garrison on condition that their lives should be saved," although the captain must go a prisoner into England. As soon as they left the steeple the mines were fired, and both church and steeple vanished in the air. The town was sacked and burnt, "not one stone being left standing, for it had ever been a noisome neighbour to England. The Englishmen had conceived such spite to it, that if they saw but a piece of timber remaining unburnt they would cut the same in pieces. The country herewith was stricken in such fear that the next day all the Kilpatricks and the Jardines, the Lairds of Kirkmichel, Aplegirth, Closeburn, Howmendes, Nuby (Newbie), and the Irrewings, the Belles, the Rigges, the Murrays, and all the clans and the surnames of the nether part of Annandale, came and received an oath of obeisance as subjects to the King of England, delivering pledges for their assured loyalty."

The invaders were again assisted by "Richie Graham brother to Fergus," and by some of the Armstrongs, Beatties, Thomsons, Littles, and other Border stragglers not dependent on any Border chief.[1]

When writing of the Borderers the English Wardens often confused Christian names and relationships, which is not surprising, when, besides the numbers bearing the same surname, the same Christian names appear even among brothers. This partly arose from the Scottish custom of naming sons after both grandfathers, and after the father. In the Johnstoun family alone the old Laird had two brothers besides himself called John; he had two sons named James, and two named John; and William of Newbie had also two sons named John. It is rather difficult to suppose that Wharton did not mean another Laird of the name, and not the stubborn patriot, when he

[1] "Sundry of the surname of Yrwen (Irving) offered to serve his Majesty with 200 men their friends, and except the bodies of Lord Johnston and John Maxwell to compel all the dwellers from the King's Majesty's possession unto the town of Dumfries to serve his Majesty if they might have entertainment being they said in poverty. . . . The King now hath prisoners the Maxwells and Johnstons who hath borne a great rule of the West part of Scotland." Wharton to Somerset, April 7, 1547. A spy reported to Sadler in "1543 that Nithsdale and Galloway were the most poor countries not able to victual themselves, and Annandale was in great poverty without corn for herself."

PLATE V

BEN JONSON, 1573(?)-1637.

wrote to the Protector: "Laird Johnstoun is a good example on these marches, for when his house was won and all his goods taken, he requested to be sworn in the King's service." It seems more likely that he was speaking of the Laird of Graitney and Newbie, whose Barony was not devastated till Lennox and Wharton invaded Scotland, and whose sturdy followers had obliged those commanders to go round by Langholm, and wait to close upon them and their Chief at Annan when the rest of the county was subdued.

Johnstoun of Lochwood was not released from an English prison till peace was made in 1550; and of him Wharton had written to the Protector: " I have despatched both my sons and my son-in-law Mr Musgrave and other gentlemen with light horsemen to make a foray in Nithsdale near Dumfries, and the part of Annandale not yet won. They have burnt nine or ten towns, and brought away prisoners, and spoil of goods with no hurt. Since I last wrote 500 lairds and gentlemen have come in, and I have in all 2400 Scottish horse. I have removed Laird Johnston from Carlisle to my house at Wharton. All his men have refused him; his own brothers and others have taken oath and given hostages for their service. They are a great band of proper men, and do good service."[1]

In Bell's M.S., preserved in the Carlisle Cathedral Library, there is a list of chiefs and their men who submitted to the English at Annan when it was burnt. It differs slightly from the lists preserved in the State papers of Edward VI., as do those lists from each other, both as to names and the number of followers. In one the Lairds of Wamfray and Elsieshields are omitted, and the Graitney Johnstouns mentioned twice. In another Lord Carlile is mentioned twice, with a different number of followers. William Johnstoun, brother to the Laird, and his three brothers are mentioned with 235 men under them. George Johnstoun (the Laird of Graitney) and those under him. Another list says the Laird of Newbie and Graitney surrendered with 122 men. George Johnstoun, called the Laird of Graitney, was a son of William of Newbie.[2]

In the next session of Parliament in Edinburgh, June 12, 1548, those chiefs who had taken an oath of fidelity to Edward VI. were declared guilty of high treason and outlawed. "William Kirkpatrick of Kirkmichael; John Jardine of Aplegirth; John Carruthers of Holmends; —— of Ros; the Lairds of Knok, of Grantoun, of Gillisbe; Grahame of Thornik; Gawyne Johnstoun of Kirkton; Johnstoun of Craigeburn; James Johnstoun of Cottis; —— of Newbie; Michael, Lord Carlile; Carruthers of Mouswald; Cuthbert Irvine of Robgill; —— of Cowquhate; Cuthbert Johnstoun of Lockerbie; James, sometime Abbot of

[1] Wharton wrote to Somerset of "the Abbot of Saisit and other chiefs of that name. . . . I have found the best sort of Scot. . . . I trust yet to cause those Johnstons to be with others a scourge to the Maxwells." (March 13, 1548).
[2] Ben Jonson (1573?-1637) believed that his grandfather was a Johnstoun of Annandale, but took service under Henry VIII.; probably he was a prisoner of war. Ben's father was born at Carlisle, lost his property and was imprisoned in Mary's reign, took Holy Orders, and died a month before the poet was born. But John*son* is found very early in England.

Saulside; and Tweedie of Drumnelzear." The Laird of Johnstoun and his son, also Maxwell, were still prisoners in England.

Only a month before the death of Henry VIII., May 17, 1547, a letter was written in the young Scottish Queen's name to remonstrate about the English invasion, and the capture of the Abbot of Dryburgh, "who was passing to the ports of France on his own affairs," and "Master John Hay sent to the most Christian King of France to perform such business as was committed unto him." They were taken on the sea by English ships of war, and imprisoned, although Scotland was nominally at peace with England and France. "Also your subjects have lately by open foray invaded our realm upon the West Borders at the parts of Annandale and there taken the Laird of Johnstoun on his own ground for defence of his lands and goods. The which unjust attempts are not only against the 'peace' foresaid; but also most unnaturally enterprised against us and our lieges without any respect unto the proximity and tenderness of our blood and mutual friendship, that should continue between us and our realms. Therefore we pray you, our dearest brother and cousin in our most effective manner to put the said Abbot of Dryburgh, Master John Hay, Lord Johnstoun and others taken with them to liberty and freedom, so that they may without any impediment freely pass on to the realm of France, or if it please them to return again within our realm," etc.

This letter, dated from Stirling, had no effect, and the ravages continued. The official list of the towns, monasteries, castles, villages, mills and hospitals destroyed by the English in 1547 is given as 287, and fills ten closely written pages of a State paper, still preserved in the London Record Office. Graitney, Sark and Cavertholme, belonging to Johnstoun of Newbie, Blacket House, Ryehill Castle, and all within fifteen miles of the English frontier are included, and Dumfriesshire was subject to the King of England for a year and a half. But in the meantime the King of France sent a contingent from Gascony to assist his Scottish allies. The English Privy Council, hearing they were expected, not only ordered the enlistment of Germans, Italians, and a Spanish corps for service in Scotland, but instructed Wharton to execute some of the pledges at Carlisle, which was done, and among others who perished was the Warden of Greyfriars at Dumfries, and the Vicar of Carlaverock, who was pledge for Lord Maxwell, his near relative.

The war spread to East Scotland, and the actual peril of the young Queen, when the enemy advanced upon Edinburgh, which was burnt, induced the Regent to send her to France in 1548, and there she was brought up. Her marriage to the delicate Dauphin Francis, who was thenceforward styled King of Scotland in legal documents, gave Henry II. the pretext for making her sign a document bequeathing Scotland to him in the event of his son's early death; and with this in view he compelled the English forces to quit Scotland by attacking Dunkirk and Calais.

A truce was signed for ten years at Norham in March 1550, when the Laird of Johnstoun was released. It provided that the Debateable Land between the Esk and the Sark should belong to neither kingdom but lie waste;

but in 1552 it was divided, the upper half including Canonbie annexed to Scotland, and the southern half with Kirkandrews joined to England. The treaty is signed by John Johnstoun of that Ilk, John Johnstoun of *Nitove* (supposed to be a copyist's error for Newbie), Charles Murray of Cockpool, and others. It was ratified on Dec. 15 by the Warden, Maxwell of Herries and the Laird of Johnstoun for Scotland, and by Sir Richard Musgrave and Sir Thomas Dacre for England.

Richie Graham was rewarded by Henry VIII. for his aid, with the lands of Netherby; but Lord Scrope, writing to Secretary Cecil in 1583, points out that the idea of thereby attaching the Graham clan to England had been frustrated, chiefly by the Lairds of Graitney and Newbie. Richie's family had been outlawed in Scotland, but Johnstoun of Graitney married one of his nieces, and the Laird of Newbie settled her brother, Arthur Graham,[1] on the Mote or Moat adjacent to Newbie, and married him to one of his own daughters, so that he was no longer sought for by the law. The couple had four sons, being brought up as Scotsmen. William Graham, Richard's brother, had married the sister of the Laird of Graitney, and Edward Irving of Bonshaw married Richard's daughter. These alliances gave the family more ties in Scotland than in England.

[1] Arthur Graham, after having his farm overrun and pillaged by unpaid mercenary soldiers, was killed by Thomas Musgrave, presumably by mistake, for Queen Elizabeth allowed his son, William Graham, £20 a year as compensation.

CHAPTER IX.

WILLIAM, LAIRD OF GRAITNEY—THE BARONY OF NEWBIE—MARGARET CRICHTON—WAMFRAY—QUEEN MARY—JOHNSTOUN—CIVIL WAR—THE QUEEN—DEATH OF JOHN OF NEWBIE—JOHNSTOUN WILLS—FEUD BETWEEN MAXWELLS AND JOHNSTOUNS—BATTLE OF DRYFE SANDS—THIRD BARON OF NEWBIE—THE KING VISITS NEWBIE—UNION OF THE CROWNS—CLAN SYSTEM REPRESSED—NOTE ON SCOTLAND.

THE sons of William of Graitney and Newbie were grown men before the Treaty of Peace. In the seclusion of his father, who was outlawed for submitting to the English, the eldest lawful son, John, seems to have signed it.

This William, mentioned as the young Laird of Graitney in 1513, appears in Acta. Dom., June 19, 1531, as having, with Andro Roryson of Bardannoch, in Nithsdale "spulzied" from the lands of Duncan Wilson in Bardannoch. Andro's mother was a Crichton, and Graitney was one of his tutors. The spoliation was probably a seizure of grain or cattle for unpaid rent. On July 27, 1532, William is described as occupying a 10 mark land in Arkilton, and was on the assize with Grierson of Lag, William Carruthers of Orchardton, John Maitland of Auchencastle, Gordon of Crauchton, Roger M'Briar of Almagill, John Kirkpatrick, Scott of Wamfray, two Douglases, Gordon of Corhead, Thomas Moffat of Knok, Walter Steward, Lindsay, Ralston of that Ilk, etc. Two years before he witnessed a Charter for Mariot, widow of Lord Carlile.

Several actions not responded to were being carried on at that time with regard to Graitney's occupation of Newbie by the Corries; but on Jan. 24, 1535, Graitney brought an action against Corrie, and another on March 6, 1535, and at last, on Jan. 20, 1536, it is stated that Thomas Corrie of Kelwood and William Cunninghame of Cunninghamehead were constituted procurators for George Corrie, feuar of Newbie, especially for the contract between the said George and William Johnstoun of Graitney. A former contract, dated Jan. 2, 1532, was referred to, as between George Corrie and Thomas Corrie, his father, free holder of the said land. The price to be paid by William Johnstoun was 23,000 marks. The witnesses are John Kirkpatrick, Ninian Crichton, James Crichton and Andrew Rorison, who sign it in 1536.

Another record of the Acta. Dom. Conc., dated 1538, is to the effect that Thomas Corrie and George Corrie, his son, show that Johnstoun of Graitney had fulfilled the agreement concerning Newbie in all points. Thomas Corrie was killed at the battle of Pinkie in 1547.

In the Charters which later transferred Graitney to Murray of Cockpool, the estate is described as about 147 acres of corn, besides woods, moss, shore, fishings, etc. William of Graitney's father is simply mentioned as Johnstoun in a suit against the Irvings in 1606, which gives the Graitney pedigree, and there it stops; but in Nesbit's *Heraldry*, compiled for the British Government in 1722, "Johnston of Graitney" is mentioned after Elphinstone as "another cadet of Johnston of that Ilk. On an old stone on the front of the house of Graitney of the date 1598 is the shield of arms of Johnston of that Ilk with the addition of two mullets." The correct date is 1573.[1]

The first regular Charter of the lands of Newbie obtained by William Johnstoun is dated Jan. 31, 1535. It is granted to William Johnstoun of Gretna and Margaret Crichton, his wife, and their male heirs by George Corrie, with the consent of his father, Thomas.[2] In case of the failure of the said male heirs, the lands to descend to the male heirs of the said couple whatsoever, and, in default of direct male heirs, to William's nearest male heirs whatsoever. The lands included "Newbie with its tower, fortress, manor, fisheries, etc., and the fisheries of New Skares with the sands of the Eden; Clout Skar, and ascending from the same to Wyldcotray; and at Wyldcotray, and the torrent called Balsucrik; and from Balsucrik descending in the waters of Annan; and from these waters to Eden and Howtyde with its pertinents. Also all and singly the lands of Barnekirk, Croftheid, Howes, Myll, Mylfield and Howmeadow, the free barony of Stapleton, Robgill with the fisheries of Stapleton, Cummertrees and its fisheries, Ellerbeck, Myddilby, Galzandleis, Hydewood, Priestwodsyde, Ruthwell, etc., lying in the Sheriffdom of Annandale, and within the stewardship of Dumfries."

These were the lands, but not Graitney, which were erected into a Barony by James V. in Jan. 8, 1542. The Crown Charter which entailed them was described by the late Sir John Holker (Attorney-General) as the most extraordinary that had ever been brought before the House of Lords. Newbie was first to pass to William Johnstoun's and Margaret Crichton's legitimate heirs; secondly to William's legitimate male heirs; thirdly to his son, George, and his heirs; fourthly to his brother, David, and his heirs; fifthly to his son, Herbert, and his heirs; sixthly to his son, John, and his heirs; seventhly to his brother, John, and his heirs. These sons, mentioned by name, and at least one brother[3] were not legitimate, as is shown by a memorandum for a Charter (March, 1543) proposing to rectify it. The relatives to whom Newbie was to descend were to bear the name and arms of Johnstoun.

[1] Mr G. H. Johnston's *Heraldry*.
[2] Another Charter, dated July 16, 1536, confers "the haill lands of Corre" as well as "the haill lands of Newbe on the laird of Gratno Willia Johnestoune and Margaret Crichton his spouse," but it seems to have made no difference to Adam Johnstoun's possession of Corrie.
[3] A legal expert was of opinion that neither brother, David or John, was legitimate, and it was a strange coincidence that the Laird of Johnstone had also two illegitimate brothers, David and John, who were legitimised.

The sasine feuing the lands of Arkilton, in Eskdale, to Ninian or Ringan Armstrong, who lived in Wauchope Castle in 1537, makes over to him "houses, woods, plains, moors, mills, and their sequels, fowlings, huntings, fishings, peats, coals, rabbits, pigeons, pigeon cotes, quarries of stone and lime, etc., to be held for ever of the grantor William Johnstoun of Graitney."

In the different deeds on the subject, it is referred to as having belonged to William's predecessors, and his great-grandson, Edward of Seafield (Wyldcotray), was one of the witnesses of its transfer to Mr Eliot in 1628. Also that in 1598 it passed from William's descendants. He probably parted with the copyhold to raise money for the purchase of Newbie.

In 1544 letters under the Privy Seal grant to William "the non-entries of Graitney with the mill thereof, and all rents since the decease of Johnstoun, his father, or any other last possessor thereof for all time to come."

Then came the fiercest English invasion of the century, when Graitney was laid waste, but perhaps in pity to his dependents he surrendered the day after the fall of Annan, and saved Newbie Tower, and further destruction in the neighbourhood.

The Graitney and Newbie estates were more compact and nearly as large as those of Johnstoun, and valued for the Crown dues at only £6 less. William mortgaged Robgill and Stapleton to Christopher Irving, and leased Sarkbrig, Conheath, and Graitney Hill to Richard Irving, probably when he was in great need after the English invasion, as it appears that at that date no rents were drawn from Newbie for eleven years.

From the time William was outlawed for submitting to the English he disappears, and probably retired a few miles to the north. Some of the Charters connected with him are signed by himself, others with "his hand at the pen," the ordinary way of signing at that time, the pen being guided by the notary. He was dead in 1565; and appears to have married after 1517, as in that year Sir John Charteris became surety for Ninian Crichton of Sanquhar in his wardship of Margaret Crichton. Her father was Sir Robert,[1] who is known in the Marquis of Bute's pedigree (Crichton being his ancestor) as the second Lord Crichton. It was a connection of which John, the eldest son of William and Margaret, was evidently proud, as he gave three of his sons, Robert, Edward and Abraham, regular Crichton names. Margaret was living when John Johnstoun, the second Baron Newbie, was returned the eldest lawful heir to his father and mother in 1565, as she had a liferent on the estate. The witnesses to the retour are John Carruthers of Holmends (Newbie's father-in-law), John Kennedy of Halleath, Robert French of Frenchland, William Maxwell of Ile, Adam Carlile of Bridekirk, Edward Irving of Bonshaw, Herbert Maxwell in Cavers, John Maxwell there, Robert Johnstoun of Newton, George Carruthers, junior of Holmends, Herbert de Powdene, John Johnstoun in Malinshaw, Adam

---

[1] His wife was the daughter of Murray of Cockpool, and his mother, Lady Marion Stewart, daughter of the Earl of Lennox. His father seems to have married a second time, as in 1527 "Dame Marion Maxwell, who had the great tierce of Lord Crichton's lands," dies, and Elizabeth Murray, his relict, claims them, opposed by Ninian Crichton.

Johnstoun de Beatok, John Johnstoun de Elsieschellis, and William Johnstoun in Hayhill. Maxwell of Cowhill was the Deputy-Sheriff.

Men did not look far for a wife when John, the second Baron of Newbie, was young. A neighbour's daughter or a cousin had the first chance. So John married Marion, the daughter of John Carruthers, the father of seven sons, and Laird of Holmends, whose lands included Wormanbie, a fief of the Laird of Johnstoun and the adjoining estate to Newbie. Marion's mother was Blanche Murray, daughter of John's cousin, the Laird of Cockpool; and another daughter of Holmends married Gilbert, second son to the Laird of Wamfray.

Wamfray, formerly owned by Avenel, Graham, Carlile, Corrie, Kirkpatrick, Boyle, Scott, and Crichton, was sold by Crichton to Laird Johnstoun in 1476. He gave it, but only in feu, to his younger son, John, who married Katherine Boyle, but appears to have left no legitimate male heirs. In 1528 Wamfray was owned by James of Pocornwell, brother-german to the Laird. Being a very poor district his retainers had the worst character for thieving and lawlessness of all belonging to the clan.[1] Possibly, like Crichton, he did not feel that it was his duty to guard the Borders; but when his brother chiefs were called out with all their able-bodied men to oppose the English, it left him great opportunities for annexing cattle and horses. It does not appear that he assisted at all in the war in 1541; and in 1546 he obtained the lands of Aldtoun and others from his second son's father-in-law, Carruthers of Holmends. The next year his "town" was burned by the enemy. He is mentioned in one State paper, but not in all, as surrendering to the English with 102 men. In 1549 his estate was erected into a Barony by Queen Mary, and settled on himself, his wife, Margaret M'Clellan, and his eldest son, James. His possession of Wamfray was as much disputed as that of his kinsman to Newbie; but in 1550 he paid Adam Scott, son and heir of Robert Scott (whose mother, John Johnstoun's widow, Katherine Boyle, had married a Scott), for his rights to Wamfray with the exception of Ryeholme.

The surviving Scottish prisoners straggled back from England when the heavy ransoms demanded for them could be paid. Cuthbert Murray of Cockpool is described by the English Warden as worth little or nothing. James, the eldest son of the Laird of Johnstoun, died soon after his release. His widow, Margaret Hamilton, niece of the Regent Arran, was re-married in 1552 to David Douglas, and made an exchange of land—Howcleuch for Harthope—with William Johnstoun, described as brother of the Laird. David Johnstoun in Nether Garvald witnessed the deed. This is the last mention of the Laird's second brother, William, who signed one document himself, another with his hand at the pen; and unless the identity of William Johnstoun of Graitney with this William is proved he left no legal descendant. The same may be said of his uncle, William, brother to Laird James (1509-24).

When the Laird returned home in 1550 he formed a bond of manrent with Wamfray, and this bound them to defend each other at home and abroad. He

---

[1] In 1530 James Charteris sues William, Thomas, David, and James Johnstoun, brothers, in Wamfray for trespassing in Drumgrey.

did not care to remain in the famine-stricken district, which his once troublesome brother was now pledged to defend, so he retired to Stirling with his second or third wife, Nicolas Douglas, the daughter of Drumlanrig, and bought a house there. But Wamfray died in 1561, and his brother took steps to reduce the power of his Barony with the aid of his second son, Robert, parson of Lochmaben. The Reformation had emptied the Church benefices, and on the Borders the patrons at once took possession of the tithes, and prevented any Reformed priest from being instituted. Lady Wamfray, who owned the liferent of the estate, had counted upon the Wamfray parsonage as her chief means of living, but Robert sold it to Sir James Carruthers, a Roman priest, and burned the tower in which she lived, seized the cattle, and "destroyed or eat her corn." She asked for the Queen's protection from her "brother-in-law, a great man having a clan of the country at his command," in 1566, but in spite of many appeals she continued to be oppressed.

Her family, the M'Clellans of Bombie, shared with Stewart of Garlies and the Maxwells the superiority in Galloway; but her father had been killed in a street in Edinburgh by Douglas of Drumlanrig in 1516, and Agnes Johnstoun, probably a sister of the Chief, had married a M'Clellan, so, as Johnstoun had a legal right to a part of Wamfray and the church patronage, his sister-in-law could hardly expect her own brother's help. Her sons, Gilbert and John, were both accused by the Privy Council of dispossessing their mother of houses at Dumfries and in Wamfray. Perhaps they claimed them to prevent her enemies turning her out.

Newbie was peaceably disposed, and possibly in agreement with his Chief he took a lease of Dundoran in Wamfray, which once belonged to his mother's family, in exchange for a holding on his own estate, where he planted his brother-in-law, Gilbert of Wamfray, who also owned land at Kirtlebrig. Newbie was obliged to support his share of 200 spearmen to guard the Border, so could employ indigent younger sons. Gilbert's elder brother, James, was dead in 1585, but it was not till 1591 that Gilbert was returned his heir at the cost of £53, in the usual manner by twelve friends and kinsmen. Up to that time he was a merchant, a most useful adjunct to a baronial property, and carried on business with Edinburgh and Dumfries. His son, Edward, did the same; while his sons, Robert, James, and John (who witnessed Newbie's Will in 1576) probably helped to look out for cruisers and danger signals,[1] which could easily be seen from Newbie Castle standing on the very edge of the Solway. Gilbert had another brother, William, who remained at Wamfray, possibly more; but prior to registers unless a younger son came before a law court no record need exist of him.

In 1542 John of Newbie witnessed a resignation by the Laird in favour of his son, James, and in 1549 he was one of four "proud and discreet men" who witnessed a Charter for Agnes Hereis, eldest daughter and co-heir of Lord Hereis. In 1550 he was one of the witnesses to the retour of Lord Maxwell.

---

[1] The English Grahams robbed the townships of Newbie and Holmends in 1575.

His father's lands were divided to provide for the numerous brothers. George had Graitney, an important but much smaller holding than Newbie; John, a younger son, received a farm in Cummertrees; and Herbert (whose sons, Adam, James, and Arthur sign a bond in 1578), a farm in Croftheid—as "gudemen" under the Baron of Newbie.

Besides the Barony Newbie inherited the church land of Kirkpatrick Fleming, and obtained a Crown Charter for it, and he bought a copyhold of Dornock part of the lands of the Abbey of Dundrennan, for both glebes intersected his Barony.

In the first session of Parliament at Edinburgh after the peace of 1552 it was proposed that an annual tax should be levied on the Borders to support a large standing army, in place of the Royal Statute of 1455 which ordained that 200 spearmen and as many archers should be maintained upon the East and Middle Marches for their defence, and that those "near the Border should have good households, and armed men as offers and to be ready at their principal place, and to pass with the Wardens when and where they shall be charged." Nearly 200 of the Border chiefs and gentlemen, including Newbie, assembled at Edinburgh to protest against this tax. They would defend the realm as their forefathers had done, but had no money. Yet as Newbie and Graitney covered a large extent of Border, the burden of defence came rather heavily upon their families.

Among the feuars of Newbie who helped in the agricultural duties were Gibsons, Hallidays, Potts, Wylds, and Raes, landowners themselves in earlier days; while the sons of the house, always armed, kept by turns a vigilant watch on the opposite shore. There were no traitors among them, so the frontier was usually crossed much farther east by the enemy. This happened only five years after the peace was signed. John Maxwell, now known as Lord Hereis, and a colleague were actually at Carlisle to arrange on the part of Scotland that she should continue at peace with England, although her ally, France, was engaging in a war with Spain, which involved the English Queen Mary as the wife of a Spanish Prince.

An English army suddenly crossed the east Borders, and Lord Hereis, to keep it out of Dumfriesshire, patriotically formed a bond of manrent, in return for the restoration of land,[1] with the head of the Armstrongs, who had assisted the enemy only seven years before and actually captured Johnstoun. Some of this clan as usual helped the English in 1557, and defeated Bothwell, the Lord of Liddesdale, who, on his side, defeated the English. Still their partial adherence to the Scots hastened the peace, which was signed in 1559.

This year the Protestants first formed themselves into a league in Scotland, and the Reformed faith was officially recognised in 1560. The young Queen a year later returned a widow to her native land, and there were hopes that she might be induced to accept it herself. Lord Maxwell and Murray

[1] The lands granted to Lord Hereis's father when James IV. hanged Johnnie Armstrong and the leading men of his clan.

with other influential men opposed her unfortunate marriage with Darnley in 1565, on the ground that it was prejudicial to the Protestant interests, also because his father had joined England in 1547. But when the old or the Reformed faith became a question of loyalty to the Queen or to the base-born Regent who supplanted her, there was a reaction on the Borders, aided by her personal attractions. She had paid a visit to Dumfries and passed a night under Lord Hereis's roof on Aug. 20, 1563; and she came again with her second husband, Henry Darnley, in 1565 with an army of 500 men. Among other recipients of her favour, John Johnstoun of Newbie received the escheat of the lands of Ryehill and a 5 mark land in Cummertrees.

The Laird of Johnstoun was a member of the Parliament which established the Reformation, but it was all the part he took in it. Still he was charged with maintaining Gilbert Johnstoun of Poldean, a fugitive accused of theft and fire-raising, and of "pressing to marry his daughter to Edward Irving of the Bonshaw's son. He was told that he was displeased with all good order as his life and doings did declare, and unless he kept his possession in a more orderly condition the Queen's Majesty will so vigorously punish him, that the West Marches shall take example and his house never forget it."

One of Johnstoun's daughters, Margaret, married Ninian Graham in 1531; and his grand-daughter had long been the wife of the Master of Carlile. Another daughter, Elizabeth, married Richard Graham.

It is easy to understand the old man's anxiety to marry all his daughters rather than let them become wards of the Crown. His niece, a daughter of Symon Carruthers of Mouswald, had killed herself rather than accept the selected husband. Bessie or Elizabeth, his youngest, seems to have married James Galloway. Two generations later the Laird could only settle on a daughter the escheat of an Elsieshields. In 1566 the Laird endowed his daughter—Irving's wife—with the rents of Wormanbie, also the copyhold of Stapleton, "the Laird of Newbie the superior."

The agitation was so great in Dumfriesshire when the Queen was sent a prisoner to Loch Leven Castle in 1567 that Parliament, in the name of the infant King James, summoned nine chiefs, including the Bishop of Wigton and the Laird of Johnstoun, to Edinburgh to consult on the best means of pacifying it. Johnstoun died at Edinburgh two months later. The Queen's escape the next year set the county in a flame, and her army of nearly 600 men was chiefly gathered from Galloway, Nithsdale, Annandale and Liddesdale, including the Chiefs of Johnstoun and Newbie with their men.

Eleven Borderers of note signed a bond to support Queen Mary—Hay, Lord Yester, Maxwell, Hereis, Edward Maxwell, Crichton, the Abbot of Dundrennan, and the Lairds of Ros, Somerville, young Johnstoun for his whole clan, and Lochinvar—while Drumlanrig, Lord Home, Glencairn, Lindsay, the Earl of Morton, and many more took the part of the Regent. The rival forces met at Langside on May 13, 1568, when the Queen's army sustained a total defeat, and, escaping on horseback through Crawford, Sanquhar, and

Dumfries to Dundrennan in Galloway, Mary crossed over to England to ask the assistance of Queen Elizabeth.

Three weeks later the Regent Moray followed up his victory by an armed progress through Dumfriesshire, to exact an oath of allegiance from the Queen's partisans. After burning two castles belonging to Gordon of Lochinvar he arrived at Dumfries on June 18, where he took possession of Lord Hereis's house and remained in it the next day, expecting the owner to do homage to him. Hereis had been there the morning before with Johnstoun, Maxwell of Cowhill, and Lochinvar, and 1000 of their men, and they cleared the town of provisions, but he never presented himself to the Regent, and it was believed that his colleagues restrained him from doing so. The "gudeman" of Hills, Fergus Graham, and Christie Irving of Bonshaw did homage for the Maxwells, Irvings, and Grahams; and Newbie, whose eldest son was killed at Langside, was pledge for the fidelity of all the Johnstouns, as the Laird's father's brother, Robert Johnstoun of Lochmaben, had been captured. This pledge prevented the Regent from burning the houses of their Chief, although he occupied them on his return journey, and gave the keeping of Lochwood to Buccleuch. On June 20 he marched to Hoddam Castle, then owned by Lord Hereis, and placed in it his ally, Drumlanrig, who had been Warden of the Borders since 1553.[1]

Holinshed (1576) says that "great hunger began to pinch in the army. A pint of wine was sold for 7s. Scots, and no bread to be had for any money." Annan, recollecting the barbarity with which it had been treated after the siege of 1547, capitulated at once when it found itself surrounded by 1000 men; and there the Regent had an interview with Lord Scrope, the English Warden. His party was in friendly communication with England all through this unhappy Civil War.

On the return journey the Regent's army captured Lochmaben from the Maxwells, and seized a large quantity of cattle near Lochwood. On June 24 (1568) it arrived at Peebles, and the next day at Edinburgh; but bands of outlaws continued to harass the country under pretence of fighting for the Queen. In the Register of the Privy Council for October 1569 a list is given of these men, and of the chiefs who were bound to arrest, or keep them in check. Under the head of Will Bell of Gretna is added "the which day John Johnstoun of Gretna obliges himself that Will Bell of Gretna shall be punished if he continues disobedient to the laws." The Lairds of Johnstoun and Newbie pledged themselves for the good conduct of the gang of Fairholm, and John Johnstoun of Graitney for the Irvings.

The Lairds of Johnstoun, Elphinstone, Newbie, and Thomas Johnstoun of Craigaburn were obliged to pledge themselves jointly and separately under pain of 2000 marks that John Johnstoun of Howgill and the "auld gang of Wamfray" should not escape. Johnstoun and Newbie were also pledges for Arthur Graham, and the first bound himself to bring the Laird of Corrie to the

[1] Carruthers of Holmends surrendered on condition that his family and followers were spared, but Kirkhous, the abode of his heir, was burnt.

Regent that Corrie might become security for those Irvings who were his tenants.

Graitney appeared with three servants and fifteen retainers when he came to meet the Regent, who, hearing that the Queen had escaped to England with Lord Hereis's assistance, at once outlawed Hereis. This Chief wrote from Dumfries in Sept. 1568 to the English Privy Council on the Queen's behalf, and started a month later for London to obtain a personal interview with Queen Elizabeth. The great rival clans were united in their loyalty, and no wonder the Reformed creed became distasteful to them when it was urged as a pretext for keeping their lawful sovereign a prisoner. Elizabeth refused to give Hereis an audience, so he went to France to plead for the intervention of Henry III. The Queen-mother, Catherine de Medicis, Mary's mother-in-law and the guardian of her youth, wrote a diplomatic letter to Elizabeth, and, speaking of her own ill health, expressed thankfulness that after all her sorrows Mary should be safe under so powerful and generous a protector. Then the news arrived of the Scottish Regent's assassination, and Hereis tried to organise a rising in Mary's favour throughout Dumfriesshire. There were plenty of informers to acquaint the English Privy Council with this attempt; and Scrope, the English Warden, received orders to lead an army across the frontier to ravage the estates of Lord Hereis and of those lairds who were particularly attached to the cause of Mary and of the Roman faith.

In a secret memorandum sent to the English Cabinet John Johnstoun of Newbie is mentioned as one of fifty-nine Scots[1] (including her groom, farrier and priest) who were still attached to, or attendant on, the Queen, and he appears to have been with her when it was written. His estate was not spared when the English orders were barbarously carried out. On April 21, 1570, Scrope reported from Carlisle that he had encamped at Ecclefechan and sent Musgrave to burn Hoddam, Graitney, Ruthwell, Calpole, Blackshaw, Sherrington, Bankend, Lochar, and old Cockpool. At the last place, in a battle with Lord Hereis, he had taken 100 prisoners, including the Alderman of Dumfries and sixteen burgesses, but had been driven back by Hereis, Carlile, Charteris, Grierson, Kirkpatrick and Carruthers. He fought them again at Cummertrees, when he captured several lairds, while Hereis, Carlile, Johnstoun and the rest "only escaped by the strength of the Laird of Cockpool's house, and a great wood and morass." Scrope's lieutenant wrote to Secretary Cecil that he had thrown down the castle at Annan and had not left a stone house standing in that town, "which was an ill neighbour to Carlisle."

The agitation continued for two years longer in Dumfriesshire, the Lairds of Teviotdale, the Scotts and Armstrongs, as well as Drumlanrig and his son-in-law, Jardine, being on the side of the infant King, and (except Drumlanrig's tenants) of the English invaders. A pestilence, consequent on the

[1] Also Kirkpatrick, Hobe Maxwell, Lord Hereis and son, James Hamilton, Lord Fleming, and Levingston.

famine which always followed these terrible wars, helped the departure of the enemy. Newbie must have been better off than some of his allies, for the splendid fisheries[1] he possessed, extending for ten miles along the coast and three up the Annan, and the saltworks on the Solway provided food for his family and dependents when there was little prospect of any other. It is not surprising that, reared in such disturbed times, some of his children and grand-children developed very combative propensities.

The Laird of Newbie, like his Chief, was related to Lord Hereis, and the marriage of his eldest son, William, in 1566 with Agnes, the daughter of John Maxwell of the Ile, made the connection still closer. But William was killed at the battle of Langside, and the young Lord Maxwell, just of age, began to revive the old hereditary feud of his family in 1574 by a dispute with some of the Johnstouns, who were now led by a young and equally hot-headed chief. Both aspired to the Wardenry of the West Marches, which carried with it the custody of Lochmaben Castle, and was likely to be soon vacant.

Johnstoun had been fined £2000 and outlawed the year before for not producing John of Graitney, who was summoned by the Privy Council to make compensation "for all attempts committed by himself, his bairns and servants in time past," and the Laird had acted as his pledge. The summons appears only to have been issued to satisfy the English Warden, for Graitney and his tenants obliged the English invaders to enter Scotland by the Middle Marches instead of by the shortest road, and probably harassed them considerably in their rear. Neither Johnstoun or Maxwell obtained the Wardenry of the West Marches on the death of the aged Sir James Douglas of Drumlanrig, but it did not alter their feeling towards each other, and the Earl of Morton, who became Regent in 1572, desired the two families to refer their differences to the Lords in Council. Each Chief appointed certain noblemen and friends to represent him in Edinburgh, any four, three, or two on either side being empowered to act for all. Maxwell selected his own kinsmen. Johnstoun also nominated relations and connections — John of Newbie, the Earl of Rothes, Sir James Balfour, Sir James Hamilton, William Livingston of Jerviswood, Thomas Johnstoun of Craigaburn, Robert Douglas of Cassogill, Walter Scott of Guildlands, and Walter Scott of Tuschelaw. They were to meet in Edinburgh on Feb. 15, 1576-7, both parties promising to keep good rule in the country during the absence of the deputies.

The disputes seem to have been settled to the advantage of the Laird of Johnstoun, who was older than his rival, for the following year he was made Warden of the Borders and knighted, an honour enjoyed by several of his ancestors. But Newbie died in Edinburgh five days before the deputies had agreed to meet.

His Chief, who had also found the air of Edinburgh too much for him in 1567, had made a codicil to his Will, which was witnessed by Newbie ; and

---

[1] There was a close time for salmon as early as Robert III., and in the reign of William III. a poacher of salmon smelt was ordered to be flogged or enlisted as a soldier.

it had been the cause of an action, in which Newbie was involved, between the widow, Nicolas Douglas, and her husband's grandson, the young Laird. The first Will, dated 1562, left Nicolas Douglas joint executor with Lord Hereis, the Laird of Drumlanrig (her father), and Johnstoun of Elphinstone. Her husband bequeathed his horse, hart, dogs and sword to Lord Hereis, desiring his heir to be guided by his counsel. Cattle, stones of cheese, butter, hay, grain, linen yarn, woollen yarn, and £200 were among his goods.

The codicil was to the advantage of the widow's own son, John, who was younger than his half-nephew, and she was accused of having forged it. It was signed with the Chief's hand at the pen. She pleaded that he was a very old man and could no longer write, so she signed it for him. Although the civil war, in which the young Chief, his father's brother, Robert, parson of Lochmaben, and others of the clan fought at Langside, seriously delayed legal affairs, a contract was registered Nov. 25, 1569, in which " John of Johnstoun, grandson and apparent heir of the deceased John Johnstoun of that Ilk, his gudesire, with the consent of John Johnstoun of Elsieshields and Robert Johnstoun in Newton, his curators [he had chosen these two for himself], on the one part, and Nicolas Douglas, widow of the said John Johnstoun of that Ilk, on the other, whereby he obliges himself to pay to her 500 marks, promising also to leave the house of Lochous to be heritably possessed by her children; and the said Laird of Johnstoun shall present John, lawful son of the deceased John Johnstoun and Nicolas Douglas, to the parsonage and vicarage of Johnstoun, and shall sustain him at the schools till he is fourteen years of age." The cautioners are John Johnstoun of Newbie, Thomas Johnstoun of Corheid (he signs his name of Craigaburn), John, Commendator of the Abbey of Salsit, and Sir Walter Scott of Branxholme.

Newbie's Will is dated Feb. 5, 1576-7, and the inventory was taken the next day by his wife and his sons, Robert and John. " The testament and inventory of the gudes, geir, sums of money and debts pertaining to the late John Johnstoun of Newbie, within the Sherrifdom of Dumfries, the time of his decease, who died on Feb. 10 the year of God 1576, faithfully made and given up by Marion Carruthers, his relict, whom he nominated his only executor in his latter Will underwritten of the date at the lodging of the late Mr James Lyndsay, within the burgh of Edinburgh upon the 5 and 6 of Feb. 1576 beforesaid, before these witnesses. Robert Johnstoun in Cummertrees, John Johnstoun,[1] grandson and apparent heir to the Laird of Holmends, John Broun of the Land (son-in-law), John Johnstoun, writer in Edinburgh, and divers others. The said John Johnstoun being sick in body, but whole in mind, submits himself, soul and body, to the mercy of God, recommending his wife and bairns to the favour, protection and maintenance of the Regent's grace, and the Earl of Angus, lieutenant and Warden of the West Marches, which he is persuaded they shall find for the good and true service that he has made, and always intended to make under the King's Majesty for ever, if it had been God's pleasure longer to continue

[1] A Wamfray.

WILL OF JOHN OF NEWBIE

his days, beseeching the said Earl of Angus that by his lordship's means it may please the Regent's grace to dispone the ward and marriage of the said John, grandson to the said Marion Carruthers, for the help of his four younger sons. He makes the said Marion Carruthers his wife, so continuing in her pure widowhood, tutrix testamentur to his grandson and apparent heir. He makes Robert, his son, his assignee to the right possession and kindness of his lands in the town of Annan, except such as is annexed and possessed with the mains of Newbie, and wills the said Robert to be good and friendly to the poor men of Annan, occupiers of the same land. He leaves to the said Robert his right possession and kindness to the Kirk and tithes of Kirkpatrick Fleming, and also makes him assignee to his lease to run of the lands of . . . within the lordship of Dundoran (Wamfray), recommending the said Robert to the favour, protection and maintenance of my Lord Hereis, beseeching his lordship not only to extend the same to the said Robert, accepting him in his lordship's service, and also to stand good lord to his wife and remaining bairns." To his fourth son, John, he leaves his house in Dumfries and money; to his brother, John Johnstoun of Cummertrees, a portion of the lands of Ryehill, and the remaining portion to his third son, Edward. To his fifth son, Abraham, he leaves lands in Middlebie, and to his son, William, lands in Stapleton. To his seventh son, David, he leaves lands in Robgill and the lease of certain lands which had been settled upon his widowed daughter-in-law and her husband on their marriage, the said David paying to her thankfully the duty contained in the said lease during her second husband's lifetime.

Newbie also left daughters—Elizabeth, married to Arthur Graham of the Moat; Marion, married to the Laird of Bardannoch; a third to John Broun of the Land; another to Charles Murray of Cockpool; Mary to John Irving. Possibly more, as the younger children are not all named in the Will.

Agnes Maxwell, the mother of the heir, was remarried to a cousin, Robert Hereis of Mabie. Her first marriage settlement, witnessed by Robert, her brother-in-law, and John of Cummertrees, is recapitulated in a Crown Charter of Dec. 13, 1579, signed at Holyrood House, confirming the local one. In it the " 5 mark lands of Mylbie, 5 mark lands of Howes, and some acres of meadows in Howmedo, lying within the parish of Annan, and half the fisheries of Stapleton " are allotted to the young couple, so soon to be separated by William's early death. The children were John and a daughter, born in 1567 and 1568. John, third Baron of Newbie, came of age, *i.e.*, was fourteen in 1581.

The income of a minor was one of the great sources of revenue to the Crown, and the wardship and marriage of an heir was sold or given to a subject as a reward for services, or a special favour, the King taking half the proceeds. At that time an estate was exhausted, not enriched, by a long minority. In the case of Newbie, the ward of the estate was given to Robert, the eldest surviving son of the late laird, perhaps, for political reasons, that the dependents, including the loyal members of the troublesome clan of Graham, might be kept together under a strong kinsman's hand to maintain peace with their neighbours, or, if need be, to oppose them. Robert received from the Crown re-grants the same year of the Kirk lands in Kirkpatrick Fleming, and the houses in Annan left to him by his father, as well as the Moat; and in 1582 he received a Crown gift of the lands of Northfield and Brigholme near Annan, and in another Charter those of Wormanbie and Gulielands. The young King, "following the good example of his noble ancestors," so the Charter runs, "in rewarding useful lieges, and solicitous for good and honest holders of the Royal lands," hereby infefts "the son of the late John Johnstoun of Newbie in lands" adjoining his nephew's property and his own inheritance. One of his neighbours is stated in the Charter to be Christopher Irving, or " Black Christie," the father of his brother-in-law, John Irving, on the land of Galabank, an estate which became the property of Robert's great-nephew, and is still owned by his descendants.

In 1578-9 the Johnstouns, including Robert Johnstoun of Newbie, John of Graitney, Thomas in Priestwodside, James Johnstoun in Croftheid, Wamfray, Elsieshields, etc., signed a bond of loyalty to the young King.

The district occupied by the clan of Johnstoun covered less ground than many an American ranche. Langholm, the Armstrong tower, is eighteen miles from Annan, Lochmaben Castle ten, Dumfries sixteen, and Gretna eight. The natural increase since the thirteenth century must have been greatly checked by war and feuds,—for the English Warden in 1583 estimated the Johnstouns at "300 sufficient men who with their Laird dwelleth towards the meeting of Annan with the river Milk, and on each side of the Annan. Betwixt the Esk and the Sark dwelleth the Johnstouns of Graitney, every which several surname (of the Border clans) defends their own." From the rent rolls, the Graitney Johnstouns must have been about twelve, but, like Newbie and the Laird, had feuars of other names. The Johnstoun lands were intersected by those of many rivals, so it is not strange that the young Chief, surrounded by enemies and by unscrupulous members of his own clan, should have leased the lands in Cummertrees belonging to his sister, the widowed daughter-in-law of Lord Carlile, now remarried to Lord Seton and come to live there among only Carliles and his kinsmen of Graitney and Newbie. His agreement to the tenants to provide him with barley, fowls and other necessaries, and he would defend them during his sister's lifetime, is signed by John Johnstoun of Newbie, John Johnstoun in Cummertrees, and Carlile of Soupilbank (1577).

John Maxwell, or Lord Hereis, died in 1582. He had been guardian to his own nephew, Lord Maxwell, as well as to the youthful Laird of Johnstoun; and Newbie had commended his son, Robert, and his other children to his protection, showing how well he had succeeded in allaying hereditary jealousies. But he hardly closed his eyes when they were revived. Maxwell refused to sell certain lands to the Chancellor of Scotland, the Earl of Arran, who enjoyed the favour of the youthful King. Maxwell's uncle was Maxwell of Newlaw, Provost of Dumfries, and the Earl in revenge obtained a Royal

Order to Dumfries, that at the election of 1584 the town should appoint a Johnstoun instead of a Maxwell to the office. On the election day Lord Maxwell, with a large body of armed followers, including some of the rebel Armstrongs, prevented Johnstoun from approaching the town, whereupon the Chancellor outlawed Maxwell, and ordered Johnstoun, as Warden, to arrest him. Symon Johnstoun was chosen Provost. But the Maxwells, with the Armstrongs, Scott of Buccleuch, Beatties, Littles, and all the outlaws of the Border, were too strong for the Warden, who was completely defeated, his castle of Lochwood burnt with the Charter chest and valuable documents connected with the clan. Lochous, owned by the Warden's uncle, was undermined; two Johnstouns of Lockerbie, a brother of the Laird of Wamfray, and some of the sons of John Johnstoun of Poldean perishing in the assault, and the country was devastated for months.

Lord Scrope[1] wrote to Walsingham on Aug. 1, 1585: "Upon Thursday last the Earl of Morton (Maxwell claimed that title) caused a gibbet to be made, and ready to be set up at Dumfries, sharply threatening Johnston, the late Warden, and all the rest of that surname of Johnstons that unless they would yield and cause Lochmaben to be forthwith delivered up to him, they should all make their repentance for the same at that pillar, and be hanged thereon."

Only a month later these contending Chiefs laid down their arms and met at a service which had been prohibited under heavy penalties for twenty-five years. A Scottish Roman priest, protected by Maxwell, made his way to the College of Lincluden, near Dumfries. A letter from the Master of Gray to Johnstoun, dated Stirling, Sept. 4, 1585, informs him "of a report having reached his Majesty and the Court that all the Johnstouns had appointed with Maxwell." "The King," he says, "disbelieved it, but desires to be advertized with certainty." Possibly the King did not wish it to be true, but the report arose from the leaders having secretly agreed to an armistice that they might meet at Lincluden for the celebration of Mass. Before the service Maxwell signed a very temporary agreement with Johnstoun to "remit freely and forgive all rancours of mind, grudge, malice and feuds that had passed or fallen between them in any time bygone." "There was a gathering," wrote Scrope, "of about 200 with divers gentlemen and others of the country . . . moreover it is said that this infection spreadeth itself into divers other places." The young Laird of Newbie was there with others of his family, and immediately afterwards he was made responsible for the Irvings of Bonshaw and their misdeeds, although Bonshaw had been claimed as a fief of Johnstoun after William of Graitney had bought the superiority and had given it up to his Chief. But Graitney had feued Stapleton and Robgill to the Irvings, and when they joined the Grahams or the Armstrongs they were stronger than the lairds. Newbie was only seventeen when he was

---

[1] He also wrote Oct. 30, 1583, that he has met Johnstoun, then Warden and Sheriff of Nithsdale, Annandale and Teviotdale. "The difficulty is he has at least four-fold to demand of me than what I required of him in redress."

fined 10,500 marks for their depredations, and borrowed it from Sir James Hamilton; but the debt eventually led to the sale of his estates. Maxwell, Gordon, and Carruthers were outlawed at the same time, but not fined.

Three years before Johnstoun had pledged himself for the good conduct of Graitney, Robert of Newbie, and Cummertrees when they were summoned for assisting at a similar service.

It is hardly possible to suppose that Maxwell took any unfair advantage of Johnstoun, but he captured Lochmaben soon afterwards, and the Warden—for he had never been superseded by the Crown—was taken prisoner to Bonshaw, a tower owned by Edward Irving, Johnstoun's "depender," but now occupied by Maxwell's followers. The captive Chief was released through the Royal intervention in 1586, but he died soon afterwards, it was said from shame and grief at his defeat, possibly accelerated by the rigours of a prison. The ward of his estate was granted to his daughter, Elizabeth (1587); and Robert Johnstoun of Newbie, Graitney, and John Johnstoun of Croftheids joined with other leaders of the clan to pledge themselves to support the young Chief.

Maxwell was again proclaimed a rebel, but his half-brother, Robert, led the feuars, who were still armed, and joined by Drumlanrig, Jardine, and Charteris made what the English Warden described as "a furious raid" on the Johnstoun lands, "coming about 8 a.m. near to the house of Bonshaw, raised a great fire and burned the Bonshaw-side, and Todholes, with another farmhouse there called Dunberton, and in short they burned along the water of Dryfe, of Annan and of Milk as much as pertained to the Laird of Johnston, and committed the like outrages to all the friends and tenants of Johnston there, carrying away with them a great booty."

In the meantime Maxwell with Scott of Buccleuch and a company of Nithsdale men, besides Beatties, Littles, and Armstrongs, marched upon Stirling, the seat of Government, assisted by families who were generally with Johnstoun, but now found it convenient to join the stronger side—the Bells, Irvings, and a troop of cavalry under George Carruthers of Holmains and his son, Charles. Their object was to depose Johnstoun's relative,[1] the Earl of Arran, who fled for his life; and the King was obliged not only to deprive him of his titles and estates but to accept the Earl of Angus, Arran's rival, in his place, and to grant Maxwell and his followers a full pardon for every offence committed since 1569. As Johnstoun was dead, Maxwell was appointed Warden in his place.

Robert Johnstoun of Newbie is mentioned in 1583 in a letter from Lord Scrope to Sir F. Walsingham as "a kinsman of the Lord of Johnstoun"

[1] He was barbarously killed by Sir J. Douglas of Torthorald in 1596. His son avenged it when he met Douglas in the High Street, Edinburgh, July 14, 1608, for although the King in Feb. 1600 describes Douglas as being "our rebel and lying at our horn for the slaughter of our umqle cousin, James Stewart" he was pardoned to assist his relative, Angus, in crushing the Johnstouns. Angus was always intriguing with the English, like so many of his race, and was perhaps accessory to the murder of Carmichael by English Armstrongs, for he protected the murderers.

who brought a letter from his Chief's wife on behalf of a prisoner in English hands. Again in Dec. 1583 "One Robert Johnstoun of Newby, a kinsman of the Laird of Johnston, came to me with the enclosed letter from the Lady Johnston (Margaret Scott), commending to me 2 gentlemen coming from the Scottish Court."

Dame Margaret Scott, as she is usually called, held a position at Court, but in 1586 fell into disgrace. Whether she or her enemies told falsehoods, an Order from the Privy Council directs that she should be tried "for making of leasings and telling of them, which may engender discord between the King and his Highness's subjects." Surrounded by her son's clansmen, and near to her powerful brother, Buccleuch, she was quite safe at Dunskellie, so there she stayed. She was in favour again in 1592, when the King granted her half the escheat of James Johnstoun of Lochous, Mungo Johnstoun of Lockerbie, Thomas Johnstoun of Craigaburn, and five more, keeping the other half himself.

The nine Lairds of the West Marches able to keep order on the Borders in 1587, as given in the 95th Act of the eleventh Parliament of James VI., included the Laird of Johnstoun, John, Laird of Graitney, Lord Maxwell, and Lord Hereis. The same were appointed Constables of the Borders in 1597, and also Johnstoun of Newbie. Graitney, whose father, George, was a younger son of William, first Baron of Newbie, seems to have been very efficient in preserving peace. The Johnstouns and Maxwells formed a band of alliance on the marriage of young James, the Chief of Johnstoun,[1] with Sarah Maxwell, the grand-daughter of the celebrated Lord Hereis. One of Johnstoun's sisters was also married to Sir Robert Maxwell of Orchardstone. The young Laird of Newbie, whose mother was a Maxwell, was married to Elizabeth, the widow of Maxwell of Carnsalloch, and the daughter of Sir Alexander Stewart of Garlies, ancestor to the Earls of Galloway[2] (her mother was a daughter of Sir James Douglas of Drumlanrig). The bridegroom had already married, when about fourteen, Marion Lidderdaill, and was left a widower with one daughter, Janet.

The unrest on the Scottish Borders was undoubtedly sustained by the imprisoned Queen's supporters, and Lord Maxwell went so far as to encourage Spain to fit out the Armada for the invasion of England. In 1583 a Scotsman, Robert Bruce, wrote to invite Philip of Spain to occupy Scotland, "and in this way bring back the Catholic faith also to England and Ireland." The execution of Mary at Fotheringay Castle was the sequence. A general mourning was ordered throughout Scotland, and it was openly said that nothing but war could blot out this stain from her shield. The Spanish Ambassador, writing to Philip in 1587, thinks that James had a secret preference

[1] He was returned heir to his father in 1588, when four of the twelve witnesses were Johnstouns — John of Graitney, John Johnstoun of Newbie, the merchant, the Laird of Elphinstone, and the Baillie of the Water of Leith (of Corrie?), James Rig of Carberry, etc.
[2] There had been earlier connections between the families. Agnes, the fourteenth daughter of Sir A. Stewart, died 1513, married a Johnstoun of that Ilk. Her aunt, Agnes Stewart, married John, Lord Maxwell, whose daughter married another Johnstoun.

for the Roman faith. "The King of Scotland," he writes, "arrived on April 12 at Dumfries,[1] to put his hand on Maxwell's collar. But he had gone the preceding night, being warned by the great lords." The Ambassador suspects the warning was sent by the King himself.[2]

A month before Maxwell actually returned to Kirkcudbright and mustered his kinsmen and tenants to act in concert with the Armada an anonymous letter in cypher was sent to King James. Bacon is accredited with it. "The King of Scotland," it ran, "ought not to undertake to avenge the death of his mother, but on the contrary to do everything possible to bring about the union of the two crowns, for if he tries to make war against this kingdom, he must consider two points. First, if the war would appear just and honest to anyone, and of the means of persevering in it; and what would be the conclusion and end; and secondly, that his pretensions to the succession might fall in the struggle." The writer, after discussing these points, concludes that the end of the war would be the ruin of Scotland, and begs the King not to attempt it.

This letter seems to have made a great impression on James; and as Lord Hereis, Maxwell's cousin, consistent with his father's principles, refused to assist any foreign invasion, the Lairds, under his influence and the Johnstouns, stood by the King. James, hearing what Maxwell was about from these loyal Chiefs, ordered him to appear before him, and on his refusal marched suddenly on Dumfries, from which Maxwell only escaped with great difficulty, and got as far in a ship as Carrick. There he was captured and finally imprisoned in Edinburgh, while his cousin, David Maxwell, captain of Lochmaben, and twenty-two kinsmen and dependents were hanged at Lochmaben and Edinburgh. This satisfied justice, and Maxwell was not only released the next year but allowed to continue as Warden, and appointed a Commissioner to assist Lord Hamilton, his father-in-law, in transacting public affairs during the King's absence in Denmark.

The wars of this century had made horses very scarce. The gift of a horse to John, brother of the Laird of Johnstoun, in 1547 is recorded in the Crown expenses; and in the list of Newbie's personal effects in 1577 only young horses are mentioned—twenty-four colts of two years old and two young mares.

The theft of a horse by Willie of Kirkhill (a Wamfray) led to fresh bloodshed. He seized on one (1592) at Gretna and rode to Wamfray on it, but a letter followed from Sir John Carmichael, the Warden, to the Chief at Lochwood—" Willie Johnstoun of Kirkhill has ane black hors of my couseing Willie Carmichael of Redmyre. It will please your lordship to cause deliver him to the Laird of Gretnay." The Chief seems to have ordered restitution at once, but Kirkhill recompensed himself by stealing a horse belonging to his neighbour, Lord Crichton. A battle ensued, in which several Johnstouns and fifteen Crichtons were killed, and, as the widows appealed to the King with

[1] The murder of Newlaw (Chapter V.) occurred during this visit.
[2] "The Lord Maxwell is in no good favour—mere dissimulation," wrote Lowther.

very lively demonstrations, Maxwell was ordered to arrest the Chief for the act of his dependent and imprison him in the castle at Edinburgh. He escaped and returned to his stronghold at Lochwood, but was proclaimed an outlaw; and Maxwell, brushing aside two agreements between the families—one signed only the previous year—formed a secret bond of manrent with Douglas of Drumlanrig, Crichton, Kirkpatrick of Closeburn, and others who agreed to support him to carry out the Royal command. According to Spottiswode, a copy of the agreement fell into the hands of Johnstoun of Cummertrees, one of the Newbie family, and he gave it up to his Chief, who scornfully received Maxwell's formal summons to surrender and prepared for battle.

Maxwell was assisted by some of the Royal troops, and mustered 1500 or 2000 men. He offered a £10 land to anyone who brought to him Johnstoun's head or hand. On hearing this, Johnstoun offered half that value, as he had not more to give, for the head or hand of Maxwell. With the junior branches of his own clan and his relatives, the Scotts of Eskdale, the Eliots, and some of the Grahams, Irvings, Moffats, and others he assembled about 800 followers. The young Laird of Newbie was an outlaw for hearing Mass, and for having his children baptized by Roman priests, and his name does not appear in the subsequent respite granted to those who took part in the fight; but as his maternal grandfather, Maxwell of Ile, was on the opposite side with eighty followers and his wife's relatives,[1] the Stewarts of Garlies, the Kirkpatricks and the Douglases, it is easy to see how Cummertrees heard of the secret bond. Robert of Newbie was with his Chief, also two Johnstouns of Cummertrees (one of whom was killed), and the Johnstouns of Graitney, of Elsieshields, Powdene, Lockerbie, Kirkton, etc. They were entrenched in a good position when the Maxwells crossed the Annan near the modern railway bridge between Lockerbie and Lochmaben, but it is said that Johnstoun disdained to take this advantage of the enemy and came down into the open plain, where the battle of Dryfe Sands was fought. Johnstoun is allowed to have handled his men with much skill, and gained a complete victory (Dec. 6, 1593). Maxwell was killed by a Johnstoun of Wamfray, the nephew of the original cause of the feud, and Douglas, Kirkpatrick and Grierson fled on horseback. The victors were at once outlawed, "no man daring," as a contemporary diarist writes, "to take any of them into his house."

Lord Scrope, writing from Carlisle to Lord Burghley the day after the battle, says: "The Larde Johnston having called together his friends, did encounter with Lord Maxwell, and hath not only killed the said Lord Maxwell, but very many of his company."

It is probable that Johnstoun's loss was heavy, for in 1594 he obtained a respite from the King for himself and only eight score surviving followers. In the preceding twelve months all the Johnstouns had need of their fortified towers; and William Johnstoun, the young "reader"[2] of Lockerbie Church,

[1] Her niece and namesake, Barbara Stewart, married Kirkpatrick of Closeburn.
[2] He had begged not to be sent there, as he was certain to be killed. He was a natural son of the Commendator of Salsit (died 1599). His effects were granted to Robert Johnstoun of Couran,

was assassinated three years after his appointment, on the pretext that he bore the name. Those respited are recorded in the following order: Sir James Johnstoun of Dunskellie, John Carmichael, Robert Johnstoun of Raecleuch, next of kin to Sir James, Symon, (half) brother to the Laird of Johnstoun, Robert Johnstoun in Brigholme, William, the heir of Graitney, and John Johnstoun in Cummertrees. Then come Johnstouns of Wamfray, Kirkton, William, Adam and James of Elsieshields, Howcleuch, Milnbank, Craigaburn, Corrie, Lockerbie, and Clochrie, besides Irvings, Moffats, Carruthers, Scotts, Eliots, Stewarts, one Chisholm, Arthur Graham, one Armstrong, and several Murrays. All offences were forgiven them except passing bad money. It was the greatest tribal fight that had ever taken place in Scotland, and it was the last.

Lord Hereis (Johnstoun's brother-in-law) succeeded his cousin, Maxwell, as Warden, but he paid no attention to the respite. He tried to capture Johnstoun's followers, till he kept the country in such a state of confusion that the King ended by superseding him with Johnstoun himself. This Chief stated that "the last unhappy and ungodly work arose out of the grit skaithis of fire, and heartless slaughters" done by Maxwell upon Johnstoun's father, "which was his death. Nevertheless he had buried these materials in his heart and entered into a hand agreement with Maxwell, when he found that he had made another bond for the wrecking of him and his friends."

Till the King sent Protestant preachers to convert Dumfries the Reformation had made little way there, still less in Annandale, but, outside, Buccleuch, Drumlanrig, Lag, Gordon, and Kirkpatrick were Protestants. Between 1594 and 1603 there are several sentences of outlawry against the Lairds of Johnstoun and Newbie, Robert, Edward and Abraham of Newbie, Charles Murray of Cockpool, and Edward Maxwell of the Ile for attending Mass, and for allowing their children "to be baptized and taught by Roman priests, and entertaining the same." That Newbie was dealt with more harshly than Johnstoun was probably his proximity to England, which brought him specially under the notice of the Warden, and the desire of the King to appear a good Protestant in English eyes. Newbie's father had been killed at Langside, but his Chief and Robert Johnstoun of Lochmaben had long been respited for "carrying their banners" on that occasion. The Roman priests had been chased from the country before the Reformed Church was ready to replace them, and both Protestants and Romanists believed that an unbaptized infant could be exchanged for a demon, and that the unshriven soul found no peace. The Presbyterians were forbidden to baptize the children of Romanists, and a Borderer's marriage was illegal if solemnised in England.

When Johnstoun was made Warden in 1596 Newbie returned to Annan, and his long delayed retour was made out in 1603. It is signed by five Maxwells, a Wamfray Johnstoun, many Brouns of Land, Roger Kirkpatrick, Stewart of Sweetheart Abbey, John Marschall, Turnour, and John Corsane, Provost of Dumfries. It alludes to the estate having been in ward for twenty-five years "or there abouts," when the Crown took the half rents.

PLATE VI.

ELSIESHIELDS, DUMFRIES.

NEWBIE CASTLE, ON THE SOLWAY, DUMFRIES.

COTTAGE ON THE GALABANK, DUMFRIES.

In *Monypeny's Chronicle*, published in 1587, sixty-four lairds and gentlemen are described as residing in Dumfriesshire and the Stewartry of Kirkcudbright. Five of the lairds were Johnstouns, viz., the Chief, Newbie, Graitney, Corrie, and Elsieshields. Nine were Maxwells, including Lord Hereis, six were Gordons, and four Douglases, including the husband of the heiress of Carlile. Among the chief men of name, "not being lairds," are the Carliles of Bridekirk and Ecclefechan, Arthur, George, and Richard Graham, five Bells, six Irvings, including Edward Irving of Bonshaw, and six Thomsons, Romes, and Gasks.

Douglas of Drumlanrig could not forgive the defeat at Dryfe Sands, and attacked Johnstoun with his "assisters" on July 13, 1597, a fight which, with the failure to arrest two rebel Armstrongs, was a reason to deprive Johnstoun of the Wardenship; but it was given to his ally, Sir John Carmichael, and Robert of Brigholme and Newbie, whose wife was a Carmichael, was made Deputy-Warden. James VI. paid a visit to Lochwood the following autumn, accompanied by his uncle, the Duke of Lennox. He went on to Newbie Castle, where he was entertained by Robert; and possibly when paying these visits discovered for himself "the wild heathen state of the men of Mid-Annandale of the baser sort," which he afterwards graphically described in a proclamation,—and no wonder, as laymen, and very unscrupulous ones, had filled the benefices for more than half a century.

At Newbie King James received Henry Leigh, the English Warden's deputy, "a Warrewyckeshire gentleman," after having held a Council with the Duke of Lennox, the Earl of Glencairn, the Prior of Blantyre, Lord Ochiltree, Lord Sempill, Lord Hereis, the Lairds of Lochinvar and "others of good account;" but, perhaps out of courtesy to his host, he sent away the Lords Hamilton, Maxwell (who was only thirteen), and Drumlanrig, all enemies to the Johnstouns. "His Majesty," wrote Leigh, "sent first Mr Roger Aston one of his chamberlains, and then Sir John Carmichael to entertain me till he rose from Council. Which done he came forth to a green and there did use me very graciously and walked up and down, and conferred with me a great while touching the state of the borders. He seemed resolved to reduce his own to obedience, and satisfy Her Majesty with justice." (Nov. 25, 1597).

Four years later Henry Leigh was taken ill at Newbie Castle, with apparently the smallpox, on his way to see the King, who was again on the Borders, but, naturally, would not send for Leigh "to come near him" when he heard of his illness. Robert Johnstoun apparently still occupied the Castle, as he and his nephew, John, are both called the Laird of Newbie; and Edward of Ryehill, Robert's next brother, who lived in Mylnfield on the Newbie estate, is called in a bond of 1603 "brother to the Laird of Newbie." Ryehill Tower was burned by the English, and a farm now stands on its site, half a mile from the Solway. Edward is mentioned by the English Ambassador as being "very inward with his chief, who is one of the most honest men in these parts."

Johnstoun told the English Warden that he did not consider all his horses of as much value as the life of one servant. Robert Johnstoun was probably the Newbie who escorted Musgrave, Lord Scrope's deputy, to visit the King in Edinburgh, and gave an introduction to Henry Leigh to be presented to the King at the Scottish capital. He also escorted Lord Sempill (who had been at Newbie Castle for twenty days) and others to Carlisle. On this occasion (1601) Scrope sent the following report to the Secretary Cecil:—

"This day Newbie came to me from the King (as he said) and protested highly that his King would be most glad of my favour, adding, that he wondered at my obstinacy. I answered, that her Majesty's orders to me were to do him all lawful service, and I was ever ready thereto. He asked if I went to Parliament. I said her Majesty had occasion for me some time here. He added that the Queen (Elizabeth) had promised his King, that in this Parliament the case of the succession should be handled, and that then there is none to succeed but his King. My reply was, that we live under so happy an estate as we hope never shall be altered, and that I trusted in God that Her Majesty's prosperous reign should continue long after his King's, and his successors were extinct. To this he replied that it was the wish of a good subject, but contrary to the course of nature; adding that if I would pawn my honour to keep counsel, he had five books come from London touching the succession, of which four he delivered to the King, the last he kept in his own custody which he would lend me to read. Upon hearing thereof, I rose up and went from him, as if I had been called in haste.

"As he will surely come again from the King ere long, I pray for Her Majesty's pleasure, whether I shall deal so roundly with him as to stop all such discourse, or hold him up with fair weather. He told me David Foulis, a man the Queen hates above all Scotsmen for that he wrote to that King at his last being here, that she was dead (whom I pray to God to preserve many years after he is rotten, and to make her estate as flourishing as she is admirable), is presently to come to her Majesty, and that he is appointed to move for the succession if he dare; yet he fears that the King will be forced to send a man of better quality than Foulis to that end."

Lord Scrope speaks of the Laird of Newbie as his neighbour; and it was the nearest house to Cumberland large enough to lodge the King, or a nobleman, with the necessary followers. Musgrave lived at Rockliff Castle. Newbie was frequented by both English and Scottish Deputies, as well as by the King, at the time that the settlement of the Borders had become a burning question if James were ever to be accepted as their sovereign by the English people. The Lords in Council even recommended to him the means by which his grandfather, James V., had rid himself of troublesome Borderers. It was always expensive to entertain Royalty, and at Newbie the estate was curtailed to pay for it. Robert of Newbie also sold his lands at Kirkpatrick Fleming, Gulielands, Northfield, the Moat, and Brigholme. The honour was dreaded by most Scottish proprietors, and the Earl of Angus allowed his house to remain dismantled, when there was hardly accommodation for himself and his wife, so that he might be unable to receive the King.

But to return to 1597, King James appears to have deposed Johnstoun, and visited Dumfriesshire in the hope of conciliating Elizabeth and her Cabinet, the first having just sent a very severe letter to him for alluding rather bitterly to his mother's death when he opened the last Parliament, the record of it having lately been forwarded to her. From Newbie he went to Dumfries to hold a Court, and in four weeks hanged fourteen or fifteen notorious thieves, and took thirty-six hostages from the Johnstouns, Armstrongs, Bells, Carliles, Beatties, and Irvings, who were charged 1s. 4d. a week each for their keep, and were to be hanged if any further outrages took place.

The English Ambassador, writing to Cecil, Oct. 12, 1599, considers that the Earl of Angus and Lord Hamilton, both related to the Maxwells, were the real cause of the troubles in Annandale and on the Borders. Lord Hereis, Johnstoun, and Drumlanrig had been arrested and imprisoned in Edinburgh. George Murray, one of the gentlemen of the Chamber, was sent to receive Lochmaben Castle from the Wamfrays for the King, and Johnstoun, who had held it as Warden, was directed to send orders to that effect. He sarcastically declined to control his dependers from so great a distance. Murray is described as "Johnston's own."

On Nov. 12, 1599, the Ambassador writes again: "On Thursday the Laird of Johnston brought in most of his pledges," and was to be released, having subscribed an assurance. This was signed by himself and his pledges, Johnstoun of Graitney and Gilbert Johnstoun of Wamfray. The Ambassador looked forward to the day of the trial, and confronting the lieutenant Angus[1] with Johnstoun, "which will be exceeding great, and may well breed a great stir," but the King was afraid of Angus and his relatives, and glad to settle the matter quietly.

In 1600 a decree of the Lords in Council charged these chiefs with the care of the Borders—Lord Home, Sir James Johnstoun of Dunskellie, James Johnstoun of Westraw (the Laird's brother-in-law), John Johnstoun of Newbie, Grierson of Lag, Kirkpatrick of Closeburn, Robert Gordon, apparent of Lochinvar, John Johnstoun of Graitney, Hamilton, various Maxwells, and Scott of Buccleuch. Before this special commission was dissolved in 1621 Newbie and Graitney had disappeared as separate baronies; and the chiefs, whose lawlessness defied the Crown, were ennobled. Buccleuch was a terror to the south of Scotland. On a report being spread that he was marching on Edinburgh, the shops were at once closed and barricaded. Gordon soon proved that he was more capable of raising a disturbance than of keeping order.

Buccleuch's exploits have been told with poetic licence by the literary members of his family. Scrope wrote that "he had ever been the chief enemy, and still is, to peace on the Borders." When he rescued Kinmont Willie from Carlisle Castle the prisoner was heavily ironed after a much later custom to prevent escape when allowed exercise, and there were not the warders and

---

[1] Angus had been made lieutenant of Southern Scotland to be superior to the Warden.

garrison of modern times.[1] The Johnstouns did not assist him, but "they lay in ambush in one place, and the gudeman of Bonshaw in another, on the pale of Scotland to have given defence to their own, and resisted the pursuers if they had followed so far."

As the new Warden had fought with the Johnstouns at Dryfe Sands, and was connected with his deputy, Robert of Newbie, another combatant in that decisive battle, the pardon of the Laird of Johnstoun followed as a matter of course. On July 2, 1600, he was acquitted of all actions since his respite for that battle, and restored to his honours (writes Birrell, the Edinburgh diarist) by a herald and four trumpets at the cross of Edinburgh. But Angus and his friends were not to be checkmated. The Wardenship was a most coveted post, and the same year Carmichael was murdered by their allies, the Armstrongs, on his way to open a Court at Lochmaben.

This murder (for the assassins were English subjects) made a great sensation on each side of the Border, and Nicolson alludes in a letter to Cecil to the anxiety felt by James VI. lest anything should prevent him from succeeding Queen Elizabeth. The Scots had been "greatly disheartened by their last war" and were in no mood for another, as they felt certain that it would end in the humiliation of their country. So to please both parties, Lord Hereis was appointed Warden, and charged to arrest and punish Armstrong, his father, brothers, and kin, as well as all professional thieves, and to avenge Carmichael's murder. He was not nearly so active in the matter as Johnstoun, who soon succeeded him as Warden and seized some notorious outlaws. There was fear that as Lord Hereis had not captured them he had a motive for it, and that they might be protected in high quarters. "The Laird," says Nicolson[2] speaking of Johnstoun "writes, as a resident and a man that will be feared . . . Johnston hath done great service in taking these men and would be thanked. He prays him (the King) to send warrant to keep them, and not to deliver them unless for justice to England, notwithstanding any warrants to be after written to the contrary; a square and honest meaning in the Laird." Johnstoun offered to meet Lord Scrope at Gretna Kirk.

On April 11, 1601, Nicolson writes that "Francis Armstrong and others, the late spoilers, have been taken by the Laird of Johnston, and he recommends that they may be delivered up to her Majesty's officers." He had displeased the King by the pressure he put upon him about these "spoilers," yet the King had sent David Murray to Johnstoun to ask if his presence was required. Nicolson and Johnstoun both wished the King to go to Lochmaben, "so that the thieves might see that their misrule displeased him, and should be punished . . . But now the Border is quiet through Johnston's diligence who hath gotten the best of the rest of the thieves, has met Mr Lowther, meets him again for justice, and keepeth those thieves to do justice with as the King shall be pleased, which he will obey. So as there is no fault in Johnston, no doubt but these late disorders shall redress and all be quiet."

[1] He blew up a private door and so entered.
[2] He encloses a correspondence between James VI. and Johnstoun.

Yet only fifteen days later James VI.[1] wrote to Lord Mar of his conference with the Laird of Johnstoun and Robert Scott, "respecting incursions by the English on the Borders, and the delay in staying the same through the absence of Lord Scrope from his wardenry; that a complaint was to be sent to the Queen, our dearest sister," about Lord Scrope, and that "a fresh man such as his father was, should replace him. The murderers of the Laird of Carmichael," said his Majesty, "were protected by the English, for some of them being pursued by our Counsellor, the Commendator of Holyrood House, and the Laird of Johnstoun were not only received in full daylight by the Grahams of Esk (Englishmen), but fortified and assisted in such sort by them as they fled in fear, that they came back reinforced by these outlaws, and turned a chase upon our Counsellor and Warden, so that they narrowly escaped with their lives. We are certified by our Warden that the said fugitives and outlawed Armstrongs have their residence now for the most part in Geordie Sandie's house, an Englishman."

Scrope wrote to Cecil that Johnstoun had "too much honour to backbite him."

As had happened before, the Scots had more grievances than the English. On April 28 Nicolson wrote to Cecil[2] that the King has had secret speeches with Johnstoun; and in August reports another Armstrong outrage, and that he cannot see how the peace will be preserved there. He wrote again that on May 25, 1602, the "outlawed Armstrongs," Carmichael's murderers, "have the last week ridden upon the Laird of Johnston's lands and carried away some of his goods," their chiefs refusing to check them, "which the Laird takes evil, and intends to take amends as he may. This I hear, and I do fear that in the end they will get life." He adds that Johnstoun and Mr Musgrave, Lord Scrope's deputy, "are the only bridles these evil men and others have. If they miscarry, both Princes will be troubled to keep those parts in order."

On Nov. 28, 1602, Nicolson writes again : " We have much ado about West Border affairs. The Laird of Johnston making odious complaints about (the sloth of) my Lord Scrope and John of Johnston (Newbie); yet if Lord Scrope please to take the opportunity he may have, with honour, he may do anything with the Laird."

Maxwell begged the King to exempt his own followers, the Armstrongs, "and broken men of the Borders, from Johnstoun's jurisdiction." Newbie was appointed in 1602, with Lord Herries and Closeburn, an assessor or adviser to his Chief.

In 1602 Graitney made a complaint to the Privy Council that having sent

---

[1] It was at this time that the King visited Newbie.

[2] Scrope writes to Cecil later "John Musgrave my deputy was lately conveyed to Scotland to the Laird of Newbie, where Carmichael his son-in-law brought him to the King a hunting, who conferred with him apart about two hours as a Scottish gentleman saw and told me. Let me not be seen in all this."

Hunsdon, Deputy-Warden, sends proof that the King had actually paid money in a private interview to Willie Armstrong of Kinmont. "Edward Urwen of Bonshaw says openly there is no confidence to be given to the King's word but they rely much on Carmichael."—*Border Papers*.

"his three sons with nine of his servants, with carriage[1] and provision to the meeting at Liddell in England, having obtained license so to do, for some venison for the banquet made by his Chief, the Laird of Johnstoun, at the late baptism of his son, Thomas Trumble of Mynto, Hector Trumble of Barnhill, and Mark Trumble of Bewlie (Englishmen) attacked and robbed them;" the carriage, bedding, and victuals were worth £240.

The same year Johnstoun, Newbie, Graitney, and other lairds signed a bond of peace, the King heading the list.

The English Crown devolved on James VI. the next year (1603); and he appointed Graitney and two colleagues (Feb. 7, 1604) to survey the Debateable Land and surrounding parts, with the view of granting or selling them to the Earl of Cumberland. The sum of £66, 3s. 4d. is charged for Graitney's expenses. In 1605 the King wrote to the Governor of York, telling him to furnish the Laird of Johnstoun with fifty more horsemen to aid in pacifying the Borders. If he had not got the money he was "to beg or borrow it." A warrant, dated Westminster, Jan. 27, 1608, also directs the Treasurer "to pay to John Johnstoun of Gretna, Scotland, £100 as a free gift and reward."

The most troublesome of the Grahams were transported to Ireland; and a special commission was convened, which sat from 1604 to 1621, to try Border causes. Strict equity was hardly to be expected, but some of those who obtained places on it took the opportunity to enrich themselves and gratify private revenge. Many outlaws, notably Christopher Irving, were hung, but others whose crimes had been equally flagrant were spared and even rewarded. One of these was Robert Gordon, the heir of Lochinvar, a Commissioner himself. In 1602, having lost a relative in a skirmish, he made a foray through Annandale, Wamfray, Lockerbie, Reidhall, Langrigs, etc., and killed Richard Irving of Graitney in his own house. A party of soldiers was sent to arrest him, but he took them all prisoners, and compelled the officer who commanded them to eat the King's warrant for apprehending him. He was outlawed, and a description of his personal appearance as well as that of Lord Crichton of Sanquhar (outlawed at the same time for the murder of a fencing-master who accidentally deprived him of an eye) was sent to Carlisle and Dumfries for their apprehension. Yet only three years afterwards Gordon was made a gentleman of the King's bedchamber, and received a gift of confiscated estates, and in 1621 he was made a baronet.[2]

The Laird of Buccleuch was ennobled in 1606. As he had got hold of much church land his son was a formidable opponent to Charles I. when the King wished to recover a portion of these lands for the maintenance of the clergy. But the elder Scott did good service by collecting a number

---

[1] Chalmers states that the first carriage in Scotland came from France with the Queen of James V., and was still the only carriage in their daughter's reign. The decreet only fined the English robbers the price of three horses, value £40 each.

[2] Baronetcies were instituted that year, and were purchased by the recipient, who, for this and other honours, was advised by the King that he had selected him as a fit person for promotion if he would take the necessary steps, *i.e.*, pay the money.

CLAN SYSTEM REPRESSED

of moss-troopers and cattle-drivers in the Middle Marches and sending them to Holland for the army of the Prince of Orange, who paid him for it. Douglas of Drumlanrig was made Earl of Queensberry; and Douglas of Angus was created a Marquis in 1633. Both received from Charles I. the gift of lands which their families forfeited in the fifteenth century, and as Lochous was escheated when its owner was hanged the King gave it to Angus. The fees paid on these transfers helped to fill the Privy purse.

Graitney's expenses were greater than the sum he received for them, but it was not only present difficulty which made him sell his estate in 1618 to John Murray of Cockpool, "one of the grooms of His Majesty's Chamber." He could not afford to sustain a yearly lawsuit against Murray, backed as he was by the King's resolve to break up a clan which was strong enough to dictate to the Crown. In 1591 a list collected by Chancellor Maitland gives Johnstoun, Armstrong, Scott, Beattie, Little, Thomson, Glendyning, Bell, Irving, Carruthers, Graham, Jardine, Moffat, and Latimer as the only families in the South-West who still have captains and chiefs on whom they depend more than on the King—and nine of these were under Johnstoun's protection.

Buchanan,[1] the Royal tutor, like Camden, his contemporary, speaks of the Johnstouns as the most important of the clans in the West—the great obstacle to the English conquest—and the King could always depend on it for promptness, loyalty, and patriotism.

In 1602 a tax was laid on every householder for the repair of the churches—"the King and Privy Council think that much of the looseness and barbarity of the Borderers arose from the want of the Gospel being properly preached to them." Johnstoun obeyed, but he and his heir were not very cordial to the first Reformed ministers who were sent to them; and those in the county who adhered to the Church of Rome usually refused to pay the tithes.

[1] George Buchanan was born in Dumbartonshire in 1506, and died in Edinburgh 1582; author of the *History of Scotland*. He was secretary in France for five years to the Earl of Cassilis, and on returning to Scotland was made tutor to the eldest natural son of James V. The King, although persecuting Reformers, thought the Franciscans were in league with malcontent nobles, so ordered Buchanan to write a satire upon them; but it displeased the monks without satisfying the King, who ordered a sharper one, hence "the Franciscan." This enraged Cardinal Beaton, and when Buchanan heard from his friends that a sum of money was offered to the King for his head he escaped from prison to England. There he found that "Henry VIII. cared more for his own security than the Reformation, and almost with one and the same fire Protestants and Papists were being burnt," so went on to the Continent. There he had many vicissitudes till recalled by Queen Mary in 1566. She made him Principal of St. Andrews and tutor to James VI.

Note.—An Englishman wrote his impressions of the Scots in 1598. He stayed "at a Knight's house (Buccleuch?) near the Borders," and, as he had been sent by the Governor of Berwick on a political errand, was entertained "after their best manner. Many servants brought in the meat, with blue caps on their heads, the table being more than half furnished with great platters of porridge, each having a little sodden meat. When the table was served, the servants sat down with us; but the upper mess instead of porridge, had a pullet with some prunes in the broth, and I observed no art of cookery or house-hold stuff, but rude neglect of both. The Scots living then in factions used to keep many followers and so consumed their revenues in victuals, and were always in want of money. They commonly eat hearth cakes of oats, but in cities have also wheaten bread. I never saw or heard that they had inns with signs hanging out, but the better sort of citizens brew ale their usual drink, and the same citizens will entertain passengers upon acquaintance or entreaty. Their bedsteads were like cupboards in the wall with doors to be opened and shut at pleasure, so as we climbed up to our beds. The husbandmen in Scotland, the servants and almost all the country, wore coarse cloth made at home of grey or sky colour, and flat blue caps very broad. The merchants in cities were attired in English or French cloth of pale colour, or mingled black and blue. The gentlemen did wear English cloth or silk or light stuffs little or nothing adorned with silk lace, much less with lace of silver or gold, and all follow the French fashion especially at Court. Gentlewomen married wore close upper bodies after the German fashion with large whalebone sleeves after the French; short cloaks like the Germans, French hoods and large falling bands about their necks. The unmarried of all sorts go bareheaded and wear short cloaks like the virgins of Germany. The lower sort of citizens' wives and the women of the country wore cloaks made of a coarse stuff of two or three colours in checker work vulgarly called pladden." He sums up, that all ranks from the Court to the country girl would not be attired like the English, and while the women preferred to follow the German, the men followed the French.

CHAPTER X.

YOUNGER SONS OF JOHNSTOUN AFTER THE UNION—CLERGY—MEDICINE—MERCHANTS—WESTRAW—THE LAIRD—CORRIE—WAMFRAY—NEWBIE—IN EDINBURGH—ATTACK ON NEWBIE TOWER—THE ESTATE PASSES TO THE LAIRD OF JOHNSTOUN—HIS MURDER—BARBARA JOHNSTOUN TRIED FOR "PAPISTRY"—HER DAUGHTERS—A ROMANTIC MARRIAGE—ROBERT OF RAECLEUCH—THE EARL OF WIGTON.

THE cruel destructiveness with which the English and civil wars had been carried on in Mid-Annandale, the sequestration of Johnstoun's estates, and the hostility of the Maxwells, who with their allies owned Galloway and half Dumfriesshire, were gradually driving the Johnstoun chiefs southward ; and after Dryfe Sands their head took up his abode at Cove or Dunskellie, near Graitney. His father began the movement by renting lands at Kelhead, between Cummertrees and Annan, from his sister Jean, the widow of the Master of Carlile, and remarried to Lord Seton. It was the weaker clan concentrating its forces. Even the sons of Johnstoun of Reidhall, outlawed for over twenty-four years, found shelter in Graitney, though the penalty was death to all who harboured criminals.

There was a want of occupation for younger sons after 1603. The regular army did not exist ; and a limited number of professional men could gain a living in so poor a country. Some went to join the Prince of Orange, others to help to found a new Empire in America. We had then no footing in India.

Speed and Monypeny, in the sixteenth century, speak of the Scottish zeal for learning ; and those who entered the professions were called Sir, a translation of Dominus, when they graduated at a university. In 1492 and 1575 Sir James Weild and Sir Cuthbert Rig, both writers, were so called in Dumfries ; in Annandale Sir John and Sir James Johnstoun were successively priests at Dornock ; Sir Edward Johnstoun, a priest at Moffat ; Sir Thomas Johnstoun, chaplain at Stirling in 1544 ; and the Abbots of Salsit, always Johnstouns, were known by the same prefix—but not the lay-parsons and lay-abbots. The custom died out when the two kingdoms were united, and Master or Mr substituted ; but landowners always preferred to go by the name of their estate.

The early physicians were called Right Hon., but they had to go to France or Italy to study. Buchanan tells us that the lairds were commonly taught surgery, to be ready when they lead their followers into battle; and that James IV. was an expert surgeon. The love of litigation common to all tribes compelled to give up blood feuds made the writer's and advocate's calling a brisk one in Annandale, but there were still amateurs selected as in the old days by each suitor to plead his cause before the courts.

One of John Johnstoun of Graitney's sons, after studying at St. Andrews, was ordained into the Reformed Episcopal Church; also Symon Johnstoun, a son of Robert, parson of Lochmaben, and John, son of the Laird of Castlemilk—but not many of the name took Holy Orders at that time, as those in Annandale were still attached to the Church of Rome. The Johnstouns about Edinburgh accepted the Reformed Faith. The old Laird of Elphinstone heard the sermon preached by John Knox at Blackfriars Church in 1558, which caused the mob to sack the adjacent monastery.

The life of a merchant had more attractions than might have been expected for a young Borderer—to act as captain of a vessel carrying goods to England, Glasgow, Ireland, and Holland, with all the chances of a sea-fight on the way; to face a lion in Morocco, like the celebrated London merchant; to be one of an armed guard in charge of merchandise through France, Germany, or Denmark, running the gauntlet among robber barons who lived on such spoil, or between the contending armies of Spain and the Dutch Republic. Favoured by Scottish soldiers of fortune in a foreign service, they not unfrequently acted as volunteers in return. It was these who, brought into direct contact with savage emissaries of Spain, helped to bring the Reformed opinions from Holland and Germany to Scotland; and they naturally spread first in the sea-port towns. Merchants were the first ambassadors to Russia, Turkey, Persia, India, and China. At this time there were Johnstouns of Elphinstone, Westraw, Newbie, Elsieshields, Wamfray, Poldean, and Clochrie engaged as merchants in Edinburgh, Glasgow, and Dumfries.

There were Johnstouns serving as officers under the King of Sweden. Among them, Matthew Johnstoun fought in the campaign in Livonia in 1564, David and John Johnstoun were in the Swedish army in 1595, and John Johnstoun in the regiment of Colonel Cobren in 1609.

When Angus was made lieutenant of South Scotland, or Dumfriesshire, he was allowed to take half the value for himself of the goods, cattle, and lands forfeited. His operations were chiefly directed against the Johnstouns, and were known locally as the Raid of Dumfries. Pitscottie says that he gained nothing by it, and spent 60,000 marks of his own. He was related to the King, who had taken steps to convert him to Protestantism; but he was out of favour in 1602, on a rumour being spread that he was a Romanist in disguise, whereupon the Presbytery placed a Reformed minister in his house for his instruction. He then openly professed his old belief, and, after imprisonment in Glasgow, he was exiled to France, where he died in 1611.

His short term of power was of lasting consequence to James Johnstoun of Westraw, who had married for his second wife, Eufemia, daughter of Sir Laurence Oliphant, Angus being the husband of her elder sister. Although only respited in 1599 " for burning the Church of Lochmaben," and for joining with Matthew Moffat in the slaughter of Alexander Baillie, Westraw was a Commissioner for regulating the Borders in 1600, with six Protestant colleagues, besides his relatives, the Lairds of Johnstoun, Newbie, and Graitney, and various Maxwells. In 1605 he was outlawed again, and in the Edinburgh Tolbooth, for rescuing some Lockerbie Johnstouns from a force under Sir John Maxwell of Pook, who, with three of his attendants, was killed. Westraw and some of the Wamfray and Poldean Johnstouns who had assisted him were released on the Laird's security, signed by Patrick Porteus and Edward Johnstoun of Ryehill.

This bond shows the strength of the ties of clanship at a time when the Crown was trying hard to dissolve them, for the Laird was actually suing Westraw for not carrying out the contract he had made when he married the Laird's sister—to rent the Johnstoun lands in Mid-Annandale. Probably Angus, now his patron and counsellor, advised him against it, exposed as these lands were to attacks from Maxwell and his allies. Maxwell himself had been lately sent to Clydesdale. Angus also supported Westraw's petition in 1607 to the Privy Council, setting forth that Lord Herries, his brother Edward, Lord Maxwell, Sir Robert Maxwell, his brother, and others threatened the petitioner's life. Maxwell and Herries were ordered to find caution for £2000.

Carmichael was equally threatened in Eskdale by the Armstrongs. In 1605 he sold Glendining to Westraw (Chapter IV.), who had difficulty in paying for it; but being near Dunskellie, he was able to renew friendly relations with the Laird; and by favour of the Crown or of the Laird's widow became one of the curators to his six-years-old heir.

Johnstoun had been loaded with fines and his lands sequestrated when, to quote the Privy Council, he was given the burden of the Wardenship in 1596, with the King's command to arrest every " dissolute and unruly person." He held it for three years, when it was conferred on Carmichael over his head, possibly owing to the lay-abbot of Salsit's complaint about his violent ejection from the Abbey lands by some of Johnstoun's followers. When re-appointed he got himself returned heir to the Barony of Corrie, and to the advowson of its Church, by the dependents of his own name and some of his neighbours—William of Elsieshields, Robert Johnstoun of Raecleuch, Robert French of Frenchland, Robert Moffat of Granton, Ninian Johnstoun of Poldean, Christopher Carruthers of Dormont, Andrew Johnstoun of Lockerbie, James Johnstoun of Hesliebrae, John Carlile of Boytath, Symon Johnstoun of Woodheid, Wilkin Johnstoun in Templand, Robert Johnstoun of Newton, Robert Johnstoun, younger of Wamfray, John Irving de Luce, and John Graham of Dryff. Nothing is said in the retour about any possessor of Corrie since his great-grandfather, who held it in ward during the outlawry of James Johnstoun of Corrie; and, as neither Elphinstone, Westraw, Graitney, Newbie, nor the Laird of Wamfray witnessed it, the retour seems to have been unjust to the sons of George Johnstoun of Corrie, who was still alive, even if Walter Johnstoun, Laird of Corrie, was dead, which is probable, and had left no sons.

CORRIE

As the Johnstouns of Corrie descend from the next brother to John of Johnstoun (1524-67) (whose direct male heirs are extinct) they are an important branch; but since the captivity of young James Johnstoun of Corrie in 1547 the stronghold of Bonshaw, which Corrie claimed, was held by the Laird, or by the Irvings, and they were reduced to a very poor position. Adam Johnstoun was Laird of Corrie in 1578. His brother seems to have joined his mercantile relatives in Edinburgh. In 1581 Geordie Johnstoun, (lay) parson of Corrie, is a cautioner with his Chief for William Johnstoun of Kirkhill and Wamfray; and in 1585 Thomas Johnstoun of Fingland (Wamfray), George Johnstoun of Corrie, Mungo Johnstoun in Lockerbie, Christie Johnstoun in Milnbank, and others are denounced by the Privy Council for assisting the Laird and his son, James, when Maxwell was Warden. Watt Johnstoun in Corrie, his brothers, men, servants, and tenants are responsible for themselves. Johnstoun was dead on June 21, 1587, and his son with the above supporters was again denounced by the Privy Council. At this time George Johnstoun of Corrie and his sons came to Mylnfield near Annan. John, called "portioner of Corrie," probably George Johnstoun of Corrie's son John, was dead in 1616. Walter Johnstoun of Corrie was among those respited for fighting at Dryfe Sands (1593).

In 1620 a bond is signed by Thomas Johnstoun, portioner of Corrie, and John, his son, witnessed it. A year later, with Marjory Hamilton, his wife, he repays money to Sir Lucas Craig of Riccarton, knight, John Johnstoun, writer, being a witness. John Johnstoun, Baillie of the Water of Leith, is "callit of Corrie" in 1608 when he lent money to the Laird, who styles him his "cusing." In 1620 Thomas Johnstoun, portioner of Corrie, borrowed money from John Johnstoun, writer. John and Alexander Johnston of Castlemilk, and Robert Johnstoun witnessed it.

George Johnstoun of Corrie, probably the son of Walter, owned Grethead or Girthead in 1623, and was sued for debt in 1628. He married Margaret, widow of William Johnstoun in Langside;[1] and in 1628 the property is made over to her with his son John's consent. John married Ann Murray, a great-niece of Nicolas Douglas, Lady Johnstoun, and died about 1652, when his daughter, Margaret, was served heir to her grandfather. George Johnstoun of Girthead, brother to John, married Elizabeth Young; and their son, George, who was Sheriff-Depute of Annandale, married Jean Johnston of Penlaw, and died 1713. Of George and Jean's three sons, Archibald, Joseph, and William, the two eldest died *s.p.* William married Helen Hamilton of Ellershaw, and died 1743, leaving four daughters. Jean, the elder, married Hugh Lawson, and left an only daughter.

George, the dweller in Mylnfield, was sued for debt in 1618; and sum-

---

[1] This inscription to their memory was moved from the wall of Johnstone Kirk to the Hope-Johnstone vault about 1858. "Heir lyes George Johnston of Girthead, and Margaret Johnston his spouse, who was laird of Corrie and lenellie descended by father and son to Adam Johnston Brother German to the Laird Johnston of Lochwood who married Sir Thomas Corri of that Ilk's only daughter and so became Laird of Corrie, and George Johnston son of the said Georg of Girthead, and Elizabeth Young his spous and all their progene since they came to Corrie."—*Records of the Corrie Family.* By J. Corrie.

moned to quit the Newbie estate by Viscount Annand in 1629. Nothing more appears of him except a monument in the old churchyard in Annan, which was legible in 1772.

In 1597 a Johnstoun of Wamfray was hung for slaying Hew Douglas "upon set purpose and forethought of felony."[1] His uncle, Gilbert of Wamfray, was one of the judges who condemned him. Gilbert's mother, Margaret M'Clellan, died in 1589; and he appears to have married a second time to a Maxwell. One of his daughters was the wife of Sir John Murray of Cockpool. Gilbert was dead before 1611, leaving Robert, his heir, John, Edward, a merchant in Edinburgh, James, and William, the last of whom was killed by Captain John Johnstoun of Lochous,[2] lay-parson of Johnstone, when he was living at Dornock, near Graitney. Lochous was tried for it and condemned to be hanged (1603).

Gilbert's brother, William of Kirkhill, known as the Galliard, was killed by the Crichtons in 1592. Another brother, John, who lived in Dumfries, obtained a respite in 1573, with Symon and James Johnstoun, brothers (probably of Elsieshields), and James Johnstoun of Corhead, for art and part in the slaughter of Adam Rae between the Court House and Market Cross of Dumfries. Gilbert's son, John of Wamfray, was made a burgess of Dumfries in 1617, with his relatives, William of Kirkhill, and William, Robert of Kirkhill's son.

Robert of Wamfray is described in a decreet in 1611 as "A gentleman of very mean rent nothing like a great baron, and his brothers, James and William, but young gentlemen without any rent or means of living." Their father's goods had been escheated and given to his relative, Sir Robert M'Clellan of Bombie, for "certain offences" in 1608, probably for receiving outlawed Johnstouns. Another brother, David, is cautioner for payment of 100 marks from Robert to Irving of Bonshaw, 1624.

An entry in the law reports, June 21, 1621, looks as if Robert was following the way of his forefathers. "Complaint of Robert Maxwell of Dinwoodie, how the Laird of Wamfray and others, and Richard Irving callit the young Duke of Hoddam came and destroyed his peats, and chased his cattle with the butt ends of their lances, so that some of them were left dead, and others broke their legs. Had to find security." But this branch did its best to improve its position by marriage. Robert's wife (Feb. 20, 1606) was Mariot Montgomery, daughter of Sir Neil Montgomery of Longham. Their daughter, Mariot, married Jardine of Apilgirth; and John, who was returned heir to his father, Oct. 27, 1641, married Mary, daughter of Sir William Douglas of Kelhead (ancestor to the Marquis of Queensberry), her mother being Lady Isobel Kerr, daughter of the Earl of Lothian. John was a member of the War Committee in 1640, and signed the Covenant. He left an only daughter, Janet, who was returned his heir, Jan. 25, 1658, her father having directed that she should only marry a Johnstoun.

George Johnstoun of Wamfray signed a marriage settlement for an Irving

---

[1] Scott much antedates the Wamfray Johnstouns in *The Fair Maid of Perth*.
[2] Half-brother to the Laird who died 1587.

of Bonshaw in 1661. He was uncle to the heiress, and great-uncle to the Chevalier Johnstone.

William, the second son of Mr Samuel Johnston of Sheens, married Janet of Wamfray. Their daughter married James Irving of Cove; and their son, Robert, succeeded his mother, Lady Wamfray, in 1701. He married Isobel, daughter of the third Lord Rollo (by his wife the daughter of Balfour of Burley), one of her sisters being married to William Irving of Bonshaw. The Irvings had a numerous family, and Wamfray and his wife appear among the witnesses to the baptism of several of the children in Bonshaw Tower; but of their own five sons only two lived to be of age. The eldest, Captain James, was served heir in 1734 to an estate deeply in debt. His brother, Robert, was captain in a regiment commanded by Colonel Marjoribanks in the service of Holland when he succeeded his brother, James, in 1746. He married his first cousin, Jean Rollo, and had a son and daughter, Robert and Mary; but as he sold his lands to Lord Hopetoun he was the last of the Johnstoun Lairds.

Thomas Johnstoun of Fingland in Wamfray was security for the Wamfrays in 1581, also for Herbert Johnstoun in Hesilbank, as well as for his own sons, William and Symon, so it seems probable that he was a younger son of the first James of Wamfray. John Johnstoun of Fingland was captured by the Maxwells in 1585, and killed when a fugitive by Jardine of Apilgirth. Abraham Johnstoun of Newbie took out Letters of Slain against Jardine; he was possibly connected by marriage more closely with Fingland than by cousinship. In 1600 Lord Herries proposed that the compromise agreed on in such matters—the humiliation, request for pardon, and money payment to the widow or nearest relative by the offender—should be accepted in this case by the Johnstouns. Abraham alone declined it, and remained at deadly feud with Jardine. When the victim's escheat was conferred on his father, he is stated to have committed suicide?

Thomas Johnstoun in Fingland, and Symon, Gavin, Geordie, and Robert, sons to the elder Thomas Johnstoun in Fingland, were among those respited after Dryfe Sands. As they were kindlie tenants it is difficult to trace their descendants. George Johnstoun of Fingland was declared by Murray in 1611 to belong to Wamfray, but to have no right to his land.

Mr David Johnstone of Mid Murthat claims John Johnstoun of Wamfray as his ancestor (whom tradition says built the house at Murthat about 1604, and that his descendants lived there ever since), but has no documents. Otherwise the Johnstouns of Wamfray seem to be extinct.

The wars with England and the heavy fines, added to the entertainment of the King at Newbie Castle, ruined the third Baron of Newbie; but his uncle, Robert, who managed the estate for the Crown while it was sequestered, sold some of his own lands and appeared at the Coronation of James VI. in Westminster Abbey. He went to London with his namesake and relative, the historian; and as Robert of Newbie is called Sir Robert, it is assumed he was knighted. The rich member of the Newbie family was his third brother, John, a merchant in Edinburgh, who owned a house in Lochmabengait, Dumfries, in 1576. He was M.P. for Edinburgh in 1581 when Robert was M.P. for Dumfriesshire; and he was one of the witnesses to his Chief's retour in 1588.

Robert of Newbie is mentioned by the English Warden as son-in-law to the murdered Carmichael. His wife must have been the Dame Sara Carmichael, Lady Johnstoun,[1] who was cautioner for John Johnstoun of Graitney in a debt to Edward Johnstoun, younger, in 1606; and they had two sons, William and Edward, and a daughter, Elizabeth. John of Newbie, the merchant, married Janet Hunter, of a family represented by the Hunter-Arundells, Co. Dumfries.[2] In 1599 and 1600 John was a Baillie of Edinburgh. In the probate of his Will in 1601 he is described as callit of Newbie, merchant burgess of Edinburgh. Besides his brother, David, and his relatives, Edward and Gilbert Johnstoun, he was associated in business with some of the merchant princes of the day—Archibald Johnstoun (Chapter V.), whose wife was a daughter of Sir John Arnot, the Lord Provost; and Nicol d ard, sometime the Lord Provost, and the father of Barbara, Edward of Ryehill's second wife. Both d ard and Arnot were connected by marriage with James Primrose,[3] the Clerk of the Privy Council, the ancestor of the Earl of Rosebery, and were declared by a decreet of the Privy Council to have had no share in the Gowrie plot.

John's Will is a long one, and every Laird's family in Dumfriesshire is represented among his debtors. The Laird of Johnstoun owed him £37, 17s. 11d.; Lady Margaret Scott, the Laird's mother, £288, 1s. 7d.; Carruthers of Holmains £317, 8s. 5d.; Johnstoun of Westraw, in two sums, £57, 6s. 10d.; and Westraw's security, Gilbert Johnstoun (Wamfray), £111 (Gilbert was also security for Lady Johnstoun, and owed on her behalf £251, 1s. 8d); James Johnstoun of Lochous £166, 10s. 1d.; John Johnstoun of Cummertrees £17, 10s.; William Graham of Blaatwood £10, 3s. 4d.; John Johnstoun of Graitney £19, 13s. 6d.; Johnstoun of Corrie £45; Douglas of Drumlanrig £380, 8s. 5d.; William Irving £200; Lord Maxwell £515, 6s. 8d.; Lady Johnstoun ot Elphinstone £23; James and Robert Johnstoun of Elphinstone £89, 8s. 7d.; Lord Crichton £100; Christian Crichton £5, 5s.; Agnes Crichton £2, 9s.; Mr Patrick Crichton £5, 16s.; David Murray of Cockpool £11, 13s.; Closeburn and his brother £77, 2s. 6d.; John Johnstoun £315, 16s. 5d.; Ninian Johnstoun; the Laird of Newbie, £30, 0s. 4d.; Douglas of Hawthornden £19, 17s. 4d.; Thomas Cunningham, a factor in Campvere (Flanders), £1810, 5s.; the Laird of Corhead £10; John Broun, elder of Land, £58, 0s. 4d.; Martha Johnstoun £29, 15s.; David Murray of Aikett £20; Lady Seton, aunt of Sir James Johnstoun, £139, 7s. 1d.; David Johnstoun of Brumehill £19, 1s. 8d.; Alexander Hunter, brother-in-law to the deceased, £93, 13s., and his wife £3, 17s.;

[1] *Reg. of Deeds, Johnstoun qra. Johnstoun*, Vol. CLV.
[2] In the *Burgh Rolls* (1575-8) John, "son to John Johnstoun of Newbie, is made free of the Burgh" with the usual fees, Symon Johnstoun being his surety. No stranger could settle without leave in the Burgh.
[3] Archibald Primrose, his son, wished to buy land in Annandale, but the old landowners combined to prevent it.

Abraham Carruthers £9, 0s. 10d.; Sir Robert Maxwell £12; Gideon Murray 10 marks; and many more in Dumfriesshire besides the representatives of other counties—Livingstons, Kers, Scotts, the tutor of Warriestoun, Ramsay, Cathcarts, Olifants, Borthwicks, Irvings, Jardines, Murrays, Maxwells, Stewarts, Carmichaels, Cockburn, Abercrombie, Armstrongs, David Wemyss, the old Lady Merchiston, Montgomery, the tutor of Bombie (M'Clellan), Fergusson, Welsh, Wilsons, Hendersons, Thomsons, Richardsons, Fleming, Hacket, Trotter, etc.—in all, the deceased was owed £12,137, 12s. On his part, he owed his brother David, £600; to Symon Johnstoun, the lawful son of the late Symon, a merchant burgess in Dumfries, 800 marks; to a burgess of Selkirk £1400; and to Lady Newbie, his mother, 525 marks. Possibly these sums had been placed in his charge as an investment, the usual way of securing money before banks were introduced.

Including the sums owed to himself, John left £19,935, 3s. 7d. after deducting the deposits. His executors were his widow and his brother, David. He divided his fortune between his widow and his children, with the exception of legacies to his mother, his brother Abraham, his sister Margaret, Lady Barndaroch, and two or three more; 100 marks "to the poor of the hospital of Edinburgh;" and 100 marks[1] to a kirk when it should be built "in this burgh of Edinburgh," and the money to remain in his executors' hands till it was built. If his widow remarried, his eldest daughter, Marion, was to be "nourished and brought up in company with Archibald Johnstoun and Rachel Arnot, his wife, until the said Marion be of perfect age or provided in marriage at the pleasure of God." His two elder sons, John and James, were in the same case to be under the guardianship of their uncle, David; the younger children, Thomas, Helen, and Janet, to remain with their mother.

John, the eldest son, was returned heir to his father in 1603, Archibald Johnstoun, as a baillie of Edinburgh, being president of the inquisition. He was married to Margaret Smyth in 1618, and his mother, a party to the contract for his marriage settlement, died before the wedding day. The parents of the bride provided 8000 marks and the bridegroom 4000 marks, all of which sum was to be invested in land and settled on them both jointly, and on the longest liver of the two. John's family had lost Newbie, and was just parting with Graitney, but he naturally turned to Dumfriesshire, and by the advice of Lord Wigton and his uncle, Duncan Hunter of Ballagan, who were securities, he invested the money in a mortgage on Sir William Douglas's Dumfriesshire property—the castle, estates, etc. of Drumlanrig—and on Kirkton and Crumhauch, owned by another Johnstoun family. Ten per cent. was to be the yearly interest, and the principal might be repaid in ten years.

The young merchant had already parted with the lands of Barboy, bought by his father in 1594.[2] A deed of Nov. 7, 1605, confirms the sale, with the

[1] In a process of 1801, Erskine stated that a mark was worth £1 sterling in 1708.
[2] In 1664 Robert was returned heir to his father, John Johnstoun. He married Jean Inglis, Aug. 2, 1661, and died *s.p.* 1684, leaving a brother, David, burgess of Cupar in Fife. Possibly there is a connection between his heirs and the Johnstons of Lathrisk and Wedderby, Co. Fife, and the Johnstons of Pitkeirie, Fife.

consent of his uncle, David, and his mother, Janet Hunter. Another family paper in 1606 shows that his youngest brother, Thomas, was dead. The other brother, James, married to Janet Wellwood, also died *s.p.* in 1616; and Janet, the youngest sister, the wife of Walter Finlayson, died in 1612.

On Feb. 13, 1617, there is a transaction between David Johnstoun, merchant burgess of Edinburgh, on behalf of his "brother's son," John, about some wine, John being then out of Scotland. In July 1617 there is another agreement about the cargo of a ship owned by John, called *The Blessing of Glasgow*, in which David, John's uncle, again appears. John signs it at Bordeaux, but it provides for his return to Scotland. He owned another ship, *The John of Burntisland*, in 1618; and in 1636 he was a merchant in London as well as in Edinburgh. His sisters, Marion and Helen, married respectively Sir John Hay,[1] and Hew Dunbar, W.S. Helen died Dec. 22, 1622. As her husband was in difficulties she left her youngest daughter, Janet, to the guardianship of her brother, John.

Abraham Johnstoun, first of Milnbie, and then of Brume, had four grown-up sons, Robert, Thomas, William, and John, living in 1622 when he was Provost of Annan, and a grandson who witnessed a legal writ. Robert, or Hobbie, of Brume was an early offender in carrying arms, and when a young boy, in 1592, was cited with several of the Newbies for using them. In 1609 he was arrested in the streets of Edinburgh for walking out with the sword and other weapons, which James VI. had strictly prohibited.

In 1595 Abraham Johnstoun of Newbie received the escheats of John and Clement Edgar of Bowhous and Kirkblan. A few years later he mortgaged Milnbie to Lady Wigton, his Chief's mother, with the right of redemption.

In 1591 the third Baron of Newbie's mother, Agnes Maxwell, with her second husband, Robert Hereis, her son and her brothers-in-law, Robert, Edward, and Abraham, were at Newbie Castle—still an escheat. Then came Dryfe Sands, when the younger man retired to Edinburgh, the influence of his mother and wife being too strong to enable him, like his uncle, Robert, to take the part of his clan. Hard pressed for money, he brought actions against his uncles, Robert and Abraham, for pasturing cattle on his lands, and using his fisheries in 1595, as a kinsman's right. Robert had to find a security for £100, and his herdsman, Bernard Wilkin, for £50. Newbie also sold part of his lands in Cummertrees and Ruthwell, the last to Charles Murray, for it was already occupied by John Murray of Cockpool. In 1603 he mortgaged Stapleton to the Laird of Johnstoun. It was afterwards sold to Raecleuch.

In 1604 Newbie was Provost of Annan, and marked his term of office by obtaining its recognition as a burgh, for it had been one in the days of Bruce. He sent the two baillies, John Galloway and Robert Loch, to represent Annan at the Convention of Royal Burghs in Perth. Lord Crichton

[1] He was Town Clerk of Edinburgh when King James revisited it in 1617. The speech he made to welcome the King was printed with a portrait of His Majesty, but is now very scarce. He was Clerk Register in 1632. He had much to do in Westminster, and Edinburgh with George Heriot's affairs.

borrowed a large sum from him which was never repaid.[1] He was sued by Sir James Hamilton for the balance of a fine, and borrowed 2500 marks from his wife's uncle, Sir James Douglas of Drumlanrig, who put him to the horn for non-payment. He died at Carlisle early in 1605, aged thirty-eight. His second daughter, Barbara, had married Sir William Maxwell of Gribton, her cousin; and Newbie was to be made over to them with its charges and debts. But as John left no lawful son, his uncle, Robert, took possession of the castle as the owner of the Barony, although his sister-in-law and her daughter, Barbara, were still living there.

A lawsuit was proceeding, when Sir William Maxwell arrived with a troop of horsemen, including Robert Johnstoun of Brume and John M'Briar, who are described in the trial as servitors of the said Maxwell; Thomas Jardine; and Charles Maxwell, who was concerned three years later in the murder of the Laird of Johnstoun; and James Jardine, servitor to Lord Herries. They were in full armour, "jacks, swords, steel bonnets, pistolets, long guns, and other weapons"; and, admitted by the two ladies, surprised the Castle of Newbie, where Robert "lay fast in bed, deadly sick," and, entering his room, shot Edward of Ryehill through the body, and wounded Arthur Johnstoun, his servitor (and cousin), in the face, turning them all out of doors with their hands fastened behind their backs.

This outrage caused more sensation than usual with a Border feud. The English Warden alludes to it; and Robert Birrell, an Edinburgh citizen, notes in his diary, March 19, 1605: "The Maxwells came to the house of Newbies, and took the house. In taking of the house sundry were wounded and hurt. They kept the house till the guard and heralds caused them to surrender." Robert was allowed to re-occupy it; and both sides appealed to the law.

Elizabeth Stewart, Lady Newbie, complained that Robert had taken and detained the tower and fortalice of Newbie, and urged that he might be compelled to deliver the same to her, "in case it be found he ought to do so, and to pay her 100 marks for his escheat and goods within forty days."

Robert stated that, having occupied the said tower and lands as present heir male by entail to the Baron of Newbie, his father, he had sown most of the oat seed in the said lands, and ought to remain till lawfully put therefrom.

A decree of the Privy Council (April 18) desired both parties to desist from interfering with the lands and house of Newbie till the case was decided. Sir William Maxwell, his wife, and mother-in-law were summoned to Edinburgh for trial (June 21, 1605) at the instance of Robert, Edward, and Arthur Johnstoun, whose advocates were Sir Thomas Hamilton, and John, the son of Edward. On Maxwell's side were his wife's uncle, Sir Alexander Stewart of Garlies, Charteris of Amisfield, and Andrew Ker of Fenton.

The record of the trial is headed—" Besieging the tower of Newbie, Shooting Pistolets, Taking Captive, etc.," and begins: "Forasmuch as by divers Acts

[1] Probably the feud between the Wamfrays and Crichtons which led to the battle of Dryfe Sands was the cause. At his trial at Whitehall, 1612, Lord Crichton said he had killed no other man but Johnstons, by the King's command, and repentance was not needed for that.

THE ESTATE PASSES TO THE LAIRD OF JOHNSTOUN

of Parliament our Sovereign Lord prohibited the wearing of pistols and hagbuts under certain pains, yet it is of truth that such is the wicked disposition of some persons who preferring their own revenge to the due reverence and obedience of his Highness's laws, they and their domestic servants daily and continually bear and wear pistols, swords and hagbuts as their ordinary and accustomed weapons. . . . As, viz., the said William Maxwell of Gribton, Barbara Johnstoun, his spouse, and Elizabeth Stewart, her mother, having a long time borne a secret and hidden malice against the said Robert Johnstoun of Newbie in respect of the depending of certain acts before the Lords and Sessioners of Council," etc.

The trial continued a week, and was prorogued till July 3, when the defendants were bound under pain of 200 marks to come up for judgment within fifteen days. Robert remained in Newbie, constantly annoyed by Gribton's followers, till Lord Herries, at the instance of the advocate, John Johnstoun, summoned Gribton to appear (Oct. 1605). Sir James Johnstoun and Robert of Newbie at the same time prosecuted Lady Newbie and her second husband, Samuel Kirkpatrick of Hoddam (brother-german to Sir Thomas Kirkpatrick of Closeburn), who, on their appearance before the Court, were outlawed.

Robert died in November, having preferred to give up his claim on Newbie to the Laird rather than to Gribton, on which Lady Newbie appealed against the sentence of "horning"; and her son-in-law pleaded that a case begun by Robert could not be carried on by Edward, who continued it on behalf of Robert's son, William.[1] John, the advocate, then took up the matter against Gribton and his colleagues, and the suits continued throughout 1606.

The intervention of the Crown in giving the wardship of the Barony of Newbie a year after the owner's death to Robert of Raecleuch, the Laird of Johnstoun's next of kin, "with the ward and marriage of all heirs of the Laird of Newbie who died in 1576," hastened the settlement under the provision of male heirs whatsoever, and the estates were made over to Johnstoun by a compact signed at Dornock, Jan. 23, 1607. Young William died at the Scots College of Douai, France (June, 26, 1607), and their uncle, Edward Johnstoun of Ryehill, quietly assumed the guardianship of William's brother, Edward. Probably the news of the boy's death did not reach Scotland for some time; and the next year Raecleuch was made tutor to Sir James Johnstoun's young son, who, when he came of age, declared that he had received nothing from the proceeds of the Newbie Barony.[2] He even went to law with Raecleuch to get back his father's favourite horse.

---

[1] Among the twelve honest and faithful men who returned William as heir to his "avi," John Johnstoun of Newbie, were James Johnstoun of Westraw, Robert Johnstoun de Newton, James Johnstoun de Chapelhill, junior, Gavin Johnstoun of Middlegill, Symon Johnstoun de Woodheid, Thomas Johnstoun in Revox, James Johnstoun de Hesilbrae. Feb. 13, 1606.

[2] From a fishing case in 1772, Viscount Stormont v. the Marquis of Annandale and others, it appears that "Sir James Johnstone of that Ilk recognized the rights of the male heir to Newbie (under the old entail to the direct heirs of William of Graitney, and his brothers, first, and after them to the heir male whatsoever, who should bear the name and arms of Johnstone), and entered into a contract with Robert, who empowered Sir James to reduce the right granted to Barbara, obliging himself to pay the expense of the

Raecleuch's mother was Marion Maxwell, "Lady Carnsalloch, elder," apparently mother to Lady Newbie's first husband. Lady Newbie occupied the Tower again for a month or two after Robert of Newbie's death, and finally left it, Jan. 2, 1606, " with all her goods and geir except seven bedsteads and one counterboard without victuals; and a garnished cellar without wine." This statement is signed at Newbie by the neighbours, Cockpool and Wormanbie, also John Johnstoun of Graitney, Robert Johnstoun, junior of Wamfray, and John Johnstoun, writer.

Raecleuch's father, Robert Johnstoun of Carnsalloch and lay-parson of Lochmaben, was second son to John of Johnstoun, who died in 1567; and, as his elder brother was captured by the English and died before 1552, Robert ruled the Barony when his father was also captured, and in his old age. A violent man, he was often put to the horn with his half-brother, John of Lochous, for slaughter and spoliation. He died at Carnsalloch in 1592, leaving several sons; the elder at the age of eleven fought at Dryfe Sands, and was now only twenty-five. The Lady of Carnsalloch died in 1601.

The murder of Sir James Johnstoun in 1608, with two poisoned bullets, by Lord Maxwell and his relative, Charles of Kirkhous, who was also nephew to John Murray of Cockpool, upset the arrangements as regarded Newbie, which the Chief meant to occupy himself. Maxwell had never given up the idea of revenging his own father's death at Dryfe Sands; and, as Lady Johnstoun, the widow, was in favour at Court, he was imprisoned when he came to Edinburgh avowedly to do it. He escaped, as people did escape from prison at that date, when they could bribe the jailor, but was later induced to sign a paper expressing his forgiveness. As he continued apparently in disgrace with the King, his cousin, Sir Robert Maxwell of Orchardston, Johnstoun's brother-in-law, arranged a secret meeting between the Chiefs, in which Maxwell was to ask for Johnstoun's intervention with the King, and all old grudges were to be wiped away. Sir James took a relation, William of Lockerbie; but Maxwell's attendant, Charles Maxwell, had assisted in the recent attack on Newbie, and, as Sir James was very friendly with Ryehill (who was badly wounded), was afraid perhaps of the effect that a reconciliation might have on himself. He told William Johnstoun that he would not have come if he had known that they were to meet Johnstouns, and suddenly shot him. William was wounded and tried to return it, but his pistol missed. He shouted treason, and Sir James, turning round, was shot in the back by Maxwell, who at once rode away, and said he had done enough when urged not to leave William alive. Sir James was propped upon his horse,

prosecution; and engaging not to sell the lands without Sir James's consent, nor to any but of the name of Johnstone, and Sir James thereby agreed to take the lands at a price to be fixed by mutual friends, if Robert were inclined to sell them." Robert's death in 1605, and the minority of his heir being prolonged by the early death of his elder son, the lawless state of the Borders, and the claims of mortgages, all combined to hasten the arrangement which made it over to the Chief; and the circumstances were asserted by the Counsel to the last Marquis to show "very clearly a relationship between James Johnstone of that Ilk and the Johnstones of Newbie."

but had only strength to say "Lord have mercy on me, Christ have mercy on me—I am deceived" before he expired.

Maxwell fled to the Continent, and was tried when absent by a special Parliament, June 24, 1609, which found him guilty of high treason for killing the Warden of the Marches, and all his goods were to be confiscated. Charles Maxwell was left free, and his brother ennobled before many years had passed.

The King had tried to reduce the influence of the Johnstouns, and continued to do so;[1] but the law gave him an interest in a minor's estate and, although away at Windsor, he appointed Raecleuch to be tutor of the Johnstoun Barony and of the heir and his sisters against the protest of their mother, who went to Edinburgh to find champions on her behalf. Lady Johnstoun declared that she knew the weakness of the tutor, and that he was unfit to govern the living or to manage the estate. She offered to give him 500 marks a year for himself, and to spend 2000 marks in reducing the debt of £50,000, which seemed likely to ruin the property, if he would give up the post. She tried by law to obtain the custody of her children, and promised to give them meat, clothes, and other necessaries, and to keep house for her son and his friends, but in vain. She secretly gave the Charter chest to the care of Edward Johnstoun of Ryehill, who owned the old castle of Annan, a strong stone house; and it was possibly by her advice that her son at fourteen chose Ryehill to be one of his curators.

The King condescended to write to Raecleuch to be careful of the pupil's education and "of the welfare and continuance of his house now fallen into decay, to be honest and faithful, and not to look for his own gain." He told the Lords of Council and Session to stay all proceedings against the heir in his minority, but this did not exempt the heir from the special Crown dues levied on a minor's estate.

Sir James had agreed to give 25,000 marks to Barbara for her claim to Newbie, and to pay all her father's debts. He also undertook to bring up her six sisters—Janet, Mary, Agnes, Christine, Elizabeth, and Jeannette—in his own house, charging himself with their education, board, clothes, and ultimate marriage, "as befits ladies of their degree." Three were already married when his death devolved their maintenance on Raecleuch.

Their mother[2] appears again with her husband, Kirkpatrick, in several actions against James Murray of Cockpool in 1610 for "non-payment of certain dues," which amounted to £5000. The younger girls married in time, but as Raecleuch had taken charge of them in Newbie Castle he brought an

[1] *Acts of Decreets*, Vol. LXXVII., fol. 2, B. Mr John Johnstoun (of Mylnfield), advocate, is given the ward of the late Laird's estate by a document dated April 12, 1608, four days after the murder. This was doubtless only pending the King's appointment, as he was Sheriff-Depute of Annandale, but it is curious that Raecleuch should have been given the ward of Mylnfield's first cousin, and Mylnfield the ward of Raecleuch's nearest relative.
[2] She gained her cause, but the King overrode the decision by a gift under the Privy Seal in favour of Sir James Murray, knight, of his own escheat and life-rent, Dec. 22, 1610. This deed refers to "the claim against the late Knight of Dunskellie by Elizabeth Stewart, Lady Newbie, relict of John Johnstoun of Newbie and Master Samuel Kirkpatrick," etc. (*Mansfield Charters*).

action for £100 to repay him for "three years' nourishment," and for providing them with silk gowns. Lady Newbie paid it.

Sir James had borrowed £10,350 from his "good friend," Archibald Johnstoun of Edinburgh, and, besides the heavy interest of the day, agreed to repay 15,000 marks in eight years (1613). The debt was bought by Raecleuch's brother, Mungo, and when a Crown Charter[1] confirmed the young Laird in the possession of Newbie, Mylnfield, and the other lands comprised in the Barony (June 8, 1609), Mungo tried to occupy part of the estate as a guarantee. The Charter disallowed the rights of the relatives who lived as kindlie tenants on the estate; and in various lawsuits carried on by James Lidderdaill for his grand-daughter, the late Newbie's eldest child, and even by the heirs of the Carliles and the Corries, it was proved what portions were legally held by Johnstouns outside the Barony. Raecleuch did not hurry to eject them, as they assisted him to withstand the new taxes and tithes.[2]

Raecleuch's protest against paying tithes to Murray (Cockpool, as he calls him), 1611, and his defence of his own conduct, shows the conditions of an estate at that time, when the rents were paid in produce. In the case of Newbie—wheat, peas, barley, oats from the cottars; salt from Priestwodesyde; malt and meal for Newbie mill; £5 in rent from Christopher Carruthers for Hardgray; and thirty salmon trout. Miskares was mortgaged to Walter Scott of Tuschelaw before the Laird's death, also Dunskellie. Souplebank was let to a Carlile, whose rent was overdue; another portion to Dame Elizabeth Carlile. He had not got enough from the fisheries to feed the keeper. He had sown and laboured with his own plough for the crop of 1609, and that was claimed by Archibald Johnstoun, of Edinburgh, for a debt owed by the late Laird. A great portion of the estate was possessed by the friends of Newbie, named Johnstoun, and others of the names of Bell and Irving, who had never paid any duty, and he could not eject them, "because the Laird of Johnstoun was never infefted in the lands of Newbie, his sole right being a contract between him and the late Robert Johnstoun of Brigholme, and of another between him and Sir William Maxwell of Gribton, taking burden upon him for the heirs of line of the house of Newbie." Raecleuch had also paid 16,000 marks to Gribton, and a compensation to the family of the murdered Johnstouns at Dalfibble (Chapter V.), as they had got none from the Maxwells.

The sentence of outlawry against Sir W. Maxwell and his wife and mother-in-law for not coming up for judgment seems to have been annulled on the payment of £62, 7s. In 1616 Barbara Johnstoun, Lady Gribton, with two of her sisters—Agnes, the spouse of John Laurie, and Jeannette, married to John Broun of the Land—were proclaimed outlaws for "holding Papistical opinions," as the Act set forth; and this penalty was duly enforced. In 1622 Barbara was a widow, resident in Paris; and her youngest son, Alexander,

[1] *The Reg. Sec. Sigilli*, Vol. LXXVIII., fol. 96.
[2] Mungo is called in one deed Raecleuch's brother-german, and in another natural brother; but that term is found in deeds earlier and of that date when the context shows that the person was a lawful heir. His son was returned his heir, and there is no other proof that he was not legitimate.

a student at Douai, died of the plague which broke out in the college. She was again in Scotland in August 1628, when "James Johnstoun of that Ilk appeared in person, and became cautioner for Dame Barbara Johnstoun, Lady Gribton, that the said Dame Barbara within the space of one month after this date shall depart and pass forth of the kingdom, and that within twenty-two days thereafter she shall pass forth of the bounds of Great Britain, and that she shall not return again without his Majesty's licence, under the pain of 5000 marks; and the said Dame Barbara appearing personally acted for herself, that during her remaining within this kingdom she shall not receive Jesuit Seminary Priests, nor trafficking Papists, nor shall travel about the country under the pain of 5000 marks, Sir James and his heirs becoming her cautioners."

Other entries in the Books of the Privy Council show that Barbara was ordered some years later to submit to instruction in the Reformed Faith. A complaint from her is registered that by their lordships' directions she had for the past three months remained in Edinburgh, " and has diligently haunted the Kirk and heard the preaching and prayers with that modesty which became a Christian, and seldom was she absent when her health would permit, as is well known to the ministers of the burgh, especially to that of the Grey Friars Kirk the parish she most frequented. Her abode has been very expensive and as the harvest is drawing near, she having the whole estate, which is but a very mean portion, in her own labouring, if she be not at home to attend it, it will be neglected to her wreck and undoing. She is willing at her home-going to continue her ordinary exercise of haunting the Kirk for hearing of sermons and as occasion serves to hear conferences, and so desires to return home. She is not resolved to embrace the religion presently professed within this kingdom, so is content to withdraw out of the country to some part where she may have the free exercise of her children."[1]

Dame Barbara was allowed to go home to settle her affairs on condition that she left Scotland within a month and the Isle of Britain twenty days afterwards. She released Johnstoun from his pledge by offering her own personal security of 5000 marks for her behaviour while she remained in Scotland. Her son, John Maxwell of Gribton, stood security for himself in 2000 marks that he would not receive any Jesuit priests. Her sisters—Jeannette, and Agnes, who was remarried to William Hereis of Mable—were also banished from the country, under the pain of 1000 marks, in company with several other members of the Maxwell and Hereis family, and Nicolas Jardine, the wife of John Carruthers of Holmains, who was himself a Protestant.

Barbara's daughters—Elspeth, Barbara "callit the Pope"—and Agnes Maxwell were summoned in 1634 for "scandalizing the Kirk and disobeying the King's laws by hearing Mass." Their cousin, Elspeth Maxwell of Conheath, who was already excommunicated for the same act, was convicted of having been married secretly, at night, to Robert Rig, by a priest with the Roman rite by the light of candles in the fields near Dumfries. Rig owned that four

[1] Lord Nithsdale's son had lately been taken from him to be brought up a Protestant.

persons were present, men and women, but as they covered their faces he could not recognise them. He was imprisoned in Edinburgh at his own charges during the King's pleasure. The ladies humbly expressed their contrition at having "caused scandal to the Kirk," and their relatives seem to have saved them from further punishment.

John Broun,[1] called of the Land, New Abbey, and of Lochhill, and his wife, Jeannette Johnstoun of Newbie, had two sons, Thomas and James, at Douai College in 1627 and 1634. The first is described in the College Record as a youth of the greatest promise who went on to serve his novitiate in Spain. Patrick Johnstoun died at Rome in 1622, preparing for the Scottish mission; and Nicolas Johnstoun was at the Scottish College in Rome in 1641. Christopher Johnstoun and Anna Gordon, spouses, left money to the College at Ratisbon for masses for their souls, and for the soul of Anna's father.

Knox had got a Bill passed as early as 1560 that Romanists not instantly abjuring their belief were for the first offence to forfeit all their goods and be whipped, for the second offence exile, for the third execution, and he ordered his followers to refuse baptism to their children. But the King qualified this outrageous act by appointing Romanist judges and magistrates; and as the Episcopalians often preferred the Pope to the Covenant these extreme penalties, which, carried out to their full extent, would have depopulated half Scotland, seem to have been only enforced in cases of treason or of friendless people. The accusers and their emissaries were very barbarous. Ogilvie, the Jesuit, was "not suffered to take sleep some days and nights with small sustenance, so that his brains being lightsome, secrets were drawn out of him" before his trial, and he spoke disrespectfully of the King. He was tried Feb. 28, 1615, with Sinclair, who had entertained him, and others who had heard him preach. Edward Johnstoun of Ryehill, a sympathiser, was one of the judges. Ogilvie was simply executed, as the sentence put it, for disloyalty to the King, but the rest were let off with fines and exile.

The aged Romanist Bishop of Dunkeld, Robert Crichton, applied for maintenance on the ground that his few remaining years would be cut short by starvation. It was pleaded for him that he belonged to an old family, so his Protestant successor's income was curtailed for his support.

Dame Barbara soon returned to Scotland, as in 1630 she was summoned by Murray with her cousins to quit the Newbie estate or pay the tithes.

The Earl of Wigton, whose name appears in several deeds connected with Newbie, having married the widowed Lady Johnstoun, was instrumental in protecting the Bishop of Galloway from the violence of the people of Dumfries, when, in 1623, the Bishop tried to carry out the King's positive command to

---

[1] In 1634 he petitioned the Privy Council for his release from prison, where he was "forthwith put for his religion" when he obeyed the order to appear in Edinburgh. He had lain there for five weeks in great misery for want He had no means to sustain his natural life, and no creature to attend him, his wife being in England and his eight children at home, sixty miles away, for the most part unable to do for themselves. He was released on condition that he left the country and never returned. At the same time Edward Johnstoun obtained an extension of protection for himself.

THE EARL OF WIGTON

insist on the Scottish ministers making use of the English book of Common Prayer. The King was advised that it would assist in permanently uniting the two countries; but Knox condemned it as Rome's illegal offspring when he was chaplain to Edward VI.: and just as the Scots would accept no English fashion in dress, but preferred the costumes of Holland and France, it was enough that the Prayer Book had been compiled in England to reject it.

The Reformation started in both countries under bad auspices. In Scotland Queen Mary's half-brother, the Regent, raised the Protestant standard to advance his own ambition. He signed a decree with Argyll and Ruthven in 1560, ordering the altars and images of saints to be broken up in the Kirk of Dunkeld. As usual, the populace went much further than their political leaders, and the vandalism,[1] now deplored by all archæologists, was carried on throughout the land. Still Episcopacy survived, but the adoption of the service books from England was the lever required by the opposition, and from this time, for the next sixty years, there was a constant struggle between the Covenanters, who would place the State under the control of the Church, and those who believed in the Royal supremacy. The defeated parties were sold to life-long slavery in the plantations of Virginia, South Carolina, and the West Indies. The cruelties committed on both sides make the seventeenth century a most sanguinary epoch in Scottish history. Dumfriesshire, wrote the Rev. A. Carlile, had not recovered from it in 1736.

[1]. Melrose, Kelso, and other abbeys on the frontier were ruined by the English in the last invasion.

CHAPTER XI.

JOHN MURRAY—THE CLAIMANTS TO THE NEWBIE ESTATE, AND THE KINDLIE TENANTS—EDWARD JOHNSTOUN OF RYEHILL—THE SONS OF THE HOUSE OF NEWBIE—DEATH OF CASTLEMILK AND MARRIAGE OF HIS WIDOW TO RYEHILL--JOHN OF MYLNFIELD—EXECUTION OF MAXWELL—GRAITNEY SOLD TO MURRAY—DESCENDANTS OF THE GRAITNEYS—MURRAY'S DESCENDANTS—RYEHILL'S LETTER TO PRIMROSE—THE GRAHAMS OF BLAATWOOD—RYEHILL'S DEATH—HERIOT'S EXECUTOR.

THE country was agitated by the search for those connected with the Gunpowder Plot, when King James remembered that Holywood was still an abbey in charge of Edward Maxwell, the Commendator, and still contained one brother, David Welsh. He dismissed them both, and gave Holywood with the lands and dues to John Murray of Cockpool, described as one of the "Grooms of his Majesty's chamber," an office introduced by James VI. As Murray had also received the lands and dues of Dundrennan, and as the two Abbots, in a Charter from William Bruce, were made superiors of Annandale, he could now override the more recent rights of Carliles, Corries, Johnstouns, and their dependents. He at once claimed feus and tithes from Newbie, Graitney, Wamfray, Castlemilk, and other properties. The King directed that Murray should put a minister into Annan and Graitney, and allow him 400 marks a year. The Cockpool family had only recently accepted the Reformed Faith, and, as the Johnstouns and Carliles in these parts still generally held aloof from it, Murray put Symon Johnstoun (brother to Robert Johnstoun of Raecleuch), married to a daughter of Sir James Douglas of Torthorald, to serve both these Kirks, as he would be protected by his relatives. When Episcopacy was re-established under Charles II. the patronage of Annan was transferred to the Earl of Annandale.

Murray's claim to the superiority of Annandale was opposed by Robert of Raecleuch, Westraw, Edward of Ryehill, Sir James Douglas (the heir of the Carliles), Carruthers of Wormanbie and Holmains, Grahams, Irvings of Bonshaw, and the Johnstouns of Wamfray and Castlemilk. The kindlie tenants, who occupied the Newbie estate to serve against the enemy if called upon by the Laird, were now asked instead to pay taxes and tithes, and refused. But after 1609, when a Royal Charter annulled their old rights, they gradually withdrew from the Barony, leaving their dependents to come to terms with Raecleuch. Ryehill left his tower at Mylnfield to be occupied by the Fareis

EDWARD JOHNSTOUN OF RYEHILL

family; David, his brother, went to Edinburgh, where he is mentioned in many writs and Wills as a witness or an executor; Abraham gave up Milnbie, but remained in Brume, just outside Newbie. The brother and heir of Captain John of Lochous—James—being next of kin to the young Laird after Robert of Raecleuch, was appointed one of the guardians.

Edward, the next brother to Robert Johnstoun of Brigholme and Newbie, ancestor to the Johnstones of Galabank and Fulford Hall, is described as "of Ryehill" when Robert Welch acts as his security for a bond in 1578, but is generally called of Newbie. He was third son of the second Baron, whose partizanship of Queen Mary precluded him from being made Governor of Annan in 1569. The Regent supported the Irvings, to whom the Queen had shown strong objection in 1566, and Edward Irving, brother to Johnstoun's son-in-law, Christopher, was appointed Governor of Annan Castle. There are several small estates still held by "kindlie tenants of the Crown," and Irving received a grant of these, including the Castle, Northfield, Gulielands, Galabank, and Mylneflat or Mylnfield. Scrope burnt Annan in 1570; but, as he had an understanding with the Regent to destroy the property of Mary's friends, possibly he spared all belonging to Irving, who had a long delayed Charter of these lands properly made out to him in 1574. But in 1583 the Warden of the Borders (Johnstoun) complained that Douglas of Drumlanrig, with Bells, Carliles, and Irvings of Mylneflat or Mylnfield, "and divers other broken men which is ever entertained by the said Laird of Drumlanrig this last half year," broke into the house of Bonshaw, and, by force, set at liberty about eighteen Bells and Irvings, notorious offenders, who were in ward there. An Order was sent by the Privy Council to arrest Jeffrey Irving of Bonshaw and Willie Irving of Mylnfield in 1583; and in 1587 Willie's escheat, including the tower of Mylnfield, was given to Edward Johnstoun of Ryehill, "father's brother" to the young Laird of Newbie. In 1597 he was appointed collector of the salt tax in Edinburgh, a great deal of salt being produced on his nephew's estate.

At the end of the sixteenth century, and beginning of the seventeenth, there is frequent mention of another Edward Johnstoun, a merchant (son of Nathaniel of Elsieshields), who married Janet Grey. After a time he is called the elder to distinguish him from Edward Johnstoun the younger (of Wamfray), also a merchant, and a partner with Gilbert Johnstoun, who married Margaret Ker, and seems to have been Graitney's son of that name who held a copyhold in Graitney. Edward the younger married Katherine (daughter of Hector Rae, an Edinburgh merchant, of Annan descent), and had a son, Francis. It was Edward of Ryehill who is described by the English Ambassador in a letter to Secretary Cecil in 1599 as being on his way to the Low Countries, and "willing to do service there for the English."

The Laird of Johnstoun at this time had been deprived of the Wardenship, which "was given to Sir John Carmichael and Robert Johnstoun of Newbie to assist him." His deprivation may have been due to an incident related in a letter from Willoughby to Cecil, Jan. 1598, that "William Home, Sir George Home's[1] brother, pursuing Edward Johnston for his escheat anent Dec. 17, and the Laird of Johnston travailling to defend Edward, the Laird and William fell to such words before the King, as the King committed them both to the Castle, but they are both out again not agreed, for they have both got parties behind them. The King supports William."

Edward defended his brother in the attack on Newbie Castle in 1605, and was shot through the body. In Dec. the same year he was a co-witness with Patrick Porteus for his Chief, that the murderers of Sir John Maxwell of Pook should be brought to trial. Edward's son was advocate for Sir James on this occasion.

The Laird of Newbie who died 1576 had left houses and land in and near Annan to his second son, Robert. Ryehill, being now tutor to Robert's son, paid off a mortgage to Jeffrey Irving in connection with the estate. Raecleuch in his defence alludes to these lands as no longer part of the Barony, but Murray desired to see the title-deeds, and Mungo Johnstoun claimed them as part of Newbie. Ryehill sent no reply to Murray, so a second summons was sent in 1610—in which he is styled Edward Johnstoun, callit of Newbie and now in Mylnfield, who was cited at his said dwelling house in Mylnfield by six knocks on his door; and that the particulars of his crop and possessions within written were certified by his son, John, and David Bell, in Annan.

With so many sons of the House of Newbie—some only kindlie tenants, others holding lands of their own adjoining the Barony—the mortgagee was confused as to what he owned, and his summons to Ryehill as well as to Raecleuch "to flit and remove with their wives, bairns, and servants—the first from Howmedow, Saltrigs, Crofthead, M———, etc.," brought a counter action from Ryehill and his nephew, Edward; and Mungo was ordered by the Court to pay him £10 for expenses. The year before Edward of Seafield released his uncle from his tutory, his cautioner being his cousin, John Broun of the Land and Lochhill, and fully acknowledged the care and integrity with which Ryehill had managed his affairs.

Edward of Seafield's retour to his brother, William of Newbie, was signed at "the vast stone house" in Annan, then occupied by John Galloway, who with Jeffrey Irving, Robert Johnstoun, John Johnstoun, vocat of Mylnfield, George Graham of Redkirk, Raes, and others witness it. The late Robert of Newbie had sold Hardrigg, Brigholme, and Gulielands, which the King gave to Mr Patrick Howat, one of his chaplains. Northfield and Galabank, owned by Edward of Ryehill, were included in the Charter; but Howat withdrew his claim on receiving compensation from the occupiers or their relatives when he found that they all held title-deeds to these lands, and were prepared to stand by them. The same title-deeds were produced in 1614 when Murray claimed that they belonged to the ancient Barony of Dundrennan.

Ryehill was Provost of Annan in 1612-13, when he lived in the "vast stone house on the old Tolbooth sted," the site of the ancient castle of Robert

[1] Earl of Dunbar.

Bruce. The next year he was married for the second time to Barbara   d ard, the widow of John Johnstoun of Castlemilk, Commendator of Holywood (*see* Chapter V.), accidentally drowned with his servant about a year and a half before while crossing the river Milk on horseback. Owing to this misfortune the people of Castlemilk tried to build a bridge over the river, but were many years in collecting money for it. Barbara   d ard's sons—Thomas, James, John, and Alexander—were under age, and, in accordance with the law, Ryehill became their guardian, but in conjunction with their grandfather, Nicol   d ard, sometime the Lord Provost of Edinburgh.   d ard had a house in Newcastle, as well as Edinburgh, after James VI. became King of England ; and his son, Nathaniel, obtained a monopoly of the fisheries on the coast of Greenland and Iceland.

Edward of Ryehill's first wife, included in several summonses for the tithes, was probably Christine Irving, who is mentioned next to him in more than one list of residents on the Newbie property, and before the name of his son, John, in 1609, and again between the name of Edward and his grandson, John, in 1610. In one document she is called "of Newbie." It seems the more likely that she was his wife, as he had a son named Christopher. That his sister married an Irving is hardly enough to account for the frequent money transactions—some to his disadvantage—which he had with the Irvings, standing security for those who got into difficulties, even for Jeffrey of Robgill, who was condemned to be hanged for marrying his brother's widow. He also owned "the vast stone house" which had belonged to Christopher Irving. In 1632 he was appointed Sheriff of Annandale over the head of the Laird of Johnstoun and James Johnstoun of Lochous, who both applied for the post. He was three times Provost of Annan, and more than once Parliamentary Commissioner, also Sheriff of Dumfries ; and was employed by the Government in unpaid services, and as a judge on the assize. He stood security several times for the young Laird as well as for his late Chief, and his name appears in nearly 100 writs as a cautioner, a witness, a principal, or a judge.[1]

On Nov. 25, 1612, the Edinburgh Records contain : " The which day Edward Johnstoun, Provost of Annan, convener of the Justices of Peace within the Stewartrie of Annandaill, promised to give in his accompt the morne to the clerk of register." In 1617 Edward was again Provost of Annan, and Convener of the Justices in Edinburgh at a trial for forgery.

After his second marriage Ryehill's duties were increased by attending to the interests of his second wife and her sons, who owned a house in Edinburgh, and the estates of Castlemilk and Flemingraw. The Murray influence was rapidly increasing. Three of the family had been Grooms of the King's Bedchamber, and purchased the title of Baronet; a fourth, Richard, was Dean of Manchester ; and a fifth, Sir Gideon Murray, farmed the taxes for Annandale.[2]

[1] The first in 1578, the last in 1640.
[2] In the petition of Lord Stormont claiming some of the Newbie fisheries in 1772, the old Newbie Charters up to 1541 were searched, and when Counsel came to the numerous

John Murray of Cockpool was created Viscount Annan, and in 1623 was made Sheriff of Annandale to enable him to evict with force all who opposed him in his new possession. The next year he was advanced to the dignities of Earl of Annandale and Lord Murray of Lochmaben. Six years earlier the Crown associated him with Lord Crichton in the wardship of the Laird of Johnstoun, so that they might benefit by the estate, although there were already seven guardians—the Earls of Mar, Lothian, and Buccleuch, James of Lochous, Robert of Raecleuch, Edward of Ryehill, and Johnstoun of Westraw. Crichton's predecessor was executed in 1612, for killing a fencing-master, by an English Court, as he was arrested in London; but his heir lent the King a large sum of money, and just before his appointment in 1617 he entertained James VI. magnificently in Dumfriesshire, and, rolling up the proofs of the King's debt into a torch, lighted him up to bed with it. Thirteen years later he was obliged to sell his estate, but a title being a valuable asset Charles I. made him Earl of Dumfries.[1]

John Murray's sister married a Maxwell, so although Sir William Maxwell of Gribton and Sir Robert Maxwell of Spots, married to Johnstoun's aunt, were "feuars of Newbie" they were not included among the defendants in the processes instituted regularly every year against the occupiers of Newbie between 1608 and 1630.

Newbie, one of the most productive estates in Scotland, was taxed £53, 6s. 8d. in 1608,—the same sum as the Barony of Johnstoun—but a supplementary memorandum raised it to £60. Ryehill was taxed £6, 3s. 4d. Among the tenants of Newbie were Dicksons and Richardsons—whose ancestors had been famous in the days of Wallace and Bruce—and the warlike Irvings, Bells, Romes, Grahams, etc., besides the Johnstouns of Wamfray, Corrie, Lochous, and Newbie, who long enjoyed the kinsman's right to occupy lands there without paying any rent.

Mylnfield, or Millfield, on the opposite side of the river to Annan, was then as large as Annan, though now reduced to about three houses. A field opposite Northfield and Galabank was also Mylnfield (Mylneflat), as the mill, which formed an important part of a landed property, as well as houses stood on it. From the description of its boundaries the smaller Mylnfield appears to be the one with the tower occupied by Ryehill, or, as a decreet states, by others in his name; and the mortgagees of Newbie claimed it. The river separated this land from that which Robert of Newbie inherited from his father, and which Edward held for his nephews, Robert's sons. With the preference a Scot always shows for territorial designations, Edward's son, John, signed himself of or in Mylnfield, and was so-called in Annan writs, though

writs obtained by Murray from 1608 onwards he observes that "Murray was a gentleman of the bedchamber to King James, and much in favour. The arts and influence of Court favourites are well known, and it is certain that in those days it was by no means uncommon for grants to be given of subjects which had been alienated from the Crown long before." In "certain decrees of removing obtained at the instance of Sir James Murray before the Steward Court of Annandale in 1613 and 1619 . . . it does not appear that the steps said to have been gone through were followed with any effect" (1772-1803).

[1] The Marquis of Bute is his descendant.

elsewhere he is styled Mr (Master) John Johnstoun, after the fashion which gave the prefix to graduates and the eldest sons of Lairds.

The career of this John of Mylnfield was a short one. He was Sheriff-Depute[1] of Annandale, and presided over the jury who returned James, the young Laird of Johnstoun, as lawful heir to his father in 1609, and for a short time had the ward of the estate. He was also Sheriff or Steward of Dumfries. In 1605 he paid 10 marks for the release of his uncle, Abraham Johnstoun, from a sentence of outlawry Lady Newbie had procured against him—first for fishing, and then for keeping from her, as she alleged, some of the Newbie rents (claimed by heirs and creditors)—and after John had taken his uncle's side at the trial for the attack on Newbie his life was not safe from the Maxwells. On July 31, 1605, Edward Maxwell of Hills and Lord Hereis had to pledge themselves for £5000, and Robert Maxwell of Dinwiddie pledged himself for the Maxwells of Gribton and Conheath with 3000 marks, not to harm Mr John Johnstoun, advocate. When their Chief was a fugitive they, in their turn, asked to be protected against the Johnstouns.

The same year John was pledge for his Wamfray cousin, Edward Johnstoun, in Edinburgh, who was accused of attacking John Broun, a goldsmith, in the High Street. It was proved that Edward and his wife, Katherine Rae, had supper with her parents, and were returning with their servants to their own lodging when the plaintiff, with an Aberdeen friend, seized Katherine, "tore her curtche and other ornaments of her head causing her nose to bleed." The husband was exonerated for inflicting severe blows on the probably drunken assailants, the Court decreeing that "the High Street at night should be a place of safety and refuge to all honest men and women, especially to the honest neighbours and inhabitants thereof." The Laird of Johnstoun, Ryehill, and Westraw were advocates or witnesses for the defence.

In 1610 John was among the Justices of the Peace for Dumfriesshire and Annandale, the other Johnstouns on the list being Raecleuch, Ryehill, and Graitney. The representatives of eleven of their colleagues—Douglas, Charteris, Stewart, Murray, Wemyss, etc.—have long since merged into the Peerage where they were not already Peers, except Kirkpatrick of Closeburn, who is a Baronet. The twelfth—Carruthers of Holmains—has no heir in the direct male line.

The deed which transferred Galabank from Jeffrey Irving to Edward of Ryehill is dated at Mylnfield. John Johnstoun of Mylnfield was a witness, and living at Galabank and also occupying Northfield and the adjacent fields in 1609 when he brought an action against some inhabitants of Annan who interfered with his fishings. The next year he was outlawed for not arresting Robert of Raecleuch in Newbie Castle, at the instance of the powerful Murray, when the Crown bestowed the property as an escheat on Mr Patrick Howat.

The five years' exile of Lord Maxwell for the murder of the Laird of Johnstoun in 1608, and his execution in 1613, eclipsed the influence of his family very temporarily, for they were widely represented in Dumfriesshire and

---

[1] This post, like that of Sheriff, Baillie, and Provost, was, says Speed, always kept in the Lairds' families.

had intermarried with the Murrays, who were trying, in addition to the title-deeds of the Dundrennan Abbey, to get a reversion of the escheat of the Earl of March in 1440. The old Charter granted to their ancestor in 1320 covered ground previously granted to Carlile; but John and James Murray based an extra claim on the retour obtained when Maxwell was Warden for their ancestor in 1494, and again in 1507, in which Rampatrick, including Graitney, Dornock, and Kirkpatrick Fleming, as well as Ruthwell, were stated as having belonged to his father. Galabank was also claimed for Dundrennan. Both the Murrays were Commissioners for the settlement of the Borders, and so was Sir James Douglas of Torthorald, whose mother, the heir of the Carliles, had been compelled to marry her cruel husband by the Regent Angus. Douglas claimed the old Carlile property, "from Wamfray to Griestna grene," and it was the object of all three to get rid of their fellow Commissioner, Edward of Ryehill. He was put to the horn, with his wife and children, for not obeying the summons in "Murray contra Johnstoun" (1609), when Robert Johnstoun of Raecleuch, tutor of Johnstoun, Edward Johnstoun (of Ryehill), called of Newbie, Christine Irving there, John Johnstoun in Mylnfield there, Robert Fareis, John Gibson, the ploughman, Abraham Johnstoun, his sons, and many others were called upon to quit Newbie.

In May 1610 John M'Briar, servitor to Maxwell of Gribton in 1605, sued the above defendants for the tithes, but instead of John Johnstoun in Mylnfield, whose name is scratched out, John the younger appears. In another summons the following year Christine Irving's name also disappears, and Ryehill and Christopher Johnstoun were living at "the vast stone house in Annan." When Ryehill married Barbara d ard in 1614 he moved to his wife's house in Castlemilk.

Barbara's father, Nicol d ard, was an intimate friend of George Heriot, the famous jeweller to the King and Queen. Heriot came of a Dumfriesshire family, and his friend and executor, Robert Johnstoun, is stated, on his monument, to belong to the House of Newbie, in Annandale.

When John of Mylnfield was outlawed by Murray for not arresting Robert of Raecleuch and the other Johnstoun occupants of South Annandale, including himself, his cousin, John Carruthers of Holmains, was made Sheriff-Depute of Annandale in his place, and a Maxwell stepped into his post as Sheriff of Dumfries. In 1611 Carruthers was displaced for the same reason, and Mr John Johnstoun of Castlemilk appointed. He found it equally difficult to arrest the lords of the soil, and applied to the Privy Council for advice. Holmains, being no longer Sheriff-Depute, refused to pay his taxes, and Raecleuch and other lairds claimed that as Holmains was no longer Sheriff they need not pay the taxes he had demanded. Castlemilk was ordered to act with severity, and to pursue and arrest one Bell who had escaped from prison at Dumfries. In the midst of his difficulties he was drowned. The eldest son, Thomas, was not long of age when, "with the consent of Ryehill, his father-in-law" (*i.e.*, stepfather), he sold his lands of Flemingraw[1] and others

---

[1] So the deeds seem to show, but his nephew, Nathaniel Johnston, says of him: "My grandmother's brother gave my oldest uncle such an education in France, &c., and encouraged

to Maxwell of Kirkhous, to whom they had already been granted by the King, and whose brother had assisted to murder the Laird of Johnstoun.

Barbara d ard died about 1621, when her second husband returned to Annan. For some time he was summoned every year to remove his goods from Castlemilk, of which his wife had the life rent, as well as from Ryehill, etc., by Douglas of Torthorald, who did not enjoy the Royal favour like the Maxwells and Murrays. King James had always been a good friend to the Maxwells, and perhaps disapproved of the unrelenting attitude of the murdered Laird of Johnstoun's nearest relations—his young son, his second cousin, Robert of Raecleuch, his mother, "the auld Lady Johnstoun," Agnes and Elizabeth, his two daughters, and his widow—for, when Maxwell after years of wandering had been arrested, the King enquired if these still persisted "in the pursuit of their petition craving justice to be executed on the forfeited Lord Maxwell," and they said they did. Maxwell's brother petitioned the Privy Council in a moving appeal, promising that the slaughter of his own father should never be brought up against any of the relatives or accomplices of the late Lord Johnstoun, and he and Lord Maxwell would forgive it if the Johnstouns would do the same by Maxwell. He proposed that Lord Maxwell should marry one of the orphaned daughters of his victim, "as owing to her father's unhappy death she had no dowry," and that the young Laird should marry Maxwell's niece (the petitioner's daughter), and he would pay her 20,000 marks as her dower, "for the better avoidance of all future enmity." It is possible that this offer never reached the Johnstouns, for the Privy Council refused to forward it as Maxwell did not send it.[1] But the refusal of the King's suggestion confirmed the Royal policy to support their rivals. Maxwell's brother and heir was created Earl of Nithsdale in 1620, apparently gratis, and lucrative posts conferred on him in an age of favouritism and bribery. The new Lady Nithsdale was niece to the Duke of Buckingham. Like her husband, she was a Romanist.

James Murray never paid the £3000 he owed to Elizabeth Stewart (Lady Newbie).

In 1612 John of Graitney obtained for himself and his heirs a Crown Charter of Graitney, where it is stated that, owing to the burning, slaughter, and devastation of these parts by their ancient enemies of England, all previous Charters were destroyed. He was probably urged to do so by Murray's claim to investigate the Charters of the owners and kindlie tenants of Annandale; and Murray stated in the document he put forth on the subject that Lochmabenstane (the old name for Graitney) had been "lately given to William of Johnstoun by the Earl of Dunbar." Lately, in the Scottish estimate of the

him in such a prodigal way of living that he involved him in great debts . . . and got him to pass all the estate to him . . . and that uncle sold the estate to . . . the Maxwells." (Brit. Mus., Add. MSS.).

Perhaps this had something to do with the trading monopoly the uncle obtained, for in 1602 he was put to the horn for debt.

[1] The King had sent word that the execution was not to be delayed as the parties concerned wished to go to extremity.

possession of an estate, might be 100 years before. One of the witnesses examined in the case of Stormont *v.* the Trustees of the Marquis of Annandale in 1772 stated that the Newbie estates "did belong to the Carliles"—yet the Carliles held it before the Corries.

In 1606 Graitney had gained a suit, long pending, over the sons of the murdered Richard Irving, who obtained the lands of Sarkbrig and Conheath, in Graitney, on mortgage from John's grandfather, William of Graitney, and they were now obliged to give them up. In the suit his pedigree is recorded and includes "Johnstoun," the father of the first Baron of Newbie (*see* Chapter IX.). The Johnstoun house at Graitney remained till 1796 (when it was rebuilt), and bore the arms of Johnstone of that Ilk over the door, with the addition of two mullets and the initials J. J. on each side.

John Murray married secondly a daughter of Gilbert Johnstoun of Wamfray. Another of Gilbert's daughters married David Johnstoun in Edinburgh.

Cavartholme came by direct male descent through the first Baron Newbie from James, Laird of Johnstoun (1513 to 1524), to John of Graitney, who made it over to his grandson, John, Nov. 10, 1613. In 1615 the copyhold of Graitney and Hailstanemuir, with their towers, fortalices, corn-mills, moors, etc., was mortgaged, but subject to redemption, to Edward of Ryehill and Barbara, his wife, for 5000 marks. David Johnstoun of Newbie probably helped to supply the money, as his consent was obtained to let Murray have these lands for 2000 marks less than his brother, Edward, had paid for them. It was but the copyhold, so this Charter was soon followed by other Charters of total resignation by John of Graitney. One of these, dated 1618, is signed by William M'Briar of Almagill, John Corsane, Provost of Dumfries, Mr Symon Johnstoun, parson of Annan, and John Johnstoun. It is followed by a new Charter from the King, granting the estates irredeemably to John Murray and his heirs to be held of the Crown for a yearly payment of £20 Scots at Whitsunday and Martinmas, doubling the feu duty at the entry of every heir (Jan. 6, 1619).

Murray, now created Earl of Annandale, obtained another Charter, in which John of Graitney, his son, William, and his grandson, John, signed away their rights to the family estate in 1623. Murray mortgaged Graitney alone for 5400 marks to his sister-in-law, Janet Douglas, widow of Sir James Murray of Cockpool, in 1634, and it was redeemed in 1637. The full payment for the estate was not made without more litigation. After serving a writ of ejectment on the feuars and kindlie tenants, who comprised two Wamfray Johnstouns, James Johnstoun of Lochous, several Grahams, and three Johnstouns of Righead, the new owner was called upon by these defendants, in conjunction with John of Graitney, his son, William, and his grandson, John, to pay the balance of 10,000 marks still owing to the late proprietor. After quoting various documents to prove that he had no title to it, Murray paid it through Edward of Ryehill during the year 1624.

Graitney's direct descendant, Colonel James Johnstone, still called himself of Graitney, when, as Provost of Lochmaben (1720), he married Isabella, who claimed the Ruthven Barony in her own right. She died in 1730, leaving a son, James, fourth Baron Ruthven. His grandson, James, dying without heirs, his sister, Mary Elizabeth, succeeded to the Ruthven Barony, and her grandson is the present peer.[1]

Murray left an only son, James, who died in 1668, when the title was extinct. James's widow married Murray's distant relative, David Murray, Lord of Scone and Viscount Stormont. Their eldest son married Marjory, daughter of David Scott of Scotstarvit, and grand-daughter, through female descents, of the elder James Murray of Cockpool, Dundrennan's brother. She also descended from the Newbie Johnstouns. This marriage united the Graitney to the Perthshire estates of the Murrays of Scone and Stormont.

In 1620 Ryehill was put to the horn and "personally apprehendit" in the street of Edinburgh, as the security for a loan to his niece's husband, Hew Dunbar, W. S.

Murray brought a yearly action for twenty years against the old and present occupiers of Newbie—in one instance only against the Wamfrays, in another against George Johnstoun of Corrie—and M'Briar of Almagill, Douglas of Torthorald, Douglas of Drumlanrig, and, later, the Earl of Nithsdale were equally persistent for rents, taxes, or tithes. The three knocks were duly given on all their doors, and each year the Town Clerk reported the same— that he met with no response. There are also four horning processes against the young Laird, Robert of Raecleuch, Edward of Ryehill, and others. Yet Robert continued to live in Newbie, and Edward to act as Provost of Annan, Justice of the Peace, and Member for the Dumfries Burghs.

Ryehill received from the Crown (Jan. 1607) a small gift of confiscated land—Stank, in Annan—belonging to George Irving, and this still remains to his descendant; and the escheat of John Broun of the Land, his nephew. He won a suit against Irving, but repaid him for the property, and he also won a suit against two Hills, who questioned his claim to Ryehill bequeathed to him by his father. Yet John Murray brought an action to compel him to give it up.

The Murrays were most unpopular. James Murray of Cockpool was

[1] The junior branches of the Graitney family survive in Dumfries and probably in other parts. The sons of John who sold the estate to Murray were William, Gilbert, and Archibald. William married his cousin, a Graham, and their eldest son, John, sold his claims, such as they were, to Robert Graham in 1637; Robert feued the estate from Murray in 1649.

The Graitneys married well-endowed wives. The younger John's widow, Elizabeth Armstrong, in 1654 settled her lands in Hoddam, Lockerbie, Redkirk, Cockpool, Blaatwood, Dornock, Ruthwell, and Graitney on her son, William. Another son, Richard, is buried with many of his kin in Graitney Churchyard.

Archibald, George, and William Johnstoun in Hoddam, in 1689, and their cousin, William Johnstoun in Dornock, owned the lands and Mains of Holmains. Johnstoun of Graitney acted as a witness at the baptism of the sixth son of William and the Hon. Emilia Irving in Bonshaw Tower in 1709; and in 1793 William Johnstone of Graitney procured the grant of a weekly market and half-yearly fair for Graitney, with the usual tolls and privileges.

In 1768 Pennant observed there was still a railed enclosure, a sort of sanctuary for criminals, near Graitney. He states that "handfisting" marriages had quite died out on the Borders, but they were revived at Gretna Green for English runaway couples when Fleet marriages were abolished. They originated in the scarcity of priests.

Sheriff-Depute in 1616. He wrote from Comlongan to the Lords of the Privy Council that he had received a summons from His Majesty, dated at Newmarket, desiring him to call upon the Magistrates and keepers of the Borders to trace out the best roads for English merchants and traders travelling into Scotland, and adds: "I summoned the Magistrates to meet me at Annan on March 8, which day they could not keep, so I appointed the 16th, but none of them would come but Edward Johnstoun of Ryehill. We therefore together examined the ground and way, and think it most fitting that the ordinary highway from Annan to the Kirk of Graitney should be used, and from the Kirk through Sark at the ford by Sark brig, and away to Carlisle, because this was the way appointed for the King's coaches and carriages, and Graitney Kirk was the meeting place of the hosts of England and Scotland —the King was escorted by Scottish soldiers to the frontier, and there English troops took their place—so the constables of Graitney and Rampatrick have been ordered to make a road 24 feet wide, according to Act of Parliament, and a dyke (wall or embankment) on each side." He says, "that the old road through Kirtle water and Sark water was full of quicksand, and many of the King's subjects perish every year, and their goods are lost when driven that way. The other road was used for the cannon from Carlisle to Lochmaben."

As trade was not encouraged between England and Scotland this order seems to have been given with a view to the King revisiting his old kingdom. When he did so in 1617 a levy of 484 horses was made to convey the Royal carriages and baggage from Dumfries to Carlisle; and Murray and Ryehill arranged it.

In 1624 Ryehill, with Carlile of Bridekirk, and other leading men on the Border were ordered to prevent malefactors from escaping to Ireland, and to disarm the Borders.

In 1626 Ryehill and Gordon of Lochinvar received orders from the Privy Council to report the names of those in the county who persisted in going about armed, contrary to the law passed by James VI., and to secure their punishment. It was hardly safe for a gentleman to do otherwise in Dumfriesshire. Two years later one of Ryehill's great-nephews[1] was murdered near Moffat, another nephew (Edward of Seafield) was "grievously wounded and left for dead" in the street of Dumfries, and his grandson, a few years before, had been run through with a poniard in Annan. Ryehill wrote the following letter to James Primrose, the direct ancestor of Lord Rosebery, and Clerk to the Privy Council:—

"Sir, After my heartiest commendation, I received a letter direct from the Earl of Mar and others the Lords of His Majesty's Council, the date thereof July 31; the effect, that I should inform myself of the general and great contempt of those who do violate H.M.'s laws in bearing and wearing of

[1] William, natural son of John, the last Baron of Newbie. John Maxwell of Gribton, described as his sister's son and nearest of kin to the deceased, took out Letters of Slain against the assassin Johnston of Willies. Yet a natural son, unless legitimised by Royal Charter, which had not been done in this case, could neither make a Will, nor act as witness on a retour, or hold any public office. Robert Johnstoun of Over Howcleuch owed money to William Johnstoun at this time.

hackbuts and pistols, contrary to this kingdom's laws. I have had occasion to be out of this part of the country for 16 days, so that their lordships' letter did not come to my hand before the night of August 18, when I came to this town, the day appointed in their honours' letter giving August 21, for me to report the diligence of my service to you Sir, as Clerk to H.M.'s Council. I have thought good therefore Sir, to excuse myself by my letter to you of the true cause as I shall answer to God, why I have not informed you of the persons acting contrary to the statutes aforesaid whereof there will be numbers more no doubt generally throughout this kingdom, if ye be well informed thereof, but the proving thereof by witnesses will be very troublesome and not easy to be done. I thought Sir the order of the Council in the probation of that cause had only to be used by the parties challenged. I entreat you to inform my lordships of this just excuse, lest they might misconstrue me in not reporting diligence in that service as becometh me according to my knowledge, and if their honours will appoint another day, I will endeavour to give the best information I can about this part of the country. But Sir I would know how the witnesses shall be charged for I conceive they must be such as can say they have seen the parties dylated [accused] bear and wear the weapons, which will be a great trouble to the people of the kingdom, and I fear followed by danger to the persons challenged, and those charging them will give but evil obedience in appearing to bear witness and small evidence for the reasons aforesaid. However Sir, I remit this to your consideration, and crave pardon for prescribing rules to the trial of the causes I am not worthy of. So committing you to the protection of the Almighty, I remain your loving friend (signed) Eduard Johnestoune of Ryehill. At Annan 9 Aug. 1626.

"To his much respected friend James Primrose, Clarke to the Secret Council, these be."

Lochinvar's answer ran: "My very honourable Lords . . . I have received your lordships' letter directing me to give up the names of such as wear hackbuts, and pistols in this country. May it please your lordships to understand that it is so ordinary in this country that it is a great difficulty to give up their names that wears, nor those that wears not, for almost every man carries pistolets. . . . I confess it is a great wrong, but that his Majesty's statutes should be observed and kept always. I would wish those corrected with lenity, for if every man that has offended in that kind must come and agree for it with the Treasury, and especially such as lie far off, it will be a great grievance to the county that is already so much grieved what with revocations and yearly taxations, and now with penal statutes that your lordships can hardly believe how the people doth grudge. But if it be your pleasure to go on with it . . . choose 4 sufficient men in every shire throughout the kingdom to compone it with such as hath offended to save such charges in their travelling as is hurtful to them and not profitable to the king, and to be done in lenity and for such as hath been wilful transgressors to be punished with greater severity both in bodies and goods." He excuses himself for his boldness in offering advice.

The penalty as ordered by the King was a fine and to lose the right hand; and shortly afterwards a petition by the Governor of the Edinburgh Tolbooth, and signed by his friends, is sent to the Privy Council, asking pardon for a James Johnstoun, whose conduct in prison had been most exemplary, and whose only fault since the last respite had been carrying pistolets. Walter Graham, a little earlier, was sentenced to be scourged through Edinburgh, to lose his right hand, and to be expelled from Great Britain for fighting in the precincts of the Parliament House while the members were sitting. But such severity could not be enforced in Annandale.

In 1618 Ryehill and the Earls of Mar, Lothian, and Buccleuch, Lord Crichton and James Johnstoun of Lochous, all curators and trustees of the young Laird of Johnstoun, brought an action against Raecleuch to compel him to turn out of Newbie Castle and give it up to the young Laird. The next year the other curators and the young Laird, with Sir John Murray, brought an action against Ryehill, his stepson (young Castlemilk), Raecleuch, and Westraw to recover the Annandale Charter chest, which was in Ryehill's charge. It was restored by Lady Wigton, the Laird's mother, to whom Ryehill had transferred it, though it contained important papers connected with the Newbie family, which have never been recovered by the heirs of the original owners.

In 1621 Raecleuch still declined to leave Newbie, whereupon, as the instrument of possession states, "the Right Hon. James Johnstoune of that Ilk for himself, and Edward Johnstoune of Ryell for himself as one of the curators to the said James Johnstoune of that Ilk, and also as procurator, and in name and behalf of the remaining persons after specified, curators to the said James, accompanied by the Sheriff-Depute and the messenger," with two Johnstouns of Wamfray, "went to Newbie, and there lawfully removed, ejected, output, and rid the said Robert of Raecleuch, —— Douglas, his wife, Robert, his son, their goods and gear forth, and from all and sundry the said lands and tower of Newbie, and admitted the said James and Edward Johnstounes to the said tower house, etc., kindling new fires within the said house," but owing to the great frost they could not dig or plough up the customary handful of earth as a sign of possession.

Raecleuch retired to Mylnfield. His daughter, Sara, was married to Fergus Graham, who with others, including Raecleuch's nephew, Robert, tried to turn the Laird out again, and a trial ensued, with no result. Raecleuch, the principal defendant, was cautioner for those who assisted him. The same year his brother Mungo died, but the son claimed the debt with accumulated interest.

Meanwhile the heir of the Newbies, Edward Johnstoun, called of Seafield (Wyldcotray), was trying to recover his father's inheritance. Hoping to enlist his uncle of Ryehill on his side, he signed a deed, witnessed by Thomas Johnstoun of Castlemilk and William Graham of the Moat, promising, if he gained his suit, he would give him proper title-deeds of Croftheid, Cummertrees, Howmedow, and certain lands in Annan, which Ryehill had occupied himself, or by others in his name, if Ryehill and his heirs "would renounce all right and title to the £10 land of Annan and Seafield, but always reserving to Ryehill and his heirs their right to the lands acquired by Ryehill from Jeffrey Irving of Bonshaw."

He must have been discouraged on this subject, for in 1623 he brought an action against Ryehill for delivering up the title-deeds of the Newbie estate and other lands to their purchasers, and for witnessing the contract between his father, Robert, and Sir James Johnstoun of Dunskellie in 1605. Two years before he was attacked by James Lyndsay in Dumfries and left for dead, covered with wounds. A passer-by seeing that he was still alive brought Patrick Young, a "chirurgeon," to assist him, and he was carried into a house, and revived.

The next year John Broun of the Land acted as Edward of Seafield's security at Jedburgh that he would appear at six days' notice to answer for any "ryot" laid to his charge (an aggressive attitude towards the Reformed clergy). John Bell of Castlebank acted as his security, and John Galloway for Mr Symon Johnstoun, the parson of Annan, that they should both keep the peace, "and not injure each other, their property, or their relatives." There were also actions against the Laird of Johnstoun, the Maxwells, Ryehill, Seafield, and others for damaging the property of recently appointed ministers, as a protest against the Reformation. The Reformers acted with a high hand in Dumfries. In 1628 there were trials for "Papistry," chiefly of priests, but two laymen were included for sheltering them. Sir William Grierson and Sir John Charteris, Sheriff and Sheriff-Depute, arrested the priests, and the populace attacked the Protestant minister of New Abbey and his family in reprisal. In 1639 James, Lord Johnstoun, was bound over before the Privy Council not to hinder, discharge, or stop any of his tenants from selling fuel and necessaries to Mr George Buchanan, the parson of Moffat.

In 1624 Edward Johnstoun parted with Seafield to his brother-in-law, John Geddes, and a little later was a witness to the transfer of the property at Arkilton to an Eliot. In 1631 he was among those occupying or claiming parts of the Newbie estate summoned by Maxwell, Earl of Nithsdale, as Sheriff, to show their title-deeds. He bought lands in Ireland, but, being a Romanist, was not allowed to settle there. He does not seem to have married, and this is the last time his name occurs.

Raecleuch was dead in 1626. His lawful children were Robert, Archibald, William, Francis, Sara, Grizel, and Dorothie. Robert, junr., signs a document from the Hospital of Annan in 1624. Robert and John are in various documents called his natural sons—possibly the two Johnstouns of that name, her tenants, who were defended in a spirited manner by Barbara Douglas, Raecleuch's widow, when accused of horse-stealing. She died in 1628. Raecleuch's brothers, Mungo,[1] Symon, William, John, and James,[2] are also mentioned. Symon, parson of Annan for fifty-five years, had a son, George, who left a son,

[1] Mungo's son, Robert, died about 1630 s.p. His daughter, Rachel, married Robert Graham of Blaatwood.
[2] The three younger are called natural sons.

John, a burgess of Dumfries, who married Agnes Carlile, 1681. This branch is supposed to be extinct.

Raecleuch borrowed money from his brother, the parson of Annan, and one of the Wamfrays in 1619; his cautioners, Robert Fareis of Mylnfield and William Gillespie, and the witnesses, Edward Carruthers of Wormanbie, Abraham Johnstoun of Mylnbie, and John Johnstoun, "callit Mylnfield."

As the young Laird was in Edinburgh when Raecleuch died, Robert, the late Mungo's son, with his sister, Barbara, took possession of Newbie Castle as a creditor. There was almost a repetition of the events of 1605 and 1618, for again Edward of Ryehill was ordered to turn them out, which he did, assisted by Captain James Johnstoun of Lochous, young Edward of Mylnfield, and others. Barbara was hurt in the scuffle, and, though obeying an order from the Privy Council, the assailants were "put to the horn"; but the Laird paid the sum due to the late Mungo to his son, Robert. The same year (1626) Edward of Ryehill, Sir J. Charteris, Sir William Grierson, and Maxwell of Kirkconnel were directed by the Privy Council to turn Christie Irving and his brother out of Stapleton, the abode of Fergus Graham of Blaatwood, Ryehill's nephew and Raecleuch's son-in-law, and to restore it to Graham. The Irvings had captured the house, and, as the summons says, "crammed it with victual and ammunition, intending to keep it as a refuge for breakers of the law." Two months later another commission was given to the Earls of Nithsdale, Roxburgh, Buccleuch, Murray of Annandale, Lord Hay, Lord Cranstoun, Sir W. Seton, and the Lairds of Traquair, Drumlanrig, Lochinvar, Lag, Amisfield, Bombie, Closeburn, and Sir John Hay to expel the Irvings, and they did so; but the Johnstoun sympathies were with Christie, for the Laird acted the next year as cautioner for two of his near relatives.

Graham appears again twenty-two years later with his wife, Sara Johnstoun, in an action against the Earl of Annandale, to whom he had sold his land, to compel him "to provide sustenance for them and their eleven poor bairns." Most of the children were of age, but the trouble was connected with a famine which resembled the terrible scarcity in 1630, when an edict of the Privy Council enacted that no food of any description should be allowed to leave Scotland under very severe penalties. "Forasmuch," it began, "as it has pleased Providence to visit this Kingdom with a most unseasonable, untymous, and late harvest, so that the corn has been universally evil win, and in many parts not yet win at all." This explains the apparent inconsistency of the law, first encouraging, then prohibiting, the trade, which was all in food, between Scotland and England.[1]

In 1648 Fergus, James, Arthur, and George Graham are among the mosstroopers found living in the Debateable Land. Probably these were some of the "poor children," if Blaatwood was not there himself, for the Civil War was in progress, and they had all taken the side of Charles I.

---

[1] So late as 1649 a law was passed in Scotland to insist on abstinence from meat in Lent, but sanitary and economical reasons were given for reviving a practice which, through "men's gluttony," so it stated, "was being disused."

In 1632 Edward of Ryehill "accepted upon him," to quote the Privy Council Record, "the Stewardship of Annandaill, and Robert Crichton of Raehills the Sheriffship of Dumfries." In 1633 he again represented Dumfries in Parliament. In 1634 he was appointed a judge with the Lord Treasurer, the Lord Privy Seal, the Archbishop of Glasgow, the Earl of Queensberry, Lord Hereis, Lord Johnstoun, Robert Maxwell of Dunwiddie, Robert Charteris, the parsons of Hoddam and Kirkpatrick, and Mr Samuel Kirkpatrick, and was made Convener of the Session. The same year he parted with Ryehill and Cummertrees to Murray, Earl of Annandale, with the consent of the Earl and Countess of Wigton, who had a mortgage on it of £2000. The deed is witnessed in the Canongate by Thomas Maxwell, Adam Johnstoun, tutor of Elsieshields, and Robert Johnstoun of Gotterbraes.

Ryehill lived chiefly in Edinburgh after 1630, but in 1636 he witnessed a Carlile Charter, and mortgaged nearly all his remaining land to Sara, Countess of Wigton, for 1000 marks. She died the same year, and Ryehill attended her splendid funeral in Edinburgh, where the deed was signed. It secured kindlie rights to his younger sons in lands bordering on Galabank. He was in Annan in 1640, when, with Almagill and Grierson of Lag, he witnessed a bond for his Chief with Sir John Charteris of Amisfield. He died before June 2, 1643, when John Johnstoun, "callit of Mylnfield," made a fresh settlement of his property, and was in possession of Stank and Closehead. In a bond signed by John, his wife, Gaylies Rig, and their son, George, John paid 2500 marks to Mr John Corsane, Provost of Dumfries, to redeem lands formerly owned by Edward of Ryehill, including the stone house in Annan.

The best known member of the Newbie family is "Robert Johnstoune, Esq., LL.D.,"[1] who died 1640. His father was probably James, a merchant in Edinburgh (died 1595). In 1612 he sued Lord Hereis as principal, and Robert Hereis as cautioner, for a debt of 3500 marks. His monument stood in Trinity Church, Edinburgh, till the church was removed (1848) for the railway. He was one of the three executors of George Heriot's Will, where he is styled Gentleman; and in his own Will he calls himself of the parish of St. Anne's, Blackfriars, London, where he filled a Government post. He left 18,000 marks to Heriot's Hospital, besides £12,000 for charitable purposes; also money to found a school at Moffat and for charities at Dumfries and to build a bridge at Annan. He left legacies to his cousins, the sons, son-in-law (Sir John Hay), and two grandchildren of John Johnstoun of Newbie (the Edinburgh merchant) (died 1601); but his principal trustee was "his Chief," the Lord Johnstoun who had visited him in London not long before Robert's death.

He was the author of a Latin *History of English and Scottish Affairs from 1572 to 1628*, published in folio at Amsterdam after his death. The book is

[1] "Dr Robert Johnstoune, of the House of Newbie in Annandale, an eminent lawier, among several sums left by him in Anno 1640 to be improven into certain pious and charitable uses in this city, did bequeathe 18,000 marks, which, according to the laudable intention of this munificent benefactor, the good town applied for advancing the charitable and religious ends of this Hospital. By which donary as by many other acts of his liberality this great donator hath propagated a lasting monument of his piety to posterity."

dedicated to Charles I.; the work, "Roberti Johnstoni Scoto-Britanni, etc.' A small portion in 1646 was translated by Thomas Middleton and published as *The Historie of Scotland during the Minoritie of James I*.[1] His admiration for Queen Elizabeth and his remarks on "the cruel fanaticism" of Knox show that he was an Episcopalian, to which, as Chambers observes, the cultivated and wealthy classes chiefly belonged in Scotland, till a strong effort was made to suppress them in 1696 and in 1746.

John Johnstoun, a writer, of the House of Newbie, was a witness to the retour of Westraw in 1634. At his house, "on the south side of the Hie St. beneath the Cross," a deed was signed by the Chief and James Johnstoun of Westraw in 1629 concerning land occupied by Gavin Moffat of Harthope.

[1] A MS. History of Scotland, in the Advocates' Library, was presented by David Johnstone, burgess of Edinburgh, as the work of his father and grandfather, in 1653. It has been wrongly attributed to Robert, who left no children.

CHAPTER XII.

JOHNSTOUNS OF KIRKTON AND WARRIESTON—CASTLEMILK AND POMFRET.

IN 1608 James Johnstoun of Beirholme was returned heir to his grandfather, Gavin Johnstoun in Kirkton. He was elder brother to Archibald, the merchant in Edinburgh, who sold his mortgage of Newbie to Mungo Johnstoun, and with his son, James, held a mortgage of Westraw.

Archibald, as has been seen, was associated in business in Edinburgh with several (Elphinstone, Wamfray, Corrie, Kellobank, and Newbie) Johnstouns. In 1595, when engaged in a suit with the English Council, King James wrote to Queen Elizabeth on his behalf. He died, Oct. 1619, and his inventory, with the debts due to him, was valued at £11,285, but of this he was owed £9,918, chiefly by Sir George Home, Lord Crichton, George Williamson, Matthew Moffat, and James Nesbit. Edward Johnstoun of Ryehill also owed him 300 marks, and Thomas Johnstoun 230 marks. His eldest son, James, married to Elspeth Craig, was dead, leaving a son, Archibald, born in 1611, to whom his grandfather left the house at Warrieston and the reversion of 21,000 Scottish marks when the Earl of Home and the heirs of the late Adam Rae should have paid their debts. Archibald left £2000 a year to his widow, Rachel Arnot, and 20,000 marks divided between young Archibald's sisters, Rachel (afterwards Mrs Burnet), Margaret, and Beatrix. Rachel was so strong a Presbyterian that she objected to her son Gilbert accepting the Bishopric of Salisbury.

The other legatees were Samuel and Joseph, sons of the testator. Joseph was only eighteen, and was to be "entertained with his mother in virtuous education and learning at the schools, in the fear of God," but, like his brother, he received 5000 marks when he came of age. The same sum to Sir James Skene of Curriehill and Dame Janet Johnstoun, his spouse (Archibald's daughter); the same to another daughter, Rachel Johnstoun, married to the late John Jaksone; 100 marks yearly to his brother John; to Robert Johnstone's son, called Archibald, £40; to Andro Johnstoun, brother to James's son (of Beirholme), £40, to Gavin, Robert, and Thomas, their brothers, each £10; to Captain Robert Johnstoun, called of Mossop, £40, and a free discharge of everything owed by him in the testator's account book; to his wife's niece, Rachel, daughter of William Arnot, 200 marks; 10 marks to each of his servants. His wife and son, Joseph, were to be his only executors, Joseph to follow his mother's counsel in everything; and he asks his "well beloved Sir James Skene, his brother James Arnot, and his faithful friend David Johnstoun to be overseers in all things concerning his Will, and his hope and confidence is that they will discharge their honest friendly duty thereunto." He also left 100 marks to help to restore the Church of Kirkpatrick Juxta, "where my predecessors bones lie."

Thomas Johnstoun (a creditor) was young Castlemilk, who, after being sued by Murray, Douglas, and M'Briar to pay rent for his own lands, besides dues and tithes, went to London, where he probably fell into the company of some of the gay young men about the Court—among whom was Richard Graham, a great friend of Charles, Prince of Wales—for there he signed the transfer of his last possession—Castlemilk. After this he entered as a captain in the army of Gustavus Adolphus, King of Sweden, where he died. His brother, Alexander, was an advocate, much employed, as his father had been, by the Laird and other relatives, and married a daughter of Wilkin Johnstoun of Elsieshields. James died *s.p.* The other brother, John, was ordained into the Anglican Ministry in Yorkshire, possibly owing to the resistance to Episcopacy in Scotland, and there he married, about 1626, Elizabeth, daughter of Henry Hobson of Ufflete. He was curate of Reidness, in the parish of Whitgift, and then vicar of Sutton upon Derwent, and had seven children at the time he was served heir to his brother Alexander, who died in Dec. 1643. He did not get much, as Alexander had lent money to his relatives—£220 to Robert Johnstoun of Stapleton, son of Robert of Raecleuch, and others—besides having had expensive tastes, for he owed £220 to a goldsmith. His only assets, except money owed him, were his library worth £200, two diamond rings worth £160, a gold bracelet worth £40, and two enamelled cups value £12.

The Vicar of Sutton, who died 1657, left eminent if rather eccentric sons, but with his double relationship to Warrieston it is strange that his eldest son, Nathaniel, was a strong Jacobite, and his youngest, Henry, became a noted Benedictine monk. Another son, Alexander, died at Mittau, in Courland.

This part of the Elsieshields family seems to have been the elder, and that of Kirkton the junior, and of the last, Archibald, Laird of Warrieston, is far the most conspicuous. He had a zealous Presbyterian in his grandmother, Rachel Arnot, as well as in his mother, Elspeth Craig, and he was educated by Robert Baillie, afterwards Principal of the Glasgow University. These Edinburgh Johnstouns, hearing of the lawlessness of their country cousins, attributed it probably to the old religion when the King saw that it was from the want of any at all.

Archibald was admitted an Edinburgh advocate to advise the Committee formed to resist Charles I.'s attempt to force the English ritual upon the Kirk. His history, which fills a controversial page in that of Scotland, is fully written elsewhere,[1] and requires a volume for itself, from the stirring events in which

[1] *Dict. Nat. Biog.*, Vol. XXX., and the authors quoted there.

he took a prominent part. Charles I. knighted him and made him a Lord of Session in 1641, when he took the title of Lord Warrieston, and the Estates voted him a grant of £3000, because he had "expended himself and his purse in public duty." He gave £2400 to relieve the needs of the Scottish army in Ireland in 1643. Carlyle calls him a "canny lynx-eyed lawyer and austere Presbyterian zealot, full of fire, of heavy energy and gloom, in fact a very notable character, of whom our Scotch friends would do well to give us further elucidation." That his sisters, daughters, and sons-in-law firmly believed in him is a great tribute to his sincerity.

Warrieston's uncles — Samuel of Sheens and Joseph of Hilton — were writers to the signet. Samuel gave 1800 marks to assist the army in Ireland. He married Helen Morison, sister of Lord Prestongrange, and was buried at Greyfriars in 1659. He sold his property in Dumfriesshire to the Laird. His eldest son married Anna, daughter of Sir James Hamilton; the second son, William, married Janet, the only child of John, Laird of Wamfray. William carried on the male line of Sheens, as only two daughters survived of his elder brother James's fourteen children, Rachel and Henrietta, who married brothers—Sir James and Sir William Johnstoun of Westerhall. The third brother, Alexander, left one daughter, Rachel.

Joseph of Hilton married Sophia, daughter of Sir Patrick Hume. His Will is dated 1638. His daughter, Sophia, married John Fairholm of Craigiehall, and was the mother of the first Marchioness of Annandale. His son, Archibald, died in 1671, under tragical circumstances. The Countess of Home entertained some intimate friends at Hirsel, the seat of Lord Home, near Coldstream, he being absent, and three of them—his brother (William Home), the Sheriff of Berwick, and Hilton—stayed the night. They spent the evening at cards, and Home, losing heavily, accused Hilton of unfairness, and Hilton answered by hitting him in the face. They apparently made up the quarrel, but in the night when Hilton was asleep Home entered his room and stabbed him in nine places. There was presumably resistance, as the Sheriff, roused by the scuffle, met Home just leaving his victim's room and received a serious wound. Home escaped on Hilton's horse. Some years later Hilton's son, Patrick (afterwards knighted and Lord Provost), was at a ball, when he was called into the lobby to speak to a stranger. The visitor told him that he had just attended the death-bed of his father's assassin, who had begged him to come and ask the son's forgiveness. Something convinced Hilton that he was the murderer himself, and he was about to stab him with his sword when Home vaulted over the staircase and escaped.

Another of the Hilton family, Major Johnston, one of Sir Patrick's nine sons, is described by Carlyle of Inveresk as being remarkable for his good looks, and many duels, yet "one of the best natured men I ever met. George II. had put a cross at his name on his behaving very insolently at one of the theatres to a country gentleman, and afterwards wounding him in a duel. In George III.'s time, John Home got the star taken off, and he was promoted. . . . Hew Bannatine had been his travelling tutor when abroad."

Warrieston was great-nephew to Margaret Craig, the mother of John Johnstoun, Laird of Castlemilk. Her brother's (Dr John Craig)[1] reputation was so great that when he failed to cure Angus it was at once assumed that the patient was bewitched, and poor old women were tortured before the King to make them confess it. His great-nephew, Nathaniel, the Vicar of Sutton's eldest son, was educated as a physician, and passed into the third class at St. Leonard's College, St. Andrews, in 1647. He took his M.D. degree at King's College, Cambridge, in 1656, and was admitted a F.R.C.P., April 12, 1687, the College of Physicians having received a Charter from James VII. He bought a house at Pontefract, where he soon had a large practice, but preferred to devote himself to antiquities and natural history, and finally came to London in 1686 as a High Tory political writer. He married Anna, daughter of Richard Cudworth of Eastfield, Yorks, by whom he had four sons. The eldest, Cudworth, took his M.D. degree (St. John's College, Cantab.) and practised at York, but died before his father, leaving a son, Pelham, also a physician, and another son, Henry, rector of Whitton, Northants, and Chancellor of the diocese of Llandaff. Pelham graduated M.D. at Cambridge in 1728, was a F.R.C.P. in 1732, practised in London, and died at Westminster, Aug. 10, 1765.

Dr Nathaniel Johnston seems to have done his duty by his sons before he gave up all means of making a living to absorb himself in his books. In 1686 he published the *Excellency of Monarchical Government*, a folio of 490 pp., beginning with ancient history. In 1687, replying to Sir W. Coventry's pamphlet, he issued *The Assurance of Abby and other Church Lands in England*, to show that even if the Religious Orders were restored in England the possessors of lands granted by Henry VIII. could not be disturbed. On July 23, 1688, he published *The King's Visitorial Power Asserted, Being an Impartial Relation of the late Visitation of S. Mary Magdalen College, Oxford;* also *The Dear Bargain, The State of the English Nation under the Dutch;* but his great work was *A History of Yorkshire*, on the model of Dugdale's *Warwickshire*, which cost him thirty years of labour. The Revolution of 1688 ruined any chance he had of a pension ; and two diarists of the day mention his poverty. One notes, May 27, 1695, " walked to the Savoy, visited poor Dr Johnston, who, by his unhappy circumstances, is little better than buried alive." The other writes, Nov. 11, 1696, " Dr Johnston gives us now some hopes to see his history brought to light. The doctor is exceedingly poor, and the chief thing that has made him so is this great undertaking of his. He now lives privately with the Earl of Peterborough, the great support of the Jacobite cause, who maintains him. He dare not let it be openly known where he is "—probably for political as well as pecuniary reasons. He died there in 1705, leaving over 100 volumes of collections written in a very crabbed scrawl, which Hearne described as a sort of shorthand. Ninety-seven volumes were bought from his grandson, and were used in editing Camden's *Britannia* and

---

[1] He was disgraced, says Burnet, because he held that James VI. died of poison. His son, John, was physician to Charles I. His father, Sir Thomas Craig, tried those accused of killing Rizzio, but by Darnley's wish only the underlings were punished. He presided over the mock trial for Darnley's murder.

Monasticon Eboracense; but his large house and other properties in and near Pontefract, with his antiques, were sold by order of the Court of Chancery in 1707.

Some of Nathaniel Johnston's MSS. are in the British Museum; among them an interesting account of his visit in 1653 to the old home at Castlemilk. He reflects that it might have been his "had it not been for the prodigality of my uncle Thomas, to whom my dear father was heir, and the wicked contrivances of my grandmother's brother, Nathaniel, it had not been sold, and the author of these collections might have been inheritor of that fair patrimony." He rode seven miles on his grandfather's estate and met with an old tenant, who told him what he had heard before from his relatives—that his grandfather, when in France for the study of Civil Law, was told by a soothsayer to beware of milk, therefore he always abstained from it. "Being a burgess in Parliament for Lochmaben, on his return from Edinburgh, having dismissed his tenants, who, by their tenure, do attend their lords in their journeys according as they appoint—the old man who related this to me was one of those who, with his half-pike or half-lance, had attended him within half a mile of the Castle, which is pleasantly situated on a hill, half a mile above the River Milk. My grandmother and some of the children were come out of the Castle; while they were expecting my grandfather home, they were the sad spectacles of his death. For the servant passing the water indifferently well, my grandfather's horse and he were drawn down the stream and both drowned."

"I have often met the old doctor's brother," wrote a correspondent to Hearne, March 23, 1773-74. "He was Prior of the English Benedictines in Paris when I was there. He fled out of England at the assassination plot, and a reward was offered by the King [William III.] to apprehend him, but he kept out of the way and died in Paris." He is elsewhere described as "a good little monk, and a pleasant and good natured man, but no writer, though long a Superior."

This was Nathaniel's brother, Henry, who had assisted Dugdale in his researches before he professed at Dieulouard, in Lorraine, for the English monastery of St. Edward the King at Paris, May 26, 1675. In the reign of James VII. he was stationed at St. James's Chapel, London, during the time that the Prince of Wales, known as the Old Pretender, was born at St. James's Palace. He remained in England till forced to fly in 1696, and held various posts at Douai and elsewhere in France; and in 1717 he secretly revisited England as Titular Prior of Durham. He died in Paris in 1723, having been employed by James VII. to translate one of Bossuet's works, published 1685, 4to. He also wrote *The History of England's late most Holy and most Glorious Royal Confessor and Defender of the True Faith, King James II.*, and replies to various controversial works by Anglicans.

Dr Samuel Johnston, the second son of the Vicar of Sutton upon Derwent, married Ann Seaman. His son Samuel, B.D. and Fellow of St. John's College, Cambridge, married Sarah Tadman, and was vicar of St. Mary's, Beverley, for more than fifty years. His younger son, William, a captain in the 48th Regiment, carried on the male line. He served under Wolfe at the taking of Quebec, and married Mary Hamilton of Tyrella, Co. Down. Their son, the Rev. William Henry Johnston, M.A., vicar of Holmpatrick, Co. Dublin, married Margaret Hamilton of Abbotstown and Holmpatrick. Their son, William, fought at Waterloo with the 51st King's Own Yorkshire Light Infantry. He married Sarah Elizabeth, grand-daughter of Sir John Dillon, Bart., and their son, William Henry, represents the Johnstons of Castlemilk, Pomfret, and Beverley, and is a Baron of the Holy Roman Empire, in right of his grandmother, Elizabeth Dillon. Mr Johnston, now of Ealing, was born in 1834, educated at Eton, and married Fanny Lewis, daughter of the Rev. Edmund Antrobus. He has issue. Of the two elder sons of the Rev. Samuel Johnston, vicar of Beverley, Samuel, D.D., Fellow of St. John's, Cambridge, and vicar of Freshwater, Isle of Wight, died *s.p.*; the other, John, M.D., of Beverley, has descendants through his daughter, who married Richard Hill of Thornton Hall, Yorks, and his grand-daughter, who married Captain Frederick Robertson.[1] Their son, Frederick, born in 1816, took Holy Orders, and was an eminent preacher and author in Brighton. When William IV. was a midshipman, cruising off Burlington Quay, he hired a gig and set off to attend a ball at Beverley. The horse fell on the way and His Royal Highness received severe injuries. He was conveyed to Dr Johnston's house in Beverley, and remained there some time, till he was quite well. When he was King an influential friend of Captain Robertson reminded him of the debt he owed to the deceased physician. The King recollected every detail of his sojourn at Dr Johnston's house, and the care bestowed on him, and inquired if he could do anything for his relatives. He was told that Captain Robertson wished to put his son into the army, and the King at once gave him a commission. From Captain William Johnston of Beverley descended the late Most Rev. Robert Samuel Gregg, Archbishop of Armagh.

[1] He saw a great deal of service, partly under Admiral Sir George Cockburn in 1813 on the coast of North America, and he received a naval medal. He was one of the founders of Cheltenham College.

PLATE VII.

ELIZABETH JOHNSTON OF BEVERLEY.
Born 1757; married Richard Hill of Thornton Hall, 1785.

W. H. JOHNSTON AS AN ETON BOY.
(ELSIESHIELDS).

CHAPTER XIII.

JOHNSTOUN OF GALABANK, "CALLIT OF MYLNFIELD."—THE FAREIS FAMILY—ACTIONS AGAINST GALABANK—YOUNG GALABANK—THE GRAHAMS—THE LAIRD OF JOHNSTOUN —JOHNSTOUN OF WARRIESTON—THE CIVIL WAR—CROMWELL—THE YOUNG EARL OF ANNANDALE—NEWBIE CASTLE BURNT.

JOHN Johnstoun, the advocate, called "in Mylnfield" in local documents, preferred a pretty face to either dower or noble birth when he married Bessie Fareis,[1] whose relatives were cottars and "dependers" of his father. She is described as the widow of John Johnstoun in Mylnfield, who, with her son, George, was among those occupiers of Newbie summoned to quit it, July 25, 1611. Edward of Ryehill received the same notice, but was living in Graitney, and John, son of Gilbert Fareis, and William Pool lived in his house at Mylnfield. The younger John of Mylnfield married Gaylies or Egidia Rig, a widow with some means, in 1622. Her first husband was Robert Loch, one of the baillies of Annan, by whom she had a son, Mark. Her sister, Marion, was the widow of their cousin, John Irving, "callit the Laird." Their father was a writer in Dumfries, and their maternal grandfather, John Galloway, the purchaser of the Rev. Patrick Howat's rights to Galabank.

Mark Loch was the first lessee of the Government post between Carlisle, Annan, and Dumfries, but it was very unremunerative. He was Provost of Annan in 1656.

The Galabank estate derives its name from an elevated mound on the side of the Annan, which in the fifteenth century was called Preditaker, or near St. Bride's, *i.e.*, Bridekirk. The mound was covered with trees till a few years ago. It passed from Bruce, Johnstoun, and others to the Irvings; and Jeffrey, the son of Christopher Irving, sold it to Edward Johnstoun in 1604. Edward mortgaged it to Galloway,[2] and John of Mylnfield acquired it in

[1] The Fareis family, once small landowners in Kindelhead, known in old days as Ferisland, consisted of Gilbert and his children—George, John, Robert, and Bessie—in 1611. Bessie married secondly Cuthbert Johnstoun of Kirk (*see* Chapter V.) Their descendants have much risen in the world; and Robert lent money to Dame Elizabeth Carlile and Fergus Graham of Blaatwood, inveterate borrowers.

[2] Galloway was the son of James Galloway and his wife, Elizabeth Johnstoun. His brother, Patrick, was a Royal Chaplain, like Howat, and father of the first Lord Dunkeld. Howat, who was made a Bishop, gave as a reason for selling Galabank in the precept for a Charter, that he "had called to mind that it is most Godly and equitable that those lands should be disponed by me to the old Kyndlie and native tenants and possessors of the said lands, and understanding that John Galloway, baillie burgess of Annan, and his predecessors since many ages past have been old kyndlies and native tenants and possessors of the said lands I herewith restore them" for an equivalent.

1624, probably with Ryehill's approval, for the sum Galloway had paid to Howat.[1] The Royal Charter to Howat constitutes it a lairdship, and it is still possessed by John's descendant.

Except as a witness in conjunction with his father to a deed, John first appears (July 2, 1611) in a Galabank Charter as "the son of the late John Johnstone in Mylnfield, who occupies, or others in his name, the land (*i.e.*, Northfield) to the east of Galabank which belonged to the late Robert Johnstone, called of Newbie." John was living in the stone house in Annan (1613-14) when his grandfather was Provost; and he was himself elected Provost in 1624. He was then living in his wife's house at Annan, as his grandfather, again a widower, had left Castlemilk and returned to the stone house. But Edward moved to Edinburgh, and John paid off the mortgages on this house and the estate of Galabank with 1000 marks, though they were soon mortgaged again. He was living at Brounehills, April 1623, and his cousin, William of Brume, is described as his servitor.

In 1618 a case was brought against him by the Provost, Baillies, and Council of Annan, who, so the indictment runs, "for the safe transport of his Majesty's subjects, and hoping to obtain money in respect of the great poverty of the said burgh (owing to the injuries of the disordered thieves and limmers of the Middle Marches) had kept a boat, and exacted dues, and now John Johnstoun, burgess of Annan, also called John of Mylnfield, and others would not let it pass their land." This action was brought in 1628 before the Lords in Council, John having been Provost in the interval, and the defendants, not appearing, were outlawed—a sentence declared to be *wrongful* by the Justiciary Court at Dumfries, and quashed.

There was an adverse judgment the same year against John and his brothers—George, Edward, and David—and Thomas Carruthers, Laird of Wormanbie, who were accused of "carrying arms and assaulting George Weild, a tenant in Mylnfield, while doing his lawful affairs in sober and quiet manner, looking for no injury to be done unto him from any person." A feud had long existed between the Johnstouns and Weilds. While Robert of Newbie was assisting his Chief in his great difficulties in 1583 the Weilds seized his lands in Annan. The Privy Council gave Arthur Johnstoun of Croftheids, one of the Newbies, the escheat of the Weild property, but they obstinately remained on the estate. John, "on his own confession," was fined £10 for the whole party by the Lochmaben court, but the pursuer, not satisfied, brought the case before the Lords in Council at Edinburgh, where, in 1618, John appeared in person and was fined £40, and ordered to be kept in prison at Edinburgh at his own expense till the money was paid.

It is unusual to find a baptism registered among the acts and decreets, but young George Johnstoun of Mylnfield and his wife, Janet Cunningham,

[1] The deed is endorsed—"A disposition of John Galloway to John Johnestoune, Jan. 15, 1624, of the lands of Gallowbank and of a tenement of land, back and fore, yard and pertinents, and a stone house in the High Street of Annan, callit of auld the auld Tolbooth Sted . . . the Sovereign of Scotland and his successors the only Superior of the land aforesaid."

took that step for their first child, William. The witnesses are John Ffareis and Adam Johnstoun (June 2, 1621); and, as no minister is mentioned, the service was probably taken by a Roman priest. George died the next year, immediately after assisting Raecleuch to regain possession of Newbie Castle by force.

His brother, John, had a narrow escape about this time. Edward of Seafield was charged with assaulting him, and the case was tried before the Privy Council in 1623. In the words of the indictment—Edward "having conceived a private hatred and malice in his heart against the said complainer, without any just cause, very craftily drew him out to the Kirkyard of the said burgh, under cover of friendship, to confer on some of their private affairs, and there, before the said complainer was aware, gave him a cruel and deadly stroke and wound through the shoulders with a long dirk, to the effusion of his blood in great quantities, and to the peril of his life." It was judged that Edward had done it, "only because the said John, as baillie of the burgh of Annan, craved the said Edward for some of the burgh mails (rates) owed by him." He was ordered to pay a fine of 100 marks to the Treasurer, the same to the Baillie, and £4 to every witness for his trouble. . An earlier grievance, in 1615, was John's refusal to appear with John Irving, called the Laird, as a witness against Raecleuch and Douglas of Torthorald when they were defendants in an action brought by Seafield for spoliation of cattle—probably for rent claimed. But two actions were pending by Seafield against Ryehill for delivering up the writs of the Newbie Barony to the tutor of Johnstoun, and also about Howmedo, which explains the attitude of Ryehill's grandson. The previous year John of Mylnfield was one of the twelve witnesses to Seafield's retour as heir to his father, Robert of Newbie.

John of Mylnfield was a careful man, for his son, George, was only a few months old when he made a deed of his property (April 21, 1623) in favour of this infant, with as much of his wife's settlement as she could bequeath without prejudice to the rights of her son, Mark Loch. It was signed by Abraham Johnstoun of Milnbie and his son, William. In a deed of 1643, property that had belonged to Edward of Ryehill, as well as to Marion Rig (Mrs Irving), sister to Gaylies, was included. It is signed by Robert Graham, son of Simon Graham of Blaatwood, merchant burgess of Dumfries, by Mark Loch,[1] by Homer Murray (the Provost), and by Wilds, Raes, Littles, Richardsons, Halidays, Tyndings, Hairs, and Galloway, burgesses of Annan, and by two grandsons of Abraham Johnstoun of Milnbie. Galabank had already been settled on George and his heirs, and in the future gave the name to this branch of the Johnstone family.

In 1631 the King's Advocate summoned John Johnstoun, "callit of Newbie," the Laird of Johnstoun, the Earl of Nithsdale, John Murray (Earl of Annandale), Barbara Johnstoun, Lady Gribton, Edward Johnstoun of Seafield, Edward Johnstoun of Ryehill, James Johnstoun of Westraw, James, his son, Viscount

[1] Mark was dead before 1678, when his daughter, Margaret, was married to James Irving of Eastrigs.

Drumlanrig, David Johnstoun of Edinburgh, Thomas Corrie of Kelwood, and others to show their titles and claims to the estates which they occupied or had disponed to other of the defendants. John of Mylnfield being Provost, was then the most prominent of his name about the Newbie estate.

As time went on old family quarrels were forgotten, and the Weild or Wyld family appear as witnesses in the Galabank deeds. Sir John Charteris (ancestor to Earl Wemyss), whose father had taken part with Maxwell of Gribton against Robert of Newbie and Edward of Ryehill, was very friendly with John of Mylnfield, who acted as the sole witness to two of his sasines in 1637, and also purchased some Charteris property in 1640. In 1634 John witnessed a Charter for David and Jeanne Irving in conjunction with James Johnstoun of Neiss and Robert Johnstoun of Stapleton. He was Provost of Annan in 1624, and from 1638 to 1643, and again in 1649, after his son's death. He was also Parliamentary Commissioner from 1640 to 1642, and from 1644 to 1647, part of that time in conjunction with his son.

Robert Johnstoun of Stapleton, Raecleuch's son, and John Johnstoun of Mylnfield, when he was Provost, and his son, George, were summoned before the Privy Council as witnesses in a dispute between Fergus Graham of Blaatwood and Mark Loch. Fergus wished to borrow 500 marks from Loch, who had signed the bond, when he took it off the table where it lay between them, and on Graham's demand refused to return it. Loch said there was a blank space on the paper which he was afraid might be used to his prejudice, and the Council decided in his favour, ordering Graham to pay Loch's witnesses £10 for their trouble. William, son to Fergus, and David Graham, also appeared.

George acted as a witness to a Raecleuch deed when he was only ten years old. He lived long enough to marry Agnes Graham, and to leave two sons, John and Edward. They occupied a house in Annan, which showed their arms and initials over the door as late as 1776. George was Provost of Annan in 1646, and also Parliamentary Commissioner for the Dumfries Burghs in 1644, 1646, and 1647, but he died the next year, still under twenty-seven, and his widow shortly afterwards married Robert Fergusson of Halhill, and brought up her sons near Dumfries.

In the legal documents signed by George, as well as by his father, he is called the eldest lawful son of John Johnstoun, now called of Mylnfield. There was a daughter, Mary, who is buried with her parents, and Barbara, married in 1648 to Lancelot Carlile.

Two once handsome stone tablets in Annan Churchyard cover the graves of John of Mylnfield and his children, but in the last thirty years they have become almost illegible. In raised letters round the edge of the earliest are the words, " Heir Lyis Ane Honest and Memorable man callit George Johnestoun Who Lived in Credit and Commendation amongst his friends, a faithful Christian in Christ. Died 21 February 1649 of age 27 years. Erected by Agnes Graham to the memory of my most tender and good husband." Next to this a stone is placed over the grave of another George, which was legible in 1771, " Heir lyes ane honest memorable man callit George Johnestoun in

THE GRAHAMS

Millfield who lived in credit and commendation and died a faithful Christian in Christ 12 November 1648 of age 70 years. Blest are they that dye in the Lord." He seems to have been a Johnstoun of Corrie. Another stone in 1771 bore the inscription, " Heir lyes ane honest memorable youth James Johnestoun in Millfield who died a Christian in Christ April 2 1651 of age 18." John of Mylnfield's name and shield were added to the first stone, and other names now illegible.

Agnes Graham was the daughter of Robert Graham, who married Rachel Johnstoun, the daughter of Mungo of Over Howcleuch. Robert Graham was brother to Simon of Blaatwood, a burgess of Dumfries. Robert and Rachel acted as security for the Laird of Johnstoun in 1622, and later he was one of the witnesses to the deed by which John of Mylnfield secured his property on his son George. He or his son was a witness, forty-six years later, at the marriage of Agnes's son, John, and lent money to John on the security of Galabank before the young man inherited it. He was Provost of Dumfries in 1643, and the younger Robert in 1670. Later the family became Grahams of Cluden.

The Grahams had made a great advance since 1603, when, in spite of the effort to insure their orderly conduct by giving the lands of Netherby to Arthur Graham's uncle, Ritchie, in 1548, his grandson, Ritchie, was pointed out by the English Warden as the great offender, and "it would cause an outcry if others were banished and he allowed to remain." " The vulgar sort," as they were called in the legal procedure, were always easily dealt with by execution, but it was the sons and brothers of the lairds who were the great obstacles to peace. " The Johnstons, Carliles, and Irvings, who were related to them," continues the report, "protected the Grahams, who fled into Scotland," so Netherby and other lands they occupied in Cumberland were made over to the Earl of that county in return for paying the expense of transporting a number of them to Ireland, because, said King James, "they do all confess themselves to be no meet persons to live in these countries, and that others of good and honest conversation may take their lands." Either this Ritchie or his son was made Master of the Horse to the King, and bought back the lands of Netherby and Liddell. He even obtained an alteration of the Scottish border, so that his own property in Kirkandrews upon Esk[1] might be English ground.

Wotton relates that, when Charles I. was on his way to Spain in search of a bride, "they could get no flesh in their inns, it being Lent. There was near Bayonne a herd of goats with their young; upon the sight whereof Sir Richard Graham tells the Marquis of Buckingham that he would snap one of the kids and make some shift to carry him away to their lodging. Which the Prince overhearing, 'Why, Richard,' says he, 'do you think you may practice here your old tricks upon the Borders?' Upon which they in the first place gave the goat herd good contentment, and then while the Marquis and Richard, being both on foot, were chasing the kid about the stock, the Prince from horseback killed him in the head with a pistol."

[1] The church was built with money given by Charles I.

Sir Richard fought at Edgehill under Charles I., and died in 1653. When Agnes and George Johnstoun were living at Annan they were only thirteen miles from her cousin's abode.

The transfer of executive authority in Dumfriesshire into the hands of a few courtiers, who hung about the King at Windsor or Theobalds to advance their own interests instead of attending to their duties in Scotland, led to an extraordinary degree of lawlessness, which the Privy Council could hardly cope with. Sir Thomas Kirkpatrick[1] sent his son Thomas to prison to keep him out of mischief, and complained to the Privy Council that he was released because he feigned illness, since which time he had continued his undutiful conduct. Elizabeth Carlile, Lady Douglas, arrested at Dumfries for a debt, was rescued from the authorities by Alexander Carlile and other armed relatives, and conveyed for safety to Annan. A case in 1633 was brought by Mr Walter Whitford, parson of Moffat (afterwards Bishop of Brechin), against the young Laird of Johnstoun, who had been married six years, for unlawfully convoking his kin and friends and assaulting people in Moffat. The Borderers seem to have had a passion for litigation, and so little discredit attached to these exploits that the Laird of Johnstoun was raised to the Peerage the same year by Charles I.

In several legal writs, years after he was ennobled, the Laird is only called James Johnstoun of that Ilk, and it was the same with his father-in-law, Drumlanrig. In 1643 he was created Earl of Hartfell. He adhered to the Royal cause during the Civil War, and was imprisoned and his estates sequestered; but after his death, and the accession of Charles II., his son James was restored to his lands and honours. When the last Murray Earl of Annandale died without male heirs, this title was given to Johnstoun, who also obtained a grant of the hereditary Stewardship of Annandale and the office of hereditary Constable of the Castle of Lochmaben.

The reign of Cromwell was disastrous to Dumfriesshire, if not to all Scotland. When the monastic lands had been distributed among the laity it was with the understanding that the new owners should help to maintain the ministers and the kirks. As this was done very inadequately, Charles I. tried to divert a portion of the rents for their proper maintenance. He also reversed the attainder of Stewart, Earl of Bothwell, which obliged Buccleuch to restore some of the forfeited lands he had received from James VI. While the Johnstouns, Grahams, and Irvings supported Charles, Buccleuch and all his clan, with others of the landed gentry who had benefited by the Church lands, ranged themselves on the Puritan side; and the entire disappearance of public registers and Charters in Dumfriesshire during the middle part of the seventeenth century shows the destruction caused by the Civil War. The taxation was excessive. The salt works on the Solway had been very remunerative to the Johnstouns of Newbie and the Murrays of Cockpool. In the first year of Charles II. (1661) an Act of Parliament relieved the salters in those parts of any payment of excise for the future. It states that "some poor people and

[1] He was a Groom of the Chamber to James VI.

PLATE VIII.

ARCHIBALD JOHNSTON, LORD WARRISTON.
(ELSIESHIELDS).

tenants in Annan, who by their industry and toilsome labour do draw salt from sand for the use of some private families in those bounds, and who, in regard of the painfulness and singularity of the work, have ever been free of any public imposition until the year 1656 or thereby, when the late usurper (Cromwell), contrary to all reason, equity, or former practice, forced from them an exaction to their overthrow and ruin, and thereby so impoverished them that they are in a starving condition."

In 1653 seventeen Commissioners of Supply were named for the county, and the Laird of Johnstoun accepted the post, though under Cromwell. The others were General Monk, the Earl of Nithsdale, Charles Howard, Grierson of Lag, Douglas of Kelhead, Johnstoun of Westraw, Douglas of Morton, the Johnstons of Corhead, Fergusson of Craigdarroch, Scott of Newburgh, Douglas of Dornock, Jeremiah Tolhurst, John Grimsditch, William Green, Crichton of Crawfordton, another Scott and Fergusson. John of Mylnfield held aloof from public matters under the Commonwealth.

The restoration of Charles II. in 1660, which was really initiated in Scotland, and particularly in Dumfriesshire, where General Monk gauged the feeling of the lairds, brought a rude shock to the Johnstoun clan, even divided as it now was in politics and religion, by the execution of Archibald Johnstoun, Lord Warrieston, with circumstances of great barbarity. He was always a staunch Presbyterian, but was appointed Charles's advocate when the Prince was in Scotland in 1640. He ventured to remonstrate with him for his irregular life, besides being present as Clerk Register at the execution of Montrose, and he was marked out for punishment as soon as the King returned to England. He was also reappointed Lord Clerk Register, after a show of reluctance, the year before Cromwell's death, and accepted a seat in the House of Peers. He was condemned by Charles II. to the scaffold and confiscation, but escaped to Rouen, where Louis XIV. gave him up; and he was imprisoned in the Tower, whence, in a miserable state of health, owing, it is said, to the treatment of his jailors, he was taken to Edinburgh. He was bled and physicked—in short, half poisoned—till he did not know his own children, in the hope that it might break down his nerve, and he was cruelly battered on the head by the guards to prevent him from addressing the mob when he was led out to the gallows. Bishop Burnet, his nephew, says that the Presbyterians depended on him more than on any man alive; but he expressed contrition for having served Cromwell, a lapse he ascribed to "fear anent the straits my numerous family be brought into." Yet Burnet held that he was enthusiastic for the Covenant, which he thought essential to Christianity, "that he had no regard to the raising of himself or his family, though he had thirteen children, but Presbytery was to him more than all the world."

Several of Warrieston's children died young, but, besides three sons (Chapter XV.), seven daughters lived to grow up. Elizabeth, the eldest, married Thomas, eldest son of Sir Adam Hepburn, and secondly Sir William Drummond, created Viscount Strathallan. Rachel married Robert Baillie of Jerviswood, himself a victim to the false charge that he was concerned in the Rye House Plot. Helen, the wife of George Home of Graden, who, after imprisonment for being a Covenanter, died of wounds received at the battle of Bothwell Bridge. His widow was fined £26,000 for nonconformity by the Sheriff of Teviotdale—really because of her devotion at Baillie's execution,[1] and that she was Home's widow, and Warrieston's daughter.

Janet, another of Warrieston's daughters, married Sir Alexander MacKenzie of Coul; and her next sister became the wife of Roderick MacKenzie. Euphan died unmarried in 1715. Margaret, who was her father's companion in the Tower, married first Sir John Wemyss, secondly Benjamin Bressey. She was imprisoned, with other Covenanting ladies, in 1674, and afterwards banished for presenting a petition to the Privy Council for freedom to be granted to their ministers to use their own form of worship.

Charles's Government restored Episcopacy to its ancient footing in Scotland, on the ground of consistency with its Irish policy, and put forth an edict to oblige all the clergy to present themselves before the Bishops, to take oaths to them as well as to the King, and to receive fresh presentations to their benefices. In the North these terms were generally accepted; but Burnet shows that it emptied the parishes in the West, which, he says, were "filled by men of the best families, not always with much learning, but leading respectable lives, and having an extraordinary hold over the laity, even the gentry, and exercising an authority over offenders equal to magistrates and judges." They had, in fact, brought in a more orderly social condition, which was not easily maintained when they were ejected. Symon Johnstoun had kept his post as Parson of Annan since 1606, by conforming to Episcopacy or Presbyterianism when required; and was married to Lady Hartfell's aunt. But he had taken oaths to Cromwell's Government, and was ejected in favour of William Baillie, who was deposed in two years and the Rev. Patrick Inglis, a graduate of St. Andrews, appointed (1664).

The attitude of the Presbyterians was stiffened by the reports that reached Scotland of the wildness of the Court, and the terrible famine which set in about this time was by many supposed to be a judgment. Donald Cargill, in 1661, describes the black, pale faces to be seen in Dumfriesshire, showing famine typhus; but three years before the county pleaded poverty as an excuse for sending no member to Parliament. Potatoes were not introduced till 1725, but quickly spread over Scotland. Glasgow diminished in population from 14,600 in 1660 to 12,500 in 1707, and other districts in the west of Scotland suffered in proportion. It has been said that the Scots wasted their corn in making distilled liquors, but very little wheat was at that time grown in the country, and, though whisky was smuggled over from Ireland and the Isle of Man, it was not much drunk by the upper classes on the Borders, as they imported wine. This is shown in the household bills of the Galabank family.

[1] She attended him in prison and on the scaffold, and even remained while all the horrible sequence to the execution of a supposed traitor was gone through, that she might collect what was left in a cloth to have it buried; the head and limbs being exposed in some public place.

The last Charter in which John of Mylnfield was concerned was in 1659. It is signed Hartfell, being a sale of land by his Chief, James, Earl of Hartfell, Lord Johnstoun of Lochwood, Moffatdaill, and Evandaill, to William M'Neish, who was married to a Carlile. John acted as sole witness. This owner of the above titles was the son of the first Earl, who had been very uncertain how to act when it became obvious that Charles I. would never accept the demands of the Covenanters. Johnstoun at first led a Covenanting band to besiege Caerlaverock, where the King was expected; and from Warrieston's letters[1] to him (1639) it appears that he had signed the Covenant, like most of the nobility and gentry. Lord Traquair undertook to bring him round, and succeeded, for he eventually marched with Montrose, Nithsdale, Murray (Earl of Annandale), and Charteris at the head of English troops to Dumfries. As the Provost was a Royalist they hoisted the Royal Standard in place of the Blue Banner of the Covenant. Both Johnstoun and Murray, who had also signed the Covenant, had expected that this would be the signal for a general rising in favour of the King in all Dumfriesshire, but it never came. Montrose thought the two were false, but in every village there were Covenanters ready to denounce a Royalist neighbour; and the younger men were not practised in the use of arms as before the Union of the Crowns, yet the remembrance of those days of fire and slaughter possibly acted as a deterrent, and the Borderers would not ruin themselves to fight on the side of the English against the Scots. Montrose withdrew to Carlisle, but Johnstoun, later, joined him with some of his own name and his tenants, and they gained a few small victories over the Covenanters. These were followed by a signal defeat at Philiphaugh, when several of the descendants of the House of Newbie, who accompanied their Chief, were left dead on the field; others of their name at once quitted Edinburgh for America, fearing the triumph of their enemies. The regiment of Dumfries, in which a few more Johnstouns were enrolled,

---

[1] From Warrieston.
"If you take this oath (to the King) you renounce the Covenant with God, you draw down His vengeance verily upon you, your house and your name, good fame, yourself and your posterity, with that stigmatising blot and blunder of a traitor to your religion, the Kirk, the liberty and freedom of this kingdom; you will be infamous in all stories and contemned both at home and abroad, whereof I am very confident you abhor the very thought worse than death. Mistake not my forewarning you of these consequences, as if I believed your Lordship would fall on them, for I protest I am not capable as yet of such an imagination; but you know my licence and liberty to be free in this business with all I love and respect."

Montrose, it seems, had been invited to Court at this time and declined, and Johnstoun is exhorted to follow his example and "do nobly as my noble Lord of Montrose has done!" The letter resumes:—

"This is my advice; but if your Lordship will go away, truly I shall be sorry for it; but I will both expect from your Lordship an answer hereunto more clear and special, whereby I may be more enabled to falsify my doubts, and answer the objections made by others against your voyage (to the Court) like as a true-hearted Johnstoun, and a true friend and servant to your Lordship and to the house of Johnstoun, and, above all, as a faithful advocate for God's Kirk, and agent for this great work of God in this land. I do faithfully counsel you and really forewarn you, as in the presence of the great God, before whom your Lordship and I will both answer, that as you love your own soul, your name, your state, your country and religion, you neither by word, or writ, undertake either to assist the King in this his course against your fellow-Covenanters, which by your solemn oath you are obliged to maintain."

fought for the young Charles II. at the battle of Worcester, and none of them lived to return.

The defeat of the Royalists at Worcester and at Dunbar made Cromwell supreme in Scotland. He ruled it like a conquered kingdom, as it was, and suspended the Constitution, even appointing English judges in place of the ancient baronial courts.

There were many specimens of gold and silver work among the Dumfriesshire families in 1640, carefully preserved as heirlooms. All this was ordered by the War Committee to be requisitioned and broken up to be coined for the army. No one, high or low, was to be spared; but if any man had an article he specially prized, he might redeem it at the rate of 56s. per oz. for Scots silver work, 58s. per oz. for English silver work, and £33, 6s. 8d. for every oz. of gold. These sums do not at all represent the real value of money at that date, but Johnstoun must have kept his, either by payment or by stealth, to judge from his son's memorial (*circa* 1661) to Charles II. In this document the second Lord Hartfell, describing his father's losses and his own, points out that all Annandale was a thoroughfare for armies marching, and especially his lands, as they bordered on England. His house at Newbie was plundered of his silver, plate, and furniture, and completely wrecked by both the English and the Scottish rebels; and troops were quartered on his estate till payment should be made of £43,000. Several of his own name in Dumfriesshire were on the side of the Covenanters—Archibald Johnstoun of Clochrie, James Johnston of Corhead, Andrew Johnstoun of Lockerbie, Wamfray, Robert Johnstoun of Newton, Poldean, and John Johnstoun of Viccarland.

The Commissioners appointed by the King to settle these claims reported that the present Earl, and his father, who died at Newbie in 1653, had given signal proofs of their loyalty, for which they had been great sufferers, " particularly in 1644, when the Marquis of Montrose came with the King's commission he did cheerfully join with him, and upon the Marquis's retreat he was made prisoner in the Castle of Edinburgh for a whole year, and was forced by the Parliament then being to pay the sum of £12,000 Scots, which, with the interest to this time, amounts to £24,400. In the following year he most cheerfully joined with the Marquis of Montrose, his Majesty's Captain-General, and after their defeat at Philiphaugh was with his sons taken prisoners and committed from several prisons to the Castle of St. Andrews, where he was tried for his life, and after an expensive and tedious process was fined 100,000 Scots pounds. If he would not pay it, both he and his sons would be executed. Before he could leave the prison he was ordered to pay to the Earl of Lanark and Colonel Lockhart £41,000, to Bogs (a Scott of Buccleuch) and Sir James Stewart £20,000, and to Sir John Brown £6000."

Warrieston was one of the "triers." He had previously proposed to exclude certain members from Parliament—Lords Johnstoun and Ogilvie, Sir John Hay, and Sir Robert Spottiswood—on the ground of their compliance with the enemies of the kingdom, and, except Johnstoun, they had protested against his appointment, as he had prejudged them. Perhaps Johnstoun hoped that

Warrieston might be lenient to his Chief. He may have been more so than his colleagues.

Besides the above sums, it was pleaded that Johnstoun was forced to pay £7000 towards arming Dumfriesshire, and by order of Parliament, £4000 to Sir William Dick as his share of a war tax. The loss of his rents and damage to his property by troops being constantly quartered there was at least £40,000, so the Committee humbly recommended him to his Majesty. Charles II. thereupon restored the Chief of Johnstoun to his father's honours and estates, adding to the previous titles those of James Murray, Earl of Annandale, who had died without male heirs in 1658. The only son of the first Earl, he had retired to England, lest as owner of the Graitney estate he should be further involved in the Civil War.

Imprisonment in Scotland seems to have been as severe in Cromwell's time as a century earlier, and Lord Hartfell never recovered from the effect, but died in 1653—seven years before the Restoration. He had been first married to Lady Margaret Douglas, by whom he had James and William ; secondly, to a daughter of Johnstoun of Elphinstone, who had no family. An item in the Newbie accounts, kept by Hew Sinclair, the factor or chamberlain, refers to this younger son, Jan. 26, 1657 : " Forty-eight torches sent to Newbie to Lieut.-Colonel Johnstoun's burial at twelve shillings a piece, is £28, 16. 0., only brother to Lord Annandale."

Lord Hartfell left the life rent of Newbie, valued at 8000 marks Scots, as a provision for his widow. The eldest son, James, created Lord Annandale, married at twenty to his cousin, Lady Henrietta Douglas, who was thirteen, died in 1679. Of eleven children two sons, William and John, and several daughters survived. The boys were educated at Glasgow, and boarded there with a connection, Margaret Hamilton, married to Mr Banantyne, related to Westraw. The young Earl came with his brother to Newbie in 1680, when he sent his Family Bible to be rebound. He had taken his degree, and was married to a girl of fourteen, his cousin, Sophia Fairholm, by the time he was eighteen. In that year—1685—Newbie Castle was burnt. The catastrophe is described in a letter from the young bride, who was sitting with the wife of the minister of Cummertrees, Lady Apilgirth, and Sophia Johnstoun, her mother (?), when the smell of burning timbers first alarmed them. The Laird of Westraw was with the Earl, and helped to try and extinguish it, but the furniture and their clothes were destroyed, and the Countess rode three miles in the night to take refuge at Kelhead with her husband's relatives, the Douglases.

In a letter to her father, John Fairholm, from Kelhead, Dec. 28, 1685, Lady Annandale wrote : " If there had been any drinking with us at Christmas I should have thought it God's judgement on us for so great a sin, but there was nobody with us but two or three neighbours, and my lord was receiving rents the most part of the afternoon, neither was anybody drunk, and my lord both then and ever since he came from Edinburgh I can bear witness has never drunk any. God pity us, for we are left without any, and make me to bear this patiently, which I willingly do for my loss if I were not afraid of something more if we harden our hearts, which God grant we may not." Sir George Maxwell and Westraw gave much assistance.

Another authority gives an account of the drunken frolics of Sir John Dalziel of Glennie and his associates, which ended "by going to Lord Annandale's house at Newbie to pay him a visit, beginning with their old pranks—burning their shirts and other linens. A little after that the house was all burnt."

It is also said that the servants in the house were amusing themselves with drinking burnt brandy while Lord Annandale was away, and his coach driving suddenly to the door, they thrust the blazing spirits under a bed, which caused the conflagration. The blaze was so great that the chambermaids at Kelhead, three miles distant, could prepare the bedrooms without candles.

For more than a generation the Annandale family had lived at Newbie Castle, only a mile and a half from the Johnstouns of Galabank in the vast stone house, as it is called in all the title-deeds, and represented as a tower or castellated building in a drawing of Annan in 1533. It covered 43 feet of ground in length by 83 in width. Lord Annandale was Provost of Annan in 1670, and again from 1686 to 1713, when James, Lord Johnstone, the eldest son, a baillie of Annan, succeeded him, as the Marquis accepted the Provostship of Lochmaben.

A great deal of the money left in trust by Robert Johnstoun, the "eminent lawyer of the House of Newbie," to his Chief for endowing schools at Johnstone and at Moffat and to build a bridge over the river at Annan, disappeared, possibly to raise men on the side of the King in the Civil War; but common report said it was used to add a modern structure to the old square tower of Newbie Castle, which was blown down in the nineteenth century.

When the new house was burnt, Lord Annandale, the grandson of the untrustworthy executor, is said to have observed that he knew it would never come to any good, because it was built with the thing that should have builded the bridge over Annan water.

Owing to the Civil War the Galabank family seem to have been almost the only members of the old Newbie family left in Annan, but Parson Symon Johnstoun's son, George, remained there, and several of the Elsieshields.

CHAPTER XIV.

JOHNSTOUN OF GALABANK—WITCHES BURNT—CIVIL WAR—WESTRAW—ELSIESHIELDS—JOHNSTOUN—JANET KIRKPATRICK—FAMINE—EDWARD JOHNSTOUN—HIS MARRIAGE, DEATH, AND WILL—WESTRAW—LOCKERBIE AND HIS DESCENDANTS—CARLILES.

ON April 4, 1665, the *Register of Retours*[1] contains the name of John Johnstoun,[1] who was declared by David Johnstoun[2] and eleven other witnesses to be the heir of John Johnstoun, lately Provost of Annan, his grandfather, in the lands of Galabank, the "vast stone house in Annan, once occupied by Edward Johnstoun of Ryehill," the lands in Stank, Gallowgait, Closehead, and some minor properties. Unless he was twin with his brother Edward, John must have been about twenty-three at this time. They were brought up near Dumfries under the auspices of their mother, Agnes Graham, and her second husband, Robert Fergusson of Halhill, and in the narrow limits of this little town witnessed many exhibitions of revolting bigotry and ignorant barbarity, for it was a stronghold of religious rivalries and superstition. Their relative, Robert Graham, was Provost of Dumfries from 1643 to 1645, when his retirement was apparently caused by having, like many other members of his family, joined the army of Montrose in support of Charles I.; and he was probably one of the two Robert Grahams who were seeking refuge in the Debateable Land in 1648. His cousin in Netherby Hall was a Royalist, and so much indignation was caused in Scotland by the barbarities of the almost naked Highland and Irish mercenaries whom Montrose had called to fight for the King, that his supporters were not safe in their own county.

John Maxwell, an Episcopalian, who succeeded Graham as Provost, is called "a Papist" for letting a Roman priest escape from the district, after a fanatical crowd had destroyed the wafers, vestments, and sacred vessels which he carried in a bag to minister to a dying co-religionist.

The Burgh accounts for 1657 include thirty-eight loads of peat, tar barrels, and stakes intended for the burning of two women accused of witchcraft. The peat alone cost £3, 12s. In 1659 nine more female victims were first strangled

---

[1] Among the witnesses to the retour are Adam Carlile, Treasurer, Robert Johnston, Dean, Mr Robert Bell of Hardrigg, Adam Johnstoun in Redgatehead (Graitney), John Johnstoun of Gotterbraes, John Murray, William Stewart, etc.

[2] David was possibly great-uncle to Galabank. He was Provost in 1678, and had a son, Robert.

at the stakes, to which they were tied, and their remains burned on the same absurd accusation. They were condemned by the English judges whom Cromwell had placed in the country, but, as Sir Walter Scott shows, the witch scare came in with the Reformation. Formerly every misfortune was attributed to the wiles of the Evil One, and it was believed that the Saints could foil him. When the law in 1560 forbade prayers to be addressed to the Saints, and every representation of them was destroyed, the people felt obliged to take the matter into their own hands, and worn-out old women were especially supposed to be Satan's emissaries. The first was burnt in Scotland in 1563, the last in 1722, a young hysterical girl. Natural laws were not understood, and medicine was at its lowest ebb. In 1680 a poor man was compensated from the offertory for losing all his live stock through a witch.

There were apparently strained relations between the elder John and his heir, whose legal guardian, as a stepfather is in Scotland, had consented to take a post under Cromwell. Robert Fergusson[1] seems to have been dead in 1670. One cause of difference was that the elder had never accepted the Reformed Faith and the younger was brought up in it.

It was only a year after John left Dumfries to live in Annan that the most desperate of the conflicts between the Covenanters and the Government, which lasted twenty-two years, was started in Galloway by a party of rough soldiers trying to extract money from an old labourer by torture. The revolt against the military soon spread to Dumfries, where a band of volunteers captured an unpopular officer and his men, and, afterwards marching to the Pentland Hills, were defeated at Bothwell Bridge by the Royal troops. The Town Council of Dumfries tried to save themselves the penalties of receiving rebels by executing two fugitives from the fight, but a few fanatics killed the Archbishop of St. Andrews, and, in spite of wholesale executions in Edinburgh and elsewhere, the Covenanters refused to attend any services but the Presbyterian, which had been illegal since 1661. In Dec. 1678 John Graham of Clavers, formerly an officer in the Dutch service, who had saved the life of the future William III. in battle and been recommended by him to Charles II., was sent to Dumfries to enforce the law. That he acted with a barbarous vigour, assisted by the Steward-Depute of Nithsdale (Sir Robert Grierson of Lag) and the Sheriff-Depute of Annandale (James Johnstoun of Westraw, who was knighted), has made his name a by-word, yet it was said that the Deputes despatched prisoners with their own swords when Clavers would have spared them. It is known as the killing time—for the frightful wounds made by the pitchforks used by the labourers, and their mutilation of the dead, brought a merciless retaliation in savage tortures, legally inflicted, as well as death. The Carruthers Lairds of Dormont, Denby, and Holmains were Nonconformists, but two of them escaped to Edinburgh and obtained the pardon of Dormont, who had been captured. Soldiers were quartered at Annan, Moffat, Lochmaben, and Dum-

[1] Robert Fergusson, brother of Alexander of the Isle, and Agnes Graham, his spouse, had a Charter in 1665 of Lags, Halhill, Dalquhan, etc. Their children were Thomas (married Susanna Maxwell, and had a son, Robert) and Agnes.

fries, at the expense of the inhabitants, till Clavers became Sheriff of Wigton, in the place of Sir Andrew Agnew, a Covenanter; and they were then moved to his headquarters in Kenmure Castle. Besides these mentioned, Colonel James Douglas, Dalziell, Sir Robert Laurie, Captain Inglis, and Captain Bruce were his colleagues; but, like Westraw, Douglas afterwards served William III.

It was in Mid-Annandale, where, according to Clavers, "they are all rebels at heart," that some of the greatest cruelties took place. John Johnstoun of Elsieshields is commemorated as

" The wicked Laird of Elsieshields
Who's left Lochmaben's pleasant fields,
To gang and sup wi' horned deils," etc.

The Dumfriesshire and Galloway lairds, having signed the Covenant[1] before it was opposed by Charles I., were probably afraid of fines and escheat unless they showed especial zeal against its followers who openly defied the Crown. In 1688 Annandale wrote that "James Johnston of Corhead informed him that two fellows, his own tenants, were supposed to be haunting field conventicles, by reason they were sometimes known to be long absent from home, and the heritors informed the Commissioners at Dumfries and desired they might be instantly apprehended."

Blanche Armstrong, the aged widow of Christopher Johnston of Persbiehall, was sentenced to transportation for having received two Covenanters, James Johnstoun[2] and William Hanna, not knowing the risk she incurred, or that they were fugitives. She pleaded for mercy, as being nearly eighty she could not endure the penalty, and that her minister would prove that she had lived regularly all her life. The Privy Council remitted the sentence, if securities could be found for £2000.

Elsieshields died before the abdication of James VII. Perhaps Galabank was fortunate that, as his father and grandfather were Romanists, he was not likely to be suspected of Presbyterian sympathies. He was a good-natured, easy-going man, who would not improve his fortunes by blackmailing or showing up his neighbours; but these troubles involved heavy expenses which ruined him. He had borrowed money on his little property before he succeeded to it from his relative, Robert Graham of Inglistoune; but was fortunate enough, in spite of his pecuniary embarrassment, to obtain the hand of Janet Kirkpatrick, daughter to the late Laird of Auldgirth, and first cousin to Sir Thomas Kirkpatrick of Closeburn. They were married at Dumfries on Feb. 2, 1670. The marriage contract is signed by his mother, his uncle (Graham), and the bride's brother (Mr Thomas Kirkpatrick). John settled his property on his bride and their children, and a few months after the wedding she made over to him all the money she had that was not settled, including 300 marks given to

---

[1] The Covenant, in its various forms, signed between 1566 and 1689, bound both clergy and laity to preserve "the absolute authority on civil matters of the State, acting through a Monarch, Parliament, and Magistrates, all of whom in spiritual concerns were to obey the Church."

[2] Possibly the same who was released from prison in Edinburgh when starving in 1690, there being no record of why he was there.

her by Closeburn. James Grierson, tutor of Lag, owed her 1000 marks of her dower, for her mother was a member of the family of the notorious Steward-Depute.

Two years later Galabank paid off his debts, and if he was again in pecuniary difficulties, a great many others in Scotland seem to have been the same. Sir William Menzies, who farmed the excise, was in arrears £6000 to the Government in 1709. He was prosecuted, and showed that from 1697 to 1705 the crops were inadequate to the support of the population, and that several thousands had actually perished of starvation, that as many more had emigrated, and that multitudes were compelled to eat snails, nettles, wild spinach, and such like for bare life. From 1696 till 1701 there were blighted crops, and in the North people sold their own children to slavery in the American plantations for food. They began to bury the dead there without sheet or coffin, for on one estate giving work to 119 persons only three families, including the proprietors, lived, and even in Midlothian we read of parishes where the proportion of deaths was one-third.

In 1699 the Government fixed the price of grain, and severe penalties were enacted against any who kept back a supply or bought up more than a fair share. The climax came in the famine of 1709. So many cultivators had been transported, their goods escheated, and their lands, trodden down by soldiers, remained barren, that it was a natural consequence. In 1706 the whole coinage of Scotland only amounted to £411,117, 10s. 9d., and of this sum £40,000 was English and £132,080, 17s. in foreign coin.

At this time the Government sold the local as well as the State taxes, and a man who had the means of paying down a sum of money for them was apt to be called upon to do so if there was no voluntary offer, and it combined the post of treasurer of the burgh. In Annan three men in succession seem to have been ruined by taking them. First Adam Carlile, one of the Bridekirks and a merchant in Annan, who was Collector and Treasurer in 1665-87; then Galabank; and then Edward Johnstoun, Galabank's brother. Galabank and Robert and James Carlile were Adam Carlile's securities when he undertook the taxes—a loss to them all. Galabank's letters from Ruthwell, Lochmaben, and other places show his pecuniary anxieties, and in one to his brother asking for assistance, he alludes to the danger of not appearing in the Kirk of his Parish on Sunday, lest he should be taken for a Covenanter. Those who did not attend were fined. He was popular, for in 1684, when the Earl of Annandale was Provost, he was chosen elder baillie, and Adam Carlile second baillie, with more votes than any one else. His handwriting in the Burgh Records is particularly good, the best in the seventeenth century. Annan possessed no school, and the baillies could not always sign their names.

In 1673 Galabank raised a loan from Bryce Blair, sometime Provost of Annan, and in 1677 from his brother, Edward. In 1680 he lost his wife, Janet Kirkpatrick, and at that time he owed his brother £373, 17s. He was left with two children, Janet and Barbara, but in a year or two was married again to Elizabeth Murray, one of the Cockpool family. The intention to provide for her made Bryce Blair obtain a legal prohibition in 1682, to prevent him from disposing of any property till he had paid his debts, although Galabank was then Provost of Annan.

On Jan. 3, 1684, Edward Johnstoun, a writer at Dumfries, was married at Ruthwell to Isobelle, daughter of Adam Carlile, formerly of Annan ; and at the same time he was admitted a burgher of Annan. He was an Episcopalian, but probably foresaw a renewal of religious difficulties with the accession of James VII. The marriage settlement is dated the same day, at Ruthwell. It begins—

"Be it known to all men by this present deed, Me Adam Carlile late baillie of Annan, forasmuch as Edward Johnstoun, brother German to John Johnstoun of Gallabank, is intending God willing to marry and his lawful wife take Isobelle Carlile my lawful daughter for his spouse in contemplation of which marriage I have already disponed to him a tenement of house and yards with the pertinents lying in the burgh of Annan, marked and bounded as is particularized in the said disposition of the date of their espousal, and therefore in confidence and contemplation of the same to be solemnized in God's Holy Kirk I the said Adam Carlile bind and oblige me, my heirs, executors and assignees to make payment to the said Edward Johnstoun and Isobelle Carlile my daughter his affianced spouse, their heirs, executors or assignees of a further sum of money," etc., this to be guaranteed by Adam's daughter, Agnes, (the spouse of John Johnstoun, burgher of Dumfries), and by Adam's brother-german, John Carlile.

The deed was witnessed by Galabank, Robert Murray, James and John Murray, James Wilson, and William Douglas, "schulemaister" (*i.e.*, tutor) in Annan. The bride was fifteen and her husband forty. There was a remote relationship, and William Graham of Blaatwood, then Provost of Annan, a relative of Edward's mother, was also married to a Carlile of Bridekirk.

Edward's Family Bible contains his name with "of" and an erasure, and the date 1653, when he was but ten years old, and probably named after his great-great-grandfather, Edward of Ryehill, who was dead about the time he was born. Then follows: "John Johnstone, son of Edward Johnstone and Isobelle Carlyle in Annan, baptized May 27, 1689; James Johnstone, son to Edward Johnstone and Isobelle Carlyle in Annan, baptized Nov. 17, 1693." Then Janet is inserted as "baptized Feb. 8, 1684-5," being the eldest of the children, and the two younger daughters, Elizabeth and Marie, are omitted. His grandson, James, adds a eulogistic paragraph about him, dated Worcester, June 26, 1755, and calls attention to the many marked verses, showing how carefully he read it.

In 1683 Galabank mortgaged his estates to his brother, who was to satisfy the creditors, particularly William Graham of Blaatwood. For a debt of £373, 9s. Graham received the first instalment of interest, £22, 7s., at once. But the next year William Craik of Arbigland, Provost of Dumfries, whose sister was the wife of Johnston of Clochrie, was the most pressing, and obtained a Royal Warrant (James VII.) directing the Sheriff of Annandale (the Earl) to denounce the debtor as a rebel from the market-place of Lochmaben, and to seize all his movable goods and gear. No official notice seems to have been taken of this warrant, and the mortgage appears to have been passed on to another creditor, from the accounts of the Sheriff-Depute, Sir James Johnstoun of Westraw, for the year 1686-87. Then came the Revolution of 1688, and the Covenanters were safe, but otherwise it hardly upset the Borders so much as the rebellion of the Duke of Monmouth, whose wife was the heiress of the great Border clan of Scott. As he had been more humane[1] than Clavers when in command against the Covenanters, many of them, besides his tenants, joined his army, which drained the district of money and supplies.

Galabank's creditors returned to the charge in 1689, and a "letter of horning," issued in the names of William and Mary, directed the sheriffs, baillies, and stewards of the Borders to seize upon John Johnstoun, "who continues and abides under the process of our said horning unslaved, and in the meantime daily and openly haunts, frequents, and repairs to kirks, markets, fairs, public and private places of meeting within this our realm, as if he were our free liege, in high and proud contempt of this our authority and laws, and giving thereby evil example to others to do and commit the like in time coming without remedies be thereto provided," etc. It is further ordered that he should be put in sure ward in a tolbooth (prison), and detained there night and day at his own expense, and, if need be, kyves or handcuffs were to be used. These letters of horning were issued twice every year without any effect till 1698, when, in addition, letters of poynding and horning were registered against the Provost of Annan (the Earl of Annandale) and the Baillies for permitting John Johnstoun to retain possession of his house and goods and to go about "unslaved."

The baillies were John himself, his son Edward, his sister-in-law's brother, James Carlile, and James, Lord Johnstoun. John's brother, Edward, was dead, and the other Edward went to London; but on May 8, 1700, John's name appears, in a minute of the Town Council, about the erection of the first bridge over the Annan, which ought to have been built long before with the legacy left to Lord Annandale for the purpose. "Ane noble and potent Earle William, Earle of Annandale and Hartfeill, said Provost of Annan, with express advice and consent of John Johnstone of Galla Banks and John Irving, both baillies, and James Bryden, grocer, and the haill Town Council and Communitie of the said burgh on the one part, and Mr Matthias Partis of Gallentyre on the other part . . . that the said Mr Matthias Partis shall immediately fall to work, and imploy, contract, and agree with workmen for building a bridge over a river at the place designed," etc. Galabank's quarry supplied the stone for the bridge, but he was obliged to sue for payment. The Earl of Annandale, as Sheriff, gave a decreet in favour of "our lovit John

[1] In an interview with the King and Duke of York, James reproached him with having saved the lives of rebels, and Charles agreed that no prisoners ought to have been taken.—BURNET.

Johnstone of Gallowbank for the payment of £400 Scots as the quarry mail of the quarry belonging to the complainer in his lands of Gallowbank, which the defendant took from the complainer for winning forth thereof the stones of the Bridge of Annan, with the sum of costs of this our precept to be added thereto in the manner underwritten." If not paid within fifteen days the defendant was to be arrested, wherever he might be, and imprisoned, and his goods seized to pay the money. This is dated Lochmaben, June 18, 1701, six days before the Earl was made a Marquis.

Galabank also gained a suit against a poacher who had fished two enormous salmon out of his part of the river, and had to pay him their value. He sold a small portion of land at Closehead, but George Blair, the son of the late Provost, was an importunate creditor, and obtained another letter of horning against Lord Annandale and the Baillies for allowing John Johnstoun to remain in free possession of his lands and goods when declared an outlaw. All these troubles, and the death of his youngest daughter, perhaps induced Galabank to retire to Kirkandrews upon Esk, in the neighbourhood of his mother's relatives. He was dead in May 1704. His surviving child, Janet, was married, Jan. 1706, "by the Rev. Edward Willshire, according to the laws of the Church of England, in the same Cumberland parish, to Richard Beattie of Milleighs."

The Episcopal Church was finally disestablished in 1696. There was a movement for restoring James VII., known as the Montgomery Plot, in 1690. Lord Annandale had mustered some of his clan to support it, and then, finding himself rather left alone, withdrew to Bath on the plea of illness. It has been alleged that he had received the patent of a Marquisate from James VII., but that his cousin, a strong partisan of the Prince of Orange, persuaded him that he had more to gain by remaining loyal to the new King. In William's Scottish proclamations he alluded to his "grandfather, Charles I., of blessed memory," not to his father-in-law, James, who was never popular in the North; but his own religious preference lay with Presbyterianism. Several Scottish incumbents had compromised themselves in the Montgomery Plot and quitted their parishes, among others Mr Patrick Inglis, priest at Annan, and his successor, James Kyneir, while the Presbyterian ministers stood by William, so the Kirk was turned into a dynastic prop and re-established throughout the country.

From 1692 there was no resident minister in Annan till 1703. Then Mr Howie,[1] the descendant of a French Protestant refugee, was appointed, and remained till his death in 1754. Just as, 135 years before, the Scots were ordered to accept the Reformation, and the priests were driven from the country, they were now expected to accept Presbyterianism or dispense with clerical ministrations.

Galabank's brother, Edward, died on Dec. 30, 1697. He was Treasurer to the burgh of Annan since 1687, and the Baillies' letter to his widow, as well as that of the Provost, exist, to show how faithfully he had fulfilled his trust. But both his brother and the Burgh owed him money, and he seems to have felt rather bitterly about it.

[1] The author of *Faithful Contendings Displayed*, quoted Chapter IX. in *Old Mortality*.

EDWARD JOHNSTOUN'S WILL

His Will, dated three days before his death, began, after the custom of the day, with a profession of the Christian faith. He gave his lands, burdened with an annuity, to his wife during her widowhood, and 300 marks to his eldest son, John. To his three daughters he left 400 marks each, and to his youngest son, James, 300 marks—the last to succeed to his lands if John died without heirs. If any of his debts were recovered the sum was to be divided between his two sons and his (wife's) nephew, George Johnstoun, whom he left co-executor with his brother-in-law, James Carlile, and he charged both to act as protectors to his wife and children "as far as they can." In case his children died without heirs, his lands were to go to James Carlile. He desired to be buried in the Churchyard at Annan. His Will was witnessed by Robert Colville, the instructor of his sons and the Presbyterian *locum tenens* at Annan; James Carruthers of Wormanbie, sometime Provost and Chamberlain to Lord Annandale; John Irving, baillie of Annan; and George Blair.

Edward's monument is the best marble in the old Churchyard at Annan, and has survived the storms of 212 years. The inscription is:—

"Heir lyes interred the corps of Edward Johnstone late Treasurer in Annan who departed this life the 30 day of December 1697 of age 54 Erected by Isobel Carlile his spous." Below are the arms of Johnstone of Annandale, and between them the inscription to Edward's wife: "Heir lies interred the corps of Isobelle Carlile spouse to Edward Johnstone late treasurer in Annan who dept. this life July the sixth 1710 of age 42. Erected by John Johnston her son."

Lord Annandale was as much pressed for money as the Galabanks, and harder on his tenants than was the custom with those landowners who habitually lived among them. He was a friend of the Duke of Monmouth, and was asked to intercede for him with King James in 1685; and it is always expensive to assist a lost cause. Sir James Johnstoun of Westraw was his agent—the same who was very prominent under Graham of Clavers (Viscount Dundee), and was even too zealous against the Covenanters to please that notorious leader. A letter to Annandale shows that he was equally zealous against non-paying feuars, when his Chief was in want of £100:—

"Moffat, Nov. 19, 90 . . . I shall be most redie to follow your Lōp's directions I have this day past sentence against all your Lōp's tenants in the several baronies for ye Mart rent except Wm. Harkness who hath presented a formal advocation from me and takes it before the Lords of the Session. I have caused number the whole goods upon the ground and taken an inventure of them, and arrested them afterwards. I have raised letters of inhibition and the two Hallidayes yt was caution in the former suspension who shall carry nothing to Ireland with them but themselves. Your Lōp's most obedient and humble servant, Ja: Johnstoun."

Directly the accession of William and Mary brought a reaction Lord Kenmure, now Sheriff of Nithsdale, arrested Grierson of Lag and imprisoned him in Kirkcudbright; but Westraw was under the protection of his Chief, and lost no time in making friends with the new Government.

Annandale's letters to his wife during those years showed the pecuniary importance it was for him to get a post under Government. The rights of the barons in Scotland were not stopped till 1748, so that he made a good deal by dues and fines, and the baronial prisons are described as having been often horrible dens. But he lost £1000 in the Darien Colony, the project of a Scotsman, much taken up by his countrymen.

Westraw was probably at this time the richer of the two. He was a minor when his father died in 1648, but was returned his heir to Dryfhead in 1654, the writ being signed at Newbie by the Earl of Hartfell, Douglas of Kelhead, Murray, and others; and he was infefted in Westerhall by the Marquis of Douglas in 1653. At the time of his father's death his uncle, William Johnstoun, was a fugitive in the Debateable Land. His mother, Isabel Scott, is said to have influenced her younger son, Francis, to take the side of the Covenanters, possibly so that whatever happened the family might keep the estate (Chapter IV.).

The younger Westraw's wife was Margaret, daughter of John Banantyne of Corhouse. The Earl of Annandale and his brother, John, were boarded with her relatives when they went to school in Glasgow before 1674; and when, a few years later, Westraw was the Earl's agent he received several letters from John, who was in Paris, begging him to intercede with his brother to send him money through Mr Graham of Annan and Mr Clerk of Edinburgh. Then in fear of being "clapt up in prison," John drew a bill of £100 on Westraw and "Bonintun." He signs his letter your affectionate cousin and humble servant, John Johnston.

Westraw seems to have been kept by his maternal relatives from joining Montrose; and in 1653 he was a Commissioner of Supply under Cromwell. He was also a member of the first Parliament of James VII. He did not follow his old chief, Clavers, when he raised an army to restore James VII., although a Johnstoun supported Clavers in his arms when he was killed at Killiecrankie in 1689—for Westraw was an officer in the Militia, embodied two months before by William and Mary to resist a possible Irish invasion. The younger Johnstoun of Lockerbie, William Johnstoun of Granton, and Andrew Johnstoun of Newton are also in the list, but not Annandale. However, the last had made up his mind in 1690 to take his seat in the first Parliament of William and Mary, the other Johnstouns from Dumfriesshire being Westraw and his son John, Corhead, Andrew Johnstoun (the younger of Lockerbie), and Granton. They were called upon to levy a tax, in case of war, for £280,000 Scots.

The eldest son of Andrew of Lockerbie married Westraw's daughter, and died before his father had made the intended provision for him. The widow's mode of obtaining it is described in the Privy Council Records in 1690. For a year or two past Mrs Margaret, supported by her father, Sir James Johnstoun of Westerhall (as the Barony was now called), and with the aid of sundry servants of her own and her father's, was accustomed to molest Andrew Johnstoun and his friends and tenants, and to threaten them. They took out a writ against the lady, but one day, in the spring, as Lockerbie's tenants were labouring their lands at Turriemuir his daughter-in-law came with her accomplices, loosed the horses from the plows and harrows, cut the harness, and beat the workmen. James, a younger son of Lockerbie, was present, and in the struggle was wounded under the eye with a penknife to the great hazard of its loss. In June a set of Mrs Margaret's friends, headed by David Carlile and his sons, William and Robert, made a personal assault on Mrs Mary Johnstoun, wife of the Laird of Lockerbie, cut her down and left her for dead, while her friend, Mrs Barbara Hill, was run through the thigh with a sword. These ladies had since lain under the care of surgeons, and it was uncertain whether they would live or die. A maid servant was also attacked by the Carliles, cruelly beaten, and nearly choked with a horn snuffbox (to stop her cries). In May Mrs Margaret's friends came and drove away the sheep and cattle from the lands of Hass and Whitwynd Hill with houndcalls, and the tenants coming to rescue their property were taken home in blankets. Not long after Westerhall's servants came to the same lands, and took by violence from Robert Johnstoun of Roberthill fourteen cows and oxen, which Sir James received into his byres, had them marked, and sold ten of them, each being worth £40. Lastly Walter Johnstoun, brother to Mrs Margaret, came with servants to the house of Netherplace at night, beat the owner, Mungo Johnstoun, in a most outrageous manner, besides squeezing the hands of his son, a boy, till the blood came from his nails. The Privy Council decided against Lockerbie for keeping his daughter-in-law out of her rights. Chambers, in his *Domestic Annals*, calls this " a fair specimen of the violence still permitted in debateable matters of property"; but it shows how wars and anarchy had lowered the standard of civilisation.

The Laird of Lockerbie in 1746 was James, whose son, William Johnstone, left two daughters. Grace, the elder, married Sir William Douglas of Kelhead in 1772, and was mother of the sixth Marquis of Queensberry. Her grandson, Robert Johnstone, inherited Lockerbie, and married his cousin, Lady Jane Douglas, in 1841. Their eldest son, Arthur H. Johnstone Douglas, was born in 1846. The descendants of the co-heiresses of Lockerbie are numerous. The younger sister, Catherine, married Colonel William Douglas in 1791.

Sir James Johnstoun of Westerhall died in 1699, and was succeeded by his eldest son, John, who had married, about 1687, Rachel, eldest daughter of James Johnston of Sheens, the last being first cousin to Warrieston and to Sophia Johnston, the mother of Lady Annandale. Westerhall was an M.P. and voted for the Union, while his Chief and Provost Johnston (Clochrie) of Dumfries voted on the other side. He died in 1711 at Tournay, when commanding a regiment of dragoons in Flanders, leaving an only child, Philadelphia, married to her cousin, James Douglas of Dornock. Westerhall was created a Baronet of Nova Scotia in 1700, and his brother, William, inherited it with the estate. A sister, Grizel, seems to have died unmarried. Sir William's wife was sister to his brother's wife, but died early in 1710. She was mother of his heir, James, and of John, the ancestor of Lord Derwent.

Sir William, like his brother, voted for the Union in the last Parliament held in Edinburgh in 1704. William Johnston of Corhead, William Johnstoun of Granton, Andrew Johnstoun of Newton, Johnston of Selkirth, Robert Johnston of Wamfray, William Johnston of Beirholme, George Johnstoun of Girthead (Sheriff-Depute), and John Johnston of Persbiehall or Craighous were also members of the same Parliament.

NOTE TO THE CARLILES.

There was no more loyal family on the Borders than the Carliles, who owned lands in the city of Carlisle when it belonged to Scotland, and one of whom, Sir Adam, received a Charter of Kinmount from the second Bruce of Annandale between 1170 and 1180. His descendant, Sir William, married Marjory, sister to King Robert I., and, according to Hume, the victory at Arkinholme in 1455 was wholly due to the Lords Carlile and Johnstoun. In 1470 the first was made a peer—Lord Carlile of Torthorald. His brother, Adam, inherited Bridekirk. But reverses began when the Master of Carlile, married to a daughter of the Master of Johnstoun, predeceased his father, leaving an infant daughter, Elizabeth. She inherited her grandfather's Barony, and the Regent Angus insisted on her marrying his relative, James Douglas, who thereupon called himself Lord Carlile. The male heir, Michael, who died in 1585, had lent money to his father, and claimed the estates. The case dragged on for fourteen years and was decided against him, and the expense impoverished all the family, who had hitherto benefited by many legal processes.

Herbert Carlile of Bridekirk and Edward Carlile of Limekilns, his brother, were living on the Newbie estate in 1605 and following years, and, with Edward's son, Adam Carlile of Murraythwaite, were summoned to quit it by the mortgagee, and to pay tithes by Murray of Cockpool. Herbert, as one of the next of kin, took out Letters of Slain against the assassin of James Douglas. After the battle of Langside Johnstoun was pledge for Alexander Carlile, while Drumlanrig was pledge for John and Thomas, brothers to Adam of Bridekirk. This Alexander was probably Alexander Carlile of Souplebank who was living on the Newbie estate in 1607, and married to a Carlile. Alexander Carlile rescued Dame Elizabeth of Torthorald from the hands of the Sheriff-Depute's officers at Dumfries in 1615, and conveyed her to a safe retreat in the Newbie Barony. There were also two Carliles, Andrew and John, living in Annan in 1591. As no Annan registers exist in the seventeenth century, the number of a man's sons cannot always be ascertained; but the tradition of the descendants of Adam Carlile of Annan and Ruthwell, that he was a Bridekirk, is probably true. All the families intermarried closely, as well as with Carruthers, Johnstoun, and Murray.

The identity is also shown by the ancient coat of arms—four Greek crosses charged with a shield bearing a saltire, and the motto "Humilitate." The Carliles are mentioned as a decayed family in 1595.

The wife of Edward Carlile of Limekilns (Bridekirk) was Margaret Young, one of the thirty-one children of Gavin Young, minister of Ruthwell, and Janet Steuart, his wife. Margaret is buried at Ruthwell, with the inscription that she died May 24, 1665, aged 48.

> "Of virtue, wit, grace, truth, love, pietie
> This woman in her tyme had store;
> On small means she upheld grit honestie,
> And in reward has endless glore."

She left several sons. Her father protected the ancient Runic Cross from total destruction at the hands of the Government iconoclasts by burying it in the churchyard. John Carlile, son to Alexander Carlile, was minister of Cummertrees in 1598; and William Carlile, son of a feuar in Kelhead, descended from Bridekirk, was the minister (1720-24).

The younger son of Edward Johnstoun and Isobelle Carlile in 1726 bought a bouse in Annan, close to the ancient churchyard, from his first cousin, Thomas Carlile, who is buried in the churchyard under an existing monument. John, elder son of Baillie James Carlile, removed to Paisley, where he married Janet Birkmyre. He died in 1772. His descendants are represented in England by the Rev. Canon Wilson Carlile, founder of the Church Army, and Edward Hildred Carlile, Esq., M.P., of the Manor House, Ponsbourne, Herts; while those of his brother, Thomas, are represented in Scotland by the Carliles of Waterbeck.

James Douglas's son, Robert, never called himself Lord Carlile; and his cousin, John Carlile, did not assume the title when deprived of the estates, so it remains in abeyance.

CHAPTER XV.

GALABANK—LAWSUITS—MARRIAGE—CHILDREN—JAMES JOHNSTONE DIES IN LONDON—RISING OF 1715—POVERTY IN SCOTLAND—SECRETARY JOHNSTON—THE FIRST MARQUIS OF ANNANDALE—HIS BROTHER JOHN—HIS SECOND MARRIAGE—THE SECOND MARQUIS—JOHNSTONE OF WESTERHALL—COLONEL JOHN JOHNSTONE MARRIES THE MARCHIONESS.

JOHN JOHNSTONE, the seventh generation of the direct male line from William of Graitney and Newbie, the eldest son of Edward Johnstoun and Isobelle Carlile, was born—the year of the Revolution—in 1688. He was nine when his father died, and received his education from the Rev. Patrick Inglis, the Episcopal minister of Annan, and from Robert Colville, the Presbyterian schoolmaster at Jedburgh, who gave tuition to the youth of the neighbourhood and an occasional service in the Kirk when Mr Inglis was deposed. In 1696 the Presbytery of Lochmaben reported that there are few settled teachers from want of salaries, and that the Presbytery of Middlebie, including Annan and six other parishes, have no salary for a teacher, and that there was hardly one that could teach Latin. But things improved as the eighteenth century advanced, and boys had to talk Latin in the burgh schools and playground, as well as, later, in the precincts of the University. The existing Scottish places of education were conducted on very rude, ascetic principles, and John never seems to have entered one. He was fortunate in not going to Moffat, which an earlier Johnstoun had endowed, for a young neighbour, John Douglas of Dornock, one of the Kelhead family, was flogged to death there by Robert Carmichael,[1] the schoolmaster, it is said, because he was being removed by his father. After his mother's death, in 1710, John enlarged his ideas by a visit to London, where Richard Beattie wrote, in 1711, that he had been for "some time."

Soon after Edward Johnstoun's death his brother, Galabank, paid a small portion of his debt to the widow, who, in 1704, when Galabank was also dead, obtained from the first Marquis of Annandale a "precept of poynding" against

[1] He was condemned to be taken along the streets of Edinburgh, and to be given eighteen sharp strokes with a whip by the hangman at three crowded parts of the city, and then expelled the country; but Chambers observes that, as boys were cruelly flogged much later, he was possibly unfortunate in the constitution of his victim. In 1790 a master at the High School in Edinburgh called his friends "to see twelve dunces flogged" on Saturday night as an amusing sight!

two of the tenants on the Galabank estate to oblige them to pay to her some overdue rents instead of to the assignee, another Edward Johnstoun, who claimed them as the only surviving son of the late owner, and on account of money he had paid for his father, including £76 to Mr Patrick Inglis. This Edward settled in London, but when he died in 1708 it appeared he was illegitimate, which seems to have been not generally known. According to Scottish law he was incapable of making a Will, and the Government claimed Galabank, Stank, the stone house, and other lands as its due. This led to litigation, which must have absorbed more money than the estate was worth. Janet, the only survivor of the marriage of John Johnstoun and Janet Kirkpatrick, claimed Galabank, as it was settled on her mother's children. Her cause was advocated at Edinburgh before the Lords of Council and Session, one of the advocates employed being John Boswell of Auchinleck, great-grandfather to the celebrated James, and it was decided in her favour. An order of the Chancellery infefted her in the estate, March 1, 1709.

Expecting this decision, Janet mortgaged Galabank to her cousin, John, for the sum borrowed by her father from his brother, and he was to pay 1d. a year to Janet, who might redeem the mortgage at any time. This was upset by another decision, Jan. 4, 1711, in favour of the Londoner's creditors. She appealed against it, while another appeal was lodged on behalf of Joseph Corrie, of Dumfries, who held an earlier mortgage on Galabank.

Joseph Corrie seems to have been a descendant of the old owners of Newbie and Corrie, whose family called itself of Newbie into the seventeenth century, and he now stepped forward to relieve the heirs of the old adversaries of his house of the last remnant of their land. The matter was hotly contested, to judge by items in the lawyers' bills—John Carlile of Limekilns and Richardson, of Edinburgh, on one side, and John Hair and Richardson, of Annan, on the other. Besides the causes mentioned, eleven processes set on foot by various claimants seem to have ruined all concerned in them except the lawyers. One creditor was Mrs Orr, half-aunt to Janet and John, being the daughter of Robert Fergusson and Agnes Graham.

In 1711 John bought off Corrie's claim to Galabank with £1000 Scots, the remaining balance of the mortgage, but he was then sued by Robert Carruthers, another creditor. The same year, in return for another 3500 marks, Janet and her husband gave up their claim to Galabank in favour of John, who was to take upon himself all further obligations connected with the estate except a small annuity to Elizabeth Murray, Janet's stepmother, which she could still pay. She declared on oath, Oct. 29, before the Baillies of Annan, that she ceded this estate with that of Stank to her cousin, "being in noways courted or compelled to do so." Her renunciation is signed by George Blair, notary, John Irving, Joseph Irving, John Johnstoun, Robert Wilson, and Bryce Tennant, and the deed of gift by Richard Beattie and several more. A similar deed is signed at Sarkbrig, Nov. 12, 1711, by Bernard Ross, Mr John Carruthers, son to George Carruthers, William Johnston of Beirholme, Joseph Murray, Janet Johnstoun, etc. Yet Mrs Beattie was not free of her father's creditors.

She appeared once more before the Lords in Council in 1713, though she was then living at her husband's home in Cumberland, where the beauty of Miss Beattie of Milleighs, her grand-daughter, is the subject of a poem in an early volume of a London magazine.

The Marquis of Annandale presided in 1713 over the inquest which declared Galabank to be the eldest lawful son of his father, and Sir William Johnstone of Westerhall, John Irving, and John Johnstoun, baillies, Robert Johnstoun, treasurer, and Matthew Fergusson, also sign it. This followed a redisposition of the house and grounds in Annan, "adjoining those of George Murray of Murraythwaite, and Thomas, son of the late Baillie James Carlile, which house was sold by the late James, Earl of Hartfell, to the late William M'Neish and his wife, Elizabeth Carlile, who redisponed it to the late Adam Carlile, who made it over to the late Edward Johnstone and Isobelle Carlile, his wife." At the same time Galabank sold his old family abode, "the vast stone house" on the site of Bruce's Castle, now covered by the Town Hall, to the Magistrates of Annan "for public purposes." He was married three days afterwards, by the Minister of Cummertrees, to Anna Ralston, daughter of the late William Ralston and Janet Richardson, his wife, of Hichill, the bride's two uncles signing the marriage contract—200 marks a year, a fourth of the annual value of Galabank was settled upon her, her own fortune being 2000 marks.

The same year John's sisters, Marie and Janet, were married respectively to John Richardson, the younger of Hichill, and to William Hair, and each bride received 500 marks from Galabank. The other sister, Elizabeth, died unmarried.

In 1714 John was much annoyed by trespassers on the Galabank estate. They pulled up his trees and broke down his fences. He attacked three of these intruders one Sunday and drove them away; but the ministers and elders ruled the Scottish parishes with a rod of iron, and were permitted to inflict heavy fines, and he was summoned before the Kirk-sessions and accused of Sabbath-breaking. He made an apology, and was shown to be otherwise an observer of the Sabbath, so the affair was allowed to drop; but the aggressors seem to have got off free, although the law was very severe as to stealing trees.[1] In 1719 John obtained "a letter of horning and poynding" against William Eliot of Eckleton, who was ordered "to defend the said John Johnstone personally or in his dwelling-place against adjudications affecting the houses and lands now in his possession within six days, the said Eliot having accused John Johnstone of being unlawfully their possessor, whereas he had received them lawfully from Richard Beattie and Janet Johnstone for certain sums of money which the said Beattie absolutely required."

This followed a final award of the Lords in Council, who confirmed John in possession of the estate; and he at once paid off the creditors who had sued the Beatties. Richard Beattie was dead in 1718, and in 1724 John sent his brother to London to make an amicable settlement with the creditors of their

[1] In 1710 a man was imprisoned four months in Aberdeen and whipped every Friday through the town for pulling up a young birch tree. Trees were very scarce in Dumfriesshire.

PLATE IX.

JAMES JOHNSTONE OF GALABANK.
Born, 1690; died 1729.

JOHN JOHNSTONE OF GALABANK, 1688-1774.

JAMES JOHNSTONE DIES IN LONDON

uncle's deceased son, to avert any more legal suits. On Oct. 30 James Johnstone wrote in a letter, beginning Dear Brother, and addressed " for John Johnstone of Galabank in Annan, Dumfries Bagge, North Britain," that he had made, with some expenditure, an end of the whole affair, and obtained a receipt from Mrs Orr, and also an order to her lawyer to deliver up to John all the family papers she had received as a security, and the legal papers connected with the suit. James wrote again, Nov. 2, when he was leaving London for Chippenham.

At the Court of Annan, Sept. 29, 1714, held by John Johnstone and John Irving on the accession of King George I., the following, after taking the oaths to the Elector of Hanover, were re-elected magistrates for the coming year: James, Lord Johnstone (eldest son of the Marquis); Sir William Johnstone of Westerhall, eldest baillie; John Irving and John Johnstone, second and third baillies; William Irving, treasurer; John Halliday, dean. John's first child, baptised Isobelle, was born the previous day; his eldest son, Edward, on Aug. 27, 1716. These were followed by Mary, June 28, 1718; William, June 27, 1720; John, May 19, 1722; Janet, June 20, 1724; Anna, May 2, 1726; Isobelle, Oct. 26, 1727; James, April 3, 1730; Adam, Feb. 27, 1732; Elizabeth, March 11, 1733; Agnes, July 28, 1735; George, Sept. 16, 1738; Richard, Feb. 21, 1740.[1] The rate of infant mortality was very high in those days, and the first little Isobelle, Mary, Janet, and Anna only gladdened their parents for eight, six, and four years, and the last for six months, when they were transferred to the churchyard and laid by the side of their ancestors. The stone covering them bears a quaintly worded inscription to their memory, and below their names that of their uncle James, "merchant in England, brother to ye forsaid Gallabanks, who dyed at ye Bleu Ancer in Little Britain, July 23, 1729, age 36. His corps is interred in ye churchyeard of St. Botolph, Aldergate, London."

Little Britain was the part of London where Scotsmen collected at that time. He owned a house in Annan, which he left to his brother, but debts of £340 English, which his brother paid. His funeral expenses were £17, 4s. 6d., exclusive of the luncheon at the Blue Anchor, which occupied the site of the modern Castle and Falcon, close to St. Martin's-le-Grand. The funeral bill, paid to William Johnston of Beirholme, then a citizen of London, includes the hire of fourteen silver sconces and satin favours, and fourteen men with wax lights, and two men with flambeaux to light the door. There were sixteen mourners.

In the midst of Galabank's troubles with lawsuits there was an agitation throughout Dumfriesshire in 1714,—the landing of Prince James Stewart being expected. He came the next year. It was not a good time to find armed followers among so poor a population; but the head of the Maxwell clan, the Earl of Nithsdale, led the Jacobites, thereby losing his title, and the Marquis of Annandale collected the Militia on behalf of George I. As he was Provost of

[1] Eight of these bore the same names as eight of the eleven children of the second Earl of Annandale.

Annan he probably controlled the feelings of the burgesses; but James Johnston of Knockhill, Fergus Graham of Mossknowe, and many others in the neighbourhood joined Nithsdale, and were transported to the West Indies to work in the plantations when the movement failed. Knockhill fought at Sheriffmuir and Falkirk; but Clan interest enabled him to return home in 1722.

Provost Corbett of Dumfries first obtained the news of an intended meeting of Jacobites on the Borders, and that their object was to capture Dumfries. He sent to the Marquis, who was there the same day, narrowly escaping capture on the road. As his brother, John Johnstone of Stapleton, was a Jacobite, he had him shut up in the town prison, and then went to Edinburgh to consult with the Government, leaving Westerhall and the other Sheriff-Depute to organise the Militia, John Johnstone, Westerhall's second son, being chosen captain of the volunteers.

Sir William Johnstone had collected a large supply of arms, but some were temporarily left near Lochmaben, and promptly seized by a party of rebels under Lord Kenmure (Sir Robert Gordon of Lochinvar). It was a disappointment to find that the Jacobites who were arrested were their neighbours and not Englishmen, who held aloof till they saw how the movement prospered. It was the same with many of the Scottish gentry, who preferred to help neither side till they felt sure which would win. Robert Johnston of Wamfray was one of several lairds who met at the Market Cross in Dumfries and, while drums were beating and colours flying, drank the King's health on their knees, every one knowing that they meant James VIII., but, as the Lady of Westerhall was nearly related to Wamfray, he escaped with a fine, although he had joined the troop of horse raised at Moffat by Kenmure on behalf of the Prince.

Kenmure, not so fortunate, marched to meet Lord Derwentwater in Cumberland, having found it impossible to take Dumfries. He was captured at Preston, and executed the same day as Lord Derwentwater, Feb. 24, 1716, happy that their rank exempted them from the horrible punishment inflicted on untitled Jacobites.

The poverty of Scotland as compared with England at that date is much dwelt upon by travellers, and is shown by the very small bribes which even the Scottish Peers most opposed to the abolition of their Parliament were willing to accept in 1700, one of them being bought over to the English side with £11, and the most exorbitant only requiring £30. In 1704 an Englishman passing through Dumfriesshire sums up his impression of the country with the remark, that if Cain had been born a Scotsman his punishment would have been not to wander about but to stay at home. Still Dumfriesshire had one source of profit not possessed farther north. The wine bills among the lairds, as well as among the English gentry, were out of all proportion to the other expenses in the eighteenth century, and before the Customs were made uniform in England and Scotland, Annan was the headquarters of an extensive trade for carrying wine, brandy, and other foreign goods into Cumberland, often on men's backs, concealed in loads of hay, sacks of wool, or sheafs of wheat. Smugglers flourished all along the coast, which was covered with small ships in their service. In 1711 a Custom House official wrote to his superior in Edinburgh, that in Ruthwell the people are such friends to the traffic, "no one can be found to lodge a Government officer for the night."

April 17, 1717, was appointed as a day of solemn fasting to avert the intended invasion of an enemy, and the threatened scarcity of bread—generally made of rye or oatmeal—owing to the severity of the weather.

In 1720 we find a complaint at the meeting of the Presbytery that the Kirk was losing its power over the people, swearing—so far as the expressions "faith" and "devil" were sometimes heard ; and in 1729 a theatre was opened in Edinburgh. A minister was suspended for attending it.

The Scots were notably a charitable people, and, though the population of Scotland was but a million and a quarter, they supported a vagrant population of 200,000 early in the eighteenth century, besides licensed bedesmen.[1] In better times there were periodical offertories in the Churches for the benefit of seamen enslaved by the Turkish and Barbary Corsairs in the Mediterranean, who had their tongues cut out or been otherwise crippled in the galleys ; others were still in need of ransom. But the epidemics carried about by the vagrants, the dearness of provisions, added to the abolition of the Scottish Parliament, sent many landowners, particularly on the Borders, to live in England. The new Marquis of Annandale began to spend most of his time in London ; and it was on the "parlour door of his lodgings in the Abbey" of Westminster that Robert Allane, Sheriff's messenger of Annan, knocked the six knocks and affixed the document showing that he had been put to the horn, because, as Provost of Annan, he had taken no steps to arrest Galabank for debt—the application having been made by Mr Patrick Inglis, the deposed Episcopalian minister of Annan. Edward Johnstone, then in London, settled this debt on behalf of his father ; but if he had not, most likely no measures would have been taken against the Provost. Annandale probably owed his promotion in the Peerage, and Westerhall his Baronetcy, to the fact of their wives being cousins to the Secretary for Scotland, James Johnston, the son of Warrieston, who was of great service to William III. and his successor. The new patent, conferring the Annandale title on heirs male whatsoever in default of direct heirs male, showed that it was intended as in days of old to reward the whole clan for its patriotism and former unpaid services, not only one branch of it.

Of Warrieston's sons who survived him, the elder, Alexander, was educated

[1] Fletcher of Salton describes the condition of the country after the Civil War with the 200,000 people left to beg, "some sorners," the dread of isolated cottages, who took food by force, robbed children of their clothes and the money they carried to pay the fees on their way to school, and even kidnapped children to be sold to merchant captains for slaves in the American plantations. Grahame, in his *Social State of Scotland*, says that this continued much later ; and that the widow of a Highland laird, who notoriously increased his income in this way, was presented to George IV. when he visited Edinburgh in 1821. "Outed" Episcopalian ministers and their families swelled the applicants for relief. The kidnapping is corroborated by an advertisement in the *New York Gazette*, May 1, 1774 :—
"Servants just arrived from Scotland to be sold on board the *Commerce*, Capt. Fergusson master, now lying at the Ferry Stairs, among which are a number of weavers, taylors, blacksmiths, nailors, shoemakers, butchers, hatters, and spinsters, fourteen to thirty-five years of age. For terms apply to Henry White or said Master."

for a lawyer, but was employed in the Secret Service of the Prince of Orange. The last heard of him is the extract from Brodie's diary, quoted in Morison's *Johnston of Warrieston*, Nov. 17, 1671—"I heard that Alexander, Warrieston's son, had brok, and through cheating, lying, wrong ways. My brother and others had suffered much by him." He had a son, Jasper of Warrieston, who left only a daughter. The younger son, James, born Sept. 9, 1655, was educated in Holland, and, having passed particularly well in civil law at Utrecht, his cousin, Bishop Burnet, gave him a helping hand. Like Burnet, Secretary Johnston was a good friend to his relations, and many of them came to London in the hope of obtaining a Government office through his influence. He is described as a tall, strong, fair-haired typical Scotsman, with much endurance at a time when the dress and mode of life in England was conducive to effeminacy. He could undertake the rough travelling a Continental journey then necessitated, and be back again in England, fit for business, after a secret conference with the Prince of Orange, before he was even missed. William III. was the great hope of the Covenanters. As the son of a Stewart Princess, with double Stewart descent through his grandmother, it was not a long step to accept him[1] and his Queen, James's daughter, in the place of James, who was never popular in Scotland. But the Secretary was considered as a friend to Scottish democracy, and insisted on an inquiry into the massacre of Glencoe. His freedom of speech is supposed to have irritated William III., who perhaps could not afford to displease Englishmen by employing Scots. Anyway, he was dismissed from office in 1696, though he continued to advise the Government. He was opposed to a separate Parliament in Scotland, and brought Annandale over to his view,— for he was again in office, for a year as Lord Clerk Register of Scotland (1704-05), under Queen Anne, but obliged to resign, and this time permanently, on account of the protection he had given to Jacobites, among them Nathaniel and Henry Johnston of Pomfret, and Annandale's brother, John, whose career only became important when it was necessary to prove that he died *s.p.* before the House of Lords.

This John (Annandale's brother) was born at Newbie in 1668, and went to school at Glasgow till he was about twelve. Then his maternal uncle, the Earl of Dumbarton, sent him to Haddington school, and gave him a commission in his own regiment as soon as he was sixteen. The pay he received was supposed to be enough for his expenses at a college in Paris, where he went to complete his education, though he shows in a letter to his brother, dated 1687, that it was not. Annandale had just got a commission in the Guards from James VII., but was never backward in helping his brother when he could afford it. John returned as a captain to England, where he was received by the Royal Chaplain, his cousin, Henry Johnston of Pomfret, into the Roman Church. The next year the Revolution began, and he joined heart and soul on the side of the King, while his brother, after some vacillation, took the oaths to William. Lord Dumbarton fled with the exiled King to St. Germains, and

[1] The *Lockhart Memoirs* state that Secretary Johnston told Lockhart he could make people's hair stand on end with revelations about the Court and Government of William III.

Captain Johnstone was arrested on a charge of high treason and committed to Newgate in 1689, just after John Johnstone, the younger of Westerhall, who managed Annandale's estate, had acted as his cautioner for a loan of £100, borrowed from his tailor in London, which was repaid. Westerhall also lent him 900 marks. Annandale himself is said to have been heavily bailed to keep him out of prison. After six months in Newgate, Captain Johnstone returned to Scotland, and a letter, dated Moffat, from Westerhall to Annandale, Nov. 19, 1690, says that his brother is staying with the Duke of Hamilton and has been strongly advised to go abroad; but it is absolutely necessary that he should have £20 for the journey. Captain Johnstone adds a letter to the same effect—that he has taken Westerhall's advice and does not want to be a burden to his family, that with £20 he would go at once to Holland, and that he has left papers with Sir John Carmichael which may be of use to the family, for whom he should be always ready to do any service in his power. Possibly the Secretary found the money, but the recipient used it to go to St. Germains, not to Holland, and remained abroad long after the term allowed for "native subjects" to make their submission. His name appears among those rebels then in France, who were liable to prosecution, in 1695, but it was removed soon afterwards through the Secretary's influence. In 1698 King James issued a warrant concerning him and his friend, Captain Livingston, who had both wished to enter the service of Venice. The King speaks of their fidelity to his cause, and that they had always comported themselves like men of honour, and he called Johnstone "a person of the first quality in our Kingdom of Scotland." In 1701 Sir George Maxwell lent him £100 to save him from being imprisoned for debt in Paris. There is some proof that he served in Prussia for a time (the Secretary had taken the Garter to the Elector of Brandenburg), but he eventually returned to Scotland, obtained a pardon under the Great Seal, and came to live at Stapleton as a Presbyterian. Still his brother thought it wise to arrest him during the Rising of 1715. This precaution enabled him to end his days in a small official post.[1]

It is often said of the Scots, that, unlike the Irish, they help each other regardless of political or religious differences. This was certainly the ex-Secretary's case; but on his marriage to a daughter of Lord Poulett he settled permanently at Orleans House, Twickenham, where he was buried, May 11, 1744, being eighty-nine at the time of his death. He more than once visited George I. in Hanover, and as he could speak Latin and German fluently both the King and his daughter-in-law seemed to have liked talking to him; and Queen Caroline often drove over to see him at Twickenham.

Major James Johnston was returned heir to the ex-Secretary, his father, in 1744. He married Lady Charlotte Montagu, but there appear to be no male descendants.

Annandale was one of the first Knights of the Thistle when the Order

---

[1] A family named Goodinge took the name of Johnstone, and claimed descent in the female line from this John, but the marriage, which was said to have taken place in an obscure part of London, could not be proved.

was revived by Queen Anne. He was also Lord Privy Seal in 1702, and Lord President of the Privy Council till 1706. His manners are said to have been courteous and pleasing. He was elected a Scottish Representative Peer in 1707, and in 1711 was Commissioner to the General Assembly of the Kirk of Scotland. In 1714 he was appointed Keeper of the Great Seal, and a Privy Councillor; and during the Rising in 1715 was made Lord-Lieutenant of the counties of Dumfries, Kirkcudbright, and Peebles. His wife (the bride of fourteen in 1682) died in 1716, and was buried in Westminster Abbey. The eldest daughter, Henrietta, had long been married to John Hope, who was created, by the ex-Secretary's influence, Earl of Hopetoun in 1703. Two younger sons, William and John, died unmarried in 1721, shortly after their father. The old Marquis astonished and disgusted his children in 1718, by going through a Fleet marriage with Charlotta Van Lore, the only child of a Dutch merchant in Westminster, John Vanden Bempdé, by his wife, Temperance, daughter of John Packer. Vanden Bempdé owned property in Hammersmith and Chiswick, and the estate of Hackness Hall in Yorkshire. He settled £300 a year on his daughter, and the reversion of his estates to her heirs, saying that he was not going to be behind anyone else in the matter, but with the provision that the inheritor of his property should take his own family name. When the Marquis died at Bath, April 21, 1721, Vanden Bempdé allowed another £300 a year for the maintenance and education of his infant grandson, George, and for the son, John, who was born six months after the Marquis's death. The ex-Secretary was among those who attended the Marquis's funeral. Sir William Johnstone of Westerhall was there on behalf of the Marchioness when the Will was read. The Earl of Orkney, Sir R. Montgomery, Colonel Graham, Jerviswood, and Lord Hope also came, but in the interest of the Marquis's elder children.

James, Lord Johnstone, the second Marquis, lived at Newbie Castle when not abroad, and was Provost of Annan in 1715. After his succession he was little seen in Scotland, and died in Naples in 1730. His stepmother had to sustain a lawsuit with Lord and Lady Hopetoun for her son, George, about the possession of the Annandale estates. In consideration of Miss Fairholm's fortune, these estates had been settled on her and on her future children after her marriage with the first Marquis; and on the death of James they were claimed as well as the title by his sister, the last survivor of that marriage, on the ground that the title went with the estates. The House of Lords in 1733 decided that the Fairholm provision was illegal on both points, the land having been settled in 1661 on the heirs male of the first Earl, and only to go to the female on the demise of all those heirs. So young George succeeded to his father's estates as well as to his title, and Lady Hopetoun inherited her mother's estate at Craigiehall. Some of the lands held by Galabank paid a trifling duty to the Marquis.

On April 27, 1700, Lord Carstairs wrote from Whitehall to Lord Annandale: "I was told your lordship wished to have Major Jhonston a Knt Baronet. I have procured his patent, and shall send it down either with this or Tuesday's packet." Westerhall was gazetted a Baronet of Nova Scotia, including a grant of land on which it was obligatory to make a settlement. His connection with Annandale became closer when his brother, Major John Johnstone, interested himself on behalf of the widowed Marchioness in the lawsuit, and before it ended in her favour he married her, so that he became guardian to the young Marquis and Lord John.

A letter from the Major to Sir James, dated from London, May 13, 1735, alludes to his stepsons as well as to his own child, Richard, born Sept. 21, 1732:—

"Sir,—I had the honour to receive your most obliging letter . . . In spite of all the discouragements my lady has met with she is determined to return to Scotland this year . . . and has not only given up Purser's Cross, but put Pell Mell in the papers and hung a ticket on the door. You have not been deceived of Lord John, he is returned to the right road, and we have all reason to believe he will persevere in it. Sir Orlando Bridgeman's son came t'other day from abroad, and saw the Marquis at Lausanne, he says he is not only the prittyest youth he ever saw but the most regular and applys the most to his books. Dick is really a very pritty child, and the best natured creature I ever saw. I heartily and sincerely thank you for your kind wishes to him and much more thank you for your advice regarding him. If I were to love him as much as I incline, and as he really deserves I should soon come to like few things else; but blessings and comfort are so seldom permanent that I shall never make my happiness depend upon anything without myself. [He speaks of taking possession at Scarsborough, *i.e.*, Hackness Hall.] Mrs Betty continues your admirer and faithful servant. Mr Michell has threatened me but done nothing, so that the time is now so short before the adjudication must take place for £6000, we take it for granted he will attempt nothing. . . . The chanceler is not to be trifled with, and Michell is already so roasted about the trust estate of Vulture Hopkins that his reputation at the bar is of the lowest. I went one morning to my lord Isla's levee but he has rather forgot me or which is worse imagines I have done somethings at which he thinks he ought to be offended. I have not returned. The Duke of Argyle very seldom sees company, but is much better than he has been. I wish with all my soul the offence may have gone no higher than *memini* but appearances are against us. Our enimys leave no stone unturned. Ld Finlater has been lately at Mr Murrays [Lord Mansfield] to retain him Hope against Annandale which you may easily imagine was refused. . . . We are yet in a storm, and how or when we shall get into safe harbour, the omniscient God only knows. Sir James Stuart of Goodtress is just come in I must therefore finish with all possible respect and esteem Sir your most affectionate brother and devoted humble servt.

"J. Johnstone.

"Offer my humble respects to Lady Johnstone and blessings to the bairns. If you think brother Walter must go into the army say so and I'll find an opportunity. My wife had begun a letter to my sister but wither she will finish it or not I cannot say company having come in upon her too. She begs her sincerest service may be acceptable to you."

To the misfortune of his stepsons, Colonel John Johnstone died in Jamaica, in 1741, of wounds received when commanding a battalion in an expedition to Carthagena.

CHAPTER XVI.

Young Galabank—The Church of Scotland—The Third Marquis of Annandale—He Presents to Moffat—William Johnstone's Death in the West Indies—Carlile of Antigua—Scottish Pharmacy—The Rising in 1745—Dumfriesshire Men who Assisted Prince Charles—The Chevalier Johnstone.

A RECENT writer on the social state of Scotland says: "Never did the Church take so high a place as in 1750 to 1770."[1] Among those who helped to raise it to that level was Galabank's eldest son, Edward. The death of the little sisters who had been his playfellows, and of two still younger before he was eleven, gave him a sober turn of mind, so he was early destined to be a minister—at that time quite as influential a post in Scotland as a Roman priest in Ireland, but by no means a lucrative one. The Presbyterian had so recently been established as the Kirk of Scotland, and ousted the Episcopalian, that its leaders resolved to keep up a high standard for their clergy, and a nine years' study and strict probation was required before the ministerial call, and Hebrew and Greek were obligatory. As to Latin, the lectures were delivered in it, and it had to be spoken in the College precincts.

Edward Johnstone's instructor before he went to College was Mr Howie, the Annan minister, from whom he learned French, as well as Latin and Greek. He matriculated at the Edinburgh University when he was sixteen, and, being an eloquent probationer of divinity, he preached several times in the College Chapel before the Professors when he was still under twenty. He took his degree of M.A. in 1739, being already tutor to Richard and Charles, the sons of the Marchioness of Annandale and her second husband, Colonel Johnstone, and he gave lessons to the sons of her first marriage, George, third Marquis of Annandale, and Lord John Johnstone.[2] While so employed he lived at

[1] Grahame.
[2] "These gentlemen," wrote his brother in 1799, "were uncommonly fortunate in their tutor, for with great literary talents, with genius, and the liberal manners of a gentleman, my brother had the highest sense of truth, justice, honour, and piety. . . . I owe much to his example, and sincerely honour his memory as my benefactor and as an honour to his family." This was not only a brother's partial estimate; "Fasti Eccles. Scotiæ" says of him: "In person he was tall and graceful. He was superior in talents, manners, and conversation, and by his knowledge and elocution was an animated and popular preacher, as well as a diligent, zealous, and faithful pastor. His sermon on the death of George II. was the only one printed in Scotland."

Comlongan Castle, which the Marchioness rented in 1737 from Lord Stormont, and at Appleby, in Westmoreland, where she spent some time every year.

The sons of Sir James Johnstone of Westerhall often visited their cousins at Comlongan, and the young tutor watched with interest their subsequent career. He also helped to teach his brothers, particularly James, who was fourteen years his junior, and stayed with him at Comlongan and at Moffat. But Annan set up a school of its own, and with an eminent master, Dr Robert Henry, the historian. James was his pupil for a short time, and though he left the school, as he says in his diary, very abruptly, it did not prevent a lifelong friendship with Dr Henry, which extended to his sons.

The despotism which Bishop Burnet describes as being exercised by the ministers in Cromwell's day had by no means lost its vigour when Presbyterianism was re-established, and the Presbyteries kept an eagle eye, far sharper than the contemporary Anglican bishops, on the conduct of the ministers. In 1743 that of Lochmaben deposed the minister of Moffat, and Sir James Johnstone of Westerhall and Mr Graham of Airth (an advocate) presented the Minister of Johnstone in his place. The Presbytery accepted him, and so did the General Assembly of the Church of Scotland provisionally. But on making their usual enquiry they declined to confirm the appointment, which lapsed to the young Marquis of Annandale, who was living at Richmond, in Surrey. He at once presented Edward Johnstone.

The Marquis, who signs his name V. Bempdé Annandale, as by his grandfather's Will the name of Vanden Bempdé must go with the English estates, wrote on Aug. 9, from Richmond, to Bryce Blair, the Provost of Annan, and to James Hoggan, a writer in Comlongan, and told them to manage all the legal part of the affair in presenting the nomination to the Presbytery of Lochmaben, and "if need be to prosecute the said settlement before all or any of the other Church judicatories in Scotland." A little later, in a letter from Paris to Westerhall, Sept. 15, 1743, he says: "I hope Galliebanks junior is settled by this time."

Edward accepted the appointment in a letter:—

"To the Rev. Moderator of the Presbytery of Lochmaben, to be communicated to the Presbytery.

"Rev. Sir,—The most honourable George, Marquis of Annandale, having done me the honour to present me to be minister of the Church and Parish of Moffat by his lordship's presentation, executed in my favour Aug 9, 1743, I do hereby declare to you and to the Rev. Presbytery of Lochmaben that I do accept of the said presentation as Law requires . . . with due submission to the Church. I am, Rev. Sir, your most obedient and most humble servant, Edward Johnstone.

"Comlongan Castle, 5 *Sept.* 1743."

There was the usual searching inquiry as to his character and antecedents, as some parishioners accused him "of employing a barber to shave him on the

Sabbath Day," and nearly four years were wasted in it. Then with a caution as to the inadvisability of so doing in future, he was declared a fit and proper person to hold the living, and the Marquis's nomination was confirmed.

Galabank's sisters died, like their parents, in middle age. He seemed to anticipate the same fate for himself, and complained of his eyes, set his wife and daughters to write his letters, and relied on his eldest son for advice as to the management of his younger children and estate. His daughter, Elizabeth, had an offer from "a very pretty laird," as she called him in a letter to her brother. The laird promised to spend every winter in Carlisle when they were married. But Edward interposed. She was already consumptive, and he did not approve of the suitor. Perhaps the disappointment hastened her end, for she only lived another year, and is buried at Annan, with an inscription to the effect that she was a pleasure to her friends, and died, regretted, in the twenty-second year of her age (1756). Her spirit and wit is often alluded to in family letters, and how she rose and spoke her mind when she thought her brother James was maligned. She appealed to James, as her favourite brother, to help her in her engagement, but his advice had already been asked, and was against it.

Galabank did not care to talk about his family. He was much tried in his youth by the legal processes in which he was involved, and in his old age thought he might have done better by following a profession, when he saw the success which many Dumfriesshire men achieved elsewhere. He sent five of his sons to College. The writer already quoted says that students could board in Edinburgh for £10 a year, and that, in 1755, the board at the best students' lodgings was 50 marks per quarter, and at the second 40; the rent from 7s. to 20s. in the session, no furniture but bedsteads and grate. All the rest had to be bought or hired by the student, who paid for his own candles, fire, and washing. He also paid £2, 2s. to the master and 5s. each for lectures to the professors; but prices had risen when Galabank's youngest son went to Edinburgh.

His second son, William, matriculated early at Edinburgh, like his senior, and studied medicine. Since 1705, when the first M.D., Dr Munro, graduated in Edinburgh, about three annually in all Scotland took this degree from 1727 to 1760, and most of them went abroad. The Russian Government, through its Ambassador, for several generations periodically applied to the Principal of the Edinburgh University to select a physician for the Russian Court; but the famous schools of Paris and Italy supplied most of the medical men required by other foreign capitals. William had no need to accept any of these posts, though they were often handsomely remunerated, as a relative, Thomas Carlile,[1] had settled in Antigua under the British flag, and offered an opening to his young countryman. Several other members of Dumfriesshire families were at

[1] Thomas Carlile, besides his estate, left £30,000 to his widow. His son died unmarried, but his daughter, Alice, married Ralph Payne of St. Kitt's, Chief Judge and one of the Council of the island. Their son, Ralph, born in 1739, was created Lord Lavington in 1795. His half-brother, John, was the well-known Admiral, whose portrait is in the Waterloo Chamber, Windsor Castle.

this time turning their attention to the West Indies, attracted by the good fortune which had followed upon the banishment to the "Plantations" of various youths who had joined in the Rising of 1715, and were too young to be hanged.

William Johnstone sailed for Jamaica as soon as he had taken his Degree. He found that Thomas Carlile had lately died, but his son, William, welcomed the young physician, and offered a post to his next brother, John, who, though only seventeen, sailed at once. The result was tragical. They were taken prisoners by the Spaniards when on a cruise among the islands, and endured great hardships in most insanitary quarters during a short captivity. They fell ill with yellow fever in Spanish Town, Kingston, where William died, Jan. 9, 1745, aged twenty-four. John recovered sufficiently to return home, but with his mind affected. William Carlile died about the same time, but whether he was with the Johnstones, and also suffered from a Spanish prison, is not recorded.

Dr Cullen went from Glasgow to Edinburgh to succeed Munro. He alluded to prescriptions which, "foolish as they were in his manhood, were preposterous in his youth." "Not long ago," he added, "the Pharmacopœia of the several colleges of Europe were a scandal to physic, and contained many things shocking to commonsense; many of them are so still. The Edinburgh Pharmacopœia, in request all over Europe, in its third edition of 1737 enumerated spiders' webs, viper's body, toads cooked alive, millipedes, snake's skin, mummy human skull, snails, Spanish flies, frogs' spawn, human blood and fat, bees, etc., some even more disgusting, and 450 vegetable simples, some of the things most difficult to get, like a stony substance found inside Borneo goats. Mummies were concocted by Jews and sold in Paris for a high price." The Pharmacopœia of the Royal College of Physicians in London retained, in 1745, viper's broth and brick oil. No wonder that epidemics raged unchecked through Europe, and the Turkish plague reached Vienna and Marseilles.

Galabank intended that his fourth son, James, should be an advocate. Several Dumfriesshire men were distinguished in the law in the eighteenth century — Lord Mansfield (born at Comlongan, and whose family owned Graitney), Sir William Pulteney (of the House of Westerhall), Sir James Kirkpatrick, Charles Sharpe of Hoddam, Alexander Fergusson of Craigdarroch, David Armstrong, Hugh Corrie, Thomas Goldie, and William Copland of Collistoun—but Erskine and James Douglas, the brothers of Sir John Douglas of Kelhead, in the neighbourhood, had taken up medicine, and Erskine Douglas with his brother Francis, a sailor, were being concealed by their relatives in 1746 for having carried arms for Prince Charles. Erskine had given up good prospects in his profession to join a losing cause, and was a local hero. His brother-in-law, Sir William Maxwell of Springkell, was Johnstone's lifelong friend. The practice of medicine as exhibited by the Douglases[1] had more adventure connected with it than the law, and James

[1] Great-uncles of the fifth Marquis of Queensberry. "Go, Jamie, and avenge Flodden," was Sir William Douglas's parting words to his son when he went to learn the composition of medicines at an apothecary's in Carlisle, where he afterwards practised.

THE RISING IN 1745

preferred it, and, like a young knight-errant, meant to try and save life by seeking for a remedy for the smallpox, which, impartially visiting the palace and the cottage, caused 60 per cent. of the infant mortality in England in 1746-50, and nearly as many in Scotland.

Lady Mary Wortley Montagu went to Constantinople in 1717, and allowed her son to be inoculated, after the custom she found prevailing in the East; but it was not readily adopted in Great Britain, and it was arranged that when James had taken his medical degree in Edinburgh, he should study for a short time in Paris, to learn the French practice in fevers, and this new mode—as far as Europe was concerned—of combating the dreaded enemy, which carried off three of his sisters and later two of his own children.

Galabank is mentioned as an ex-Provost of Annan, but it is not quite clear which year he served.

It was in sight of his house, and over the bridge at Annan, that the wearied and disappointed army of Prince Charles Edward, in 1745, continued their retreat from England, where they had not found the support they had been led to expect. No Prince had visited Annan since James VI. stayed at Newbie Castle and hunted in the neighbourhood, although Charles I. was anxiously expected at Caerlaverock Castle when it maintained a siege on his behalf. Some volunteers undertook to guard the bridge, but fled at the first sound of the pibroch; and as part of the Prince's army halted for the night on Galabank's land, James, the eldest of his sons at home, then fifteen, conveyed away all his horses in front of the cavalry by the bridge to Limekilns, the house of a relative, Carlile, who was attached to the cause of George II., lest their seizure should compromise the owner in the eyes of the Government.[1] In an autobiography, written in his old age, James relates how he returned in the morning "in time to see the march of the clans towards Dumfries. The Prince walked at the head of the Clan Macpherson, which defeated the Duke of Cumberland's troops in a skirmish, and gave some check to the advance of the punitive force." He describes Prince Charles Edward as "tall, fair, and his whole demeanour, affable and princely. Though possessed of courage and address, he had not enough to succeed in his arduous undertaking. He was not forward in battle, and left the field at Culloden too soon (but his friends obliged him to do so). In repassing the Esk, Dec. 21, on his retreat, he carried on a high horse a Highlander behind him, and returned back again and brought a second in like manner; this was gracious, and encouraged his people to pass the river, which was breast high. The vanguard of their horse, under Lord Kilmarnock, suddenly drew up the same day before my father's door, accompanied by Mr Lawson," etc.

[1] In *Glimpses of Peebles*, by the Rev. A. Williamson, there is a letter from the Marchioness of Annandale, then a widow for the second time, dated Jan. 17, 1746, from Comlongan Castle, describing the Highlanders on their march: "My dear boys," she writes, "being at home, was an amusement to me in such disturbances as this country was in when they returned on Dec. 21, the day my house was visited by 3 A.M., when a captain and five men entered the house and stayed till 7. They asked for arms and horses—the former I had none. Then they went to the stables and would have taken all my mares but Mr Hoggan pleaded hard for them, and said I was afflicted with gout, and had no way

The next time that young James met a member of the Royal House was in the Bishop's Palace (now Deanery) at Worcester, when he and his three eldest sons were presented to George III. and Queen Charlotte.

The Risings of 1715 and 1745 cost Dumfriesshire as much as if she had actively supported them, and the stoppage of a chief bank at Ayr, which had a branch in Dumfries, caused a complete stagnation of commerce, except in the illegal form in which it was conducted on the southern coast.

Yet, poor as the country was, the Rebellion of 1745 could only be crushed out in Scotland with the aid of Dutch and German troops. These mercenaries or conscripts seem to have been more civilised than the rabble with which the press-gang and the prison recruited the British army at that date. The license permitted to the victorious soldiers left the northern parts of the country a famine-stricken waste, but as the Militia alone secured the loyalty of Dumfriesshire, it suffered less from the exactions of the avengers of Gladsmuir.

Galabank must have found it hard to pay the sum of £100 which was demanded of him towards a forced loan raised in the county for Prince Charles Edward; in fact he gave it in the form of a bond, for which his securities were Thomas Kirkpatrick and Robert Laurie. Bryce Blair, the ex-Provost, also gave £100. There was great sympathy with the movement even among those who did not care to risk the penalties for high treason, or, if treated more leniently, to be sent as slaves to the Southern States of North America. The Prince lodged at two houses in Dumfries; one is the Commercial Hotel, where he held a levee on his return from England. The town was fined £4000 sterling for an attack made in the street on one of his Highland followers. He is said to have lodged in both the Buck Hotel and the Blue Bell at Annan on his return, and some of his followers, camped in Galabank's field, went to carouse in the Queensberry Arms. There they heard Carlile of Bridekirk, a staunch Hanoverian, express his opinion very freely on the respective merits of King George and their young leader. They arrested him, and compelled him to march with them to Dumfries, where he asked for an interview with the Prince, and told him why he came there. The unfortunate Charles replied, "Sir, I commend you for it, and if some of my pretended followers had been so firm

of exercising but in the coach; which prevailed with them so far that they left four, but the odd one they took, and two of H——'s best horses, which I was sorry for, as it is a loss to his business, and after they got plenty of meat and drink they all went to Sir W. G——'s who lost some horses too. After the morning was over I had another visit of forty more who came at 2, and made the same demand as the former; but as I had time I sent the best of my mares out of the way, and by that means saved them, but they threatened to shoot one of Mr H——'s workmen, if he did not tell where my mares were, for they said they knew I had five and a shelty; but the man said, he knew not where they were which pacified them. Then they slipped round the parks and got a poor old dragoon of Mr H——'s. . . . And after eating and drinking thirty-four of them marched off, but the other six who was not so able to go on to Dumfries said they would lie here. . . . They were away by 6 A.M., after a good breakfast of meat and cheese, ale, good brandy, and was so civil as never to set their foot in the House, sent their service to me, and thanks for their good entertainment, and told my boys who were much entertained with them, that they were namesakes For M'Donalds which they were, was the same as Johnstone. But I own I was very glad when my cousins were gone. . . . All the effects were really Triffells to what my neighbours suffered. . . . I hope we shall never see them more for they ruin wherever they go."

in my cause as you are to George, I now should have been on the throne of my fathers." He was at once released, and as the Duke of Cumberland, who was on his road to the North to attack the Prince's army, heard of it, he sent for Mr Carlile and offered to relieve him of the heavy debt on his estate if he would assist him with all the information he could, but, to the distress of Mr Carlile's nearest relations, he refused even to meet the Duke. His estate passed out of the hands of his family, owing to the general ruin caused by the failure of the local banks after the insurrection was suppressed.

Dumfries received the gift of some confiscated estates in recognition of its townspeople having seized a baggage waggon left in the mud near Ecclefechan as the Prince's army marched South. The Highland soldiers in charge were only armed with pikes and scythe blades, so easily taken prisoners.

A few in the county were reported for their share in the movement—two Johnstones of Knockhill, James Irving, junior of Gribton; "Edward Irving of Wysbie guided the rebels from Ecclefechan to Graitney, on their way to Carlisle; William Johnstone of Lockerbie was very assisting to the rebels in their march through Annandale; William Irving of Gribton refused to drink His Majesty's health and is supposed to have forced his son into the rebellion; John Henderson of Castlemains imprisoned at Carlisle for drinking treasonable healths was set at liberty and made Governor of the Jail by the rebels" (he was executed at Carlisle); Gavin Broun, the two Douglases, the Earl of Nithsdale, and many Maxwells, including Sir William of Springkell, who "had entertained certain rebels and provided them with horses"; Sir John Douglas was kept for a short time in the Tower, but his brothers were left alone after a trifling search.

One of Prince Charles's aide-de-camps at Culloden was a scion of the House of Wamfray, the only son and eighth child of James Johnstone, a merchant in Edinburgh (a Jacobite), and his wife, Cecile Hewit. The younger James was baptised in Edinburgh in 1719; and in 1738 visited his uncles, General Douglas and Hewit in St. Petersburg, but his father declined to allow him to enter the Russian service. The same objection did not prevent the youth from joining Prince Charles Edward at Perth in 1745; and he became aide-de-camp to Lord George Murray, till Prince Charles made him one of his own, and he remained with the Prince till the end. Lady Jane Douglas, a distant relative of his mother, had always been kind to him, and, in spite of hair-breadth escapes, he safely reached her house at Edinburgh, and was concealed there for two months. After a secret interview with his father, he went to London, but, probably dismayed by the fate of other captured insurgents, he left England for Holland disguised as Lady Jane's servant, thence to Paris to join the Prince, and received 2200 livres out of 40,000 given by the French Court for Jacobite refugees. He entered the French marines, went to Louisbourg, and obtained promotion; but when Louisbourg was captured by the English, he fled to Quebec, and assisted Montcalm against the English. On the capture of Quebec, General Murray kindly ignored his nationality, and sent him back with other captured officers to France. His parents were now dead, as well as his favourite sister, Cecile, the wife of the sixth Lord Rollo, so he remained in Paris till the Revolution deprived him of his pension; but he had relatives there, one of whom, the President of the Scots College, sold to Messrs Longman in 1820 his MS. of the *History of the Rebellion in 1745-46*.

The Chevalier de Johnstone died about 1798.

CHAPTER XVII.

"Within the bounds of Annandale
The gentle Johnstones ride,
They have been there a thousand years,
A thousand years they'll bide."—*Old Ballad.*

JOHNSTONES OF WESTERHALL—SIR WILLIAM—HIS SONS—SIR JAMES MEETS DR SAMUEL JOHNSON—SIR WILLIAM PULTENEY—GOVERNOR JOHNSTONE'S CAREER—JOHNSTONE OF ALVA—GIDEON JOHNSTONE AND MRS JORDAN—LADY OGILVIE—MISS JOHNSTONE.

THE Johnstones of Westerhall increased their property in the eighteenth century, and after the death of William, first Marquis of Annandale, were the most influential of the name in Scotland, as James, the second Marquis, lived chiefly abroad. There were serious quarrels between these two, partly because the Marquis had sold hereditary estate to Westerhall, and Sir William of Westerhall, with very profane language, tried to reconcile the Marquis to his son. He was therefore much annoyed when Marquis James made an entail of his property—settling it first on the heirs of his sister and aunts, after his own male and female heirs, and then, in the event of the failure of his grandfather's direct heirs, to Colonel James Johnstone of Graitney and his male heirs—without any mention of the Westerhalls, except to annul the succession of any heir who married into that family. He also ignored his half-brothers, George and John, or any other Johnstone. The settlement was signed at Ferrybridge, in Yorkshire, Oct. 1, 1726, witnessed by William Johnston (younger of Corehead) and others.

Sir William was M.P. for the Dumfries Burghs for nearly twenty years. He died 1728, leaving four sons—James, John, Archibald, and Walter. John was a major in Brigadier Phineas Bowles's regiment of Dragoons at the time he married Charlotta, Dowager-Marchioness of Annandale. Archibald, a surgeon in the Hon. Lieutenant-General Howard's regiment of Foot, died 1748. His Will describes him as a widower, late of Westerkirk, North Britain. He appointed his brother, Walter, guardian to his children, John and Jane, till they should be twenty-one. Walter was also in the army, and served under the Duke of Cumberland in 1745-46.

The eldest brother, the third Baronet, was an advocate and Provost of Lochmaben when elected to represent the Dumfries Burghs in 1743. He married Barbara Murray, daughter of Alexander, fourth Lord Elibank, and had eight sons and six daughters. The following letter from William, Marquis of Annandale, was on the birth of his third son :—

"Whitehall 21 off *April*, 1720.

"Cusin,

"I congratulate you heartily upon the birth of your son. I wish my lady a safe recovery and all healthe to the childe. I thank you for the compliment of his name and assure you as I have ever been a true friend to the family so I shall ever continue to do you and yours all the particulars that lie in my power for nobody shall ever wish your prosperity, and the good of your family more than I shall do. My wife [second] gives your lady her humble service and I hope next summer they shall be known to one and other. My service to Lord Elibank and all the good family. I hope your father will do all in reason and justice that can be expected of him. I am cusin your true friend and servant, Annandale."

Sir James died in 1772.

His eldest son, James, the fourth baronet, was born about 1719, and educated at Leyden. He married a widow, Mrs Merrick, née Louisa Coleclough, and was a lieutenant-colonel in the army, and M.P. for the Burghs; but chiefly noted for his good nature, his excellent qualities as a landlord, and for the suggestion of the first bridge over the Esk.

As an M.P. he brought in a Bill to regulate the sale of flax and wool, and acted as chairman of many committees. Dr John Moore, father of the hero of Corunna, described meeting him at a party at Hoole's, where Samuel Johnson was a guest, when a case was being tried by the House. Johnson inquired if the Baronet was going to hear it. Sir James said he should not, for he paid little regard to the arguments of Counsel at the Bar of the House. The author of the Dictionary asked, "Why?" "Because," was the reply, "they argue for their fee!" "What is that to you, Sir," said Johnson, "you seem to confound argument with assertion," and he proceeded to explain the difference. Some of his admirers applauding, surprised the old man, who added, "Sir, the illustration is not mine, it is Bacon's."

In his father's lifetime Major Johnstone, when quartered at Edinburgh, had a sad duty to perform. A rumour was started that seventy Highlanders, enlisted for Lovat's regiment, were to be drafted into a Lowland corps, so they refused to embark for England. They must have felt very strongly about it, as a Highlander was sentenced a year before to 1000 lashes for mutiny, and was only let off on condition that he would serve beyond the seas; but the General Commanding ordered five officers and 200 of the Fencibles, under Major Johnstone, to march to Leith, where they found the Highlanders on the shore ready for action. The Major drew up his detachment so as to prevent escape, and the orders he must obey were translated into Gaelic by the sergeant, but the answer was they would neither surrender nor lay down their arms. One Highlander, trying to escape, was bayonetted, and a fierce battle began. As the Highlanders had only a few charges they lost over forty in killed and wounded. The rest were taken prisoners, while the Fencibles lost two killed and one wounded, besides Captain J. Mansfield. A court-martial on the survivors, many of them badly wounded, condemned them all to be shot, and they were already drawn up for execution when a pardon from the King was announced, as two of them had been distinguished under the Duke of Cumberland in 1746. One fainted away, and the weak, shattered condition of all is described as exciting so much sympathy that it would not have been safe to carry out the sentence.

From some lines in an epistle to Robert Graham, only found in one edition of the Poet's works, it appears that Sir James assisted Burns in his pecuniary difficulties :—

> "What Whig but melts for good Sir James,
> Dear to his country by the names,
> Friend, patron, benefactor.
> Not Pulteney's wealth can Pulteney save
> And Hopeton falls, the generous brave,
> And Stewart bold as Hector."

William, Westerhall's third son, was educated for the Scottish Bar, and entered it in 1751. In 1762 he was appointed Secretary to the Poker Club in Edinburgh, but he removed to London, when he married the heiress of the first Earl of Bath, whose large fortune obliged him to take her name, Pulteney. That the fourth son, George, born 1730, a man of strong character, a bold and noted duellist, was early sent into the merchant service is not surprising—whipping having been almost abolished as a punishment for youth in Dumfriesshire since the tragical death of his connection, young Douglas—but it was not unusual to let a boy learn seamanship on a merchant vessel, the only training he had before qualifying with a very slight examination for a commission in the Navy. When George Johnstone passed for lieutenant, Feb. 2, 1749-50, he was described as *apparently* twenty-one, as having served six years at sea, part of the time in the merchant service, and the rest in eleven different ships under different captains. Yet he had distinguished himself notably in the *Canterbury*, under Captain David Brodie, at the attack on Port Louis, March 8, 1747-48, when he boarded a fireship and made fast a chain by which she was towed off clear of the squadron. He was also in the *Lark*, with Captain John Crookshanks, on her meeting with the *Glorioso* on July 14, 1747, and on leaving her is said to have challenged, fought, and wounded Crookshanks, who had refused to give him a certificate. In Oct. 1755 he became a lieutenant, and was appointed to the *Sutherland*, from which he was moved the next year to the *Bideford*, on the West Indian Station. While in her he is said to have killed the Captain's clerk in a duel. On Feb. 22, 1757, he was tried by court-martial for insubordination and disobedience, but was only reprimanded in consideration of former gallant behaviour; and was advanced to post rank in 1762. He injured his foot and ankle at Chatham while waiting for the arrival of the *Hind*, to which he had been appointed, and kept his bed twelve weeks, so was superseded and placed on half pay.

In 1763 he was appointed Governor of West Florida, which had been ceded by Spain, Colonel Grant having been put into East Florida. As the nomination of two Scotsmen was severely commented on by an organ of the press, Johnstone wrote to challenge the writer, who did not come forward, and on threatening some one connected with the paper he was bound over before a magistrate to keep the peace. He fought a duel with Lord George Germain, but neither was hurt. At that time, through his brother William's interest, he was M.P. for Cockermouth, and in 1774 for Appleby.

In 1778 Johnstone was one of the Commissioners, which included Lord Carlisle, for adjusting affairs with America, but he is said to have offended the American members by offering a bribe, and Congress passed a resolution that it was incompatible with its honour to hold any manner of communication with the said George Johnstone, especially upon affairs in which the cause of liberty and virtue were interested. He was obliged to resign; yet he appears in the Biographical Dictionaries of distinguished Americans, having been Governor of Florida, in which capacity he gave very prudent advice as to the dealings of white men with the natives. He was a ready speaker, and attacked abuses with characteristic vigour; in one instance the payment of large salaries for small special services easily performed and cutting down the scanty pay of the men who really did the work.

In 1780 Johnstone was made Commodore and Commander-in-Chief of a small squadron, to be employed on the coast of Portugal, with his broad pennant in the 50-gun ship, *Romney*. The next year, with a squadron, he was sent to convoy the East India merchant ships as far as the Cape and to attack it. He seems to have been surprised by the French fleet and did not gain the complete victory it was hoped that his ships would have secured. The French got first to the Cape, after which it was almost impossible with the means at the command of the General and the Commodore to make the intended attack. But five Dutch East Indiamen came in their way. Johnstone secured four of them and returned with his prizes to England in his own ship, leaving the rest of the squadron to go on with the troops (which were to have assisted in the attack on the Cape) to India, except H.M.S. *Isis*, which had sustained some damage. He put its captain, Evelyn Sutton, under arrest. This involved the Commodore in trouble to the end of his days. Captain Sutton, deprived of a share of the prize money in addition to this reproach, brought an action against him for false imprisonment, and obtained a verdict for £5000 damages. In a new trial an appeal was dismissed; in a further trial the verdict was reversed, but the House of Lords confirmed it. The Governor did not live to hear the final judgment, and Sutton never got the money awarded to him.

Governor Johnstone married Charlotte Dee, and carried on the direct line of Westerhall, being great-grandfather of the present Baronet. His wife, after his death, married Admiral Nugent.

John, born 1734, the fifth son of the Laird of Westerhall, was the founder of the House of Alva. He went out at the age of sixteen to Fort William or

PLATE X.

JOHN JOHNSTONE OF ALVA, 1734-95.
(WESTERHALL).

Calcutta as an artillery officer (*History of Bengal Artillery*). Some time after his arrival he fell ill, and owed his recovery, under Providence, to the care of an elderly lady, Miss Warwick, the daughter of a deceased East India merchant, who took him into her house, and having no near relation except a brother, whom she believed to be dead, she adopted the youth as her son. She died soon afterwards, leaving him all she had. As it was over £100,000, Johnstone retired from the Service, and meant to go home and buy an estate in Scotland. He was waiting at an inn in Calcutta till a ship sailed homeward, when he met a new arrival, Captain Warwick, and, attracted by the name, made inquiry, and found that he was the long-lost brother of his benefactress. When sure of his identity, and that he had no idea his sister had left anything, Johnstone told him that she died rich, and had made him her trustee till her heir was found, so that now he would hand it over to the rightful owner. When Warwick learned the real facts from the Will he offered to divide the money with Johnstone, but this offer was refused, and Johnstone gave up the idea of going home, and took a clerkship in the H.E.I.C.S. His brother, Patrick, had also a post in Bengal.

The conditions of life in India were very different to the present day. The French and Dutch had large possessions there, and were our rivals in the influence they exercised over the native rulers. In Bengal the Companies paid rent to the Viceroy of the Great Mogul; and among a peacefully disposed people the British population were all traders, with a small military force. Mere boys went out straight from the severe discipline of the eighteenth century schools and found horrible Asiatic punishments inflicted by the Mogul's officials, and bribery and corruption rampant. It was not strange if they imbibed some of the views of the place, and the modern ways of counteracting the baneful influence of the climate were not understood. That an angry Englishman suffering from the loss of his baggage should write to a native Prince and order him to impale the thieves is impossible now. It seems to have surprised no one in 1768.

The Viceroy of Bengal, who was our friend, died in 1756, and was succeeded by Surajah Dowlah, his grandson, a boy of eighteen, who, finding that a rich native he wanted to plunder was protected in Calcutta, marched with a large army against Fort William. The news of his atrocities preceded him, and the Governor and Military Commandant escaped; the fort was taken, and 146 British captives were shut up on a tropical night in a dungeon 20 feet square. The guards looked through the air-holes, mocking their sufferings, and only twenty-three survived. Among the corpses drawn out in the morning was that of Patrick Johnstone, Westerhall's sixth son. He was buried with his comrades in a pit hastily dug; and it was only, thanks to the female relatives of the Nabob, that any of the survivors were released.

John Johnstone is mentioned as one of the fugitives collected at Fultah—the port where a few British ships took them on board. His name is among those saved at Dacca. In a letter, dated in 1765, to Lord Clive he exculpates himself from a charge of disclosing confidential transactions, preferred against him by Governor Drake. In this letter he says he had been "remanded to the artillery, his former" occupation, and served with the army till 1765, when he returned to Calcutta. The date is, however, uncertain.[1]

To return to 1757. Clive received the rank of Lieutenant-Colonel in England, and arrived in Bengal with a punitive force. He reached Plassey. The French had joined the natives, and the combined force seemed overwhelming. With Clive's army were 100 artillerymen, eight 6-pounder guns, and two howitzers, commanded by Captain Jennings. Johnstone volunteered to command a large field gun, and kept back Meer Jaffir, who, with a native force, was advancing nominally to join the British. Meer Jaffir had accepted bribes to separate a large force from Surajah Dowlah's army and bring them over to Clive. But on the eve of the battle he made no sign that he would keep this promise, and was believed to be prepared, if the British faltered, to join the victors. Johnstone probably acted in accordance with instructions or with well-founded distrust in keeping him back, while Clive felt it was convenient to accept Meer Jaffir's excuse, and to place him, as his tool, on Surajah Dowlah's throne. The great treasures of Bengal, now at Clive's disposal, were the chief source of the wealth which he and some of his followers obtained.

Johnstone's obituary, in the *Gentleman's Magazine*, states that "he was chief of the province of Midnapore during the arduous contest with the Nabob Cossun Ali Khan," as well as a prominent member of the Bengal Council. The Warwick episode is a proof of his upright character, and the simple life he lead when he came back to Scotland was very unlike the ordinary idea of a returned East India magnate.

Clive went back to England, for the second time, in 1760, and passed a year in seclusion on account of his health. Reports of insubordination among the native soldiers and princes reached the East India Directors, and he went back in 1764 with new regulations and fresh men, whom he formed into a Committee, to be superior to the ruling Council of Bengal, which consisted of his old colleagues. Up to this time the Company permitted its officials to receive payment from the natives, and to increase their slender stipends by trade and presents. All this was to be changed. He found that Meer Jaffir was dead, and replaced by his son, Najamud Dowlah, and that the Council had exacted from the young Prince twenty lakhs of rupees. Clive vigorously attacked the members, and showed that the new regulations declared this practice to be illegal. As he had recently received the thanks of the Houses of Parliament, an Irish Peerage, and a grant of £300,000, Johnstone, who was his chief opponent, naturally reminded Clive of the money he had himself accepted from Meer Jaffir, thereby establishing a precedent, and that no censure had been suggested for it. Meer Jaffir had also left Clive £70,000, but Clive made use of this legacy to found the Pension Fund for Retired Officers in the Bengal Service, and their Widows and Orphans.

Owing to this dispute with his chief Johnstone retired from the Council, and returned to Scotland with £300,000. He is said to have spent about a

[1] Buckle's *Bengal Artillery*.

ninth of it in the Alva, Hangingshawe, and Denovan estates. He was little more than thirty, with three brothers in Parliament, and they did not let the matter rest. He had also a friend in Holwell, one of the survivors of the Black Hole, who, in a pamphlet to refute "criticism on historical events," speaks of "Mr Johnstone's spirited and sensible letter to the East Indian Proprietors affording the strongest support to his reasons, for by that Gentleman's indefatigable labour it appears that in the district of Burdwan only he had increased the revenue to the annual value of £116,727."

Scotland was very unpopular at that time in England, partly owing to the Rising in 1745. This was seen in the opposition to Lord Bute. In the present difference public opinion went with Clive, and the Committee which was appointed by the House to inquire into East Indian affairs would have collapsed for want of a plan if it had not been supplied by Governor Johnstone, who pointedly directed it against Clive himself. In a very long and dignified speech Clive defended his own conduct, and said that, when he thought of the rooms full of gold, diamonds, and other treasure which he had passed through, and which victory had placed in his power, he could only wonder at his own moderation. According to Sir C. Wilson in his *History of India*, he was answered by "Governor Johnstone in a speech of great violence," declaring that all the evils that had arisen were the natural result of Clive's action when Governor of India (March 1772).

Eventually the House resolved that Clive, as Commander-in-Chief, had received large sums of money from Meer Jaffir; but when it was asked to affirm that Lord Clive had abused his powers, and set a bad example, the amendment was rejected, and Wedderburn moved that "Lord Clive did at the same time render great and meritorious service to his country."

This was passed without opposition, but Clive, in bad health, never seems to have recovered from the annoyance. It has been thought that it was the cause of his unhappy end, but James Johnstone, of Worcester, who had prescribed for him some years before, maintained that, when suffering from acute Indian liver, he had been ignorantly advised to try the wrong Spa for his disorder, which had consequently produced extreme depression and temporary delirium. He had also for some time past taken opium for sleeplessness.

John Johnstone, returning to Europe, lived quietly on his beautiful Scottish estates till he was elected M.P. for the Kirkcaldy Burghs. This took him occasionally to London, but country pursuits seem to have been his chief interest. He was left sole executor to his brother, the Governor, whose affairs were in a very complicated state. He married Elizabeth Caroline, daughter of Colonel Keene, and niece of Sir Benjamin Keene, Minister at the Court of Madrid, and of Dr Keene, Bishop of Ely. Their only son, James Raymond, married, June 20, 1799, Mary Elizabeth, sister of Sir Montague Cholmeley, Bart., and the only daughter, Elizabeth, was the wife of James Gordon of Craig.

John Johnstone of Alva died Dec. 10, 1795, aged sixty-one. His brother,

Alexander, a lieutenant-colonel, died *s.p.* 1787. He is mentioned in this letter from his eldest brother to their father :—

"Dearest Sir,
"Brother Alexr. was quite recovered when the last ships came away, but excessively chagrined at being left behind. A gentleman of his acquaintance told me that he was more disordered in mind than body. All the Knights of Nova Scotia have been applying for grants of the lands mentioned in their patents on record in the Parlt. House, Edinr. If you could get yourself served heir male to Johnston of Elphinstone I will get you your grant, and without your being at one shillings expence will put at least £1000 in your pocket, providing your 100,000 acres (one share) lies near a navigable river; at any rate it will do much more than pay the expence.

"George, I believe, will get a government. I am told I shall get rank. I ever am, dearest sir, your most affectionate and dutiful son, Jas. Johnstone.
"*March* 1, 1763."

Captain Gideon Johnstone, another of Westerhall's sons, married the celebrated Mrs Jordan, when she was still a girl acting at Leeds, about 1779. He was the only admirer who led her to the altar, and when, in her last lonely and poverty-stricken days in France, she called herself Johnstone, it was the one name to which she is believed to have had any legal claim. He had probably met her first when she was acting in Dublin and Cork, but, as he died abroad, she continued to act with the stage name of Jordan. She was the mother of the Fitz Clarences and the ancestress of the Duke of Fife.

Of Sir James Johnstone's daughters, Barbara married Lord Kinnaird, and Charlotte married James Balmain. Both left descendants. The adventures of another daughter, Margaret, form an interesting chapter in Burke's *Family Romance*. She was married to David, Lord Ogilvie, the eldest son of the Earl of Airlie, and induced her husband to join the banner of Prince Charles in 1745 on the ground that, so long as his father remained at home, he perilled neither rank nor property by heading the clan. She kept him up to the mark by riding with them to Culloden, and took charge of a led-horse in case her husband should want it during the battle. Towards the end of the day he rode up to tell her all was lost, then mounted the fresh horse, and reached the coast in time to catch a Norway fishing boat, by which he escaped through Denmark to France, while his wife, stupefied with fatigue, anxiety, and disappointment, was taken prisoner.

Several ladies shared Lady Ogilvie's prison in Edinburgh Castle, but were all released while she was detained, because "so much mischief had been done by women taking an active part in the Stewart cause, and persuading their husbands to join when they would otherwise have stayed at home, that it was necessary to make an example of the one who was foremost in rank and influence." She was tried and condemned to be executed in Edinburgh in six weeks; but it seems probable, from the unusual length of time allowed, that a remission was expected. She anticipated it by leaving the prison disguised in

PLATE XI.

MARGARET JOHNSTONE, LADY OGILVIE.
(WESTERHALL).

her laundress's clothes, and at Abbey Hill found horses and baggage waiting for her. Thence she proceeded by easy stages to Dover, seeing everywhere a caricature supposed to be herself, with the reward offered for her capture. She joined her husband, who had entered the French service, but died in France when only thirty-three. She left two children—David, Earl of Airlie, and Margaret, who became the wife of Sir John Wedderburn, Bart.

Two little sisters, Elizabeth and Henrietta, died young, but another Elizabeth lived to old age, a favourite with her younger relatives, to whom she was known as Aunt Betty, and with a large circle of friends. At that time the ladies of a family were still allowed to use the Scottish accent, though with boys it had to be checked if they were to enter public life. Dean Ramsay relates that Miss Johnstone was extremely indignant when, on the death of her brother, his widow proposed to sell the old furniture at Westerhall. As she described it, "the furniture was a' to be roupit, and we couldna persuade her. But before the sale came on, in God's gude Providence she just clinkit off herself." She came into possession of Hawkbill, near Edinburgh, and died there. When dying, a tremendous storm of rain and thunder shook the house. In her own quaint, eccentric spirit, and with no thought of profane or light allusions, she looked up, and, listening to the storm, quietly remarked, "Sirs, what a night for me to be fleeing through the air."

CHAPTER XVIII.

YOUNG GALABANK VISITS FRANCE—SETTLES IN WORCESTERSHIRE—LORD LYTTLETON—GALABANK'S WRITINGS—CORRESPONDENCE WITH HIS FAMILY—MANY DEATHS—THE MINISTER OF MOFFAT—LETTERS TO AND FROM THE WESTERHALLS—LORD JOHN JOHNSTONE—DEATH OF THE LAST MARQUIS—HIS AFFAIRS—GALABANK'S FAMILY.

JAMES JOHNSTONE, the eighth in descent from William, first Baron of Newbie, was born at Annan, April 14 (O.S.), 1730, and named after his father's only brother, who died in London the previous year. He was the fourth son and ninth child of Galabank and his wife, who survived all their sixteen children, except this son, his elder brother John, and Isobelle, the widow of Adam Murray of Belriding.

James's first recollection of his mother was being tenderly nursed through an attack of small-pox, and the prayers she offered up by his bedside for his recovery. He matriculated at Edinburgh in 1747, and spent his vacations in study at Annan, Moffat, and in Dr Blencowe's house at Whitehaven, where he learned the composition of medicines and their effect. During the Session at Edinburgh, he studied anatomy under the second Munro (who was also instructor to the first anatomist of his time, John Hunter), besides attending some of the best medical lectures of the day. Edinburgh was famous, as she is now, for her medical science, but there were only sixty students in all in 1750. Her schools were the resort of Dutch, Polish, Swedish, and Danish pupils; yet it was still such a disadvantage in England to be a Scot, that Dr St. Clair from Edinburgh, settling in Dover, was not consulted by a single patient during six months, and then left England altogether to take up a Professorship at Leyden, which he had been offered a year before.

Johnstone graduated simultaneously as M.A. and M.D. in 1750,[1] and before he was twenty-one was admitted a member of the Royal Medical Society of Edinburgh. Only his brother William, who was still younger, and himself were ever appointed at so early an age. A month later his brother, Edward, gave him a letter of introduction to an old college friend, Mr Coburn, a merchant in Dublin, as the ship, in which a place had been secured, touched

[1] Oliver Goldsmith took his degree the next year. Dr Darwin, Dr Withering, and other eminent Englishmen had Edinburgh degrees.

there between Whitehaven and Havre. Edward spoke of James as being on his way to continue his studies in Paris. " I am sure I have your good wishes," he adds. "The business of physician is crowded here, your advice and countenance to my brother is what I may expect; and if in the course of things he should possibly want any money on his return, will you answer his application to the sum of £10, £15, or £20, and I will repay it. May I hope to see you at the Manse of Moffat," etc.

It was autumn when James went by diligence from Havre to Rouen. His diary shows the novel impressions of the most civilised and luxurious kingdom in Europe on a youth who came from the country of all others where an educated class was most hardily reared. The religious paintings in the churches especially interested him, for he had never seen anything like them before. He comments on the extraordinarily bold language of the Press and its rebukes to Royalty, under a Government professing to be an absolute despotism, but he dwells little on the evils disfiguring its administration and its cruel punishments,—and, no wonder, for only $17\frac{1}{2}$ miles from his home some of the followers of Prince Charles Edward were executed four years before, with the special barbarity which the English law adjudged for high treason, and their decaying heads still hung on the gateway of the old Castle at Carlisle.

"Having proceeded sometimes by land and sometimes by the barges on the Seine to Poissy," he writes, "I there quitted a very mean man to whom I was introduced at Rouen, and who was going to take the degree of doctor of physic at Rheims. He condescended to ride a horse I hired to carry my portmanteau; and I was heartily tired of his company and services.

"At Paris, I rejoined Dr Monro and Dr Colin Drummond, and by my banker Mr Isaac Vernet of Geneva, I was introduced to Daniel le Clerc, grandson of the famous author of the *History of Medicine*, and to several medical students. By the usual means and premium, I obtained permission to visit the patients in the Hôpital de la Charité, and there I was given the opportunity of becoming a practical anatomist. [This was impossible in Britain at that date, except by stealth.] M. Faget was the chief surgeon. I attended practical demonstration of the most important branches of medicine and surgery, as well as the lectures of M. Ferrein in Anatomy, and M. Rouelle in Chemistry, which enabled me to compare the lectures and doctrines of these two gentlemen with those of Macquair on Chemistry, and Winslow on Anatomy, at Edinburgh.

"I visited the different magnificent libraries in this city on the days they were public, particularly the Bibliothèque Royale, and that of the Abbé of St. Germain, where I consulted several different works, and viewed various curiosities, also the exquisite paintings in Natural History in 100 volumes, carried on at the expense of the Kings of France, from the time of Louis XIV. But I chiefly read and made extracts from papers relating to medicine in the later volumes of the *Memoires de l'Academie Royale des Sciences*.

"At other times I viewed the magnificent palaces in this Royal city and its environs; the noble entrances; and the ready permission given to see these palaces, and the gardens, was pleasing and striking. The pictures in the Palais Royale belonging to the Duke of Orleans, those of Rubens in the Luxembourg, and the immense magnificence of Versailles, and the Royal State of the Court of France, to which I was often witness, alike impressed me, for I had seen nothing to approach them. The rural seats of Marly and St. Cloud, and the machine contrived to force up the water to supply the basons, and innumerable jets d'eau, which crowd the gardens; the grand review of the household troops of France by the King in May, 1751; and the enchanting palace of Chantilly, made me return to England inclined to compare what I saw in London less favourably perhaps, with objects so interesting by their novelty and grandeur."

Six years later the fascination which France had exercised on the young man was rudely dispelled by the atrocious tortures and execution by wild horses to which an unhappy lunatic, who had scratched the King with a penknife, was condemned by the highest Court in Paris, and which was approved by the votes of all the Royal Princes who heard the sentence. It sent an appalled shudder through this country, and alienated a large number of Britons permanently from any sympathy with the Royal House of France. The day had gone by when such deliberate barbarities were approved even by the French populace.[1]

Johnstone observes in his journal that nowhere did authors write so much about liberty as in France, where it was less apparent than in any country he had ever read of. He gives some statistics worth quoting, as it is difficult to find them elsewhere. Paris was two leagues in length, and enclosed 960 streets, containing 22,000 houses. The streets were lighted by 5532 lanterns. Most of the houses had four or five storeys, and many six or seven. There were 750,000 inhabitants, amongst which were 150,000 servants. The town was divided into twenty different quarters. His studies took him into the Hotel Dieu, a magnificent hospital which was said to have been founded in the year 660, and enlarged and enriched by many Kings of France down to Henry IV. The spacious wards and passages, so important for its salubrity, were counteracted by the narrow streets and houses which crowded it on three sides; but 8000 sick were tended there by the Sisters of Mercy. The Monastery of the English Benedictine monks was in the Faubourg St. Jacques, near the Grand Chatelet and the great Market.

The Code Frederick was promulgated in Berlin while Johnstone was in Paris, and was the subject of much discussion, a desire being openly expressed that it should be naturalised in France. "The Parliaments of Paris," he writes, "have ever been remarkably firm in using the few privileges which still belong to them by the permission of their sovereigns. As they have the liberty of making representations against such edicts from the throne as they judge inconsistent with the fundamental laws of the Kingdom and prejudicial to the welfare of the king and people, so their language on these occasions is not

[1] It was by no means the only horrible sentence which was carried out in the reign of Louis XV.

wanting in frank patriotism, and they have even administered something like a lecture and a rebuke to the reigning Prince." He gives a specimen.

Johnstone left France in July 1751 for Dover, and took the coach to London, by Canterbury and Rochester. London seemed small and poor compared to Paris, but then it only reflected the difference between the two kingdoms. England, with Wales, contained a population of 7,000,000, and France more than 30,000,000, while our Indian possessions consisted of scattered Colonies, often threatened by the French and Portuguese; we had no footing in China, the Mediterranean, Ceylon, Eastern Canada, or the Cape, but we could boast of possessions in the West Indies, and of a large American Colony, now part of the United States, already anxious to part from us in the middle of the eighteenth century.

Johnstone stayed a short time in London, and went by sea to Newcastle-on-Tyne, and thence to Annan, passing on the road several parts of the remains of the old Roman wall. He found his brother just returned from Worcestershire, where, having preached in Kidderminster at the *Parish* Church, he was convinced that the young physician would be very well received, for there was none nearer than Worcester. The constant prevalence of fever, and the death of 103 children in six weeks of the preceding year, in Kidderminster, from a complaint now known as diphtheria, and which the apothecaries could not cope with, had made the need urgently felt. Dr Priestley, well known in Worcestershire, had praised the medical thesis which James wrote in Latin for his medical degree. He was only twenty-one, but set off at once for the scene of his future work, and arrived at Kidderminster, Sept. 12, 1751. It was his ambition to practise in Edinburgh when Kidderminster, with his assistance, should be restored to health.

The road from Annan to Worcestershire in the middle of the eighteenth century was a well-beaten track, the first 17 miles being the chief difficulty. People either went by Longtown to Carlisle or by the sands, crossing both the Solway and River Esk. On the south bank of the river, opposite the fording place, there was a little Public-house forty-five years later, with this inscription on it:—

"Gentlemen, here take a guide
To either Scotch or English side
And have no cause to fear the tide."

With £20 in his pocket, young Johnstone travelled on horseback, with a led-horse to carry his baggage, the cheapest way of travelling at that time, except on foot, and between the Esk and Carlisle it was an agreeable ride along the east bank of the Eden. The approach to the Cumbrian city was very fine, the two branches of the Eden, crossed by bridges of seven and four arches, appeared in view, forming a triangle, and the Cathedral and Castle lying to the south-east. He halted at Preston, then redolent of the same sinister memories as Carlisle, and where the ghastly heads of Scotsmen were seen over the prison entrance. The journey from Annan to Kidderminster, through Birmingham, was 219 miles.

When Edward Johnstone was in Worcestershire, two months before, Lord Hopetoun, living at Raehills, near Moffat, gave him an introduction to Sir George (the first Lord) Lyttleton of Hagley, which lies 4 miles from Kidderminster, a poet and a Cabinet Minister, although, according to his undutiful son and heir, all England was shaking its sides with laughter at his mismanagement of the national finances. However that might be, he was an important friend, and it was acting on his suggestion that Edward advised his brother to settle in the Midlands. Finding a congenial literary spirit in the young Scot, the noble poet inserted one of Johnstone's compositions, "Ferdinand Cortez and William Penn," in the volume he published anonymously, *Dialogues of the Dead*. In the fifth edition three more were added from the pen of Mrs Montagu. After Lyttleton's death, Johnstone published anonymously in 1788 *A Second Dialogue of the Dead between Ferdinand Cortez and William Penn*, bound up with a reprint of the first, and with an essay on the abolition of the slave trade, to which the second dialogue referred. The copy in the British Museum has the name of the author in his son John's handwriting.

The essay on the slave trade, written more than a generation before its abolition, and when Johnstone was fifty-nine, was entitled "A Scheme for the Abolition of Slavery without Injury to Trade and Navigation." The author quotes from a speech of Mr Wilberforce the terrible statistics of the loss of life and excessive suffering entailed by this trade, and observes that "the first thing to be done is to remedy the evils of the passage, by limiting the number conveyed in ships of various sizes; and the heaviest penalties to be exacted when the number is exceeded. The disposal of the newly arrived slaves in the plantations should be with the provision that from 1790 they were to become servants with indentures only for a term of years; the term to be settled by Act of Parliament. That all born after 1790 should be free born subjects of Great Britain, maintained and placed out as apprentices at the expense of the owners of the estates to which they do and shall belong; but that all these servants, infants, and apprentices should be protected and regulated by and under the laws now in force for the regulation of poor apprentices and others in Great Britain."

Sir William Pulteney, one of the most eminent of British barristers, wrote to Johnstone, Feb. 27, 1788: "As to what you say about the negroes there is a great deal more difficulty in doing what could be wished in the matter than appears at first sight. I could state a great many objections which seem to me unanswerable to the plan you suggest, but perhaps something may be thought of. The matter is under the consideration of the Board of Trade who are taking evidence, and obtaining every species of information."

The first of Johnstone's publications (in 1756) was on the fever epidemic, which, with diphtheria, was almost chronic in Worcestershire. He had seen diphtheria, then called putrid sore throat, and a sort of low typhus in Annan and its neighbourhood, where he had learnt the absurdity of treating it in ill-fed people with the lowering system and profuse bleeding, which was still the English as well as the Scottish practice in all kinds of fever; and he adopted an opposite method. The Annandale fever of which he speaks is alluded to in the *Old Statistical History of Scotland* as being brought by the wild people from the mountains when they came to beg in the towns, and that they contracted it from the scantiness and bad quality of their food, particularly from eating the flesh of animals which had died of disease or old age (not entirely extinct in the Highlands). The *New Statistical History of Scotland* refers rather jeeringly to this statement, and asks, Who are these savages, and where are the mountains? Of course the high parts of Annandale, Nithsdale, and Lanarkshire are meant. Scott answers the query about the "savages" in *Guy Mannering*, where he describes the numerous gipsies amounting, early in the eighteenth century, "to 200,000 people, recruited, as they had been, from others whom famine, oppression, or the award of war had deprived of the ordinary means of subsistence." Fletcher of Salton adds : " There were besides a great number of poor families very meanly provided for by the Church boxes, who with others, living on bad food, fall into various diseases."

Johnstone dedicated his book to Dr Whytt, in Edinburgh, and Dr Thomas Shortt, late in Sheffield. Coming from a country where cattle and sheep were reared for export, and where, as usual in exporting districts, very little of that produce was eaten among the inhabitants, who chiefly lived on porridge and fish, he thought the working class of Kidderminster, employed in weaving carpets in their small unventilated rooms, consumed too much meat in proportion to their other food, and that the meat was frequently tainted and unwholesome, and therefore sold cheap to the poor. In Dumfriesshire there was a provision in the indentures of apprentices that they should not be expected to dine on salmon more than three days in the week, as by the time salmon reached the apprentices it was very stale.

Johnstone supposed it was the same with meat in Kidderminster, but later in life he thought this early essay was too much mixed with theory. The food of the poor in England was different to the present day. Wheat was always dear, and often unattainable when there was a bad harvest. A Parliamentary report, forty years later, showed that in Dorset, Pembroke, and several other counties in England the labourers for years ate no wheat, but lived on barley bread, and in Shropshire, Cheshire, and Lancashire potatoes were the daily fare, and bread a luxury for Sundays. As to bacon and meat, they hardly knew the taste of it. Imported tea, coffee, cocoa, and sugar were beyond their means, but they made tea out of various British herbs. Johnstone gave fruit to counteract the disposition to fever—rhubarb when it was in season, and dried currants and raisins when there was nothing else. He overthrew the theories he had learnt as a student, adopted antiseptic methods—fumigated the patient's room and the surrounding passages with mineral acid vapours, ordered the windows to be kept open in the sick room, gave bark (quinine), port wine, and acids very liberally in every stage of life, insisted on scrupulous cleanliness, allowed copious draughts of cold water, barley water, and other fluids, and refused to bleed, or to prescribe debilitating remedies. His book was to advocate this novel practice.[1]

The fine weather enjoyed in 1753 seemed to restore the district to health, but the wet summer of 1755, followed by a mild, wet winter, ushered in another outbreak of fever with increased severity. Early in November the great earthquake which laid Lisbon in ruins occurred. Johnstone says it shook the whole eastern limit of the Atlantic Ocean, and was felt from Africa to the remote coasts of Europe. "Precisely at the time which corresponded with the general commotion, in a profound calm, the waters of Severn and some fishponds in our neighbourhood were tossed and agitated in a manner which astonished the spectators." In another book, on the second outbreak of fever, he refers to the illness of Queen Anne's son, the Duke of Gloucester, whose death caused as much dismay in the three kingdoms as that of the Princess Charlotte in 1818. He imagined from the rapidity with which it ran its course that it was the same, so fatal to the children in Kidderminster in 1750. Dr Ratcliffe was called to see the Duke the day before he died, and predicted that he could not live through the next day. He said the two attending physicians deserved to be whipped for their treatment of the Royal invalid. It would have been interesting, adds Johnstone, if this celebrated physician had told us the course he himself would have pursued if summoned earlier.

Johnstone's books excited more interest in London than in the country, but they were severely criticised in spite of his success. They made a favourable impression on Lord Lyttleton, who had rather ignored him since his imprudent marriage. He invited him to stay at Hagley to meet a select party of some of the leading men of the day as well as Mrs Montagu, with whom he and his children became very intimate later on.

A young physician who refuted the traditions of Boerhave, in which he had been educated, and of his followers, Munro and Cullen, and thought his own observations the best guide was certain to be opposed, and Dr Cameron and Dr Wall, of Worcester, old-fashioned practitioners, were great rivals. Cameron and MacKenzie, both Scots, were the earliest physicians to the Worcester Infirmary when it was opened in 1745. Cameron's father was an "outed" Episcopalian in Edinburgh. John Warner, Bishop of Rochester, a theologian and antiquarian, founded four scholarships in 1666 at Baliol College for Scotsmen, but provided that when the scholars had taken their degree "they should return to Scotland in Holy Orders, that there may never be wanting men to support the ecclesiastical establishment of England in the North." When William III. abolished Episcopacy the trustees allowed the youths to choose their own professions, and Cameron was the first to profit by it. He partially adopted Johnstone's views, and is described by Johnstone as being sometimes right, often wrong, and always positive. Dr Wall was a local man, combining medicine with art, and is generally mentioned with

[1] It is needless to say this is according to modern lights, but Johnstone advocated it sixty years before it was generally adopted in this country, and still later on the Continent.

Johnstone as the discoverer of the efficacy of Malvern air and water. He married a Sandys, first cousin to Lord Sandys, and Cameron's wife was a well born Roman Catholic.

"The reputation of a physician," wrote Johnstone, "is in some proportion to the size of the place he lives in, besides the Worcester physicians had for a long time been in high repute in the provinces. Their opposition stimulated me to support my theories by study and diligent observation; and as my success was obvious I acquired fame."

It was possibly a remark in one of his brother Edward's letters that he never meant to marry, and should leave to James the task of carrying on the line, which encouraged the last to ask if their father could allow him enough to make a marriage settlement. He wished to propose to a young lady "whose family was known to his parents, and as a most desirable connection, and in antiquity had no superior in Scotland." He seemed certain of being accepted if he could make a settlement. He wrote to Galabank, who, as usual, left the decision to his eldest son, who wrote :—

"Moffat, 20 *March*, 1753.

"I was favoured with yours and one to your Papa, which I delivered. . . . Your father, who is aged and infirm, devolves the solution of it on me, and I am divided between regard for you and tenderness for my younger brethren, to whom I must consider myself as the guardian. . . . I advised with two of my friends and confidants, and both yours very sincerely, one of them being my lord's agent (Ronald Crawford), who is known for his good heart and just sentiment, and can you doubt of his regard for you? Yet he was utterly against the notion. . . . 'Your father,' he said, 'has other children to whom he behoves to do justice. The doctor's education has already stood him £700, and yours not much less. While the doctor remains unmarried he is one of the children of the family. Prudence requires that he be assisted till he is established in his profession; but when the second or third son of a family marries he sets up a separate interest, no longer being of much benefit to the root from which he sprang' (this is given in Scottish law terms). As it is, the younger children's portions may be cut off without encroaching on the family estate, and you seem as likely to inherit as any of us. If my father and I were called off, or if I married and left no child, you are next in the succession. . . . Yet such is my regard for the worthy and pious family to which the young lady belongs, that I would do any reasonable thing to make the matter easy if it is what you both wish. I hope there may be no lasting difficulty, and that with the views you have in life, which are worth something, and your industry and attention to your profession you may still succeed.

"I am always, dear doctor, your affecte. brother and most humble servant,
"Edward Johnstone."

Another letter on the same subject crossed this. Edward again told his brother that the education of both had cost their father £700 for each, and that the younger children had a right to expect the same. He reminded his junior of his youth and good prospects, for he had been well received in Worcestershire by the County families, and was already thinking of taking a house in Worcester. If he waited a few years he could make a settlement for himself without drawing further upon their father, and that to encroach on his estate was the last thing either of them wished.

The lady's name does not appear in these letters, but a later one shows that she was one of the eight children of Sir Thomas Kirkpatrick of Closeburn, who died 1771. Yet before the end of the year the young physician sent money to his brother to arrange a settlement in the way of life insurance with an Edinburgh lawyer, for he was married on Sept. 10 at Lower Myton, near Kidderminster, to Hannah, the daughter of Mr Henry Crane, an old-established carpet manufacturer, who also owned a small estate, which he farmed, in the neighbourhood. It was "came, saw, and conquered" with the young lady; and her father, finding his daughter's affections were engaged, was first persuasive and then threatening, for, with the easy confidence of youth drawn into an intimacy with a lively family, Johnstone had lamented that some years must elapse before he could marry his Scottish love. He in fact found himself engaged and hurried to the altar before he was at all prepared for it. His parents sent their blessing in an affectionate letter, and his father and Edward added the advice about being a good husband, which was certainly followed during forty-eight years of married life.

His friendship with the Crane family began the previous January, when the eldest son of the house died at the age of twenty-seven, and, either from grief or from the same complaint, the bereaved mother lay for several weeks on what appeared to be her death-bed. Johnstone was called in, and her recovery, under Providence, was attributed to his skill and care. The first time she was able to attend her usual place of worship was made the occasion for a thanksgiving service combined with a delayed funeral sermon for her son. It was preached by Mr Fawcett in the same church which had been served by her grandfather, Richard Serjeant,[1] who was evicted from the living of Stone, in Worcestershire, in 1662, when, with others of the clergy, he signed a petition to Charles II. asking him to close two "lewd" theatres opened in London after the Restoration, and much patronised by the Court. In most of those cases the dismissed ministers set up a little conventicle of their own, and their children drifted into Nonconformity.

The Cranes originally came from Norfolk, where they were related to Sir Richard Crane of that date, and are found in the Register as inhabitants of the

---

[1] "At Stone was silenced Mr Richard Serjeant, formerly my assistant, a man of such extraordinary prudence, humility, sincerity, self-denial, patience, and blamelessness of life that I know not, of all the years that he assisted me, of any one person in town or parish that was against him, or that ever accused him of saying or doing anything amiss. So that though many excelled him in learning and utterance, yet none that I ever knew, as far as I could judge, in innocency and sincerity, which made him beloved of all above many abler men."— Baxter, p. 93, Part III.; and earlier, p. 88, Part I.: "He became a solid preacher, and of so great prudence in practical cases that I know few therein go beyond him, but none at all do I know that excelleth him in meekness, humility, self-denial, and diligence. No interest of his own did ever seem to stop him in his duty," etc.

PLATE XII.

JAMES JOHNSTONE OF WORCESTER, M.D., 1730-1802.
(GALABANK).

HANNAH, WIFE OF JAMES JOHNSTONE OF WORCESTER.
Died 1802.

Foreign of Kidderminster as far back as Queen Elizabeth; but with the disabilities under which Nonconformists laboured at that time it was a social mistake for Johnstone to connect himself with the Cranes and Serjeants. Edward made their acquaintance when he visited Kidderminster, and thought them desirable friends for a young man far away from his own people, but he changed his opinion, to judge from a letter to his brother, Oct. 1753.

In March of the previous year Edward wrote to James that their sister, Isobelle, then about twenty-three, was married on the 10th to Mr Adam Murray of Belriding. "She had other offers, but had satisfied herself that this was the best. Murray seemed a good sort of man; he was well connected, belonging to the same house as Cockpool and Lord Stormont, and had £1200 of his own, which, with the £200 she received from her father, would enable them to live in a cheap country, where his little estate produced all the necessaries of life."[1] He was thankful to see her settled, as his own health had become very precarious, and he gives his brother the particulars in confidence. He hoped some day to ride over to Bewdley, where James was then living, as he wanted a thorough change; but this journey never took place, for every year increased his work and responsibilities.

On May 8, 1752, Adam Murray wrote to thank his brother-in-law for a kind letter on his marriage, and hopes that he may soon be able to offer him the same congratulations, "for I think the noble name of Johnstone seems to be on the decay, so I want you to improve your line. I heartily wish you good success in that and all your undertaking. You have done much considering the short time you have been in England."

On June 10, 1754, Edward wrote to James that their sister Murray had just given birth to a daughter, and soon congratulations were sent by post at the advent of James's son and heir. Mrs Murray wrote an affectionate letter prophesying that, as Edward seemed disinclined to marry, this little James "would be Galabank." The grandparents both wrote, of course delighted, and Galabank, also referring to Mrs Murray's baby, fervently thanked Providence for all His mercies to them. On Nov. 27, 1754, he adds: "Your mother has sent by Mr Marschal a table cloth and half a dozen table napkins; they are Dantzic damask, marked with your mother's name for our daughter-in-law, and a pair of silver buckles and a silver spoon for your son, our grandson. We are all pretty well in health, and are always glad to hear that you are; also your wife and child. Your affectionate parent, John Johnstone."

The bride of seventeen developed into a matron of a very shy and retiring disposition, an excellent wife and mother, but averse to society, and preferring to remain at home when her husband and children visited their friends. Much taken up with her own relatives, she never accepted the invitation to visit her parents-in-law at Annan. She thought it would be soon enough when she had to live there, for her husband always hoped to end his days in his native land.

[1] The tenants held their plots with the provision that they should work a certain number of days for the laird.

In a letter to his brother, James alludes to the family of his first attachment. "I was much touched," he wrote, "by Sir Thomas Kirkpatrick's message. I had thought that I must have passed entirely from his recollection"; and again, on Nov. 9, 1755, he wrote: "A few days since (Oct. 8, N.S.) my wife was happily delivered of another son. As the first bore his father's name, his mother and grandmother desired that he might be named after Mr Crane's son—who died lately, in the flower of his age—Thomas Crane, and that is his name. I had indeed thought of another on our own side, but could not refuse so tender a request; and I have the greater pleasure in giving it, that it is the same as Sir Thomas. It was very obliging of him to write the letters I had the honour to convey, but under the rose the persons they were directed to have been but little my friends if they have asked anything of Sir Thomas on that account. It would be using him well to let him know it, otherwise it is better to take no notice of the matter. Upon the experience of four years' practice in the world I have found the friendship of men a variable thing, but most gratefully acknowledge the goodness of God in raising me up such as have been unexpected supports and helps. I live easily, but I don't know that I am likely to be rich."

Johnstone alludes in his letter to a slight he thought he received from one of the Johnstones, who passed through Bewdley without seeing him, and the coolness of Sir George, afterwards Lord Lyttelton. With regard to the first Edward expresses surprise, "as he is courtesy itself, and we never lose an opportunity of extolling him, but do not let it prejudice you against his family, who wish you every possible success, and are worthy of your homage"; and as to the second: "A fortnight ago Mr Bower, author of the *Lives of the Popes* and the *Historia Literaria* (with whom this time four years I became acquainted at Carlisle when I was attempting to negotiate your business),[1] on his way to Edinburgh did me the honour to call on me. He and his lady were so good as to breakfast at the Manse, and to promise to make it their lodging in case at any time they should be again upon the road. I had seen in the papers that 'Sir George Lyttelton, cofferer to his Majesty,' had named 'Mr Bower to the office of Master of the Buck Warrants, a profitable post.' This gave me room to speak with Mr Bower about the nature of his office, etc. He told me he was, at Sir George's invitation, to spend some weeks with him at Hagley, where a new house was begun.

"I took the opportunity to mention you, and gave Mr Bower your address, and took his and his lady's promise to call on you. Mr Bower is a great

---

[1] Archibald Bower, a Scot, born 1686, educated at Douai, and at one time adviser to the Spanish Inquisition. He became a convert to Presbyterianism, as he alleged, from having witnessed the horrible torture of two innocent men, one of whom died, the other became insane; but the last eight years of his life were spent in refuting the charge of being an emissary of the Jesuits throughout his career. Anyway, he returned to the Roman Faith and then became an Anglican, but seems to have induced others to join the Roman Church. In 1748 he was made Librarian to Queen Caroline. Lyttelton took him to visit Lord Chatham, and obtained the post alluded to for him. Besides other works he edited the *Universal History*, where his acquaintance with the writings of the Jesuits is shown in the history of Japan, Tartary, etc. He married the niece of Bishop Nicolson. Died 1766.

favourite of Sir George, and a sensible, well-bred man. I told him your father-in-law was in the political interests of that family, as I certainly believe I have heard. Mr Bower, I am persuaded, will do you no harm. . . . Having been lately employed at Mouswald on a Sacrament occasion, Mr M'Millan[1] of Torthorwald was my colleague. His son, Surgeon M'Millan, who has attended the Physical College at Edinburgh for two years, is now in hope of work. I think the young gentleman pleads your acquaintance, as his father does that of relation to you. The favour they ask is, if there be any town or village where a young man might probably shine as a surgeon apothecary, you will oblige them much by soon letting them know. . . . Your scheme for building rather frightens me. You may not always wish to remain in the same place, but if it is necessary, build,"[2] etc. On May 8, 1754, Edward wrote from Edinburgh of the death of "old Mossop," and adds : "The General Assembly now sits. The Earl of Hopetoun, our Commissioner, makes a more splendid appearance than all his predecessors. Each day of the Session he has been supported by several of the nobility, and sometimes by the sixteen representative lords, among them the Dukes of Argyle, Hamilton, Queensberry, Athole, etc. The street between his lodging in the Bank Close and the High Church always lined with six companies of the Castle Regiment, beside the City Guards, who, with their standards, etc., do him honour as the representative of the Sovereign, and the ceremonie and entertainment falls not short. We have not much business. . . . I leave this place in about eight days for Moffat." He promises to send a printed sermon he had preached before the Lord Chief Justice and Lord Minto at the opening of the Circuit Court in Dumfries, April 12, 1754, entitled " Truth and Justice."

"22 July 1754. I expect by the return of the post to hear that Lady Betty Hope, eldest daughter to our Commissioner, the Earl of Hopetoun, and grand-daughter to William, Marquess of Annandale, the toast for beauty, good sense, and modesty of all the Caledonian fair, is married to Lord Drumlanrig, eldest son of the Duke of Queensberry, as yesterday the proclamation of banns would be finished. Last week I had the honour to kiss the bride's hand on her way through Moffat, after paying a visit under her Papa and my lady's protection to her future domains. This is truly a good marriage, and unites in one interest a very great number of families of estate and influence." On Aug. 13 he writes that Lord and Lady Drumlanrig were coming to Moffat on their way to Tinwald House, the property of the Duke of Queensberry, "and we are not without hopes of keeping them prètty much in Scotland, which is sure to be agreeable to the Hopetoun family." The same letter alludes to " Henry Home's (Lord Kames) curious philosophical pamphlet," and the answer to it by Dugald Stewart. The uncle sends his affectionate compliments to his sister-in-law and nephew, adding : " It shall not be long before he has something from the Land o' Cakes, but of what kind is uncertain, and it is unlucky that

[1] One of this family was the original of Scott's Maxwell of Summertrees in *Redgauntlet*. Scott had met him in his youth. (*See* Chapter V.).
[2] James did build, for his own residence, a substantial house with grounds outside the town.

except perhaps once a year I never see any person who could be depended on to carry anything, and then often he has no place for it except a small mouse hole in the crowded bags of some very thrifty merchant." Shortly afterwards the uncle bought a silver spoon for 45s. for the child, and found a trusty messenger going South, who, however, would not take it lest he should be robbed on the road! The same letter relates how he had been asked to meet the Drumlanrigs at Lord Hopetoun's, and once more had the honour of kissing the hand of " Caledonia's fairest daughter."

Only two months later Lord Drumlanrig was killed by the discharge of his own pistol on his way to England. Edward Johnstone alludes to it as accidental. His bride only survived him a year and a half, and, leaving no child, the Queensberry dukedom (after being held by a distant relative, who died in 1810) merged into that of Buccleuch, the Marquisate going to his cousin, Sir Charles Douglas.

On Nov. 10, 1755, Edward wrote: " I congratulate you on the exploit of Major-General Johnson[1] [in Virginia], for his name originally is Johnston, whose ancestors in the time of Oliver Cromwell were a colony from this country. What a pity that so fine an officer had it in his power to do so little. We are told that we have twenty to one in that part of the world more than the French, and yet in every action we might almost say sans hyperbole that les messieurs are twenty to one against us. This being his Majesty's birth-night, I have ordered a bonfire and ringing of bells, etc., and my people are instantly drinking the loyal healths and 'Success to brave General Johnston,' and at every round they hurra, 'Up with the Johnstones.' Our poet says, 'Johnston has done what Braddock failed to do—routed the Indians, scourged the faithless crew.' And we all wish that you were there to cure his wound."

The *Life of George Washington* states he was a major in the Colonial Militia " under the unfortunate General Braddock." James's letter on the subject crossed his brother's. " In America the safety of our Colonies seems to depend upon New England, and General Johnson has retrieved the respect to our arms which Braddock lost by his inconsiderate rashness and obstinacy. A

[1] Sir William Johnson, as he spelt his name, held a Colonial commission. He was born in Ireland in 1715, the son of Christopher Johnson of Warrentown, Co. Down, and his wife, Anne, sister of Admiral Sir Peter Warren, who took up a large tract of land near the Mohawk river, in British America, and made his nephew the manager. Johnson, by firmness, justice, and honesty, acquired a greater influence over the six united Indian tribes than any Briton had done before. In 1748 he was appointed General of the New York Colonial Forces to oppose the French on the north frontier. Peace intervened, but he was ready to act when the war broke out again In 1755, with these Indians, aided by provincial Militia, he defeated the French, who also had Indian allies, at Lake George, and saved the colony from invasion, being wounded in the hip early in the action, but remaining in the field. He "went far to counteract the ill effects of Braddock's defeat" (*Dict. Nat. Biog.*). He received the thanks of both Houses of Parliament, a grant of £5000, and a baronetcy. In 1760 he led the Indians, under Amherst, to the advance on Montreal and the capture of Canada, for which he received a grant of 100,000 acres. There he lived, in baronial and pasha-like style, improving his estate. He died at his house, near New York, in 1774. His son, John, who claimed knighthood when he came to England—the old privilege of a baronet's heir—commanded Colonial troops on the British side during the Revolutionary War. The baronetcy is represented by his descendant.

powerful faction is forming before the meeting of Parliament to oppose the payment of the subsidy his Majesty has stipulated with the Czarina [Elizabeth] for her troops for the protection of his Majesty's German dominions. The disagreeable observations of some leaders in the House of Commons upon a late altercation in the Ministry is the cause of this designed struggle in which we hope the Pilot of our State [Pitt] will not be so much disconcerted as to draw off his attention and the force necessary to be exerted against the common enemy." Nov. 9, 1755.

Shortly after this Adam Murray and his wife both wrote to Johnstone about Murray's health. He treated the symptoms as lung disorder, contrary to the local opinion. On Feb. 25, 1758, Edward wrote: " I ought to have acknowledged yours long ago. I am sure the sequel will be my apology for I have been taken up with the affairs of the late Mr Adam Murray of Belriding who died on Monday Dec. 26 of an abscess in his lungs which carried him off in not more than 6 weeks from the first appearance of a cough—he and his family looked on it as only a common cold as in appearance he was a clear strong man till within 10 days of his death. [The usual symptoms and sudden death are then detailed.] Dr Gilchrist was sent for, but in his dialect it was all over. He was a very sensible honest gentleman and by his death his family lose a prudent husband and an indulgent father—the youngest infant is nearly 8 months old. The eldest is in her 5th year. They are fine children—were inoculated with the smallpox about the middle of their father's illness for all the while it was only looked on as a cold; and he had the satisfaction to see the eldest recovered before he died. The day after, the youngest was seized with a feverish disorder (this was three weeks after the inoculation), next day about 20 spots appeared. Dr Fergusson the surgeon who attended pronounced this to be all the smallpox she would ever have. Your nieces Marianne and Bessie are both pretty, the eldest has the complexion of her father, black eyes, etc. but poor little Bessie is a veritable Duchess of Hamilton[1] only a great deal more vivacity than her Grace. After all inquiries I think the estate will be clear to your sister and her children as Murray's personalty is equal or superior to the debts, but you may believe I have had uncommon anxiety and fatigue with these matters. He was a member of a very ancient family.' He ends as usual with compliments to his sister-in-law and the boys, the youngest, born the previous September, having been named after himself.

Galabank might have foreseen that this child would carry on the male line of his family, for he was so pleased at his birth. " I received your letter," he wrote, "with the good account of your wife and the son you have named Edward. The next day I sent the letter to your brother. If please God he be spared he will be of use to one of your sons in his education. We will welcome one of your sons and shall do for him as if he were our own. I pray God to spare you and your wife to be good parents and a blessing to your three sons, and that He will bless them and make them comforts to you. We are all

[1] Miss Gunning.

in good health; but your brother's weakness returned upon him three weeks ago. Let us hear frequently and write 'by way of Kendal and Chester.' I hope when your son comes here this country air and the colder climate will agree with him. We are all greatly pleased with the name of Edward. Your mother anticipated it. I hope he will prosper the better, and that God will preserve him in his young and tender years. Your affecte father, John Johnstone, Nov. 2, 1757."

On Oct. 29, 1759, Edward wrote from Annan about their mother, whom James had prescribed for during a temporary illness, and adds: "With regard to —— I could not with any countenance speak of him to the friends whose interest he had in a manner cast at his feet—but I have tried another interest and am promised that as soon as Parliament sits down a member shall be warmly applied to for a commission. Meantime if by your English interest you can do anything, if a commission can be got, I'll consent in that case to your drawing on the family to the extent of £50 sterling. I waited at Moffat many weeks hoping to have seen my Lord Lyttelton. He did not pass Moffat at the time of my being there. One night in this town an equipage with six horses drew my attention. It was the Scots Earl of Glenorchy. Lord Hopetoun told me he should either see Lord Lyttelton at Buxton where his Lp was to drink the waters or Lord Lyttelton would come to Hopetoun house. I expect to see Hopetoun in a few days and then I shall know if his Lp was at Hopetoun House or not. . . . The report at this moment is that Monsieur Thurot with a squadron of 6 or 7 ships of the line with transports containing several thousand men has sailed to the north of Scotland and that an English Admiral is in pursuit.[1] A little time will discover this, but the gallantry of the Scots will not suffer them to come to your distance. We should have done better had we been put on equal terms, and permitted a national militia." The political allusions in these letters are all in cypher, Latin, or French.

The person vaguely alluded to seems to be Adam, Galabank's fifth son. He was started as a partner in Manchester with a "considerable merchant," recommended by a Scottish relative; but was robbed by highwaymen just outside Manchester of a fairly large sum of money, and a little later his partner absconded, leaving joint liabilities which had to be defrayed by Adam's share of the assets. He set off to London where he hoped to hear of his partner, but did not keep his family informed of his address, and for some weeks they did not know it. During this time Captain James Johnstone, the heir of Westerhall, kindly wrote to his brother, Gideon, a lieutenant in the Navy, who was staying in Park St., Grosvenor Square:—

[1] The fleet was defeated at Carrickfergus, Feb. 28, 1759, by Captains Clements and Logie. Thurot was really O'Farrell, a Jacobite agent. Lord Lyttelton arrived at Raehills with his son, Tom, and it is amusing to read the opinion of this young Etonian of fifteen, formed from the Scots he met (including several Johnstones) at Moffat, Edinburgh, and Inverary Castle. "Their virtues," he wrote to Mrs Montagu, "are courage, prudence, economy, and hospitality, the last universally practised. Good breeding the Scots all possess, and there is not in the north such a character as the English country squire, whose whole life is spent in the laudable customs of hunting, swearing, drinking, and sleeping. Scotch ladies are very handsome and very sweet tempered, etc."

"Dear Brother,—You was so obliging as to promise to take aboard a young Gentleman of my recommendation I presume so far on your kindness to me that you will exert yourself in favour of this Gentleman your namesake in getting him with you if he chuses the sea or in desiring good Sam Swinton to carry him to Colonel Coote if he likes Bengal, and in doing everything else in your or my power to serve him. If he can think of anything Mrs Johnstone can do you will show her this. I am ever my dearest Gid most affectely yours, Ja. Johnstone, Sunderland, Jany. 21, 1759."

Gideon offered a junior officer's place on his own ship, but Adam could not be found before the fleet sailed. John, afterwards of Alva, was already distinguished in the East India Company's service. He was twenty-five at this date, and two years before commanded a gun at Plassey. Some time earlier he wrote to James at Worcester to ask him to find out the price of any Scottish estate on the market. To him Edward applied, March 1759:—

"Dear Sir,—Your eldest brother and my worthy friend Capt. James Johnstone was so good as at my request to write several recommendatory letters in favour of a brother of mine who proposes to go to the Indies. The gentlemen he particularly wrote to were Colonel Coote and Major Robert Gordon now going on an expedition to that [your] part of the world. In the hurry the Capt. was then in and by a misfortune he since met with of having his right arm hurt he could not conveniently write, but with the letters delivered to me some time ago by a private hand he commanded me to write to you myself in obedience to which I presume to take that liberty. [After detailing Adam's misfortunes, he adds.] The Lad nevertheless is of good character and has both integrity, activity and resolution, and as he is a *Johnstone* remotely related to your own family I humbly recommend him to your protection. I am now the Minister at Moffat and though you were but young when I had the pleasure of seeing you I am confident you will remember me and permit me without flattery to tell you that the goodness of heart which your face indicated and the strong resemblance you early bore to your uncle Colonel John Johnstone gave promise of your future fortunes such as I thank God on your behalf as a youth whom I loved, has happened, and which I hope may continue till you return after a series of success a comfort to your friends, and an honour to your Native country. It is on good authority I tell you that Sir James, my lady, and your other relations in this part of the world are well. Without further words I think I can expect everything that is reasonable from your kindness. Humbly recommending you to Him who is the confidence of all the ends of the earth I am my dear Sir your most obedient and affectionate servant, Edwd. Johnstone.

"To John Johnstone Esq. at Calcutta."

A year later Edward wrote to his friend, the heir of Westerhall (whose good fortune, he told his brother, in marrying a most estimable lady with £600 a year was not even equal to his merits), March 16, 1760:—

"Dear Captn.,—I received with pain last Friday night by our friend Mr Hoggan the first accounts of your having actually sailed for India where may God protect you, and whence may you return with Health and Honour or to borrow your own words with the plunder of many a Nabob. The unfortunate Lad I did myself the honour to write to you about was absent when my letters arrived at London so lost the recommendations you kindly gave him. As he has been unsettled ever since the moment I heard you had sailed for India I tried to find him, not doubting that if he proceeds to India and can be so happy as to arrive where you are that you will consult his promotion as much as if any friend were present to remind you. Your friends in this country are all well. Hoggan had the pain to hear that his eldest son who by the death of the former had become Captain of his ship has been carried into Martinico after a brave resistance. I doubt not you will pay them measure for measure if the wishes or prayers of any person for the safety of another avail, then will you be safe and happy and return to the old Thorn-tree in all the splendour of triumph and success. That this may happen whether I live to see it or not is again the earnest prayer of Dear Capt. Johnstone your most affectionate and obliged humble servant Edward Johnstone.

"*P.S.*—I have enclosed this letter to my brother Dr Jas. Johnstone desiring him to ship Adam for the East Indies where I doubt not under your protection he will do well."

James had already offered to take his brother and find a place for him, and Edward replied that with his family (he had now five sons) it was too much to expect; but before this letter could reach India Adam obtained a commission in the Scots or North British Brigade.

For the first time since 1745 an order came to recruit 2000 men in Scotland for the British Army. The Johnstones were anxious to show their loyalty, and Edward, at Moffat, and his brother, Richard, spared no pains to induce suitable persons to join. Adam was sent with a portion of these recruits to Aberdeen to embark with his regiment for Bremen, under orders to serve with the Hereditary Prince of Brunswick and the Hanoverian troops on the side of Frederick the Great in the Seven Years' War. Adam's last letters to his father and brothers only a few days before his fatal wound are rather touching, as he seems conscious of the trouble he had caused his relatives. To James he wrote from Brimar Lake, May 29, 1760:—

"Honoured Sir,—Perhaps it may not be disagreeable to you to hear from me as I am now a great distance from you—we landed here a few days ago all in good health and spirits and began our march for Munden immediately, a place where our baggage is to be lodged in His Majesty's German dominions, and then to proceed to the Grand Army. In my last I was a little confused and now I am in haste and have only just time to correct my last concerning the agent of the Regiment,—that is I did not tell you where he lived. It is Channel Row I think. I hope you will be so good as to get the money I wrote for and send it to John Calcraft Esq. in the above place, Westminster, and advise me of it by a letter and direct to me as before in Prince Ferdinand's Army in Germany. Pray write soon and oblige honoured Sir your humble servant, A. Johnstone."

He was only two years younger than James, whose medical books he had taken some trouble to make known to the doctors in Manchester, and in his letters from thence addressed his brother as Hon. brother. The extra stiffness showed there had been coolness. But a little later the gallant Scots strewed the ground of a lost battle near Wesel with their dead, including Ensign Johnstone. They were engaged from 5 A.M. till late at night, and this defeat, in which so many Scots suffered, was a final argument with Lord Bute, Prime Minister to George III. (who had just ascended the throne), when he advised his Sovereign to withdraw from the support, financially and otherwise, which Great Britain had hitherto given to King Frederick of Prussia against Austria and Russia in the Seven Years' War.

As a rule we make little of our reverses, and an account of this battle is only to be found in private letters and biographies; but it was a very hard campaign. The Marquis of Granby, who led the British contingent serving under Prince Ferdinand, wrote to the Duke of Newcastle (who succeeded Lord Bute) in Jan. 1761: "In Germany it is not like in Flanders, one battle, tranquillity for the rest of the campaign, with great plenty of all sorts of wine, etc. and good and early winter quarters."

Isobelle Murray wrote the particulars of their brother's death from his wounds to James (Dec. 14, 1760), and said that if she had had her way he never would have been sent out there; but like a true Presbyterian she adds that it was "the will of Heaven that he should have been unhappy a while and we should be disappointed," and then fills up her letter with ordinary news. Their eldest brother was gone to Edinburgh to get a sermon printed which he had preached on the death of the King (George II.); Richard, the youngest of the family, was spending the winter there studying for the law; Agnes, their sister, was still keeping her brother's house at Moffat; and John, "le pauvre incapable," seemed to miss the lively Dick, but they had got a new manservant who could play, and that was a mercy for him. Dr Gordon was going to England, and Sir William Maxwell of Springkell had died not long before, and poor Mrs Turner had lost her son. "Your old friend Mr Jaffray, who preached in Annan the day before you went away from it, is minister of Ruthwell, my old parish. Our father and mother are both a little tender, though they are as well as people of their years can expect; my father is much troubled with a cough, but can walk and go about his affairs as much as ever he did. Your friend Mr Spearman is in Edinburgh about that book, and poor man has much need of all that will arise from it. I am very glad you have served him with so many subscribers. He often speaks of you with great pleasure. Your parents send their blessing to you and your family, and my daughters desire their duty to their uncle, aunt, and cousins. May God long preserve you all for blessings to one another is the constant prayer of your affectionate sister and humble servant, Isobelle Murray."

Letters passed between the brothers about an occupation for Dick, whom Edward described as "a lad of much spirit and sense who cannot be put to anything mean," and his sister, "as very sober, and very promising." His parents wished to keep him at home. James suggested an appointment in Jamaica, or medicine. To stay at home would end with the estate being divided to provide for him, and it was only valued at £2000 sterling in 1750. It was a subject which gave James some uneasiness. He was an exile from home, working to support himself and his family; why should not Dick do the same? But after his experience of the West Indies for his sons no wonder that Galabank declined an opening there. In 1755 Edward wrote to James :—

"I came to Annan about 10 days ago at your father's request. He fancyed himself ill, but is I think quite well. I came in time to prevent his making any settlement dishonourable to himself and hurtful to the legal and proper representation of his family and this I made no scruple to tell him that failing his heir-at-law ought to devolve in the natural course on the next, setting aside those whom debility and incapacity have rendered unfit. And I hope I brought him to think more justly. I don't chuse to divide a small estate nor to settle it on the youngest and most inexperienced Branch of the Family; yet property is so precarious here that some there ought to be to look after it. I have put our Father on a plan of giving all suitable encouragement to his youngest if he behaves himself but I could not consent to divide it on his behalf, as I want the estate to go to the heir at law and what I mean by that you'll understand but keep this to yourself. Old people must be treated with tenderness nor will they be wrong if it is not by false glosses and insinuations." He then refers to current politics, and alludes to his own failing health, ending with, "now dear Esculapius I hope Mrs Johnstone and the boys are all that you and I most sincerely wish them, and offer them my most respectful and affectionate compliments." Later he reminds his ambitious brother that his numerous sons will be against his ever taking up a title.

At the end of a letter, in answer to one from James asking him for information about Scottish estates, and after saying (1755) that the Duke of Queensberry gave £18,600 for Tinwald, and that Alva is in the market, he says that, without having any children of his own, he has the care of a large family, and, combined with his clerical duties, is worn out by riding backwards and forwards to Annan and Ruthwell about the Galabank and Belriding estates. The living of Moffat was one of the best in Scotland, and the incumbent filled inspectorships and other offices connected with the Kirk, which alone involved a good deal of travelling. He had "become a dissenter," he wrote, "in England," as he was directed by the Presbytery to supervise the restoration of a Presbyterian Chapel in Cumberland, and to collect the money. His reports on various subjects were printed by the Presbytery, which also published several of his sermons.

With reference to Galabank's settlement of his estate, and having been over to Annan to arrange a tack of two farms—Closehead and Gladsmuir—to a Mr Nelson, Edward wrote to James "it would be sinful and vain to suppose that I shall much longer direct these matters." He had been prohibited by Dr Rutherfurd from reading anything whatever—even the Bible—and had engaged an assistant to preach for him. He tells his symptoms to his brother, as to "a medical father confessor." The levy of recruits which provided "many stalwart sons of Mars, if you in England will but find officers fit to command them," and the administration of the oath of fealty to the young King George III., in which, as magistrates, he and his father took their share, and other public matters, with the improvement in the health of Lord Annandale, who was now able to play at whist with his mother every night, the loss incurred by his own father through a dishonest agent, and the necessity of providing another home for his unfortunate brother, John, filled up his latest letters.

"I congratulate you," he wrote, July 5, 1760, "as I do all my countrymen on the behaviour of the troops at Quebec, mostly Scotsmen and headed by a young, but brave and sharp-sighted officer. Your remotences will perhaps make you unaware that General James Murray is youngest brother, or youngest but one to Lord Elibank consequently is a brother of Lady Johnstone of Westerhall and I have been told by good authority has all the peculiar vivacity of her family and a happy mixture of penetration and solidity, shown in his masterly letter to Pitt."

On Jan. 15, 1761, less than five weeks after the news of Adam's death had arrived, he suddenly lost his sight, followed the same night by slight delirium, his mind running on the affairs of the Marquis and the Johnstones of Westerhall; and he expired the next day after only thirty-six hours' illness. His sister, Agnes, was with him. It was a terrible blow to James, too far off to attend the funeral, and he had thought his brother over fanciful about himself; but there was a very large gathering of friends and relatives when he was laid to rest in the old church, near the pulpit, at Moffat.

Among numerous letters of condolence on the occasion to Galabank one came from Captain (later Sir James) Johnstone of Westerhall, dated Hillington, near Lynn.

"*Jan.* 24, 1761.

"My dear Sir,—Would to God I could minister the least comfort to so worthy a Father mourning in the deepest anguish of heart, the best the most dutiful of sons. Permit me to mingle my tears with yours. I have lost a kind and affectionate Friend whose life and even his last moments was spent supporting the Johnstones. How tenderly must I feel his loss. How dear to me is his memory; who expiring wished me success and prayed for my welfare with his last breath. Alas my dear Sir I judge from myself what you must feel. May God of His Infinite Goodness support you under this heavy this unexpected stroke may you see all your other children flourish and multiply and may you never have cause to shed a tear is the wish and prayer of dear Sir your much obliged and most grateful humble servant, Jas. Johnstone. My best wishes to

Mrs Johnstone when you think it will be proper to make them and to all the rest of your Good Family."

Edward was insured in the Ministers Widows' Fund of the Church of Scotland, in whose books it is recorded that he died unmarried, leaving no children, and that his heirs were "his brothers and sisters, particularly Mr Richard Johnstone, writer in Edinburgh, to whom apply."

The allusions in Captain Johnstone's letter possibly referred to the differences between the Hopetoun and Westerhall families. Edward had done his best to act as mediator, as they partly arose from the friendship between the Westerhalls and the Dowager-Marchioness of Annandale, their near connection. The Marchioness had a charge of £1000 a year on the Annandale property. The young Marquis had attained his majority, and her second son, Lord John Johnstone, was elected to represent the Dumfries Burghs in Parliament when he was still only twenty. This took the young men to London, where they had inherited property from their grandfather, Vanden Bempdé, and, with the pride of a new Member using his own frank, Lord John dated from the Speaker's room in the House of Commons his receipt to Bryce Blair at Annan for £277, 4s., lent by the Presbytery of Lochmaben to the Marquis, adding in a second letter from New Bond Street, Nov. 19, 1741, his hope "that the good Harvest will make the tenants pick up, and that the rents and arrears may be got with more ease." There was one petition already before the House to unseat the Member for Westminster, but he hoped to be let alone. As an acknowledgment of the kindness that Dumfries had always shown to his family, and to himself in particular, he presented it with a picture of King William and Queen Mary, "who are of course particularly interesting to me," and added that he meant to do all the good he possibly could for the Burghs. But his career was cut short by consumption. The Marquis, who seems to have been very warm hearted, and not the born idiot that he is sometimes represented, took the invalid to the south of France, and wrote to Edward Johnstone as well as to his mother reports of his progress. But a new writ was issued for the Burghs of Annan, Dumfries, Kirkcudbright, Lochmaben, and Sanquhar in the room of Lord John, now deceased, Dec. 21, 1742. The Marquis visited Scotland the next year, and gave Edward Johnstone a Greek Testament which had belonged to his brother as a memento. His signature to the official paper presenting Edward to the living of Moffat was the last he affixed to any legal document, but a statute of lunacy was not actually granted till Feb. 9, 1747. In this it was stated that he was living in the Parish of Hammersmith, and, although enjoying lucid intervals, had been "incompos mentis" since Dec. 12, 1744; but it only applied to the English property, and there was a deadlock in the Annandale estate owing to the friction between the two families. The Marchioness's jointure was unpaid, and houses were falling to ruin in Moffat and Annan. At last, in 1758, Lady Hopetoun and her son, as nearest heirs to the Marquis, obtained the declaration of his lunacy in Scotland, and the second Earl of Hopetoun became curator of the Scottish property, a private Bill being passed to give him full powers. It was in virtue of that Bill that Newbie was a little later sold to Neilson, a member of an old local family, and Moffat provided with suitable accommodation for those who came to use its far famed medical waters. Captain Richard Vanden Bempdé, as his mother's representative, assented to it.

The Marquis lived till April 27, 1792, under the charge of a doctor in Annandale House, Chiswick, and was buried in a nameless grave in Chiswick Churchyard. A historical lawsuit disposed of his estates according to English law, as it was decreed that his long unbroken residence in England made him an Englishman, not a Scot. Hackness Hall and the English property went to his half-brother, Richard, an officer in the 3rd Life Guards, and the Scottish estates to the third Earl of Hopetoun. Of the £415,000 personalty, a third went to each of his half-brothers and to the descendants of his half-sister, Henrietta. Richard was created a Baronet in 1795, and an Act of Parliament annulled a clause in Vanden Bempdé's Will obliging the owner of his English property to assume the Dutch name after Johnstone. Richard's grandson was made Lord Derwent in 1881.

It does not appear that the doctor revisited Scotland till after his brother's death, but he went there in the spring of 1761. He was still hardly thirty-one, but had a very wide practice—a good deal by letter—and had made most of the experiments necessitated by his medical books, particularly those on the nerves. He disdained to follow the custom of the day and obtain subscribers beforehand, and it was a great deal of trouble and expense to circulate his books. His brother's published sermons, being criticised by the *Edinburgh Review*, were more remunerative. He had a house in Worcester as well as Kidderminster, and visited Lichfield, Tamworth, Sutton Coldfield, Bromsgrove, Solihull, Nuneaton, Stafford, Shrewsbury, Bath, Wolverhampton, Warwick, and Birmingham professionally. At the last place he made acquaintance with Samuel Johnson, of Dictionary fame, at his friend Hector's in the Old Square. Lord Chesterfield, Lord Hertford, Richardson (the novelist), James Boswell, Lord Clive, Mrs Foster, Milton's grand-daughter, Mrs Siddons, Sir William Pulteney, Governor Johnstone, and Lady Huntingdon were among many eminent people who consulted him. His mother wrote very anxiously in June 1759 as she heard he was ill and was afraid that, like Edward, he was killing himself with study; she begged him to remember that his health was more precious than the best book he could write. He did not neglect his old home. He was constantly asked to send some prescription for Beatties, Neilsons, Irvings, Hairs, and other families in and around Annan, and did it gratuitously; and his parents would see no local doctor for themselves, but relied entirely on him. His father once begged him to send no more presents but keep his money for his children. He often wished he was nearer, for it was a very tragical ten years. First his favourite sister, Elizabeth, dying of consumption. Edward, writing to him the opinion of the Carlisle physician that there was no hope, adds, "if you could write a letter to her it would so please poor Lizzie, and tell her anything about her little nephews or your wife to amuse her." Then the poor "Antiguan's" vagaries, alluding to his brother John, then Adam's difficulties and heroic end, Edward's sudden death,[1] and now Agnes, who had been with him spending her time between Moffat and Annan, could not recover from the shock, and was dying. All thoughts of pressing his father to settle his property so as to exclude John vanished when he arrived at home and saw the state she was in. He felt he could do so little, yet so much was expected from him.

He shared his post-chaise back to Kidderminster with a friend. In a letter which followed immediately, Richard hopes that "the noble squire and yourself arrived safely at Kidderminster and found your dear wife and family well. I got back," he adds, "on Sunday morning after a very disagreeable and fatiguing ride, for my horse tired several times and it was with the greatest difficulty I got into Wigton the night I parted with you and crossed over in the Bowness boat next morning. I found poor Aggie much as when you left. Dr Gilchrist has been sent for to this town and came to see her but she is weaker and can with difficulty walk from the bed to the fire and cannot now go out on horseback. She is very grateful to you for the care and concern you showed about her and sends her blessing to you all. Her distress makes me wonder if I can go back to Edinburgh this session or not. You'll no doubt write to her at once, it will please her and be a satisfaction to us all. Nothing has happened but old mother Blair is dead to the great grief of all concerned. Mrs Murray obeyed your orders about her children and they are now well. Remember us all most kindly to the good Squire and to Mrs Johnstone and your five boys. Your horse is recovering. I dress its foot myself every day. Your most affectionate brother, Richard Johnstone."

James found an overwhelming amount of business awaiting him, and Richard wrote again a fortnight later:—

"Dear Brother,—I wrote long ago, and we looked for news from you with great impatience, particularly poor Aggie would have been glad to hear from you before she dies. She is now extremely weak [he details her symptoms] and surely within a few days of her death. She fell away every day after you left us perceptibly and her cough is so violent she gets almost no rest, yet she bears all with a wonderful resolution. The other day she showed me her poor arm and said 'Dick, the churchyard worms will get nothing off me compared to what they had off old Mother Blair.' She speaks of death with the utmost composure and resignation. O doctor what severe shocks are these! The flower of our family to be cut off. I enclose a letter from Dr Gilchrist," etc. (June 19, 1761).

Then came another dated July 4: "My two last letters will have prepared you for this. Our dear Sister Aggie died on June 28 between 12 and 1 a.m. She was a perfect skeleton but retained her cheerfulness and resolution to the last. As death is inevitable it is a comfort to reflect that never was a girl so beloved, nor I believe more deserving. She is lamented by all who knew her.

---

[1] "She was then in the bloom of youth, spirits, and beauty," wrote James, "she was in every point of view an amiable and valuable relation, and a great loss to us."

GALABANK'S FAMILY

She was interred in the burial place of our family on Wednesday last. All the gentlemen in the country round attended her to the grave. Her death is a particular loss to our weak family, for she was a surprising fine girl. Our father and mother are pretty well. . . . Either of your Scottish boys [*i.e.*, with the family names] is desired with great earnestness. It would be the greatest comfort to the old people and to Mrs Murray and me to have one of them to represent their father and mother at Annan, and they bid me assure Mrs Johnstone and you that they will be as careful of him as if he were their own son, and you may depend upon Mrs Murray's care and mine. I should be very glad to visit you and Mrs Johnstone after the harvest, and carry back one of your pretty boys. God bless and long preserve you and your wife and children, to all of whom I beg you will remember me in the kindest manner. Yr. affecte brother and obedt. servt., Richard Johnstone.

"*P.S.*—A chaise and everything that could make poor Aggie's life agreeable was got for her."

Five months later Richard wrote from Annan: " Dear Brother,—I was at Westerhall the other day where I was most cordially received by all that good family. My Lady J. was vastly well pleased with the basket, she had not done admiring it when I left them [of Worcester porcelain]. They all inquired for you and your family in the kindest manner, and my Lady desired her hearty thanks for your pretty present. She will be extremely glad to hear from you. You must direct her letter to the care of the Postmaster of Carlisle. They did not know where Mr R. J. [of Hackness Hall] is. Hoggan says he is in Yorkshire but I will be able to send you the address, and Major Johnstone's after I get to Edinburgh. The Major is now there where I hope he will remain all winter. He is a very warm friend. I received your last packet some time ago, but have been so tossed about that I could not answer them. I am to set off for Edinburgh in a day or two. I have got John's confirmation and approbation of the settlement as strongly wrote out as possible and I think there cannot be the least doubt of their validity. I am obliged to trouble you with a piece of ceremony I did not expect, but such is the exaction of my Lord H—— that till you who are one of the executors give my father a full power to receive your part and discharge the same he will not pay it. [He encloses a form and describes how it is to be filled in and returned to their father]. The old Gentleman's eyes are rather tender but he says it is old age. Mr Gott was quite transported with the present you sent him. I dined with Mr Beattie's mother the other day. She spoke much of your friendship for her son. Tell Jamie I have not forgotten to write to him but shall do so as soon as I get settled in Edinburgh . . . your affectionate brother and sincere friend, Richard Johnstone."

The old people might well feel alarmed when any of their children were ill, and both wrote in some consternation, having heard that James was suffering from fever, in May 1762. In July his father wrote again to express thankfulness at his recovery. Richard was studying in Edinburgh. Would James advise him? They were hoping to see James at Annan, and that he would bring his son. This was little Edward. His grandparents particularly wished to see him on account of his name, recalling not only his late uncle but Galabank's father, who was still regarded with filial reverence. "I am sure Neddie must be a pretty boy," wrote poor Agnes not long before her death, "we all want to see him." Mrs Murray wished to effect a temporary exchange, and to take entire charge of Edward if one of her daughters might go to England and be under the care of her uncle and aunt. So Edward was taken to Scotland by his father, and remained there four years, when he was brought home lest he should pick up the accent, which was fatal to a career in England. Thomas wanted to join his brother, and wrote to his grandmother to show how well he could write; but he was viewed with less favour, having a Crane name, though he went to Scotland a few years later, and his amusing flow of conversation was appreciated by his relatives.

On Sept. 2, 1766, Galabank wrote to his son: "The man has come for Neddy in great haste to go with him in a post chaise. He is a very pleasant boy. I gave him 10/- to buy playthings. May the Lord bless you and your wife and all your children, and may He prosper you in your business." Besides Neddy, Henry, John, and Anna were added to the family. Richard wrote to his brother that their parents were particularly pleased at the two last, like Neddy, having been given old family names. Galabank adds in a postscript that there is a dearth of coffee in the county, as it can neither be bought in Annan or elsewhere.

James was over-anxious, his Scottish relatives thought, about the family estate, and in Oct. 1758 his eldest brother, in answer to two letters, waived the matter aside, saying he had not assurance enough to advise their father any further, as it was not in human nature to care to be hurried in these matters, and he went on to talk of Richard's future. He was having him educated in Scottish law, but as there was no opening for practice at home would his brother advise in the matter. James replied: Their father ought to set his house in order and do justice to his children for his own honour and the peace of the family. That if his elder was afraid of speaking in a matter of right and justice he hoped he would not fail to tell their father, as a message from himself, what he—James—thought about it. No one could be so blind as to think it unreasonable or unnecessary. This brought a severe letter from his mother, as if he had been ten years old. She said he distressed his father, who always meant to do him justice, and was uncivil to his brother Edward. There the matter rested till after Edward's death, when the invalid, whom Edward had observed "must be supported as a burden Providence has laid on the family," suddenly recovered, and was able to sign a resignation of his rights, as the eldest living son, and to come home.

It is evident by some of the letters in 1761-62-63-64 that things were not at first settled quite in accordance with James's wishes. But in 1762 he was impressed with his father's "great cleverness in the knowledge of business, and great steadiness in the disposition of it." He knew the old man had signed deeds with a lawyer earlier in the day, but it was not till late in the evening that it was given into his hand with the remark, "Son, I most willingly deliver you this deed, and I only fear that I shall keep you too long out of it." The deed was the usual resignation of the estate in favour of James, reserving the life rent, but with a small portion detached for Richard.

In March 1764 the old man wrote that his eyes were very dim so that he could only read large writing, that he was now seventy-six, and anything James and Richard agreed upon should be done. James must let Richard have all the stone he wanted from the quarry for the house property he owned; and his mother was hurt that he did not mention her. Again on July 29 Galabank thanks his son and young James for their letters: " I am glad you are restored to health for the sake of your family and your business in South Britain. All tolerably well considering everything. I shall send you some salmon as soon as I can get it. Let no business here trouble you. Let your son stay here till you come, and write always and affectionately to your mother. Give Richard your advice with respect to your wife and children. Bless all your sons and my little namesake and thank James for his letter. My eyes are so bad I cannot look into my writs, and no one shall till you and Richard are both here together. Farewell."

The tenants of Galabank's farms held them at a smaller rent on condition that they provided a certain number of days' work for getting in the landlord's harvest, for shearing, for loading hay, and for cutting turfs or peat to supply the landlord's house with fuel. This distributed all round did not come hardly on the tenants. The provision made in the lease of a public-house that it was to entertain soldiers for six weeks every year was in force up till 1765 on Galabank's lands, and probably much later. One of the farms rented by John Irving was bound to cut and bring in sixteen carts full of peat, and eight carts full of turfs every year. The tenants kept their own premises in repair. Sheets, blankets, and the material for clothes were all spun and woven on the estate. It was arranged that the lands should be feued to James, who wrote, Dec. 4, 1764:—

"My dear Parents,—I received long ago your letter and very lately the salmon, for which and for all favours I thank you sincerely. I have been somewhat long in answering your letter, but you who know the heavy burden which a large family entails upon the mind will judge of my cares who have that burden as well as many more arising from my business. It has pleased Almighty God to restore me to better health than I had in the spring and to preserve me though exposed to much danger in attending poor families here labouring under an infectious fever. I desired Mr Palmer to raise me a great quantity of quick in your garden in order to plant new hedges in your grounds. . . . I desire also that some day labourer may be employed to dig a trench between the thorns in the Galabank dyke next the road, and I desire that some of the hazel nut trees may be rooted up skilfully and planted in the spaces so as to complete some of the fence. This I hope will not be neglected and that some person of skill will be desired to direct the best manner of executing my design, which is part of a plan (of which I shall be able to judge of the success when next I see you) I have formed for fencing the Galabanks. I enclose two letters to be forwarded to Richard in Edinburgh. I sincerely wish him well and nothing can prevent me from doing everything in my power to serve him but his own folly. I can never be a friend to anyone who shall be so far my enemy and the enemy of the dignity to which your family may arrive, who shall try to impair or diminish the estate of Galabanks to its lawful successor, but all such views I hope will be no more thought of. Richard prosecutes his studies as he informs me with a view of being a chirurgeon rather than a physician, which last was my advice, but a life of action and business is not to be objected to in any way. I send you letters from my children. They would be glad to receive a letter from Galabank or any of his family. . . .

"I was more sorry to hear of the long hopeless illness of my cousin Jeanie Hair than of her death, which I hope and believe has changed her condition infinitely for the better. I condole with her brothers to whom present my kindest respects, and tell James Hair that I received his letter . . . and if I can have a clear view of the case and can in any prudent way be the means of extricating him from his difficulties I shall do it with my whole heart. . . . My wife sends her compliments to you and to my sister and her children, and wishing you all every happiness this world (how properly called a vale of tears) can afford I am with the sincerest duty and affection your dutiful and affectionate son, J. Johnstone.

"*P.S.*—I hope to amuse Galabank when I see him with a history of his family and memoirs of his ever respected son the Minister of Moffat, which I have in M.S. and which would make a pamphlet of a tolerable size."

Although money came to Galabank and more was owed to him, both his sons said he had the credit of being richer than he really was, and, according to his son Edward, he was surrounded by hangers-on and dishonest employés or agents, who preyed upon him, and he could not be induced to proceed[1] against a debtor. Edward had helped with necessary expenses, but before James would do the same he must be assured that his descendants would reap the benefit. Richard was offered a cadetship in His Majesty's Navy, and also a commission in the Guards, but declined both to please his mother. Not originally wishing to be a medical man, he gave up the law to study for it, as there was an opening for a surgeon in Dumfriesshire. Again urged by James, he took up medicine instead of surgery, and went to practise for a time

---

[1] The result of experience, as these cases appear in the list of inhibitions :—
  1740. John Johnstone of Gallabank *v.* William Carlile of Bridekirk for himself and as representing his father, the late Adam Carlile, and Sibella Bell, his wife.
  1752. John Johnstone of Gallabank *v.* Mr Walter Cork, minister in Cummertrees.
  1752. John Johnstone of Gallabank *v.* John Henderson of Broadholm, Robert Irving, and William Johnston, younger of Lockerbie.
  1755, Nov. 28. John Johnstone of Gallabank *v.* Sir John Douglas of Kelhead, Bart. (ancestor to the Marquis of Queensberry).
  1755, Dec. 24. Sir John Douglas put to the horn at the suit of John Johnstone of Gallabank.

under Dr Finlay to complete his education in London. But small as London then was compared to the present day, its atmosphere was noted for its ill effect on the youth from the North. Richard showed symptoms of consumption, and set off by post for Annan. A letter to James from their father gives the end :—

"Annan, *April* 4, 1769.

"Dear Dr,—This comes with the afflicting news of my dear son Richard's death. He came from Shield in a very weak condition, with a man in the chaise to take care of him. He lived here only 14 days; he died 28 March at 10 o'clock at night, was interred March 31 . . . there was a good attendance of friends. There is one thing more I have to acquaint you with; two poor houses built in front of the Closehead Farm; magistrates and council are determined to roup them to the highest bidder. Your brother, if he had lived, would have bought them if he could for a low price, not for the sake of the houses, but to protect the farm Provost Hardie has. He was your brother's good friend in putting off the sale as long as possible on account of this illness at London, therefore if you have a mind to buy them, write to Provost Hardie to befriend you in that matter, for it is believed Provost Anderson and his friends want to buy them to serve John Oliver, his brother-in-law. I have no son alive now that can help me but yourself. I pray that God may bless you and your wife and children. Send me the answer by post, and oblige your parent. John Johnstone."

The ten years of misfortune were not over before Mrs Murray's daughter, Elizabeth, had joined her father and little brother David in the vault in Ruthwell Churchyard. Her mother for some years past had taken her every summer to Moffat Spa or to try the whey cure at Belriding. But a brighter period seemed to dawn when Marianne, the surviving child, was engaged to James Lockhart of Lee and Carnwath, a General in the Austrian service, a widower with one daughter. Since the Rebellion of 1745, in which his family were involved, obliging him to enter a foreign army, he succeeded to family estates, and was in Dumfriesshire arranging his affairs when he met Marianne. They were married early in 1770 at Galabank's house. The want of repair and the old man's refusal to have anything done is alluded to in letters from time to time; but in 1769 James began to put the whole property into good condition, and his sister wrote on Oct. 16, 1769 :—

"We have heard nothing about the Closehead of late. I spoke to Provost Hardie, and he says he will not let them meddle with your dyke. As to the masons, they are so busy with this great house none of them has had time to make out an estimate of such a wall as you want, but the ground is set out long ago, so you may build as you please. Your father begs you to take care that Sir John Douglas don't drag you in too far, for he is very intent to have the dyke lifted. I told the schoolmaster he might have his half year's salary, and he says he never was paid that but once a year. I think myself greatly obliged to you for expressing yourself so kindly towards Marianne. You shall never find me ungrateful. Your bill came in good time; indeed, if it had not been for advancing poor Richard money I had not been in any strait. Bushby told me the day he was doing your business, that your bills were as good as the bank. Our harvest is not concluded. It was wet all August and most of September, but good ever since. Mr Thompson died about a fortnight ago, and Captain M. succeeds him. He has left Miss Douglas £500 if Mrs Hardie has no child. . . . We are all glad to hear of your Lordship's welfare, and hope to see your eldest son some time before he goes to Edinburgh. Marianne will write to you both. You are desired by the old lady and gentleman to write oftener. They send their blessing. Marianne joins in my affectionate wishes for you, your wife, and all the bairns. I am, your affectionate sister and humble servant, Isobelle Murray."

Annan reminded Miss Wordsworth in 1803 of a town in France or Germany, from its large houses, too big for the present population, and the paintings representing various trades over the shop doors. Since then the houses have been divided or rebuilt.

CHAPTER XIX.

JOHNSTONE OF GALABANK—WORCESTERSHIRE—YOUNG JAMES IN SCOTLAND—
HIS LETTERS—EDINBURGH.

WHILE the cycle of misfortune was sweeping over Galabank's family the home in Worcestershire had not been spared. The only but terrible alternative to the smallpox scourge at that time was inoculation. Little Edward and Henry had undergone it, and as Edward had the complaint mildly the baby, Anna, was inoculated from him, but it gave her convulsions, and she died. The two next, John and Mary, were not inoculated, but John, aged four, took the smallpox and died, Aug. 1767. A sixth son, one of the family landmarks, born Oct. 22, 1768, was also called John, and for him and his junior, Lockhart, their father again tried inoculation, with success, in 1772.

The four elder boys were educated first at the Kidderminster Grammar School under the Rev. John Martin, the schoolfellow at Westminster of Horace Walpole and Lord Mansfield. Founded by Charles I., it was patronised by most of the neighbouring County families for their sons, and for so small a school sent out an unusual number of eminent men. The young Johnstones also studied at home under the Rev. Job Orton, and afterwards at Daventry under Dr Ackworth. The eldest, now sixteen, was preparing for Edinburgh, and destined to relieve his father as early as possible of some of his work. He wrote from Daventry, April 14, 1770:—

"We shall finish philosophy in a week or two, and then Dr A. intends to begin anatomy! You told me when I was with you there was no occasion to study it here. I am afraid Dr Ackworth will think it disrespectful if I do not, and it cannot do me any harm, but I leave it to you to determine. I saw in the paper lately the death of the member for Stafford. I hope your friend Mr Pulteney will be chosen in his place. I shall answer my mother's letter very soon. Pray give my duty to her, love to my brothers and sister. Your dutiful son, James Johnstone."

Young James went to Edinburgh with Dr Ackworth's testimony, after three years' study of his character, that he was one of the most ingenious and promising young men he had ever known, with a remarkable quickness of insight and aptitude for literary work.

He left Worcestershire in September, and stayed three nights in Birmingham at the " Hen and Chickens," New Street, to buy a horse for his journey at the Autumn Fair, and saw a bull baited in the Bull Ring. This much annoyed his father, who had signed a petition to the Houses of Parliament some time before to abolish bull-baiting and cock-fighting,—the Bill to that effect being thrown out on the ground that they were manly, national sports! The elder James did not fail to let his son know his displeasure. The next letter, after an apologetic one, was dated from Dumfries, Oct. 10:—

"Hon. Sir,—I came to Dumfries this morning and delivered the deed to Mr Bushby to be registered, and have this moment received the two copies, one of which I send. He began to write out the settlements some time ago, and discovered a mistake which will require a considerable alteration. The mistake is that the houses are held not of the town of Annan but of Lord Hopetoun.

"I reached Annan about seven o'clock on Saturday night, and found my grandparents quite well. Mrs Murray is gone to Dryden, and will remain there some time.

"They intend to set the in-fields immediately, and the out-ones as soon as they know your conditions, which they desire you to send as soon as possible.

"Neither my grandfather, grandmother, nor John Irvin can tell me how many acres the lands amount to. By Tate's account, he would not tell them, but promised that he would send you the plan a long time ago. I shall call on him and ask about it.

"I called at Mr Anderson's for the memorandum. He could not give it me then, but has promised it before I go out of this country. I asked when the common[1] was to be enclosed and divided. He said they would very likely come to a conclusion next winter.

"This is all the answer I can give you at present to the articles you desired me to enquire after. . .. I shall not have an opportunity of looking at the several parts of our property till next week, when John Irvin will finish his harvest, which he cannot possibly leave now.

"Mr Bruce Johnstone has been confined to his bed for this week past with a bad fever. He is now better, and desires his compliments to you. I am afraid he will not recover in time for me to have his company to the Birns.

"Please to let me know whether you will have me do anything relating to the stone intended to be put up to my uncle's memory at Moffat. My grandmother seems very desirous of having it done as soon as possible.

"My horse performed his journey exceedingly well, but I am afraid will not bring so good a price as we might have got for him in England. Several persons who pretend to be judges have passed their judgment upon him, but none of them set a higher value than four guineas.

---

[1] The dispute about the Common led to the case of the Magistrates of the Burgh *v.* the Curators of the Marquis of Annandale, Carruthers of Holmains, Johnstone of Galabank, etc., in 1771, and these were also defendants in a fishing case brought by Lord Stormont in 1772.

"Give my duty to my mother, love to brothers, etc., and respectful compliments to all friends.

"I am, yours dutifully and affectionately, J. Johnstone."

"Annan, *Oct.* 21, 1770.

"Hon. Sir,—I received yours of the 15th yesterday, and I suppose you would have mine of the 10th soon after yours was sent.

"I have frequently visited the Gallabank, and more especially that part of it where the plantation ought to be. I have examined it closely, and cannot find a single plant except nettles and other useless weeds. I do not know the reason, but Irvin says the place is too cold, and that they should be planted in some warmer place, and not put there till they have grown pretty large.

"I have been with Anderson at least ten times about that paper. He told me that it must be signed by a majority of the Magistrates and Council, and that he must give in a fresh petition, which he has at last done, and got signed by eleven of them, but not without letting me know that a bowl of punch was a necessary article. Tate does not know how to send the plan he has nearly finished to you. The best way I could think of was to send it by a parcel from some of the booksellers to London, as he can easily convey it to me at Edinburgh. I asked him how many acres it was, but he could tell me nothing about it only that I should see by the plan.

"I cannot find that Mrs Murray has had any money from my grandparents or applied for any, but my grandmother tells me that she has spent no less than £200 in preparations for her daughter's marriage, £100 of which she borrowed of a person in this country and £100 in Edinburgh, and for that reason wants you, I suppose, to pay her the £200 due at Gallabank's death.

"Gallabank has been excessively busy till last night with his harvest. He and my grandmother desire their love to you, and will be glad to hear from you.

"I shall set out to Edinburgh early to-morrow and get to the Crook, ten miles beyond Moffat, if I can. You shall hear from me as soon as I get to Edinburgh, and am a little settled."

His father gave orders that the hedges on the Galabank should be replanted, but, according to a letter from his agent at Dumfries, the thorn trees were all stolen in 1773. "It seems that thieving is practiced in the Royal burgh, but the magistrates have not yet been able to find the thieves."

"Edinburgh, *Oct.* 27, 1770.

"Hon. Sir,—I should have written to you before, but was unwilling to do it without having it in my power to let you know that my box was come and my horse sold, neither of which I can do at present. My horse, indeed, I hope to dispose of this evening, as there is a person coming to look at him who wants such an one, though horses sell very low at this time (when there is such a number coming in). I hope my box will soon be here, as they expect several

London vessels at Leith in a few days. There are but two there, both of which are lading for their return.

"Messrs Wallace and Billingsley had been looking out for lodgings for me before I came, and showed me several from the prices of 2s. 6d. a week to 6s. The one I have taken will cost me 4s. a week. There is a dinner provided in the same house for a set of eight or nine at 5s. a week, and I find my own breakfast, supper, fire, candles, etc. I have a tolerably good room with a small closet for my books, and a bureau. The person I take them from is a widow, and seems a good sort of woman. One other person lodges in the house, and he is an Irish physician.

"I came here about 4 p.m. on Tuesday, and went to Dr Henry's soon after, but he was not returned from London. I called again this morning, and found him. I shall dine with him to-morrow. I went to Dryden on Thursday and met with a very polite reception from both the General and Mrs Lockhart, who desired me to make an apology to you for her not writing. She told me that she had begun to write twice, but was called away, and will write to you very soon.

"I have seen but little of Edinburgh yet, though by the appearance of it, and what I have been told, there must have been great alterations and enlargement since your time. They have been repairing that part of the bridge that fell. The three arches standing are the largest I have ever seen. Give my duty to my mother, love to brothers and sister, and respects to all friends, etc.

"*P.S.*—Direct to me, if you please, at Mrs Gilchrist's, in the College Wynd, Edinburgh."

"Edinburgh, *Dec.* 4, 1770.

"Hon. Sir,—I am ashamed to acknowledge the receipt of your two letters, the last of which I ought to have answered almost a week ago. I should have writ to you on Sunday, but I went to Dryden on Saturday and was detained there longer than I intended, so that I did not come home time enough for the post. I spoke of your friend Mr Rae more than once, though I did not mention him to the General with any reference to a living, but I desired Mrs Lockhart privately to use her influence with him, and if she does as she promised, no doubt she will succeed, for the General does not seem disposed to deny her anything she asks. They behave extremely kindly to me, and desire me to come *sans ceremonie* as often as is convenient to myself. I have never said a word to any of them concerning the £200.

"Your objections to my lodging occurred to me when I first came to it, and for that reason I took it for only a week at a time, but now I have had between five and six weeks' trial of it, I do not find it liable to those inconveniences. The dinner in the house is not open to anybody, but a set who constantly come to it, and stay no longer than just while they are eating, for it is a constant rule to drink nothing but small beer. There are indeed some of the company not very agreeable, but these I have no connection with in the least, and I do not find any place where, upon the whole, I should do better; at least I am sure any of the public ordinaries are infinitely worse. I have never gone to taverns, oyster houses, etc., or joined in any kind of extraordinaries, nor intend it, for I find the necessary expenses, even with the utmost care, must be great. I have hitherto kept a regular account of all my expenses, and shall continue to do it, and hope to keep such a one as will give you and myself satisfaction. I am very sensible of the importance of frugality and the justice of your observation, that great expenses are commonly closely connected with idleness and its consequences, and I shall want no greater motive to engage me to it than the examples of yourself and Lord Lyttelton.

"I wrote to Tate as you directed me, and let Gallabank know in a letter I wrote to him since, so that when they see him they may remind him of it.

[Then follows an abstract of the lectures he had attended.]

"I have spoken both to Donaldson and Kincaid concerning your book. They seem but indifferent about it. If you choose to put all of them in the hands of one person let it be Donaldson. The spirit of any of them in disposing of them will depend very much on the profit you allow them."

"Edinburgh, *March* 12, 1771.

"Hon. Sir,—I dined yesterday with Dr Henry.[1] . . . Your books arrived very safe with the *Success*, though many goods were spoiled, owing to the ship being leaky. I got them about a fortnight ago, gave fifty to each of the booksellers in Edinburgh, and have sent twenty-four to Foulis in Glasgow, with a letter to let them know that if they could dispose of more I would supply them. I gave one to General Lockhart, Dr Monro, Dr Rutherfurd, and Professor Stewart.[2] . . . I gave one also to Dr Black, as I have the honour to be a little acquainted with him, the rest I have deferred till I receive Mrs Montagu's letter to Dr Gregory, which I hope you will get soon.

"I have spoken to Mrs Murray on the business you desired me. She desires that you will write to London yourself for my uncle's books, and seems to be much offended at you for setting so small a value as 30s. upon them, and says they must be worth more than that if you value them at no more than farthings each. I say as little as possible to Mrs Lockhart on this subject, as I know it is a disagreeable one to her as well as myself.

"Before I left Annan I desired John Irvin, if my grandfather should be seized with any sudden or violent illness, to let me know it by a letter put with his own hand into the Post Office of Dumfries, which he promised me to do.

"My stock of money is getting very low. I have but £1, 6s. 6d. remaining, and shall be very much obliged to you for a supply as soon as is convenient.

"This is my last frank. Be so good as to send me some other if you have any that will serve."

Richard had left his sister his executor and residuary legatee, but the elder James had lent him money and books, and there were bills for his rooms in London, and for a suit of Court mourning for the mother of George III., and

[1] A Scottish minister, at that time attached to St. Giles', Edinburgh, the author of a *History of Great Britain in the Reign of Henry VII.* and other works (1718-90).
[2] His son was Dugald Stewart, Mathematical Professor (1753-1828).

other expenses due to Mr Veitch, a relative of the late member for the Dumfries Burghs. He had assisted Dr Finlay, and Mrs Murray thought that money was due from him to Richard, but no one seems to have asked, and James ended by paying up everything.

"Annan, *Aug.* 31, 1771.

"Hon. Sir,—I have received your letters, and am very happy to find you so well satisfied with the execution of the business you directed to be done, and am sorry that it is not in my power to send you copies of the deeds, etc., as you desired both in your letters. Neddy's writing is very intelligible, and only wants a little practice to perfect himself in shorthand writing. The reason of my not sending you the booksellers' offers was that I had none to send in the least worth your acceptance. I offered them to him for 1s. each copy, but he said he could not think of dealing with me on such high terms. I told him I would not give them much lower, but keep them to advertize next winter. I was the less solicitous to sell them as I have great hopes of their going off next winter. Dr Gregory gives the *Institutions*, and I do not doubt but he will mention it honourably.

"The sum I borrowed of Dr Henry was £7, 7s. I will be much obliged to you, if convenient, to send it to him immediately. I intend writing to him this evening. His *History* has sold exceedingly well in Edinburgh. When at Dumfries I enquired of Thomas Bushby, who is cashier to the Bank, as well as of his brother John whether the assignation was intimated, and he assured me that it was, but there is a further necessary step he required the other notary to take, *i.e.*, writing the execution on the back of the original copy with the names of the notary. The person in whose hands the money is and another third person subscribed. This was done at Sir William Maxwell's and Mrs Moore's, and I desired Bushby to get the same done at the Bank. He promised me to do it last Thursday. I saw him in Annan on Wednesday, and shall be at Dumfries the beginning of next week myself, when if he has not done it I will take care to have it done.

"Gallabank desires me to tell you he has paid James Moffat 40s. for the dyke at Closeheads, and that there is as much as will cost 20s. more remaining to be done.

"This is all the business I have to write to you about, and have only to add that, as some persons through whose hands your letters sometimes pass to my grandfather and grandmother are not likely to put the best construction upon your words, I would wish when you write to them that you would cautiously word any expressions which may be misconstrued to your disadvantage, and when you mention General Lockhart will you be so good as to give him his title,[1] because when you write only Mr Lockhart it is misconstrued either as a wilful disrespect or pride. I know you will excuse me mentioning these trifles, as an attention to them may be a means of further promoting that family peace which you are so desirous of establishing.

[1] This was not usually done when the title was a foreign one.

"It is now time for me to inform you of the way I employ my time here. I brought Haller from Edinburgh with me to endeavour to make myself master of it before I return there, but find it not so easy a task as I imagined. I generally read the whole morning till twelve o'clock, and after that go and talk Latin, and read with John Irving, the blind man, whom you know to be an excellent Latin scholar. I am acquainted with everybody in the town that I wish to be, and am commonly out every afternoon.

'I bought the *Comparative View* last winter, and have read it over and over; it is a book in every respect worthy of its author. I cannot express its worth in stronger terms, and with all who are acquainted with Dr Gregory it cannot bear a higher character. When you see Mrs Montagu at Hagley, I beg you will present my best acknowledgements to her for the honour she has done me in introducing me to that excellent man, and my duty to his Lordship, if you think proper. I visited your friend Mr Gath[1] last Sunday. He is very well. The old people here ask a great many questions about home. My love to Neddy and all my brothers and sister."

"Annan, *Oct.* 11, 1771.

"Hon. Sir,—I received yours of the 20th ult. with the agreeable news of the birth of Lockhart on the 12th, and heartily join all friends here in wishing that the increase of your family may prove an increase of your happiness. I have not been able to go to Dumfries on account of the harvest till yesterday, when I went to receive the interest at the Bank.

"I made inquiry about John's confirmation, but the office can give no answer without searching the Register, and unless you can give the exact time it will be attended with much expense. . . . I am sorry I cannot, in spite of repeated solicitations, send you copies of the writings, etc., you desired, but my grandfather cannot look them out himself and will not allow me to do it. He once said he might let me have them if Mrs Murray was away, but now she has been at Locherwood some days he has altered his mind. Not a day passes but my grandmother has something to say about the monument. She is very angry at it being put off so long, and still persists that it shall be of marble, or (says she) 'I will send a man on purpose to pull it down the moment it is put up.'

"I read to Gallabank your letter. He says he has no money, but will try to spare enough to supply me to Edinburgh, though I am afraid it will be little enough as the good old man seems to have the prevailing passion of his years growing pretty fast upon him.

"The sale of Sir John Douglas's land will be next Tuesday. Mr Dickson will attend it on your account. He expresses great readiness to be of any service to you in his power.

"You ask what sort of a schoolmaster we have. As a schoolmaster I know little of him; but he is a very sensible man, has read a good deal, and is in his

---

[1] Minister of Graitney, an author, and noted for the strictness with which he ruled his flock.

behaviour much of a gentleman. He has not so large a school as his predecessor I am informed had; not for want of equal or superior merit, but for want of a certain degree of assurance which the other possessed, and not adapting himself to the conversation and company of the lower class of people."

The population had diminished during the eighteenth century, and in 1772 Annan only contained 500.

Galabank objected to a monument at Moffat at the time of his son's death, and said he would put the name on the family vault at Annan; but nine years later, by his mother's wish, James took it in hand, and paid £25 for the handsome marble monument attached to the piece of the chancel wall of the old church left standing at Moffat, which bears this still legible inscription:—

> P. M. Reveredi Vivi
> Edwardi Johnstone, A.M.
> (Vetustae apud Annandie familiae de Gallabank
> geniti) pastoris et conneionatoris olim in hac
> pareccia per Annos quartuor decim celeberrimi
> Qui obiit 16 Januarii 1761 aetatis suae 46
> Hoc posnit
> Jacobus Johnstone, M.D.
> Delita spargens lacryma
> farillam fratris amici.

Below are the family arms and motto, with old Galabank's name.

CHAPTER XX.

Johnstone's Books — Death of Lord Lyttelton — Correspondence with Mrs Montagu—Thomas's Illness—James's Letter—Settles in Worcester—Galabank's Letter and Death—Edward's Illness—In Edinburgh—Letters from Drs Cullen and Gregory—In Birmingham—Samuel Johnson and Dr Priestley—Visit to the Lockharts—Assemblies at Sutton Coldfield—Mrs Montagu's Letter—Gordon Riots—The Jail Fever—Death of Young James—His Character—His Father removes to Worcester—Members of the Literary Society—The Assize.

THE result of Johnstone's experiments on the ganglions of the nerves were at first privately printed and presented to several physicians— among others to Baron Haller, the Swiss medical Principal of the University of Gottingen, who began a controversial correspondence with the author which lasted from 1761 to 1775. He was no vivisectionist, for, when speaking of his experiments with kittens and rabbits, he says they must be made immediately after the animals are killed; but with frogs he thought they could easily be deprived of sensation, and that this should be done before proceeding further. Dr Lyttelton (brother to Lord Lyttelton), who was Dean of Exeter and then Bishop of Carlisle, President of the Antiquarian Society, presented Johnstone's pamphlet to the Royal Society, and, with supplementary articles, it was printed in Volumes LIV., LVII., and LX. of the *Philosophical Transactions* in 1764. Another essay refuting objections appeared in the *Encyclopædia*, and both are favourably mentioned by Dr M'Kittrick in his *Commentaries on the Principle and Practice of Physic*, and also by Dr Tissot in his *Traite des Maladies Nerveuses*. Frederic Casimir seems to have adopted the whole system in a work published at Mannheim in 1774, and Dr Kolpin, of Stettin, translated it into German, the work being entitled *Versuch uber den Nussen der Nervenknotten von James Johnstone.*

Of this book the author wrote: "Solitary and indeed casual study produced my first sketch on the uses of the ganglions of the nerves, a subject on which no one had even plausibly conjectured anything probable. From this arose the little notice taken of it by the anatomists in this kingdom. No one had any idea of it; no one could pretend any claim to the discovery; on this single subject there was no room for wrangle—*more anatomico*—so one of the most important discoveries of the age has been but little noticed, at home especially, yet it is the key which unlocks the functions of the heart."

Johnstone continued to the last four years of his life to publish, in the organs of the Medical Societies of Edinburgh and London, remarkable cases that had come under his notice and the result. He was the recipient of the first medal presented by the London Society. In all he brought out seventeen books and essays, apart from writings on non-medical subjects. He was a member of the Philosophical and Literary Society of Manchester and of the Philosophical Society of Bath, and wrote in their journals. But his most important discovery was perhaps the treatment of fevers, and the arrest of infection by sulphuric or muriatic acid mixed with common salt placed in an open jar in the patient's room. He used it seventeen years before Guyton Morveau purified the Cathedral of Dijon with a similar mixture, and twenty-two years before Dr Carmichael Smyth corrected contagion in Winchester Prison in the same way. He even advised it to disinfect his father's house after his sisters and brother died of consumption in 1756, 1761, and 1769.

When George, Lord Lyttelton, was dying in May 1773, he told Johnstone to write minute particulars of his illness to Mrs Montagu, and also of a conversation on Christianity and his spiritual state, which he began by telling the Doctor that he was going to make him his confessor. Dr Samuel Johnson, in his *Lives of the Poets*, gives a part of the letter, and Miss Warner, in her *Notes to Original Letters*, gives the whole. Johnstone had to defend himself from some critics who accused him of revealing the secrets of a death-bed, which ought to be as sacred to the physician as to the priest, and he explained that he acted entirely by Lord Lyttelton's command.[1] Lady Lyttelton, the deceased's daughter-in-law, confirmed this statement to several of her friends, and she was a constant attendant at her father-in-law's death-bed.

Mrs Montagu's reply to Johnstone's "excellent" letter showed she appreciated it. "Lord Lyttelton," she wrote, "was enabled to be in death, as in life, the best of examples to mankind. The solemn event is often attended with such disorder of body and mind that the wisest and best men only show the weak and frail condition of humanity . . . and rather inform the spectator what he is to suffer than how to support suffering. This excellent, incomparable man was a noble instance how virtue, integrity, and faith rob death of its sting, the grave of its victory. . . . My house when he appeared in it was a school of knowledge and virtue to the young. . . . But as such a friend is the best worldly gift Heaven bestows, I most gratefully acknowledge the goodness of God in having permitted me to enjoy such a friend and such an example, and submit with humble resignation to the stroke that deprives me of a much greater good and advantage and honour than I ever could merit. I am glad that all that human skill and care could do was done to prolong a life so valuable to us, and that in you he had the consolation of the friend he

[1] In the so-called fictitious letters of Thomas, Lord Lyttelton, occurs: "When you are here I will amuse you with a pamphlet which is a complete physical or rather anatomical reply to those who defend the right of self-murder; it is a treatise on the Ganglions of the Nerves by a Dr Johnstone, a physician in my neighbourhood; it is written with the pen of a scholar, and possesses throughout a most perspicuous ingenuity. This gentleman attended my father in his last illness, and was not only his physician but his confessor."

loved as well as the physician he respected and trusted. I wished we lived nearer to each other, that I might hope to inherit some part of the friendship you had for this deceased friend. I will hope so far that if ever it is in my power to be of any little service to you or yours you will command me. If your son should go abroad to finish his studies it is not impossible I might be of some use in getting recommendations to persons whose acquaintance might be of some little use, as I have a pretty extensive acquaintance among foreigners. The character I heard of Mr Johnstone, your son, both from good Lord Lyttelton and Dr Gregory,[1] makes me sincerely congratulate you on the pleasing hopes you may reasonably indulge of his success in the world. He has been very unfortunate in losing two such friends, but his father's character and his promising genius will do everything for him."

The younger James graduated at Edinburgh in Sept. 1773. His papers and debates before the Medical Society of Edinburgh were considered by Dr Cullen and Dr Gregory as remarkably clever, and he acted as clinical clerk to Gregory to prepare cases for the lectures at the Infirmary. His thesis, "De Angina Maligna," was recommended to the attention of physicians by Dr Cullen, for, as he said, it was based on his father's observations. It was the subject of much congratulation in his family; and of two letters from his aged grandmother to her son in Worcestershire, in the second of which she says: "I pray indeed that James, Thomas, and Edward may be as you say good men. Your father, if he is spared, rests upon what you say as to the land, and we will be glad to see you here if it be with your convenience. Your father and I are both in our ordinary state of health, but we can get no money from Mr B—— or Mr C—— though the last has owed us £10 since June." (Nov. 5, 1773.)

Six months earlier she wrote: "You told me in your last that Thomas was ill of fever and that the young doctor was waiting on him. I am heartily sorry to hear it, and beg you will write and tell me how my grandson is, directly you receive this as I am very impatient to hear. May God bless you and all your family. I am dear son your affectionate Mother.

"Annan, *May* 9."

Young James had gone by sea from Edinburgh to London by his father's desire to look after Thomas who had been put into a merchant's office, and fallen ill. He wrote from London, April 30, 1773: "My brother has been gradually mending every day since I wrote last, but is not yet able to sit up above half an hour in the day. His spirits are exceedingly good and he is as lively in conversation as ever. I called at Mr Pulteney's on Wednesday last but he had gone to Shrewsbury. He is expected home in a day or two so I shall call again. I have been twice to Mrs Montagu but was so unfortunate as not to meet with her at home. Lady Valentia has received your letter; she desires me to tell you that she cannot leave town till May 6 but wishes to have the children removed to Mr Vicary's and inoculated as soon as you

[1] Mrs Montagu was related to Dr Gregory's wife, daughter of the fourteenth Lord Forbes.

think it proper. She will be with them before they sicken. I hope my uncle and Aunt Crane had a safe journey home, remember me affectionately to them as well as to my mother, Your dutiful son, etc."

And on May 7, 1773, he wrote again :—

"Hon. Sir,—I received yours this morning and (as you will see by the cover) have since been with Mr Pulteney. He sent me a very polite card of invitation to dinner to-day, and received me with great civility. On my way home I called at Mrs Soley's. That family is all in mourning for Mrs Marriot who died a fortnight ago. I was with Heydinger before dinner and have written to the Bishop that the copy is not complete, and that he expects others in six weeks time. Tom is daily recovering strength; he sat up eight hours to-day. Dr Fothergill urges his going into the country. If you think it proper that he should come in a post-chaise by short stages, I have no doubt that he will be able to do it by the end of the week. If you approve, I must ask you to send me a small bill for £5 more. I shall be on the look out for a third person to lessen the expense.

"Mr Fuller had engaged a person to go with him to Birmingham before he knew of my coming to Town. I went last night to see Garrick in the character of Hamlet the former part of the evening and I never was more entertained in my life. It is impossible to do justice to the merit of this inimitable actor. After the play I went to Ranelagh and stayed till mid-night. I have no time to lose and will see as much as I can, so at present lead a complete life of dissipation. Present my duty to my mother and respects wherever they are proper, from your dutiful son, J. J."

After taking his degree James took his father's place at Worcester, and in the summer of 1774 was elected Hon. Physician to the Infirmary of that city. His colleague was Charles Cameron, educated at Eton and Baliol, the son of the elder Johnstone's rival, whose failing health had obliged him to resign the post. James took a house in Foregate Street, and a poetical letter from his twelve-years-old brother, Henry, who visited him, describes very fully occupied days of business and harmless amusement.

He was sworn in as special constable on the occasion of a local riot, and served with the Worcestershire Militia when it was called out. His friend, Dr James Gregory, coming to see him, he wrote to his brother "Ned" to join them under canvas. The regiment was afterwards moved to Warley, where a fatality occurred in the death of the senior officer, Major Clements, 1778.

The following year a commission in the Army was bought for Henry Johnstone.

Galabank's last letter to his son was dated Jan. 15, 1774. "Worthy Doctor," he wrote, "this day I received your letter and you have given me good council not to disturb my own mind in the affair of the burgh land that they speak of exchanging; my mind is not to exchange anything till your mother and I are dead. Take good care of the rights that you have from me for the

sake of your family, and I wish your spouse and children a happy New Year and many of them. This is all, from your affectionate father and mother.
"John Johnstone.
"I can get no interest from Mr Corrie Carlile paid. When you write to me be so good as to write to him and ask for regular payment. We have had a cold hard winter."

The old man survived till the next October, when he had a slight stroke which affected one arm. He said at once that it was the forerunner of death, and that he would neither see a doctor nor take any remedy. "Did they wish him to live to be 100 years old and a burden to everybody?" was his answer when his wife and daughter urged him to give himself a chance. His son did not arrive till the end had already come, Oct. 14, and it gratified him to see the respect in which his father was held by all the neighbourhood. "His word was as good as another's bond," and "Scotland never bred a more honest man," were common observations, and repeated in the funeral sermon by the Rev. W. Moncrieff.[1] He was in his eighty-seventh year, and the oldest freeholder in Scotland.

His Will was dated May 18, 1769. He left no debts, but £214, 3s. 4d. was owed to him by Mr William Corrie Carlile of Bridekirk. Except a small charge on his property for his son, John, and some special furniture to his daughter, Isobelle, besides an elbow chair, and six chairs, and a rococo bookcase to his grand-daughter, Mrs Lockhart, and a large silver spoon and silver tankard to his grandson, Edward, he left all else—"lands, crops, stock and utensils of husbandry, furniture, window curtains, pictures, prints, looking-glasses, beds, tables and chairs"—to his daughter, Isobelle, and his son, James. The Will, signed by himself and his wife, was witnessed by George Hardie, Provost of Annan, John Bushby, writer in Dumfries, and John Anderson, notary.[2]

His son speaks very warmly of him in his diary, and expresses thankfulness that he did not live to see the unfortunate end of his grand-daughter's marriage with General Lockhart, which was solemnised in his house after the Presbyterian fashion, which had crept in since he was married himself. No change was made in the establishment while the widow lived, but on June 18, 1776, her son records: "This morning died my dear affectionate mother, Anna, in the 81st year of her age." "My active feeling mother"—as he calls her elsewhere. "She was eight years younger than her husband. In the last year of her

---

[1] Only three ministers have succeeded him in Annan to the present day—his son, the Rev. J. Monilaws, and Dr Crichton.

[2] His monument in Annan Churchyard bears the inscription below the names of the children who had predeceased him. "Here also is interred the venerable father of this numerous family John Johnstone Esq. of Gallabanks, representative of the Johnstones of Milnfield and Newbie Castle, and an antient cadet of the Johnstones of Johnstone. He died the 12th day of October 1774 aged 86 years and 4 months.
"The hoary head is a crown of glory if it be found in the way of righteousness.
"Also Anna Ralston his relict who died the 18th of June 1776, and in the 81st year of her age.
"All flesh is grass."

Q

life the usual infirmities of eighty years added to other complications made her patiently but earnestly look for death, the great remedy of incurable discomfort."

"Respecting family claims after my mother's death," he wrote rather later, "I settled everything due to my sister or her daughter, and have her discharge in ample terms with those of her daughter and General Lockhart, and I now remain sole male representative, and by deed as well as heirship sole claimant to the real and personal property anywise belonging to or derivable from my father."

Sir James Johnstone of Westerhall witnessed Galabank's deed of settlement.

The bills for the various family funerals show the difference in the value of money 130 and 140 years ago. The mourners often came from long distances, and in so hospitable a country they were of course entertained. The Presbyterian ministers said prayers and gave exhortations in the house, but the coffin, borne by relatives from the churchyard gate to the grave, was laid in the ground almost in silence. The previous generation was buried with the Episcopal service, for Edward Johnstone died only a year (1697) after the Presbyterian Kirk was established by law, and it had not then supplied a minister for Annan. But the entertainment in every case was much the same. For six dozen of wine supplied at Richard's funeral £5, 8s. sterling was paid. On the occasion of his mother's, "sixteen gentlemen dined at the Queensberry Arms Hotel in Annan for 16s.," four ladies for 4s., ten tenants for 5s., the wine being supplied from the house of the deceased; the porter they drank amounted to 5s., and horse hire 4s. 6d., for the churchyard was very near. There was a larger attendance when Galabank was buried, and the bill for dining the mourners and pall-bearers at the Hotel was £2, 2s. "Servants eating" was 8d. and beer; ale and porter 4s. 8d., wine being supplied from the house. Two guineas was paid "for an Achievement of the Arms of Gallabank, and all materials by me, Lewis Cleghorn," to put over the house door, and 4s. 6d. for the frame. A coffin was £1, 5s.

At another of these funerals, when fourteen gentlemen were to dine at the Queensberry Arms at 1s. per head, the dinner consisted of a ham and chickens, a roast leg of mutton, a pigeon pie, fish, a dish of flounders, besides tarts of various kinds, the wine and beer being extra, and 1s. for a dish of veal cutlets. Crape was 1s. 6d. a yard, ribbon 8d., cloth for a bombazine gown £1, 7s., white crape for a coffin pall 4s., a flannel shroud 15s. 6d., tape 2d. a yard, a set of white and gold coffin handles and letters 4s. 6d., mourning paper 10d. per quire, sealing wax 4d. a stick, cloth 5s. 8d. a yard, black silk thread 2s. per oz., almonds 1s. 8d. per lb., carraway seeds 6d., currants 7d., and raisins 6d. per lb., cheese 4d., etc.

A letter from young James on the occasion of his grandfather's death, dated Kidderminster, Oct. 21, 1774, shows that he had undertaken to look after his father's practice during his necessary absence. After giving details of the health of various people, he says: "We have this moment received yours from Warrington, and rejoice to hear that you reached that place so well.

Having gained your point on the first day, we are encouraged to hope that you were not much later than the appointed time on Thursday at Annan.

"My mother desires to join me in assuring you that we are very impatient to hear of your arrival at Annan and of the situation in which you find my good grandmother. We most cordially sympathise with you both. We hope you will not forget to offer our respectful duty to the worthy old lady, and let her know how anxious we are to have more pleasing accounts of her. There is a letter to you from Mr Pulteney. It contains no more than you know already, and I will answer it. Also one from General Lockhart to tell you that my cousin Mary Anne had a daughter born on the 15th, and that both are doing well. He regrets not having seen Neddy, and hopes he is quite well."

Edward's studies were interrupted by serious illness. He had assisted his father during the vacation in his work among the poor in Kidderminster and the neighbourhood, where there was an outbreak of typhus fever,[1] and he caught it. In after life he attributed his recovery, under Providence, to his father's skill and his mother's care and perfect obedience to his father's orders. As his younger brothers and sister were in the house, three of them quite little children, muriatic acid poured on common salt was placed in a jar on the stairs, and everyone who passed up or down was directed to stir it up with a stick. The efficacy of this new remedy was proved by no one in the house, including the servants, taking the complaint. "My brother," wrote John Johnstone in after life, "recovered almost miraculously from the last and worst stage of this dreadful fever. The muriatic vapour was kept rising continually in the room, and not one of the family, at that time consisting of sixteen persons, was infected;" but the boy, for he was not eighteen, was a long time before he got up his strength, and his future sphere of action was decided by his father thinking it desirable that he should live in a bracing climate.

General Lockhart, a man of the world who had won his title and the Order of Maria Theresa by his campaign in Poland, seems to have had a sincere regard for his wife's young cousins. He wrote to congratulate Johnstone when Edward was completely recovered, often asked him to Dryden when he was at Edinburgh, and later, when he was appointed Governor of the Austrian Netherlands, invited Edward to spend a month with them at the Viceregal residence.

As Edward was his father's executor, and destroyed all his own letters home while preserving those of his elder brother, only his careful note-books and thesis for his medical degree exist as memorials of his College life, but the letters of Dr Cullen and Dr Gregory to his father show that it was very creditable. The first wrote from Edinburgh, July 3, 1779:—

"Dear Sir,—An esteem and regard for your character very readily engaged my attention to your sons, who came to be our pupils here, and I cannot now

[1] Fever that the elder called putrid, the younger called typhus.

dismiss the last of them without telling you that tho' it was a regard for you that first engaged my attention, yet the good qualities I soon observed in the young Gentlemen themselves would have effectually secured it, tho' they had been otherwise unknown to me. I must say of both of them that they soon discovered very excellent parts, and have always given so much application to study, and shewn such correct and polite manners, that they have engaged both my affection and that of all their other Preceptors. I am fond by this testimony to do justice to the young men and to give you the pleasure which I am confident you will receive from it. I congratulate you heartily on your happiness in two such sons, and assure you I am with great affection theirs, and with great respect and esteem, dear Sir, your most obedient servant.

"William Cullen."

Dr Gregory's letter, dated July 4, says:—

"Sir,—As your son is now going to leave Edinburgh after three years spent at our College, I cannot suffer him to depart without conveying to you my assurance that his Behaviour here, both in respect of his private conduct and his application to his studies, has been such as his best friends would have wished. Of this, and of his proficiency in his studies, all the Professors are perfectly satisfied, but I think myself better entitled than any other to assure his father of it, as I have had more particular opportunities of being acquainted with him than any of them could have, as I was not only frequently favoured with his company in the domestic circle, but also had his assistance in the capacity of my Clerk at my last course of chemical lectures, in which office his attention and judgement were such as to give me the highest satisfaction. So far as I can judge he has as good a title to success in his profession as personal merit can give him. Your most obedient humble servant,

"J. Gregory."

Edward attended his grandmother's funeral at Annan, and visited that part once more on his way home in 1779 to see his invalid uncle, John, who lived sixteen years after the death of his mother broke up the family home. It was a tribute to the skill and kindness of his brother, who placed him under suitable care in Annan, that, as John approached seventy, the cloud over his mental powers seemed to pass away, and he finally succumbed, a practically sane man, to failure of the heart in 1792—a few months after Lord Annandale's decease at Chiswick.

No grass grew under the feet of the young Galabanks, and within three months of his admission to the Royal Medical Society in Edinburgh Edward was appointed an honorary physician to the newly built General Hospital in Birmingham, and his name appeared on a brass plate on a house in New Street, then the fashionable residential quarter of the rising village,—for it was nothing more. His colleague and senior was Dr Ash, but Johnstone admitted the first patient, a fact of which he was rather proud in his later life. He was very soon connected with the philanthropic associations in the town; but he could play as well as work, as appears in a letter from the younger Dr Gregory, dated Cambridge in 1780, in which Gregory refers to Johnstone's frequent attendance at the dances given in the Assembly Rooms at Sutton Coldfield, seven miles distant, and imagines that the attraction must be either Miss G., one of the Galton family, who were then living at Great Barr Hall, or else Miss Jesson, a scion of an old Warwickshire family, who afterwards became Mrs Lynch. Gregory wishes that he could change places with him.

In the *Birmingham Directory* for 1783 Edward Johnstone is set down as living in Temple Row. The house was larger than the one in New Street, and just opposite St. Philip's Church, now the Cathedral. He selected it because it was on the highest ground in the place.

He had unsuccessfully tried to introduce his father's system of arresting contagion with muriatic acid mixed with common salt in the hospitals at Edinburgh when they were filled with the Duke of Buccleuch's Fencibles suffering from fever. The physicians were not accustomed to be instructed by their students, and raised a trivial objection to a second trial of it; but in Birmingham he at once proved its utility, and it continued in practice till replaced by the more convenient and less obtrusive modern disinfectants.

He also followed his father's new system of treating fevers. The first time he was called in by an apothecary to see a woman apparently dying from the effects of three weeks' typhus fever he called for the first stimulant that could be brought. It was a jug of ale. He gave some to the patient, while the apothecary looked on as astonished as if the young physician was pouring poison down her throat, and was still more surprised when she raised herself to take the jug in her own hand for another draught, and she recovered.

A coach ran between Worcester and Birmingham along the Bristol road, and Edward often went on the top of it to see his brother and consult with him about the serious cases that came before him. His father also came frequently to Birmingham. He was intimate with Edmund Hector, the kind friend of Samuel Johnson, and who lived in the Old Square, close to Temple Row. Johnson stayed with Hector, after his last visit to Lichfield, about two months before he died.

In Boswell's *Life of Samuel Johnson* he contradicts an assertion made by Dr Parr, that the author of the *Dictionary* had ever met Dr Priestley, on the ground that when visiting a College dignitary at Oxford Johnson turned his back and left the room on the appearance of a notable Nonconformist. Boswell admits that he knew very little of his friend's movements during the last year of his life, but Edward Johnstone told his friend Mr Hill that he was present when such a meeting took place. Samuel Johnson was a dying man, suffering from dropsy, when he reached the Old Square, but he wished to return to London. Hector, unwilling to let him travel alone, and finding that Johnstone was going to visit Dr Parr, who had only arrived at Hatton Vicarage the previous Easter, asked him to let the invalid accompany him, and to arrange that he should make Hatton the first stage of his journey. Dr Priestley also came there, and it was the one occasion when they met at Dr Parr's. Samuel Johnson, aware of his own condition and softened by it, was as civil as his nature permitted to his fellow-guest. He rested again at Oxford at the house of his friend Dr Adams, thence went by the public coach to London, Nov. 16, 1784. Less than a month later he died.

In 1781 Edward Johnstone visited his cousin at the Viceregal residence of the Austrian Governor of the Netherlands at the Hague, her husband, Count Lockhart,[1] having recently been appointed to that post. This part of Europe in 1725 was restored to the House of Austria, represented in 1781 by Joseph II., Emperor of Germany, which was then an elective monarchy. Edward stayed a month with the Lockharts at Utrecht, the Hague, and Spa, and brought home a map of Spa and some very handsome books on Flanders and Brabant.

On Jan. 4, 1781, Mrs Montagu wrote to Johnstone: "I shall take every opportunity of mentioning your son at Birmingham to all my friends with esteem, and indeed one never declines doing justice when it gratifies one's private affections as it does mine where your family is interested. I beg my affectionate compliments to my young friend. I did not know till you told me that he was going to assume the grave character of a married man, but I heartily congratulate both you and him. . . . I have been building, near Portman Square, a house[2] I purpose to inhabit next winter. I assure you it will owe many of its decorations to Birmingham and its neighbourhood. The arts seem to be rising to a high degree of perfection in England, but the late horrid violences and outrages which have been committed in London too plainly prove that if we are polished in matters of taste we are savages and barbarians in principles and manners." This alludes to the riots instigated by Lord George Gordon in June 1780 to oppose what was known as the Catholic Relief Bill, a Bill warmly supported by the Whigs or Liberals of that day. It began on June 2, the next day the Chapels and numerous private houses of the Romanists were pillaged and burned, as well as Lord Mansfield's and those of prominent Whigs. Thirty-six fires were blazing at once, the jails, including the King's Bench, Bridewell, and Fleet, were broken open and the inmates released, the Bank attempted, and for six days the Civil Law was overpowered. Then the Militia from various counties arrived to reinforce the Horse Guards, nearly 500 rioters were killed and wounded, and many others tried and executed. Lord George Gordon was acquitted; but in six years a warrant was issued against him for libelling Marie Antoinette. He escaped to Birmingham, where he was concealed for some weeks, then captured, and died of fever in Newgate (1787) while awaiting his trial.

Two years later all Johnstone's friends joined him in mourning over the

---

[1] Madame D'Oberkirch, governess to the Grand Duchess Paul, afterwards Empress of Russia, wrote an account of a visit she paid in 1782 with the Grand Duke and Duchess to Utrecht, where they were entertained by "Lady Lockhart." "The Lockharts," she adds, "are an ancient Scotch family, of whom one member was Ambassador from Cromwell to the Court of France. The Grand Duke [Emperor Paul 1796-1801], who is very well informed, did not fail to make a delicate allusion to this personage."

[2] The large detached house now owned by Lord Portman.

death of the eldest son of the house. Nash, in his *History of Worcestershire*, Dr Valentine Green in his similar work (both authors were acquainted with him), give very sympathetic accounts of young James's career; and Howard, the philanthropist,[1] in his *State of Prisons*, alludes to his premature end: "In the course of my pursuits I have known several amiable young gentlemen, who in their zeal to do good have been carried off by that dreadful disorder the gaol fever, and this has been one incentive to my endeavours for its extirpation out of our prisons. I shall mention one affecting instance which happened here [Worcester] of a young physician falling a sacrifice to this distemper through a benevolent attention to some prisoners afflicted with it—Dr Johnstone, jun., of Worcester. He attained at an early period to great and deserved eminence in his profession, and will be ever regretted as a physician of great ability and genius, and as one of the most pleasing and benevolent of men, prematurely snatched from his friends and country." The *Biographical Illustrations of Worcestershire* gives a similar sketch of his career. "A much lamented martyr to a noble discharge of duty," wrote Dr Barnes of him in the *Manchester Memoirs*, Vol. II. The Governor, his wife, and the surgeon had all died of the fever which had broken out in Worcester Castle, then used as a jail, and the panic caused by it made it difficult to supply their place. Young Johnstone offered himself, and was at once accepted by the Magistrates, and for a short time was in charge. He was most successful in rescuing debtors as well as criminals with his energetic use of disinfectants and wholesome diet, and removal to better quarters of those who had not yet been affected,[2] and in his treatment of the sick. "He went into cells and dungeons full of pestilential contagion," wrote Dr Green, "and restored health to the miserable sufferers, but his own invaluable life fell a sacrifice. He was seized with the dire contagion, and, fully persuaded that the event must be fatal, he was conveyed to his father's house, there to receive the last attentions of parental skill and affection. He died Aug. 16, 1783, aged twenty-nine, a lamented victim to the discharge of one of the most dangerous duties of his profession. The oldest rarely attain to greater skill and knowledge, and the youngest enter not into the world with more innocency, or leave it more sincerely mourned.

"Dr Johnstone's manners were as remarkably cheerful and pleasing as his abilities and knowledge were great and extensive. To these were superadded great sweetness of temper, mingled with vivacity and sensibility. He had vigour of body which seemed to promise a longer life, but by his premature death verified an old observation, 'Immedicis brevis est aetas et para senectus.'"

The Governors of the Worcester Infirmary in their Yearly Report in 1784

[1] He sent presentation copies of his works to Johnstone.
[2] "He ordered the cells to be fumigated with brimstone, and in the apartments of the sick the acid air was kept constantly rising. The prisoners were fresh clothed, their old clothes were burnt, and their hair cut off. They had fresh straw to lie upon every night, were allowed 2 lbs. of currants each every day, and had diluted vitriolic acid water for their common drink, and before the new clothes were put on each prisoner was obliged to wash himself all over in tubs of water placed in the open court of the prison."—*Account of the Discovery of Mineral Acid Vapours, etc.*, by John Johnstone, M.D., 1803.

Apparently the old Castle, which was close to the Cathedral, had never been modernised.

state: "It would be unpardonable to overlook the mournful occasion of this election of physicians by the death of Dr Johnstone, jun., who for nine years served this charity with great assiduity, humanity, and skill, and who fell a memorable sacrifice by his attendance on another public service."

The elder Johnstone tried his favourite disinfectant while his son was ill in the house, and proved its efficacy by no one taking the fever except Henry, who had driven from Worcester in the same carriage with the invalid; but as he had been in the best of health and not overtaxed by his duties he recovered.

Only four days after his son's death Johnstone offered to take his place as physician to the Worcester Infirmary, and was at once appointed. His parents-in-law were dead, also his friend Mr Orton, and his son Edward advised him to leave Kidderminster with its now tragic associations. He removed in the autumn to a house in the Foregate Street. His son was buried at Kidderminster, but a marble monument, with a Latin inscription by Dr Parr, was put up in Worcester Cathedral to his memory. From all parts of the kingdom letters of condolence poured in. Young James was engaged to be married to a sister of his colleague, Dr Russell, whose son, Sir John Pakington, was the first Lord Hampton of Westwood. They were also related to the family of Earl Somers. The lady wrote a touching monody on her dead betrothed. She ultimately married.

Johnstone's hopes had soared high with regard to the marriage of his eldest son; and in a letter when he was but twenty-one gives him advice how to proceed in the courtship of a young lady visiting Ombersley, and in whom the fond father thought he had discerned a predilection for young James—an instruction in moral gallantry he calls it, advised him how often to pay a visit, how long to stay, and when he might offer to kiss her hand. But at the back of the letter are the words "disappointed," whether on his son's part or the young lady's does not appear. In a postscript Johnstone adds that Lady Valentia (daughter to the first Lord Lyttelton) writes to him that the business they have gone upon will end without expense, and that he had "a very friendly letter from Miss Baines about the death of the Bishop (owing to a fall from his horse in Bath), an event which concerns me as I fear no successor will be equally my friend" (Dec. 14, 1774). This was not the case, as he was very intimate with the next Prelate, the Hon. F. North, and on familiar terms with Dr Hurd, whom he already knew as Bishop of Lichfield and Coventry, when he was appointed to Worcester in 1781.

Kidderminster is fourteen miles from Worcester, and is described in 1783, the year that Johnstone left it, as containing 1180 houses and 5749 people. It owned 1700 looms in 1773, but hardly 700 in 1780, owing to the Cranes and another manufacturer having retired. The compiler of these statistics says: "It returned two members in the Parliament 23rd of Edward I., but luckily for the trade of the town has since then had nothing to do with politics."

Worcester, an ancient city of about 11,000 inhabitants, in 1783 was the most attractive town in the Midlands, in spite of the terrible epidemic which had overshadowed it and fresh symptoms of rioting in the county which had brought out the Worcester Militia—among them two of the Johnstones. There was very good society in the city and county. Charles, the elder brother of the more celebrated Richard Brinsley Sheridan, and an M.P. in Ireland, came to live in the Foregate Street not long before Johnstone's death, and was introduced by him to a literary circle founded by Mr Dunster, a poet and author, who was Rector of Oddingley and Naunton Beauchamp in 1775. The other members between that date and 1802 were Sir Edward Winnington, James Johnstone, the Rev. Reginald Pyndar of Hadzor, Mr Dandridge of Malvern, Colonel Barry, Dr Russell, Rev. J. Carver, Prebendary of Worcester, Mr Coombe, author of *Dr Syntax*, Dean Swift, a relative of the author of *Gulliver*, and his relation Theophilus, Mr Ingram of the White Ladies, Worcester, Mr Berkeley of Spetchley and his chaplain, Mr Philips, the author of the *Life of Cardinal Pole* (both Romanists), Edmund Lechmere, Dr Goodinge, Master of the College School, Holland Cooksey, and Captain Clements, R.N. They met periodically at each other's houses, and are called by Chambers "a bright constellation of men of genius and talent who were the boast of this city and its environs in the last half of the eighteenth century." Mr Burney, uncle to the author of *Evelina*, also lived close by, and gave dancing lessons.

In Johnstone's diary he speaks of the "agony" he had experienced in the death of four lovely infants, but this—his eldest son—was a loss of a more serious kind, and "it was aggravated by the discovery of the embarrassment of my second son and by the difference which arose about this time between my niece and her husband."

There was quite a panic in London as to the sanitary condition of Worcester, and the Judge, Sir F. Buller, writing to condole with Johnstone, asked him to give a candid opinion as to the safety of holding the Lent Assize there or taking it to Bromsgrove. Johnstone reassured him, and stated that numbers whom his son had attended in the jail had recovered, and that no serious illness remained except one or two cases of fever at Droitwich. "The Judge gave a strong charge to the Grand Jury to reform their jail, and did not fail to mention with due concern and deserved honour the character and death of my son."

By Johnstone's advice the County Hall was fumigated during the whole of the Assize, as well as the jail, and the prisoners again supplied with new clothes. Alterations were also made in the jail, but "on too narrow and parsimonious a plan."

The account of Droitwich and its springs, in Nash's *History of Worcestershire*, was by young James, and that of Kidderminster and the character of Baxter by his father.

CHAPTER XXI.

VISIT OF GEORGE III. TO WORCESTER—THE KING'S ILLNESS—JOHN JOHNSTONE—DEATH OF THE SECOND LORD LYTTELTON—MRS MONTAGU'S LETTER—SIR WILLIAM PULTENEY AND THE ELECTION—GOVERNOR JOHNSTONE—HIS ILLNESS AND DEATH—THE ELECTION FOR DUMFRIES—WESTERHALL—DR PARR—MR ORTON—MISS PULTENEY—EDWARD JOHNSTONE—DR ASH.

ON August 5, 1788, at 8 P.M., George III. and Queen Charlotte, with their daughters, Charlotte, Augusta, and Elizabeth, arrived at the Bishop's Palace in Worcester (now the Deanery) to attend the Music Meeting (the Festival of the three Choirs). They drove from Cheltenham, having only three days before driven thirty-seven miles to Hartlebury Castle and back to visit Bishop Hurd in his country seat. The Bishop had been tutor to the Princes George (afterwards King) and Frederick, and one of the Royal Chaplains; and since he had been at Worcester he had confirmed Prince Edward and Princess Augusta in St. George's Chapel, Windsor, and preached there before the King on Christmas Day.

The King was partial to Hurd, and offered him the Archbishopric when it was vacant in 1785, but he answered that "several greater men than himself were content to die Bishops of Worcester, and he wished for nothing else."

At 10 A.M. the day after the King arrived the Corporation and their Recorder, Earl Coventry, came and kissed hands, after which the King held a levée in the Great Hall. Johnstone and his sons, Edward, Thomas, and Henry, were presented by the Bishop. After the custom of the day, the King made a remark to each, and asked Edward at what time he left Birmingham. It was over by 11 A.M., when their Majesties walked across to the Cathedral preceded by the various functionaries and Bedesmen, who on great occasions went before the Bishop. Then came the King between the Bishop and Earl of Oxford, followed by the Royal ladies and the suite. After Matins and a sermon, the Music Meeting began. The two next days the Sovereigns attended service in the private Chapel of the Palace, and then adjourned to the Music Meeting, and on the last day the King gave £200 to the Charity. When they left for Cheltenham, Aug. 9, the King gave the Bishop £300 for the release of debtors in Worcester Jail and £100 for the city poor.

The King's appearance was rather a shock to Edward, who, less reserved

JOHN JOHNSTONE

than his father, told an intimate friend that the King must be either intemperate or going out of his mind, and that the former was precluded by his well-known character. In less than three months the opinion proved correct, and the King was *non compos mentis* for about the same period.

Johnstone observes in his diary that Dr Hurd was the fourth Bishop of Worcester with whom he had been acquainted and the third whom he had attended professionally. His greatest pleasure in Worcester, he alleges, was derived from the Bishop's instructive and pleasing conversation; and with his family he was accustomed to spend every Christmas at Hartlebury. His fifth son, John, was preparing to enter his own profession. He had taken his degree at Merton College, Oxford, and then went to study medicine in London. His letters[1] from St. Martin's Street give the latest details of the King's illness direct from Dr Heberden and Dr Warren, and the opinion of outsiders that he could not live, which checked the manœuvring about a Regency, till, in February, he unexpectedly recovered, though he had been bled enough to turn most people into idiots.[2]

Johnstone had offered to send his son Edward to Oxford instead of Edinburgh, but Edward had spent some years of his childhood in Scotland, and preferred Edinburgh, where a shorter time was required before taking the M.D. degree. John was still an M.B., although a Fellow of the Medical Society of Edinburgh, when, on Nov. 1, 1793, he was unanimously chosen Hon. Physician to the Worcester Infirmary. The Governors present were Lord Sandys, Rev. Dr Nash, Rev. Mr Cooke, Mr Kelly, Mr Lawson, Mr Lygon, and Mr Foley.

His father, in a short speech, thanked the Governors for this expression of their "confidence in the third election of a physician in my family to serve this charity . . . and I flatter myself my son will not disappoint my hopes and your expectations."

John assisted his father for a year in Worcester, and was very popular. It was a great annoyance to the elder when his son, by the advice of Edward, resigned his post, Dec. 1794, and removed to Birmingham to help his brother, whose practice extended to Tamworth, Lichfield, Derby, and the neighbourhood of Shrewsbury and Wolverhampton. Possibly, as there were other physicians in Worcester, the young men saw that the fact of a third of the family coming there was not looked upon complacently by their rivals. Forty years later this happened in Birmingham. Johnstone's non-lowering system was in 1795 still opposed by the Royal physicians and others in London, and all over

[1] In one of these he describes a visit to the British Museum (only recently opened), where he saw the original Magna Charta, the South Sea Curiosities brought by Captain Cook, the Roman Antiquities, etc. "Among the annoli [rings] there is not one either so large or so perfect in gold as yours." This is a Roman Governor's ring found on the Borders, still possessed by his great-great-nephew.

[2] It would have been much to the advantage of the King if Johnstone had been his physician. Those about him hardly knew what to do for fear of *lèse Majesté*, and the specialist who was summoned had old-fashioned methods long exploded, and of which Johnstone was a great opponent. More than one who suffered from nerves, and was afraid of being shut up in an asylum, came to live in Kidderminster to be protected by Johnstone from such a fate. The retreat founded by the Quakers near York was the one enlightened home for the insane at that period.

the country; and those in or near Worcester who preferred the Johnstone method sent for John after his father's death.

Among these was the Marquis of Hertford, at Ragley. Johnstone took his son to call there, and said he hoped that when he retired the Marchioness would send for the young man. John was fair and very youthful looking, and Lady Hertford replied rather contemptuously, "What! that boy a doctor!" "I hope I may be grey," said John, "before your ladyship has need of my services." "Well done!" said she, "You ought to go to Court," and they were afterwards great friends.

In 1779 Johnstone became a magistrate for Worcestershire, and was often called to serve on the Grand Jury. He was a warm politician of the kind then known as Whig, like all Scotsmen who were not Jacobites, and the Lytteltons were the same. The second Lord Lyttelton, chiefly known to fame on account of the ghost story connected with him, consulted Edward Johnstone, then under twenty-three, a few months before his death, and was told that his symptoms were those of a stroke. "You are the first who has been bold enough to tell me that," he said, "but I know it." He had been very friendly with Johnstone senior, but avoided him after receiving a caution as to his mode of life. "His death," wrote Johnstone, "amazed the public more than it did me, who knew his feeble constitution and impressive mind. The letters which bear his name have much of his manner and many internal marks of being genuine, though they have been publicly denied by his executors."

A letter from Mrs Montagu to Johnstone, Jan. 4, 1781, alludes to it:—

"I was extremely shocked at the sudden death of Lord Lyttelton, and it made the deeper impression from the unusual circumstance of the dream or vision. Would to God he had given to repentance the three days he passed rather in the dread of death than an endeavour to divest it of the sting of unrepented sin and folly. . . . From what cause I know not this young man believed in ghosts and the appearance of departed souls while he doubted, or rather as a doctrine disbelieved in, the soul's immortality. On this subject he allowed the same thing to be and not to be. He denied the existence of the departed soul, and yet told you when it had appeared. Whenever I think of the poor young man I comfort myself in an opinion that he was to a certain degree insane. I remember his excellent father saying to me, with tears in his eyes, that he was obliged to consider this circumstance, so terrible in most cases, as an alleviation of his unhappiness. . . . People urge that Lord Lyttelton's dream had not any supernatural cause, because it does not appear to have had any effect, but this argument has little weight with me. There may be many ministering spirits, many subordinate agents between man and the Great Omniscient. . . . It is probable from the peculiar turn of this young man's mind that a ghost's warning would have more effect than the preaching of the Apostles had they been alive, and if not on him, still that the atheist should have borne testimony in this singular manner to the existence of a spirit endowed with power and faculties so superior to humanity as to foreknow what in its highest perfection of nature and science no man can—the hour of his own and another's death—may make a deep impression on many libertines and freethinkers.

"I cannot agree with you that his lady might have reclaimed him. A woman who marries a most vicious and profligate rake, knowing him to be such, and promises to love, honour and obey such a wretch can with an ill grace discountenance the character to which she promised affection, respect and allegiance. Lord Lyttelton was not really as bad as the character represented of him, the lady had heard all the stories told of him, his behaviour to Mrs Dawson . . . she perfectly knew. You will say she intended to reform and reclaim the rake. Such a hope the vain credulity of youth and a first love might entertain, but failing in the first attempt I cannot wonder she did not make a second. The story you mention of the Duke of Saxony is very striking, it gives me great delight to find he made so excellent a use of the mysterious whisper of his guardian angel.

"I shall be very happy to enjoy as much of your society as you spare me when you can come to London, which I rejoice to find you think of doing. It seems to me that such a tribute is now and then due to our great metropolis though your engagements in the country will not allow you a long residence."

Johnstone took the warmest interest in the Shrewsbury election in 1774, when Sir William Pulteney opposed Mr Leighton, who was supported by the great Lord Clive,[1] and Mr Noel Hill. The very limited suffrage at that day made the influence of a few men important, and many Liberal votes were secured through Mr Orton and Mr Gentleman, great friends of Johnstone, and Presbyterians. Sir William Pulteney wrote confidently in June 1774, but hurried down to Shrewsbury hearing that the other side had assured the Dissenters that Pulteney, who was known to be their friend, would get in elsewhere if not successful in Shropshire. But in a letter to Johnstone, Sept. 24, 1774, he says that he shall not be in Parliament at all unless he gets in there. "Mr Gentleman," he adds, "seems to think that I shall not have a vote from Lawrence but I hope you have the means of fixing him." On Oct. 6 he wrote from Shrewsbury: "I shall be very glad to see you here as soon as possible, as I think it may be of consequence. I think it will be very proper to bring along with you the letter wrote by L. to Mr Orton, in which he desires that you may not insist upon his promise, and also all the letters to yourself in order to be shown to Mr Gentleman."

The usual amenities at elections were indulged in, and the opposition asserted that Sir William was mainly supported by a Scotch Dissenter. Johnstone answered that he was a Scotsman, and proud of it; but that he was not a Dissenter, for he had been a member of the Established Church in Scotland, as he was a member of the Established Church in England.

[1] M.P. for Shrewsbury till 1774, being an Irish peer.

The polling day was put off, as it used to be in old days, and was suddenly fixed for Oct. 11. Sir William wrote on Oct. 13:—

"The hurry of yesterday prevented my writing as I intended and I write now in great haste on the first scrap of paper I can find. The Poll is not ended but will close to-day. The event will be that by the Mayor's rejecting a good many of my good votes and admitting others against me in the same or worse circumstances I shall lose the return by five or six votes, but I shall not only have a great majority of the freemen but a certainty of getting the return set aside even upon the footing of the burgesses by a petition. Mr Mitchel, Crawford, Barrett, Rev. Fownes, Mr Symonds and Thomas Mason voted for me, but James Mason and two of their Shearmen, Gittens and Lawrence and Benjamin Davies against me, which would have given a majority to me even on the Mayor's plan. I beg my compliments to Mr Orton, whose friendship I shall never forget. Yours with much regard. William Pulteney."

Before Johnstone received this he had set off for Annan to attend his father's funeral, but, as anticipated, Sir William gained the seat.

Another letter from him, dated London, June 19, 1781, thanks Johnstone for his congratulations on Pulteney's brother, "the Governor," having beaten a French squadron at Port Praya. "It gives great satisfaction here as it promises to secure the object of his expedition [to take possession of Cape Town], for the French fleet will be obliged to touch at the Brazils to refit and water and by that means he will get before them to the Cape of Good Hope. I shall be glad to assist your son when he arrives in his object of promoting [raising] a company [of soldiers], but I know of no channel except by means of the agents of regiments. I am glad he has already got one step."

Four years later the correspondence is engrossed with reports of Captain George Johnstone's last illness.

The first intimation of its hopeless character appears in a letter from himself to Warren Hastings, who had resigned the Governorship of India and returned home to defend himself when he was impeached before the Houses of Parliament. Edmund Burke, in a speech lasting three days, accused Hastings of injustice and oppression of the native princes, and of unduly enriching himself and his friends. The Governor wrote from Taplow, Oct. 6, 1785:—

"If it were possible to arrest the decrees of fate your elegant and affectionate letter would have stopped the current of my disease, as it is with all the charm of words it could only produce a momentary cessation from the most cruel pains that a man has ever suffered. Without admitting womanly fears or vain delusive hopes it is clear to me that the period of my dissolution is not far distant, whether it may be within two weeks or two months is a question, but that it will happen on or about those periods I am myself satisfied. I grow daily worse and weaker and all the causes or symptoms which have reduced me continue to rage in a double degree.

"It is pleasing to me that you receive in the manner you have expressed my feeble endeavours in the public cause in the discussion of a subject in which you stood the principal figure. If I was a chief instrument in warding off the blow of ignorance and oppression, whose arms were both lifted up against you, I glory in the deed, lying in the condition in which I describe myself in which there ought not to be any guile. I was anxious after your arrival to have discussed what had passed here and in India in the presence of Major Scott, to show that whatever has occurred either with respect to you or to him that I had acted a fair and consistent part agreeably to previous public declarations, and that the reason you find such a total reversion in the Power in India and in the Power of Indian affairs at home respecting persons and things from what you had reason to expect was due to meanness, duplicity and perversion of understanding in those whom you deem and not without reason your best friends. This was why I frequently solicited Major Scott to procure me the honour of meeting you not at a hasty dinner but such a meeting as would be required thoroughly to go over such subjects. It was natural for you to wish to see your most private and intimate connections first. The time is now past, as I am totally incapable of any public business, and, confined to my bed, I am unable to look for any necessary papers. The favour you had shown my son[1] made me anxious to convince you that in the generous communication of good offices I had not been capriciously wanting . . . your letters convince me that you must be satisfied my conduct has not been unfriendly to you." He spoke of the various times he had voted against Hastings being recalled with a vote of censure, but adds that "after all our labours, all our struggles the power of the East India Co. was entirely thrown into the hands of John Robinson; and Henry Dundas is now absolute Lord Paramount of East Indian affairs."

A month after this letter Sir William wrote to James Johnstone from London:—

"I intended to have come here by way of Worcester from Shropshire above a month ago on purpose to have paid you a visit, but some business in Northamptonshire obliged me to take that road. My brother the Commodore, better known as the Governor, has been for a long time afflicted with a hard swelling in one of the glands of his throat . . . and often very great pains which distract his head and has much disturbed his rest at night. He has had all the advice that this place affords and has tried various remedies without success . . . when he was at St. Helena on his way from the Cape of Good Hope it went almost entirely away. . . . . His strength has greatly failed him, but when he is not in pain his spirits are very good. He has been advised to try Malvern waters, but could not go there on account of business at the proper season; he is desirous of going now, and my reason for troubling you is to know whether at the village of Malvern any tolerable accommodation could be had at this time of year, and whether if the waters are fit for his case he is likely to be disappointed of their effects in winter. I see by Dr Wall's pamphlet

[1] In his Will he describes George Lindsay Johnstone, James Primrose Johnstone, Alexander Patrick Johnstone, and Sophia Johnstone as his natural children.

that they have been used with success even in winter, but I have heard lately such accounts of the cold and exposed situation of Malvern that I wished to know whether in his reduced state there may not be hazard in going there so late in the year. He is very much set upon it, and the experiment is worth trying if there be any probability that the waters at this time can be of service. He means to go abroad about Xmas for the sake of a warm climate, and he has been advised if Malvern fails to try Venlo's vegetable syrup. I own I wish him to try Malvern, and I wish him to have the benefit of your advice. Hoping I may hear from you by return of post as my brother thinks of setting out next Tuesday I am, dear Sir, your most obedient. William Pulteney."

As Johnstone's reply was favourable, the next letter, dated Nov. 29, 1785, from the Worcester Hotel, says: " My brother has bore the journey tolerably well. We have travelled slow, but one of the days he was too much fatigued by coming thirty-five miles from Oxford to Broadway. We go to-day to Malvern. I write this to give you a caution. He has met with so many disappointments from the faculty that he has said, and repeated it since we got out from London, that he had hopes from Malvern water, but would have nothing more to do with physic or any who belonged to it. As that was his temper I did not inform him that I had wrote to you, but only mentioned it to Mrs Johnstone [the invalid's wife] and the rest of the company, and therefore you must come to him as a family friend and not as a physician, and leave him either to talk to you or not about his complaint. We can give you all the information you will want, and we can contrive that he shall follow your plans without being fretted about it. Our great endeavour is to keep up his spirits, and it is surprising that under so much pain and loss of strength he is not more nervous and irritable."

On Dec. 22 Sir William wrote from Great Malvern: "I think my brother is going on well, but he is not very governable, and has over-fatigued himself with exercise beyond his strength and by eating more than he ought, but we are now all combined to keep him in order, and I hope will be too many for him. He has been on horseback two days at the top of the highest mountain, and walked down with only the help of a stick. He has had no pain till last night, but he eats enough to give a man in health a fever. We beg you will come to us to dinner on Monday, and bring Miss Johnstone and your sons, as we have some venison, and will try to make a little dance if my brother is well. If Colonel Hume will do us the honour to come with you we shall be glad of his company."

The invalid had not left Malvern many days when Johnstone heard again from his friend. "My brother," he said, "stood the journey very well, and all the inn-keepers on the road remarked how much better he looked; on Wednesday night there was an alarm about him, and Mrs Johnstone sent an express to me from Taplow which arrived at mid-night. I set out immediately and carried Sir George Baker with me. Before we arrived he was better and Dr Lind had arrived from Windsor. He proposed coming to town to-day. I enclose a strange letter I received to-day with my answer, which I must trouble you to read and send. I beg my compliments to Mrs and Miss Johnstone and the young gentlemen. I heard from Laura yesterday. She is well at Sudbro'."

They came to Malvern again the following August, and when the Governor wished Johnstone good-bye he said, " I do not mean to compliment your heart, but I am sure that if it had been in the power of medicine to cure me it would have been done by your skill." They adjourned to Clifton, where the lady wrote on Feb. 1 :—

"I have the pleasure to acquaint you that the Governor goes on pretty well. He has had the honour of receiving a letter from you which he means to answer very soon; at this moment he is a little hurried, as his cause comes on to-morrow before the Lords Mansfield and Loughborough—I mean the Sutton prosecution. May I trouble you, Sir, to put a direction upon this note, and have it delivered at the China shop that Miss Johnstone was at with me in Worcester, and this other note at the Glove Manufactory opposite the Hop Pole. I beg you will remember me with kindness to Mrs, Miss Johnstone, and the rest of your good family, and begging forgiveness for the liberty I have taken, hope you will believe me to be your most humble servant.
"C. Johnstone."

A letter from Miss Pulteney, written a few days later, thanks Johnstone for sending " a piece of news which gave us so much pleasure. I can say little about my uncle, who now talks of going abroad. He is at present at Taplow, twenty-five miles from town. Papa joins me in best compliments to all your family. I hope Miss Johnstone has danced a great deal this winter."

Miss Dee wrote on April 4 to thank Johnstone for settling Mr Wheeley's wine bill, and would send the money by the first person going to Worcester. "I am sorry I did not know that the 14th was your birthday, as we might have met half way and celebrated it together, as it happens to be mine too. Is it true that Lady Huntingdon[1] is to go to Vienna? Surely her zeal is great, and if we do not all go to Heaven it is not her fault. I am sorry I cannot give you a good account of the Governor. He grows weaker and weaker. My sister is well. So is Jock, and all join in kind compliments to you and yours."

The last letter that "the Governor" wrote to Johnstone was to enclose one from his brother-in-law, Lord Kinnaird, " granting the request I made to him at your desire in favour of Dr Beattie, to whom I beg my compliments. All of the family desire their compliments to you and yours. I am sorry I cannot add any favourable account of my own health; upon the whole it seems resolved I should wait the issue at this place, where the air has certainly agreed with me better than any I have yet tried, and as to Jock and my sister Nellie, it has quite restored them. Your little book, *Ikon Basilicon*, I receive

[1] Johnstone was not disposed to laugh at Lady Huntingdon. She wrote to him to obtain religious privileges for the prisoners in Worcester Jail, and he cordially agreed with her.

as it was meant, a token of your friendship, but you should not have robbed your library of so valuable a composition. I am, with respect, dear Sir, your obedient and obliged servant. George Johnstone.
"Bristol, *Nov.* 14, 1786."

During the last few months of his life Governor Johnstone added repeated codicils to his Will—some with his own hand, some dictated to Miss Dee. As his elder brothers had no sons, he knew that his heir would be eventually well provided for, and he left him only £200 a year, with a stipulation that he was to be brought up in Scotland from the time he should be six years old. He left his wife £500 a year, and various legacies to those whom he said had been very kind to him during his long illness. His chief anxiety seemed to be for the future of the illegal scions of his house, although the eldest was well provided for in the Civil Service of the H.E.I.C.S. He left £5000 among the younger three, his swords, and the most valuable of his personal treasures. He desired to be buried at Westerkirk, and that his bearers should be chosen from the villagers. They were to be given new suits of clothes, and £10 was to be spent in drink, to be distributed in Westerkirk, on the day of his funeral.

On May 25, 1787, Miss Dee wrote:—

"Mine is the melancholy task to acquaint you of the death of my brother and your relation, Governor Johnstone. He departed this life yesterday morning at nine. It will be pleasing to you to know, what will ever be a comfort to us, that he died perfectly happy and easy, not an instant of delirium, and watched his own dissolution to the end. His exit was as truly great and edifying as it could be, and a more blessed end I never saw, heard, or read of. He died like a lamb, and had no pain or crisis, as we had expected . . . The only thing on his mind was that long tedious cause, and that, thank Heaven, he lived to enjoy and see the most honourable conclusion to in his favour. It came on in the House of Lords on the 22nd, when it was given for him by the unanimous opinion of the Judges and also by a division of the Peers, and he felt the satisfaction of knowing that not only the law but the opinion of the House had done him justice."

A letter from the same, dated Taplow, June 27, 1787, adds that the funeral took place at Westerkirk, where "he was laid by his father, according to his directions, and there was a very respectable attendance of friends. My sister is as well as we can hope. Jackey is stout and well and merry; happily for him he is too young to know the magnitude of his loss."

Sir William Pulteney also wrote to Johnstone:—

"Notwithstanding the little hope for some time past which could be entertained of my brother's recovery his death was a shock to me, but he died with so much satisfaction that his honour was vindicated that it afforded me much consolation. He was indeed an ornament to his country, and the delight of his friends. . . . Tell me if I gave you my pamphlet on the Sutton case. If not, I will send it to you."

A few years later Sir William wrote from Edinburgh describing his nephew, Jock, who was with a tutor preparing for the University.

The following is from Westerhall (Sir William's brother) when he stood for the Dumfries Burghs :—

"My dear Doctor,—I well know the ardent attachment of all your family to mine. Mr Lawson and his brother-in-law are not so sanguine in my interest as we could wish. A line from you would make them both my friends. Do, my dear doctor, write to them immediately, and add to the obligation already conferred on your sincere, grateful, and affectionate   James Johnstone.

"Annan, *March* 18, 1784."

Sir James was elected and kept the seat till 1790, when he was defeated by Captain Miller in the famous contest of "the Border Knight and the Soldier Laddie," sung by Burns. When the poet found that the Duke of Queensberry [1] was backing Captain Miller he openly took Sir James's side :—

"Up and waur them a', Jamie,
Up and waur them a';
The Johnstones hae the guidin' o't,
Ye turncoat Whigs awa'."

Shortly before, Sir James replied to a letter from Worcester :—

"London, *May* 11, 1789.

"Dear Doctor,—No man can be more sensible than I am of the attention and kindness that you and all your family have always testified to me and mine. . . . It would give me infinite pleasure that the Bill I am bringing in would be of the smallest service to you and give you a vote for the county. I think, from the experience of thirty years, I have a pretty good guess who you would choose for your representative, but the Bill I am bringing in will make no alteration whatever either in the qualifications or in the present mode of election. It goes no further than to take from the Sheriffs of Scotland a discretionary power of executing the writ of election when they think proper, either in one week or in six months, and obliging them to execute the writ exactly in the same time that is allowed in England. I take it very kind your having wrote me on this subject, as it gives me an opportunity of explaining my Bill. I shall be ever happy to hear from you, and still more so if you can suggest anything in my power by which I can prove to you the gratitude and affection of, dear doctor, your much obliged humble servant.

"James Johnstone."

A secret memorandum [2] to the Government showed that, owing to the

---

[1] "I am too little a man," wrote Burns to Graham of Fintry, "to have political attachments . . . but a man who has it in his power to be the father of his country, and is only known there by the mischiefs he does in it is a character that one cannot speak of with patience."

[2] It describes the resident landowners: "Sir Jas. Kirkpatrick, a lawyer; Sir R. Grierson, has a brother a merchant in Glasgow; Charles Sharpe of Hoddam, a lawyer, Keeper of the Harriers to the Prince of Wales; Patrick Miller of Dalswinton, made his fortune as a banker

restricted suffrage and the many lairds who lived in England or were disqualified, there were only fifty-two names on the electorate in Dumfriesshire in 1788.

Johnstone corresponded with his brother's old pupils, the Vanden Bempdé Johnstones. The second, Charles, stayed with him in Worcester, and after inheriting a third of Lord Annandale's personalty retired from business as a Hamburg merchant, and settled first in Pembroke (where he had a numerous family) and afterwards near Ludlow. His son Charles lies buried, by his own wish, next to Johnstone's younger son, Lockhart, in Hindlip Churchyard, near Worcester.

Johnstone left on record his view of the characters and preserved the correspondence of most of the eminent men he was acquainted with, and many of whom he had attended professionally—two Viscounts Dudley and two sons; Lord Foley and his numerous family; Sir Edward Winnington, whom he speaks of most warmly; four Bishops of Worcester; two Lord Lytteltons; Richard Ingram of the White Ladies; John Murray of Murraythwaite; Dr Erasmus Darwin; Mr Mynors; Dr Withering; Dr Seward; Dr Priestley; Dr Samuel Johnson; James Boswell; the Marquis of Hertford; Lord Yarmouth; Graham of Blaatwood, who died at ninety-six, and recollected his great-grandparents, George Johnstone (died 1649) and Agnes Graham; three Bishops of Lichfield and Coventry; Mr Stedman, the Vicar of St. Chad's, Shrewsbury, to whose son, Henry James, he stood sponsor; and many others. He shared his son's admiration for Dr Parr, and describes him as "a man of ancient probity and purity of manners, a modern theologian without servility, though one of the most accurate and distinguished scholars of his age, still only curate of Hatton, though his great talents ought to be employed in some great and important work of permanent interest to mankind." According to John Johnstone (Parr's biographer) the admiration was mutual. In a letter from Parr to the elder Johnstone, with an introduction for Professor Porson

---

at Edinburgh; George Milligan Johnston of Corhead and George Johnston of Cowhill, both new proprietors who made their fortunes as merchants; Sir Robert Herries, a banker in London; Alex. Fergusson of Craigdarroch, advocate; David Armstrong, advocate; Wm. Copland of Collistoun, advocate; Robt. Maxwell, his affairs much embarrassed; Archibald Goldie in Shaws, of Tinwald, and brother—doubt if they will swear; William Pulteney, Esq., of Bath House; Sir James Johnstone (Westerhall), a very independent, honest character; Richard Bempdé Johnstone, son of the late Col. Johnstone; John Mackie of Palgowan, Revenue officer in England; Jas. Carruthers of Wormanbie, no children; Wm. Elliot of Arkleton; Sir Wm. Maxwell of Springkell; Wm. Jardine of Apilgirth; R. Henderson; R. Wightman; Dr Jas. Hunter, physician; Hugh Corrie, W.S.; Thos. Goldie, writer; Lord Annandale, insane; Duke of Queensberry, no children—commanding interest; John Carruthers of Holmains, no children; Geo. Kirkpatrick, a bachelor; John Johnstone of Denovan, brother to Westerhall, immensely rich; Wm. Campbell, W.S.; Rev. Dr A. Hunter of Barjarg; John Hunter, W.S.; John Murray of Murraythwaite; Peter Johnston of Carnsalloch, English barrister; Hon. Jas. Veitch, Lord of Session; the Duke of Buccleuch; John Bushby, sheriff's clerk; Jas. Irving of Gribton; Lord Stormont; Charles Charteris-Wellwood Maxwell, etc." Persons were disfranchised who, within a year of an election, had been twice present at divine service where the pastor had not taken the oaths to Government or did not in express words pray for the King, his heirs, and successors by name, and for all the Royal family. The oaths to Government included the assertion that the heirs of James VII. had not the slightest claim to the throne.

and a young student of Merton College who wished to see Worcester, Parr writes: "I thank you for the instruction I have received from your writings, and beg leave to assure you that I consider my friendship with Dr [Edward] Johnstone of Birmingham as one of the happiest circumstances of my situation." John says of his father: "His personal appearance, always dignified, was in his last years *visuque et auditu juxta venerabilis*. His mind was replete with knowledge and inventive, and his character full of originality and fire. Dr Parr has done justice to his accomplishments in every place where he could express an opinion."

Johnstone speaks warmly in his diary of the Rev. Job Orton, who published several books, and left Shrewsbury to live in Kidderminster, near his friend. He suffered from nervous depression, for which Johnstone prescribed regular occupation, and allowed him to assist in the education of his sons. Dr Hugh Blair, minister of the High Church in Edinburgh, corresponded with Johnstone and sent him all his sermons. His theological library was a very large one, and, from the marginal notes, the books—most of them presentation copies—were carefully read.

A letter from Miss Pulteney, afterwards Countess of Bath, asks Johnstone to obtain admission to the Worcester Infirmary for a blind fiddler. The man went back to Montgomeryshire, cured of an injured knee and with his sight restored by an operation, as Johnstone at once saw that he suffered from an old case of cataract. On this, Sir William asked him to receive a gamekeeper of seventy who was becoming blind, and the man was cured. These were followed by many more from Sir William's extensive estates, till Worcester became quite famous for its oculists. After Johnstone's death his son, Edward, admitted outlying cases sent by friends into the Birmingham hospital, which soon rose to fame, although his colleague, Dr Withering, persisted in treating consumption by bleeding and low diet, and Dr Ash's practice was so eccentric that the elder Johnstone thought it only to be accounted for by his subsequent insanity.

CHAPTER XXII.

BIRMINGHAM—THE RIOTS—EDWARD JOHNSTONE—DR PARR'S LETTERS AND PAMPHLET —THE DISSENTERS—MRS WEBSTER OF PENNS—SUNDAY SCHOOLS—FAMINE— MARRIAGE—FORMER OWNERS OF FULFORD HALL—LOCKHART—GALABANK—DEATH OF MRS E. JOHNSTONE.

IN 1778 Birmingham, occupying a corner of three counties, contained 8042 houses; more than double those of Manchester. According to the mode of estimating the population at that time—six to a house—the inhabitants were set down as 48,252, including neighbouring villages connected with it by isolated houses standing in orchards and gardens. Edward, Duke of York, came there on Oct. 1765, and danced at a ball held at No. 11 in the Old Square. He said a town of such magnitude ought to have a bigger ball-room with a better entrance, for it stood in a back-yard; and this remark stimulated the erection of Dadley's, afterwards Dee's Hotel, with its ball and concert room, in Temple Row. The Lunar Society, which met there, at Great Barr Hall, Sutton Coldfield, and other places, was so called because it assembled when there was a full moon. Writing to Edward Johnstone, Dec. 16, 1788 (see *Edgbastoniana*, Feb. 1884), the poet and naturalist, Dr Erasmus Darwin, says: "I was in Birmingham yesterday, and meant to have waited on you to return the visit you once favoured me with at Derby. I dined at the Hotel with the Philosophical (lunar) Society and was sorry to see no physician there but Dr Withering. How does this happen when philosophers are liberal-minded and agreeable and there are so many ingenious of the faculty at Birmingham?"

The members of the Society were: Matthew Boulton; Dr Erasmus Darwin; Dr William Small, Physician and Chemist of Virginia; Thomas Day, author of *Sandford and Merton*; Richard Lovell Edgworth; Dr William Withering; James Watt, F.R.S.; John Baskerville; Rev. Dr Joseph Priestley; William Murdoch; Rev. R. A. Johnson, of Kenilworth; Samuel Galton; Mr Samuel Galton, jun., his son; Dr Stoke; Captain James Keir (Secretary).

As Birmingham has played an important part in the political life of the Empire for over eighty years, it is worth while to look back when she was only a village governed by the old Baronial Court system, with her High and Low Bailiffs, and when the County families took houses there in the winter to enjoy the balls at the Assembly Rooms and the excellent hunting in the neighbourhood, and when it troubled itself little about politics and returned no member to Parliament. Sutton Coldfield, seven miles distant, was an ancient town, with a parish extending many miles over parks and halls, and between them Aston, a country village, with its Elizabethan Manor-house and picturesque old Church, filled with Holt, Holden, Caldecott, and Bracebridge tombs. On the west side Edgbaston Hall and Park, two miles away, had been bought from the heiress of the Middlemores, married to Lord Falconer, by an East Indian nabob, Sir Richard Gough. It was a noble effort for so small a town when it planned that fine structure St. Philip's for its second church, now the Cathedral. It had been ten years building when the money fell short, and Sir Richard Gough applied to Sir Robert Walpole to ask for assistance from the King, who gave £600; and, in gratitude, the Gough crest—the boar's head—still surmounts it. The Blue-coat School was founded at the same time, to bring up the children of impecunious members of the Church of England, and the same names appear on both committees. But the chief manufacturers and the richest people were Nonconformists—notably most of the Lunar Society—and there was a large sprinkling of Romanists, who were quietly allowed to maintain their priests and places of worship in the district, at a time when their very existence was contrary to law. Even in 1791 neither Romanists nor Nonconformists could sit in Parliament or hold any office under Government, yet paid church rates and the enormous taxes of the day. They had their own schools and colleges, for they could not enter Oxford or take degrees at Cambridge; and the public grammar schools, from Eton downwards, were entirely directed by Churchmen and taught by clergymen.

It was not strange if the interests of the Nonconformists were not those of Churchmen, and if they viewed the downfall of the Established Church and of monarchy in France with a hope that it might bring about some amendment in British law as regarded themselves. Those in Birmingham organised a dinner to be held at Dadley's Hotel in Temple Row on the second anniversary of the capture of the Bastille. The tickets were 5s., including a bottle of wine, and about twenty-three toasts were to be drunk. The usual loyal ones, then, "The Prosperity of the glorious form of Government ratified in France on July 14, 1790," "The Majesty of the People," "The Rights of Man," "The United States: May they ever enjoy the liberty they have so honourably acquired," and ten more, all desiring peace with France and the whole world; yet no one was more shocked and astonished than Dr Priestley, the promoter of this dinner, when Louis XVI. and his Queen were guillotined.

The majority of Englishmen had not forgotten nor forgiven the American Secession, and the whole prosperity of Birmingham was bound up in its manufacture of implements of war; so the working class was easily made to believe that it would starve if there was a long peace.

As Edward Johnstone's mother was of a Nonconformist family, he had many dissenting acquaintances, which had long included Dr Priestley; but among his intimate friends were the Rector of St. Philip's, Dr Spencer, at whose house he first met Dr Parr; Charles Curtis, the Rector of Birmingham and Solihull; the Stewards; and others well known as Tories and Churchmen. He did not attend the dinner, but his house in Temple Row being very near, the railings in front were pulled up and his windows broken by a few rioters brought over from the mining districts to make a disturbance when the Dissenters sat down to dine at three. They proceeded to demolish two Meeting Houses, and to attack some shops with cries of "Down with the Dissenters!" "Hurrah for Church and King!" till they were dispersed by Mr Curtis. But the next day, led by the Town Crier, they were increased by crowds in the town, and a mob accustomed to cock-fighting and bull-baiting was sure to be a brutal one. The owners of threatened property tried to buy it off with money, ale, beer, and expensive wines, but this made matters worse, and for nearly a week there was a reign of terror, Tories and Churchmen suffering as much as Dissenters.

It took the rioters two days to pillage Edgbaston Hall, for it was so strongly built they could not burn it, though the occupant, Dr Withering, like most physicians, was a philanthropist. His botanical and zoological specimens were destroyed, while the old coachman sat crying helplessly in the coach-house. Dr Priestley's house and unique chemical laboratory and library were burnt, but he and his family had already left it. Edward Johnstone[1] offered to shelter him at Moor Green, a house he had just taken in Worcestershire, but as Moseley Hall, the residence of Lady Carhampton, was burned down close by, Dr Priestley thought it wiser to leave the neighbourhood. Washwood Heath, Bordesley Hall, Spark Brook, Showell's Green, Baskerville House, and other buildings were laid in ashes, and the rioters spread over the country to King's Norton, Kingswood, The Leasowes, Hales Owen, Northfield, and Bromsgrove. It is notable that the suburb occupied by manufacturers was unhurt. It was not till the sixth day that any military arrived, but the respectable townspeople were mustered under Captain Edward Carver, who arrested the leaders when they were intoxicated, and produced something like order. Many house-holders fled to Sutton Coldfield, for they could not trust their own servants.

There were no police in the country at that time, but the residents in Birmingham had for two years past supported a night patrol, partly volunteers. Many years later a single watchman kept guard over the whole parish of Edgbaston. Colonel de Lancey, who first appeared with a troop, brought a sympathising message from the King: "His Majesty heard with the greatest concern of the terrible scenes that had taken place in his loyal and industrious town. Such was His Majesty's anxiety to provide for its security that he had given orders for a vast number of troops to march from different quarters for its relief." On being assured that Captain Carver had quelled the riot, Colonel de Lancey sent notice of it in the hope that the troops might be stopped, but the 1st Dragoon Guards and the 11th Light Dragoons arrived the same night, and were quartered on the inhabitants.

[1] "A wise and worthy man," wrote Dr Parr of him to Lord Leicester, "whose firmness in seasons of difficulty and danger would stand even comparison with your own."

Captain Carver (afterwards Colonel)[1] is buried in St. Philip's Churchyard, in the same vault with his parents, his brother (Colonel Henry Carver), and their sister (Mrs Steward). The Carvers owned property near Birmingham in the reign of Edward III., and were engaged on every good work in the town during the eighteenth century,—as members of the Committees which built St. Philip's, the Blue-coat School, and the General Hospital, and as Governors of King Edward's School. The Stewards were Tories; but the Carvers must have been Whigs, as they were at the dinner held to commemorate the centenary of the Revolution of 1688. That dinner probably suggested the one in 1791, but it appears from Dr Parr's letters to Edward Johnstone that much had been done to prevent it. One of the Berringtons of Little Malvern, a Romanist family, being asked to join by Dr Priestley, declined on the ground that "Catholics" were in better odour with the Government than Dissenters. He might have added, as he was a priest, that the Revolutionists were sending the Bishops and clergy out of France, and that they were being received as brethren by the Anglican Bishops and clergy and given shelter in their houses, while the Dissenters had nothing to do with them.

Dr Parr speaks of Edward Johnstone in his writings as a skilful physician and a very enlightened man, and to him (Aug. 10) he wrote of the infatuation of the county, " Where all ranks approve of the riots. Only two exceptions agreed with me in lamenting the unsocial pride which prevented the Dissenters from attaching themselves to any party, and of course excluded them from the protection of every party. In the London Riots the King said he would do his duty, though the magistrates had not done theirs. Does he say so now? I hear on the best authority that great care had been taken by the Sheriff not to put on the Grand Jury any person suspected of a bias in favour of the Dissenters. One of his friends told me so. . . . I saw the chaplain, who dined the other day with Sir George Shuckburgh, who, as other men are, is an open apologist and a secret exulter, and he told the preacher that he had a fine field, etc. I said I will hear your sermon, and if you utter one word unbecoming your office I will communicate it to those by whom you will be chastised without appeal. . . . Are not these alarming symptoms of the general temper of the country. The gentlemen, the clergy, the farmers all say, Why punish the rioters? Were they not acting for the King? Is not Dr Priestley so and so?

"Dr Johnstone this is most important. Pray meet me on Tuesday at Solihull or somewhere before the Assizes come on. Indeed, dear Sir, you will see at last that my judgement on the conduct of the Dissenters is deep and solid. . . . God bless you. . . . The Chaplain is a sensible, popular, but Toryish clergyman. I believe he will keep his word and be wise."

[1] Carver was invalided from wounds, including the loss of an eye.

"There is something scandalous," wrote Catherine Hutton, "in putting on the Committee the justices who first lighted the firebrands of the mob. All the Committee whom I know are the professed enemies of Dissenters except Mr Carver, who I believe is the enemy of no man."

Carver's brother-in-law, Mr Steward, a barrister, was thanked by the Committee for assisting as a magistrate. He died suddenly in the Court at Warwick while conducting a case.

A collection of newspaper extracts of the day show that the press, without exception, supported the rioters, some of its organs pointing out that Dr Priestley's opinions, not being Anglican or Christian, were illegal, as the law protected the Church, and he had therefore put himself outside the law. Edward's answer seems to have been more indignant with the promoters of the riot than Parr quite approved, for he wrote again:—

" Dear Sir,—You are a philosopher with the spirit of a religionist. Let me entreat you to use your influence to obtain the mildest measures possible in punishing the rioters, who were misled and inflamed we know by whom and by what means. A declaration to this purpose will do immortal honour to the sufferers, and direct the scorn of all good men from the rabble to the proper objects. Anticipate the mercy of the crown by your own . . . this will be wisdom and virtue. I entreat you, dear Sir, to use healing and moderate persuasions for the peace of the country . . . above all praise were the friendly exertions of my parishioners in quelling the reports which held me out as a Presbyterian."

To his brother John, who was at Oxford, Edward wrote (the letter is endorsed by John, "when I was trying for Merton," 1791):—

" Dear John,—The agitation of mind which our late terrible riots occasioned has made me unfit for anything; you will have seen full accounts of these in the papers, and I shall only add that Government seems inclined to take the matter up with spirit, and that there is little doubt of the business being investigated fully and the secret encouragers[1] being detected and punished. But say nothing, when I see you I will tell you more. However I have not been inattentive to your interests. [He mentions the votes he has secured.] Notwithstanding all these promises success is very uncertain, and if we are prepared for the worst the pleasure of attaining the object will be the greater. It is a satisfaction to have done everything we could. Let me see you on your return, and do not fail to write if chosen. Your paper deserved a better fate, but the sentiments it contains are too open, too refined, for the age and country in which we live. At present Truth is the greatest libel that can be spoken, and the avowal of those undoubted rights of mankind, placed in such a striking point of view by Locke, and will render his name immortal, is a crime of the deepest dye for which our houses are to be burnt and ourselves chased from Society, whilst the principles which have actually caused two Rebellions against the King and Constitution are cherished and those who profess them rewarded, Yours affectionately,   E. Johnstone."

A year later Edward Johnstone became a member of the Liberal Club in London, and subscribed £100 to Mr Fox, who was in pecuniary difficulties.

The Dissenters were so convinced that the riots had been got up by Government to show the danger of democracy, and by those interested in bringing about a war with France, that they began to organise a second dinner

[1] Among these was supposed to be Lord Aylesford, who lived at Packwood.

on the third anniversary of the taking of the Bastille. Dr Parr's forcible rhetoric, and the courage with which he inveighed against oppression or vice in all stations of life, gave him great influence in the Midlands. He even contradicted the Prince Regent, when dining at Carlton House, on the respective merits of the two Bishops who had educated the Prince. He wrote to Edward Johnstone, May 14, 1792 : " Private. At our Quarter Sessions I was told that the Dissenters intended to meet again in July, but I thought it impossible till I heard it again yesterday and believe it. Dear Sir, I am frozen with horror. . . . If it is so, grant me a great request. Some thoughts occurred to me last night which I will throw into a friendly pamphlet, and by to-morrow I will finish it. It shall be printed by Thomson at Birmingham, who must be told to finish expeditiously. I hope that you or your brother will correct the press, my name must not be known."

The next day he wrote again : " This letter shall not depend upon the Dissenters not having made up their minds to dine, for I shall publish it if they have taken any step to give alarm, and I am doing them a substantial act of friendship if they are wise enough to think so."

John, less engaged than his brother, undertook to correct the press, and to him Parr wrote in a familiar strain (he was not twenty-four), very unlike the formal manner (the fashion of the day) in which he addressed the elder brother : "You must know John that the Socinian writers publish their books in Holland or Poland with the quaint names of Eleutheropolis or Irenopolis, and I think it won't be amiss to imitate them in the title page (though to be sure, my boy, very few of your Oxford doctors will understand it), let therefore the title run thus, 'A letter from Irenopolis etc. etc.,' . . . ten copies must be disposed of to the Prince of Wales, Duke of Portland, Earl of Dartmouth, Mr Mackintosh (Sir James), Mr J. Tweddell, Dr Priestley, Mr Wakefield, Rev. Mr Martyn, Lord Grey, and Mr Fox. You have done well, well, well."

The result was :—

" At a meeting of the Committee appointed by the Societies belonging to the new and old Meeting Houses in Birmingham—

"Resolved unanimously, that the thanks of the Committee be respectfully presented to the Rev. Dr Parr for the candour and benevolence he has displayed in the eloquent and energetic pamphlet lately addressed to the dissenters under the title of 'A letter from Irenopolis to the inhabitants of Eleutheropolis.' William Russell, Chairman."

With the Resolution this letter was posted :—

" Birmingham, *June* 23, 1792.

"Rev. Sir,—It is with much satisfaction that I enclose the resolution of a Committee who represent as honest and independent a body of men as the kingdom contains. Smarting under unmerited suffering and disgrace, they are feelingly alive to every generous attempt to restore peace and order in this distracted town. Their thanks naturally follow your excellent and nervous address, and I assure you they are deeply sensible of the dignity of your sentiments and the uprightness of your intentions; and that they will long retain their gratitude and respect for a character which so forcibly delineates the man of honour, the Christian and the good citizen.

"I am gratified by the present opportunity of begging you to accept my fervent wishes for the prolongation of your valuable life, and for the still further extension of your sphere of usefulness and enjoyment, and of assuring you that I remain with very high respect, Rev. Sir, your sincere and obedient.

"William Russell."

Considering the severity of the law at that date,[1] the Dissenters had cause to complain of the sentences passed by the magistrates—the Rev. Dr Spencer (Rector of St. Philip's), Mr Carless, Captain Carver, and the Rev. Charles Curtis. Only fifteen were committed to the Assizes, and when they were tried at Warwick great efforts were made to save them. One of the judges, Lord Chief Baron Eyre, observed that never in his life had he seen so much rancour and ill blood. In the end three were executed; but of the claims preferred for property destroyed during the riot only £26,961 were allowed.

Several of the burnt houses were left in ruins for many years, and residents, like Lady Carhampton (who was taken to Canwell by Sir Robert Lawley), neither owners of property nor attached to Birmingham by profession or business, quitted the place altogether, and it was many years before it recovered its prosperity. The terrible distress of 1800-1 was an indirect consequence of the riots.

There is another undated letter to Edward Johnstone from Parr about this time. Madame Belloc observes that Parr had been a tutor very early to boys who were statesmen before he was middle-aged, and that he continued to influence them. "Mr Mackintosh (Sir James) came hither on Thursday and he will be glad to see the town and avail himself of your hospitality. If you will meet him in your chaise at Hockley House I will attend him on horseback and we will dine together, and he can go on with you to Birmingham. I never saw so philosophical a mind at his time of life mingled with so much delicacy of spirit and strength in elocution. . . . In truth, my good friend, the Dissenters have such narrow views . . . so visionary and inexperienced, yet so rash, that society has no confidence in their policy. Pitt will oppress them, insult them, yet retain them for his shifting purposes. Had they possessed your firmness, temper and penetration what is bad would not have happened nor could. Yours sincerely and respectfully. S.P."

One of Edward's friends was Mrs Webster[2] of Penns, a very pretty country house six miles and a half out of Birmingham. Her husband met with an accident, which caused his death, in 1788, when hunting with the Warwickshire hounds in Chelmsley Wood, accompanied by the Rector of Solihull, who had

[1] For attending a political meeting in Edinburgh a West Indian proprietor was sentenced in 1794 by a Scottish jury to fourteen years banishment to Botany Bay. He died very soon after landing from the hardships of the voyage.

[2] Her father was Mr Parkes, the banker at Warwick. She was great-aunt to Madame Parkes-Belloc.

breakfasted with him. He owned Hawford at Ombersley, near Worcester, where he probably became acquainted with the Johnstones, and he was on the Committee and one of the earliest subscribers to the General Hospital in Birmingham, and left it £50. He and his father were at the same time Governors of Lench's Trust, an old Birmingham charity, so as Edward was connected with most of the philanthropic societies in the town they often met. After his death, leaving a young widow with four little children, Johnstone helped her in the management of her affairs. As a Presbyterian, her property was in danger during the riots. A secluded lane about a mile long led from the house to the high road between Birmingham and Lichfield, and a report came that a mob was entering the lane. A neighbour, Mr Lloyd-Davies, who rented Pipe Hayes during the minority of the Rev. Egerton Bagot, sent over to invite Mrs Webster to take refuge there, and she at once walked to his house by a field path with her children, the youngest carried by the maid, Molly, while the butler carried one of the little boys. The plate chest was lowered into the small lake in the grounds before they started, and furniture and everything of value packed away in cellars and hay-lofts. That evening, as she was waiting for dinner with other guests in the drawing-room, a Colonel, just arrived from London, who was watching the smoke, coloured with flame, mixing with the clouds in the direction of Birmingham, quietly observed, " I hope they are well roasting all the Dissenters." The poor young widow heard it.

The rapid march of the 13th Light Dragoons from Nottingham *via* Lichfield to Birmingham is supposed to have saved Penns. They crossed the top of the lane, followed by numbers from Sutton Coldfield, and the rioters beat a quick retreat. Although the horses were taken up from grass they marched fifty-three miles in one day.

One effect of the riots was to strengthen the hands of those who advocated the education of the working class. In 1784 a meeting had been held in Birmingham to discuss Sunday schools, started elsewhere,—some say by Mrs Montagu, others by John Pounds. Those who attended and headed a subscription list were Edward Johnstone, still only twenty-seven, the most sanguine as to their result; the Rev. C. Curtis, who quoted his brother's famous joke as to the three R's; the Revs. John Riland (rector of Sutton Coldfield), Thomas Price, John Clutton, C. L. Shipley, and J. Turner; and Messrs W. Bedford, W. Villiers, T. Simcox, R. Lloyd, W. Holden, I. Westley, and T. Lutwyche. Within a year 1400 children were admitted to these new schools, and 500 were catechised in the churches. The masters and mistresses were all paid, and the scholars were much increased in 1788.

The destruction of property in 1791 was followed by the invariable result— very hard times for the poor, which in 1800 became famine. In 1793 a rumour spread abroad that malignant fever prevailed in Birmingham. It was contradicted at once by Edward Johnstone and nine other physicians and surgeons. In 1795 one of the Cabinet, the Duke of Portland, wrote to Mr Heneage Legge of Aston Hall to commend the prudence and liberality of the upper class in adopting measures of relief. " It is," he added, " to the exertions and liberality of gentlemen in general that Government must look in the present distress for effectual relief for the country at large." The taxes were enormous, and enough munitions of war having been collected, and economy being urgent, all Government orders were stopped for a year in 1800. A wet summer spoilt the harvest, and no foreign corn was imported. A subscription depôt was opened, which supplied good meat—soup at 1d. a quart to the poor, who were seen eating potato peelings picked out of the gutters. In 1799 the poor-rate was levied sixteen times, but in the terrible winter of 1800-1 no child born in the working class in Birmingham is said to have lived. The nobility and gentry came forward to do their duty. There were liberal distributions of loaves and meat on different days from the larger houses, including those of the Johnstones, and George III. set the fashion adopted here of forbidding flour to be used in the kitchen for any purpose than bread. All kinds of wild fruits and herbs were suggested for fattening pigs instead of meal. The youth of that day grew up with an ingrained economy as regarded food. They recollected hearing their fathers say as they sat down to a meal that they felt as if they could hardly eat when they thought of the hungry poor. The quartern loaf was 2s. 2d., and this state of things prevailed more or less till the battle of Waterloo.

The Inniskilling Dragoons, as well as a battalion of Volunteers, were quartered in Birmingham throughout the year 1800 for fear of riots, and the press-gangs were active, for men were too dispirited to enlist voluntarily. "Working men were always in rags, and guns were being proved morning, noon, and night. The street posts were made of old cannon, and bread was a luxury which the country labourer only got on Sunday." This was the recollection of an old inhabitant of the first twenty years of the nineteenth century in the great Midland Metropolis.[1]

The matrimonial project referred to, rather too soon, in Mrs Montagu's letter failed or was put off, and Edward Johnstone was thirty-six before he married Catherine Wearden of Olton Hall, Solihull. By the death of her parents, and lately of her only sister, Letitia, whose illness had long delayed the wedding, she was left alone in the world, and through her mother had inherited the estate of Fulford Hall, in the same parish. This lady, *née* Letitia Holden, was the descendant of Sir Cresswell Levinge[2] (1627-1701), Attorney-General in 1679, on one side, and on the other of a county family owning considerable estates in the Midlands. The first of the Levinge family was Archbishop of Canterbury in 1005, and he crowned King Canute. Sir Walter Levinge, his collateral descendant, accompanied Richard I. to the Crusades.

[1] When statistics were collected in South Staffordshire in 1815 the male population exceeded the female by one-third. The compiler supposed that the conditions of life in the mining districts were too hard for women to support them.
[2] His brother spelt the name Levinge and Levinz, so did their father. The *Reports of Sir Cresswell Levinz*, two volumes published in 1702 in black letter, were republished in 1722 and 1792. He represented the Crown in various trials of supposed Popish plotters in 1677-79. His uncle, Robert Levinge, was hanged for supplying Charles II. in 1650. His sister was Maid of Honour to the Queen of Bohemia, daughter of James VI., and some of the thick brocade dresses she wore, and her travelling chest with the German Custom House mark on it, still exist.

This Knight's descendant was living at Baddesley Ensore, in Warwickshire, in 1434. One of his great-grandsons migrated to Derbyshire, and was ancestor of the baronet of that name. The Levinges who remained in Warwickshire owned Fulford Hall in the reign of Queen Elizabeth. Sir Cresswell Levinge's children were William Cresswell and Catherine. His grandson is described as a gentleman of Westminster in 1720 and a K.C. The elder daughter of the K.C, who inherited Fulford Hall, married one of the Holdens, who then owned Erdington Hall (Wood End); and their only daughter married the Rev. Thomas Wearden, who came from Lancashire to hold a mastership at King Edward's School in Birmingham in 1747, but resigned it when he married to take the Rectory of Solihull.

The Holdens, like the Carvers, were people of substance in the district when a tax was levied by Edward III. for the war in Scotland. Fulford Hall was left to Mrs Wearden, while her brother, much younger than herself, inherited Erdington Hall. The Weardens lived at Olton Hall, and when Mrs Wearden was left a widow, about 1781, she took a house for the winter in the Old Square. There Edward became acquainted with them. The sisters were highly accomplished. Catherine had lived much in London with her aunt, Mrs Caldecott, her uncle being a K.C.; but she was much worn by her sister's long illness, and Edward's father was less pleased with the marriage than his son expected, as he hoped to re-establish a strong family on his little Scottish estate, and at present his only grandson was Thomas's very delicate boy.

Thomas, after losing £2000, which his father gave him, as well as his wife's money in business, had taken Holy Orders. He married, in Aug. 1779, Sarah Hale, a descendant of the eminent judge, Sir Matthew Hale; and from a letter asking Dr Parr to preach for his charity schools at Bewdley, he seems to have been an earnest clergyman, at issue with most of his congregation on the advisability of teaching the labouring class to read and write, though he pointed out that it would make them better servants. He held several livings, as pluralists were then allowed, and his father thought he had done enough for him, compared to what he was able to do for his other children, also that Thomas, as an Episcopal clergyman, could not legally officiate in Scotland, so ought not to live there. On hearing of Edward's engagement, he offered to settle Galabank on Edward as his part of the marriage settlement, for his son had lent him £2000, to be repaid at his death. Edward declined, urging the prior right of his elder brother. The offer was repeated after Edward's first child was born, and again refused, but the old gentleman was not to be dictated to as regarded Thomas, and it appears to have been left to Edward as late as 1795.

Lockhart, the youngest brother (except William, who died young), was reading for the Bar, and his father in 1790 wrote to him about a Chancellor's living. Lockhart, a spoiled child, who took far more liberties with his parent than the elder sons ventured to do, replied: "The Chancellor [Thurlow] has not resigned, nor is he likely to quit his office for some time to come. Immediately upon his last quarrel with Pitt he disposed of about forty vacant livings. This was the prevailing report this day week. Besides the disagreeable rubs he has met at Court, he has been much vexed by a favourite daughter marrying without his consent. In a temper always fretful these accumulated disappointments have produced so great an irritability that he is barely tolerable. Judge, then, whether a letter from Worcester will not have the greatest effect. In writing to him, the living of Baynton should be the first in the letter, that he may see its purport at a glance."

Johnstone sent his letter, and Lockhart wrote: "I took it to the Chancellor's House in Great Ormond Street. He is in the country, nor do the servants know when he will be in town. I left the letter and half-a-crown to the care of one of the servants, who faithfully promised to deliver it the instant he could."

Another letter from Lockhart alludes to the medal adjudged by the Royal Medical Society to his father for a treatise on scarlet fever. He inquires after Mrs Siddons, whom Johnstone was attending, and laments that she had left the stage before he came to town. He describes debates he had heard in the House of Commons, in one of which Eldon was at his best. Lively and amusing, Lockhart got anything he wanted out of his father, who, on his tenth birthday, had written to Edward fondly describing his cleverness, and that he was growing "very handsome." He was started under good auspices, as, besides the patronage of Sir W. Pulteney, he was intimate with some of the future lights of the Bar—Mr Pearson, afterwards Advocate-General of India; Erskine, who asked him "to spend two days with him at Hampstead, where he was going for fresh air"; Mackintosh (Sir James), who, "when I dined with him, seemed to have given up the French Revolution." He alludes to the death of the Marquis of Annandale, and to a rumour that "Sir James Johnstone of Westerhall will succeed to his titles." He was evidently fond of saying unpleasant things.

Edward's marriage settlements were arranged in accordance with his wishes, the bride's estates and £17,000 being settled on their joint heirs, failing which, entirely on himself. This was her wish, as she had no heir-at-law except her uncle, Thomas Holden of Erdington Hall. He was of extravagant and dissipated habits, having quarrelled with her father, the late Rector of Solihull, because he had warned him of the consequences; and she was anxious that Fulford Hall should in no event revert to him. Mr Mynors and Mr L. Withering were the trustees. Edward wrote to inform his mother that the wedding was to take place at Solihull:—

"Dear Mother,—I hope the things I have sent will be sufficient for the purpose I intend, if not, I do insist on your informing me of everything you want, and also that you do not on any account use what I send for any other than yourself. I know the generosity of your temper has been such as to lead you at all times to deny yourself to accommodate your family, but it becomes them in their turn to take care of you, for they owe much to the unceasing tenderness which you have shown them both in sickness and health. I hope you will not think that I was guilty of inattention to you at the beginning of the business I am about to engage in. I assure you I particularly desired my father to inform you, and would have written if I had supposed he would have neglected it. I think you will approve the choice when you know the object. We shall be married on Tuesday morning. I desired Thomas to come over to perform the ceremony. We mean to dine at Hagley, and if you will come with my father and meet us it will give us great satisfaction. Pray do come if you can. I shall hope to see as many of the family as are either able or disposed to come; the more there are the better I shall be pleased. On Wednesday we will come to Worcester. What we shall do afterwards I am uncertain. If I thought it would be convenient to Thomas we would go there, but that I shall find out from himself. Mary is at present at Hay Hall. If there is anything else we can do for you, pray let us know, etc."

The bridegroom was so late that the bride grew very nervous, and the good-natured Rector (Rev. C. Curtis) mounted the tower himself and put back the clock when the hands were dangerously nearing twelve. The Solihull Church Register records that "Edward Johnstone of the parish of St. Philip Birmingham and Catherine Wearden of this parish were married in this Church by license this 2nd day of October in the year 1792. By me T. C. Johnstone, Rector of Hope Bagot, in the presence of Mary Johnstone and Charles Curtis."

After the wedding tour they retired to Moor Green,[1] in Worcestershire, which lies conveniently near to Birmingham and to the Fulford estate. The same year they employed Eginton of Handsworth to paint the window in Aston Church to the memory of Letitia Wearden, who was buried there in a vault with her parents, and with the Caldecotts.

On Feb. 13, 1794, Mrs Edward Johnstone gave birth to a daughter. It was feared that the child would not survive the day, and her father went to find a clergyman to baptise it. He met the Rev. Charles Pixell and brought him in, and the child was named Catherine Letitia Wearden. Mr Pixell was at that time Curate of St. Martin's, under Mr Curtis, and his father was Vicar of Edgbaston, so they were probably old acquaintances, and the friendship between the two families still continues. In 1796 another daughter— Hannah Maria—was born, the last of her mother's children who survived more than a few hours, and her grandfather, afraid lest his Scottish property should go off in a female line, as had twice occurred, to the family misfortune, began to think of a resettlement. Henry was in Edinburgh on military service, and his father directed him to see an advocate on the subject, thinking that Edward's formal renunciation would be necessary, and sending a draft of the new resignation which he wished to make.

The advocate's comments on the document were uncalled for, such as reminding Johnstone that the dates must be in writing, not in figures, as it was only a memorandum for a charter; but there were other signs that John-

---

[1] It has been occupied by Mr Joseph Chamberlain, M.P.

stone was then an over-worked man in failing health. Henry was a light-hearted bachelor, in character resembling his father's great-uncle, John, who left Galabank to be scrambled for by his creditors; but John, still a bachelor, was a careful, steady, and ambitious man, and never gave any trouble to his parents. He was an M.D. of Oxford, and his medical essays were widely discussed in the profession. In acuteness and energy he closely resembled his father and eldest brother, and, like most of the contemporary members of his family, shone in conversation. It was not strange that the old man fixed his hopes on this son as the most likely to carry on the line with male descendants able to keep up the family traditions. The advocate informed him that no renunciation on Edward's part was necessary, as the existing deed was a revocable one, and no further step seems to have been taken till 1799. Possibly, recollecting his remonstrance with his own father, he did not wish to take so strong a step without much thought.

Meanwhile Edward did nothing to alter his father's views, and events seemed to justify them. Thomas died in Oct. 1799, leaving daughters and the one delicate boy. Edward's wife became a confirmed invalid. He had settled John in his town house in Temple Row, where their sister, Mary, came to reside with him, for Edward, absorbed in domestic cares and his duties as a land-owner and a magistrate, seemed inclined to withdraw altogether from his profession and leave it to his brother, while their father continued abnormally active. When, in 1799, Johnstone resigned his honorary post at the Worcester Infirmary on the score of age, Dean Onslow begged him to reconsider it, for to all appearance he was in good health. But he only consented to remain till a successor could be found. Edward's daughters would each have a much larger income than the Scottish estate brought in. So in 1799 a document was deposited in the Scottish Register House resigning Galabank to his sixth son, John, with a charge of £400 towards the maintenance of Thomas's family. He stated that he made this settlement for certain reasons, but does not seem to have told either of his sons the particulars of it.

The eldest child (afterwards Mrs Crompton) of Mrs Webster of Penns had a pleasing recollection of the home at Moor Green. Edward had driven over to Penns to see her mother, and invited the young girl of fifteen to come back with him for a few days' change of air. She remembered in her old age the kind, gentle face of Mrs Johnstone and the pretty little fair-haired, rosy-cheeked Catherine, who was brought down by her nurse in her white lace frock and blue sash to wish her parents good-night after the late dinner, and to sit on her father's knee for a few minutes to share in the dessert. A long period of weak health ended in a chronic malady, and on April 4, 1801, Mrs Edward Johnstone was buried in Aston Church by the side of her parents and sister, Dr Parr taking the funeral service and insisting on the elaborate ritual to which he was very partial. The last few years of the elder Johnstone's life seemed crowded with tragedy.

CHAPTER XXIII.

The Aufreres—The Lockhart Tragedy—Thomas Johnstone—Letters—King Edward's School, Birmingham—Young James—Little Hannah—Johnstone of Worcester—Death of Mrs Johnstone, followed by that of her Husband—Mrs Murray.

IN Johnstone's diary there is an entry, Dec. 1792: "I learn that my great-niece, Mary Anne Matilda, gave birth to a daughter, Nov. 17, at Heidelberg, and that the child was named Louisa Anna Matilda, after Louisa, a Princess of Prussia, who with Mrs Aufrere, her mother-in-law, are to be Godmothers." This great-niece was the wife of Anthony Aufrere of Hoveton, York, and the daughter of Mrs Lockhart.

Catherine Hutton [1] wrote from Malvern Wells a few years later: "I have been a great favourite with a most elegant and clever woman who is gone, and from whom I have a long letter. She was a Lockhart of a Scottish family famed for many things. [Here follows an account of their exploits.] The great-grandfather of my lady collected a number of papers relative to the attempts of the Stuart family whom he favoured. These are now published price five guineas by Anthony Aufrere, Esq., her husband, and I have a note from her to her cousin, Dr Johnstone of Birmingham, desiring him to lend them to me. The father of Mrs Aufrere (descended from Cromwell's sister) was a general officer in the Austrian service, who routed the Poles in defiance of the orders of his commander. He then rode post to Vienna and carried the tidings of his disobedience to the Empress Maria Theresa, laying two flags which he had taken at her feet and acknowledging that his life was forfeited. He was made a Count . . . which honour his daughter now enjoys though she does not assume it, and the two Polish flags were added to the family arms and are now painted on her carriage."

General Lockhart had taken his young and beautiful wife to, what her relatives affirmed from her description was the worst court in Europe. She was presented by Lord Stormont, the Ambassador, as his own relation, and the Emperor, Joseph II., stood sponsor at the baptism of her first son, who was named Joseph, and died an infant. She was much attached to her uncle and first cousins, her only near relatives, and stayed with them both at Kidder-

[1] *Reminiscences of a Gentlewoman.*

minster and Worcester, acting as godmother to Lockhart. In a letter written to her uncle when the child was about seven she says: "I hear little Lockhart wants to be a sailor. I am sure he is much too pretty and delicate for such a profession." Her cousin, Mary, stayed with her in Scotland, and remembered an unpleasant scene between the Lockharts, after which Mrs Murray, who was also there, said to her very impressively, "Mary, never marry for a coach and six."

Mrs Lockhart returned from the trying climate and hot rooms of Vienna, and appeared at St. James's, when George III. remarked, in a stage aside, "Mrs Lockhart—Mrs Lockhart *was* a pretty woman." Her husband, in love with a younger woman, began to look about for a cause for divorce, more easily obtained in Scotland than in England. Johnstone had a heart-broken letter from his niece, and remonstrated very strongly with the General, whom he imagined chose to believe mere gossip; but the poor wife died very suddenly in 1787, it was believed from an overdose of opium. Her husband at once married Annabella Crawford, but the child of this union—James—only lived a few months, and General Lockhart died himself in 1790 at Pisa, aged sixty-one, of disease of the brain,—which was perhaps his excuse.

Mrs Lockhart left a son, Charles, born in 1778, who succeeded to his father's title and property, but he died of consumption, unmarried, in 1802, when the estates passed to his cousin, Macdonald Lockhart.

Thomas Johnstone was presented to the living of Fisherton Anger, near Salisbury, in 1798, and relinquished Hope Bagot, which Sir William Pulteney wanted for another friend, in exchange for the livings of Winkfield and Aston Botterell. He was very popular, and preached for charities all over the diocese, when his father delighted in going to hear him. He was now in comfortable circumstances, and very active. His death was a totally unexpected blow.[1]

Aston Botterell, *Sept.* 30, 1799.

"Dear Sir,—I am requested by Mrs Johnstone to inform you of the melancholy event which happened here last night. Your beloved son and my most worthy friend and intimate acquaintance, Mr T. C. Johnstone, departed this life at 7.30 yesterday. I was sent for but arrived too late to take my last farewell. I found the whole family in tears looking to me for help which I was unable to afford them. It was one of the most trying moments of my life. Mrs Johnstone hopes to see you this evening or to-morrow morning. In the meantime I will give every assistance in my power. I am your most obedient humble servant.

"(Rev.) J. Purcell."

Johnstone sent Lockhart to Aston Botterell, and wrote a very agitated letter to Edward, who sent this undated reply:—

"Dear Sir,—The melancholy event of poor Thomas's death is indeed most awful and unexpected. John went to him on Thursday and stayed till Friday afternoon. He represented him as having had a bad inflammatory sore throat

---

[1] Before presenting the living again Sir W. Pulteney wrote to ask Dr Johnstone if he imagined there could be anything unhealthy about the house or neighbourhood to cause it.

. . . lanced by Mr Wheeler, by which he was much relieved, and, though low and weak, did not think him in much danger. He went again early yesterday morning so that Lockhart would meet him at Aston Botterell. This event does indeed throw a most serious care and duty upon us, and you may be sure I shall not shrink from taking my portion of it. I promised the poor fellow some years ago[1] that if anything happened to him I would take care of his son, and I mean most religiously to perform that promise. Whether he should come here immediately or remain at his present school till Christmas we will concert together as well as the destination of the other parts of the family when we have had more time for calm consideration. . . . I have myself had a very bad cold and slight sore throat but am now well, and Catherine had so severe a cough that I had some fear of croup, but thank God, it is entirely gone. Mrs J. is as well as can be expected. I sincerely hope you and my mother will be supported under this very severe affliction, and that the comfort you will receive from the surviving branches of your family will compensate the heavy losses you have sustained. I am, with the truest sympathy, your dutiful son. E. J."

Worcester, *Oct.* 1799.

"Dear Edward,—The remains of my dear son were yesterday committed to the earth in the Chancel of Botterells Aston. He has left all his brothers a legacy of his fair fame, and the care of his children with sufficient documents to secure £90 a year in the funds for his wife's maintenance, and after her death a provision for the surviving children, of whom I intend to take care of two of the younger ones without neglecting any of them.

"I enclose his Will for your consideration and after administration. It must be recorded in Doctor's Commons some time. Though cut off in the midst of his days Thomas had the satisfaction to find himself possessed of means for the enjoyment of life, had it been continued. God's Will be done on Earth as it is in Heaven. The thread is a measure for a ring for Mr Davenport. Inscription ob. 29 Sept. 1799 et. 44. I dare say the family will not be hurried out of their present residence.

"We are well. I mention this lest you should hear a strange report which alarmed the people here this morning,— that I was drowned near Pershore. I was uncommonly sound asleep in my bed when your mother came to tell me that the Mayor and Corporation had sent a message of inquiry on the subject, and I went to the Cathedral to dissipate the anxiety which had possessed the public mind. In fact two horses of the Star and Garter were drowned.

"I beg you and all my family will guard against the mischief of quick walking up an ascent, especially after a meal. I know nothing so likely to force the blood to the lungs to that degree as to produce a violent inflammation of

---

[1] Thomas proposed in early life to a lady, who accepted him, but her letter never arrived. He thought she had treated his offer contemptuously, and after a time married Miss Hale. Later, he met the other at a dance, and an explanation followed. He was never cheerful afterwards.

the lungs. By this, not attended to in the beginning, your brother has fallen. The pulmonary system and the lesser circulation has been shown to be the most assailable part of our frame. Temperance in action, in thought, and in regimen, are indispensably necessary to conduct you all to the age of threescore years and ten, to which with a frame originally feeble has arrived your affectionate J. Johnstone.

"Remember us all most kindly to your wife and children. I daresay she will have a good time. Let her be assured of this, for it is as probable as that ripe fruit shall drop from the tree. You may be sure of my care of the documents I speak of which are actually in my hands."

Edward adopted his little niece Catherine, who was six months younger than his eldest child, and his wife's God-daughter. It was arranged that his nephew, James, should live in Temple Row under the care of his aunt, Mary, and receive his education at King Edward's Classical School. The widow and the other children found a temporary home with the old Doctor in Foregate Street, where she lost the child born soon after her husband's death.

King Edward's School, in Birmingham, was endowed with part of the lands seized by Henry VIII. from the Hospital of St. Thomas and the Guild of the Holy Cross. The Hospital was included in a Priory on the site of the Old Square, and when the Square was pulled down to erect the present buildings parts of the walls and many bushels of human bones were excavated. As the country was left without means of education when the monasteries were suppressed, Henry's successors established grammar schools, and as the masters were educated by monks they followed the same kind of teaching,—almost exclusively Latin, Greek, and mediæval literature. In Birmingham the School occupied the old building of the Guild; the masters were always to be clerical graduates of Oxford or Cambridge, and the Board of Governors, who elected themselves, were members of the Church of England till the last quarter of the nineteenth century, when the old Charter was remodelled. As time went on and the funds increased an English school was added for boys intended for a commercial life, and elementary schools all over the town to give a useful education to both boys and girls. Many eminent scholars have been educated in the Classical School, including some distinguished military and naval men, Carey, the translator of *Dante*, several bishops, and an Archbishop of Canterbury. In 1852 this department contained 150 boys, but far less in 1800.

Young James was transferred to this school in January 1800, and showed the same capacity for study that his father and uncles had done before him; but the Register of the Cathedral notes: "May 10, 1804. Buried James Johnstone. Aged sixteen." His little sister Catherine, the only one who lived to be sixty, as well as his cousin Catherine had a fond recollection of his youthful good looks and his gentle disposition. A cadetship in the H.E.I.C.S. had been procured for him, and his outfit was already obtained by his sanguine uncle, John, though his more experienced uncle, Edward, was convinced that he was consumptive, and would never reach manhood.

Three weeks before the death of his wife in 1801 Edward Johnstone retired from his post of Honorary Physician to the General Hospital, Birmingham, and his brother, John, was at once elected to fill his place. After her death he took his two children for change of air to Leamington Spa, accompanied by the faithful nurse, who was a poor relation of his mother's family. Leamington was then a little village with less than 300 inhabitants. One of the children caught scarlet fever; her father and the other child took it from her, and little Hannah,[1] the youngest and healthiest of the two, died Oct. 23. She was buried in the old Churchyard at Leamington.

From Dr Johnstone to his son:—

"Worcester, *Oct.* 26, 1801.

"Dear Edward,—It grieves me that you who have always been the comfort of your parents, and all that belong to us, should now be called to drink so deep from the cup of affliction. I partake it with you, but hope you will invite the topics of comfort which must occur to you as a man of experience and as a Christian, and also those diversions from mournful thoughts which arise from business. What to our feelings is distress in the death of infants is generally Providential mercy; to the deceased certainly so; why then do we mourn that this dear tender plant is withered at an early period of life? It is the lot of 500 in every 1000 that are born to die before the age of five. In this affecting event let us trust in the Lord with all our hearts and not lean on our own understanding. He has done it; that should both quiet and comfort us. I hope your own health will be restored, and it is a great mercy that Catherine's is recovered. You must by this day's post have seen my invitation to you and Catherine to come here as soon as your health will permit, and I hope it may be done with advantage to your health and Catherine's. Dr Parr at the same time can indulge us and his other friends with his society. You may be sure I am most deeply and most gratefully impressed with a sense of his kind and sincere most friendly offices: in every thing else the great man appears, in his conduct to us, the eminently good man; present my kindest and best respects to him and attend to his advice and consolation. It gives me great satisfaction that he is with you and promoted your return to Birmingham. I hope the Being, Who chastises us, yet reserves brighter days for my children and their aged parents, who remain ever affectionately yours, J. Johnstone.

"Our love to Mary, John, Catherine, and Cattie."

About a month before Johnstone wrote in his diary: "If I have not been a very profitable servant to the public, it is certainly contrary to strenuous efforts on my part long continued. It is easier, says De la Bruyére, for a person known in the world to obtain celebrity for a work of moderate merit,

---

[1] A precocious child, born at Moor Green, Dec. 18, 1796; baptised in Moseley Church by the Rev. Dr Parr, Oct. 2, 1798, her sponsors being General and Mrs Amherst and her Aunt Mary.

than for a work of the first merit by an obscure person to make its way. This observation is proved every day; it supports the vanity of disappointed obscurity, and should not be forgotten by some who flutter on the wings of celebrity."

Dr Crane, who succeeded him in Kidderminster, spoke with the greatest admiration of Johnstone's skill in checking outbreaks of fever which from time to time appeared. After young James's death, when the elder had removed to Worcester, the Magistrates requested him (1785) to visit the Workhouse at Kidderminster, where something like jail fever had broken out, and he at once stopped its progress and cured the sick. He had a weak chest in his youth, and his old age was distressed with asthma; and although he continued to protest against bleeding, with a few exceptions, as being useless and generally mischievous, he tried it on himself very frequently to be fit for his work. His wife died March 3, 1802, and his diary, March 9, records:—

"This day my dear companion, the tender nurse of eleven children, is conveyed to the tomb at Kidderminster to sleep with her father and five of her children. Thomas lies at Aston Botterells."

At the beginning of April he went to sit on a Commission of Lunacy in Birmingham, his opinion being considered of special value in such cases, and from thence, within three days, he travelled about the country in his carriage on professional duties nearly 200 miles. Only five days before his death he went to Bromsgrove, thirteen miles distant, and three days later was requested by a husband to come and see his wife. "Sir," he said, "I am a dying man, but the end of usefulness is the end of life, and if my daughter can come with me I will go."

"That my father did not actually die in his carriage was all that could be said," wrote John Johnstone. He drove home and was lifted out on to the couch, on which he expired the next day, April 29, 1802. His biographer speaks of his vivacity and cheerful conversation with his family up to the last day of his life, and that, "seeing his end approaching, he prepared for it with the same firmness as if he were about to take a long journey. His intellect was clear, his mind calm, and he expired at Worcester after a short, and in no wise painful, struggle in the 73rd year of his age."

Berrow's *Worcester Journal*, April 29, 1802, says: "This morning died at his house in Foregate Street, James Johnstone of Galabank, M.D., well known in this city and county for his humanity and eminent skill during an extensive practice of more than half a century, for the firmness and uprightness of his moral demeanour, the variety, extent, and depth of his knowledge, the warmth of his affections and the steadiness of his attachments. But his fame is not confined within the sphere of his personal activity, his genius is consecrated to posterity by an immortal physiological discovery, and the improvements he has introduced into the science and art of healing will ever rank his name among the benefactors of mankind."

There were also sympathetic notices and biographies in Aris's *Gazette*, the *Monthly Magazine*, and the *Gentleman's Magazine*. The two last had obituaries of Mrs Johnstone,[1] in which her quiet unobtrusive life and devotion to her family were described. Her husband[2] was buried by her in the vault at Kidderminster, May 3, 1802, and commemorated by a tablet in Worcester Cathedral, with a Latin inscription, placed on the south wall, just above the tablet to his eldest son.

Directly after his father's funeral John went to Annan to look at his estate. He paid a visit to his aunt, Mrs Murray, the only survivor of his father's family, at Dumfries, and found her very depressed, her grandson, Count Charles Lockhart, being lately dead. She gave him her father's Family Bible and other books and law papers of much importance which her brother had wanted, and never saw all his life. A letter from a Dumfries minister to John announced the end.

"Dumfries, *Dec.* 10, 1808.

"Sir,—Your respectable and worthy relative and my friend the late Mrs Murray of Belriding, by a disposition executed by her in my favour as executor, among some other small bequests has made the following, 'To my nephew, Doctor John Johnstone, Physician in Birmingham, six silver table spoons and a divider with eleven tea spoons and a pair of tea tongs, all marked with the old names of his family. Item, Miss Mary Johnstone, sister to the said Dr John Johnstone, my two gold rings and the box which contains them.' . . . Our late venerable friend was interred agreeably to her own desire in the tomb of her husband.[3] I trust everything relative to her last illness and funeral has been conducted in a manner that will give satisfaction to her relatives.

"Adam McCheyne."

[1] Aris's *Gazette*. "Died March 3, Worcester, in her 69th year, Mrs Johnstone, wife of Dr Johnstone of that City, and mother of the Drs Johnstone of this town. Her affectionate kind-hearted disposition, genuine unaffected piety, and unwearied attention to all the duties of her station, conciliated the love and esteem of all about her, and will make her to be long remembered with gratitude and respect."

[2] Many anecdotes are told of his practical illustration of his theories. When visiting a girl's school, after warning the schoolmistress to open the dormitory windows, he saw that his orders had not been obeyed. He at once poked out the glass with his gold-headed cane. He strongly objected to the extreme severity of the law hanging men for fifteen offences besides murder. One evening he put a table outside his house to make an astronomical observation, and, while he was bringing out his telescope, a thief ran away with it. He would not allow any search to be made for him, lest it should be a case for Botany Bay, adding, "Well it is a no-table observation." His son Edward some years later was robbed by his butler of two large silver salvers, but simply dismissed the man without prosecuting him or recovering his property, as hanging was the penalty for stealing from a master. When young, the elder Johnstone was bitten by a dog supposed to be mad. He cut out the part with his pocket knife.

[3] On the Murray family vault in Ruthwell Churchyard :—

"Also the body of John Adam Murray of Belriding, son of the above David Murray and Mary Carlile, who died Dec. 27, 1757. Aged 43.

"And of his son David, who died aged 9 weeks, July 1753.

"Here lies Elizabeth Murray, daughter to Adam Murray and Isabella Johnstone of Belriding, a child of very hopeful disposition, cut off by the will of God in the 9th year of her age, 1765.

"Here also lies the body of Isabella Johnstone, widow of Adam Murray of Belriding, aged 81, who survived her husband more than 41 years, died Dec. 4, 1808."

CHAPTER XXIV.

Dr Carmichael Smyth, and John Johnstone's Defence of His Father—Wilberforce's Letter—John's Second Pamphlet—Sir W. Pulteney's Letter—House in Foregate Street—Belsham's Letter—Edward's Second Marriage—The Pearsons—Dr Withering—Visit to Portugal—Johnstones of Westerhall—John's Marriage—Edgbaston Hall—The Monument—Visitors—Edward Irving—Thomas Carlyle—The Children of Edgbaston Hall—Letters—The Adult School—The Rent Dinner—Eminent Artists.

IN 1795 one of the King's physicians, Dr Carmichael Smyth, a scion of the old Border family of Carmichael, described in a pamphlet how he had purified the Winchester Barracks, filled with Spanish prisoners during an epidemic in 1780, with what he believed was a new discovery of his own—the use of vapour raised by acid mixed with salt. Johnstone read the pamphlet, and makes this comment in his diary upon the claim Dr Smyth put forward as to priority of invention: " I hope I may be excused in presenting to posterity my claim to an early use of marine acid to destroy contagion in putrid fevers. [He gives the dates of the publication of his book on the subject in London (1758), and of his son's (1779).] Ever since that time it has been constantly directed by me to be used in workhouses, gaols, and in private practice, with a success which has recommended it in this country. I do not mean to deprive M. Morveau and the French chemists and physicians, nor Dr C. Smyth of the honour due to them for applying and extending this invention. But I also have a claim to assert invention; and perhaps the spark struck by me may have kindled a more splendid blaze. What I recommended in the obscurity of my retired situation may gradually have made its way to the attention and experience of these learned men, aided by a more extensive and correct knowledge of chemistry. Nevertheless, I also am an inventor."

In Feb. 1802 Dr Smyth petitioned the House of Commons for remuneration for purifying the Winchester Barracks in 1780 and the Union Battleship with what he called his own discovery—the use of vapour raised by acid mixed with salt. Johnstone was too ill and occupied to exert himself in the matter, but his son John, anxious that his father should have the credit due to him, wrote a paragraph in the *Morning Chronicle*, March 12, 1802, pointing out that his father had used that mixture for the same purpose during the prevalence of malignant fever in Kidderminster in 1756, and published a book on the subject, quoted in Germany and France, and of which a whole edition had been sold out; that since then it had been in common use not only among the apothecaries but among the shopkeepers and manufacturers of Worcestershire; that the younger James quoted his father's book in his thesis, "De Angina Maligna," printed at Edinburgh in 1773, and added his own views as to the success of this mode of correcting contagion in a publication in 1779; that when Edward was a student at Edinburgh the men's portion of the hospital was filled with soldiers of the Duke of Buccleuch's regiment suffering from typhus fever, and the young man recommended his father's invention, which Dr Hope at once ordered to be used, but discontinued it the next day as it made some of them cough. Nothing daunted, Edward alluded to it in the next medical exercise set him by Dr Hope as to how to cure a suppositious case. No notice being taken of this anonymous paragraph, except that Dr Carmichael Smyth procured Johnstone's *Book on Fevers*, John, by the advice of Sir William Pulteney, wrote to Mr Wilberforce, who had presented Dr Smyth's petition to the House, and also to Mr Addington, the Prime Minister (afterwards Lord Sidmouth), himself the son of a physician, and to Sir Joseph Banks. He said he did not wish to stop or divide the grant claimed by Dr C. Smyth, but it was not just that his father's discovery should be entirely ignored. Wilberforce answered from the House of Commons, March 23: "Dr Johnstone's character, I assure you without a compliment, gives too much weight to whatever comes from him not to make me desire on every ground of receiving any elucidation he can give to any subject."

Johnstone died while the Committee was sitting, and a letter from Dr Percival, of Manchester, to John observes: "You have vindicated the claim of your late excellent father to a very important discovery in a manner which does honour to your abilities, candour and filial piety, and I am confident that the public will approve your exertions on this occasion, and that even my friend Dr Carmichael Smyth will find in what you have done no cause of umbrage or complaint."

The matter might have rested there, even when the Committee gave the solicited reward to Dr Smyth, had he not written to Wilberforce, with something like a sneer, that James's death, and Edward's and Henry's illness, proved the inefficacy of their father's treatment.

This was in answer to John's pamphlet, "Account of the Discovery of the Power of Mineral Acids in a State of Gas to Destroy Contagion" (March 1803), which he forwarded, with copies of his father's and brother's books on Fever and Diphtheria, to the Committee presided over by Mr Wilberforce, through Sir William Pulteney. The last approved of John's zeal in the matter, but reminded him of the critical state of public affairs, which prevented any private question from receiving notice at that moment.

John, being absorbed with business consequent on his inheritance of Galabank and his large practice, did not hear of Dr Smyth's letter, or that it had been printed after the Parliamentary custom, till his father's old friend,

Sir John Wrottesley, M.P., Co. Stafford, told him of it. Simple and straightforward himself, he had believed that the facts only required to be made known to be accepted. He was too late in the field, and his father's reputation was too near his heart, to argue the subject to the best advantage. He was apt to overload his gun, and in 1805 he published a crushing reply, to which his brother, Edward, contributed a long letter.

It is not for a moment to be supposed that Dr Smyth did not quite believe, in 1795, when he wrote on the subject, that the acid vapour had never been used before. He was a hard-worked man of sixty in 1802, with a numerous family to put out into the world, and had evidently not kept himself up in current medical literature to the same extent as his rivals. His cause was gained by Dr Lind, of Windsor, asserting that he had *never heard* of this antidote till Dr Smyth wrote in 1795, and by a quotation from a very old book to the effect that no one had yet found any means of arresting contagion in fevers.

Sir William Pulteney and one or two other Scottish friends had been very cool with John since Galabank was bequeathed to him over the head of his nephew and elder brothers, and Sir William even declined further correspondence with him, but put off this frigid attitude after a visit to Edward at Ladywood House, where they met. John sent him his second pamphlet, which was acknowledged.

'London, *March* 30, 1803.

"I received yours of the 22nd two days ago, and have read with great satisfaction the paper you sent me on the comparative merit of your father's discovery of the muriatic acid for destroying contagion and of nitric acid for the same purpose. I forwarded it with your letter to Sir Joseph Banks for the Royal Society; and I should think that even if it should be published, as I trust it will, by the Society, yet that it ought also to be published as a separate treatise, not only for the honour of your father's memory, but for giving very important information to mankind on a subject of very great importance. I approve very much of the style and manner in which you have detailed the particulars concerning this matter. I am, etc. William Pulteney.

"To Dr John Johnstone, Birmingham."

It was declined by Sir J. Banks on the ground of it being controversial; but shortly afterwards John was made a Fellow of the Royal College of Physicians, and of the Royal Society. He had already received a medal from the Royal Medical Society of London for his *Essay on Mineral Poisons*, published in 1793.

Although the two brothers had differences a little later, Edward declined to make Galabank a cause of quarrel, for he had always treated John paternally in the assistance he had given him, but he felt it, and Henry and Lockhart took his side. The house in Foregate Street was advertised in 1804 as "Those Extensive premises situate in Foregate Street, Worcester, entirely freehold, and recently occupied by Dr Johnstone, which are well calculated for a Gentleman's habitation or any other purpose where a considerable number of rooms are wanted. Also a large seat in St. Nicholas's Church" (over which, on Johnstone's death, a hatchment had been placed). The reference is to the lawyer, or to the executor—"Edward Johnstone, M.D., Ladywood, near Birmingham." The coachman, Tolley, was taken on by Edward, and the butler by John.

This old house, with the family crest—the spur and wings—interlaced on the iron gates, stood detached in walled grounds on the site of the Foregate Street Station, and was removed to make the railway in 1849.

The house occupied by Johnstone in 1755 in the Tything was left to Lockhart, who sold it, but later bought another there, and ended his days in it.

A letter from Belsham, the historian, to Edward shows that his old schoolfellow was contemplating a second marriage:—

"Hackney, *Oct.* 1, 1802.

"My dear Sir,—I called yesterday at the Equitable Assurance Office, where agreeably to your desire I promised, vowed, and subscribed certain things in your name, all of which I trust that, like a good churchman, you will think yourself bound to believe and to do. They gave me a receipt for you, which I take the liberty to enclose. I am sorry you should think it necessary to apologize for employing me upon this occasion, as I hope you will take for granted that it will give me very great pleasure to transact any business for you in London as far as lies in my power.

"I regret that you have given up the intention of going to France, as it will deprive me of the pleasure of seeing you and your lady on the way. But I hope that the visit to Hackney, though deferred, is not laid aside. I presume the knot will soon be tied, and my earnest wish and prayer is that it may be productive of all the happiness which it appears to promise to the latest period of human life.

"Dr Parr is in town, and I hope the report is true that Sir Francis Burdett has presented him to a valuable living in Huntingdonshire.

"With my best compliments to your sister and brothers, I am, dear Sir, your affectionate friend and servant. Thomas Belsham."

The Peace of Amiens in May 1802 had caused a rush of English travellers to France, but its rupture within a year consigned many of these to prison or exile for twelve years, as Napoleon, contrary to international law, prevented them from leaving the country. Among others so detained was the eldest son of Lord Hertford and the Greatheds of Guy's Cliff, Warwick.

An entry in the Register of Tettenhall Church, Staffordshire, records, Oct 5, 1802:—

"Edward Johnstone, Widower, of the Parish of Birmingham, and Elizabeth Pearson, Spinster, of this parish, were married in this Church by licence. Witnessed by [the bridesmaids] Jane Elizabeth Matilda Hooke [afterwards married to the bride's eldest brother] and Mary Davies."

Mr Pearson of Tettenhall Wood, the bride's father, died in 1796, three years after a visit to Portugal for the benefit of his health. An incident is worth recording. Two ladies of his own name, who believed him to be their nearest if not only relation, lived near to him. He managed their affairs; they regarded him as their heir, and so certain were they that he would succeed as heir-at-law that the survivor left only an informal Will in his favour. He was taking possession when another came forward, claiming to be a nearer relative to the deceased. He had no evidence to prove it, and as the case was tried it was on the point of being decided for Mr Pearson, when the latter, making a final search in his own family papers, found that his rival was right. He at once stopped the legal proceedings on the ground of this discovery, and the other took the property. As coal was found under it some years later, it changed hands for £90,000. His eldest grandson and heir (General Hooke Pearson, C.B.), when he related this, added, "Still I would rather my grandfather had acted as he did."

The Pearson family had been friends of the Johnstones for ten or fifteen years. They lived two miles from Wolverhampton, and were related to Dr Withering of Edgbaston Hall and to Mr Hector, Samuel Johnson's friend, in the Old Square. In the *Life of Dr Withering* he is described as "paying a visit to his esteemed relatives, Mr and Mrs Pearson of Tettenhall Wood; in that sweet retirement he for a few months benefitted by every assiduity which the most refined friendship could suggest; and which he again experienced at a later period, when the same amiable family so materially conduced both to his pleasure and comfort in a foreign country."

The Pearsons also paid many visits to Edgbaston Hall, where Edward used to meet them, and, in 1791, the eldest daughter was staying in Moseley (two miles off) when her relative's house was besieged for three days by the Birmingham mob, because Dr Withering was a Liberal and advocated the admission of Romanists and Nonconformists to the rights all now equally enjoy. It was only saved by the arrival of the military. Much damage was done, but, like Edward Johnstone, he did not apply for compensation from the already over-taxed town. His medical theories were opposed to the Johnstones on the subject of fever, and his mode of counteracting a tendency to consumption was low diet and bleeding. His relative, Mr Pearson, had suffered so much from this system as a delicate child that, after taking his degree of M.A., his health never enabled him to follow a profession, and as in the summer of 1792 he had consumptive symptoms it was arranged that, accompanied by his wife and daughters and two elder sons, he should join Dr Withering in spending a winter in Portugal.

The Pearsons arrived at Edgbaston Hall from Tettenhall, Sept. 14, 1792, and set off the next day as far as Worcester, whither they went by slow stages to Malvern, Cheltenham, Bath, Clifton, and Teignmouth to Falmouth, and embarked, Oct. 24, on the Lisbon packet. Byron described its discomfort some years later, and as the Barbary corsairs were then the terror of the Mediterranean, so that Portugal was the favourite resort for English invalids, every vessel bound in the autumn "for the Tagus was inconveniently crowded

PLATE XIII.

EDWARD JOHNSTONE, M.D., 1757-1851, AND HIS WIFE, ELIZABETH PEARSON.
(GALABANK).

with valetudinarians, and in this instance fifty-nine persons were stowed in a ship of about 300 tons burden." The voyage took eleven days, and Mr Newport, one of the passengers, entertained them with impromptu verses as they entered the Tagus, specially referring to the three Graces of Staffordshire, as the Miss Pearsons were called.

After six weeks in Lisbon, the Pearsons and Dr Withering joined another English family in taking a large house—St. Jozé de Riba Mer—five miles out of the extremely dirty capital, and on the road to Cintra. There the young ones danced or held an amateur concert every night, and studied natural history in the day. The seniors visited some of the hospitals for consumption in Portugal, and, from its extreme prevalence in this lovely climate, felt convinced that it was contagious, and spread by the foreign invalids. On May 14 they sailed for England, escorted by an armed cruiser, as war had just been declared with France. The vessel was chased out of its course by a privateer, and was three weeks on the road.[1] Sea-sickness and real privation compelled many of the passengers, including the Pearsons, to remain some time at Falmouth before they began their journey to the Midlands. Among those who called on them were the Fox family, with whom they kept up a correspondence for many years.

On returning to Tettenhall, Penelope, the second daughter of the Pearsons, married Mr John Tayleur of Buntingsdale, Shropshire, his father being still alive; and the youngest, Anne, married the Rev. Richard Warner, of Bath, a theologian and antiquarian of European celebrity. Before Elizabeth's engagement her second brother, Thomas, one of the clergy of Bath Abbey, married Sarah, the daughter of an old friend and neighbour, Mr Gibbons; and the youngest, Edward, was united at St. George's, Hanover Square, to Lucy, the sister of Sir Thomas Hesketh. Only John, a rising barrister in London, remained at home, and he was engaged, and when Mrs Pearson saw a prospect of settling her eldest daughter she gladly gave up Tettenhall to this son, and went to live with the Warners in Somersetshire.

Edward Johnstone had left Moor Green soon after his first wife's death, intending to retire to Leamington, but, strongly advised by Dr Parr to continue his profession, he removed to Ladywood House, which then stood in picturesque grounds among fields, with two or three detached houses near. Now the grounds are covered by streets, one called after him, if the house itself still stands.

On the rupture of the Peace of Amiens a third battalion of Loyal Birmingham Volunteer Infantry was formed in 1803. They paid for their own arms and equipment. Lord Dartmouth, who lived at Sandwell Park, close by, was the Colonel; Henry Johnstone was appointed Lieutenant-Colonel; and among the other officers were John Wilkes, Wyrley Birch, Jervis, Attwood, William Withering, E. Thomason, Bellamy, Meredith, Lloyd of Bingley, Moore, Cope, Francis Eginton, Rabone, Steward, Whitmore, Linwood, John Parkes, Webb,

[1] The captain had broken his parole when a prisoner, and prepared to blow up his ship rather than surrender.

Williams, Dixon, Sheppard, Grafton, Wilding, Walker, and Vale. On Nov. 21, 1803, they were inspected on their Parade ground, where Broad Street now stands. Drs Edward and John Johnstone, Thomas Smith, John Carmichael, Robert Bree, George Edward Male, Francis Rogers, and William Gilby offered to attend all Volunteers gratuitously, and published a letter with advice how to preserve their health and efficiency. The necessity of temperance, personal cleanliness, regular hours, and active sports could not be more strongly advocated at the present day.

Besides subscribing three guineas each for the Volunteers, for whom large sums were raised in a month, all the ladies in the neighbourhood made flannel clothing for the troops. Lady Dartmouth provided 120 garments, others altogether 5000; 9000 canal boat and coach owners offered their services in case of invasion, which was talked of as so likely that little Catherine Johnstone and her cousins selected the cupboards and closets they should hide in if Bonaparte got so far inland.

From 1797 onward, money was raised in Birmingham for the widows and children of the gallant men who fell at Camperdown, Trafalgar, Waterloo, etc. It had always been a loyal town, praised for its patriotism by Samuel Johnson in 1768, when it petitioned the King to tax the American Colonies.

Sir William Pulteney Johnstone succeeded to his brother's baronetcy of Westerhall[1] in 1794. He was reputed to be the richest commoner in England, and more than once refused a peerage. He had served in seven successive Parliaments when he brought in a Bill to abolish bull-baiting, after a visit he paid to the Edward Johnstones at Ladywood, where the matter was doubtless discussed, as bulls were regularly baited in the Bull Ring and Gosta Green for the entertainment of the denizens of the Black Country, who poured into Birmingham on those occasions.

The Bill was not passed till 1835, being opposed on the ground that it was a manly, British sport! Sir William married, a second time, the widow of Andrew Stuart of Castlemilk in 1804, and died the next year, but lived long enough to act as godfather to young Edward Johnstone, born at Ladywood, April 9, 1804.

His daughter, Henrietta Laura, who was created Countess of Bath in 1803, died in 1808, leaving no heir. Her husband, General Sir James Murray, who had seen much service in the West Indies, survived her three years. His conduct of military operations in Sta. Lucia, where Henry Johnstone served under him, was the subject of an inquiry, to which Sir William alludes as very uncalled for in a letter to Dr Johnstone in 1795.

The *Gentleman's Magazine*, in recording Sir William Johnstone Pulteney's death at Bath House, Piccadilly, June 29, 1805, says: "He had been in a very dangerous state for several days past, but his immediate decease was the result of an operation. In private life he was remarked chiefly for his frugal habits, perhaps the more striking as he was supposed to be the richest commoner in the kingdom. His funded property amounted to nearly £2,000,000, and he

[1] The late Westerhall only left an illegitimate son, James Murray Johnstone.

was the greatest American stockholder ever known (1805). He had the greatest borough interest of any gentleman in the country, and of course his friendship was courted by all parties. In the latter part of his life he was remarkable for his abstemious manner of living, his food being composed of the most simple nourishment, chiefly bread and milk. In his own rooms very little fire was used, not from economy, but because he declared his health to be the better for it. Sir William's character has been much mistaken by the world. He was penurious only as to himself. All his servants enjoyed comforts unusual in most other families. His nephew, the heir to his title and entailed Scottish and West Indian estates, comes in for about £10,000 a year. His Shropshire estates go to the Earl of Darlington, and if no will is forthcoming, the lady he married about two years ago will inherit a third of his personalty." He paid £120,000 for an immense tract of land in Tennessee, which, managed by agents, who sold off portions of it separately, had become very remunerative. He had bought Over Wormanbie and other properties from the Hope Johnstones, and founded the Agricultural Professorship at the Edinburgh University.

There was a grand funeral in Westminster Abbey. The procession left Bath House, preceded by two pages, then eight horsemen, two more pages, and the hearse, drawn by six horses all covered with escutcheons, four pages on each side, followed by eighteen mourning coaches, each with six horses, having two pages on each side, and the horses covered with escutcheons. In the first was the deceased's son-in-law, Sir James Murray, and the young baronet, Sir John Lowther Johnstone of Westerhall, then about twenty-two. The other seventeen carriages contained many of the nobility, the Bishop of Chichester, and Andrew Cochrane Johnstone (no relation to the deceased, but had taken the name). The Rev. Dr Dakins took the service, after which there was a consultation as to whether the vault ought to be made deeper, for the coffin came within five inches of the surface. The relatives decided to let it be as there was just room for the stone. The obituaries differ as to Sir William's age, which was about eighty-six.

His nephew, the only legitimate son of "Governor" Johnstone, was returned heir male to his uncle, William, in 1809, when his cousin, Lady Bath, was dead, after having been returned heir male to his uncle, Sir James, in Oct. 1805. Sir James had presented a petition to the House of Lords, claiming the honours and titles of the Marquis of Annandale as heir male whatsoever, June 12, 1792, immediately after the death of the last Marquis. But when Sir James died in 1794 his brother and successor dropped the proceedings. They were resumed, just before Sir William's death, by his heir on June 17, 1805. On both occasions the petition was opposed on behalf of the third Earl of Hopetoun, great-grandson of the first Marquis of Annandale in the female line. Dr Johnstone believed himself to have a nearer claim than Westerhall, but the two families had been very friendly for at least three generations, and other reasons prevented him coming forward, particularly as he imagined that the Lords would give the Earldom, which was granted to male or female heirs, to the undisputed eldest female, and would not also revive the Marquisate.

Sir John Lowther Johnstone married Charlotte Gordon[1] of Cluny, Jan. 17, 1805, but died six years later in 1811, aged twenty-seven, leaving a son, George Frederick, and two daughters. It is understood that his trustees were empowered to sell some of his Scottish property to provide for the younger children, and Mr Graham of Annan, knowing that Dr John, as he was commonly called, wished to increase the Galabank estate, wrote to advise him about it. John had married, in 1810, Anna Delicia,[2] only daughter of Captain George Curtis, and niece of his friend, Mr Curtis, the Rector of Birmingham and Solihull, and of Sir William Curtis, the well-known Lord Mayor. He proposed to invest some of his wife's settlement money in these lands—Relief, Burnswark, Woolcoats, and Axletreewell, and empowered Graham to buy. Graham writing to William Johnstone, a writer in Edinburgh, asked him to attend the sale there, June 28, 1815, and secure them if they could be had for £15,600 free of auction duty, the sellers paying the cost of conveyancing. "This is the utmost Galabank is inclined to give for the property, and it is considerably more than the lands have been valued at by anyone except myself. Indeed no one valued them more than £14,000, and I am afraid I may have advised him to go rather too far." The agent exceeded his powers by offering the price without excepting the costs, but Galabank never thought of escaping from the bargain on this ground and accepted it, when the Curtis trustees declined to allow the money to be invested in Scotland. At a time when the Bank of England had only paid in paper for eleven years there was probably difficulty in borrowing the sum required. He was ignorant of Scottish Law, and it was strained to its full extent. He offered to pay all expenses the Westerhall trustees had been put to, including the auction expenses on both occasions if the estates were put up again, as he "was unable, from the absurd objection of his own trustees, to complete the purchase."

He was at that time in very large practice, and before railways the journey to Edinburgh was not an easy one. It is impossible not to feel that this position and his employment of agents, the Edinburgh one being very careless, was taken advantage of in the terms of sale, which he assumed would be those in common use. The Westerhall agents gave him no option to find the money and keep the lands, when thirty days were spent in a slowly conducted correspondence. The terms of the sale gave three alternatives to the vendor—the last and highest bidder was obliged within thirty days to grant bond for the price offered by him (with a sufficient cautioner), payable in Edinburgh, or incur the penalty of a fifth part more than the price, as well as the interest;

---

[1] She married secondly Richard Weyland of Woodeaton.
[2] Writing to the first Lord Leicester (Coke of Holkham) Dr Parr describes his guests at dinner : "Mrs Corry, handsome, sensible, and a Whig; Mrs John Johnstone, equally beautiful, quite as accomplished, quite as amiable, and the Whig daughter of a Tory Captain ; Miss Mary Johnstone, less young, less handsome, equally if not more sensible, and a most resolute Whig; Tertius Galton, a semi-demi quaker in religion, a semi-beau in dress, a lover of wonders and of rarities in science, and by profession a Whig," etc.

the vendor might either insist on the completion of the purchase by the last bidder with this penalty, or he might treat with the previous bidder, obliging Galabank to pay for the extra expense and loss; or he might consider the lands unsold, put them up again for sale, and only amerce Galabank for his failure to complete the purchase by the costs of the first auction. The vendor preferred the third course, and, after receiving payment of the first auction expenses, claimed the costs and penalties which would have been his due if the lands had been offered again to the previous bidder, and also the fine for which Galabank would have been liable if he had completed the purchase. The vendor put them up again at the previous price, and, finding it too high, petitioned the Lords in Council and Session in Nov. 1815 to be allowed to lower the upset price; and then sold Relief and Burnswark at a reduced price, holding back the rest. He brought an action against Galabank and his agent for £3129, 6s. 2d. as penalty for not originally completing the purchase, and also for £5000 for damage sustained by the Westerhall estate from selling the lands at a smaller price (to a friend), and for any loss that might be sustained in the future sale of the remainder.

The defendant showed that the petitioners had deliberately preferred the alternative of declaring the sale void, and making the most of the lands by separating them, but Lord Reston adjudged, Jan. 20, 1818, that the defendant, Dr John Johnstone, domiciled in England, was liable for the sum claimed, and also for any difference between his original offer and the price for which the remaining lands may be sold. He again appealed, pointing out that this decision enabled the Westerhall trustees "to carry on a speculation upon these lands on the extraordinary footing that they were to draw the benefit while he had all the loss" (June 3, 1818). But the Lords, undoubtedly annoyed at the Curtis trustees thinking land in Scotland an unsafe investment, upheld the previous decision, and John had to pay the costs, which, in the end, mounted up to over £18,000. The affair was so mortifying that his wife induced him, for the recovery of his spirits, to take a few months' holiday in London, on the pretext of education for their two daughters, who received music lessons from the Abbé Liszt and drawing lessons from the artist, Mulready.

The Curtis trustees were very short-sighted. They preferred an estate in the Vale of Evesham, with a house, mentioned in Shakespeare as "Haunted Hilboro'." This was sold by one of John's representatives for under £4000 a few years ago (it was valued at £16,000 in 1868); and land in Annandale now commands a fancy price.

Edward invested his second marriage settlement in the estate of Dunsley Manor, near Kinver, and in a farm at Upton Snodsbury, lying in both East and West Worcestershire. For some years he put a bailiff into Dunsley, and kept the farm of several hundred acres in his own hands. Edgbaston Hall[1] was

[1] Edgbaston Hall, says Dr Withering's biographer, was a spacious and commodious mansion, surrounded by a park, affording an interesting combination of wood, water, and undulating lawns. "There, launching upon the unruffled surface of the lake, he devoted a summer's evening to angling, whilst the swan 'with arched neck proudly rowed with oary feet,' or, attended by Newfoundland dogs, he would inspect his beautiful herd of French

vacant in 1805, and his wife had pleasant associations with it, and wished to live there. They moved to it from Ladywood in 1806, just a fortnight before their second son, James, was born, April 12. It was then two miles out of Birmingham, which could only be reached across fields or down Sir Harry's Road into the Bristol Road, part of the old Roman way from Derby, Lichfield, Birmingham to Worcester and beyond. The adjoining parish was Northfield in Worcestershire, and the stream which empties into a lake of thirty acres in Edgbaston Park was the boundary of Worcestershire and Warwickshire. The situation was unique, planted on the highest tableland in England, the ground sloping from the house to the lake, and beyond it the Lickey Hills rising in the distance; the ancient Church, now enlarged till it is like a little cathedral, still backed by the old trees of the Hall, as it was in Camden's day, with the park and its magnificent foliage. The park still covers 120 acres, though portions have since been detached for villas. The rent was £300 a year, and Johnstone lived there forty-five years.

Only one house was then in sight between the lake and the Lickey Hills, and that has given its name to the road. It was a lonely farmhouse, where a priest lodged before 1780, when it was a felony for a Roman priest to live in England, and the penalty of death if he celebrated Mass. Everyone in the neighbourhood knew that he lived there to officiate for the benefit of his co-religionists, who met on Sundays and festivals, but no one showed him up; and when the "Catholic Relief Bill" was passed Edward Johnstone and Dr Withering, who were then in command at the General Hospital, directed that the Roman priests should be allowed equally with other denominations to visit members of their Church in the Hospital. In London this privilege was not granted till eighty years later.

A few years after his marriage John removed from Temple Row to Monument House, so called from a tower built in the garden to enable a former owner to see his estate on the other side of the Lickey. A footpath across fields connected it with Edgbaston Church and Hall, and before the chimneys of Selly Oak intercepted the view the old grey tower of Northfield Church could be seen from the stile which stood at the corner of Church Road and the modern Westbourne Road.

The Johnstones, like their father, were very sociable, and much given to hospitality. At Edgbaston Hall there were two large dinner parties regularly every week, and the family on other days seldom dined alone. The list of guests, who came from all over the county, as well as from Worcestershire, was long preserved, and the name of young Mr Webster of Penns often occurs. A few years later his eldest daughter, the beauty of the neighbourhood, married James, the younger son of Edward Johnstone. They carried on the male line of the Johnstones of Newbie and Galabank.

The John Johnstones at Monument House entertained even more of the

cattle, or observe the sagacious habits of the interesting colony in the rookery in early spring, or later, when necessary, to reduce the too numerous progeny." Such Edgbaston was, within the memory of the writer.

outside world, as they were nearer the town. When Birmingham had neither a Mayor nor a Member, it was customary to select an influential resident near Birmingham, and to ask him to receive a distinguished foreigner when he was desirous of seeing the world-renowned manufactories. Englishmen and Scotsmen came with introductions. Two old Roman roads cross Warwickshire and the central position of Birmingham in coaching and posting days brought everyone through it who was going from London to Wales, Derby and the North-West, yet the town was still so unimportant that in 1820 it was seriously proposed that the London coach should leave the Birmingham mail bags at Stonebridge to save the long hill which leads up to it.

Dr Johnstone's father had obtained, through Sir William Pulteney, a commission for an Irving; and a more humble member of that warlike clan, but who became more celebrated—the Rev. Edward Irving—stayed at Edgbaston Hall on his way to pay his first visit to London. His striking appearance, real religious enthusiasm, and great eloquence deeply impressed all who met him, and subsequently made a convert of the only surviving daughter of the house to the "Catholic Apostolic Church" when she stayed in London with some friends of her stepmother's, and with them attended his services. After her death a voluminous correspondence with Irving on religious subjects was burned. It rather cooled his friendship with her father, but he was always warmly received at Monument House by the John Johnstones, where he met their son-in-law, Dr Hook, who, in a published letter, has left a testimony to his sincerity, though he calls "Irvingism" the High Church gone mad. Henry Carey, Thomas Carlyle, and his brother John were also visitors at the Monument and at Edgbaston Hall.

Dr John Johnstone in 1815-16 took the young Russian Grand Dukes, Nicholas, afterwards Emperor, and Michael, who each gave £100 to the Hospital, round that admirable institution when it stood in Summer Lane; the younger talked agreeably, but the elder was shy and silent—perhaps not a good English scholar.

Gladstone, the future Lord Sherbrooke, the Peels, Lawleys, Adderleys, and many other Eton and Winchester boys, afterwards noted, travelled to Birmingham on the top of the coach and breakfasted in the early morning at the "Hen and Chickens." Lord Sherbrooke and his brothers generally broke their journey here for a few days to visit their cousins, the Websters, at Penns. Young Gladstone, with characteristic impatience, seems to have conceived a horror of Birmingham, from the weary wait in New Street till the Liverpool coach was ready to start.

There was living in Birmingham at that time an adventurer, Andrew James Cochrane, eighth son of the eighth Earl of Dundonald. He took the name of Johnstone when he married Georgiana, daughter of the third Earl of Hopetoun, so his son and daughter appear in the long entail of the property now owned by Mr Hope Johnstone. He had served in the army in India, when he was made a Colonel in 1797, and Governor of Dominica. "His rule was marked by tyranny, extortion, and vice. He drove a brisk and profitable trade in negroes, and kept a harem."[1] He was recalled in 1803 and his commission suspended. He and his subordinate accused each other of peculation, and the result of a court-martial obliged him to leave the army. He published a Defence, and, being a Liberal, Mr Whitbread presented a petition to the House on his behalf, and he was returned for Grampound, in Cornwall, in 1807. He was unseated for bribery, and through the influence of his brother he got a post in the Customs in the Leeward Isles, but, after a course of bribery and corruption, broke his parole and escaped to England. He joined a gun manufactory in Birmingham, where he made guns for 17s. each for the Spanish Government, having received £3, 3s. for each; and from several Spanish colonies he had large remittances and goods, for which he engaged to ship arms and ammunition, but never did so. His first wife died in 1797, and he married the daughter of the French Governor of Guadeloupe, but at this time she was obliged to divorce him. He ended by spreading false news for speculative purposes, and contrived to get his nephew, the celebrated Lord Dundonald, accused of it, while he fled the country—1814—and disappeared.

A ball was given at Edgbaston Hall on the evening of Oct. 5, 1811, when the two sons of the house, Edward and James (already privately baptised), and their little sister Elizabeth were received into the Church by the Rev. C. Pixell, Vicar of Edgbaston. Elizabeth was named after a sister who had died, aged fifteen months, of pneumonia. The second Elizabeth, born May 7, 1811, lived till July 28, 1814, when she died very suddenly of croup. Another son, Charles, was born on the night before the battle of Waterloo, June 17, 1815.

Charity was not forgotten in the midst of amusement, for no mendicant was turned away empty-handed from the back gates. As this was widely known, a very miscellaneous collection came—Bohemians; Roumanians, who found that here their curious Latin dialect could be understood; Frenchmen and others, who were prisoners for years in England, and when the war was over preferred to remain. Once a group of self-styled Frenchmen, having received the customary dole, wished "Long life to your Honour" in an unmistakable Irish accent as they went away. There was no parish school at that time in Edgbaston, and Dr Johnstone built a lodge, which still stands, though the entrance it was intended to command has long been closed. The lodge combined a school, where the keeper of it, with the ladies of the family, used to teach as many girls as could come; and they were given a neat dress, such as was then worn by the working class. In his own large servants' hall any men who wished to learn to read and write were invited to come on Sunday evenings, and they were taught by the master of the house, his sons, and their tutor, and any friend who might be staying with them. The scholars paid a penny a week, nominally for pens, ink, and paper, but it was returned with interest at Christmas when they all had supper at the Hall,—a lesson in investment. This adult school, and the anxiety the men showed to learn, made a great impression on some of those who stayed at Edgbaston, and were

[1] *Dict. Nat. Biog.*

destined to play an important part in the future, notably on Sir Rowland Hill, the founder of the Penny Post.

The Rent Dinner, which took place at the autumn quarter, was an imposing occasion. The farmers dined in the dining-room, the cottagers in the servants' hall, and they were as well entertained as if they had been in the peerage. Never was there a more indulgent landlord as regarded the rents, but it began to be too much considered as a matter of course that he could afford to do without, and when he died some of his cottagers had paid no rent for twenty years. He gave all the shooting rights to the tenants, but this plan had its disadvantages.

It was a great boon to the neighbourhood, which at that time had no public park, that Dr Johnstone allowed people to walk in his park every week-day if they gave their names to his butler. David Cox, Creswick, Elijah Walton, and other artists made their first sketches in Edgbaston Park. The late Miss Ryland of Barford, whose benefactions are a household word in Warwickshire, as a young girl used to come with her governess to draw the magnificent trees. In winter, when the lake was frozen over, thousands skated on it. The present occupant of the Hall, Sir James Smith, in spite of the immense growth of the town, generously admits the public on these occasions for a charge of 6d., which he pays over to the local charities.

CHAPTER XXV.

Scarcity in 1816—Employment Found for Starving Workmen at Edgbaston—Dinner at Lord Hertford's—Colonel Henry Johnstone—Lockhart—The Peace of 1814—The Advocate-General of India—Death of Dr John and Dr Edward Johnstone — Their Heirs — Dr James Johnstone — Mrs Buckley (Westerhall) — General Sir James Johnstone — His Heirs and other Relatives.

THE year 1816 closed with almost a repetition of 1800-1. The war with France was over, and the country had to pay for it. Everything was taxed, from almanacs and windows to coffins, the necessaries of life being included, so that everyone might pay their share. The manufactories had for years been employed in feeding, clothing, and arming our large army and navy, and now both were reduced to the lowest point, and the Government—the great employer—drove numbers of officers and men into civil life, and crowds of mechanics were turned off. The harvest failed, and foreign wheat was heavily taxed. Edward Johnstone made many improvements in the grounds of Edgbaston Hall to help the otherwise unemployed. He added a sunk fence between the lawn and the Park, carried the drive in a circle round the grounds, enlarged the lake, and added a small one on the other side of the Park. When the men had done a moderate day's work they were given a good supper in the servants' hall. Parliament voted a large sum, to be spent in building churches, as a thankoffering for the close of the war, but the payment was deferred some years owing to bad times.

Christ Church, an imposing building which stood opposite the future Town Hall, was already finished and consecrated in 1800. Edward Johnstone took great interest in it, as the ground floor was to be entirely free and unappropriated. He was one of the first Committee of the Mechanics' Institute, and in 1812 was one of the Committee for the establishment of the Deaf and Dumb School.

The description that Bishop Butler (of Lichfield) gave of John Johnstone in his obituary notice in the *Gentleman's Magazine*, 1837, applied as much to the elder brother. "He held a distinguished station among the most eminent of his professional brethren, not only in the town and neighbourhood of Birmingham, but to a much greater distance than provincial celebrity usually extends." People did not go to London for everything at that time, and the medical works then published by London physicians show that they were not in advance of the Johnstones if the survival of the systems which the latter inaugurated is a test. The Court physicians considered themselves at the head of their profession, but two, if not more, of those who attended George III. and his successor had not gone through the regular medical education, though very clever men. But from the year 1800 Edward Johnstone became more of an amateur than his brother. He learned Anglo-Saxon when he was fifty, with a view of completing a history of the Anglo-Saxons on much the same lines that Freeman afterwards carried out. His library filled the ground floor of the east wing of Edgbaston Hall, and contained a good collection of classical, historical, and geographical works, a large portion of them collected by his father, and here he spent many hours in the week; but the illness of his wife and of his youngest son, as well as the stirring politics of the day, in which he always took very great interest, interfered with his literary pursuits, and the result of his work is still only in MS.

In 1814 John dined with the Marquis of Hertford at Ragley to meet the Prince Regent and his brothers, the Dukes of York, Clarence, and Kent. As soon as the ladies had left the table the Prince Regent asked his opinion as to a mysterious attack with which he had been seized, and which gave him intense pain, five years before. He had sent at once for Sir Walter Farquhar,[1] who was laid up with the gout, and returned a message that the Prince should be "bled profusely," but by the time it came the pain was gone, and his doctors were unable to account for it. He gave minute particulars, and Johnstone told him what he believed to be the cause. When George IV. died, sixteen years later, Johnstone wrote to Sir Herbert Taylor and to Sir Henry Halford to ask for a report of the *post-mortem* examination, and it proved that he was perfectly correct in his diagnosis.

In 1817 John Johnstone was one of the Committee presided over by Lord Dartmouth for the foundation of an Orthopædic Hospital; and both he and his brother were on the Committee for the establishment of the Society of Arts in 1821.

Henry Johnstone died at Edgbaston in 1811 and was buried in the old Churchyard. He had served for thirty years when he retired, invalided, as Lieutenant-Colonel, with many interruptions from bad health, since he suffered from typhus fever, caught from bringing his brother James in a carriage from Worcester to Kidderminster. Before that date he even stood three years in the West Indies—where his regiment, the 91st, was decimated by fever and war—without being the worse. Sir William Pulteney wrote to his father that he had seen Henry in London, just after his return, looking extremely well, and was glad to hear that he attributed his good health to following the advice Sir William had given him on the West Indian climate. His father bought his lieutenancy, and he was employed in recruiting for a year and a half in England, when the result of fever incapacitated him for present duty, and he

[1] Sir Walter Farquhar's grandson, afterwards Dean Hook of Chichester, married Anna Delicia, eldest daughter of Dr John Johnstone.

was on half-pay till 1787. He again was ordered to the West Indies with the 66th Regiment till 1791, when he was permitted to raise an extra company of sixty men for the chance of a Spanish war, which gave him his promotion to Captain,—raising a company being no small expense to the officer. He marched the men from Worcester to Edinburgh to join the 94th Regiment, and embarked at Dunbar for Portsmouth *en route* to Gibraltar, where, after a year, they went on to the Cape. In 1798 he was allowed to go home on a certificate of extreme ill-health from the Governor, Sir James Craig, and a year later, being promoted to Major, received orders to join the 45th Regiment in India. He fell ill in London on his way, and a certificate from Sir Lucius Pepys to H.R.H. the Duke of York gave him leave of absence, and in 1800 he went on half-pay.

In 1803 the Major was appointed Lieutenant-Colonel of the Loyal Birmingham Volunteers, but employed later in the extra recruiting service, in which he was always very successful. In 1809 he wrote to Edward from Preston, Dec. 5, 1809:—

"I have been stationed at this place for eighteen months, and I was only moved from Gloucester from being senior to the inspecting field officer there, and ordered to the regiment then at Manchester, where, finding I should be also senior, the Officer Commanding got an order to move me immediately to this place on the recruiting service. I have not met an officer of higher rank since my arrival here, but I find from a confidential letter of the paymaster of the regiment that changes are about to take place which will place me in the 1st Battalion, and that I must join it in Portugal. This I should wish to have done, for with my present rank I may benefit by it, but unfortunately a monitor has come which I fear will impede my purpose. [He gives his symptoms, which were similar to those preceding the death of his uncle, Edward, at Moffat.] You will, I am sure, not impute cowardice to my charge, though I may be obliged to retire, but I will thank you for your opinion, as no step is yet taken. My life here has been an active one, and I have claims on my country—at least many less deserving have been provided for.

"I hear John is soon to be married. As to Lockhart, I know nothing of him. I think the most idle person in the family might have given me a letter. [He was godfather to Lockhart's eldest daughter.] I thank you for the notice you took of my little boy. I request my best remembrances to Mrs Johnstone [here the seal is torn out] and the three children. I remain, yours very truly,

"H. Johnstone.

"Dr Johnstone, Edgbaston, near Birmingham."

Lockhart lost a great incentive to work by marrying a lady from Bath, Elizabeth Greene, with some money; by obtaining an easy post, a commissionership in bankruptcy, and being early made a bencher in Gray's Inn. Mrs Greene was a Joliffe, a well-known family in Hampshire, and her husband, a merchant at Poole, had served the office of High Sheriff. Lockhart was married at Bath

Abbey, and took a house at Kempsey, but went straight from Bath to Ladywood House to pass the honeymoon. They came with post horses, and when crossing a very lonely part of the Lickey Hills were stopped by highwaymen, and the boxes fastened on to the back of the carriage were carried off. These contained the best part of Mrs Lockhart Johnstone's very handsome trousseau, and were never recovered. Yet on that road a gibbet, with the bones of a man hung in chains for highway robbery and murder, still remained.

Peace being made with France and Napoleon sent to Elba, Lockhart took his eldest daughter to a convent school at Rouen, where her grandmother was educated in pre-revolution times; but when Louis XVIII. fled from Paris in 1815, and the British Government still refused to recognise Napoleon, there seemed a prospect of another long war, and he at once set out to bring her home. As the mail packets had stopped, he hired a fishing boat at Southampton and went up the Seine.

After the battle of Waterloo little Hannah returned to the convent, then removed to Paris, and for three years more her companions were the daughters of the marshals and general officers who had so long fought against this country. Her cousin, Catherine, had been educated since 1805 at the school of a French refugee, Madame Dupont, in Russell Square, which had not been long built, and cornfields and gardens still covered the sites of Woburn and Tavistock Squares, and all beyond to Islington and Hampstead. This kindly mentor was as enthusiastic as any Englishwoman over the victories which restored Louis XVIII., and seems to have gained the permanent affection of her pupils. Having no children of her own, she went to the Foundling Hospital and selected the prettiest she could find for an adopted daughter, and young Eliza Dupont, as she was called, grew up in the School. When the Allied Sovereigns came to England in 1814, Madame Dupont with her twelve pupils were conspicuous among those who greeted the visitors in front of Buckingham Palace and at the various entertainments where they were present; but the event abruptly closed the establishment, for Madame returned to France.

From Edward Johnstone to his daughter:—

"Dear Catherine,—I suppose you will have been so much occupied by the rejoicings for peace, and the arrivals of Kings and Emperors, that you will scarcely have had time to think of us country people, and indeed I am very glad you have an opportunity of witnessing such interesting scenes. We have had splendid illuminations in Birmingham. Edward and James saw them both on Monday and Tuesday, and on your return will give you a better account of them than I can. I write now to inquire when your vacation begins, as Mrs Mynors [of Weatheroak Hall] has a friend coming from London about the end of the month, with whom you may travel if you have made no other arrangement. . . . We unite in best remembrance to Madame Dupont, and love to yourself. Yours affectionately, E. Johnstone.

"Thursday, *June* 9, 1814."

Mrs Johnstone's brothers had been at Shrewsbury School, where they were badly fed, and several of her relatives were at Eton in the days of Dr Keate. The tales which reached Edgbaston of that eminent master's liberal use of the cane prejudiced her against any school for her boys, and they were educated by private tutors, but in these they were exceptionally fortunate. Mr Thomas Wright Hill, born at Kidderminster, had remained in Dr Priestley's house when the owners escaped from it, and the brave young man faced the rioters alone, but was unable to prevent its destruction. He established a school near Birmingham, and his third son, Rowland, the future founder of the Penny Post, was engaged to teach the young Johnstones at Edgbaston Hall. When his father required his services on the transfer of the school to Hazlewood, the Rev. James Yates, an eminent classical and linguistic scholar, took Mr Hill's place, and prepared both boys for Trinity College, Cambridge. The elder, Edward, matriculated in Oct. 1821, and James in Oct. 1823, both of them at the age of seventeen, and the younger[1] showed the sense which always distinguished him by preferring not to be entered as a fellow-commoner, like his brother, but as an ordinary undergraduate. He would have chosen the army as his profession, and was very anxious to go to India, but it was settled, without consulting them, that Edward was to be called to the Bar and James to take up medicine.

Mrs Johnstone's eldest brother, afterwards Advocate-General of India, acquired so much distinction at the English Bar that, had he remained at home, the highest honours seemed likely to fall to his lot. He would never plead a cause as innocent unless he really believed it. His nephews recollected his arrival late one night from Shrewsbury when the Assizes were on. He had accepted a brief for a man accused of murder. When he examined the evidence he felt convinced of his guilt, so he took post horses and came to Edgbaston to consult Dr Johnstone on the symptoms of insanity, as the only ground on which he could defend him. Dr Johnstone decided that the man was certainly out of his mind, and his brother-in-law set off again in time to attend the Court the next day, and saved the murderer from the gallows by proving him to be insane.

In 1832 Dr Johnstone was again appointed a magistrate, but declined to act on account of his age (seventy-five). He was at that time absorbed in the progress of the Medical School. Its foundation was proposed by Mr W. Sands Cox, who felt that the usual means of educating a surgeon was very inefficient, being merely sent as a pupil to some medical practitioner to be instructed by his conversation and by watching his practice at the

---

[1] Letter from Mrs Pearson in Bath to Dr Johnstone, after a visit from his son James :—

"My dear Sir,—I will not encumber you with a letter, dear James is commissioned with loves, respects, and best wishes, but he would not like to carry what I am anxious to send to you, the delight we have in seeing in him as excellent a young man as you, his dear mother, or ourselves could wish. I could fill my sheet in his praise, not only from his grandmother but all the family, but I will hasten to add the name of your obliged and affectionate friend,
"E. Pearson.
"Bath, 23 *July* 1831."

hospital. "The plan," wrote Aris's *Gazette*, Nov. 22, 1825, "has met with the approbation of Dr Johnstone, Dr Pearson, and other distinguished practitioners." In 1831 it was enlarged by a museum and library. ". . . Handsome donations have been presented already," says the same paper, "by the Earl of Dartmouth, Viscount Hood, Sir Eardley Wilmot, Sir Astley Cooper, Francis Lawley, James Taylor, Dr Edward Johnstone, the Low Bailiff, etc." Edward Johnstone was made President; his brother John, also a generous donor, Vice-President; and Edward Johnstone, jun., of the Inner Temple, was one of two legal advisers. The Rev. Dr Warneford gave the Chapel. The first stone of the Queen's College, into which it developed, was laid, Aug. 18, 1843, by Edward Johnstone, who, during eighteen years, was never absent from the meetings of the Council. In 1836 the Council deviated from its course by fixing its anniversary meeting on his eightieth birthday. He was the first Principal of the new College, and when he retired in 1845 Lord Lyttelton took his place.

In 1840 Dr Johnstone helped to found the Queen's Hospital in Birmingham, and was Honorary Physician till his death. He was a great supporter of the dispensary for supplying medical and surgical attendance on the poor at their own homes, and though he had long retired from his profession, and took no fees, his advice was valued and always given gratuitously to rich and poor —a great boon to those who could not afford to pay for it; but the last condition was the rule at that period with physicians, and much later, for there are no philanthropists superior to those in the medical profession. His son James, as Honorary Physician to the Birmingham General Hospital for thirty years, completed a period of 116 years, in which his father, grandfather, uncles, and himself had given their unpaid services for the good of their fellow-creatures.

Few men could have had more peaceful declining years than Edward Johnstone, with a daughter devoted to him and most dutiful sons. Not a day passed, except Sunday, when he did not drive in his old-fashioned yellow carriage and pair to his younger son's abode in the Old Square; and his son's family spent every Sunday and the summer months at Edgbaston Hall.

When the Laird of Galabank resigned the post of Honorary Physician to the General Hospital, his nephew, James, was unanimously elected to fill it. At the age of twenty-eight James was made an F.R.C.P., and later declined an F.R.S. Like his uncle, John, he was early appointed a Governor of King Edward's School. His marriage with Maria Mary Payne, eldest daughter of Joseph Webster of Penns, J.P. for cos. Warwick, Worcester, and Stafford, took place at Sutton Coldfield Church, Jan. 7, 1834.

The birth of five grandsons, besides grand-daughters, in the grandfather's lifetime was a cause of great congratulation. The large party entertained at Edgbaston Hall for the christening of the first grandchild at the old Parish Church included her mother's parents, Mr and Mrs Webster of Penns, Mrs Webster's father, Sir Peter Payne,[1] and two of his daughters, many uncles

---

[1] Son-in-law to the Stewards of Winson Green (Chapter XXII.), M.P. for Bedfordshire, and the author of political pamphlets.

and aunts, young and old, the John Johnstones, the Lockhart Johnstones from Worcester, and many other relatives. Dr John Johnstone's two daughters had both been married at Edgbaston Church from their uncle's house—the elder, Anna Delicia, to the Rev. Walter Farquhar Hook, afterwards Vicar of Leeds and Dean of Chichester;[1] and the younger, Agnes Mary, to the Rev. Henry Clarke,[2] Rector of Northfield and Cofton Hacket, parishes which, at that time, extended from the Lickey to Edgbaston Park.

That the eldest grandson should be called James, after his elder brother, the family hero, had long been settled by the grandfather, who lived to recognise the early promise of the future representative of his house. It was enough to bring Johnstone of Worcester out of his grave if he could have known that, after all his anxiety lest his own father should divide Galabank or leave it away from the direct male heir, it was to pass out of the Johnstone family, to a female branch, which would probably value its own distinguished English name and its long English descent[3] more than its Scottish ancestry. The younger of John Johnstone's daughters, Agnes Mary Clarke, inherited the Scottish estate. She died at Malvern, aged ninety-one, in 1905, when, as she left no children, Galabank passed to Mrs Hook (née Acland-Troyte), the widow of the Rev. Prebendary Walter Hook, Rector of Porlock, second son of the Very Rev. Walter Farquhar Hook, Dean of Chichester, and Anna Delicia Johnstone, his wife.

John Johnstone of Galabank predeceased his brother, Edward, Dec. 28, 1836. He was an active magistrate for Warwickshire and Worcestershire, and among his most intimate friends were Sir Henry Halford, M.D., Dr Maltby (the Bishop of Durham), the Rev. Dr Parr,[4] Dr Routh (the President of Magdalen College), and Bishop Butler of Lichfield. He gave the Harveian Lecture (in Latin) before the Royal College of Physicians in 1819; and Bishop Butler regarded him as "a scholar among scholars," and wrote of "the extraordinary ascendancy he gained over the minds of his friends. In private society he was lively and agreeable, instructing it by his talents, animating it by his cheerfulness, and refining it by his taste." His wife survived him thirty-two years. They were both buried in the chancel of Northfield Church.

The following is from an article on Edgbaston Hall in Feb. 1884 in *Edgbastoniana*, a local magazine. After describing Dr Edward Johnstone's

[1] See his *Life*, by his son-in-law, the late Dean of Winchester.
[2] Fifth son of Major-General Sir William Clarke, Governor of Seringapatam, who died there, 1808.
[3] Acland of Columb-John, Co. Devon (*see* Burke's *Baronetage*).
[4] In Langford's *Modern Birmingham* appears: "The year 1837 opens with the record of the death of a very able and useful gentleman, Dr John Johnstone. . . . He practised as a physician in this town upwards of forty years, and among the members of his profession he must be placed in the first rank. With deep learning he possessed an acuteness of intellect, an insight into character, a decision of mind, and a kindness of manner eminently valuable in every relation of life, but more peculiarly important in that of a physician. The confidential friend and biographer of Dr Parr was himself a scholar of no ordinary acquirements, and his biography of that celebrated man displays sound judgment, refined taste, and classical learning."

parentage, his philanthropy, and the death of Mrs Johnstone in 1823, it adds:—

"It is pleasant to think of the long extension of his useful life, which continued till Sept. 4, 1851, when he wanted but a few days of completing his ninety-fourth year. The writer of this notice was at the Hall on the day of his funeral. Never before, probably, had the old place seen so remarkable a gathering of the notable men of Birmingham within its walls. . . . The tolling bell of the quaint old Church intensified the solemnity which prevailed. The grandeur of the park, solemn and still at all times, was, on that morning, mellowed with the softness of waning summer. The sombre shadows 'neath its majestic trees, the writer well remembers; and he recollects that a solitary artist patiently sat in front of his canvas, far away down the sloping lawn.

"The occasion was no common one in 1851. . . . Dr Johnstone was followed to his grave in the ivy-covered church, near which he had so long lived, by a large assemblage of his brethren, and the officers of the hospital he had himself served in more than seventy years before. When we entered the venerable porch and enquired of some of the 'elder brethren' the early history of the patriarch of medicine in this town, a strange awe pervaded the mind on being informed that we were about to consign to the dust the remains of one who had witnessed the first decade of the reign of George III., and admitted the first patient into the wards of the General Hospital."[1]

The last funeral that had taken place from the Hall was that of Mary, sister to Dr Johnstone, in 1841, and seven years earlier that of his son, Charles. His daughter inherited her mother's estate of Fulford Hall in Worcestershire and Warwickshire. The Dunsley Manor estate, Co. Stafford, went to Edward, and, failing direct heirs, was entailed by his father on James and his eldest son. An estate in Worcestershire and lands, Co. Stafford, were left to James. The elder brother, born April 9, 1804, graduated M.A. (Trinity College), was called to the Bar in 1828, but never practised, being chiefly engaged in literary and philanthropic pursuits. With the poet Campbell, Lord Dudley Stuart, Lord Ilchester, and others he founded in 1832 the "Literary Association of the Friends of Poland." It was non-political, but assisted many of the exiles of the Polish Revolution to gain their livelihood, and even to obtain Government posts. On his sister's death in 1860 he inherited Fulford Hall, and in 1876 put in a claim to the dormant Marquisate of Annandale against that of Sir Frederick Johnstone of Westerhall. Mr Hope Johnstone again advanced his claim as direct heir in the female line, but it was dismissed on the ground of the superior claim of the male heirs whatsoever, and the other cases in 1881 on the score of inconclusive evidence. Edward Johnstone died unmarried at Worcester, Sept. 20, 1881. As his brother James predeceased him, Fulford

[1] *Modern Birmingham* also gives an appreciative notice of Dr Edward Johnstone. Those who look into the causes of longevity may be interested by the fact that he neither smoked nor took snuff, and was a very temperate man. He died from a slight cold, but was otherwise in perfect health. A notice in the local paper on his eightieth birthday spoke of the purity of his life and conversation. He recollected hearing the bells rung for the Coronation of George III.

Hall and Dunsley Manor went to his nephew, the late Major-General Sir James Johnstone, K.C.S.I.

The younger brother, James (*see ante*), graduated M.B. at Trinity College in 1828, and M.D. 1833. From Cambridge he went to Edinburgh to attend Dr Munro's lectures. The sons and grandsons of his father's fellow-students at the University gave him a warm welcome to Scotland, where he enjoyed the genial hospitality of several country houses, danced at the Edinburgh balls, and, having very good introductions, afterwards looked back on this period as one of the happiest in his life. He saw Sir Walter Scott take his seat in Parliament House when, as the great novelist wrote, his head was full of *Anne of Geierstein*. Johnstone later went to study in Paris, where the leading surgeons were Baron Larrey, Guilliet, and others, who had shared in all Napoleon's campaigns. The last crowned sovereign of France, Charles X., was still on the throne, and his niece and daughter-in-law, the Duchesse d'Angoulême, presided at the Tuileries. British visitors were admitted to great state functions on showing their visiting card. Among other persons of note, Johnstone became acquainted with the poet Longfellow, who was making the tour of Europe with his friend Dr Storer.

At this time Johnstone fully hoped to settle in London. He had studied at St. Bartholomew's Hospital, and went to Hastings for six months to acquire knowledge of the disorders of the chest, which, at that time, were supposed to be specially benefitted by a sojourn in this mild resort. Hastings must have reminded him of Annan in the days of his forefathers, for it was the headquarters of a flourishing smuggling trade, when luggers were actually unloaded on the beach, in front of the houses, while the Preventive Service men were at dinner. He left Hastings for London, where the leading members of the medical fraternity advised him to remain, as a physician was much required who had particularly studied phthisis. He had even chosen a house, but in obedience to his father's wish he came to Birmingham, where he settled in one of twenty-four substantial abodes, built in 1698 by a pupil of Sir Christopher Wren, and which formed the now defunct Old Square. He was the first Professor of Materia Medica and Therapeutics at the Queen's College, and Extraordinary Physician to the General Hospital for thirty years. On the visit of the British Medical Association to Birmingham in Sept. 1856 he was chosen President.

In 1831 Asiatic cholera was brought to Poland by the Russian troops, who came from Astrakhan to quell a Polish insurrection, and it spread through Europe. It reached Britain in 1832, causing great mortality. Dumfries alone had 540 deaths. A temporary hospital was established in Birmingham for cholera patients, to which James Johnstone was appointed Honorary Physician. Many suspected cases were admitted, but he was always of opinion that not one of real cholera had appeared in Birmingham, which, in later panics, was made quite a health resort. At the first notice of its approach Dr John Johnstone printed and circulated, gratis, a sheet of advice as to how to avoid it.

The best known of James Johnstone's writings are: *A Therapeutic Arrangement and Syllabus of Materia Medica, 1835*, which had an extensive circulation, and *A Discourse on the Phenomena of Sensation as connected with the Mental, Physical, and Instructive Faculties of Man.* He was Senior Governor of King Edward's School in Birmingham for some years, and his classical attainments and strong opinions on the subject of education gave him a prominent voice in the development of this important foundation, and the establishment of the commercial and elementary schools for both boys and girls, in addition to the original Classical department, which has educated so many distinguished men. He also filled other public trusteeships in Birmingham, but refused several times to be either a county or burgh magistrate. Johnstone was also chosen for the Harveian lecturer at the Royal College of Physicians, but it was in a year of domestic anxiety, and he declined it.

When dining at Solihull Rectory with Mr and Mrs Archer Clive, Dr and Mrs James Johnstone met Mrs Buckley, the eldest daughter of the late Sir John Lowther Johnstone, who, on hearing the name of her fellow-guest, at once recognised him as the descendant of her grandfather's and uncle's great friend. Mrs Buckley, who still retained some of the good looks which had made her the beauty of the London season when she was introduced, had, through a piece of girlish obstinacy, failed to make the brilliant match which was expected, and married a clergyman (her cousin) at the end of the year, to pass the great part of her life, perhaps as happily, in a village. She was staying with an aunt in London, and, returning from a drive, disappeared for two hours, and declined to give any reason for it. Young girls were very strictly watched and educated in those days, and though it transpired too late that her errand was an act of kindness it was enough to injure her. Her daughters, to some extent, inherited her charms. Two were married on the same day, June 14, 1859, to Messrs G. E. Ranken and R. A. Farquharson, and the youngest, Lilias Charlotte, a month later to Edgar Disney.

It was not till 1832 that Birmingham demanded a representation in Parliament, and by a meeting of 100,000 men on Hall Hill alarmed the Government lest there should be a repetition of the riots of 1791; and the Reform Bill was passed at once. Some years later the new borough set up a mayor, town council, and magistrates. In 1839 what seemed likely to be a serious disturbance began. Johnstone, among others, was sworn in as a special constable. Railings were pulled up and houses battered in the Bull Ring. No regiment was in the town, and a troop of Scots Greys were summoned from Coventry. A county magistrate was secured in Mr Webster. He happened to be riding from Penns to Edgbaston Hall (nine miles) to see his daughter (who, with her children, had gone there for the summer), and passing through Birmingham found the town in unusual confusion, increased by fighting men from South Staffordshire. He waited till the military arrived, and in company with the officer, the Hon. G. M. Yorke (afterwards Rector of St. Philip's and Dean of Worcester), rode at the head of the troop to the Bull Ring, where he read the Riot Act,[1] and the mob dispersed. This was the last time

[1] When Mr Muntz, one of the earliest M.P.'s for Birmingham, died, John Bright, who had lost his seat for Manchester, was nominated as a candidate. He was too ill to appear. As

that the Riot Act was read in Birmingham. When a borough—now a city—it continued its upward progress.

Langford's *Modern Birmingham* alludes to the last of the Johnstones of Galabank who practised as a physician—James, born at Edgbaston Hall April 12, 1806, and died at Leamington May 11, 1869: "His sound sense and high principles of honour, with unflinching truthfulness, gave him a high position in his profession, and he was looked upon as an example of all that is kind and courteous in manners. Modesty as to his own acquirements and knowledge was sometimes carried to an excess, and therefore prevented his opinion from gaining the confidence to which it was entitled." Here we differ from the talented writer. Dr Johnstone was aware—what thoughtful physician is not?—that medicine is fallible, and that there are cases beyond all human aid. In these he declined to take a fee, and gave the reason; and if hopeful relatives turned to another doctor, who promised a speedy cure, he was not surprised. Like his father and uncle and other physicians of their date, he took no fee from ministers of religion, whether the Established clergy, the Fathers of the Oratory, including Cardinal Newman, the priests at Oscott, and Cardinal Wiseman, the Nonconformist minister, the Jewish rabbi, or the members of the Romanist Sisterhoods in Dudley, Handsworth, Mary Vale, and other places in the neighbourhood. The Anglican Sister had not then arrived. The writer already quoted adds: "It is impossible to convey the high esteem in which Dr Johnstone was held." His portrait, by Roden, now hangs in the Birmingham Hospital. Mrs Johnstone predeceased him (April 23, 1859). Of their thirteen children, five sons and seven daughters survived them.

The eldest son, James, was at that time a Captain in the Bengal Army, and Political Agent at Keonjur during the minority of the Rajah. Born 1841, he was the last cadet appointed to the H.E.I.C.S. in 1858. Arriving in India during the closing days of the Mutiny, he served with the 73rd in pursuit of the rebel armies, and was afterwards stationed in Assam. Thence he was moved to Keonjur, where the pains he took to plant the first seeds of civilisation in what is now the diocese of Chota-Nagpore, and which was then desolated by an insurrection against the Rajah, is recorded in the reports of Superintendent Ravenshaw to the Lieutenant-Governor of Bengal in 1869. He founded schools, out of his own means, for both boys and girls, and 900 children attended them before he left for England to recover from malaria fever, which was very prevalent till he opened out roads and cut away jungle in this hitherto

he afterwards pathetically said, he had been reduced to the condition of a young child. As his unbending peace principles were inconsistent with the fact that Birmingham was the chief producer of the weapons of war, Mr Webster's second son was asked to oppose him. Mr Bright was well served by Mr Parkes and George Dawson, the great leader of democracy in the town, who asserted that "it was absurd to choose an untried and younger man because he was born in the neighbourhood and was highly respectable, when they had the offer of the greatest orator of his age." Baron Webster was very popular from his extreme good temper and kindness of heart. He was an active J.P. for the town and two counties since he was twenty-one, was a D.L., and Captain of the Q.O. Staff. Yeomanry; but as two more candidates appeared, he gracefully retired to avoid dividing his party.

neglected province. When the Rajah was of age the Agency, for economical motives, was abolished, but the work he began smoothed the paths of the missionaries who, a few years later, settled in those parts.

"Keonjur," says the Government Report of India for 1870-71, "continues under the able administration of Captain Johnstone, who was mainly instrumental in restoring the country to quiet three years ago." He superintended the cultivation of flax and rice and proved it a success, and "at his own expense formed a valuable herd of sixty cows and several young bulls" to improve the native breed of cattle, and distributed them gratis when he left. ". . . Captain Johnstone's sacrifices for this end [education and civilisation], and for his charge generally, are," wrote the Lieutenant-Governor of Bengal in 1872, "His Honour believes almost unique."

Johnstone's education was begun by his able and accomplished mother, and after a short time in the Classical Division of King Edward's School, Birmingham, then containing 150 boys, he went to a military college in Paris. As previously shown, the monastic system still clung to the old English classical schools. In Birmingham, theology and the higher classics were well taught in the Classical Division, but other science was optional or had to be learnt at home, so the education was only useful to the sons of the gentry or to those intended for the learned professions, particularly the clerical. But all that is changed now. At that time young James was absorbed in astronomy. He fitted up an old telescope of his father's with new glasses, and took nightly observations from his bedroom window at the top of the house, and when only thirteen discovered a new comet on its progress, not yet visible to the naked eye. He wrote to the Astronomer-Royal, Mr J. W. Hinde, describing the position in the heavens of the approaching star; and the Astronomer, not aware of the youth of his correspondent, replied in a few days—when it was nearer—that Johnstone was perfectly correct as to where its place must have been when he first saw it, although he had not observed it so soon himself.

Experiences in Manipur and the Naga Hills, by Major-General Sir James Johnstone, K.C.S.I., published after his death, gives an account of his life there as Political Agent. The bomb-proof residence which he built and the liveried native servants he had trained, with the beautiful garden, were among the inducements to the unfortunate Mr Grimwood to apply for the post. Johnstone had twice borrowed the native army, and conducted it, by forced marches, for the rescue of Europeans—first to the besieged town of Kohima, leading it

---

[1] The printed Official Reports (1869-71) to the Lieutenant-Governor of Bengal contain: "Captain Johnstone hopes very shortly to be able to dispense with the greater part of the Special Police Force at Keonjhur. He appears to take very great interest in his work, and to be sanguine of success" (1870). His first official report "has much interesting matter regarding the people, and shows that he has taken great pains in bringing them into the present peaceable and apparently loyal condition. Nearly one half of Captain Johnstone's time has been occupied in Khedda (catching wild elephants), operations which have been successful and profitable to Government, and totally unconnected with that officer's duty in Keonjhur. Of Captain Johnstone I cannot speak too highly; his management has been efficient, and he has exercised careful and constant supervision over the Rajah and his estate, to the material improvement of both."

through hundreds of hostile Nagas; and then into Burmah, where the war of annexation endangered the unprotected European trading centres near the Manipur frontier. He did this, knowing their position, before he was officially informed of the declaration of war. Yet he had always an enemy in one of the Princes, known as the Senaputtee, the evil genius of Manipur. Johnstone had more real knowledge of medicine than the native doctors, and prescribed for cholera patients with approved British remedies when he was only a Lieutenant in Assam. But Calcutta was the nearest place where a British resident physician could be found, and there he was obliged to bring his wife for medical advice, and it ended by taking her to Europe. He returned for a few months to Manipur, and then hastened back to England, to leave it again as a widower, after making the best arrangements for the care of his three young children.

His return to Manipur was of vital importance to its peace, for the natives, of the same race as the Burmese, to whom they once belonged, were naturally stirred by the Burmese war. Then came his march into Burmah, not only for the safety of the Europeans but to keep the Manipur army employed under his own eye in a useful work instead of in a foolish struggle against the British power, urged on by its enemy in the Palace. A very eminent General, then in India, not knowing the double reason, said that Johnstone ought to be tried by court-martial for risking the lives of his soldiers (all natives) in such a foolhardy expedition,—but he saved British lives, and brought his men safely back to Manipur.

In Jan. 1887 Johnstone was gazetted a K.C.S.I. and received the honour of Knighthood at Windsor Castle, when he had a most kind, congratulatory letter from General Sir Harry Prendergast, V.C., the late Commander-in-Chief in Burmah. At this time he was living in the Midlands, having rebuilt Fulford Hall; the old, half-timbered Manor House, which would have outlasted many more modern buildings, had been pulled down when the property was left to the care of an agent. The beneficial effect of a resident landlord was soon felt by the tenants.

In Sept. 1890, when Mr Grimwood was in charge at Manipur, a Palace revolution took place, the Maharajah was dethroned by the Senaputtee, and the next year the Chief Commissioner was sent to arrest him and to put another prince on the throne. Mr Quinton, Mr Grimwood, Colonel Skene, and others were invited into the Palace and there murdered. It was due to intrigues, which hardly required the great muster of troops ordered up to quell the outbreak. The Senaputtee sent his followers to destroy the grave of Sir James's infant son, Arthur, who had died in 1879 (also the Sanatorium which he had built), for mere spite, as he knew that Johnstone had urged the Government to exile him, years before, for his cruelties. Johnstone offered his services to the Government to restore order, but they were refused, and severe punitive measures were taken. Many despairing letters from the dethroned Rajah and others who had been loyal throughout came to Johnstone to ask him to intercede for them. "O for a moment of Colonel Johnstone's presence at such a crisis," wrote a British official to the *Pioneer*. "One strong word, with the ominous raising of the forefinger, would have paralysed the treacherous rebel." A question was asked in the House of Commons about the recent appointments to Manipur, and a member of the Cabinet answered that the (Liberal) Government did not care for men of genius, but preferred to work with men of mediocre ability!

Probably the Government was aware of the service which Johnstone had done for the Unionists in Worcestershire and Warwickshire, and he was Chairman of the Committee that nominated Austen Chamberlain as the candidate for East Worcestershire—his first constituency. He did not live to know that the energy and money he had spent on Manipur was not all thrown away, but a most pleasing tribute to his memory was received by his son, Captain Richard Johnstone, in 1908. Manipur, long in disgrace, was restored to a position of independence as a protected state; and Sir Lancelot Hare, the Lieutenant-Governor of Eastern Bengal and Assam, with suitable ceremony went to instal the Maharajah on his throne. He further proceeded to unveil a bust of Johnstone in the English School, and, in the accompanying speech, said "it was very gratifying to him to see that Sir James Johnstone's memory was held in such esteem in the valley which he loved so well. Certainly," he continued, "it would be difficult to name anyone who has done more for Manipur, or who was more devoted to its people, or had a greater regard and affection for the country. It is very fitting that this memorial should be erected, and, of all the places where it could be placed, none is more suitable than this School, which was founded by him and in which he took so much interest. Among the many good works he did for Manipur none, perhaps, was more important and far-reaching than his work as a pioneer of education in this State. Of Colonel Sir James Johnstone's work in Manipur from 1877 to 1886 it is not necessary to say much. The splendid work he did at the time of the rising in the Naga Hills in 1879, and when the war broke out with Burma in 1885, is well known. The care with which he protected the interests of this State, when the boundaries between Manipur and Burma were laid down, has also been of great advantage to Manipur."

Colonel Shakespear, the present Resident, sent an account of the ceremony to Captain Richard Johnstone, and enclosed a letter signed by Tombi Singha, Ango Singh, and ten other native scholars:—

"Johnstone School, Manipur.
"*Feb*. 15, 1908.

"Sir,—We never knew that Sir James Johnstone, K.C.S.I., had a son living till the other day, when a beautiful bust of your kind father was unveiled by his Honour the Lieutenant-Governor of Eastern Bengal and Assam, and when Colonel Shakespear, the Secretary of Johnstone School, mentioned the fact to us, which we were delighted to hear.

"At first there was no English School in Manipur, but when your kind father came here he got the consent of the Maharaja of Manipur, and established an English School for the good and the improvement of Manipuri youths. He left, at the same time, 1200 rupees, the interest of which the School is still enjoying. The School was named Johnstone Middle English School, after the Founder. We look upon your father as our benefactor, just as the Bengalis do upon 'David Hare.'

"The Manipuris now value education as much as the Bengalis do; and it is to your father's great kindness that the means had been provided for the education of Manipuris. We shall ever be thankful to him, and hold your father's name in reverence."

Colonel Shakespear also wrote to Captain Johnstone:—

"The School has striven well, and there are now about 150 boys.

"Your father's name is still remembered here, and I am sure you will be glad to hear that a bust, which is said to be an excellent likeness of him, has been placed in front of the School, and was unveiled a few days ago by the Lieutenant-Governor. I enclose the speech he made on that occasion.

"The bust was made from the picture in your father's book by a Punjabi workman employed in the construction of the Rajah's palace."

Johnstone had entirely recovered his health, which had suffered much from malaria fever in India. He was a magistrate for two counties, and took a prominent part in county affairs. His house contained the good library[1] collected by previous generations, and to which he added unique Oriental books and MSS. In June 1887 (the Jubilee) he feasted 600 of the agricultural population, and gave them each a cup of Minton's work as a souvenir. He married, in 1872 (at Sutton Coldfield Church), Emma Mary Lloyd, whose father was at that time M.P. for Plymouth, and living at Moor Hall, in Warwickshire. She died in 1881, and *Experiences in Manipur*, not published till after his death, was a memorial to her. Two sons and a daughter survived her. Johnstone's name was set down for a Colonial Governorship, when his career of usefulness was cut short by a fatal accident, not five minutes' walk from the lodge at Fulford Hall. He was a splendid horseman; but his horse appears to have been startled by some dogs springing out of a cottage. It was seen to race wildly towards home, then apparently reared, for the ground showed signs of a struggle. The rider's whip was grasped firmly, but he never recovered consciousness.

The event evoked universal sympathy. The Worcester and Birmingham papers recalled the career of his forefathers. "His family has taken a prominent part in the social and public life of the Midlands for a century and a half," wrote the Birmingham *Daily Post*, "and has produced several eminent physicians." He was engaged to assist the next day at the annual meeting of the Conservative and Unionist Association at Stratford-on-Avon, and the Marquis of Hertford, when announcing the catastrophe, spoke of the excellent work that Sir James had done for the Unionist cause in Warwickshire. A

[1] A portion of it was presented to the Birmingham Reference Library.

little later Lord Leigh alluded to him, at a meeting, as a great and public loss.

"I have never known," wrote his father-in-law (Mr Sampson Lloyd), "any one who combined so many noble traits of character, the deeply sincere, though unpretending Christian believer, the brave soldier, the man of highest honour in all things, the useful magistrate and public man, the kind, true friend. His loss can of course never be replaced in this world. Happily he was especially fitted for a sudden call—if that had to be." His children were:—

I. James, died 1873.

II. Richard, now of Fulford Hall and Dunsley Manor, born at Samagooting, Assam, June 1874, educated at Winchester College and Trinity College, Glenalmond, Captain in the 1st Battalion King's Royal Rifle Corps, was in the Chitral campaign, and severely wounded at the battle of Talana Hill, South Africa, also in the besieged Ladysmith. He married Catharine Florence May, daughter of Admiral Sir Robert Harris, K.C.B., and has a son, James, and two daughters.

III. Edward, born 1875, served in the Imperial Yeomanry and the South African Constabulary during the Boer War.

IV. Arthur, died 1879.

V. Emma Mary.

The brothers and sisters of the late Major-General Sir James Johnstone:—

I. Edward, settled in Canada, born 1842. Married and has issue.

II. Charles, Vice-Admiral (retired), of Graitney, Co. Surrey, born 1843. Married Janet Schonswar, only child of George Schonswar, and has (1) George, Lieutenant, R.N.; (2) Janet Schonswar; (3) Mildred Elizabeth Dryad Schonswar; (4) Cicely Catherine Schonswar; (5) Frances Lucy Schonswar; (6) Winifred Barbara Schonswar.

III. Richard, M.A. (Trinity College, Cambridge), late Rector of Moreton Sey, Stone, and Yoxall, born 1845; died 1894. Married Imogen Isabella Twysden, daughter of the late Walter Hele Molesworth, barrister-at-law. Left (1) Andrew, Lieutenant, R.N.; (2) William; (3) John; (4) Hugh; (5) Edmund, R.N.; (6) Richard Michael; (7) Delicia Mary, married F. Fox, Co. Devon; (8) Frances Benetta.

IV. Thomas, died in India.

V. Maria Mary Payne, married Theodore Rathbone, J.P. (late of Inniskilling Dragoons), of Backwood, Co. Cheshire, who died 1890. Left Mary, now of Backwood.

VI. Elizabeth.

VII. Catherine Laura.

VIII. Janet Emma, married Rev. F. Bigg, M.A. Has four sons and five daughters. The eldest daughter, Maria Mary, married to Rear-Admiral F. Stopford.

IX. Fanny Matilda, died in India, married the late Horace Boileau Goad of Simla. Left Lockhart, Deputy-Superintendent of North-West Provinces Police, India, and five other children.

X. Harriet, married, first, J. E. Lloyd, barrister-at-law, died 1882; second, Rev. W. O. Peile, M.A.

XI. Gertrude and Lucy (twins), died young.

The heirs of John Johnstone of Galabank, 1768-1836:—

I. Anna Delicia, married the late Very Rev. Walter Farquhar Hook, Dean of Chichester. She died 1871. Their children—

(1) James (Rev.), died *s.p.* (late 60th Rifles), married Gertrude Hargreaves. She married, secondly, Rowlands Venables.

(2) Walter Hook (Rev. Prebendary of Wells), born 1839, Rector of Porlock. Married, 1864, Mary Dyke Acland-Troyte (now of Galabank). Died March 27, 1899, and left—1, Walter Acland, born 1867; 2, Arthur James (Rev.), born 1877; 3, Mary, married Rev. Bruce Harrison; 4, Anna Delicia, married James Taylor, New Zealand; 5, Katherine Frances, married Rev. R. Lloyd; 6, Lucy; 7, Agnes Joanna.

(3) Cecil Hook, Rt. Rev. Bishop of Kingston, born Dec. 1844, married Edith Turner.

(4) Augusta Agnes, married the late Ven. Archdeacon George Anson.

(5) Anna Delicia, married the late Rev. A. Empson, Rector of Eydon. Left—1, Walter, barrister-at-law, New Zealand, married Agnes, daughter of John Acland; 2, Cecil (Rev.); 3, Mary, married Rev. Robert Wylde; 4, Mabel, married A. Rowden, K.C.; 5, Evelyn, married Rev. A. Tisdall; 6, Beatrice.

(6) Charlotte Jane, married the late Very Rev. W. R. W. Stephens, Dean of Winchester, who died 1903. Has—1, Charles; 2, Cecil, married Rev. C. Cooper; 3, Helen, married Major Percival Barry; 4, Catherine.

II. Agnes Mary (*see ante*).

The heirs, now extinct, of Lockhart Johnstone (born 1771, died at Worcester 1861):—

I. John (Rev.), U.S.A., married Eliza Windsor, died 1894. Left Janet, died *s.p.*

II. William Greene, Lieutenant-Colonel (retired) Madras Army, died at Worcester 1887.

III. Hannah, died 1880.

IV. Janet, died 1893.

WESTERHALL, DUMFRIES.

ALVA HOUSE, CLACKMANNAN.

CHAPTER XXVI.

JOHNSTONES OF WESTERHALL—ALVA—DERWENT—FRANCIS JOHNSTON'S
DESCENDANTS.

THE revenues of the Baronets of Westerhall must have been much increased by the portion which reverted to them from the great wealth of Sir William Pulteney. His nephew and heir, Sir John Lowther Johnstone, left three children—George Frederick, seventh Baronet; Charlotte Margaret, already mentioned as Mrs Buckley; and Anne Elizabeth, married to the Rev. Edmund Estcourt. Sir George was born Dec. 1810, and married, Oct. 24, 1840, Lady Maria Louisa Elizabeth Frederica, daughter of the first Earl of Craven. He died from the effects of an accident on horseback, May 1841. The next male heir was Mr Johnstone of Alva. But the Baronetcy remained in abeyance till Aug. 5, 1841, when the widow gave birth to twin sons—the present Baronet, Sir Frederick John William Johnstone; and Colonel George Charles Keppel Johnstone, late Grenadier Guards. Colonel Johnstone, who is his brother's heir, married, 1875, Agnes, daughter of Thomas Chamberlayne of Cranbury Park, Hants, and has George Thomas Frederick Tankerville, born Aug. 1, 1876, married, 1901, Ernestine, youngest daughter of the late Lieutenant-Colonel Alan Roger Charles Cust, and has a son and three daughters — Frederick Alan George, Laura Adeline, Violet Florence Ernestine, Dorothy Frances Catherine.

Colonel Johnstone is a J.P. of Hants, and lives at Rothsay, West Cowes, Isle of Wight. His younger children are—Charles John, late Lieutenant, Rifle Brigade, born Dec. 20, 1877; Agnes Louisa Barbara Snowflake; Rose Mary Adeline Dagmar Amelia.

Sir Frederick Johnstone sat as a Conservative for Weymouth, 1874-85. He was one of several young men specially selected by the late Prince Consort to be companions to the present King when, as Prince of Wales, he went to Oxford. His marriage to Laura Caroline, widow of the fourth Earl of Wilton, took place in June 1899.

At the time of Sir George's death a petition[1] had been presented to the

---

[1] The learned Counsel claimed for his client the sole representation of the Johnstone family in the male line, and this brought forward other claimants to prove their male descent.

House of Lords for permission to assume the honours and dignities of the last Marquis of Annandale, but it was again opposed by Mr Hope Johnstone, the direct descendant through the females of the first Marquis, and by several other claimants. His mother carried on the suit on behalf of her infant son, and it was finally thrown out in 1844. In 1876 Sir Frederick presented another petition to be allowed to assume the dormant dignities, and was opposed by Mr Hope Johnstone and also by Mr Edward Johnstone of Fulford Hall. Judgment was given against all the claimants in 1881.

Sir Frederick has been a very noted member of the Turf Club. His ancestral mansion in Dumfriesshire is beautifully situated, enclosed by woods and surrounded by steep hills. The mausoleum of his family, in the churchyard, is surmounted by a handsome dome supported by massive pillars. At Glendining, another part of the Westerhall estate, a profitable antimony mine was opened in 1760, but not regularly worked till Sir William Pulteney inherited the property. Sir Frederick's other residences are The Hatch, near Windsor, a villa on the Riviera, and his town house in Arlington Street.

Lady Maria, widow of Sir George Frederick Johnstone, married, secondly, Aug. 1844, Alexander Oswald of Auchencruive, Co. Ayr, M.P., who died Sept. 6, 1868. She died Oct. 1858.

Failing the heirs of Colonel George Johnstone, the House of Alva, coming from the third Baronet of Westerhall, is next in succession to the Baronetcy. James Raymond Johnstone, only son of John Johnstone of Alva, was born June 4, 1768, and married, June 20, 1799, Mary Elizabeth, sister to Sir Montague Cholmeley, Bart. They had eight sons and eight daughters:—

I. James, born 1801.

II. John, born 1802, Colonel H.E.I.C.S., married, June 18, 1845, Caroline, daughter of the Rev. Charles Pannel. Their daughter, Harriet Augusta, married Sir Robert Buxton, and left children. Colonel Johnstone embarked at Madras for Singapore with half his regiment in 1854. The ship was never heard of again, and there were suspicions of foul play.

III. Montague Cholmeley, born 1804 (Major-General), married, Dec. 31, 1844, Leonora Louisa, daughter of General Sir Henry Somerset, K.C.B., great-grand-daughter of the fifth Duke of Beaufort. He died 1874, leaving—

(1) Somerset James, Lieutenant (retired) R.N., born Aug. 29, 1846. Married, first, 1875, Cassila, daughter of W. Johnson. She died 1886, having had— 1, Fitzroy Augustus, Lieutenant Indian Army, born July 1878; 2, Emily, married Herbert Algernon Adams, R.N. He married, secondly, 1887, Isabel Ann, daughter of Joseph Mappin, and has—3, James Montagu, born 1889; 4, Malcolm Bruce, born 1893; 5, Catherine Octavia.

(2) Montague George, D.S.O. (Frampton, North Berwick), J.P., Major (retired) Royal Scots Greys, Lieutenant-Colonel late commanding 3rd Battalion Militia Yorkshire Light Infantry. Served with Bechuanaland Expedition, 1884; South African War, 1899-1901. Born March 21, 1848. Married, July 10, 1880, Agnes, widow of Captain Robert Johnston Stansfeld, daughter of Joseph Harrison, D.L., J.P., Co. Lancaster. They have—1, Montague Joseph

JAMES RAYMOND JOHNSTONE OF ALVA.
(WESTERHALL).

MARY CHOLMELEY,
WIFE OF JAMES RAYMOND JOHNSTONE OF ALVA.

Charles Somerset, late Lieutenant 2nd Dragoons, born June 1882, married Victoria Stewart; 2, Reginald Fitzroy Lewis, born 1884, Second Lieutenant Cameron Highlanders; 3, Violet.

Colonel Montague Johnstone was educated at Cheltenham, where he won in one term the class Mathematical, Divinity and German prizes. In athletics he won the boxing belt and other trophies. He was not only the last Cornet to be gazetted to the Royal Scots Greys, but the last officer to buy his Cornetcy and Lieutenancy. In 1880 he was made extra Aide-de-camp to the Lord-Lieutenant of Ireland, and four years later was appointed to the Headquarter Staff in Sir Charles Warren's expedition to Bechuanaland, where he helped to raise the 2nd Mounted Rifles, for which he obtained 400 volunteers. He saw much hard service in the South African War, taking part in all the operations in which Lord Methuen's Brigade was engaged (1899-1901). He commanded the Lambeth Palace Camp at the King's Coronation.

(3) Francis Fawkes, Lieutenant-Colonel late Bedfordshire Regiment, born Aug. 1849. Married, first, 1878, Henrietta, second daughter of James Sullivan, and had—1, Montague, born 1880, died unmarried 1907; 2, Mary Louisa, married, 1897, P. Kitchin; 3, Frances Geraldine. He married, secondly, 1887, Harriet, widow of Captain Greg and daughter of Richard Sargent, and has— 4, Charles, born 1889.

(4) Robert Fitzroy Maclean, late Major 4th Hyderabad Lancers, born Sept. 30, 1859. Married, 1898, Mary, widow of F. A. Beauclerk and daughter of Admiral J. B. Dickson.

(5) Frances Mary (10 Newbold Terrace, Leamington).

(6) Fanny Louisa, died 1895, married her cousin, John Pitt Muir Mackenzie.

(7) Edith Olive, married, 1883, Captain Edmund George Reilly, B.S.C., who died 1887. A son, Noel.

(8) Mysie Caroline, married, 1886, Frederick Gomer, and has children.

(9) Maud, married, 1904, Stanley Davies.

IV. George Dempster (Rev.), Captain (retired) H.E.I.C.S., born March 13, 1805, Rector of Creed, Cornwall. Married, Sept. 1, 1842, Mary Anne, daughter of the late John Hawkins of Bignor, in Sussex, and niece of Sir Christopher Hawkins and Colonel Sibthorp. Died 1867, having had—

(1) George Herbert, born June 1, 1843; died young.

(2) John Heywood of Bignor Park, Sussex, J.P., M.P. for Horsham Division, 1893-1904. Born May 18, 1850. Married, 1878, Josephine, daughter of the late J. Wells of Bickley, Co. Kent, and died Oct. 10, 1904, leaving—1, George Horace, now of Bignor Park and Trewithen, Co. Cornwall, born Jan. 8, 1882; 2, Frances Grace, married, April 19, 1904, George Bernard Hill; 3, Margaret Ruth.

(3) Mary Catherine, the only daughter of the Rev. George D. Johnstone, married, April 23, 1874, John Gwennap Dennis Moore of Garlenick, Co. Cornwall, and has—1, Herbert Tregosse Gwennap, Captain R.E., served in South Africa, 1899-1902; 2, Waldo Alington Gwennap, Captain Welsh Regiment;

3, Charles Wilfred Gwennap, Rev., M.A.; 4, Hartley Russell Gwennap, Lieutenant R.N.; 5, Irene Mary Juanita Gwennap.

V. Charles Kinnaird Johnstone-Gordon, born Sept. 25, 1806, Captain in the E.I. Co.'s Navy, Knight of the Persian Order of the Lion and Sun. Married, May 1838, his cousin Elizabeth, only daughter of Francis Gordon of Craig, by whom he had four daughters, of whom the eldest, Elizabeth Mary, married, Sept. 8, 1857, Hugh Scott of Gala (who died Dec. 9, 1877), leaving issue. At the death of Mrs Johnstone's father, 1857, Captain Johnstone assumed the name and arms of Gordon on succeeding to the estates of Craig and Kincardine, Co. Aberdeen. The Gordons of Craig are descended from Patrick Gordon of Craig, who fell at Flodden (1513), and whose grandfather, John, was younger brother of Sir Adam Gordon.

VI. Henry Wedderburn, born April 15, 1810, Commander R.N. Married, Nov. 13, 1857, Sarah, daughter of John Walter; died Dec. 30, 1865, leaving—

(1) James George, born Dec. 22, 1859. Married, 1896, Mary Margaret, daughter of Thomas Duff. He died *s.p.* 1900.

(2) Montagu Henry, born Oct. 2, 1861; died *s.p.* 1891.

VII. Robert Abercrombie (Rev.), Rector of Ingrave, Essex, born July 8, 1811. Married Anne, daughter of Joseph Walker, and died *s.p.* 1867.

VIII. Francis William, born May 25, 1818, late Captain in the Army, and Lieutenant-Colonel 2nd Lanarkshire Militia. Married, Jan. 10, 1844, Maria, daughter of Peirce Mahony. He died Aug. 9, 1888, having had—

(1) Montagu, born Sept. 28, 1844.

(2) Peirce de Lacy Henry, M.A., Oxon., born 1848. Married Jessie, daughter of James Sime.

(3) Alice Jane, died 1906, wife of her cousin, Peirce O'Mahony.

(4) Edith Lucy, married, 1888, Leonard Barnard, and has issue.

IX. Caroline Elizabeth, married, June 23, 1829, Rev. John Hamilton Gray of Carntyne, Co. Lanark, by whom (who died June 1867) she had an only daughter, Maria, who married, 1852, John Anstruther Thomson of Charleston, Fife; died 1883. Mrs Hamilton Gray acquired literary reputation by her historical works on Etruria and Rome. She died Feb. 21, 1887.

X. Sarah Emily, died unmarried 1891.

XI. Mary Anne, married, 1839, James Dewar, and died Sept. 1892, leaving—

(1) James Raymond Johnstone Dewar, Major R.A., late Bengal. Married Caroline Emily, daughter of General R. Phayre, C.B.

(2) Arthur Robert Johnstone Dewar, New Zealand Local Force, and three daughters.

XII. Catherine Lucy, died unmarried 1866.

XIII. Sophia Matilda, married, Aug. 28, 1832, Sir John Muir Mackenzie, Bart., of Delvine, Co. Perth. She died Jan. 29, 1900, leaving issue.

XIV. Jemima Eleanora, married, Feb. 16, 1848, Lord Frederick Beauclerk of Grimsby Hall, son of the eighth Duke of St. Albans. She died Oct. 14, 1877, leaving—

(1) William Nelthorpe. (2) Frederick Amelius.

Lady Frederick Beauclerk. Rev. Robert Johnstone. Emily Johnstone. Rev. George Johnstone. Miss Lucy Johnstone. Mrs Dewar. Lady Muir Mackenzie. Charles Johnstone. John Johnstone. Mrs Hamilton Gray. Capt. Harry Johnstone.

Mr. Kiug Harman. Octavia Johnstone. Mr Johnstone of Alva. Colonel Frank Johnstone. General Montague Johnstone.

THE SIXTEEN CHILDREN OF JAMES RAYMOND JOHNSTONE OF ALVA AND MARY ELIZABETH CHOLMELEY, HIS WIFE.
(WESTERHALL).

XV. Mary Cecilia (twin with Jemima), married, May 17, 1837, the Hon. Lawrence Harman King-Harman, second son of the Earl of Kingston. He assumed the name of Harman on succeeding to his grandmother's (the Countess of Rosse) estate of Newcastle, Co. Longford. She died Jan. 11, 1904, leaving issue.

XVI. Charlotte Octavia, married, first, May 1845, James Harrison Cholmeley, Major, 8th Hussars; died *s.p.* 1854. She married, secondly, Oct. 9, 1867, Francis Bernard Pigott of Eagle Hill; died 1875. She died March 26, 1898.

Mr Johnstone of Alva died April 7, 1830, and was succeeded by his son, James, in Alva and Hangingshaw, born July 4, 1801, J.P. and D.L. of Clackmannan, Stirling, and Selkirk, M.P. for Clackmannan and Kinross from 1851 to 1857. Married, first, Jan. 9, 1846, the Hon. Augusta Anne Norton, daughter of the Hon. Fletcher Norton, Baron of the Exchequer in Scotland and sister of Fletcher, third Lord Grantley. She died 1859, leaving—

(1) John Augustus James of Alva, born 1847; died *s.p.* 1890.

(2) Caroline Elizabeth Mary, now of Alva.

He married, secondly, May 5, 1862, Sarah Mary, daughter of Lieutenant-Colonel L'Estrange of Moystown, King's County. The British residents in Brussels in 1861 recollect the keen competition between Mr Johnstone and a foreign Royal Prince for Miss L'Estrange's hand. The children of the second marriage were—

(3) James Henry L'Estrange, M.V.O., Major R.E., of the Hangingshaw, Selkirk, J.P., Order of the Osmanleh, President of the Egyptian Railway Board, born Aug. 8, 1865; died 1906. He married, 1891, Amy Octavia, youngest daughter of the late Andrew Wauchope, and had—1, John Andrew born May 1893, heir to his aunt; 2, Henry James, born 1895; 3, Andrew Wauchope, born 1903.

(4) Henry Beresford, B.A., Oxon., born Jan. 26, 1871, Vice-Consul at Addis Aluba, late Assistant Collector, Rabai, East Africa.

(5) Gilbert Lumley, late Lieutenant R.F.A., Sub-Inspector Hausa Force, Africa, born April 16, 1872. Married, 1907, Florence, daughter of A. Fincham.

Mr Johnstone died Feb. 24, 1888. The eldest son, John Augustus James Johnstone of Alva, Co. Stirling, J.P., born May 3, 1847, married, May 1868, Emily, daughter of the late R. W. Crossling. He died *s.p.* April 1, 1890, and was succeeded in Alva by his sister, Caroline Elizabeth.

The Vanden-Bempdé Johnstones of Hackness Hall, represented by Lord Derwent (Sir Harcourt Johnstone), descend from John, second son of Sir William Johnstone, second Baronet of Westerhall, by his marriage with Charlotta, Marchioness of Annandale. Their two sons — Richard (created a Baronet), an M.P. in the Irish Parliament, and Charles, of Pembroke and Ludlow—have been described. The Marchioness spent the last few years of her life with her daughter, Charlotte Henrietta, at Turnham Green, Chiswick, to be near her unfortunate son, and he was often well enough to stay in the same house. She lived quietly from choice, but it was no isolation. Sir

Robert Walpole, the Princess Amelia, and several of the nobility lived in the Tudor and Queen Anne houses, planted among magnificent trees, for Chiswick was one of the most beautiful districts in England, and a favourite drive with George II. from Kensington Palace. The house and park of the Duke of Devonshire, built and laid out after the pattern of a smaller Versailles, was close to Annandale House, and it was only five miles from Pall Mall, where the Marchioness had passed her early life. She died there Nov. 23, 1762. Her daughter survived till Feb. 17, 1789, predeceasing her half-brother, the Marquis, whose guardian she virtually became. She left her brother, Charles, her sole executor.

Sir Richard Johnstone of Hackness Hall married, first, Catherine, daughter of James Agnew of Bishop Auckland. She died *s.p.* 1790. He married, secondly, 1795, Margaret, daughter of John Scott of Charterhouse Square, London (who married, secondly, William Gleadowe), and had (1) John, his heir; (2) Charles, M.A., Canon of York, born 1800; (3) Margaret, married her cousin, George; (4) Charlotte, married William Fenton Scott; (5) Laura, died 1817.

Sir Richard died 1807, and was succeeded by his son, John, second Baronet, born 1799. Married, 1825, Louisa Augusta Venables Vernon, daughter of the Archbishop of York and his wife, Lady Anne, sister of the Duke of Sutherland. They had:—

(1) Harcourt, born 1829, created Lord Derwent 1881. Married Charlotte, daughter of Sir Charles Mills, and has issue.

(2) Henry Richard, born 1830, took the name of Scott. Married, 1866, Cressida, daughter of W. Selby Lowndes, and has—Henry Lister, J.P., and others.

(3) Caroline, married, 1848, the Marquis of Abergavenny; died 1892. Left issue.

(4) Elizabeth Margaret, married, 1855, Sir Thomas Erskine Perry.

(5) Blanche Maria, married, 1859, Robert Swann of Askham, Co. York.

(6) Georgiana Emily, died unmarried 1863.

Sir John Vanden Bempdé-Johnstone died in consequence of a fall out hunting in 1869.

His brother, Charles (Rev. Canon), and his wife, Amelia, daughter of the Rev. R. Hawksworth, left:—

(1) Charles, Vicar of Hackness, born 1828.

(2) Frederick Richard, born 1829; died *s.p.* 1900.

(3) William John, born 1833; died 1855.

(4) Arthur George, born 1837; died *s.p.* 1871.

(5) Charlotte Frances, married Edmund Walker.

(6) Laura Georgiana.

(7) Caroline, and other daughters.

Harcourt, first Lord Derwent, succeeded his father 1869. Lady Derwent died 1903. Their children are:—

(1) Francis, J.P., Deputy-Lieutenant, late Captain 2nd Life Guards, born

1851. Married, 1880, Ethel, daughter of Henry Strickland Constable of Wassand, Co. York. By her, who died 1891, he has—1, Sibell; 2, Freda, married eldest son of third Earl of Listowel, and has issue.

(2) Edward Henry, born 1854. Married, 1896, Hon. Evelyn, daughter of fifth Viscount Clifden. Died 1903, leaving—1, Leopold, born 1897; 2, George Harcourt; 3, Patrick Robin Gilbert.

(3) Cecil, C.E., born 1856.

(4) Alan (Sir), K.C.V.O., married, 1892, Antoinette, daughter of J. W. Pinchot, of New York. Has Harcourt, born 1895.

(5) Louis, born 1862. Married, 1891, Gwendoline Mary Talbot, and has—1, Granville Henry, born 1891; 2, Robin Talbot; 3, Dorothy Ethel; 4, Joan Gwendoline.

(6) Gilbert, born 1865. Married, 1897, Rachael, daughter of Colonel the Hon. Archibald Douglas Pennant. Has—1, Mark, born 1900; 2, Felix.

(7) Hilda, died 1853.

(8) Edith.

(9) Mary.

Charles,[1] of Ludlow, the second son of Lady Annandale by her second husband, Colonel John Johnstone of Netherwood, was born in London, July 15, 1736, and is registered as baptised in the parish of St. George's, Hanover Square, on the 20th. Died 1805. He married Mary, daughter of John and Mary Beddoe of Haverfordwest, Pembroke, in 1778. The bride was seventeen, the bridegroom forty-two, and they had eight sons and six daughters. The eldest:—

(1) William, born Oct. 1779 at Haverfordwest, was educated at Charterhouse and Cambridge; Rector of Culmington, Salop. Married, 1804, Catherine Brome, and died *s.p.* 1856.

(2) Charles Philipps, born Nov. 6, 1780, his second name, that of his godfather, Sir Richard Philipps, Lord Milford. He was a Captain in the 3rd King's Own Dragoon Guards, and married, 1807, Frances, youngest daughter of James Harrison of Cheadle Bulkley, Co. Chester, and by her, who died at Newbold Manor, Co. Stafford, 1844, he had eleven children. He died in Worcester, March 8, 1863, and was buried in Hindlip Churchyard. His eldest son—1, Charles James, born 1809, Fellow of Caius College, Cambridge, Physician to the Foundling Hospital, London, died unmarried March 26, 1838. He is buried in the Chapel of the Foundling, with a marble tablet to his memory by Lough; 2, William Henry, born 1812, drowned when bathing in the Mersey, 1828; 3, Parker, R.N., born 1813, died unmarried 1842; 4, a son, died an infant; 5, Vanden Bempdé, born May 10, 1819, Cantab. in Holy Orders, died April 15, 1859, buried at Itchen Stoke, Hants. He married, April 12, 1855, Louisa, daughter of Jonathan Scarth, Esq., of Shrews-

---

[1] He wrote down his recollections of the Macdonald followers of Prince Charles Edward quartering themselves at Comlongan Castle, and their theory as to the connection of Johnstones and Macdonalds from two daughters of a chief named Haliday—so called because he chose Saints days for raids into England—marrying the progenitors of the two clans.

bury (of an old Yorkshire family). Their children were—Vanden Bempdé, born at Hurstmonceaux Place, Co. Sussex, Feb. 11, 1856, married, 1897, Minnie Sarah Gratton; Charles Julius, M.A., born at Brighton June 1857, married Mary Gertrude, daughter of E. Madoc Jones of Glentworth, Oswestry, died 1904, leaving Charles Arthur, born 1887, Francis Edward, Richard Noel, William Robert Parke; 6, Frances Maria, died unmarried 1866; 7, Margaret Eliza, died unmarried 1892; 8, Laura, died unmarried 1891; 9, Emma, died unmarried 1905; 10, Georgina, died unmarried 1900, who for some years superintended the education of the children of the eighth Duke of Argyll; and 11, Susan, died unmarried 1899.

(3) John, third son of Charles Johnstone, of Ludlow, born Feb. 1783, married, 1813, Agnes, only child of the Rev. George Hutton. Was Captain in the 3rd and 5th Dragoon Guards in the Peninsular War, A.D.C. to the Duke of Wellington, and settled at Mainstone Court. He died, 1870, at The Cliffe, near Ludlow, and was buried in the family vault in Culmington Churchyard, Salop. His children were—1, John Hutton, died unmarried 1842; 2, George Henry, Rector of St. Nicolas, Sutton, Co. Hereford, M.A., Trinity College, Cambridge, died *s.p.*; 3, Geoffrey Plantagenet, died unmarried 1855; 4, Charles Octavius, a merchant at Moulmein, Burmah, died unmarried; 5, Robert Bruce at Rangoon, died *s.p.* 1854; 6, Agnes Charlotte; 7, Laura Maria Henrietta, died unmarried; 8, Louisa Rebecca, married, 1847, Humphrey Salwey of Ashley Moor and The Cliffe, Ludlow, and died 1906, leaving a son, Theophilus, and two daughters; 9, Anna, married, 1849, The MacGillicuddy of the Reeks, Kerry, Ireland, and had nine children.

(4) George of Broncroft Castle, 5th Dragoon Guards, born 1784. Married, first, 1815, his cousin, Margaret, daughter of Sir Richard Vanden Bempdé Johnstone, and had—1, Anne Georgina, died *s.p.* He married, secondly, Jane, daughter of Hugh Edwards of Borthwynog, Dolgelly, and had—2, Charles Edwards, married, 1848, Jane, daughter of James Abel, died *s.p.*; 3, Hugh Edwards John George, married Mary Tudor, died *s.p.*; 4, Catherine, married Thomas Knox Holmes, and died *s.p.*; 5, Marianne, married William Stutfield, and had George Herbert, barrister-at-law, and other children. George Johnstone died at Folkestone 1856.

(5) Richard James, born 1793, married Miss Gilder, and died 1850, leaving— 1, Richard, Colonel Bombay Army, born 1825, died 1888, married, 1874, Anna Maria Clayton, daughter of S. W. Clayton of Ryde, and had Richard Harcourt Vanden Bempdé, born 1875, died 1892; 2, Frederick Charles Johnstone, born 1828, died 1907, married, 1860, Helen Kathleen, daughter of Colonel Alexander, and had Frederick Alexander, born 1865, John Villiers, born 1873, and four daughters; 3, Edmund John, born 1832, drowned off Cape Coast Castle 1868, married at the Cathedral, Port Louis, Mauritius, to Agnes, daughter of Thomas Gulliver, R.N., 1856, and had Charles Frederick Dale, born 1858, Richard James Annandale, born 1865, and Kathleen Matilda, married to Captain James P. Agnew of Bishop Auckland, Co. Durham; 4, Francis Edward, born 1840, died *s.p.* 1873, Captain H.E.I.C.S.; 5, Georgina Maria, married, 1856, to Edward

William Cates, and has three sons; 6, Augusta Jane; 7, Matilda Lucy, married to Marshall Christie, and has three sons and three daughters; 8, Louisa Amitié, married to Rayner Alexander, and has issue.

(6) Bempdé, born 1794, R.N.; killed at the siege of New Orleans, 1815, s.p.

(7) James.

(8) James Pulteney, died young, 1799.

(9) Charlotte, married, 1800, Admiral Sir Charles Knowles, Bart., G.C.B., and has descendants; died 1867. Her sons, Francis (Sir) and Henry, died young, were twins.

(10) Maria Henrietta, married, 1803, the Rev. Denham Cookes, Rector of Astley, Co. Worcester, and had issue. She died 1873.

(11) Catherine, married, 1809, Captain Baugh, R.N., and had issue.

(12) Louisa, married, 1813, Colonel Sir William Parke of Dunally, Ireland, and had issue.

(13) Jane, married, 1815, the Rev. Philip Jennings, D.D., Archdeacon of Norfolk, and had issue. (These two sisters each lived to be ninety-two.)

(14) Laura Sarah, died unmarried.

Francis Johnstoun, the merchant in Clydesdale outlawed for taking part with Richard Cameron in the Sanquhar Declaration in 1680, is conjectured to have been probably the same as Francis, brother to James Johnstoun of Westerhall (died 1699), and the father of Francis (born 1669, died before 1712) who married Agnes Brown, and was father to James, whose second son, Francis, settled in London and died there in 1828, having married Elizabeth Ellis. This Francis and Elizabeth had seven children—1, Thomas Francis and 2, Francis William, died young; 3, James, barrister-at-law, died s.p.; 4, Edward, born 1804, married Harriet, daughter of Charles Alexander Moke, M.D. (of the family of Moke of Thourout, in Flanders), and his wife, Martha Masterson; 5, Henry, an artist; 6, Thomas, died s.p.; 7, Elizabeth, married, first, Captain E. Blackwell, second, Rev. A. Maister.

Of the above sons, Edward Johnston and his wife, Harriet, left a large family—1, Charles Edward (1829-1908), married Mathilde, daughter of Judge Eustis of New Orleans, and left children; 2, Francis John (*seq.*); 3, Horace James, second Secretary H.M. Diplomatic Service, died s.p. 1866; 4, Hamilton, Lieutenant 9th Lancers, died s.p. 1873; 5, Reginald Eden, Deputy-Governor of the Bank of England, married Alice, daughter of the Rev. C. Eyres, and has issue; 6, Cyril Earle; 7, Harriet, married, first, Hardman Earle, second, Major James Lyle Thursby; 8, Eliza Fanny, married Admiral Sir E. Inglefield; 9, Eweretta, married Colonel Charles A. B. Gordon; 10, Edith, married the Rev. W. St. Aubyn; 11, Constance, married John Archibald Shaw-Stewart.

Francis John, born 1831, married Caroline, daughter of Sir Hardman Earle, first Baronet. Their children—1, Bertram Masterson, died s.p. 1890; 2, Francis Alexander, born 1864, married Audrey, daughter of Ernest Alers-Hankey; 3, Horace James Johnston, Colonel, D.S.O., married Florence Hope,

x

daughter of William Browne-Clayton of Browne's Hill, Co. Carlow, and has Francis William and Patrick James; 4, Caroline Margaret, married Richard Heywood Heywood-Jones of Badsworth, Co. York; 5, Violet Mary, married Henry Offley Wakeman; 6, Harriet Monica, married Captain Charles Wyndham Knight, D.S.O.; 7, Mildred Earle, married Ernest Perceval Alers-Hankey; 8, Vera Cecilia.

Besides the above, there are existing descendants of James and Robert Johnston (the last a minister), whose father, James, born 1701, married to Jean Clark, was grandson of Francis, the bold Covenanter. The younger James was born 1755; died 1828. He married Mary Spiers, and lived for forty years in Dalquharran Castle as factor and land surveyor to the Laird of Dunore. His poetical and literary tastes were developed amid romantic surroundings, where his sons, Thomas and James, were born. Thomas is now represented by Thomas Johnston of Balvaig, Dumfries. James was educated as a minister in the Church of Scotland, but ultimately joined the Baptist sect, which required almost as much courage as for his ancestor to become a Covenanter. His son, Francis, born 1810, and brought up at the High School, Edinburgh, followed in his father's footsteps, which, in spite of a brilliant University career, checked the exercise of his talents in a wider sphere. He married Eliza Broad, from Yorkshire. They had seven sons and two daughters. The eldest son, James, died 1909, leaving five daughters, the eldest married to Dr John Balfour of Portobello. The Rev. Francis Johnston's younger daughter, Helen Eliza, married Mr Penman, and has one son—Frank Garfield Penman, B.A. Cantab., born 1884. Her father died 1880, and is buried in the Grange Cemetery, Edinburgh.

CHAPTER XXVII.

JOHNSTONS OF ELPHINSTONE — WISHART AND KNOX — YOUNGER SONS — SALTON — COUSLAND — JOHNSTONS OF NEWTON — EDINBURGH, ETC.

THE Johnstons of Elphinstone were early impoverished by a succession of lawsuits. Sir Alexander Elphinstone was killed at the battle of Piperdean in 1435, and his only child, Agnes, who married Gilbert of Johnstoun, was opposed in her possession of his estates by the male heir who generation after generation carried on a lawsuit up to 1581. These Johnstouns were among the first Reformers. John Knox was born in the neighbourhood of Elphinstone Tower, and in 1544 was living at Ormiston, and tutor to Francis and John, the sons of Hew Douglas of Longniddry near Tranent, and to the son of the Laird of Ormiston. George Wishart, who had been ministering to the plague-stricken town of Dundee, was forced to leave it by Cardinal Beaton, the Archbishop of St. Andrews, and took refuge with Knox at Ormiston. The Cardinal with the Regent Arran and an armed suite came to Elphinstone Tower, and sent orders to Bothwell (the Sheriff) to arrest the Reformers (Jan. 1546). Wishart made no resistance, for Bothwell promised that he should suffer no bodily hurt, but the Cardinal, hoping to secure Knox, kept Wishart for a short time imprisoned in Elphinstone Tower, where a rent in the wall was long shown by the country people as a sign of the Almighty's displeasure at the martyr's fate.

It is probable that Andrew Johnstoun, the old Laird of Elphinstone, enabled Knox to escape to England, for the Cardinal, disappointed at not having more than one prisoner, took Wishart to St. Andrews, where he was strangled and burnt at the stake in front of the Cardinal's palace. Bothwell revenged it three months later by procuring the Cardinal's assassination; and Andrew Johnstoun supported Knox when he returned to Scotland. One of his family, John Johnstoun, witnessed Knox's Will, May 13, 1572, and Andrew's son, John, was present at the Reformer's death-bed.

On Sunday, Nov. 23, 1572, during the afternoon sermon, Knox, says his biographer, became so ill that his secretary, Richard Bannatyne, "sent to the Church for John Johnstoun of Elphinstone, who immediately came to his bedside; and many more arrived when the sermon was over. From that time till Monday night, Nov. 24, Mrs Knox, Bannatyne, Campbell, Johnstoun, and

Dr Preston—his most intimate friends—sat by turns with the dying man till he expired."

Andrew Johnstoun of Elphinstone witnessed an agreement in 1561 between James or John, for he is called both in the deed, the Abbot of Salsit, and Margaret, the widow of Johnstoun of Wamfray, and her elder sons, James, Gilbert, and William, in which the Abbot, moved, as he says, "by pity and reuth for the said Margaret and for her bairns, was content to pay 100 marks yearly for two years for support to hold them at schools where they may learn knowledge and letters, and further, in remembrance of the good deeds and thankfulness done to the said Abbot by the late James of Wamfray; but if the abbeys and ecclesiastical benefices decay by taking away the lands the said Margaret and her children must pay back a portion of it." James Johnstoun of Kellobank was the witness.

In 1553 representatives of the Peerage, Knighthood, and gentry of Scotland were ordered to meet the English commissioners of equivalent rank on the Borders to discuss the terms of peace. Andrew Johnstoun of Elphinstone appears among the Knights. Two of his sons were named John, the one who attended Knox's death-bed, and another a merchant, who was for some time a Romanist, and had a son educated at Douai for the priesthood. His eldest brother, James, was his cautioner for £1000 that he should have no communication with traitors and exiles. His name appears several times in public affairs in Edinburgh, where he joined with George Heriot, Arnot, and others in trying to reform the Edinburgh Corporation, but those individuals whom his party elected would not act. Another of Andrew's sons, Mr Adam Johnstoun, a commissioner for Lothian and Provost of Crichton, declined to subscribe to the Act of Pacification signed at Perth. He and eight other ministers were ordered to appear before the King, who, report said, was "a Papist," but however that might be, it was the King's policy just then to conciliate his future Romanist subjects, who were still numerous in England, and were issuing pamphlets accusing him of conniving at his mother's fate. Three of the ministers obeyed the order and were convinced by the Royal arguments. Adam was one of those put in ward for contumacy. In 1584 they were ordered to leave Edinburgh, and not to print or circulate their views. Mr David Chalmers was appointed Provost in Adam's place, and both carried on lawsuits against the other. Adam was dead in 1607, when his widow, Bessie Borthwick, and his son James are mentioned in John Johnstoun of Elphinstone's Will. As Clerk of the Privy Council this John had taken the oath of secrecy in 1561.

The political intrigues in which the Johnstouns of Elphinstone were mixed up were all to further the Protestant cause. In 1565 "Mr John Johnstoun, writer, was respited for assisting the Earl of Moray in his treacherous dealings in England and France," *i.e.*, when Moray went to London and Paris to find a Protestant husband for Queen Mary instead of Darnley. He was probably the Elphinstone whom Moray sent from Paris to confer with Queen Elizabeth's Ministers. The murder of Rizzio was in the same interest. James Johnstoun, who was respited in 1571 for acting as Squire to Claud Hamilton at the battle of Langside and bearing arms for the Queen against the late Regent, seems also to have been an Elphinstone, his zeal as a Reformer having succumbed to his loyalty.

Buchanan states that Scrope's invasion in 1570 was chiefly directed against "one Johnston . . . whose lands he ransacked; but Johnston himself with a few of his companions, being well acquainted with the passes of the country made a shift to escape from the horse that pursued him. John Maxwell had gathered together 3000 men out of the neighbourhood yet durst not adventure to come to his aid, but only stood upon his own guard." This was John of Newbie (*see* p. 74), but James of Elphinstone came to the assistance of his clan at that period, and was one of the sureties for Johnstoun of Corrie. Having married a Melvill, he was not likely permanently to desert the Protestant camp.

The Elphinstone family took a different view of the Reformation to that of the Johnstouns of Elphinstone, and it was chiefly to remove one of the first from the councils of the King, with all who had been excommunicated by the Presbytery for "Papistry," that a party of the Reformed clergy at the head of a threatening mob collected round the Tolbooth (Dec. 17, 1596), where the King with the Queen was presiding over a Session of Parliament. It was confronted by another party, including Edward Johnstoun of Ryehill, William Little (called the Laird), Thomas Hunter, and others, who probably saved the building from being wrecked. The Provost and Baillies escorted the King down the street safely to his palace, and the Court left the next day. But from Stirling Castle the King issued a decree declaring the Provost, Baillies, and whole body of the Burgh of Edinburgh to be held guilty of the tumult. He directed that they should "repair to the Tolbooth and be examined by warding, torture, or any manner of means to find out the most pernicious offenders." He reproached the clergy, "who ought to have been emissaries of peace."

As the summons was not obeyed, another proclamation was issued against four of the Edinburgh clergy and against Edward Johnstoun and his colleagues, ordering their goods to be escheated. It was complained that they had friends who took care of their possessions. Finally the King, perhaps learning that no one had intended to injure him, respited most of them. John Johnstoun of Elphinstone was among those whose effects were ordered to be escheated.

Ryehill was probably mistaken for an Elsieshields [1] of the same name, a well-known Protestant merchant, but as he did not appear he was proclaimed a rebel and his escheat given to Sir George Home. Ryehill brought an action against

---

[1] Some time before, a ship with cargo belonging to this Edward Johnstoun (whose father and brother being named Nathaniel, was perhaps related to N. Udward) had been captured by pirates in the Tyne, and he applied to the English Admiralty for compensation. James VI. supported the claim, and Elizabeth, overruling the decision of the Admiralty, ordered that the loss should be repaid. The Queen quoted this case in the correspondence about Buccleuch's capture of Armstrong, and said that as she had taken Edward's word against the advice of her counsellors, so her officers' version of the circumstances of Armstrong's capture should be accepted rather than that of Buccleuch.

Home for seizing his house, which led to the scene described by the English Warden (*see* p. 112). A year later Ryehill received a post in the Customs.

James Johnstoun of Elphinstone died Dec. 16, 1594. He married, first, Margaret Ruthven, March 1550, and had two sons, Patrick and John. He married, secondly, Janet Melvill, by whom he had James, Robert, and John.

The inventory of his goods and debts was given up by his son, John, and his daughter, Martha. The witnesses, Patrick Johnstoun (his son), Allen Cubie in Preston, Mr Robert Johnstoun (his son), Ninian Weir (notary), and others. His wealth consisted of corn, cattle, and sheep; and his tenants in Ballincrieff, Cousland, and other places, Thos. Rae, Peter, William, Janet, and Thomas Johnstoun, were in arrears with their rent. But he had many creditors and owed part of a daughter's dowry (Lady Glenegiis); £130 to his brother, John; £48 to his brother, Mr Adam Johnstoun; £48 to Mr James Johnstoun, merchant; £30 to Elspeth Johnstoun for her bridal gown; £80 borrowed from his son, Mr John Johnstoun; and he owed his tenants of Cousland and others for malt, fish, and necessary provisions. In his Will, written in Edinburgh, possibly in George Haldin's house as he owes rent to him, the Laird of Elphinstone leaves John and Martha his executors, "to be counselled by the advice of their mother and of my brother John . . . Because," he adds, "my son, Mr James, has behaved himself most proudly and rebelliously towards me, his father, and offended me grievously as is notoriously known to all his friends . .. . I declare that I will no ways have him to share any part or portion of my goods and gear, but debar him simply therefrom and from the name of a son, and for all benefits which he might have had through me." He had already made over Leuchie and Ballincrieff to his son, Robert, and as John and Martha are the only children he has not provided for they are to divide what is left when his debts are paid. He empowers John to continue an action against Lord and Lady Gowrie for the rent of the lands and Mains of Cousland, and he bequeaths Cousland to John, and his daughter Marion to the guardianship of the Laird of Wedderburn, that he may suffer her to get no wrong in her marriage with the Laird of Cockburn.

There had been an action going on since 1591 between William Bonar of Rossie and Elphinstone about a contract of marriage with Jean Johnstoun, the latter's daughter, as apparently the Laird declined to give up the title-deeds of Bonar's estate, which was settled on Jean and which Elphinstone had himself obtained by escheat. But in his Will he states that Bonar is doing "his honest duty to his wife and children," so that Robert, to whom he leaves the title-deeds in trust, is not to use them for his own profit, and to have no power to do anything with them without the advice of his brothers, Patrick and John, and of his uncle, John. He constitutes Patrick his eldest son, but the disinherited James was the eldest son of the second wife. In 1603, immediately after her death, "Master James Johnstoun is returned heir to his father, the late James Johnstoun of Elphinstone."

There was not much but land for any of them, and Bonar of Rossie continued his suit against the trustees. In 1603 Elphinstone's widow, Janet

Melvill, died, her only executor being Elizabeth Haldin, the widow of her stepson, John. John also died in 1603, and in his Will describes himself as brother german to Patrick. His eldest son, Gilbert, was returned his heir, and in 1619 signed a bond of reversion to Mr David Home of Godscroft and Barbara Johnstoun, sister of the said umquhile Mr John, his spouse, of an annual rent of 60 marks payable yearly forth of the lands of Godscroft. The deceased Mr John had lent money to one of the Homes.

Patrick Johnstoun of Elphinstone died in 1606. He married Elizabeth Dundas, and left 7000 marks to his eldest daughter, Barbara. His Will mentions the children who were minors, Robert, Patrick, Martha, and Mary, but Samuel was returned his heir and is also called young Patrick's eldest brother in Elizabeth Dundas's Will, 1610. Ninian and John Johnstoun "sometime in Dalkeith," owed her money.

In the Will of John Johnstoun in "ye pans," in Preston parish 1597, he speaks of money owed him by " J. Johnstoun now of Elphinstone."

In 1605 a bond was signed at Carlaverock, in which Mr John Home of Godscroft is surety that Mr James Johnstoun, portioner of Ballincrieff, shall not harm his brother, Mr Robert Johnstoun, Susanna Hamilton (his wife), or Robert Hamilton of Bathcat. Witnesses, Alexander Cranstoun, brother of Sir John Cranstoun; George Haldin, servitor of Elizabeth Haldin, relict of Mr John Johnstoun, brother of the said Mr James. In another bond James Cochrane is surety for £1000 that Robert Johnstoun and his wife should not hurt his own brother James; and Robert and Patrick Hamilton pledge themselves each for £1000 to the same effect. In 1607 the Captain of the Guard is ordered to arrest Mr James Johnstoun, portioner of Ballincrieff, son of the late James Johnstoun of Elphinstone, and inventory his goods for a debt of 360 marks.

His brother, Robert, was put into Haddington Jail for debt, but contrived to make his escape in 1614.

John Johnstoun in "West Pans of Musselburgh," Robert Douglas of Musselburgh, and Hew, his brother, had to find caution for threatening Mr Patrick Henryson in 1607. John was one of the Johnstouns of Salton. William Johnstoun in West Salton died in 1578, leaving four sons—Robert, Thomas, James, and John—besides a grandson, George Dewar. Robert, the eldest, died in 1586, and left his brother, John, executor and adviser to his children—Margaret, Agnes, Robert, William, Christian, Marion, and Jean. The younger Robert died in 1598, having married Agnes Gourlay, their eldest son being John. John, the elder, had two sons, David and Alexander, in 1601, when his first wife died. He married, secondly, Agnes Allan, and had by her George, Robert, Helen, and Janet, all minors when he died in 1606. His son, Alexander, called of West Pans, died in 1643. His elder brother, James, died in 1611, leaving by his wife, Christian Porteous, Robert, James, David, Marion, Agnes, and Katherine. David died *s.p.*; but James was living in 1631. James Johnstoun of Salton was alive in 1675.

Peter Johnstoun in Cousland, mentioned in James of Elphinstone's Will as a debtor, died in 1600, leaving by his wife, Jane Sympson, James, Alexander

Helen, Gilbert, and Janet, and "the Laird of Elphinstone to be adviser to his spouse and bairns." Peter was also father of Alison, married to John Noble of Inveresk, and of William and Isabel, by a previous marriage to Janet Wood, who died 1566. Janet Wood owed money to John, brother to the Laird of Elphinstone, and to her daughter Alison and John Noble.

Edward Johnstoun in Cousland, married to Agnes Hunter, was brother to Thomas the younger, and probably to Peter. He mentions three sons in his Will, but only William, the eldest, by name. Thomas the elder, and younger, and Alexander Johnstoun in Dalkeith are witnesses (1628).

There were more victims in South-East Scotland than in Dumfriesshire to the witch scare which discredited the Reformation, and in 1609 Giles Johnstoun, the widow of John Duncan of Musselburgh, was accused of witchcraft. She eloquently defended herself, never having been so wicked, she declared, as to have any dealings with the devil. It was seldom that such an assurance was enough without torture to prove it, but Giles had some powerful influence to help her, for the Privy Council relieved the ministers of Inveresk, Crichton, Borthwick, Newbattle, Cranston, and Lasswade, before whom she was charged, of any further responsibility and took it on themselves. A similar case of interference occurred in 1629, when the Provost and Baillies of Dunbar had to find caution for 500 marks to appear before the Privy Council and answer for arresting William Johnstoun, James Williamson, and others in Dunbar as "idle and masterless men."

The frolicsome youth of the period could make itself extremely objectionable to the industrious citizen, and the action of the Provost may have been only a precaution.

The descendants of George, the brother of Sir Adam Johnstoun of Elphinstone, have never been traced, nor of any son that Sir Adam may have had younger than Gilbert and Andrew. In the absence of proof elsewhere, they may presumably have existed in the families of Johnstoun settled in and around Elphinstone, who bore the same Christian names, and after the custom of the day would have had the first claim to feu the estates. Some of the descendants of the elder James of Elphinstone and his brothers, of John, the son of Robert of Leuchie, of Gilbert and other sons of John Johnstoun of Carlaverock and Elizabeth Haldin, have not been proved to be extinct, and possibly appear in David and Patrick[1] Johnstoun in Preston in 1634; Patrick, a farmer in Elphinstone in 1687; Robert of the same place in 1694; and James, who was returned heir to Robert; and in the Johnstouns of Newton. James Johnstoun of Newton Grange, in a deed registered March 9, 1634 and signed at Preston Pans, lent £83 Scots to John Baptie in *Lufuresmure*.

This James of Newton Grange was presumably related to David Johnstoun, whose son John's name is recorded on the baptismal register at Newton in 1629. David's younger children were Agnes, Patrick, Margaret, James, and

---

[1] The name Patrick, so often found among the Elphinstone Johnstons and their connections, came from Patrick of Dunbar, uncle to the first of this branch, who perished when his sovereign, James I., was murdered.

JOHNSTONS IN EDINBURGH

Jean, the various witnesses being several members of the Veitch family, Andrew Young, and Thomas Baillie. The children of William Johnstoun, Patrick, and two James's are also on the baptismal roll at Newton, 1638, 1640, and 1652.

David Johnstoun's eldest son, John, married, Nov. 12, 1658, Janet Akers, their children being Agnes, 1659, William, 1662, Alison, 1664, James, 1665, and John, 1667; the several witnesses to their baptisms were John Johnstoun, Alexander Davidson, William Gray, David Anderson, James Johnstoun, James Raith of Edmistoune, and Robert Harvie.

It was in 1666 that Sir Archibald Primrose obtained possession of Elphinstone Tower, and procured the retour of Sir James to his father, Sir John Johnstoun, to enable him to part with the property. Lady Johnstoun and the first Lady Primrose were sisters, co-heiresses of the Hon. James Keith of Benholme, and Sir Archibald had a mortgage to its full value on the estate. Another son of the late Sir John, to whom his father had left a small portion, was apprenticed in 1663 to Robert Hamieson, merchant in Elphinstone.

The Newton Johnstons flourished after the extinction of the main branch of Elphinstone, and William, the son of John of Newton and Janet Akers, married Margaret, daughter of John Handiside, July 5, 1694, and left six children — Hew, baptised 1695 (the witnesses being John Johnstoun and Robert Simpson), William, James, John, Margaret, and Robert.

James, baptised April 7, 1700, married, May 15, 1719, Agnes, daughter of Richard Web. He was a writer, like his ancestors, and was admitted a burgess of Edinburgh in 1731. Of his three children, James, William, and Andrew, the youngest, also a writer, baptised Feb. 14, 1731, left descendants. He married, July 4, 1760, Jean, daughter of Daniel Brown, in Elginhauch, and died Dec. 25, 1799. She survived nearly five years. Their children were: (1) Margaret, born 1761; died 1838. She married Archibald Wilson, who died 1837. (2) John, a banker, died *s.p.* 1788. (3) Jean, born 1766. (4) Peter, born 1768 (he was in the same class with Sir Walter Scott at the High School, Edinburgh). (5) Alexander, Royal Navy, born 1769, wounded twice at Camperdown, 1797, and was drowned about 1810. (6) Andrew, born July 2, 1771.

Andrew, the youngest son, was a writer. He married, 1798, Isobel, daughter of Archibald Keith of Newbattle, and died Jan. 3, 1844, his wife having long predeceased him. Their children were: (1) John, M.D., born Dec. 8, 1798; died *s.p.* Jan. 30, 1820. (2) Archibald, Fleet Surgeon Royal Navy, born Dec. 20, 1800; died *s.p.*, at Lisbon, Dec. 22, 1843. (3) Sir William, born Oct. 27, 1802. (4) Alexander Keith, LL.D., born Dec. 28, 1804. (5) Jean, died 1835, married Archibald Douglas. (6) Margaret, married Captain George Hewett Ainslie, son of Colonel Ainslie of Teviotgrove, and brother to Colonel Bernard Ainslie, C.B., who commanded the 93rd Highlanders, the "Thin Red Line," at the battle of Balaklava. (7) Isabella, married George Gulland; two of their grandsons are Dr Lovell Gulland and John W. Gulland, M.P. for Dumfries Burghs and a Junior Lord of the Treasury. (8) Thomas Brumby. (9) Adam Coulston, died young. (10) Helen Marion, died young.

Of these sons William was educated at the High School, Edinburgh. He was twice married--first, to Margaret, daughter of J. Pearson, of Fala, who died 1865 ; secondly, to Georgiana Augusta, daughter of William Ker of Gateshaw, and widow of the Rev. William Scoresby. After filling various public posts in Edinburgh he served in the office of Lord Provost (1848-51). His brother, Alexander Keith, was an eminent geographer—appointed to that office for the Queen—and he travelled round Europe and in Palestine, meeting the best known foreign travellers and geographers, among them Humboldt, while he was planning the *Physical Atlas of Natural Phenomena and Gazetteer*, and a list of publications occupying a column in the *Dictionary of National Biography*. The two brothers founded the firm of W. & A. K. Johnston, of Edinburgh and London, and while the elder was knighted, the younger received the LL.D. degree from the University of Edinburgh, and was awarded the Patron's or Victoria Medal from the Royal Geographical Society, of which he was a Fellow, as well as of the sister society in Paris, and a corresponding member of those of Vienna, St. Petersburg, Bombay, and America. Sir William was elected a Fellow of the Antiquarian Society in 1852, and retired from business in 1867, to live on his own estate at Kirkhill, in Midlothian. There he died Feb. 7, 1888, and was buried in the Grange Cemetery.

His brother, Alexander Keith, died of a sudden illness at Ben-Rhydding in 1871. He married Margaret, daughter of Robert Gray, by whom he had eleven children, six surviving him. The eldest son, Alexander Keith, born in 1844, was educated at the Edinburgh Institution and Grange House School, but early settled in London, where in 1868 he was elected a life member of the Geographical Society, and was employed in its service. He went as Geographer with an expedition for a survey of Paraguay, and published a book on the subject, besides relating his experiences to the British Association in 1875. He was next, in 1879, sent as leader of the Society's expedition to the head of Lake Nyassa, *viâ* Zanzibar. He was soon prostrated with illness, and, though with great spirit he continued to direct his colleagues from the stretcher on which he was carried in a dying state, he expired about 120 miles from the coast, and was buried under a tree. He had already published eight important books, and four more appeared after his death.

Thomas Brumby, D.L., the younger brother of Sir William and Alexander Keith, born 1814, died 1897. He married Jane Ruddiman, daughter of Thomas Ruddiman (of the Latin Grammarian's family). She died March 23, 1892. They had six sons and three daughters: (1) Archibald, married Amelia, daughter of Philip Whitehead, and has two sons and two daughters. (2) William, died unmarried 1863. (3) Thomas Ruddiman, married Alice, daughter of John Beale Mullins. (4) James Wilson, died 1906, married Mary, daughter of Joseph Whitaker, and had a daughter. (5) John Keegan, died *s.p.* 1901 ; married Sarah, daughter of Hugh Taylor. (6) George Harvey, married Ellen, daughter of James Bentley Ashton. (7) Helen Jane, married Rev. Francis, son of Rev. William Shepherd, and has issue. (8) Margaret Isabella, married Francis James, son of Rev. John Tobin, and has issue. (9) Rossie Marr, married James, son of John Stevenson, who died 1899.

The Rev. William Johnston of Carlaverock (Hadds.), who died on Dec. 14, 1670, at Haddington Abbey, was removed by the magistrate from his benefice at Lenelle "for adherence to the Presbyterian Government." His wife, Isabel Maitland, was related to the notorious Earl of Lauderdale, and his debtors were all members of local families, related to Salton, Cousland, and Newton. Another minister, John Johnston, in the Presbytery of Dunfermline, was deposed in 1684 for being "too much affected to Episcopacy, and for recommending a superstitious and erroneous book called *The Whole Duty of Man.*"

The Rev. Andrew Johnston, minister of Salton (1791-1829), was the son of Andrew Johnston in Dalkeith, where he was baptised in 1763. He married Mary, daughter of the Rev. William Crombie, minister of Spott, and had seven sons and three daughters. The eldest married the Rev. John Ramsey, minister of Ormiston and Gladsmuir.

Andrew Johnston in Dalkeith, though in humble position himself, was reputed to be the descendant of ministers for five generations.

The fourth generation of a London family is said to be unknown, and so late as the middle of the nineteenth century the rate of mortality in Manchester was higher than at the battle of Waterloo. The first doctor from Edinburgh who went to Kidderminster, Dr Mackenzie, soon left it on account of its unhealthiness some years before a Johnstone went to practise there, but the effect of Edinburgh itself on the members of the Dumfriesshire families who settled in it during the seventeenth century was greatly to reduce the average of life. Are any of the many Johnstons and Johnstones now found in Edinburgh, Leith, and the suburbs, descendants of the nephews or cousins of Archibald, the merchant, who died in 1619? It would be interesting to prove it. His eldest son, James, the father of Archibald of Warrieston, died young, and Warrieston's eldest grandson, Jasper, a brewer, who died in 1707, left an only daughter, Mrs Wood. The elder Archibald's youngest son, Joseph, who was Clerk Register, and bought Hilton, Co. Berwick, died at thirty-seven. His son, Archibald, and his grandson and great-grandson, both Joseph, were returned heirs to Hilton in quick succession; Robert, the brother of the second Joseph, in 1695. Another brother was Sir Patrick. Robert died May 1748, and his son, Wynne, was returned his heir, and was heir to his uncle, John, in 1758. In 1783 Robert was returned heir to his great-grandfather, Joseph, and in 1810 to his mother, the widow of Wynne Johnston.

Sir Patrick Johnston of Hilton, Provost of Edinburgh, married Mary Kinnear. His house was attacked by the mob when the Union was proclaimed in 1707, as he was one of the Union Commissioners. Of his nine sons the second, Captain George, left a son, James, a retired General, who died in 1797, having married Lady Henrietta West. Their son, Major H. George Johnston, was the father of Lieutenant-Colonel Frederick Johnston, who registered Arms at the Lyon Office in 1844. He lived at the Albany, Piccadilly, in 1862.

The death of Captain George Johnston, son of Sir Patrick, is recorded at

Monkstown, near Dublin, on June 7, 1770. "He was father of General James Johnston, now Lieutenant-Governor of Minorca, and of the present Lady Napier, and of Mrs Johnston of Hilton."

General Johnston gave up the command of Minorca before its capture by the combined forces of France and Spain in 1782; but he published a defence of General Murray and the officers who headed the little garrison, stricken down by fever and want of the proper supplies. The Balearic Isles had been offered to the Empress Catherine of Russia if she would assist Great Britain in the war with America—an offer which seems almost incredible, but will be found in the diplomatic memoirs of the day, for at that time it was our only post in the Mediterranean east of Gibraltar. Even after her refusal the garrison was not reinforced, and in this neglected condition it had no chance.

Patrick, another son of the Provost, was made a citizen of Edinburgh in 1708.

The Johnstons of Eccles, Co. Berwick, also appear likely to be descendants of one of the Lord Provost's nine sons. James Johnston of Eccles married Miss Thomson, and died about 1810. He farmed his land, and brought up many children. The eldest, James, joined the 99th Regiment when it was raised, and served in the Peninsular War with honourable mention. He married his first cousin, Jane Trotter of Dunse, and she accompanied him to the Mauritius, where several of their ten children were born, and where for some years he held a command. He retired a Colonel in 1836, and settled at Portobello, near Edinburgh. He died in 1850, aged seventy. Of his sons, (1) Colonel Patrick Johnston, born April 10, 1822, died 1898, served with the 99th and 32nd Regiments, and in New Zealand, and left six sons and one daughter; the eldest living is Matthew, M.D., born 1859, of Wribbenhall, Shropshire. (2) William, died in Australia, leaving issue. (3) Margaret, married Colonel Archibald Baldwin, Madras Army, left four sons, all in the Army, and a daughter. (4) George, Lieutenant-Colonel Royal Marine Light Infantry, born Feb. 23, 1838; died at Bath 1888. Married Laura Margaret Goding, and left one son, George Arthur Johnston, born 1871, barrister-at-law (Trinity College, Oxford), J.P. for Berks, author of *Small Holdings and Allotments*, and *On the New Agricultural Act*. He married in 1894 Lilian Hooper, great-niece of Archbishop Temple. They have two sons and a daughter.

Colonel James Johnston possessed the tattered colours of his regiment. His son, Colonel Patrick Johnston, presented them to St. Giles' Cathedral, Edinburgh, when H.R.H. the Duke of Cambridge received them from his hands. The elder Colonel's brother, Dr George Johnston, of Berwick-on-Tweed, was a well-known writer on natural history. He married Miss Charles, the daughter of a distinguished Peninsular officer, and left a son and two daughters—Mrs Barwell Carter and Mrs Maclagan, the last married to a brother of Archbishop Maclagan. Three of their sons are missionaries in China.

The elder Archibald Johnston's grand-nephews mentioned in his Will (1619)—Gavin, Andro, Robert, Thomas, and Wilkin—lived more or less in Edinburgh, and were probably his employés. Some of their names, and those of their children and grandchildren, appear in Edinburgh records to the end of the seventeenth century and later, when they seem to have become extinct in the male line. David Johnstone of Newbie, the merchant, Archibald's "faithful friend," appears to have married a third time, and died very old in June 1644. His daughter Geillis, wife to a Johnston of Elsieshields, died Oct. 1643. He had bought land in Preston and Galloway, and left descendants. In 1640 he lent money to the Laird, the bond being signed by his "nevoy" John, a writer.

Gilbert Johnstone of Graitney, the merchant, left John (and probably other sons), in Edinburgh, 1620.

Agnes Johnstone, wife of Patrick Spens, was returned sole heir to her brother, Robert, the historian and donator to Heriot's Hospital.

CHAPTER XXVIII.

JOHNSTONS OF CARNSALLOCH—JOHNSTONES OF SAUGHTREES—OF BEATOK—ROUNDSTONEFUTE, ETC.—IN FIFE—STRAITON—WALES—PROMINENT MEMBERS OF THE CLAN—OF AYR—IRELAND—AMERICA—NEW ZEALAND—ORKNEY.

PART I.

ABOUT 1752 James Maxwell, a Jacobite, sold Carnsalloch to Alexander Johnston, from London. It stands a few miles above Dumfries, on the left bank of the Nith. His son and heir, Peter, was at the English Bar, and, as Peter[1] is an uncommon name in the Johnston family, Peter Johnston, of York, called Esq., who had a sasine of Stank in Dornock in 1751, was perhaps a relative. This family use the Westerhall shield, so apparently claim to be cadets of that illustrious house.

In 1688 there is a sasine to Robert Johnstoun in the lands of Carnsalloch—probably the copyhold; and in 1720 Robert Johnston, late Dean of Dumfries, and Jean Cannon, his wife, resign these lands to Robert M'Clellan of Bombie. In 1753 there is an action by Alexander Johnston of Carnsalloch v. William Maxwell, Esq., of Dalswinton, and another in 1761 by the same plaintiff.

Family tradition adds that from one of the nine children of an ancestor—Robert Johnstoun—descended Patrick, born 1634, married, 1660, Jane, daughter of Francis Scott of Thirlstane. Their fourth son, Patrick, born 1667, married, 1698, Jane, daughter of Samuel Brown. The eldest son (or grandson), Alexander, married, 1748, Janet, daughter of James Gordon of Campbelton, Kirkcudbright, was M.P. for Kirkcudbright, and had: (1) Peter, his heir. (2) Alexander, born 1750, married, 1774, the Hon. Hester Maria, his cousin, only daughter of Lord Napier, and had—1, the Right Hon. Sir Alexander Johnston, Chief Justice of Ceylon, heir to his uncle in Carnsalloch; 2, Major-General Francis Johnston, C.B., born 1776, died 1844; 3, Samuel, died 1798, Paymaster to the Forces in the West Indies.

Peter Johnston of Carnsalloch, born 1749, was one of the subscribers to an early edition of Burns. He was M.P. for Kirkcudbright and a Commissioner

[1] In the Glasgow Register, Archibald, son of Peter Johnstoun and Mary Elphinston, was baptised Dec. 1635. Peter is dead in 1651, having had six daughters and four sons. This Peter seems to be one of the Clauchrie family.

of Bankruptcy in England. His next brother, Alexander, obtained a civil post under Lord Macartney at Madras, and settled at Madura in 1781. On his way out, with his wife and eldest son (born in 1775), he sailed in one of the ships convoyed by Commodore George Johnstone, but they were attacked, off the Cape Verd Islands, by the French squadron under Admiral Suffrien. One of the enemy's frigates engaged the Indiaman which contained his party, and, with permission of the Captain, Alexander Johnston took the command of four of the quarter-deck guns. His wife refused to leave his side, and held her six-years-old son by one hand, while in the other she grasped a thick velvet bag containing, with other things of particular value to her, a gold filigree case enclosing the *heart* of Montrose. This had been given to her by her father, Lord Napier of Merchiston, having been handed down in his family since a friend of the Napiers at midnight opened the grave where a few remains of Montrose had been buried after his execution, and brought it to Lady Napier, his nephew's wife, as a precious relic. A French shot struck one of the guns, killed two sailors, knocked over the amateur gunner, and shattered the box in his wife's reticule to pieces, severely wounding Mrs Johnston's arm, and bruising the muscles of the little boy's hand, so as to make it difficult for him at times to hold a pen for the rest of his life. But the French were repulsed, and immediately after Commodore Johnstone came on board and "complimented them both in the highest terms for the encouragement which they had given to the crew."

"My father," wrote Sir A. Johnston to his daughters from Great Cumberland Place on July 1, 1836, "was in the habit of sending me every year during the hunting season to stay with some of the native chiefs who lived in the neighbourhood of Madura for four months at a time, in order to acquire the various languages and to practise the native gymnastic exercises. One day, while I was hunting, my horse was attacked by a wild hog which we were pursuing, but I succeeded in wounding it so severely with my hunting pike that the chief soon killed it." Probably young Johnston was accompanied to the chief's house by Swartz, the missionary, and Munro, afterwards Sir Thomas, who are said to have educated him. "This was the chief, so celebrated throughout the Southern Peninsula of India, who thirty or forty years ago rebelled against the authority of his supposed sovereign, the Nabob of Arcot, and who, after behaving with the most undaunted courage, was conquered by a detachment of British troops and executed, with many members of his family,"—a necessity to be regretted, as, from Johnston's account, he was an upright and civilised native.[1]

At the age of eleven, young Johnston obtained a cornetcy of dragoons, but, as the regiment was ordered on active service, he resigned, and returned

[1] A new case was made for Montrose's heart in India, and it was kept in the drawing-room at the Residency in Madura; but, with the idea that it was a talisman, a native stole it and sold it for a large sum to the chief at whose house young Johnston visited. When the last distinguished himself by wounding the hog the chief asked what he could do for him in return, when Johnston told him about the relic, and begged for it again. It was at once restored.

to Europe with his parents to study law at Gottingen. He was called to the Bar, and went on circuit till he was unexpectedly introduced to Fox, who obtained for him the Advocate-Generalship of Ceylon, which had just been annexed. In 1805 he was made Chief Justice, with a very acceptable rise in salary, as he had married the daughter of Lord William Campbell, son of John, fourth Duke of Argyll. He was recalled to advise the British Government in 1811 on certain points to be embodied in the new Charter to the H.E.I.C.S., and was knighted by the Prince Regent before returning to Ceylon as President of the Legislative Council. He advocated trial by jury, popular education, and the employment of the natives, with due respect to the religion and customs of Buddhists, Brahmins, and Mahometans. When he returned to England in 1849 Earl Grey declared, in the House of Lords, that his conduct in Ceylon alone had immortalised his name.

Sir Alexander Johnston inherited Carnsalloch on the death of his mother in 1849, but he represented the Dumfries Burghs in the Liberal interest shortly after the death of his brother, who died in 1837. He was made a Privy Councillor, and chiefly by his advice the judicial committee of the Privy Council was established as a Court of Appeal in Colonial litigation. He was appointed a member of that Court, but declined to take the salary attached to it, as he had already declined to accept the salary when acting as an Admiralty judge. His services were acknowledged in a petition to the House of Commons by the leaders of native society in Bengal,—for he always supported the rights of the natives. He was influential in founding the Royal Asiatic Society, of which he became Vice-President, and was examined at some length before a Committee of the House of Commons with regard to the natives of India in 1832. He died in London, March 1849, and was buried at Carnsalloch. He left four sons and three daughters.

The eldest son, General Thomas Henry Johnston, Colonel of The Berkshire Regiment, D.L. and J.P., born 1807, succeeded his mother in 1852 and died 1891, when his brother, Patrick Francis Campbell, inherited the estate. He was a Commissioner of Charities in England, and also sent on a special mission to Portugal, born 1811, died 1892, having survived his younger brother, Alexander Robert Campbell Johnston, who was born at Colombo, Ceylon, entered the Colonial Civil Service, and went to Mauritius in 1828. In the absence of the appointed Governor, Sir Henry Pottinger, Mr Johnston was Acting Governor at Hong-Kong (June 1841), when the British flag was first hoisted, until the close of 1842. His conduct was highly commended in despatches, and he was made an F.R.S. for his contributions to the natural history of China. He retired from the Colonial Service in 1852, and became a J.P. for Suffolk, where he lived at the Grove, Yoxford. He died on the Raphael Ranche, Los Angelos, California, Jan. 21, 1888, having married, 1856, Frances Helen, daughter of Richard Bury Pelham, and left seven sons and two daughters.

The eldest son, Captain Archibald Francis Campbell Johnston, now of Carnsalloch and Dornal, succeeded his uncle, Patrick, in 1892. He married, 1884, Edith Constance, daughter of the late Captain Shaw, R.N., Lieutenant-

JOHNSTONES OF SAUGHTREES

Governor of Malacca. His brothers and sisters are Augustine Conway Seymour, Godfrey, Louis, Ronald, Alexander Napier, Roderick, Charlotte, and Mary. Their father's youngest brother, Frederick Erskine, R.N., born Oct. 1817, married, 1855, Clementina Frances, daughter of Vice-Admiral Henry Collier, C.B., and had seven sons and five daughters. He died 1896. His surviving children are: Henry Francis, born 1857, Lieutenant 91st Highlanders; Herbert, born 1862; Frederick and Bruce (twins), born 1864, Captain R.A. and Captain R.E.; Gordon, also Captain R.A., born Nov. 1866, married Aileen Lucy, daughter of Edward Courage of Shenfield Place, Essex; Seymour, Captain K.O.S.B. (twin with Gordon), married Olive Cecil, daughter of Sir James Walker, Bart.; Louisa Charlotte, married W. H. Trollope, son of the late General Sir Charles Trollope, K.C.B.; Frederika Maria; Paulina.

A family of Johnstone in Lancashire came from Saughtrees in Wamfray, where John and Nicol Johnstoun in Saughtrees appear in 1605. William Johnstone in Saughtrees married Grizel McMillan, 1767, and had thirteen children, some of whom are buried at Annan with their parents. The eldest son, James, married Nicolas, daughter of Robert Maxwell of Castlehill, Provost of Lochmaben. This James was a surgeon at Harrington, in Lancashire, where he died 1823. His son, William Maxwell, also a surgeon at Harrington, married Jane Clark Nicholson, and died 1856, aged sixty, leaving James Alexander Maxwell Johnstone, born June 16, 1844 (M.A., Cantab.), Vicar of Astley, near Manchester. Married Catharine, daughter of the Rev. J. Birchall, 1873, and has two sons and five daughters.

Johnston of Beatok came off the Poldean group. Adam and his sons, Herbert and John, appear in 1549, when they held the lands of Beatok and Newpark, in Nether Kirkpatrick. Some of the name were at Dryfe Sands, and took part with the clansmen in other battles. David Johnstoun owned Beatok in 1703, and Adam Johnston received a charter of it in 1737. As the last was the defendant in numerous lawsuits, it is not surprising that he is described as late of Beatok in 1753. He was sued in 1743 by Captain William Johnston of Corhead; Lieutenant James Johnston, his brother, and Sophia Johnston, their sister, relict of George Milligan, surgeon in Moffat; by Thomas Proudfoot in 1744; by John Ewart; by Ann Johnston in Craufurd; in 1745 by Robert Johnston, surgeon in Moffat; in 1746 by Jean Copland, widow of David Johnston of Beatok; and by her daughter, Rachel, in 1747, when he was living in Moffat. In 1753 Adam Johnston is the plaintiff with Sophia and Margaret, daughters of the late David Johnston of Beatok—their mother and their sister, Rachel, being dead—against William Scott of Beatok. Adam was married at that time to Betty Carruthers, Sophia to George Carruthers, and Margaret to Gilbert Johnston in Leadhills. A suit was carried on separately in 1762 by John Johnston, writer in Moffat, and Adam Johnston, against William Scott of Beatok. The family is still represented.

The Johnstouns of Rowantrieknowe, Rowantriebrae (*see* p. 43), or Roundstonefute, also belong to the Poldean branch, and have still a representative in Mr William Johnston of Alderwood House near Thornliebank, whose grandfather, Provost William Johnston of Sanquhar, sold his little property on Moffat Water and settled on the farm of Clackleith in Nithsdale. He was first elected a member of the Town Council of Sanquhar in 1765, and served as Provost from 1791 to 1793. He was a boon companion of Robert Burns, described by the poet as the trusty and worthy "Clackleith," and, perhaps playfully, as "that worthy veteran of original wit and social iniquity"; but he appears to have been among the mistaken friends who helped to bring Burns to an early grave, as it is reported that he was one of another trio, including Burns, who repeated the drinking competition of Friar's Carse at Sanquhar. "Occasional hard drinking," wrote Burns, "is the devil to me. Taverns I have totally abandoned; it is the private parties among the hard-drinking gentry that do me the mischief." Yet William Johnston lived to be eighty-seven, and his eleventh child, Susan, to be 101. His wife, who predeceased him, was Susanna M'Adam of Craigengillan. He is described as an excellent scholar, a musician, and a collector of old ballads and local songs, and "much respected in the district."

Among their many children the twelfth and thirteenth were distinguished— John, who died Sept. 1, 1880, aged ninety-nine, and is buried in Old Cumnock Churchyard, and William, born in 1782, who died on board the *Atholl* troopship and was buried at sea 1836. John was intended to succeed his father in his farm, but the stirring events of the time and the patriotic songs filled him with a desire to serve at the seat of war, and he ran away from home to enlist in the Marines at Liverpool. He was severely wounded on the *Colossus* at the battle of Trafalgar,—a wound which troubled him for the rest of his life, and in 1814 caused him to be discharged when serving on the West Indian Station, but without a pension. Later he received one of £27, 10s. yearly from Greenwich Hospital. He was at first warmly received by his father and lived at home, where he was made a Baillie of Sanquhar in 1815, but, owing to a quarrel which ended in his father disinheriting him, he opened a school near Cumnock, and partly supported himself with his pen. He contributed to Dr Simpson's *Traditions*, and wrote a long poem on Lord Nelson, in which he forcibly describes the battle where he had himself taken a part. His eldest son is the present William Johnston of Alderwood House, now aged ninety-one, but the younger generations springing up seem to make it improbable that this sprig of an ancient tree will die out.

William, the younger son of the Provost, obtained a commission in the Army in 1805, and was transferred as Lieutenant to the Rifle Brigade the next year. He was with his regiment at Copenhagen under Lord Cathcart, and at Rolica and Vimiera in the Peninsula, in the Corunna retreat, at Ciudad Rodrigo and Badajoz, and later at Waterloo. At Badajoz he commanded a storming party with ropes and nooses intended to drag down the bayonets and swords which formed a *chevaux de frise*, but he and his party were all shot down before they arrived within throwing distance; and Johnston so severely wounded that he was invalided home. He was still only a lieutenant, and did not get his company for some time afterwards. He was wounded at Quatre Bras, but able to serve at Waterloo in the "Fighting Light Division" under Picton. He obtained his majority in 1829, and two years later retired on half-pay, with no letters to put after his name or any other recognition of his services. Local interest obtained for him a Colonial magistracy in 1833, but ill-health obliged him to resign it two years later, and he expired on his way from the Cape at the age of fifty-four. There is an appreciative notice of him in the *United Service Magazine* for March 1837; and a brother officer, Capt. Kincaid, writing of him in *Random Shots from a Rifleman*, when Johnston was lying wounded in his tent after Badajoz, says: " I . . . never set my eyes upon a nobler picture of a soldier."

Mr John William Johnston, of the firm of Johnston, Horsburgh & Co., Papermakers, London, has a story of his ancestor which might have suggested Harry Bertram's capture in Scott's *Guy Mannering*, viz., that when a child playing on the shore of the Solway in charge of a nurse he was stolen by smugglers and taken to Holland. There, according to this legend, he learned papermaking, and returned to practise it in Scotland, where the first paper mills were built on the Water of Leith in 1675. A tomb in Lasswade Churchyard bears an inscription to Marion Craig, wife of James Johnston, Papermaker, Springfield, who died 1743, aged fifty-nine, and to John, their son, died 1750, aged twenty-eight. Below, another James Johnston is recorded, probably grandson or great-grandson of the above James, and also a Papermaker at Springfield, who died, aged eighty, in 1872, and his wife, Elizabeth Bertram, died 1865. Their younger son, George, died on his way home from India in 1869, aged thirty-eight. The elder son, John, born 1828, married Elizabeth Simpson, and migrated from Springfield, Polton, near Edinburgh, to the paper mills at Peterculter, Co. Aberdeen, where his son, John William, now carrying on the business in London, was born. The latter's eldest son is John William Simpson Johnston.

The only daughter of Sir Alexander Munro, Bart. of Ross, Isabella Margaret, married the Hon. H. Butler, son of Lord Dunboyne, and she and her husband took the name of Johnstone as she was heiress to her uncle, General Johnstone of Corehead. Their son, Henry Alexander Butler-Johnstone of Auchen Castle, Moffat, was born 1837 and educated at Christchurch, Oxford. He was Member for Canterbury for eight or nine years from 1862, but died *s.p.*

Dr William Johnston, living in Jamaica in 1793, claimed a relationship with the Corehead family. His nephew and heir, Captain William Johnston, died *s.p.* These were connected with a family from Tundergarth. Thomas Johnston of Crawshalt, married to Janet Dobie, died in difficulties, and their eldest son, John, went out as a surgeon to St. Elizabeth in Jamaica. He died at Dumfries about 1795, leaving a daughter, Mrs Moore, who, when a child, had sat on the knee of the last Marquis of Annandale at Chiswick, and he told her she would some day be a Marchioness! Her grandson is Mr Edgar T. Briggs of Holmwood, Weybridge. Of John the surgeon's five brothers only James, a merchant in Maxwellton, left sons, and William, W.S., left a daughter, who married a physician in Ireland.

Two Johnstons are found in Fife in the eighteenth century, David Johnston, advocate, son of David Johnston of Lathrisk, who recorded Arms in 1797; and Andrew Johnston of Pitkeirie, who was First Magistrate of Anstruther Easter, died 1765.

The last Johnston of Lathrisk and Wedderby—George—died *s.p.*, and his estates went to Mr Maitland Makgill Crichton, born 1880, a descendant of Mary Johnston, daughter of David, who died before 1810. She married, in 1794, Charles Maitland.

From Andrew Johnston of Pitkeirie, who died 1765, have descended five generations called Andrew. The second was of Rennyhill; the fourth was M.P. for St. Andrews, and sold Rennyhill in 1853, and went to live at Holton, Suffolk. He married Priscilla, daughter of the late Sir Thomas Fowell Buxton, and died 1862. His eldest son, Andrew, born 1835, now of Forest Lodge, Woodford Green, married, 1858, Charlotte Anne, eldest daughter of the Rev. G. Trevelyan, and had a daughter, who died an infant. Mr Johnston was educated at Rugby and University College, Oxford. Was High Sheriff for Essex in 1880, Chairman Quarter Sessions, and County Councillor, and M.P. for South Essex, 1868-74.

James Johnston of Straiton, Linlithgowshire, the son of the Rev. James Johnston, minister of Stonehouse, recorded his Arms in the Lyon Office (1672-77), and died about 1685. Another James Johnston of Straiton, W.S., flourished 1702-20. Robert Johnston, who died before 1716, is probably the intermediate generation, and his son was succeeded by his brother, Alexander, 1742, who left a son, Alexander, and a daughter, married to Sir William Hamilton, Bart. The last Alexander died 1793, leaving two sons—Alexander, died 1796; and James, who married a Baillie of Polkemmet, and had a son, James Johnston of Straiton, who was at one time M.P. for Stirling. He died 1841, and his nephew, Robert Hathorn Johnston Stewart of Physgill, Co. Wigton, born 1824, was returned his heir. Mr Johnston Stewart married Anne, daughter of Sir William Maxwell of Monreith. Captain Robert Hathorn Johnston Stewart, M.V.O., is the present representative.

Lieutenant-Colonel Samuel Henry Nairne Johnstone of Coedfa, Carnarvonshire, second son of Samuel Johnstone of Liscard, Co. Chester, and his wife, Eliza, daughter of William Pennell, late Consul-General in Brazil, born 1832. Married Emma, daughter of Peter Clutterbuck, Esq., of Red Hall, Herts. He is a J.P. for Denbigh and Carnarvon.

Sir Harry Hamilton Johnston, G.C.M.G., K.C.B., Gold Medallist, Zoological, Royal Geographical, and Royal Scottish Geographical Societies; Trustee of the Hunterian College, Royal College of Surgeons; Vice-President of the Royal Geographical Society, of the Royal Anthropological Institute, and of the African Society. Born at Kennington, London, 1858. Son of John Brookes Johnston and Esther Letitia Hamilton, his wife. Married Hon. Winifred Irby, daughter of fifth Lord Boston. Educated at Stockwell Grammar School and King's

PROMINENT MEMBERS OF THE CLAN

College, London, student Royal Academy of Arts, 1876-80, and was medallist of South Kensington School of Art. He studied painting in France. He travelled in North Africa, 1879-80; explored Portuguese West Africa and River Congo, 1882-83; led a Royal Society Expedition to Mount Kilimanjaro, 1884. H.M. Vice-Consul in Cameroons, 1885; Consul for Province of Mozambique, 1888; and founder of the British Central Africa Protectorate 1889; Consul-General in Regency of Tunis, 1897-99; and Commander-in-Chief of Uganda Protectorate, 1899-1901. Has published essays on the "Tunisian Question," "Life of Livingstone," "River Congo," "History of a Slave," "The Nile Quest," "The Uganda Protectorate," "The Colonization of Africa by Alien Races," and others. He lives at St. John's Priory, Poling, Arundel.

James William Douglas Johnstone, late Inspector-General of Education, Gwalior State, Central India, born at Murree, Punjab, 1855. Son of late Major-General Henry Campbell Johnstone, C.B., of the Indian Staff Corps. Educated at Edinburgh Academy and University. Principal of Daly College, Indore, 1855, and lent by Government of India to Gwalior State as tutor to the Maharajah Scindia, 1890. Besides other posts, he was employed on famine duty in 1897 and 1900; and accompanied the Maharajah to England in 1902 to attend King Edward's Coronation.

Colonel Francis Buchanan Johnstone, D.S.O., born 1863. Son of David Johnstone of Croy, Row, Dumbarton. Married, 1887, Edith Arethusa Padwick. Entered the Royal Artillery in 1882, and served in South Africa.

Rev. J. O. Johnston, M.A., Vicar of Cuddesdon and Principal of Cuddesdon College, born at Barnstaple 1852. Son of Rev. G. Johnston and his wife, Elizabeth Morgan. Educated at Barnstaple Grammar School and Keble College, Oxon. Author of *Life and Letters of H. P. Liddon, D.D.*, and other works.

Rev. Hugh William Johnston, Rector of North Cray, Hon. Canon of Canterbury, head of the Irish family of Redemon. His daughter married Dr Ridgeway, Lord Bishop of Chichester.

Alderman Charles Johnston, of the City of London.

John Lawson Johnston was in business in Edinburgh in early life, and afterwards removed to London, where he acquired a fortune from a useful invention. He rented Inverary Castle after the death of the late Duke. His son, George Lawson, married, in 1902, a daughter of Lord St. John of Bletsoe.

George Hope Johnston, fourth son of Francis Johnston of Handsworth, Staffs., born 1841. Married, 1867, Emily Wilkinson. J.P., Staffs.

Among many eminent ministers, the Rev. David Johnston, born 1734, must be noted. Appointed to North Leith in 1765, and made a D.D. of Edinburgh in 1781. He was the founder of the Blind Asylum in Edinburgh in 1793, and was appointed Chaplain in Ordinary to George III. in Scotland the same year. At the request of a sailor's wife he wrote to Napoleon and asked him to release her husband, then a prisoner in France. Dr Johnston received an answer from Talleyrand that the request was granted and the man would be sent home. One of Campbell's poems is founded on this incident.

The handsome group of cottages in Johnstone Park, Dumfries, was built by

David Johnstone of Righead and Ann Jardine, his wife, for the widows and daughters of Johnstones who had been business men in Lockerbie and Dumfries. A sundial has lately been erected in Johnstone Park as a memorial of the founders, and of Mr Boyd, who bequeathed £3614 to the same fund.

Alexander Johnston, born at Edinburgh 1815, died 1891. Started as a portrait painter, but is known more by his historical pictures in the National Galleries of Edinburgh and London. His son, Douglas, a musician of great promise, predeceased him.

Two branches of the Johnstouns settled in Ayrshire, one traditionally from Westraw,[1] the other from Caskieben.

Arthur Johnstoun and his wife, Janet Otterburne of Ayr, were dead in 1481, and their son, Alexander, caused a mass to be said for their souls. Alexander appears again in 1511 and 1525. William Johnstoun's death is recorded at Ayr in 1515, and that he had paid for masses to be said for the souls of his brother, Thomas, and for Thomas's wife, Alison Raith. Adam Johnstoun was living in Ayr in 1524, and Andrew in 1535. Adam and George Johnstoun about 1598 bought lands from Fareis in Ayrshire; and in 1624 a contract, dated at Newmilns in the barony of Loudoun, Ayr, regarding burdens on lands in Loudoun, is signed by George, son and heir to William Johnstoun in Newmilns. In 1653 George and Christopher Johnstoun, living in Ireland, have a money transaction with John Osborn, late Provost of Ayr.

John Johnston, or Johnstone, of Ochiltree, Ayrshire, an officer in the Army, died there about 1818. A deed of Oct. 1817 shows that he had married Elizabeth Cust, a sister of Sir Edward Cust of Barnard Castle, Ochiltree, who survived him till 1852, when, in accordance with his settlement, a small sum of money was divided among the surviving descendants of his brother, Alexander Johnston, an officer in His Majesty's Service, and barrack master in the Tower of London, who had died in 1829, having married Esther Tanner, Nov. 1, 1781. Of their ten children four have surviving descendants. The eldest son, Lieutenant-Colonel William Johnston of the 26th Cameronians, C.B., born 1787, died on his way home after serving in the Chinese War (1841), and was buried at the Cape of Good Hope. His widow was drowned in the wreck of H.M.S. *Conqueror* on the coast of France, having been given a passage in it to England. They had five children. The second son, Surgeon-General Thomas Blackadder Johnstone (who added the "e" to his name) served in the Bombay Presidency for forty years, and retired to live in Edinburgh. His brothers were: Alexander, died *s.p.*; John, a Captain in the 26th Cameronians; William Paul, a Solicitor in Chancery Lane; and a sister, Isabella, who married James Cunningham, Jan. 27, 1824, and whose children settled in Australia. George Johnstone, son of Thomas Blackadder Johnstone (who married Mary Jane Rubens), is the present representative. He married, 1882, Catherine, daughter of the late William Cadwallader Foulkes.

[1] The recorded cadets of Westraw before 1600 are: Adam, younger son of Matthew (died 1491); John, son of Herbert (died 1555); Gavin in Westoun, second brother of James Johnstoun (died 1570); Robert of Westraw Mains, died 1589, leaving descendants; and his brother, David, in Westraw.

PART II.

"Here's to the Johnstons and the Johnstons' Bairnes,
And to them that lies in the Johnstons' Airnes."
—*Kilmore Toast.*

IT is not unlikely that scions of the two Ayrshire families of Johnstoun settled in Ireland before 1620, but the name first appears there in official documents between that date and 1646. Edward Johnstoun, a merchant in Edinburgh, of the House of Wamfray, was one of the earliest who bought an Irish estate. He died soon afterwards, leaving a son, Francis. John Johnstoun in Edinburgh applied for land there after the Rebellion of 1641, but Captain Walter Johnstoun, a Royalist, was already in Fermanagh, and Thomas and John Johnstoun settled in Lowtherston, Fermanagh, at the time of the massacre of the British settlers on Oct. 23. In the Betham-Phillips M.S., 1718, it is stated that "260 Johnstons were enlisted at the beginning of the War of 1641, under that gallant and wise man Sir William Cole."

Several other Dumfriesshire names were among the immigrants, and as Christopher Irving, whose mother and son-in-law were Johnstouns of Newbie and of Beirholme, was a proprietor and a commissioner for levying fines there in 1630, probably many members of the clan joined him.

James Johnstoun, of Co. Fermanagh, borrowed £48 from Katherine Cockburn in Edinburgh. The bond is dated at Moffat, 1623. Another bond, dated at Marjoribanks, Annandale, 1627, and witnessed by James Johnstoun of Wamfray, disposes of lands in Moffat by Janet, widow of the late George Johnstoun, portioner of Moffat, to their son James; another James Johnstoun in Drumadown, Co. Fermanagh, and John Johnstoun in Moffat, called of Vickerland, are cautioners for the payment. They were all relatives, and of the Poldean, or Powdene, branch.

The Scottish settlers were obliged to be Protestants and to become English subjects, and were released from the obligations or protection of either English or Scottish law. Many Grahams and a Herbert Johnstoun were sent there as a penal settlement, turned loose among the ancient Romanist lords of the soil, to live, if they chose, their old brigand life. They were foredoomed to come in conflict with the natives. The massacre was carried out on the plan of the Sicilian vespers. At a given moment all the immigrants were to be murdered. The horrors of this action, the retribution which followed, and the Cromwellian Settlement of Ireland, have never been forgotten to the present day.

The Johnstouns of Gilford, Co. Down, claim descent from James of Johnstoun (1509-24) through his second son, named Robert, but although in the older Peerages Robert is mentioned, he cannot be traced in extant legal documents. He is said to have married a Carruthers, to have died about 1572, and to have had issue, James, married to an Irving, and died in 1589. James is stated by the traditions of this branch to have left issue, William, who married a M'Dowall of Gillespie, Co. Wigton, and died in 1608, leaving Richard, Adam, and David. Richard married a Muir, and left David, ancestor of the Johnstouns of Duchrae in Galloway, and of Ballywillwill, as well as of Gilford.

This David, known as "in Orchardtoun" in the Duchrae pedigree (*see* p. 27), and the ancestor of the M'Dowall Johnstons, is believed to have married Margaret Vans,[1] the wife of Lochinvar's brother, James Gordon, whom she pursued for divorce in 1621. Her mother was a M'Dowall. David was a Captain in Colonel Leslie's army, which, with his brother William, he joined in 1640. They served under Leslie in Scotland and England till he was taken prisoner, when the Johnstons, including Thomas and James, believed to be also David's brothers, escaped to Ireland. They were settled in Down when Oliver Cromwell took the command of the army in Ireland in 1649, and carried on his devastating campaign against the Irish Romanists and the Scottish Royalists. David's return to Scotland was probably hastened by himself, William, John, James, and Adam Johnston being placed on the list of Scots whom the Government proposed in 1651 to transplant from Antrim and Down to Munster. His friend, Sir Godfrey M'Cullock of Myrton, was one of those appointed with Graham of Clavers to enforce the test in Galloway. Probably David and his brothers had shared in the defeat of Leslie at Worcester, 1651. Captain William Johnston lent money to Colonel Ludovick Leslie about 1653. James Johnstoun, merchant in Edinburgh, witnessed it.

Captain David Johnston in Orchardton, Galloway, and Co. Down, borrowed money from his eldest son, William, in 1680. The cautioner to the bond was Sir Godfrey M'Cullock, who was executed at Edinburgh in 1697 for the murder of William Gordon. When arrested he was concealing himself under the name of "Johnstoune." In 1685 William obtained a tack of lands, called the Park, in Netherlaw, owned by Sir George Maxwell of Orchardton, who owed him money, and who also possessed the lands of Ballycastle, Co. Antrim, which he eventually lost through a dishonest agent, Maxwell of Cuil. Perhaps the agent was responsible for the grievance stated in a letter written from Ballywillwill by William in Netherlaw to Maxwell of Munches, when the writer was evidently an old man (1705-6). It is not unlikely that this William in Orchardton and Netherlaw was father, not brother, to the wife of Captain James M'Dowall, and to Richard (who succeeded through a clause in his brother-in-law's Will to M'Dowall's property of Gillespie in Wigton), as well as to William in Netherlaw, described as Mrs M'Dowall's brother.

Captain David Johnston, in the parish of Donagh, who appears in the Irish Roll of the first subsidies in or about the year 1661, and who is said to have died at Donagh in 1675, was probably nephew or son to the elder David. Thomas, brother to the elder David, was Captain of Grenadiers, and is said to have been killed at the battle of Aughrim in 1691, *s.p.;* but confusion is often made between two generations, when marriages were very early and families

[1] Her brother, Patrick Vans of Barnbarroch, married Grizel, sister to Sir James Johnstoun of that Ilk, and widow of Sir Robert Maxwell of Spots, Orchardton.

very large. Thomas Johnston signed the address from Londonderry to King William, July 29, 1689. William Johnston in Netherlaw, Captain David's eldest son, wrote from Ballywillwill, May 16, 1705, to Maxwell of Munches:—

Dear Sir,—I received yours, and am glad that Sir George Maxwell is cum home. As to Hodam's accounts and mine I left them with you as I came out of Dumfries at your own house. . . . I desired Beley Gordon when I came away to speak to you for them, but he told me he did, but could not get them, so you have an account of what payments that I paid except 40 pounds of reparation of houses and 31 pounds that Hoddam got in the use of a bond I asined him for the payment of the 1000 mark bond which I was due for the stock of the Parke, with 21 pounds worth of butter and chies he got in Dumfries. . . . But I have much to get from Sir George Maxwell. He cased take a cow and a bulock out of the Parke and killed them when my Leddy Nidsdil was in Kirkcudbright as also 1000 marks penalty, Sir Robert (Sir George's father) was bound in for the performance of the bargain he maid with me for the Netherlaw Parke and 200 marks a year he maid me pay Ruscoe (Hew M'Guffock) by breaking his own tack to me. All of which I hope he will take to his consideration, and not put me to so great lose as to Gelston. . . . I am in no ariers with him and I wish he were due me as little."

In a second letter from Ballywillwill, March 1706, to Sir George Maxwell, William reminds him of the account he sent in his letter to Munches by John Halliday:—

". . . I received yours in January (1706) wherein you say you expected that I would a gone over when Munches wrote to me. But truly I am grown very tender and sickly so that I dare not venture upon so grait a journey." He refers to his visit to Hoddam, and his expenses which he hopes Maxwell will repay, and adds that his "brother is in good health and gives his humble service to you, and so doth he who is your most humble servant,
William Johnston."

The Gilford pedigree states that Richard of Erny, Co. Monaghan, the ancestor of that Irish branch, led a number of his tenants into Londonderry and served during the siege. He had estates in Cos. Armagh, Down, Fermanagh, and Monaghan. He married Susanna, second daughter of Lieutenant or Captain William Johnston and his wife, Susanna, daughter of Captain John Magill, and had William of Gilford, born 1682, Captain Royal Irish Dragoons, knighted 1714, married Nichola, daughter of Sir Nicholas Acheson, Bart., died 1772; their children were Richard, Acheson, William, George, and Henrietta, married to William, son of William Johnston of Woodpark.

Richard, born 1710 and died 1759, married Catherine, daughter of Rev. John Gill. They left Richard, born 1743, created a Baronet; and Robert, married Jane, daughter of Rev. Hamilton Traill; besides daughters. Sir Richard married, 1764, Anne, sister to Sir William Alexander, by whom he had: (1) William, second Baronet, born 1765, High Sheriff of Down 1788; died *s.p.*

1841. (2) Mary Anne, married, 1794, John H. Burges of Woodpark, Co. Armagh, whose descendant now owns Gilford. (3) Catherine, married J. M. Ormsby, half-brother of the Countess of Limerick.

Besides Richard, William Johnston in Netherlaw had a brother, Archibald, Rector of an Irish Parish, who was attainted. According to the Gilford pedigree, William's son, Richard, took the name of M'Dowall before his own, and had a son, William M'Dowall Johnston of Ballywillwill, Co. Down, and of Gillespie, in Scotland. William married Rebecca, daughter of the Rev. G. Vaughan. Their son, the Rev. George Henry M'Dowall Johnston, was born in 1779, and married, 1811, Anna Maria, daughter of the second Earl of Annesley. He died *s.p.* in 1864, when his lands went to his sister, Mary Jane, married to William Young. Their son, William, married the daughter of Sir Neal O'Donnell, Bart., and left two sons, who both served in the Crimea. George Henry died unmarried, but William (Captain) succeeded in 1882, when he assumed the name M'Dowall.

The Rev. Samuel Arnot, Vicar of Tongland, escaped with his brother to Ireland in 1674 to avoid arrest by the emissaries of Clavers, David Arnot selling his property at Barcaple to Hew M'Guffock of Rusco, the same who leased Netherlaw to William Johnston. Barcaple was only six miles from Orchardton, in Buittle, and close to Bargatton, where a branch of Sheriff-Depute Grierson's family lived.

Robert, a younger son of William Johnston, remained at Nether Barcaple,[1] where he brought up a large family. Some of them were scattered, in all probability joining their relatives in Ireland.

The Johnstons of Kilmore descend from William, an architect from Scotland, whose claymore is still preserved by his heir, and who superintended the repair of the public buildings injured in the Rebellion of 1641. He married Miss Campbell, who died in Derry during the siege. His sons, William and Alexander, served at the siege of Derry, and are both buried in Armagh Cathedral. Alexander married Ellinor Fleming. Their son, William, married Susanna, daughter of the Rev. Nathaniel Weld, and settled at Bordeaux, where his descendants remain. Edward, the son of the elder brother, born 1700, married, 1720, Mary, daughter of Captain John Johnston of Drumconnell, Co. Armagh. Captain John's eldest daughter married, about 1707, John Crossle of Armagh, and their male descendants are still represented. The Captain had served at the siege of Derry, and was attainted by the Parliament of James VII. His son-in-law, Edward, died 1771, leaving a son, William Johnston of Armagh, born Feb. 1728, married, 1757, Margaret Houston, and had: (1) Richard, of Eccles Street, Dublin, born 1759, married, 1789, his cousin, Susanna, daughter of Robert Barnes (who was uncle to Sir Edward Barnes, G.C.B., M.P., formerly Governor of Ceylon, and subsequently Commander-in-Chief in India), died *s.p.* (2) Francis married Anne, eldest daughter of Robert Barnes, died *s.p.* He was first Treasurer and then President of the

---

[1] In the Nether Barcaple family, David was baptised in 1699. He had brothers, William, Thomas, Andrew, etc.

Royal Hibernian Academy of Painting, Sculpture, and Architecture, which he founded, and laid the first stone of the Academic edifice in 1824, which was built at his expense. (3) William, married Margaret, daughter of John Arthur Donnelly. (4) Andrew, President of the Royal College of Surgeons, Ireland, married Sophia, daughter of George Cheney of St. Stephen's Green, Dublin, and Hollywood, Co. Kildare.

Andrew's son, Richard Johnston, late Rector of Kilmore, born 1816, married Augusta Sophia, daughter of the Rev. George Hamilton, son of the Bishop of Ossory. She died 1860. Mr Johnston died 1906, having married, secondly, Hester, daughter of Robert William Lowry, J.P. and D.L. of Pomeroy, and thirdly, Olivia Frances Hall-Dare. By his first wife he left: (1) George Hamilton, Lieutenant-Colonel, late East Yorkshire Regiment, born 1847. (2) Andrew Edmund, born 1848, married Mary Constance, daughter of John Samuel Graves of Woodbine Hill, Honiton, Devon, and has George Paul Graves, born 1881; Catherine; Isabel; Constance. (3) Francis Burdett (Rev.), born 1850, Vicar of Waltham Abbey, Essex. (4) Henry Augustus, barrister-at-law, J.P., Co. Armagh, born 1851. (5) Sophia. (6) Isabella. (7) Augusta.

Kilmore, the seat of Colonel G. H. Johnston, stands on a hill seven miles from Armagh. The house is a museum of art and historical relics, among which is the organ brought by Handel to Dublin in 1741, on the occasion of his Oratorio—"The Messiah"—being performed. The family pictures include portraits of some of the Burney family, Susan Burney having married Colonel Molesworth Phillips, great-grand-uncle of the present owner of the estate; Sir Philip Crampton and Chief Justice Doherty, direct descendants of Captain John Johnston of Drumconnell; Nathaniel Weld Johnston, and William, son and grandson of William Johnston, who settled at Bordeaux; Hugh Hamilton, D.D., F.R.S., Dean of Armagh, and later Bishop of Ossory; Major-General Robert Ross, the hero of Bladensberg; Walter Shirley, Bishop of Sodor and Man; George Hamilton, M.P. for Belfast, Solicitor-General for Ireland, a Judge of the Irish Court of Exchequer; Major-General Sir Edward Barnes, G.C.B., M.P.; Right Hon. Sir Henry King, Bart., M.P.; Thomas Cromwell, Earl of Essex; John Paulet, first Marquis of Winchester; and Sir John Seymour, maternal ancestors of the present owner. There are also marble busts of the Marquis of Wellesley and the Duke of Wellington.[1]

[1] Last but not least are the mementoes of the eminent architect, Francis Johnston (1761-1829), whose three-quarter length portrait, with that of his wife, hang on either side of a splendid clock in the spacious hall. Opposite the entrance is a large picture of the Lower Castle Yard, Dublin, showing the Old Chapel and the Birmingham Towers, in all of which Francis Johnston superintended the modern alterations (1807-16). He lived at Armagh from 1786 to 1793, presiding over the erection of the Cathedral Tower. Later he held the post of Architect and Inspector of Civil Buildings in Dublin, where his munificence and the important works he executed are recorded on a silver trowel, now displayed in the hall at Kilmore. It is inscribed: "His Majesty King George IV. was graciously pleased, on the 6th day of October 1822, to constitute and appoint the Royal Hibernian Academy of Painting, Sculpture, and Architecture. Francis Johnston, Esq., then Treasurer and now President of the body, laid with this trowel the first stone of the Academic edifice on the 29th day of April 1824. This building, elegant in design, spacious in extent, and costly in execution, he raised and perfected at his sole and proper expense, and with it endowed the members of the

The Johnstons of Drum, Co. Monaghan, come from Hugh of Killevan, who flourished in 1678. They appear to have died out in the direct male line, but are represented by female descendants.

The Johnstons of Carrickbreda and Knappagh, Co. Armagh, descend from James of Tremont, a Presbyterian minister who left two sons, James of Knappagh and Carrickbreda, who died 1728; and Joseph, who lived till 1778, and married Anne, daughter of Joshua M'Geough of Drumsill. Both brothers have living male descendants. The elder left two houses he had built in Armagh to his son James. His great-great-grandsons, James, born 1809, and Arthur, married respectively Anne, daughter of Charles Hudson, and Sarah Call, daughter of Thomas Whittier of Exeter. The third brother, John Joseph of Tremont, married and left two daughters. James Johnston's only son died at fourteen, but Arthur, who died in 1847, left James, born 1827, married Mary, eldest daughter of James Daly, of Castle Daly, Galway; and Sarah Maria, who married Arthur Alexander. Mr Johnston, a J.P. and D.L. for Co. Armagh, was High Sheriff 1874-75. He was educated at Prior Park College and Edinburgh University. He died 1879, leaving James, born 1861, J.P. for Armagh; married the daughter of Charles G. Corbett, C.E., of Dublin. Mr Joseph Atkinson, D.L., of Crow Hill, Co. Armagh, represents the Knappagh branch.

The ancestor of Sir William Johnson (*see* p. 196), was Christopher Johnston of Kilternan, Co. Dublin, who died 1683, and whose name points to a probable relationship to Andro Johnston of Beirholme and his Irving wife. Christopher's grandson, John, was Governor of Charlemont, Co. Armagh. A

Academy, and their successors for ever. Anxious to record their sense of his liberality, his Academic brethren have here inscribed these circumstances, and present this mark of their gratitude to a worthy, munificent, and patriotic benefactor, 1828." In the centre of the blade are the figures representing Sculpture, Painting, and Poetry; on the right is an easel with a design of the front of the Academy; and in the background a view of the General Post Office, which was built from the design of Mr Johnston, to which Poetry is calling the attention of Sculpture and Painting. Sculpture is resting her right hand on the head of a bust of Mr Johnston, and gazing with rapt attention at the design placed on the easel. The whole is surrounded by a serpent, tail in mouth, representing Eternity. Underneath is some handsome scroll work, copied from the cornice over the pillars of the Post Office, and above a group of objects emblematic of Science, Music, Arts, and the Drama, in the centre of which is a harp, surrounded with a wreath of laurel and oak leaves. In the same case is a bronze medal, on one side the head of Francis Johnston, after the bust by Smythe; on the other, "Academy House, erected at the expense of Francis Johnston, Esq., 1824"; round the border, "Royal Hibernian Academy, incorporated by Charter 1824." The medal is by Woodhouse, after the cast struck by the Royal Irish Art Union to distribute as prizes to their students. Above the trowel case is the only engraved copy known to exist of the portrait, by Martin Cregan, of Francis Johnston, which hangs in the Council Chamber of the Royal Hibernian Academy. Here are several portraits and engravings, among them Webber's picture, engraved by Bartolozzi, of the death of Captain Cook, wherein is represented Lieutenant-Colonel Molesworth Phillips, who shot Cook's murderer. On the other side of the window is the engraving of West's picture of the death of Wolfe, in which is depicted Colonel George Williamson, father of Lieutenant-General Sir Adam Williamson, a near relative of Lieutenant-Colonel Phillips. The four busts are Francis Johnston and his wife, *née* Anne Barnes, Sir William Verner, Bart., K.H., Major 7th Hussars—who is stated to have been on the staff of the Duke of Richmond, and to have issued the invitations for the ball at Brussels, being wounded at Waterloo—and his wife, Lady Verner. Sir William was a near relative of Francis Johnston. The (smaller) sarcophagus is a replica of the one in Dublin Castle with the Johnston Coat of Arms impaling Barnes. The same Arms are displayed (of Francis Johnston and his wife) on a window in Armagh Cathedral.

portrait of John exists in the possession of Colonel Wade-Dalton, Co. Yorks., a descendant of his nephew.

There were also descendants of Lockerbie Johnstons, Mungo, of Co. Monaghan, and George Johnston, in Fermanagh, about that date.

Mr Joseph G. Johnston, of Rathmines, Dublin, tells a story which shows there was one point at least in which the Scottish settlers could sympathise with the native Irish. In the outlying districts the Irish distilled their national spirit, poteen, without troubling themselves to pay the duty. The narrator's great-grandfather, Joseph Johnston, of Corran, or Cairn Hill, Co. Cavan, was a farmer, and heard that the Government officials were about to arrest a poteen distiller. He sent one of his boys to go as fast as possible to warn the man, and the boy passing the revenue officers on his return heard the exclamation: "We are undone, that's a young Johnston I know, from his long nose and dress."

The Johnstones of Snow Hill descend from William Johnstone, a Scot, who married Prudence, daughter of William Goodfellow. Their son James, of Co. Fermanagh, married Joanna, daughter of Gunnis of Donegal. The sons of this Irish union—James of Snow Hill, married Anne, daughter of a Johnston of Leitrim, died 1808; and Christopher, a surgeon in the 17th Lancers, who was father of another Christopher, Colonel in the 8th Hussars. The elder brother, James, died 1808, leaving John Douglas; Andrew, Lieutenant in 8th Hussars, died *s.p.* at Calcutta, 1810; Margaret, married Captain W. Johnston; and Mary, married Francis Lloyd.

John Douglas Johnstone, born 1769, married, 1798, Samina, daughter of Samuel Yates of Kildare, and died 1842, his eldest son, James Douglas, having predeceased him, leaving by his wife, Charlotte Devereux, a son, John Douglas, who succeeded his grandfather at the age of three. The next brother, Richard, died in Canada in 1840. The third, John Douglas, born 1809, Major-General, C.B., served throughout the Crimean War, and lost an arm at the Redan, June 18, 1855. He married, 1830, Caroline, daughter of Rev. A. O. Beirne, D.D., and left a son, John Douglas of Snow Hill, born 1838, and two daughters, Samina and Caroline. His uncles and aunts were—Samuel Yates, born 1815, barrister-at-law, died *s.p.*; Anna Douglas, married her cousin, Francis Lloyd; Samina, married William Worthington.

Colonel John Douglas Johnstone, J.P., married Hon. Augusta Anna, daughter of twelfth Lord Louth. He was High Sheriff of Fermanagh, 1899.

The first of the Johnstons of Ballykilbeg, William, married, 1760, Ann Brett of Killough, great-great-granddaughter of Francis Marsh, Archbishop of Dublin, a cousin of Edward Hyde, grandfather of Queen Mary and Queen Anne. William's son, another William, died in 1796, having married Mary Humphrey. Their son, John, married, in 1828, Thomasina, daughter of Thomas Scott, and left William, M.P. for Belfast, late Inspector of Irish Fisheries. By his third wife, Georgina Barbara, daughter of Sir John Hay, Bart., he had Lewis Audley Marsh, married Emily Sophia, daughter of Rev. Thomas Jones, died at Hong-Kong, 30th September 1909; and Charles, married Vera, daughter of General Jelikovski.

The Rev. William Henry Johnstone (the son of James Johnstone and Catherine Evans, married Nov. 5, 1811), was Chaplain and Professor at Addiscombe. He married Anna Maria Davies, and had eight children. Two sons survive—the Rev. Charles James Johnstone, married, and has children; and Colonel James Robert Johnstone, born Jan. 1859, C.B., married Eleanor, daughter of Rev. E. Pitman, and has two sons. He served in Egypt and China.

Ralph William Johnstone, M.D., born at Kingstown, Co. Dublin, 1866. Son of late Robert Johnstone, Q.C., County Court Judge of Laputa, Co. Dublin. Author of several medical works.

His brother is Captain Robert Johnstone, V.C., late Imperial Light Horse, dangerously wounded at the siege of Ladysmith. He was born 1872. Educated at King William's College, Isle of Man.

Sir John Barr Johnston, Kt., born 1843. Son of John Johnston, Beragh, Co. Tyrone. High Sheriff of Londonderry, 1900. Married Isabel Weir; has one son and three daughters.

The Johnstons of Glynn, Co. Antrim, are found there in 1672, and George Johnston of Glynn, who was attainted in 1689 by the Parliament of James VII., is said to have been a near kinsman of Captain John Johnston of Drumconnell. William, the son of George Johnston of Glynn, was High Sheriff of Antrim in 1723. He is supposed to have been the elder brother of James, who married Elizabeth, daughter of James Leslie, son of the Bishop of Down, and great-grandson of George, Earl of Rothes. James Johnston died 1707, leaving Henry and George, besides six daughters. George left a son, Robert. The elder son, Henry, born 1694, married, 1724, Ann Stewart, and left James, drowned at sea on a voyage from St. Croix; Adam Blair; and four daughters. Adam married, 1760, Margaret, daughter of Robert Johnston of Kinlough House, and of Aghadunvane, Co. Leitrim, and died 1782. She died 1821. Their children were: (1) Robert, died *s.p.* (2) Henry Leslie, Captain Royal Marines, died at Ajaccio, 1794. (3) James, killed in a mutiny at sea near Penang, 1805; (4) Peter Leslie, Lieutenant, died *s.p.* (5) William, midshipman, drowned. (6) Randal. (7) William M'Donnell. (8) Adam Blair, died in the West Indies.

Randal, born 1777, married, 1806, Isabella Anna Jane, daughter of George Birch of Ballybeen, Co. Down. Three of their five sons, Adam, James, and Randal, died *s.p.*; Robert married Anna Causer, and died in the West Indies, 1840. George Birch succeeded his father. Of the daughters, Isabella Jane married her cousin, James Walker; Margaret married Michael Andrews, died 1905; Sarah Hill married William Purdon, died 1908, leaving issue.

George Birch Johnston, born 1811, married, 1856, Jane Waring, daughter of Thomas Kelly Evans. He died 1885 leaving: (1) Randal William, born Sept. 8, 1858, late Captain K.O.S.B. and Hon. Major 5th Battalion Royal Irish Rifles. (2) Thomas Kelly Evans, born 1860, Colonel Royal Field Artillery; married, 1891, Margaret Ross, daughter of Archibald Gray, and has Randal William M'Donnell and Margaret Gray. (3) George Birch, born 1866. (4) Charles M'Garel, born 1876. (5) Elizabeth Thomasina Evans, married, 1884, Rev. R. Lauriston Lee, and has issue. (6) Isabella Eva. (7) Charlotte Maria.

JOHNSTONS IN IRELAND

Robert Henry Johnstone of Bawnboy House, Co. Cavan, J.P. and D.L., born 1849. Married, 1892, Mary Elizabeth, only child of Thomas Blackstock, and has a son, Arthur Henry, born 1893. Mr Johnstone is the eldest son of the late Captain John Johnstone, 70th Regiment, who died 1864, by Isabella Eccles, his wife, daughter of Captain John Jameson, 70th Regiment.

The Will of James Johnston of Aghamulden, Co. Fermanagh, was proved in 1676. He is supposed to have been agent to Sir Gustavus Hume. His sons, Robert and John, married daughters of James Weir, of Co. Sligo. From Robert descend the Johnstons of Kinlough, and from John the Johnstons of Brookhill, Co. Leitrim. The late Captain Forbes Johnston, of Brookhill, born 1829, married the daughter of Rev. T. Low, and died Nov. 5, 1904. He left Forbes, born 1859, and other issue.

The senior branch is represented by Robert's great-great-grandson, James Johnston of Kinlough House, Leitrim, J.P., D.L., High Sheriff, 1884 (only son of the late William Johnston of Kinlough, J.P., D.L.), born 1859. Married, 1890, Rebecca, daughter of Maurice C. Maude of Lenaghan Park, Fermanagh, and has Robert Christopher, born 1896.

The Johnstons of Magheramena Castle, Co. Fermanagh, where they settled 200 years ago, are believed to come off the Johnstons of Caskieben, Co. Aberdeen, through a branch settled in Ayrshire. The late representative, Robert Edgeworth Johnston, was son of the late James Johnston, born 1817 (and High Sheriff in 1862), by Cecilia Edgeworth, his wife. He was born 1842, and married, 1873, Edythe Grace, daughter of John Reynolds Dickson of Tullaghan House, Co. Leitrim. Their son, James Cecil Johnston, born 1880, is now of Magheramena Castle and Glencore House, Co. Fermanagh.

William, living at Donagh in 1650, seems to be the first recorded of the Johnstons of Fort Johnston, Co. Monaghan. His son, Baptist, was second in command at the battle of Glasslough in 1688. Their cousin, Hector, left a son, James of Stramore, who left a son by Marjory, his wife, George of Fort Johnston, who was born 1728, married Margaret, daughter of Sir Richard Baxter, and died 1818, leaving two sons, John, M.D. of Cork, married sister of Sir Anthony Perier, died *s.p.*; and Thomas, who succeeded to the estate. The late representative, the Rev. Walter Johnston, born 1823, died May 20, 1901, Rector and Prebendary of Connor, married Fanny, daughter of the Rev. Henry Murphy, 1857, and had Henry George, born 1860, and other children.

The Vicar of Ballynahinch about 1681, Thomas Johnston, educated at Aberdeen, ancestor of the Johnstons of Portmore, has many descendants. His grandson, John of Ballinderry, had a great-nephew, William, born about 1758, who married Hannah Ferris (probably descended from the Scottish family of Fareis) about 1781 or 1783. William was employed under the agent of the Marquis of Hertford, and was a lieutenant in the Ballinderry Yeomanry. He left five sons, of whom James, Thomas, John Moore, and Philip left sons. John Moore's eldest son, John (died 1897), was a wholesale tea merchant, and an Alderman of Belfast. The second son, James, died the same month as his brother, and was head of the linen firm of James Johnston & Co. Their uncle, Philip, was a partner in the firm of Johnston & Carlisle, and Chief Magistrate of Belfast in 1871. Philip's elder daughter, Hester, married the Rev. Francis Graham; the younger, Maude, married Edward Jenkins, author of *Ginks's Baby*. The sons, Samuel and David, are partners in a flax spinning mill.

The grandsons of John Moore Johnston are: John Moore, died 1909; Philip Henry, LL.D., a Solicitor; William Hope; Robert Stewart, LL.B., Administrator in the Bahamas; Alfred; and two daughters—children of the eldest son, John, by his wife, Lucinda Stewart. The issue of James, the second son, by his wife, Elean, daughter of Hugh Moore, are: John Moore, Hugh Moore, James Hope, William, Philip, and four daughters.

One branch of the Kellobank and Beverley family settled in Ireland about 1770, Captain William Johnston, who married a Hamilton of Tyrella (*see* p. 132). Their son, the Rev. William Henry Johnston, M.A., incumbent of Holmpatrick, Co. Dublin (1770-1835), married Margaret, daughter of James Hamilton of Abbotstown and Holmpatrick (descended from the brother of the first Viscount Claneboye), and left William, father of Mr William Henry Johnston of Ealing; John of Hacketstown; Henry, Rector of Ratoath; and Charles, emigrated to Australia. The Rev. Henry Johnston married Emily, daughter of Stuart Craufurd of Bath. Their elder son, Col. Henry Stuart Johnston, J.P., late in command of the Royal Meath Militia, has two sons and two daughters. The second, William Stuart, left a daughter, Belinda, married Mr Pitman of Bath.

Colonel Percy Herbert Johnston, Medical Corps R.A., C.M.G. Son of the late Surgeon-Major J. W. Johnston. Married Agnes, daughter of the late General J. M. Perceval, C.B. Educated at Queen's College, Cork. Served in the Afghan War, 1878-79; the Hazara Expedition; and South Africa, 1899-1902.

The first Johnston of Woodpark was George Johnston, a Solicitor at the time he closed a mortgage upon Woodpark and took possession. A tradition asserts that he went over to the exiled King James at St. Germains. His descendant, Major Nicholas George Johnston, was forced to sell his property, part of which was bought by his brother, the Rev. John Beresford Johnston, whose descendants still hold it. Mr Johnston's eldest grandson, the Rev. E. A. Johnston, was appointed Vicar of St. Edmund's, Dudley, 1904.

George Johnston of Co. Monaghan, being executor to the first Johnston of Woodpark was probably related to him. The latter died 1724. His third son, Gabriel, died in London *s.p.*, 1752. His second son, Joshua, married, 1718, Elizabeth, daughter of Lord Blayney, High Sheriff of Armagh, 1722. Their sons were: William George Cadwallader, Robert Joshua, Boulter, and Gabriel. William was Colonel in the 63rd Regiment, died 1795, leaving one daughter.

A Johnston family, settled at Coshocton in Ohio, U.S.A., came from near Dungannon, Tyrone, in Ireland. Margaret, daughter of the Rev. Joseph Kerr, and widow of David Johnston, brought their five children to Pittsburg in 1818. She married secondly, James Renfrew of Coshocton, where four of her children married into the family of Humrickhouse, who had braved the Indians then dominant in Ohio and made their home among its dense forests. The eldest son of David Johnston, John, was a member of the Convention in 1849 which framed the present constitution of Ohio, and a little later was elected a member of the National Congress at Washington. He died, aged sixty-one, in 1867. The second son, Joseph, was an elder in the Presbyterian Kirk for forty years, and settled in New York city, where he lived to be eighty-seven, and where his sons, David and John, remain. The third son, William, died 1860, aged fifty-one, leaving three sons and three daughters. The eldest of these, James Renfrew, who married Anna Hogle, farms his own lands at Coshocton, and has been an elder of the Presbyterian Kirk forty-two years. He has two sons, Frederick and James, and a daughter, Margaret. His brother, Thomas, is a consulting engineer to two important railway companies at Pittsburg.

PART III.

THE JOHNSTONS OR JOHNSTONES IN AMERICA.

WHILE Johnstons from Ireland assisted the British Government against the French in America, those escaping from Scotland after the defeat of the Jacobites were equally keen in helping the Americans to independence.

It would require the evidence of registered documents in public keeping—the only evidence which a Committee of Privileges in the House of Lords will accept—to refute the common belief that John Johnston, as he generally spelt his name, the brother of the first Marquis of Annandale, left no legitimate direct heirs. But an American family claim descent from this John, on the ground that a written uncertified statement made by Gilbert Johnston of Brompton, Cape Fear, North Carolina, in 1790, when he was sixty-five, calls himself grandson to John Johnston of Stapleton. Some of his descendants infer that this John Johnston was the brother of the first Marquis of Annandale (*see* p. 162). The statement is:—

"My grandfather John Johnston of Stapleton, officer in a Scottish regiment in French service, married Elizabeth, her father Gabriel Belcher, French Protestant. Their children were, 1. John, he and only son died in North Britain. 2. Gabriel, Governor of North Carolina. 3. Gilbert my father. 4. Samuel lived in Onslow, N. Carolina. 5. Elizabeth married Thos. Keenan at our home Armagh. My father married Caroline. Her grandfather George Johnstone, Armagh 1724. Children, Gilbert, Henry, Caroline, Gabriel, Robert, William, Isabel, John. I married Margaret Warburton, North Carolina, 2 June, 1750. Children, Hugo, Gilbert, Jean, Isabel. Henry died Catawba County, son James, Col. in war. Caroline married William Williams, son

William. John lived in Bertie, N. Ca. Gabriel married Janet McFarland, son Francis killed, Lieut. Mother and Aunt Francis died Brompton. My father to Ireland after 1715. Got my lands through George Gould. Barfield tories burned my house to cellar. Was at Culloden with father, he wounded, came to Cape Fear 1746. My father died 1775. Marion, two Horrys and Francis Huger met Folsome and Giles my house, all chose Marion, bar Folsome. Hugo took my men with Marion 1780. All horsemen. Francis Huger, and James often at my house. John Rutherford a tory.

"Writ by my hand for Susana 8th day of March 1790

"Signed Gilbert Johnston Gentleman."

The above Gilbert is stated to have died in 1794. It was at his house in 1780, we are told, that General Marion signed the commissions for the celebrated band of Marion's men. All the sons and nephews of the family seem to have taken part against the British in the American War.

It is also stated by the descendant of Gilbert senior that his second son, Henry (born 1727), married Margaret Knox. Henry's son, James, was a Colonel on the Staff of General Rutherford during the American Revolution. He commanded a force in two engagements, and married Jean Ewart. James's fourth son, William, M.D., married Nancy, daughter of General Peter Forney, and died in 1855. He left five sons: (1) James, a Captain in the C.S.A., who married Miss Todd. (2) Robert, Brigadier-General, married Miss Evans. (3) William, Colonel, married Miss Gage. (4) Joseph Forney, born in Lincoln Co., North Carolina, 1843, married Miss Hooper. The last was a Captain in the Confederate Army, with which he served (1861-65), and was four times wounded, but at the end of the war went to Selma, and now practises law in Birmingham, Alabama. He was Governor of Alabama (1896-1900), and in 1907 was elected a Senator of the United States for Alabama. The youngest brother, (5) Bartlett, was an officer in the Confederate Navy. Altogether they were wounded twenty-one times, but all survive except William.

Robert, fourth son of Gilbert senior was an attorney and civil engineer. His son, Peter, was also being educated for a civil engineer, when he left his school to enter as a lieutenant in the legion which Colonel Henry Lee recruited in Virginia. He afterwards practised law in Virginia, and must have been the same as Peter, the father of General Joseph Eccleston, who is called by his son's biographer the grandson of a Scot; and in 1780 when Lee's legion arrived at Farmville, in Prince Edward's County, just before Christmas, Peter threw aside his lesson books to mount a horse and join the cavalry. Later, having greatly distinguished himself, Peter Johnston turned his sword into a pen, and became Judge of the South-Western Circuit in Virginia, and Speaker of the Virginia House of Delegates. He married Mary Wood, a niece of Patrick Henry, Secretary of State to General Washington in 1795. Their eighth son, Joseph Eccleston Johnston, was born in 1807, and was educated among the men who had fought against the British in 1777-83. This probably led him to choose the army as a profession, and in 1829 he graduated at the Military Academy of

West Point. He had served with the Federal Army in all its campaigns, and been severely wounded, up to the time that the Southern States declared for independence. He was then Lieutenant-Colonel and Quartermaster-General, but, a Virginian educated with Virginian funds, he thought it his duty to throw up his commission and join the South, where he was born, against the North. As he chose the losing side he was involved in all its disasters, but is looked upon as the most experienced and skilful General in the war. He married Louisa M'Lane, whose grandfather served as a Captain under Washington. He died in 1891. Dr George Ben. Johnston, of Richmond, Virginia, is his grand-nephew.

The next brother of Gilbert senior is said to have been Samuel, who married Helen Scrymgeour, and came to Onslow County, North Carolina, in 1736. His son, Samuel, was the Naval Officer of North Carolina in 1775, Treasurer during the Revolution, and Governor of North Carolina from 1787-89. He was President of the Convention that finally adopted the Constitution for this State, which stood for sixty years unchanged. He was the first Senator elected by North Carolina to the United States Congress in 1789. He died in 1816 and his son, James, was the largest planter in the United States on his death in 1865.

The elder Samuel's second son, John, was a Captain of Light Horse in the Revolution. He died in 1790, and his descendants live in North Carolina, Texas, and Canada.

The senior representative of this branch of Johnston is Huger William of Idlewild, Georgia ; married, 1871, Emma O. Johnstone. They have many children and grandchildren. He is great-grandson of Hugo, born 1751, died 1795, and of Susanna Barefield, his wife—first cousin to her husband, who was eldest son of Gilbert Johnston, junr. (died 1794).

The latter part of this family history, including the children and brothers of Gilbert junior can be proved, but so far this is not the case with the first part, and inaccuracy is only natural when a worn-out old man describes family links of ninety years before from memory alone. He may have mixed up his grandfather with his great-grandfather in calling him John Johnston of Stapleton, for Stapleton, a part of the Graitney parish, contained many Johnstons, some of whom settled in America, and also sent out soldiers of fortune to foreign lands. The unusual name of Gabriel might very probably be introduced by a French connection. But a different parentage to that in Gilbert's statement is shown for Gabriel, and Samuel Johnston, the husband of Helen Scrymgeour, in *Fasti Scotiæ Eccles.*, and in the collections of Robert Riddell Stodart of the Lyon Office, Edinburgh. The Rev. Samuel Johnston,[1] who graduated M.A. of Edinburgh in 1677, was successively minister of Southdean, Roxburgh, in 1690, and of Dundee in 1699. He married Isabel Hall, and two of their children, Gabriel and Samuel, were baptised at Southdean in 1698 and 1699. Three

---

[1] He was older than the Hon. John Johnston, who was not born till 1668 ; but if he came from the Elsieshields' branch, as seems probable from his name, or if his father was John Johnston of Stapleton, possibly of Graitney, his descendants would be equally of Annandale.

more were baptised at Dundee, viz.: Elizabeth, Dec. 2, 1700; Nathaniel, Dec. 27, 1702; and Joseph, May 4, 1709.

Mr R. R. Stodart adds that Gabriel had another brother, John. There may also have been Gilbert, a name found among the Graitney, Elphinstone, Newton, Elsieshields and Powdene Johnstouns—probably among them all. John is described as a Surveyor-General; Gabriel, as being educated at St. Andrews, and afterwards a Professor of Hebrew and Oriental languages in the New College of St. Andrews. He resigned, and emigrated to America, where he was appointed Governor of Carolina. Samuel, junr., married Helen Scrymgeour, and two of their sons were baptised at Dundee—Samuel, Dec. 22, 1733; John, Aug. 14, 1735.

It is likely that the migration of these Johnstons to America was caused by Jacobite sympathies, particularly if they went by way of Armagh, where the Woodpark Johnstons shared their views and were perhaps connections. Armagh was also a convenient place for testing the support that a Jacobite attempt was likely to find in the west of Scotland. Without admitting the claim put forward by their descendants that Gilbert senior, Gabriel, and Samuel were the sons of John, the brother of the first Marquis of Annandale, it may readily be conceded that they were a valiant and sturdy family, pushing to the front in politics and battle, and carrying on the motto and best traditions of the clan in the New World.

General Albert Sydney Johnston was the son of a physician, John Johnston, whose father was Archibald, the descendant of a Scottish family long settled in Connecticut. He was born in Kentucky, 1803, and graduated at West Point, but, throwing up his commission, entered the Confederate Army as a private. He was killed in the Civil War, 1862. Josiah Stallard Johnston, an Author, is his nephew; and William Preston Johnston has published his biography.

Robert Matteson Johnston, Professor of History, is the author of *The French Revolution, The Roman Theocracy and the Republic*, and other books.

Alexander Johnston, A.M., is noted for his works on American history and politics.

William Andrew Johnston is a Historical Writer.

Thomas Crawford Johnston, an Essayist in California.

W. W. Johnston (New York), Author.

Richard Malcolm Johnston, Author.

Richard Holland Johnston, Author.

William Dawson Johnstone, of Chicago, son of Rev. James Arthur and Jannette Johnston, is Librarian at the Bureau of Education, Washington.

Charles, the son of William Johnston, M.P. for Belfast, was born at Ballykilbeg, Ireland, and passed into the Bengal Civil Service. He was invalided home two years later, and became an Author. He married Georgina Barbara, daughter of Sir John Hay, Bart., and is President of the Irish Literary Society, New York. He lives at Flushing, New York.

George Ben. Johnston, Surgeon, graduated in the City of New York College, 1876; LL.D. of St. Francis Xavier College, New York; ex-President of the Richmond Academy of Medicine and Surgery. He lives at Richmond, Virginia.

Edward Robert Johnston, Editor, born at Utica, New York, 1849.

William Pollock Johnston, Professor at Geneva College, Beaver Falls.

Swift Paine Johnston, born at Chicago 1857. Son of James Johnston of Chicago. Professor of Moral Philosophy since 1898 in Dublin University.

Henry Phelps Johnston, Professor of History in the City of New York College, and Author, born 1842.

Rev. James Wesley Johnston, Pastor at Brooklyn, Theological Writer.

George Doherty Johnston, Author.

William Agnew Johnston, Justice of Supreme Court, Kansas.

Julia Harriette Johnston and Mary Johnston, Authoresses. The last is the daughter of Major John Johnston, a lawyer and ex-soldier of the Confederate Army.

Hugh Johnston (Rev.), Baltimore, born in Canada, Author.

Right Rev. James Stephen Johnston, D.D., Bishop of West Texas, born 1843. Son of James Stephen and Louisa C. B. Johnston. He served four years in Lee's army. Was ordained in 1870.

Harold Whetstone Johnston, Professor of Latin, Indiana University.

Thomas William Johnston, of Kansas City, Writer and Journalist.

Robert Daniel Johnston, Lawyer.

Mrs Maria Isabella Johnston, Lecturer.

The American descendants of the Johnstons of Hazlebank and of Duchrae have already been described.[1]

PART IV.

FOR a long time the Hudson's Bay Company in Canada only employed Scots and Norwegians, supposing that Englishmen could not stand the climate. When Canadians of Indian descent call themselves Bruce, Johnston, M'Nab, etc., they need not have come from those families, as it was the custom when an Indian was baptised for him to take the name of his European sponsor. But the real Johnston is found in all our Colonies.

John Johnston, a Poet, in Manitoba.

William Andrew Johnston, of Blanshard.

The Hon. H. Johnston, in New Brunswick.

The Hon. Walter Woods Johnston, of Wellington, New Zealand, was born in London 1839. Married at Wellington, 1868, Cecilia Augusta, second daughter of Forster Goring, of Wellington (fourth son of Sir C. F. Goring,

[1] Since p. 44 was printed Dr Christopher Johnston has found a sasine in the Register House, March 21, 1662, confirming the connection between Hazlebank and the Poldean branch.

Bart., of Highden, Sussex), and has issue—Hon. C. J. Johnston of Homewood, Wellington, New Zealand; and Hon. J. Johnston. This family claim descent from that of Annandale through an Ayrshire branch.

Robert Mackenzie Johnston, Author, Tasmania.

S. Johnston of Ornu Whero, Hawke's Bay, New Zealand.

Alexander James Johnston, Chief Justice of New Zealand for 1867 and 1886, and puisne Judge of the Supreme Court, New Zealand, was the eldest son of James S. Johnston of Kinnellar, Aberdeenshire, where he was born 1820. He was called to the Bar in the Middle Temple 1843, and, after serving as Deputy Recorder of Leeds, went to New Zealand in 1859. There he was noted for his quiet dignity during the Maori trouble, objecting to summary trials by court-martial instead of by the ordinary tribunals. He died in England in 1888.

The Johnstouns who appear in Orkney in 1677 claim to be a branch direct from Annandale, but Alexander Johnstoun was a merchant in Wick in 1627, pointing more to a descent from Caskieben.

Robert Johnstoun of Birsay flourished in 1677. His son, Richard, a merchant in Stromness, died before 1707, having married, first, Helen Manson, secondly, Marjorie Cursetter, by whom he had a son, John, born 1690, who, as well as his father, bought several houses in Stromness and other small estates. John died 1757. He married a Londoner, Marjorie Crafts, and of their three sons only the eldest, Joshua, has male descendants.

Joshua Johnston of Outbrieks was a lawyer in Stromness, born 1720. Married, 1749, Margaret Halcro, the heiress of Coubister. Their son, John, married his first cousin, Jane, daughter of Dr Henry Taylor, of Quebec, and his wife, Anne Johnston. He sold his father's property; but of his four sons only James left descendants. One of his five daughters married Captain Nugent; another, the Rev. W. Smith; and Ann Matilda, the Rev. S. Stock, Rector of Killanley, Ireland.

James, born 1798, died 1887, married Margaret, daughter of Lieutenant James Robertson, R.N., and had: (1) James of Coubister and of Ophirhouse, J.P. and Vice-Convener of Orkney, born 1846; married Sarah Sophia, daughter of the Rev. David Ferguson, and has James Halcro, born 1891, and four daughters. (2) John Nugent, died 1901; married Jeanie Fergusson Johnston, and left four children. (3) Charles Stewart Still, born March 1850; married Elizabeth, daughter of General Gairdner, C.B., and has issue. (4) William, died *s.p.* (5) Henry Halcro, Lieutenant-Colonel R.A.M.C., M.D., C.B., born 1856; author of medical and other books. (6) Alfred, born 1859; married Amy Leslie. (7) Ann. (8) Jane, married the Rev. John Steill.

CHAPTER XXIX.

THE JOHNSTONS OF THAT ILK AND CASKIEBEN—ARTHUR JOHNSTON, THE POET—
IN CORSTORPHINE—PERTHSHIRE.

FROM the Johnstones of Dumfriesshire, with all their branches in England, Ireland, and elsewhere, we turn to one of the oldest families of the name long settled in Aberdeenshire, and probably the ancestors of many Johnstons in London, Edinburgh, and the North.

According to Sir William Fraser, the most authentic documents show that the Johnstons of Caskieben changed the name of their lands to Johnston, and took the name from these lands. He thought there was no proof of a connection with the Annandale family, but the scarcity of papers in 1380 makes this opinion hardly conclusive,[1] for it was before 1380 that Helen, co-heiress to the Earl of Mar, brought the land now called Johnston to her husband, James de Garviach. Their son, Andrew, gave it to his daughter, Margaret, when she married Stiven Cherie, surnamed "the Clerk," a scholar living in the reign of David II., and the name was assumed by her descendants.

The chief of the fifth generation, William Johnstoun, married Margaret, daughter of Meldrum of Fyvie, and was killed at Flodden in 1513. His son, James, married Clara, daughter of Barclay, Laird of Gartley, and died in 1548. Their son, William, married Margaret, daughter of Hay of Dalgety, and was killed at Pinkie, the year before his father's death. His son, George, succeeded the grandfather, married Christian, fourth daughter of William, seventh Lord Forbes, and had six sons and seven daughters. Of these, the fifth son was

---

[1] Sir William Fraser was of opinion that the Elsieshields Johnstons were not related to the main branch because Warrieston used a different crest, but they certainly claimed a relationship, and the Chief of Annandale in Warrieston's time believed in it.

Sir William says of the Graitney family: "The Lord Chancellor held that Wm. Johnstoun of Graitney, from whom Mr Edward Johnstone claimed, was not a Johnstone of Annandale." The writer was present, and heard the discussion on which this is based. The opposite Counsel enlarged on the great distance of Gretna from Lochwood, suppressing the fact that Wormanbie in Annan and Cavartholme in Gretna were among the Laird's oldest properties; and the Lord Chancellor, not claiming to be a Scottish genealogist, said that it seemed as if they might be another family. Later on—July 19, 1881—the Lord Chancellor said to the same Counsel: "We did not doubt in the case of Mr Edward Johnstone that it was probable that the stock from which he came and that of Westerhall were the same [as the Marquis's], but he did not prove it."

Arthur, M.D., physician to James VI. and Charles I., who holds amongst the Latin poets of Scotland the next place to Buchanan (*see* Sir W. D. Geddes' *Musa Latina Aberdonensis*, New Spalding Club, 2 vols., 1892 and 1895). He was educated at the Burgh School at Kintore, and in 1608 went to Padua, where he graduated M.D., and also to Rome, after which he settled in Sedan, the seat of one of the six Protestant universities in France. He practised medicine in Paris in 1619, but, returning to Scotland before the coronation of Charles I., he was introduced to Archbishop Laud, who invited him to London. There he published one edition of his Latin translation of the whole Psalter in verse. He was married to a Frenchwoman, and, secondly, to a Gordon. He died at Oxford, when visiting a married daughter, 1641, having had thirteen children.

His next brother, William (M.D.), married Elizabeth Irving of Drum, and was also the father of a large family. He was the first Professor of Mathematies in the Marischal College and University of Aberdeen. His Latin verses are about to be reproduced in the third volume of the *Musa Latina Aberdonensis*.[1] His eldest brother, John, married Janet, daughter of Turing, Laird of Foveran; he died 1614, and was succeeded by his son, George, created a Baronet of Nova Scotia by Charles I.[2] George's son, George, sold Caskieben in 1660 to Sir John Keith, who changed the name to Keith Hall, now the seat of the Earls of Kintore. His son, John, third Baronet, was hanged at Tyburn in 1690 for assisting in the abduction of Mary Wharton, an heiress, by his friend, Captain the Hon. James Campbell. Being the only offender arrested, he paid the penalty. The title went to his cousin, John, who bought Cordyce, Co. Aberdeen, and changed its name to Caskieben. Sir John followed the fortunes of Prince James in 1715, and was present at the battle of Sheriffmuir, where his only son was killed by his side. The bereaved father, not venturing to go home, retired to Edinburgh, where he died 1724. He married Janet Mitchell.

The succession passed to the descendant of John (died 1614) by his second wife, Katherine, daughter of William Lundie of that Ilk in Fife, the fifth Baronet, William, being the son of John Johnston of Bishopstown and his wife, Margaret, daughter and co-heiress of John Alexander, merchant, burgess of Aberdeen. Sir William, who was an advocate, married Jean, daughter of James Sandilands of Craibstone. He had two sons in the Navy—William, his heir; and Alexander, who perished, with his ship's crew, off the coast of Scotland. As he sold the last remnant of the family estate, his son, William,

---

[1] Another member of this family, John (whose ancestor was Gilbert, a grandson of Stiven), was Professor of Divinity at St. Andrews in 1593. His great-grandfather, Alexander of Crimond, was alive in 1540. When the Annandale Chief was outlawed for the battle of Dryfe Sands John received a grant of a third of the benefices in Annandale from James VI. on condition that he put "Godlie ministers in the parish Kirks." He does not seem to have claimed his share from the old owners, and he died in 1611. His wife, Katherine Melvill, and their two children predeceased him. He was a poet and historian.

[2] There is a payment in 1646 by Sir George Johnston to "James Douglas, Keeper of the Tolbooth of Canongate, for 2586 marks Scots for meat and drink, chambermaill and borrowed money, together with other necessaries, for my use the time of my incarceration."

who succeeded him in 1750, bought and entailed the estate of Hilton, near Aberdeen. By his wife, Elizabeth, daughter of Captain William Cleland, R.N., the sixth Baronet had eleven children, most of whom predeceased him. He died in 1794, aged eighty-two. His heir, William, served in seven battles against the French in India. In 1798 he raised a regiment of Fencibles—the Prince of Wales's Own—which was reduced in 1802. By his second wife, Maria, daughter of John Bacon of Friern House, Middlesex, he had three sons and four daughters. He was elected M.P. for Windsor in 1832, and died at The Hague, 1844.

The eighth Baronet, Sir William Bacon Johnston, was for some years an officer in the 1st (Royal) Regiment of Foot. Having obtained the consent of the three next heirs—his brother, Captain Arthur Lake Johnston (who died *s.p.* 1853), and his third cousins, David Morice Johnston and Alexander Johnston, W.S.—he disentailed the estate of Hilton, which, after his death, was sold by his trustees. Sir William married Mary Ann, daughter of William Tye of Mendlesham, Suffolk, and died in 1865, when his only son, William, became the ninth Baronet, the fifteenth in lineal male descent from Stiven de Johnstoun.

The senior branch of the Caskieben Johnstons descends from John Johnston in Standingstones, afterwards in Bishopstown, the younger brother of the fifth Baronet. John married Isobel, daughter of John Marnoch in Balnagask, and had a son, John Johnston in Boginjoss, afterwards in Cairntraddlin, Kinnellar, who died at Milbowie, Skene, 1770. He married Margaret, daughter of William Chalmers. Of their children, two sons left male issue:—

I. William Johnston of Viewfield, merchant in Aberdeen; died in 1832. By his wife, Catharine, daughter of David Morice of Tullos, Kincardineshire, he left three sons:—

(1) David Morice Johnston, Solicitor in London; died *s.p.* 1863.

(2) Alexander, W.S., married Christina Martha, daughter of John Leith Ross of Arnage, Co. Aberdeen; died *s.p.* 1880. He printed at Edinburgh, in 1832, *A Genealogical Account of the Family of Johnston of that Ilk, Formerly of Caskieben.*

(3) Robert, merchant in Aberdeen, married Mary, daughter of George Hadden, merchant in London, and died in 1887, leaving two sons—1, William of Newton Dee, Aberdeenshire, C.B., LL.D., M.D., Colonel (retired) Army Medical Staff. He married, in 1882, Charlotte, daughter of James Arnott of Leithfield, Kincardineshire, and of Edinburgh, W.S. 2, George of Garlands, Ewhurst, Surrey, formerly planter in Ceylon; married, in 1876, Agnes Elizabeth, daughter of the Rev. Richard John Sparkes, M.A. Oxon., Rector of Alfold.

II. The youngest son of John Johnston and his wife, Margaret Chalmers, in early life went to sea, but later occupied the farm of Mains of Balquhain, in the parish of Chapel of Garioch, Aberdeenshire, and died in 1845. By his wife, Margaret Inglis, he had nine children, but of his four sons only William, merchant in Aberdeen, married and left issue. William died in 1866, having had by his wife, Ann Craig, a family of ten children. William, the eldest son, was killed in a hurricane at Navy Cove, Mobile, Alabama, U.S.A., in Sept. 1906, leaving a widow, several daughters, and three sons—Thomas Alexander, born Dec. 15, 1857, married and has issue; John; Curtis Laudiner.

The most ancient branch of the Johnstons of Caskieben seems to be that of Corstorphine, whom, tradition says, founded the earliest inn in Scotland, and had settled in that village in the fifteenth century. Their names occur as buyers of grain from the Elsieshields Johnstons settled in Edinburgh early in the seventeenth century. Patrick Johnstoun appears in Corstorphine in 1625. John and Janet Johnstoun, spouses, were living there in 1680. The monuments in the ancient Churchyard, headed by a verse from St. John's Gospel, record the death of John Johnston of Corstorphine in 1707, aged thirty-seven, and of his wife, Mary Dick, aged seventy-four, in 1747. Their son, William, a brewer, died March 1768, aged seventy-two. His wife, Margaret, the daughter of David Douglas of Gilletts, Co. Fife, predeceased him at the age of fifty-five. They had several children and grandchildren, who died before them—Andrew, the eldest son, in 1748, aged twenty-two. But David inherited his father's business, and lived to be seventy-nine. He married Margaret, daughter of the Rev. Henry Lindsay, minister of Perth. Their second son, Henry, a surgeon in Edinburgh, born 1767, died 1845, married Isabella Nicholson. The names of the sons and daughters of these two, though buried elsewhere, are engraved over the ancestral tomb:—

David Johnston, M.D., born 1801, died at Bath 1870; buried at Phillack, near Hayle, Cornwall. Henry J., Surgeon H.E.I.C.S., born Jan. 4, 1804, died at Bath, April 27, 1865; buried in Lansdowne Cemetery. James, M.D., born 1816, and Anne Ramsay Douglas, his wife, died Jan. 1894. Henrietta, born 1802, died 1880. Margaret Lindsay, born 1807, died 1893.

A window in the church is dedicated by James Dunsmore Johnston, M.D., J.P., to the memory of his relatives interred there between 1707 and 1898.

In the diary of a tour in Scotland (1843), Dr David Johnston is mentioned as a benevolent landowner in Corstorphine, the son of David Johnston, a merchant in Gibraltar.

The Senator of the College of Justice from 1905, Henry, Lord Johnston, was the eldest son of the above Henry Johnston (died 1865) and his wife, Elizabeth Lilias, daughter of the late Sheriff Duncan Campbell. He was born 1844; educated at Glenalmond, and is a B.A. Trinity College, Cambridge; Scottish Advocate, 1868; Q.C., 1897; Sheriff of Ross, Cromarty, and Sutherland, 1891-98; of Forfar, 1898-1905. Married, 1873, Mary, daughter of David Small of Dundee. His brothers are: Colonel Sir Duncan Alexander, C.B., K.C.M.G.; educated at Trinity College, Glenalmond; Director-General of the Ordnance Survey, 1899-1905; Hon. Secretary Royal Geographical Society, etc. etc. He married Clare Millicent Mackenzie in 1883, and lives at Branksome, Eastbourne. Colonel David George, late of the Royal Munster Fusiliers; and James Charles, who was Manager of the Prairie Cattle Company (twins).

JOHNSTONS IN PERTHSHIRE

Robert Mackenzie, M.D., born 1856, Consulting Surgeon at the Edinburgh Royal Infirmary, late Lecturer to the University of Edinburgh; married Amy, daughter of Henry Younger, D.L., of Benmore, Argyllshire; author of papers in various professional journals. William Campbell, W.S. Mary Jane. Henrietta Milligan.

Of the Johnstons of Kincardine Castle and Montrose, James, born 1802, eldest son of James Johnston of Kincardine Castle by Sarah Pelling, his wife, succeeded 1807, and married Matilda Crowe of The Abbey, Co. Clare. He entered the Royal Navy, but later went to the Edinburgh University, and was called to the Bar. His son, James, born 1839.

James Johnston of Sands, Perthshire, born 1812, was the son of Lawrence Johnston by Mary Wellwood, his wife; succeeded 1838. Married Margaret, daughter of the Rev. Christopher Nicholson, and had Laurence, now of Sands, born 1856, married Mary Curtis, is J.P. for Cos. Perth and Fife. His brother, Christopher Nicholson, born 1857, K.C., Sheriff of Perthshire, 1905, Procurator of Church of Scotland, 1907. He married Agnes Warren Dunn, and contested Paisley in the Conservative interest, 1882.

An Act of the Scottish Parliament under Charles II., Aug. 21, 1663, states that on the petition "of Mr David Johnstoun alias Souter, student in Divinity on behalf of himself and his Kinsmen of the name in Perth and Forfar, Mentioning that the petitioners predecessor and his brother of the surname of Johnstoun in the year 1460 (as they are informed) came from Annandale to Scone in Perthshire upon some discontent, and there attended the owner of that place for a long time and assumed to themselves the surname of Souter, that they should not be noticed for the time. One of the brothers dying without issue, the other surviving for his good deportment was married to a Gentlewoman, from which marriage proceeded divers honest men who are grown into considerable families, whereof the petitioners are descended, and being desirous that they should be restored to their true and ancient surname of Johnstoun . . . they are permitted to resume it." These were the Soutar Johnstons to whom a monument is erected in the Perth burying-ground, recording the names of every generation from James, who died at Scone Palace in 1510, to John, who died in 1814—all burgesses, and some of them members, of the Glover Incorporation in Perth.

Stewart Soutar Johnston, son of the above John, claimed the Annandale titles at the election of a representative peer for Scotland in Holyrood Palace in 1824, and, no opposition being made, his vote was recorded. He had been an outrider to George IV. when the King visited Edinburgh; but died *s.p.* in Canada 1846. His papers were brought back to Scotland and handed over to his cousin and nearest of kin, William Reid, a contractor in Meadowside, Dundee. His son, William Reid, F.S.A.Scot., of Meadowside, Dundee, presented several interesting historical memorials of this now extinct branch to the Sandeman Museum of Perth in 1904.

TYPICAL JOHNSTOUN ARMS.

The lower part, or "field," is charged with a saltire, or St. Andrew's Cross. The upper part is called a "chief," and is charged with three cushions. The Crest above the shield shows the winged spur.

HERALDRY.

THE earliest armorial seal of the Johnstouns is that of Sir John de Jonestone, who swore fealty to King Edward I. in 1296. It shows—*Two garbs or wheat sheaves, and a canton covering a third garb in dexter chief.* These Arms, apparently founded on the Arms of Comyn (who bore three garbs), do not again occur in the Johnstoun Family.

The typical Johnstoun Arms are made up of those of Bruce and Randolph, both Lords of Annandale.

Bruce bore—*A gold shield charged with a saltire or St. Andrew's Cross, and a chief* (or upper part of the shield), *both red.*

Randolph bore—*A silver shield charged with three cushions surrounded by a Royal tressure, both red.*

JOHNSTONES OF ANNANDALE.

These Johnstones combined the Arms of Bruce and Randolph, but altered the colours to *A silver shield charged with a black saltire, and a black chief charged with three silver cushions.* The CREST was *A star;* and the MOTTO, "*Light thieves all,*" alluded to the office of Warden held by the Johnstone Chiefs.

William Johnstone, second Earl of Annandale, and later Marquis of Annandale, recorded Arms in 1694. He then changed the colours of the "chief" to *red and charged it with three gold cushions,* and quartered the Johnstone Arms with those of his wife, Sophia Fairholm—*Gold charged with a red anchor.*

The SUPPORTERS of the shield were: Dexter, *A silver lion with a blue tongue and crowned gold;* Sinister, *A silver horse with red harness and saddle.*

The CREST was altered to *A gold winged spur*, and the more dignified MOTTO adopted—"*Nunquam non paratus.*"

According to Robson's *British Herald*, the illegitimate Johnstons of Corehead and Lochhouse bore—*Silver, on a red invecked saltire a gold spur, and on a red engrailed chief three gold cushions.* CREST: *A gold spur without wings.* MOTTO: "*Ad arma paratus.*"

JOHNSTONS OF ELPHINSTONE.

These Johnstons adhered to the original Arms—*A silver shield charged with a black saltire, and a black chief charged with three silver cushions;* but sometimes they added *a silver rose in the centre of the saltire*, and at others quartered the Johnston Arms with those of Seton, Elphinstone, and Buchan.

JOHNSTONES OF WESTERHALL, ALVA, AND HACKNESS.

The Johnstones of Westerhall bore at first the same Arms as Annandale, but later they adopted—*Silver, a black saltire, in base a red heart crowned gold, and a red chief charged with three gold cushions.* The heart was added to commemorate the services of this family in defeating the Douglases in 1455, the crowned heart being that of King Robert Bruce borne by the Good Sir James Douglas, at least part of the way, to the Holy Land, and a representation of it added to the Douglas Arms. CREST: *A gold winged spur.* MOTTO: "*Nunquam non paratus.*"

ALVA.

The Johnstones of Alva add *a black annulet or ring above the saltire* in the Westerhall Arms.

One cadet of Alva adds *a gold portcullis in the centre of the saltire* of the Alva Arms, and another adds *five silver fleurs-de-lis on the saltire.*

HACKNESS.

Johnstone of Hackness, a cadet of Westerhall, and now Lord Derwent, bears—First and fourth quarters the Arms of Westerhall, quartered with those of Vanden Bempdé in the second and third quarters. CREST: *A gold winged spur.* SUPPORTERS: Dexter, *An ermine lion crowned gold;* Sinister, *An ermine horse saddled and bridled red. Both Supporters charged on the shoulder with a gold shield bearing a red winged spur.* MOTTO: "*Nunquam non paratus.*"

JOHNSTONES OF NEWBIE AND GRETNA.

The Johnstones of Newbie bore in 1604—*Three stars, and on a chief three cushions.*

In 1648 their Galabank descendants bore—*The saltire on the field, with the three cushions in chief.* In 1772 their Arms were recorded—*Silver, a saltire wavy black, a red star in chief, a red rose in base, and two green garbs in the flanks; a red chief charged with three gold cushions.* CREST: *A winged spur proper.* MOTTO: "*Nunquam non paratus.*" These Arms were again recorded 1871, the only difference being that *the saltire has straight edges.*

The illegitimate Johnstones of Gretna bore—*A saltire between two stars, one in chief and the other in base.* CREST: *A man armed cap-a-pie on horseback brandishing a sword.* MOTTO: "*Cave paratus.*"

JOHNSTONS OF ELSIESHIELDS, ETC.

JOHNSTON OF KELLOBANK. In *Familiæ Minorum Gentium* given as—*Silver, a black saltire; on a red chief two gold wool packs* (or cushions).

JOHNSTON OF BEIRHOLM. Nisbet gives—*Silver, a saltire and chief red, the last charged with three gold cushions, all within a silver bordure.*

JOHNSTON OF WARRIESTON. Burke's *Armory* gives—*Silver, a black engrailed saltire; on a red chief three gold cushions.*

JOHNSTON OR JOHNSON OF WROXEL, ISLE OF WIGHT, claiming descent from Sheens, recorded in Lyon Office 1735—*Silver, a black saltire, in base a blue mullet, and on a red chief three gold cushions.* CREST: *A spur, winged silver.* MOTTO: "*Sic paratuo.*"

JOHNSTON OF HILTON recorded Lyon Office 1672-77—*Silver, a black engrailed saltire; on a red engrailed chief three gold cushions.* CREST: *A sword and dagger proper, hilted gold, crossing each other saltireways with points uppermost.* MOTTO: "*Paratus ad arma.*"

JOHNSTON OF CASKIEBEN.

At first this family bore Arms quite different to those borne by the South Country Johnstones. In 1550 they bore *A blue shield, charged with a bend between a stag's head erased in chief, and three cross crosslets fitchy in base silver.* In 1630 *three stags' heads erased* appear in chief in place of the one above mentioned.

This family recorded Arms in 1695—1 and 4—the Arms of the South Country Johnstones—*Silver, a black saltire; on a red chief three gold cushions.* 2 and 3. *Blue, a gold bend between three stags' heads erased silver, attired gold, in chief, and three cross crosslets fitchy gold in base.* CREST: *A phœnix in flames proper.* SUPPORTERS: *Two savages wreathed about the middle with laurel.* MOTTO: "*Vive ut postea vivas.*"

Colonel William Johnston, C.B., heir-presumptive to the Baronetcy, recorded the same Arms in 1903, with the addition of *a gold bordure* round the Arms.

Major James Johnston, said to be descended from Caskieben, recorded Arms in 1764—*Silver, a black saltire, in chief and base stags' heads proper, and in the flanks blue cross crosslets fitchy.*

OTHER JOHNSTONS.

SCOTLAND.

JOHNSTON OF BLACKWOOD. Nisbet's *Heraldry* gives—*Silver, a saltire and chief black, the latter charged with three gold cushions.*

JOHNSTON OF CARNSALLOCH uses same Arms as Westerhall.

JOHNSTON OF CLAUCHRIE recorded Arms 1672-77—*Silver, a saltire invecked black with a pellet* (black disc) *in each flank; on a red chief three gold cushions.* CREST: *The sun rising behind clouds.* MOTTO: "*Appropinquat Dies.*"

JOHNSTON OF COWHILL uses same as Westerhall.

JOHNSTON IN EDINBURGH (Newton, Midlothian) recorded 1887—*Parted per pale. Silver and black, a saltire counter-changed; on a red chief three gold cushions.* CREST: *A winged spur, gold.* MOTTO: "*Ready Aye Ready.*"

JOHNSTON OF GORMUCK recorded 1680-87—*Silver, a saltire and chief nebuly, the latter charged with three silver cushions.* CREST: *A pierced mullet, blue, within a green wreath of laurel.* MOTTO: "*Securior quo paratior.*"

JOHNSTON OF LATHRISK recorded 1797—*Silver, a black saltire within a bordure engrailed blue; on a red chief a silver mullet between two gold cushions.* CREST: *A gold spur with silver wings.* MOTTO: "*Semper paratus.*"

JOHNSTON OF PITKEIRIE recorded 1755—*Silver, a black saltire; on a red chief three gold cushions. All within a green wavy bordure charged with three bezants* (gold coins or discs). CREST: *A gold winged spur.* MOTTO: "*Assiduitate,*" and later "*Nunquam non paratus.*"

JOHNSTON OF POLTON recorded 1676—*Silver, a wavy saltire and chief black, the latter charged with three silver cushions.* CREST: *A spur proper, winged silver.* MOTTO: "*Sic paratior.*"

JOHNSTON OF STRAITON (?) recorded 1672-77—*Silver, a black wavy saltire; on a red engrailed chief three gold cushions.* CREST: *A hand proper holding a bezant.* MOTTO: "*Ex sola virtute honos.*"

JOHNSTON OF WARDMILNES recorded 1672-77—*Silver, a black saltire, a red escallop in each flank; on a black chief three silver cushions.* CREST: *A hand proper holding a red escallop.* MOTTO: "*Sine fraude fidus.*"

ENGLAND AND FOREIGN.

JOHNSTON UND KROEGEBORN, formerly of Craigieburn, uses—*Silver, a black saltire; on a red chief three gold cushions.* CREST: *A winged spur, the wings coloured quarterly red, silver, gold, and black.* SUPPORTER: *A silver lion.* MOTTO: "*Nunquam non paratus.*"

JOHNSTON IN LONDON, formerly of Edinburgh, recorded 1897—*Silver, on a black saltire the golden sun, in each quarter of the field a red dagger; on a red chief three gold cushions.* CREST: *A gold winged spur.* MOTTO: "*Nunquam non paratus.*"

JOHNSTON IN VENICE, formerly of Duchrae, recorded—*Silver, a saltire pean* (black with gold ermine spots); *on a black chief three gold cushions.* CREST: *A gold winged spur.* MOTTO: "*Nunquam non paratus.*"

IRELAND.

JOHNSTON OF KILMORE—*Silver, a black saltire, in chief a green shamrock, and in base a red heart crowned gold; on a red chief three gold cushions.* CREST: *An arm in armour charged on the elbow with a red spur rowel, and holding a sword erect.* MOTTO: "*Nunquam non paratus.*"

JOHNSTON IN ARMAGH AND DUBLIN—1 and 4. As Kilmore, above. 2. Cheney. 3. Hamilton. CREST and MOTTO: As Kilmore.

JOHNSTON IN DUBLIN—*Black, a bend, and in sinister chief a tower silver, all within a bordure gobony silver and blue.* CREST: *A horse walking, per fess silver and black.* MOTTO: "*Festina lente.*"

JOHNSTON OF KNAPPAGH AND GLENAULE, CO. ARMAGH—*Silver, a black saltire; on a blue chief three gold cushions.* CREST: *An arm in armour holding a sword erect.* MOTTO: "*Nunquam non paratus.*"

JOHNSTON OF LITTLEMOUNT, CO. FERMANAGH—*Silver, a black saltire between a shamrock in chief and flanks, and a red heart crowned gold in base; on a red chief three gold cushions.* CREST: *A winged spur.* MOTTO: "*Nunquam non paratus.*"

G. H. J.

INDEX

INDEX.

Abel, Elizabeth, 304
,, James, 304
Abercrombies, 100
Abergavenny, Marquis of, 302
Acheson, Nichola, 329
,, Sir Nicholas, Bart, 329
Ackworth, Dr, 213
Acland, Agnes, 296
,, John, 296
,, of Columb, John, 286
Acland-Troyte, 286
,, Mary Dyke, 296
Acts of Decreets, 105
Adams, Dr, 230
,, Herbert A., 298
Adderley Family, 277
Addington, Mr, 267
Agar Ellis, Hon. Evelyn, 303
Age, coming of, 77
Agnew, Captain J. P., 304
,, Catherine, 302
,, James, 302
,, Sir Andrew, 147
Ainslie, Colonel Bernard, 313
,, George H., 313
Airlie, David, Earl of, 183
,, Earl of, 182
,, Lady, 17
Akers, Janet, 313
Albany, Duke of, 7, 8, 10, 39, 52
Alers-Hankey, Ernest Perceval, 306
Alexander, Anne, 329
,, Arthur, 332
,, Colonel, 304
,, Helen Kathleen, 304
,, John, 344
,, Margaret, 344
,, Rayner, 305
,, Sir William, 329
Allan, Agnes, 311
Allane, Robert, 161
Almagill, 125
Alva, Johnstones of, 298
America, Johnstones in, 27, 28, 44
American War, 337
Amherst, General, 196, 263
Anderson, David, 313
,, John, 225
,, Mr, 214, 215

Anderson, Provost, 211
Andrews, Michael, 334
Angoulême, Duchesse d', 288
Annan, 78
,, burned, (1570) 111
,, Castle, 62
,, destroyed, 52
,, First bridge over the, 150
,, John Murray, Viscount, 114
,, Ministers of, 151
,, Provostship of, 13
Annand, Viscount, 97
Annandale, Bruce, Lord of, 50
,, Charlotta, Marchioness of, 175, 301
,, Charter Chest, 122
,, Dowager Marchioness of, 204
,, Earl of, 110, 124, 148, 149, 150, 153
,, Earldom of, 138
,, Estates, settlement of, 164
,, Feuars of, 42
,, First Marquis of, 337, 340
,, George, third Marquis of, 164, 167, 168, 169, 175, 204, 205, 228, 244, 256, 323
,, James, Earl of, 143
,, ,, second Marquis of, 164, 175
,, John Murray, Earl of, 114, 118
,, Lady, 154
,, Lord, 37, 143, 144, 152, 153, 203
,, Lordship of, 1, 7, 8
,, Marchioness of, 167, 168, 171
,, Marquis of, 16, 103, 156, 158, 159, 160, 161, 162, 163, 168, 214
,, Marquisate of, 273, 287
,, Marquises of, 57
,, Sophia, Marchioness of, 129
,, Stewardship of, 125
,, Titles, claim to, 347
,, V. Bempdé, 168
,, William, Earl of, 150
,, ,, ,, first Marquis of, 143, 151, 164, 175, 176, 195, 273
Anne, Queen, 162, 164, 190, 333
Annesley, Anna Maria, 330
,, Earl of, 330
Angus, Archibald, Earl of, 10
,, David, Earl of, 19, 20, 21
,, Earl of, 53, 56, 58, 76, 77, 80, 86, 87, 88, 130
,, Regent, 155

INDEX

Anson, Archdeacon George, 296
Antrobus, Fanny Lewis, 132
„ Rev. Edmund, 132
Apilgirth, Lady, 143
Arbroath, Lord of, 21
Arcot, Nabob of, 319
Argyll, Duke of, 165, 195, 304
„ Earl of, 109
„ John, Duke of, 320
Arkinholme, Battle of, (1483) 10, 155
Armada, The, 81, 82
Armagh, Archbishop of, 132
Armorial Bearings, 349, 350, 351, 352, 353
Armstrong, 84, 309
„ Blanche, 147
„ David, 170, 244
„ Elizabeth, 119
„ Francis, 88
„ Johnnie, 53, 58, 71
„ „ hanged, 55
„ Murder of Symon, 55
„ Ninian, 68
„ of Kinmont, Willie, 87, 89
„ Sander, 61
Armstrongs, 40, 48, 52, 53, 54, 62, 74, 79, 80, 85, 87, 88, 89, 91, 95, 100
Arnot, 308
„ David, 330
„ Helen, 33
„ James, 128
„ John, 34
„ Lord Provost Sir John, 33
„ Rachel, 33, 100, 127, 128
„ Rev. Samuel, 330
„ Sir John, 99
„ William, 127
Arnott, Charlotte, 345
„ James, 345
Arran, Earl of, 58, 78, 80
„ Regent, 57, 60, 69, 307
Ash, Dr, 228, 245
Ashton, Ellen E., 314
„ James Bentley, 314
Aston, Roger, 85
Athole, Duke of, 195
Atkins, Janet, 35
Atkinson, Mr Joseph, D.L., 332
Attwood, Mr, 271
Auchinleck Chronicle, 8, 18
Aufrere, Anthony, 259
„ Louisa Anna Matilda, 259
Aughrim, Battle of, 328
Augusta, Princess, 234
Avenel, 69
Aylesford, Lord, 250

Babtie, John, 312
Bacon, John, 345
„ Lord, 82, 176
„ Maria, 345
Bagot, Rev. Egerton, 253
Baillie of Jerviswood, Robert, 139
„ of Polkemmet, 324

Baillie, Robert, 128
„ Slaughter of Alexander, 95
„ Thomas, 313
„ William, 140
Baillie's execution, 140
Baines, Miss, 232
Baker, Sir George, 240
Baldwin, Colonel Archibald, 316
Balfour, Dr John, 306
„ Laird of, 34
„ of Burley, 98
„ of Burlie, Sir Michael, 17
„ Sir James, 75
Baliol, King Edward, 4
„ „ John, 2
Baliols, 1, 2
Balmain, James, 182
Balsucrik, 67
Banantyne, Mr, 143
Banatyne, Margaret, 153
„ of Corhouse, John, 153
Bankend, 74
Banks, Sir Joseph, 268
Bannatyne, Hew, 129
„ of Brochtoun, Sir James, 16
„ Richard, 307
Barclay, Clara, 343
Bard, Mrs, 28
Bardannoch, Laird of, 77
Barefield, Susanna, 339
Barnard, Leonard, 300
Barndaroch, Lady Margaret of, 100
Barnes, Anne, 330, 332
„ Major-General Sir Edward, 330, 331
„ *Manchester Memoirs*, 231
„ Robert, 330
„ Susanna, 330
Baronetcies instituted, 90
Barrett, Mr, 238
Barry, Colonel, 233
„ Major Percival, 296
Baskerville, John, 246
Bath, Countess of, 245, 272, 273
„ Earl of, 177
Battle Abbey Roll, 2
Baugh, Captain, 305
Baxter, 233
„ Margaret, 335
„ Sir Richard, 335
Beacons on the Border, 6
Beaton, Cardinal, 91, 307
Beattie, Dr, 241
„ Elizabeth, 37
„ Mr, 207
„ of Milleighs, 158
„ „ „ Richard, 151
„ „ Richard, 156, 157, 158
Beatties, 62, 79, 80, 87, 91, 205
Beauclerk, Frederick Amellus, 300
„ Lord Frederick, 300
Beaufort, Duke of, 298
Becker, Anna, 41
Beddoe, John, 303

INDEX

Beddoe, Mary, 303
Bedford, W., 253
Beirne, Caroline, 333
  „   Rev. A. O., 333
Belcher, Elizabeth, 337
  „   Gabriel, 337
Bell, Andrew, 55
  „   John, 55
  „   of Castlebank, John, 123
  „   of Gretna, Will, 73
  „   of Hardrigg, Robert, 145
  „   Roland, 55
  „   Sibella, 210
Bellamy, Mr, 271
Belloc, Madam, 252
  „   „ Parkes-, 252
Bells, 56, 62, 80, 85, 87, 91, 106, 111, 114, 116
Bell's MS., 63
Belsham, Thomas, 269
Bempdé, John Vanden, 164
  „   Vanden, 204, 205
Berkeley, Mr, 233
Berrington Family, 249
Bertoon, Robert, 51
Bertram, Elizabeth, 323
Betham-Phillips MS., 327
Bigg, Rev. F., 295
Billingsley, Mr, 216
Birch, George, 334
  „   Isabella, 334
  „   Wyrley, 271
Birchall, Rev. J., 321
Birmingham in 1778, 246
  „   „ 1800, 254
Birrell quoted, 88
  „   Robert, quoted, 102
Black Hole of Calcutta, 179
Blacket House, 64
Blackshaw, 74
Blackstock, Mary Elizabeth, 335
  „   Thomas, 335
Blackwell, Captain E., 305
Blair, Bryce, 148, 149, 168, 172, 204, 206
Blair, George, 151, 152, 157
Blantyre, Prior of, 85
Blayney, Lord, 336
Blencowe, Dr, 184
Bligh, Admiral, 24, 25
Blind Harry's *Life of Wallace*, 3
Boerhave, 190
Bonaparte, 272
Bonar of Rossie, William, 310
Border Papers quoted, 89
  „   Raids, 51, 52, 53
Borders, Defence of the, 71
  „   Johnston, Warden of the, 9
  „   Religion on the, 91
  „   Sir John de Johnstoun, Warden of the, 4
Borthwick, Bessie, 16, 308
  „   Tutor of, 16
Borthwicks, 100
Boston, Lord, 324
Boswell, James, 157, 205, 244

Boswell of Auchinleck, John, 157
Boswell's *Life of Samuel Johnson*, 229
Bothwell Bridge, Battle of, 146
  „   Earl of, 33
  „   Lord, 307
  „   of Liddesdale, 55
  „   Lord of Liddesdale, 71
Boulton, Matthew, 246
Bower, Archibald, *Lives of the Popes*, 194, 19
Bowes, Sir Robert, 56
Bowles, Phineas, 175
Boyd, Mr, 326
Boyden, James, 150
Boyle, 69
  „   Katherine, 69
Braddock, General, 196
Brandenburg, Elector of, 42, 163
Brechin, Bishop of, 138
Bree, Robert, 272
Bressey, Benjamin, 140
Brett, Ann, 333
Bridgeman, Sir Orlando, 165
Briggs, E. T., 323
Broad, Eliza, 306
Brodie, Captain David, 177
Brodie's Diary, 162
Brome, Catherine, 303
Broun, Gavin, 173
  „   James, 108
  „   of the Land, John, 76, 77, 99, 106, 108, 112, 119, 123
  „   Thomas, 108
Brouns of Land, 84
Brown, Agnes, 23, 305
  „   Daniel, 313
  „   Jane, 318
  „   Jean, 313
  „   of Lochhill, John, 112
  „   Samuel, 318
  „   Sir John, 142
  „   „ Patrick, 47
  „   Clayton, William, 306
Bruce, 133, 341
  „   Captain, 147
  „   King Robert, 62, 101
  „   Lord of Annandale, 50
  „   Marjory, 155
  „   Robert, (1583) 81
  „   William, 2, 3, 110
Bruce's Castle, 158
Bruces, The, 1, 4
Brus, Robert de, 1, 2
Bruyére, De la, 263
Buccleuch, Duke of, 196, 229, 244, 267
  „   Earl of, 114, 122, 124, 138
Buchanan, 52, 344
  „   George, 91, 123
  „   quoted, 5, 54, 93, 309
Buckingham, Duke of, 117
  „   Marquis of, 137
Buckley, Mrs, 297
Buller, Sir F., 233
Burdett, Sir Francis, 269

INDEX

Burges, John H., 330
Burghley, Lord, 83
Burke, Edmund, 238
Burke's *Family Romance*, 182
Burnet, Bishop, 130, 139, 140, 162, 168
   "   "   quoted, 150
   "   Gilbert, Bishop of Salisbury, 33, 127
   "   Mrs, 127
   "   Robert, 33
Burney, Mr, 233
   "   Susan, 331
Burns, Robert, 24, 243, 322
   "   "   quoted, 177
Bushby, John, 218, 225, 244
   "   Mr, 214
   "   Thomas, 218
Bute, Lord, 181, 201
   "   Marquis of, 68, 114
Butler, Bishop, 280, 286
   "   H., 323
   "   Johnstones, 323
Buxton, Priscilla Fowell, 324
   "   Sir Robert, 298
   "   Sir Thomas Fowell, 324
Byrne, of Elsieshields, John William, 32
   "   "   Theodore Edgar Dickson, 32
   "   Theodore Edgar Dickson, 33
   "   William, 32

Calcraft, John, 200
Caldecott, Mrs, 255
Caldecotts, 257
Calpole, 74
Cambridge, Duke of, 316
Camden quoted, 2, 91
Camden's *Britannia*, 130
Cameron, Charles, 224
   "   Dr, 190, 191
   "   Richard, 23, 305
   "   "   Covenanter, 23
Campbell, Captain James, 344
   "   Elizabeth, 44
   "   "   Lilias, 346
   "   Lord William, 320
   "   Miss, 330
   "   Mr, 307
   "   Sheriff Duncan, 346
   "   the poet, 287
   "   William, 244
Camperdown, Battle of, 272
Cannon, Jean, 33, 318
Canute, King, 254
Carey, Henry, 277
   "   Mr, 262
Cargill, Donald, 140
Carhampton, Lady, 248, 252
Carlaverock, 50
   "   Castle, 59, 171
Carless, Mr, 252
Carleton, Sir Thomas, 60, 61
Carlile, 4, 8, 69, 74, 116, 125, 141, 171
   "   Adam, 145, 148, 149, 158, 210

Carlile, Agnes, 124, 149
   "   Alexander, 138
   "   Alice, 169
   "   *Arms*, 155
   "   Dame Elizabeth, 106
   "   David, 154
   "   Elizabeth, 133, 138, 158
   "   Isobelle, 149, 152, 155, 156, 158
   "   James, 148, 150, 152, 158
   "   John, 18, 49, 149
   "   Lancelot, 136
   "   Lord, 2, 18, 19, 46, 47, 52, 66, 78, 155
   "   "   Michael, 34, 63
   "   "   William, 18
   "   Mary, 265
   "   Master of, 72, 93
   "   of Annan, 155
   "   of Boytash, John, 95
   "   of Bridekirk, 59, 61, 68, 120, 149, 155, 172, 173
   "   "   William, 210, 211
   "   of Limekilns, 155
   "   "   John, 157
   "   of Murraythwaite, 155
   "   of Ruthwell, 155
   "   of Soupilbank, 78
   "   of Souplebank, 155
   "   of Torthorald, 155
   "   "   William, 5
   "   Rev. A., 109
   "   Robert, 148, 154
   "   Thomas, 158, 169, 170
   "   William, 47, 154, 170
   "   "   Corrie, 225
Carliles, 2, 8, 22, 53, 87, 110, 111, 118, 137, 154
   "   Note to the, 155
   "   of Bridekirk, 85
Carlisle, Lord, 178
Carlyle of Inveresk quoted, 129
   "   quoted, 129
   "   Thomas, 277
Carmichael, 95, 266
   "   James, 22
   "   John, 51, 84, 272
   "   Murder of, 80
   "   murdered, 88, 89
   "   of Redmyre, Willie, 82
   "   Robert, 156
   "   Sara, 99
   "   Sir John, 19, 82, 85, 111, 163
Carmichaels, 100
Carnsalloch, Lady, 104
Caroline, Queen, 163, 194
Carriages in Scotland, 90
Carruthers, 4, 29, 53, 74, 84, 91, 146, 155
   "   Abraham, 100
   "   Betty, 321
   "   Christopher, 106
   "   Elspeth, 46
   "   George, 157, 321
   "   Janet, 32
   "   John, 10, 157
   "   Katherine, 40

INDEX

Carruthers, Marion, 76, 77
" Miss, 327
" of Dormont, Christopher, 95
" of Holmains, 52, 99, 110, 115, 214
" " George, 80
" " John, 107, 116, 244
" " Thomas, 8, 9
" of Holmends, 69, 73
" " John, 47, 62, 63, 68
" " Marion, 69
" of Mouswald, 63
" " Archibald, 46
" " John, 45, 48, 49
" " Symon, 7, 18, 52, 72
" of Orchardton, William, 66
" of Wormanbie, 110
" " Edward, 124
.. " James, 152, 244
" " Roger, 46, 54
" " Thomas, 134
" Robert, 157
" Sir James, 70
" " Symon, 46
" Symon, (1494) 54
Carstairs, Lord, 164
Carter, Mrs Barwell, 316
Carver, Captain, 252
" " Edward, 248, 249
" Colonel Henry, 249
" Family, 255
" Rev. J., 233
Casimir, Frederic, 221
Cassilis, Earl of, 91
Castlemilk, Laird of, 46, 52
Cates, E. W., 305
Cathcart, Lord, 322
Cathcarts, 100
Catherine, Empress, 316
Causer, Anna, 334
Cecil, 87, 88, 89, 111, 112
" Secretary, 65, 74
Chalmers, David, 308
" Margaret, 345
" quoted, 90
" William, 345
Chamberlain, Austen, 293
" Joseph, 257
Chamberlayne, Agnes, 297
" Thomas, 297
Chambers, Robert, quoted, 126, 156
Chambers's *Domestic Annals*, 154
Charles Edward, Prince, 170, 171, 172, 173, 182, 185, 303
" I., King, 90, 91, 114, 124, 126, 129, 130, 137, 138, 141, 145, 147, 151, 171, 213, 344
" II., King, 23, 110, 138, 139, 142, 143, 146, 254, 347
" VI., King, 5
" X., King, 288
" Miss, 316
Charlotte, Princess, 190, 234
" Queen, 172, 234

Charteris, 4, 29, 74, 80, 115, 141
" of Amisfield, 8, 52, 102, 124
" " Robert, 10
" " Sir John, 125
" Robert, 125
" Sir J., 124
" " John, 68, 123, 136
Chatelherault, Duke of, 20
Chatham, Lord, 194
Cherie, Stiven, 343
Chesterfield, Lord, 205
Chevy Chase, John de Johnstoun at, 5
Chisholm, 84
Cholera in Great Britain, 288
Cholmeley, James, H., 301
" Mary Elizabeth, 181, 298
" Sir Montague, Bart., 181, 298
Christie Marshall, 305
Claneboye, Viscount, 336
Clarence, Duke of, 281
Clark, Jean, 306
Clarke, Major General Sir William, 286
" Rev. Henry, 286
Clayton, Anna Maria, 304
" Florence Hope Brown-, 305
" S. W., 304
Cleghorn, Lewis, 226
Cleland, Captain William, 345
" Elizabeth, 345
Clement VII., Pope, 30
Clements, Captain, 198, 233
" Major, 224
Clerc, Daniel le, 185
Clercson, Andrew, 18
Clerk, 153
" Margaret, 17
Clifden, Viscount, 303
Clive, Lord, 179, 180, 181, 205, 237
Clout Skar, 67
Clutterbuck, Emma, 324
" Peter, 324
Clutton, John, 253
Coal Working, Early, 13, 15, 16
Cobren, Colonel, 94
Coburn, Mr, 184
Cochrane, Andrew James, 277, 278
" James, 311
Cockburn, Katherine, 327
" Laird of, 310
" Sir George, 132
Cockburns, 100
Cockpool, Old, 74
Code Frederick, 186
Coke of Holkham, 274
Colclough, Louisa, 176
Cole, Sir William, 327
Colles, Frances, 28
Collier, Vice-Admiral Henry, 321
Colville, Robert, 152
Comins, 1
Conheath, 118
Constable, Ethel, 303
" Henry Strickland, 303

INDEX

Cooke, Rev. Mr, 235
Cookes, Rev. Denham, 305
Coombe, Mr, 233
Cooper, Rev. C., 296
   ,,   Sir Astley, 285
Coote, Colonel, 199
Cope, Mr, 271
Copland, Jean, 321
   ,,   of Collistoun, William, 244
Corbett, Charles G., 332
   ,,   Provost, 160
Cork, Rev. Walter, 210
Corrie, 49, 69
   ,,   Adam de, 54
   ,,   Barony, 9, 53
   ,,   Elizabeth, 44
   ,,   Family, 54
   ,,   George, 9, 66, 67
   ,,   ,,   de, (1484) 54
   ,,   Herbert, 9
   ,,   Hugh, 170, 244
   ,,   Ivon, 51
   ,,   James, 54
   ,,   Janet, 36
   ,,   Johnstouns of, 95, 96
   ,,   Joseph, 157
   ,,   of Corrie, George, 47
   ,,   ,,   Robert, 9
   ,,   of Kelwood, Thomas, 9, 66, 67, 136
   ,,   of Newbie, Thomas, 56
   ,,   Sir Thomas, 96
   ,,   ,,   ,,   de, 53
   ,,   Thomas, 53, 55
Corrie Family, Records of the, 9, 96
Corries, 2, 3, 4, 8, 66, 106, 110, 118
Corry, Mrs, 274
Corsane, John, 84, 118, 125
Courage, Aileen Lucy, 321
   ,,   Edward, 321
Cousland, Johnstons in, 311
Covenant, The, 139, 141, 147
Covenanters, The, 27, 146, 153
Coventry, Earl, 234
   ,,   Sir W., 130
Cowquhate, Laird of, 63
Cox, David, 279
   ,,   W. Sands, 284
Crafts, Marjorie, 342
Craig, Ann, 346
   ,,   Dr John, 34, 130
   ,,   Elspeth, 33, 128
   ,,   John, 130
   ,,   Margaret, 34, 130
   ,,   Marion, 323
   ,,   of Riccarton, Sir Lucas, 96
   ,,   Robert, 34
   ,,   Sir James, 282
   ,,   ,,   Thomas, 34, 130
   ,,   Thomas, 33
Craik, Grizel, (1732) 26
   ,,   Janet, 25
   ,,   of Arbigland, William, 27, 149
Crampton, Sir Philip, 331

Cranchlay, Laird of, 50
Crane, 208, 224, 232
   ,,   Dr, 264
   ,,   Hannah, 191
   ,,   Henry, 191
   ,,   Sir Richard, 192
   ,,   Thomas, 194
Cranstoun, Alexander, 311
   ,,   Lord, 124
   ,,   Sir John, 311
   ,,   ,,   William, 12
Crauford, Margaret, 31
Craufurd, Emily, 336
   ,,   John, 49
   ,,   Stuart, 336
Crawford, Annabella, 260
   ,,   Mr, 238
   ,,   Ronald, 191
   ,,   Sir Ronald, 3
Craven, Earl of, 297
   ,,   Lady Maria Louisa Elizabeth Frederica, 297
Cresswell, Catherine, 255
   ,,   William, 255
Creswick, Mr, 279
Crichton, 4, 29, 69
   ,,   Adam Johnstoun, Provost of, 16
   ,,   Agnes, 99
   ,,   Christian, 99
   ,,   Dr, 225
   ,,   James, 66
   ,,   Lord, 51, 72, 82, 83, 99, 101, 114, 122, 127
   ,,   ,,   on killing Johnstouns, 102
   ,,   Maitland Makgill, 324
   ,,   Margaret, 67, 68
   ,,   Ninian, 66
   ,,   of Brunstoun, John, 13
   ,,   of Crawfordton, 139
   ,,   of Drylaw, 13
   ,,   of Kirkpatrick, Robert, 50
   ,,   of Raehills, Robert, 125
   ,,   of Sanquhar, 8, 9
   ,,   ,,   Lord, 50, 90
   ,,   ,,   Ninian, 56, 68
   ,,   Patrick, 99
   ,,   Robert, 51
   ,,   ,,   Bishop of Dunkeld, 108
   ,,   ,,   de, 47
   ,,   ,,   second Lord, 68
   ,,   Sir William, 7
Crichtons, 2, 97
   ,,   in Nithsdale, 50
   ,,   Maxwell attacks the, 50
Crimond, Lord, 33
Crombie, Mary, 315
   ,,   Rev. William, 315
Crompton, Mrs, 258
Cromwell, Oliver, 138, 139, 140, 142, 143, 146, 153, 168, 196, 230, 259
   ,,   Thomas, Earl of Essex, 331
Crookshanks, Captain John, 177
Crossle, John, 330

INDEX

Crossling, Emily, 301
    „   R. W., 301
Crowe, Matilda, 347
Crusade, a Johnestoun goes to the, 2
Cubie, Allen, 310
Cudworth, Anna, 130
    „   of Eastfield, Richard, 130
Cullen, Dr, 170, 190, 223, 227, 228
Culloden, Battle of, 171, 173, 182, 338
Cumberland, Duke of, 171, 173, 175, 177
    „   Earl of, 90
Cumyng, Janet, 26
Cunningham, Elizabeth, 25
    „   James, 326
    „   Janet, 134
    „   of Dargavell, John, 26
    „   Thomas, 99
Cunninghame, William, 66
Cursetter, Marjorie, 342
Curtis, Anna Delicia, 274
    „   Mary, 347
    „   Rev. Charles, 248, 252, 253, 257
    „   Sir William, 274
    „   Trustees, 275
Cust, Colonel Alan A. C., 297
    „   Elizabeth, 326
    „   Ernestine, 297
    „   Sir Edward, 326
Cuthbert, Catherine, 35

Dacre, Lord, 51, 52, 54, 55, 58
    „   „ attacks Borders, (1573-74) 52
    „   Sir Thomas, 65
Dakins, Rev. Dr, 273
Dalrymple, John, 18
Daly, James, 332
    „   Mary, 332
Dalziel, 147
    „   Laird of, 50
    „   Murder of William, Laird of, 51
    „   of Glennie, Sir John, 144
Dandridge, Mr, 233
Darien Scheme, 153
Darlington, Earl of, 273
Darnley, Henry, Lord, 13, 71, 72, 308
    „   Murder Trial, 130
Dartmouth, Earl of, 251, 285
    „   Lady, 272
    „   Lord, 271, 281
Darwin, Dr, 184
    „   „ Erasmus, 244, 246
David I., King, 1, 2
    „   II., King, 4, 5, 343
    „   Prince, 45
Davidson, Alexander, 313
Davies, Anna Maria, 334
    „   Benjamin, 238
    „   Mary, 269
    „   Stanley, 299
Day, Thomas, 246
Deaths from Starvation, 148
Debateable Land, The, 50, 55, 90
Dee, Charlotte, 178

Dee, Miss, 241, 242
Denellourt, Sebastian, 16
Derwent, Lord, 154, 205, 301, 302
Derwentwater, Lord, 160
Devereux, Charlotte, 333
Dewar, George, 311
    „   James, 300
Dewar's, Mrs, *History*, 23
Dick, Mary, 346
    „   Sir William, 143
Dickson, Admiral J. B., 299
    „   Edythe Grace, 335
    „   John, 32
    „   „ Reynolds, 335
    „   Mr, 219
Dicksons, 114
Dictionary of National Biography quoted, 128
Dillon, Sarah Elizabeth, 132
    „   Sir John, Bart., 132
Dirleton, Earl of, 32
Dixon, Mr, 272
D'Oberkirch, Madame, 230
Dobie, Janet, 323
Doherty, Chief Justice, 331
Donaldson, Mr, 217
Donnelly, John Arthur, 331
    „   Margaret, 331
Dornock, 116
    „   Johnstoun Priests at, 93
Douai College, 108
    „   „ Jonathas Johnstoun at, 16
Douglas, 17, 19, 20, 29, 51, 58, 66, 115, 128
    „   Anne Ramsay, 346
    „   Archibald, 313
    „   „ Earl of Angus, 10
    „   Barbara, 123
    „   Captain Alexander, 37
    „   Colonel James, 147
    „   „ William, 154
    „   David, 7, 69, 346
    „   „ seventh Earl of Angus, 19
    „   Earl of, 5, 6
    „   Erskine, 170
    „   Francis, 170, 307
    „   General, 173
    „   Hew, 311
    „   „ Murder of, 97
    „   James, 34, 155, 170, 171, 172, 344
    „   Janet, 118
    „   John, 307, 333
    „   Katherine, 30
    „   Lady, 138
    „   „ Henrietta, 143
    „   „ Jane, 154, 173
    „   „ Margaret, 143
    „   Lord James, 7
    „   Margaret, 49, 346
    „   Marquis of, 91, 153
    „   Mary, 97
    „   Miss, 212
    „   Murder of Earls of, 7
    „   Nicola, 70, 76, 96
    „   of Angus, 91, 94, 95

Douglas of Bonjedward, 49
„ of Cassogill, Robert, 75
„ of Corhead, George, 40
„ „ Margaret, 13
„ of Dornock, 139
„ „ Archibald, 24
„ „ James, 154
„ „ John, 156
„ of Drumlanrig, 59, 61, 70, 72, 73, 74, 75, 76, 80, 83, 84, 85, 87, 91, 99, 111, 119, 124, 155
„ „ Sir James, 81, 102
„ „ „ William, 50, 100
.. „ William, 47
„ of Hawthornden, 99
„ of Kelhead, 139, 143, 153
„ „ Sir John, Bart., 210
„ „ „ „ 170
„ „ „ William, 97, 154
„ of Longniddry, Hew, 307
„ of Morton, 139
„ of Musselburgh, Robert, 311
„ of Spott, Jean, 15
„ of Tofts, Archibald, 14
„ of Torthorald, 119, 135
„ „ Sir J., 80
.. „ James, 110, 116
„ Pennant, Hon. Archibald, 303
„ „ Rachael, 303
„ Rebellion of, 7, 8, 9, 18
„ Robert, 155
„ Sara, 37
„ Sir George, 56
„ „ John, 173, 211, 219
„ „ William, 170
„ William, 149
Douglases, Johnstone, 36
Draffan, Siege of, 20
Drake, Governor, 180
Drinking Competition, 24
Drumlanrig, Lord, 195, 196
„ Viscount, 136
Drummond, Dr Colin, 185
„ Sir William, 139
Dryfe Sands, Battle of, 19, 21, 30, 33, 35, 42, 49, 83, 85, 88, 93, 96, 98, 101, 102, 104, 321, 344
Dudley, Viscount, 244
Duff, Mary Margaret, 300
„ Thomas, 300
Dugdale, 131
Dugdale's *Warwickshire*, 130
Dumbarton, Earl of, 162
Dumfries, 78
„ Burghs, Johnstoun M.P. for, 32
„ Earl of, 114
„ Johnstoun Provost of, 154
„ Raid of, 94
„ William Johnstoun Commissioner of Supply for, (1685) 37
Dunbar, Battle of, 142
„ Earl of, 48, 55, 112, 117
„ George, Earl of, 10

Dunbar, Hew, 101, 119
„ Janet, wife of Adam Johnstoun, 10
„ Lady Janet, 45
„ Patrick, Earl of, 3
„ „ of, 312
Dunboyne, Lord, 323
Duncan, John, 312
„ of Cousland, Edward, 14
Dundas, Elizabeth, 14, 311
„ Henry, 239
Dundee, Viscount, 152
Dundonald, Earl of, 277, 278
Dundrennan, 116
„ Abbey, 116
„ Abbot of, 72
„ Barony of, 112
Dunkeld, Bishop of, 108
„ Lord, 133
Dunn, Agnes Warren, 347
Dunster, Mr, 233
Dunwedy, Thomas, 46
Dunwiddie, Laird of, 52
Dupont, Eliza, 283
„ Madame, 283
Dyndum, Thomas, 45

Earle, Caroline, 305
„ Sir Hardman, Bart., 305
Eccleston, General Joseph, 338
Edgar Atheling, 1
„ George, 25
„ of Bowhous, 101
„ of Kirkblan, 101
„ Robert, 32
„ Theodore, (1738) 32
Edgeworth, Cecilia, 335
„ Richard Lovell, 246
Edinburgh, Board of Students in, 169
„ James Johnstoun, Bishop of, 15
„ Johnstons in, 99, 313, 314
Edmonstone, 23
Edward I., King, 2, 3, 7, 232
„ III., King, 249, 255
„ VI., King, 61, 63, 109
„ Prince, 234
Edwards, Hugh, 304
„ Jane, 304
Eginton, Francis, 271
„ of Handsworth, 257
Elibank, Alexander, fourth Lord, 175, 176
„ Lord, 203
Eliot, 68
„ of Eckleton, William, 158
Eliots, 83, 84, 123
Elliot of Arkleton, William, 244
Ellis, Elizabeth, 305
Elizabeth, Princess, 234
„ Queen, 73, 74, 86, 87, 88, 126, 127, 193, 255, 308, 309
Elphinston, Mary, 318
Elphinstone, Johnstouns of, 12, 307
„ Sir Alexander, 307
„ Tower, 307

INDEX

Elsieshields, Johnstouns of, 29, 33
Empson, Rev. A., 296
England, Food in, 189
  ,,   in Eighteenth Century, 187
  ,,   Johnstouns get "safe conducts" to, (1485) 5
Episcopacy abolished, 190
  ,,   in Scotland, 110
  ,,   restored, 140
Episcopal Church disestablished, 151
Erroll, Earl of, 5
Erskine, Mr, 256
Essex, Thomas, Earl of, 331
Estcourt, Rev. Edmund, 297
Evans, Catherine, 334
  ,,   Jane Waring, 334
  ,,   Miss, 338
  ,,   Thomas Kelly, 334
Ewart, Jean, 338
  ,,   John, 321
Eykyn, Ellen, 33
Eyre, Chief Baron, 252

Faget, M., 185
Fairholm, John, 143
  ,,   of Craigiehall, John, 129
  ,,   Sophia, 143, 164
Falconer, Lord, 247
Falkirk, Battle of, 160
Famine in Scotland, 148
Fareis, 110, 335
  ,,   Bessie, 33, 133
  ,,   George, 133
  ,,   Gilbert, 133
  ,,   John, 133, 135
  ,,   of Dalfibble, James, 33
  ,,   of Mylnfield, Robert, 124
  ,,   Robert, 116, 133
Farquhar, Sir Walter, 281
Fawcett, Rev. Mr, 192
Ferguson, Rev. David, 342
  ,,   Sarah Sophia, 342
Fergusson, 100
  ,,   Agnes, 146
  ,,   Captain, 161
  ,,   Dr, 197
  ,,   Matthew, 158
  ,,   of Craigdarroch, 24, 50, 139
  ,,   ,,   Alexander, 170, 244
  ,,   of Halhill, 145
  ,,   ,,   Robert, 136
  ,,   of the Isle, Alexander, 146
  ,,   Robert, 146, 157
  ,,   Thomas, 146
Ferrein, M., 185
Fife, Duke of, 182
  ,,   Johnstons in, 100, 324
Finlay, Dr, 211, 218
Finlayson, Michael, 17
  ,,   Walter, 101
Fitz Clarences, 182
Fleming, 100
  ,,   Elinor, 330

Fleming, Lord, 74
  ,,   ,,   Michael, 41
  ,,   Mr, Q.C., 53
Fletcher of Salton, 189
  ,,   ,,   quoted, 161
Flodden, Battle of, 51, 53, 57, 343
Flogging, 156
Foley, Lord, 244
  ,,   Mr, 235
Folsome, Mr, 338
Forbes, Christian, 343
  ,,   Lord, 223
  ,,   William, seventh Lord, 343
Forney, General Peter, 338
  ,,   Nancy, 338
Forsyth, Janet, 24
Foster, Mrs, 205
Fothergill, Dr, 224
Fotheringay Castle, 81
Foulis, 217
  ,,   David, 86
Foulkes, Catherine, 326
  ,,   William Cadwallader, 326
Fownes, Rev., 238
Fox, Charles James, 250, 251
  ,,   F., 295
  ,,   Family, 271
  ,,   Mr, 320
Francis II., King, 31
Fraser, Sir William, 53, 343
  ,,   ,,   ,,   quoted, 4
Fraser's *Annandale Book*, 22
Frederick of Prussia, King, 201
  ,,   Prince, 234
French of Frenchland, 68
  ,,   ,,   Robert, 95
Fulford Hall, Johnstones of, 295
Fuller, Mr, 224
Funerals, 226

Gage, Miss, 338
Gairdner, Elizabeth, 342
  ,,   General, 342
Galliard, The, 97
Galloway, Bishop of, 108
  ,,   Earls of, 81
  ,,   James, 72, 133
  ,,   John, 101, 112, 123, 133, 134
  ,,   Lordship of, 7, 8
  ,,   Patrick, 133
Galloways, 135
Galton, Miss, 229
  ,,   Samuel, 246
  ,,   Tertius, 274
Garviach, James de, 343
Gask, Andrew of, 45
Gasks, 85
Gates, Eliza, 44
Gath, Mr, 219
Geddes, John, 123
  ,,   Sir W. D., 344
Gentleman, Mr, 237
George I., King, 159, 163

366   INDEX

George II., King, 129, 167, 171, 201, 302
  „   III., King, 129, 172, 173, 201, 203, 217, 234, 254, 260, 281, 287, 325
  „   IV., King, 161, 281, 331, 347
Germain, Lord George, 178
Germany, Johnstons in, 42
Gibbons, Sarah, 271
Gibson, John, 116
Gibsons, 71
Gilby, William, 272
Gilchrist, Dr, 197, 206
  „   Mrs, 216
Gilder, Miss, 304
Giles, Mr, 338
Gill, Catherine, 329
  „   Rev. John, 329
Gillespie, William, 124
Gillisbe, Laird of, 63
Gittens, Mr, 238
Gladsmuir, Battle of, 172
Gladstone, W. E., 277
Glasslough, Battle of, 335
Gleadowe, William, 302
Glencairn, Earl of, 85
  „   Lord, 72
Glencoe, Massacre of, 162
Glendynings, 91
Glenegiis (Gleneaglis), Lady, 310
Glenorchy, Earl of, 198
Gloucester, Duke of, 190
Goad, Horace Boileau, 295
Goding, Laura Margaret, 316
Goldie, Archibald, 244
  „   Thomas, 170, 244
Goldsmith, Oliver, 184
Gomer, Frederick, 299
Goodfellow, Prudence, 333
  „   William, 333
Goodinge, 163
  „   Dr, 233
Gordon, 29, 84
  „   Anna, 108
  „   Dr, 201
  „   Elizabeth, 300
  „   James, 318, 328
  „   Janet, 318
  „   John, 300
  „   Lord George, 230
  „   Major Robert, 199
  „   Miss, 344
  „   of Cluny, Charlotte, 274
  „   of Corhead, 66
  „   of Craig, Francis, 300
  „   „   James, 181
  „   „   Patrick, 300
  „   of Crauchton, 66
  „   of Lochinvar, 39, 55, 59, 60, 72, 73, 85, 120, 121, 124
  „   „   Robert, 87, 90
  „   „   Sir Robert, 160
  „   Riots, 230
  „   Sir Adam, 300
  „   William, 328

Gordons, 2, 85
Goring, Cecilia Augusta, 341
  „   Forster, 341
Gott, Mr, 207
Gough, Sir Richard, 247
Gould, George, 338
Gourlay, Agnes, 311
Gowan, Donald, 26
Gowrie, Earl of, 310
  „   Plot, 99
  „   William, Earl of, 14
Grafton, Mr, 272
Graham, 56, 69, 153
  „   Agnes, 136, 137, 138, 145, 146, 157, 244
  „   Arthur, 65, 73, 84, 124, 137
  „   Colonel, 164
  „   David, 136
  „   Elizabeth, 20
  „   Fergus, 61, 62, 73, 122
  „   George, 124
  „   James, 124
  „   John, 23
  „   Mr, 274
  „   Ninian, 60, 72
  „   of Airth, 168
  „   of Blaatwood, 123, 244
  „   „   Fergus, 124, 133, 136
  „   „   Simon, 135, 137
  „   „   William, 99, 149
  „   of Claverhouse, 146, 147, 150, 152, 153, 328, 330
  „   of Cluden, 137
  „   of Dryff, John, 95
  „   of Fintry, 243
  „   of Inglistoune, 147
  „   of Mossknowe, Fergus, 160
  „   of Mote, 65
  „   of Netherby, 65, 145
  „   „   Ritchie, 137
  „   of Redkirk, George, 112
  „   of the Moat, Arthur, 77
  „   „   William, 122
  „   of Thornik, 63
  „   „   Robert, 47
  „   Rev. Francis, 336
  „   Richard, 72, 128
  „   Richie, 62, 65
  „   Robert, 51, 60, 119, 135, 137, 145, 177
  „   Sir John the, 3
  „   „   Richard, 137, 138
  „   Walter, 122
  „   William, 65, 136
Grahame, *Social Life of Scotland*, 161, 167
Grahams, 83, 85, 90, 91, 110, 114, 118, 138, 327
  „   English, 70
  „   of Esk, 89
  „   of Thornik, 60
Grain, Price of, fixed, 148
Granby, Marquis of, 201
Grant, Colonel, 178
Grantley, Fletcher, third Lord, 301
Gratton, Minnie Sarah, 304

INDEX

Graves, John Samuel, 331
  ,, Mary Constance, 331
Gray, Archibald, 334
  ,, Margaret, 314
  ,,   ,, Ross, 334
  ,, Rev. John Hamilton, 300
  ,, Robert, 314
  ,, William, 313
Greathed Family, 269
Green, Dr, quoted, 231
  ,, Valentine, 231
  ,, William, 139
Greene, Elizabeth, 282
Greg, Captain, 299
Gregg, Rev. R. S., 132
Gregory, Dr, 217, 218, 219, 223, 227, 228, 229
  ,,   ,, James, 224
Gretna, 78
  ,, Destination of, 67
  ,, Green, 48, 116
  ,,   ,, Marriages, 119
  ,, Kirk, 88
  ,, Tower, 45
Grey, Janet, 111
  ,, Lord, 251
Gribton, Lady, 106, 107, 135
Grierson, 74, 83, 330
  ,, James (Lag), 148
  ,, Marion, 32
  ,, of Lag, 66, 84, 87, 124, 125, 139, 152
  ,,   ,, Sir Robert, 25, 27, 146
  ,, Sir R., 243
  ,,   ,, William, 123, 124
Grimsditch, John, 139
Grimwood, Mr, 292
Guilliet, M., 288
Gulland, Dr George Lovell, 313
  ,, George, 313
  ,, John W., M.P., 313
Gulliver, Agnes, 304
  ,, Thomas, 304
Gunning, Miss, 197
Gunnis, Joanna, 333
Gunpowder Plot, 110
Gustavus Adolphus, King of Sweden, 34, 128

Hackbuts, Wearing of, 120, 121
Hacket, 100
Hackness Hall, Johnstones of, 301
Hadden, George, 345
  ,, Mary, 345
Haddington, Lands in, belong to Johnestoun, 3
Haddon Rig, Battle at, 56, 57
Hair, James, 210
  ,, Jeannie, 210
  ,, John, 157
  ,, William, 158
Hairs, 135, 205
Halcro, Margaret, 342
Haldin, Elizabeth, 311, 312
  ,, George, 310, 311
Hale, Miss, 261
  ,, Sarah, 255

Hale, Sir Matthew, 255
Haleday, 45
Halford, Sir Henry, 281, 286
Haliday of Brumehills, 39
Halidays, 135
Hall, Isabel, 339
Hall-Dare, Olivia Frances, 331
Haller, Baron, 221
  ,, Mr, 219
Halliday, 3, 152
  ,, Andrew, 18
  ,, John, 48, 159, 329
Hallidays, 4, 71
Halyburton, Ellen, 10
Hamieson, Robert, 313
Hamilton, 87
  ,, Anna, 129
  ,, Augusta Sophia, 331
  ,, Claud, 309
  ,, ,, and John, 20
  ,, Duchess of, 197
  ,, Duke of, 163, 195
  ,, Esther Letitia, 324
  ,, George, 331
  ,, Hugh, 331
  ,, James, 22, 74
  ,, Lord, 19, 46, 82, 85, 87
  ,, Margaret, 69, 132, 143, 336
  ,, ,, (Angus), 19
  ,, Marjory, 96
  ,, Mary, 132
  ,, of Abbotstown, James, 336
  ,, of Bathgate, Robert, 311
  ,, of Eldershaw, William, 37
  ,, of Ellershaw, Helen, 96
  ,, of Preston, Sir John, 14
  ,, of Tyrella, 336
  ,, Patrick, 311
  ,, Rev. George, 331
  ,, Robert, 311
  ,, Sir James, 75, 80, 102, 129
  ,, ,, Robert, 16
  ,, ,, Thomas, 102
  ,, ,, William, Bart., 324
  ,, Susanna, 14, 311
  ,, Thomas, 30
Hamiltons, 21
Hampton of Westwood, Lord, 232
Handel, 331
Handiside, John, 313
  ,, Margaret, 313
Hankey, Audrey, 305
  ,, Ernest Alers-, 305
Hanna, William, 147
Hardie, George, 225
  ,, Mrs, 212
  ,, Provost, 211
Hare, David, 294
  ,, Sir Lancelot, 293
Hargreaves, Gertrude, 296
Harknes, Murder of John, 43
Harkness, William, 152
Harris, Admiral Sir Robert, 295

Harris, Catherine Florence May, 295
Harrison, Agnes, 298
,, Frances, 303
,, James, 303
,, Joseph, 298
,, Rev. Bruce, 296
Harrogate, Dr Thomas Johnstone in, 37
Hartfell, Earl of, 15, 138, 143, 153
,, James, Earl of, 141, 142, 158
,, William, Earl of, 150
,, Lady, 140
Hastings, Warren, 238
Hawkins, John, 299
,, Mary Anne, 299
,, Sir Christopher, 299
Hawksworth, Amelia, 302
,, Rev. R., 302
Hay, Georgina Barbara, 333, 340
,, John, 64
,, Lord, 124
,, Margaret, 343
,, of Yester, Lord, 42
,, Sir John, 101, 124, 125, 142
,, ,, ,, Bart., 333, 340
Heberden, Dr, 235
Hector, Edmund, 229
,, Mr, 270
Henderson of Broadholm, John, 210
,, of Castlemains, John, 173
,, R., 244
Hendersons, 100
Henry I., King, 1
,, II., King of France, 64
,, III., King of France, 74
,, IV., King of France, 186
,, VIII., King, 52, 54, 55, 56, 57, 58, 59, 61, 63, 64, 65, 91, 130, 262
,, Dr, 216, 217, 218
,, Patrick, 338
,, Rev. Robert, 168
Hepburn, Sir Adam, 139
,, Thomas, 139
Hereis, Agnes, 70
,, Janet, 45
,, Lord, 71, 72, 73, 74, 75, 76, 77, 78, 81, 82, 84, 85, 87, 88, 115, 125
,, Mungo, 30
,, of Mabie, Robert, 77
,, ,, ,, William, 107
,, Robert, 101, 125
Heriot, 116
,, George, 101, 125, 308
Herreis, 29
Herries, 3
,, John, 5
,, Lord, 22, 30, 32, 89, 95, 98, 102, 103
,, ,, John, 59
,, of Hoddam, Lord, 9
,, of Terregles, David, 47
,, ,, ,, Lord, 51
,, Robert, 25
,, Sir Robert, 244
Hertford, Lord, 205, 269

Hertford, Marquis of, 236, 244, 281, 294, 335
Hesketh, John, 271
,, Lucy, 271
,, Sir Thomas, 271
Hewit, Cecile, 173
Heydinger, Mr, 224
Heywood-Jones, Richard, 306
Highland Soldiers, Rebellion of, 176
Hill, Barbara, 154
,, George Bernard, 299
,, Mr, 229
,, Noel, 237
,, Richard, 132
,, Rowland, 284
,, Thomas Wright, 284
Hills, 119
Hobson, Elizabeth, 128
,, of Ufflete, Henry, 128
Hoddam Castle, 73
,, Duke of, 97
Hog, Amabel or Agnes, 12
Hoggan, James, 168
,, Mr, 171, 200, 207
Hogle, Anna, 337
Holden Family, 255
,, Letitia, 254
,, of Erdington Hall, Thomas, 256
,, W., 253
Holinshed quoted, 8, 57, 62, 73
Holker, Sir John, 67
Holmes, Thomas Knox, 304
Holyrood House, Commendator of, 89
Holywood, Bryce Johnstoun, Minister at, 37
,, Commendator of, 110
Home, 55
,, Alexander, 13
,, Countess of, 129
,, Earl of, 56, 127
,, George, 15
,, ,, Lord, 13
,, Henry, 195
,, Lord, 72, 87, 129
,, of Godscroft, David, 16, 311
,, of Graden, George, 140
,, of Wedderburn, 17, 20
,, ,, ,, Sir David, 15
,, Sir George, 112, 127, 310
,, William, 112, 129
Homes, 17, 19
Hood, Viscount, 285
Hook, Dean, 281
,, ,, Walter Farquhar, 286
,, Dr, 277
,, Mrs, 286
,, Prebendary Walter, 286
,, Rev. Walter F., 296
Hooke, Jane Elizabeth Matilda, 269
Hooper, Lilian, 316
,, Miss, 338
Hope, Dr, 267
,, John, 164
,, Lady Georgiana, 277
,, Lord, 164

Hope, Margaret, 26
Hopetoun, Earl of, 164, 195, 196, 204
„ Lady, 164, 204
„ Lord, 98, 188, 198, 214
„ third Earl of, 205, 273, 277
Hopkirk, Agnes, 14
„ James, 14
Horry Family, 338
Houston, Margaret, 330
Howard, Charles, 139
„ Lieutenant-General, 175
„ R., 27
„ *State of Prisons*, 231
Howat, Patrick, 112
„ Rev. Patrick, 133, 134
Howie, Mr, 37, 151, 167
Hudson, Anne, 332
„ Charles, 332
Huger, Francis, 338
Humboldt, 314
Hume, Colonel, 240
„ quoted, 155
„ Sir Gustavus, 335
„ „ Patrick, 129
„ Sophia, 129
Humphrey, Mary, 333
Humphreys, Mary, 28
Humrickhouse Family, 336
Hunsdon, 89
Hunter, Agnes, 14, 312
„ Alexander, 99
„ Arundells, 99
„ Dr A., 244
„ „ James, 244
„ Janet, 99, 101
„ John, 184, 244
„ of Ballagan, Duncan, 100
„ Thomas, 309
Huntingdon, Lady, 205, 241
Huntly, Earl of, 34, 56
Hurd, Dr, 232, 234, 235
Hutton, Agnes, 304
„ Catherine, 249
„ „ *Reminiscences of a Gentlewoman*, 259
„ Rev. George, 304
Hyde, Edward, 333

Ilchester, Lord, 287
Illegitimate Johnstouns, 67
Inglis, Captain, 147
„ Jean, 100
„ Margaret, 345
„ Patrick, 151, 161
„ Rev. Patrick, 140, 156, 157
Ingram, Mr, 233
„ Richard, 244
Irby, Winifred, 324
Ireland, Johnstouns in, 27
Irvine of Robgill, Cuthbert, 63
Irvines and Irvings, 56
Irving, 29, 106
„ Christie, 124

Irving, Christine, 113, 116
„ Christopher, 36, 68, 78, 90, 111, 113, 133, 327
„ David, 136
„ de Luce, John, 95
„ Edward, 111
„ „ (Bonshaw), 72
„ Elizabeth, 344
„ Gavin, 47
„ George, 119
„ Jeanne, 136
„ Jeffrey, 112, 133
„ John, 77, 133, 135, 150, 152, 157, 158, 159, 209, 214, 217, 219
„ Joseph, 157
„ Miss, 332
„ Mrs, 135
„ of Bonshaw, 48, 51, 56, 65, 68, 85, 88
„ „ Christie, 73
„ „ Edward, 79, 80, 89
„ „ Jeffrey, 111, 122
„ „ John, 36
„ „ Robert, 97
„ „ William, 97, 98, 119
„ of Cove, James, 98
„ of Graitney, Richard, 90
„ of Gretna Hill, 31
„ of Gribton, James, 173, 244
„ „ William, 173
„ of Mylneflat, William, 111
„ of Mylnfield, William, 111
„ of Robgill, 56
„ of Wysbie, Edward, 173
„ Rev. Edward, 277
„ Richard, 68, 118
„ Robert, 210
„ „ Duke of Hoddam, 97
„ William, 47, 99, 159
Irvings, 60, 62, 83, 84, 87, 91, 100, 114, 124, 137, 138, 205
„ of Bonshaw, 110

Jacobites, 340
Jaffray, Rev. Mr, 201
Jaksone, John, 127
James I., King, 7, 10, 312
„ II., King, 6, 7
„ III., King, 8, 9, 10
„ IV., King, 10, 11, 57, 71, 94
„ V., King, 19, 39, 52, 56, 57, 58, 60, 67, 90, 91
„ „ goes to the Borders, 55
„ VI., King, 2, 48, 72, 81, 82, 85, 86, 87, 88, 89, 90, 91, 98, 101, 108, 109, 110, 112, 113, 114, 127, 130, 138, 171, 254, 309, 344
„ „ visits Scotland, 120
„ VII., King, 131, 147, 149, 151, 152, 153, 162, 163, 244, 330, 334
„ VIII. (?), King, 160
Jameson, Isabella Eccles, 335
„ Capt. John, 335
Janvils, 2

INDEX

Jardine, 1, 2, 29, 52, 80
„ Ann, 326
„ James, 102
„ Jane, 26
„ Nicholas, 107
„ of Apilgirth, 30, 39, 97, 98
„ „ John, 25, 63
„ „ William, 45, 46, 244
„ Sir Alexander, 52
„ Thomas, 102
„ William, 46
Jardines, 3, 62, 74, 91, 100
Jeanville, Geoffrey de, 2
„ Seigneur de, 2
Jelikovski, Vera, 333
Jenkins, Edward, 336
Jennings, Captain, 180
„ Rev. Philip, 305
Jervis, Mr, 271
Jerviswood, 164
Jesson, Miss, 229
John, Gilbert, son of, (1191) 3
Johnson, Dr Samuel, 176, 205, 222, 229, 230, 244, 270, 272
„ Rev. R. A., 246
„ W., 298

Johnston, Johnstone, Johnstoun, Jhonestoun, Johnestoun, Johnestoune, Johnnestoun, Johnnstoun, Jhonston, Johnstown, Jonestone, Jonestoune, Jonistun—
Adam, 135
„ of, (1464) 5
Aghadunvane, Robert, of, 334
Aghamulden, James, of, 335
Alderwood House, William, of, 322
Aldtoun, James, of, (1546) 69
Alexander, Author, 345
„ Painter, 326
ALVA—
Elizabeth, 181
James Raymond, of, 181
John, of, 178, 179, 180, 181, 199
Johnstones of, 298
America—
Emma O., in, 339
Gilbert, in, 338
Johnstons in, 337
Andrew, 54
„ Cochrane, 273
„ Rev., 315
Annan—
Abraham, Provost of, 101
Edward, Provost of, 113
John, M.D., in, 38
„ Provost of, (1745) 37
Johnston Builders in, 38
„ Provost of, 112, 145
Symon, Parson of, (1618) 118, 123, 124
William, in, (1729) 37
William Joseph, in, 38
Annandholme, Gavin, of, (1605) 42

Johnston, Johnstone, Johnstoun, etc.—
Archibald, (1521) 13
„ Merchant, 33
Arkilton, William, of, (1532) 66
Armagh—
Johnstons in, 329
William, in, 330
Arthur, 326
„ Poet, 344
Auchinleck, Patrick, in, (1576) 35
Auchinsbork, George, of, (1513) 51
Auchinskeoch, George, in, (1513) 35
Auchinstock—
James, in, (1576) 35
John, in, (1618) 35
William, in, (1576) 35
Auldgirth, Roger, in, (1561) 25
Ayill (Isle), John, of, (1483) 23
Ayr, Johnstons in, 326

Ballincrief, Ballincrieff, James, of, 311
Ballykilbeg, Johnstons of, 333
Ballywillwill—
William, of, 27
„ M'Dowall, of, 330
Balmaghie, John, in, (1749) 27
Baltimore, Johnston in, 341
Balvaig, Thomas, of, 306
Barbara (Lady Gribton), 106, 107, 108
Bartycupen—
David, 51
John, in, 51
Bawnboy House, Robert Henry, of, 335
Beatok—
Adam, of, (1565) 69, 321
David, of, 321
Rachel, 321
Beech Hill, John, of, 37
BEIRHOLM, BEIRHOLME—
Andrew, 36, 127, 332
Archibald, of, 37
Charlotte, 37
Gavin, 127
Grizel, 37
James, of, 36, 37, (1608) 127
Janet, 37
John, (1621) 36
Marie, 37
Robert, 127
Thomas, 127
„ of, (1618) 36
William, (1685) 37
„ of, (1723) 37, (1704) 155, 157, (1729) 159
Belfast, Johnstons in, 335, 340
Beverley—
John, 132
Johnstons of, 336
Samuel, Rev., 132
William, Captain, of, 132
Birmingham—
Doctor, in, 259
Edward, in, 257, 258

Johnston, Johnstone, Johnstoun, etc.—
  Bishopstown, John, of, 345
  Blanshard, William Andrew, of, 341
  Boginjoss, John, in, 345
  Bolton, John, Dr, in, 37
  Bordeaux, Johnston in, 331
  Brackenside, Brakinside, Breckonside—
    James, of, 42, 43
    Thomas, of, (1438) 45
  Brakenhill, Thomas of, (1496) 29
  Brakenthwaite, Gilbert, de, of, 4
  Briggs, James, of, 32
  Brigholme—
    Robert, in, (1594) 84
    „ of, 85, 106, 111
  Brompton, U.S.A., Johnston of, 337
  Brooklyn, Johnston in, 341
  Brotis—
    David, of, (1511) 45, 46, 54, 60
    John, of, (1476) 45
  Bruce, 214
  Brume—
    Abraham, of, 101, 111
    John, 101
    Robert, 101
    „ of, 102
    Thomas, 101
    William, 101
    „ of, 134
  Brumehill—
    Bessie, 43
    David, (1553) 42, (1611) 43
    „ of, 99
    Grizel, 43
    Helen, 43
    James, (1553) 42
    „ in, (1574) 30
    John, 43
    Johnstouns in, 42
    William, (1553), 42, 43
  Bryce, Dr, (1805) 37

  Cairn Hill, Johnston of, 333
  California, Johnston in, 340
  Canada—
    Anne, in, 342
    Johnstons in, 341, 342
  Carlaverock—
    John, of, 312
    William, Rev., of, 315
  Carlisle, William, in, (1745) 27
  CARNSALLOCH—
    Alexander, 318, 319
    „ of, 318
    „ Robert Campbell, 320
    „ Sir, of, 318
    Archibald Francis Campbell, of, 320
    Francis, Major-General, 318
    Patrick, 318
    „ Francis Campbell, of, 320
    Peter, of, 244, 318

Johnston, Johnstone, Johnstoun, etc.—
  CARNSALLOCH—
    Robert, 318
    „ of, (1592) 104, 318
    Samuel, 318
    Thomas Henry, General, of, 320
  Carrickbreda, Johnstons of, 332
  Carterton, Gawyne, of, (1621) 42
  CASKIEBEN, Johnstons of, 343, 344, 345
  Cassila, 298
  Castle Robert, George, of, (1649) 25
  Castlehill—
    James, of, (1714) 23
    Thomas, in, (1714) 23
  Castlemilk—
    Alexander, 113, 128
    „ of, (1620) 96
    James, 113, 128
    „ of, (1493) 47
    John, 94, 113
    „ of, (1599) 35, (1620) 96, 113, 116, 130
    Johnston of, 34
    Thomas, 113, 128
    „ of, 122
  Catherine Letitia Wearden, 257
  Cavertholme, William, of, 53
  Chapelhill—
    James, in, 40
    „ of, 39, (1581) 41, (1606) 103
    Charles Vanden Bempdé, 244
  Chevalier, 98, 173, 174
  Chicago, Johnstons in, 340
  Christopher, 108, 116
    „ Dr, 340
  Clackleith—
    John, 322
    William, of, 322
  Clauchrie, Clochrie, Clouthrie—
    Alexander, of, (1678) 25
    Archibald, of, (1644) 25, 142
    George, 25, (1690) 26
    James, 25, 26
    John, (1594) 25
    „ of, (1673) 25, (1690) 26 (1633) 27
    Johnstons of, 25, 149
    Margaret, 26
    Thomas, 26
    „ of, 24, (1594) 25
    William, 27
  Clydesdale, Francis, in, 23, 305
  Co. Down, Johnstons in, 327, 329
  Coedfa, S. H. Nairne, of, 324
  Comlongan, John, in, 24
  Corehead, Corhead, Corheid —
    General, of, 323
    George Milligan, of, 244
    Gilbert, in, (1582) 41
    „ of, 22, (1563) 40, 42
    James, 321
    „ of, 97, 142, (1688) 147

Johnston, Johnstone, Johnstoun, etc.—
  Corehead, Corhead, Corheid—
    John, in, (1577) 40
    Robert, of, 42
    Sophia, 321
    Thomas, of, (1587) 40, (1584) 42, (1569) 76
    William, Dr, 323
      „ of, (1704) 155, 175, 321
  Corran, Joseph, of, 333
  CORRIE—
    Adam, of, 9, 53, (1536) 56, 57, 60, 67, (1578) 96
    George, 137
      „ of, (1585) 60, 95, (1581) 96, 119
      „ Parson of, (1581) 96
    James, of, 60, (1547) 95, 96
    John, 96
    Johnstouns of, 95, 96
    Thomas, Portioner of, (1620) 96
    Walter, of, 95, (1593) 96
    Watt, in, 96
  Corstorphine, Johnstons in, 346
  Cottis, James, of, 63
  Couran, Robert, of, 83
  Cousland—
    Edward, 14
    Johnstons in, 14, 311
    Thomas, 14
    William, 14
  Cowhill—
    Charles, Admiral, of, 25
    George, Major, 24
      „ of, (1789) 24, 244
    Johnstons of, 24, 25
    William, of, (1831), 25
  CRAIGABURN—
    Francis, 41
    George, 41
    Gilbert, 41
    James, 41
    John, 40, 41
    Symon, 40, 41
    Thomas, 41
      „ of, 39, (1581, 1587) 40, (1584) 42, 73, 75, (1569) 76, (1592) 81
    William, 41
  Craighous, John, of, (1704) 155
  Craufurd, Ann, in, 321
  Crawshalt, Thomas, of, 323
  Crichton, Adam, Provost of, 16, 308
  Croftheid, Croftheids—
    Adam, 71
    Arthur, 71
      „ of, 134
    Herbert, in, 71
    James, 71
      „ in, (1579) 78
    John, of, 80
  Croy, David, of, 325
  Cuddesdon, Rev. J. O., of, 325

Johnston, Johnstone, Johnstoun, etc.—
  Cummertrees—
    John, in, (1577) 78, 84
      „ of, 71, 77, 99
    Johnstoun of, 83
    Robert, in, (1577) 76
  Dalkeith—
    Andrew, in, 315
    John, in, 311
    Ninian, in, 311
  Dargavell, John, of, 26
  Daubate, David, of, (1476) 45
  David, (1597) 17, (1476) 45, 126, 128
    „ Captain, (1685) 27
    „ Rev., 325
  Denovan, John, of, 244
  District occupied by Clan, 78
  Donagh, David, in, 328
  Dornock, William, in, (1689) 119
  Douglas, Musician, 326
  Drumadown, James, in, 327
  Drumconnell, John, of, 330, 331, 334
  Drumgrey, James, of (1618) 35
  Dryfesdale, James, of, 36
  Dryfhead, James, of, (1581) 40
  Dublin, Johnston in, 341
  Duchrae—
    Robert, 27
    William, in, 27
  Dumfries—
    Francis, Baillie of, (1728) 23
    James, Burgess of, 30
    John, 149
      „ Baillie of, (1728) 23
    Provost of, 154
    Robert, Dean of, 33
      „ Provost of, 26
    Symon, 100
    William, Surgeon in, (1740) 24
  Duncan, A., Sir, Colonel, 346
  Dundee, Johnstons in, 339, 340
  Dunduff, William of, 25
  DUNSKELLIE—
    James, Sir, of, 22, (1594) 84, 87, 105, 106, (1605) 123
    „ Sir, of, Murder of, 104
  Dunwoodie, Johnston of, 34

  Eccles, Johnstons of, 316
  Edinburgh—
    Archibald, in, 33, 99, 100, 106, 127, 315, 316
    Beatrix, in, 33
    Cecile, in, 174
    David, in, 118, 136
    Gavin, in, 43
    George, in, (1655) 36
    Gilbert, in, 22
    James, in, 33, 34, 125, 127, 173, 315
    „ Bishop of, 15
    „ Burgess of, 39
    John, Commissary Clerk of, 16

INDEX 373

Johnston, Johnstone, Johnstoun, etc.—
  Edinburgh—
    John, Writer in, 76
    Margaret, in, 33
    Rachel, in, 33
    Robert, in, 34
    William, in, 34
  Edward, 157, 168, 169
    ,, Sir, Priest, (1577) 30, 93
    ,, Writer, Marriage Settlement of, 149
  Elizabeth, 133
  ELPHINSTONE, ELPHINSTOUN—
    Adam, 13, 308, 310
    ,, of, 10
    ,, Sir, of, (1507) 12, 312
    Agnes, 13
    ,, of, 10, 12, 13
    Alexander, 22
    Andrew, 312
    ,, of, (1526, 1549) 12, 16, 17, 59, 307, 308
    , of, his daughters, 13
    ,, of, his sons, 13
    Anna, 15
    Barbara, 16, 311
    Elizabeth, 15
    George, 312
    ,, de, (1463) 47
    ,, of, (1463) 12, 47
    Gilbert, 311, 312
    ,, of, 45, (1513) 51, 307
    ,, Sir, of, (1472) 10, (1501, 1513) 12
    Helen, 15
    James, 13, 14, 16, 17, 99, 308, 310
    ,, of, (1566, 1588) 13, 14, 17, (1565) 19, 309, 310, 311, 312
    ,, of, his sons, 14, 16
    ,, Right Hon., of, 14
    ,, Sir, Bart. of, 313
    ,, ,, third Bart. of, 15
    Janet, 13, 16
    Jean, 15, 310
    John, 13, 14, 16, 17, 307, 308, 310, 312
    ,, callit of, 17
    ,, of, (1581, 1599, 1607) 16, 17, 307, 308, 309
    ,, Sir, Bart. of, 313
    ,, ,, second Bart. of, 15
    Johnstoun of, 76, (1588) 81
    Johnstouns of, 12, 94
    Jonathas, of, (1581) 16
    Laird of, 73
    Margaret, 13, 15
    Marion, 310
    Mariot, 15
    Martha, 310, 311
    Mary, 15, 311
    Patrick, 14, 311
    ,, in, 312

Johnston, Johnstone, Johnstoun, etc.—
  ELPHINSTONE, ELPHINSTOUN—
    Patrick, of, 17, 310
    ,, of, his children, 15
    Rachel, 16
    Robert, 13, 14, 17, 99, 310, 311
    Samuel, of, 16
    ,, Sir, Bart. of, 311
    ,, ,, ,, of, his children, 14, 15
  ELSIESCHELLIS, ELSIESHIELDS—
    Adam, (1594) 30, 31, (1616) 32, 84
    ,, Tutor, of, 125
    Alexander, of, (1693-1702, 1738) 32
    Archibald, (1480) 29, (1577) 30, (1616, 1630) 32
    Edward, 111
    Gavin, of, 10, (1555, 1577) 30, (1707) 32, 36, (1723) 37, (1498) 46
    James, (1594) 30, (1616) 32, 34, 84, 97
    John, (1616) 32
    ,, of, (1536, 1574) 30, (1688) 32, (1565) 69, (1569) 76, 147
    Johnstouns of, 26, 29
    Marion, of, (1738) 32
    Nathaniel, of, 111
    Nicolas, in, 31
    Robert, 31, (1616) 32
    Symon, 97
    Wilkin, 30
    ,, of, 31, (1616) 32, 128
    William, (1594) 30, (1616) 32, 84
    ,, Murder of, 31, 32
    ,, of, (1594) 30, (1616) 32, 34, (1536) 56, 95
  Elspeth, 310
  Ernemynie, Symon, of, 60
  Erny, Richard, of, 329
  Esbie, Gavin, of, 18, (1485) 29, (1707) 32, (1514) 39
  Evandaill, Lord, of, 141

Fermanagh—
  Johnstons in, 329, 333
  Walter, Captain, in, 327
Fingland—
  Cuthbert, (1605) 42
  Gavin, 98
  Geordie, 98
  George, of, (1611) 98
  John, (1605) 42
  ,, of, (1585) 98
  Nicholas, (1605), 42
  Robert, 98
  Symon, 98
  Thomas, in, 98
  ,, of, (1605) 42, (1585) 44, (1581) 96
  William, 98
Flemingraw, Thomas, of, 116

Johnston, Johnstone, Johnstoun, etc.—
　Fort Johnston, George, of, 335
　Foulderis, Fouleduris, William, of, (1577) 30, (1513) 51
　Francis Buchanan, 325
　　,, Covenanter, 306
　Fulford Hall—
　　Edward, of, 298, 343
　　James, Sir, 292, 294, 295
　　Johnstones of, 295
　　Richard, Captain, 293, 294

G., Rev., 325
GALABANK—
　Adam, 159, 198, 199, 200, 203, 206
　Agnes, 159, 203
　　,, Death of, 206, 207
　　,, Mary, 286
　　,, ,, Clarke, 286
　Anna, 159, 208, 213
　　,, Delicia, 281, 286
　Arthur, 292
　Barbara, 148
　Catherine, 263, 272, 283
　Charles, 278, 287
　David, (1665) 145
　Edward, 148, 149, 150 (1697) 151, 159, 167, 168, 184, 185, 188, 191, 192, 193, 195, 196, 197, 198, 199, 200, 202, 203, 205, 206, 208, 210, 213, 218, 219, 223, 224, 225, 226, 227, 228, 229, 230, 232, 234, 235, 236, 237, 246, 247, 248, 249, 250, 251, 252, 253, 254, 255, 256, 260, 261, 262, 263, 265, 267, 268, 269, 270, 271, 275, 276, 278, 280, 281, 282, 283, 284
　　,, Death of, 203, 204
　　,, Dr, 245, 272, 285, 286, 287
　　,, Will and tombstone of, (1697) 152
　Elizabeth, 149, 158, 159, 169, 205, 278
　George, 159, (1649) 244
　　,, of, 135
　Hannah, 263, 283
　Henry, 208, 213, 224, 231, 234, 257, 258, 267, 268, 271, 272, 281, 282
　Isobelle, 159, 184, 225
　James, (1693) 149, 152, 159, 168, 169, 170, 184, 185, 186, 213, 214, 215, 216, 223, 226, 232, 233, 239, 262, 264, 267, 276, 278, 281, 283, 284, 285, 286, 287, 288

Johnston, Johnstone, Johnstoun, etc.—
GALABANK—
　James, Dr, 187, 188, 189, 190, 201, 202, 203
　　,, of, (1802) 264
　　,, Sir, Major-General, 287
　　,, Tombstone of, 159
　Janet, 148, (1685) 149, 151, 157, 158, 159
　John, (1689) 149, 152, 159, 170, 184, 203, 206, 208, 213, 219, 225, 227, 235, 236, 250, 251, 258, 261, 262, 263, 266, 267, 276, 277, 282, 285, 286
　　,, Dr, 264, 265, 268, 269, 272, 273, 274, 275, 278, 279, 280, 281, 286, 288
　　,, of, (1665) 145, 146, (1684) 149, (1689) 150, 151, 156, 157, 158, 159, 193, 210, 225, 286
　　,, Death of, 225
　　,, Heirs of, 296
　Lockhart, 213, 219, 244, 255, 256, 268, 282, 283, 286, 296
　Marie, 149, 158
　Mary, 159, 213, 258, 263, 265, 274, 287
　Richard, 159, 200, 202, 204, 206, 207, 208, 209, 210, 211, 212, 217, 218, 226
　Thomas, 208, 223, 224, 234, 255, 258, 264
　William, 159, 169, 170, 184, 255
Gavin, 42
　,, of, 18
George (1617) 17, 144, 152
　,, Harvey, *Heraldry of the Johnstons*, 6
Georgia, Johnston in, 339
Germany, Johnston in, 42
Gilbert, 111
　,, de, 3, (1464, 1485) 5
Giles, a witch, 312
Gilford, Johnstons of, 329
Gillespie, William M'Dowall, of, 330
GIRTHEAD, GRETHEAD—
　Archibald, 96
　George, of, 96, (1704) 155
　Jean, 96
　Joseph, 96
　Symon, of, (1515) 39
　William, 96
Glasgow—
　John, in, 26
　　,, Baillie of, 26
　　,, Professor of Medicine in, 26
Glenquotto, James, of, (1581) 41
Glynn, Johnstons of, 334
Gotterbraes, Gotterby, Gutterbraes—
　John, of, (1745) 37, 145
　Robert, of, (1624) 37, 125

INDEX

Johnston, Johnstone, Johnstoun, etc.—
  GRAITNEY, GRETNA, GRETNO—
    Archibald, 119
    George, of, 48, 63, 66, 71,
    Gilbert, 119
      " de, (1450) 45
      " de, de, (1453) 8
      " of, 317
      " Sir, de, de, 10
    James, Colonel, of, (1720) 118, 175
    John, of, 19, (1615) 48, (1569) 73, 75, (1579) 78, (1587) 81, 87, (1608) 90, 94, (1606) 99, 104, (1612) 117, (1613) 118
    Johnstoun of, 87
    Michael, in, 47
    Richard, 119
    Thomas, of, (1493) 47, 51
    William, (1594) 84, 119
      " of, 9, 48, 51, (1515) 52, (1524) 53, 54, 55, 57, 66, (1535) 67, 68, 69, 79, 103, (1623) 118, (1793) 119, 343
      " of, made a Baron, (1542) 56
      " Young Laird of, (1513) 9
  Granton—
    James, of, (1739) 43, 44
    William, of, 153, (1704) 155
  Greskin, Archibald, of, 30
  Gumenbie, George, of, (1655) 36

  HACKNESS HALL—
    Charles, 167
    " (of Ludlow), 301, 303
    Harcourt, Sir, Bart. of, 301
    John, Sir, second Bart. of, 302
    Johnstones of, 301
    Richard, 167
    " Sir, Bart. of, 301
  Halleaths—
    Agnes, 24
    Andrew Scott, of, (1901) 24
    David, (1739) 24
    George, (1739) 24
    John, (1739) 24
    " of, 24
    Johnstouns of, 24
    Nicolas, (1739) 24
    Samuel, (1739) 24
  Handsworth, Francis, of, 325
  Hannah Maria, 257
  Harry Hamilton, Sir, 324
  Harthope, David, of, (1523) 20, (1520) 39
  Hayhill—
    John, of, (1504) 47
    William, in, (1565) 69
  Hazlebank, Hesilbank—
    Christopher, in, 44
    Gilbert, (1585) 44
    Herbert, in, 44, 98

Johnston, Johnstone, Johnstoun, etc.—
  Hazlebank, Hesilbank—
    Symon, (1585) 44
    Thomas, (1585) 44
  Hennaland, Thomas, of, (1584) 42
  Henrietta, Lady, 205
  Henry Campbell, 325
  " Lord, 346
  Herbert, of, (1487), 48
  Hesilbrae, Hesliebrae, Hesliebray—
    Adam and James, in, (1595) 35
    James, of, 95, (1606) 103
    William, in, 31
  HILTON—
    Archibald, of, 315
    " of, Death of, 129
    Frederick, Lieutenant-Colonel, 315
    George, Captain, 315
    Henry George, Major, 315
    James, General, 315
    Joseph of, 33, 127, 128, 129, 315
    Major, 129
    Patrick, 316
    " Sir, 129, 315
    Robert, 315
    Sophia, 129
    Wynne, of, 315
  Hoddam—
    Archibald, in, (1689) 119
    George, in, (1689) 119
    John, in, (1504) 47
    William, in, 48, (1689) 119
  Holmends, John, (1577), 76
  Holywood—
    John, Abbot of, (1613) 34, 36
    " Commendator of, 113
  Hope, 298
  " Mr, 277, 287
  Howcleuch, Mutilation of Gilbert, in, 43
  Howes, Archibald, of, (1630) 32
  Howgill, John, of, (1605) 42, 73

  ILK—
    Adam of, 5, (1448) 9, (1484, 1488, 1504) 10, (1498) 18, (1504) 19, (1502) 22, (1488-1509) 46, 47, (1508) 48, 53, 54
    " of, his sons, (1448) 45
    " Lord of, (1413) 5
    " Sir, (1453) 8
    Agnes, 70, 117
    Archibald, of, (1450) 45
    Elizabeth, 72, 80, 117
    Gilbert de, (1296) 3, (1347) 4
    " de, Sir, 3
    " of, (1450) 45
    " Son of John de, 4
    " Son of Thomas de, 4
    Grizel, 328
    Henrietta, 164
    Herbert of, (1450) 45
    Hugo de, (1285) 3
    Humphrey, (1502) 47

INDEX

Johnston, Johnstone, Johnstoun, etc.—
  Ilk—
    James, 69, (1542) 70, 111
     „ of, (1516) 9, (1504) 10, (1624, 1629) 22, (1450) 45, (1509-24) 48, (1588) 81, 96, 104, 107, (1609) 115, (1621) 122, 138, (1524) 327
     „ Sir, of, (1595) 35, 36, 103, 112, 154, 328
     „ Son of Adam, (1503) 9
    Jean, 93
    John, (1296) 3, 43, 57, 76, (1547) 82, 153, 162, 163, 164, 175
     „ de, (1385) 5
     „ de, Sir, (1285, 1296) 3
     „ Hon., 143
     „ Laird of, (1484) 12
     „ of, (1459) 5, 9, (1483) 10, (1586) 19, (1450) 45, (1476, 1498) 46, (1496) 47, 49, (1524) 53, 65, 76, (1524-67) 96, (1567) 104
    Johnstone, Lieutenant-Colonel, 143
    Johnstoun of, (1597) 30, 33, 59, 60, 61, 73, 75, (1593) 83, 85, 87, 91, 117
     „   „ imprisoned, 55, 56
    Margaret, 72
     „ of, 21
    Master of, 58
    Patrick, of, (1450) 45, (1542) 47
    Robert, 43, 327
    Sophia, 154
    Symon, 57, 84
     „ of, (1498) 46
    Thomas (1296) 3
     „ de, (1452-63), 5
     „ Sir, Chaplain, 93
    Walter, (1296) 3
    William, 57, 63, 69, 164
     „ of, (1408) 10, (1485) 29, (1450) 45, (1478) 46, (1523) 48
  Indiana, Johnston in, 341
  Ireland—
    Anne, in, 333
    Herbert, in, 327
    John Douglas, in, 333
    Johnstons in, 326
    Marjory, in, 335
    Mary, in, 330
    Susanna, in, 329
    William, Captain, in, 328
  Isabella, 265

  James, (1421) 5, (1511) 30, 122, 127, 147
    „ Boorman, 28
    „ Chevalier de, 173, 174
    „ Clerk-Deliverer, (1597) 17
    „ Hon., 143
    „ Laird of, (1513-24) 118
    „ Lord, (1639) 123, 144, 150, (1714) 159

Johnston, Johnstone, Johnstoun, etc.—
  James, Lord Ruthven, 119
    „ Sheriff of Lanark, (1535) 20
    „ Sir, 99, 103
    „   „ Priest, 93
    „ Son of Archibald, Merchant, 33
    „ William Douglas, 325
    „ Janet, 310
    „ Jeannie Fergusson, 342
  John, (1421, 1464) 5, (1597, 1617) 17, (1476) 18, (1504) 19, 99, 157, 158, 159, 244
    „ Baillie of Water of Leith, 96
    „ Barr, Sir, 334
    „ Brookes, 324
    „ Colonel, 244
    „ Dr, (1645) 28
    , Herbert, 28
    „ Hon., 337, 339
    „ Humphreys, 28
    „ Lawson, 325
    „ Lord, 167, 204
    , M.D., 231
    „   „ Author, 41
    ,, Rev., 315
    „ Sir, (1587) 33
    „   „ Priest, 93
    „   „ Son of Gilbert, 4
    „ Son of Laurence, (1502) 47
    ,, Taylor, 28
    „ William, 323
    „ Writer, (1624) 22, 96
  John*son*, *see* Douglas of Bonjedward, 49
  Johnston, Horsburgh & Co., 323
  Johnstone, Lay Parson of, 97
  Johnstoun—
    Robert, of, (1484) 10
    „ Tutor of, 19
  Joseph, Senator, 338

Kansas, Johnston in, 341
Katherine, 40
Kellobank—
  Alexander, 34
  James, of, 34, 308
  John, 34
    „ of, (1572) 34, (1599) 35, 36
  Johnstons of, 34
  Nathaniel, 34
  Robert, 34
  Thomas, 34
  William, of, 34
Kelton—
  Ann, 26
  Mary Ann, 26
  Robert, of, (1706) 26
Kentucky, Johnstons in, 340
Killevan, Hugh, of, 332
Kilmore, Johnstons of, 330, 331, 332
Kilternan, Christopher, of, 332
Kincardine Castle, James, of, 347
Kinlough House, Robert, of, 334

Johnston, Johnstone, Johnstoun, etc.—
  Kinnellar, James S., of, 342
  Kirk—
    Archibald, in, (1574) 30
      „   James, and Cuthbert, in, 33
    Cuthbert, of, 133
  Kirkhill—
    John, (1605) 42
    Johnstons of, 42
    Robert, (1605) 42
      „ of, 97
    William, (1605) 42, 97
      „ of, (1581) 96, (1592) 97
    Willie, of, (1592) 82
  Kirkton—
    Gavin, in, 127
      „ of, (1526, 1555) 30, 63
    Herbert, (1526) 30
    James, of, 30, 33
  Knappagh, Johnstons of, 332
  Knockhill—
    Andrew, of, (1672, 1745) 36
    George, of, (1655) 36
    James, of, 36, 160
      „ Leslie, of, 23
    Johnstones of, 173
  Knokilshane, Walter, in, 25

  Lady, 99, 108, 165
  Laird of, 33, (1514) 39, 41, 42, 43, (1513) 51, 52, 53, 57, 61, 63, 64, 69, 72, 78, 81, 88, 89, 90, 95, 96, 99, 101, 102, 103, 111, 112, 113, 122, 135, 137, 138, 139
  Lanark—
    James, of, 20
      „ Sheriff of, (1535) 20, 39
  Langshaw, Francis, of, (1714) 23
  Langside—
    John, 96
    Margaret, 96
    William, in, 96
  Langwodend, John, of, (1581) 41
  Lathrisk, David, of, 324
  Laurence, (1436) 60
      „ of (1438) 45
  Leadhills, Gilbert, in, 321
  Leuchie—
    Andrew, of, 12
    Robert, of, 14, 312
  Lilias, 36
  Liscard, Samuel, of, 324
  Lochmaben—
    Captain, of, 3
    James, Parson of, 39
    Provost of, (1616) 32
    Robert, of, 73, 84
      „ Lay Parson of, 19, 104
      „ Parson of, 14, 70, 76, 94
    Symon, 94

Johnston, Johnstone, Johnstoun, etc.—
  Lochous—
    James, of, (1618) 35, 42, (1592) 81, 99, (1632) 113, 114, 118, 122, 124
    John, of, (1603) 97, 104
      „ Captain, 111
  Lochwood—
    Johnstoun of, 63
    Lord, of, 141
  Lockerbie—
    Alexander, (1675) 36
    Andrew, (1689) 36
      „ of, (1678) 36, 95, 142, 153
    Catherine, 154
    Cuthbert, in, (1559) 36
      „ of, 30, 63
    David, (1739) 36
    Francis, 36
    George, (1739) 36
    Grace, 154
    James, 36, 154
      „ in, 36
      „ of, (1746) 154
    Johnstouns of Lockerbie, 36, 79
    Mary, Mrs, 154
    Mungo, (1701) 36
      „ in, 96
      „ of, 21, (1678) 36, (1592) 81
    Robert, (1739) 36, 154
    Symon, 36
    William, 21, 36, 154
      „ of, (1608) 104, (1752) 210
  London—
    Charles, Alderman of, 325
    Francis, in, 305
    Johnstons, in, 305
    William, in, (1726) 37
  Lord, 22, 64, 125, 142
  Lowtherston, John, in, 327

  Major, 207
  Malinshaw—
    Archibald, of, 30
    John, in, (1565) 68
  Manitoba, Johnston in, 341
  Margaret, 23, 60
  Margaret Vanden Bempdé, 304
  Marjoribanks—
    Adam, of, (1618) 36
    Andrew, of, (1580) 31
    William, of, 30, 36
  Martha, 17, 99
  Mary, 257
  Maryland, Johnstons in, 44
  Matthew, (1504) 19, 55
      „ de, (1464) 5
  Maurice, Sir, (1521) 13
  Maximilian von, 42
  Middlegill—
    Gavin, of, (1606) 103
    James, of, 34, 36, 41
      „ of, Murder of, 43

Johnston, Johnstone, Johnstoun, etc.—
　Milkymoss—
　　James, of, (1605) 42, 43
　　Symon, of, (1515) 39
　Milnbank—
　　Andrew, in, (1602) 36
　　　„　of, (1681) 36
　　Christie, in, 96
　　Christopher, of, 36
　　John, 36
　Milnbie, Mylnbie—
　　Abraham, of, 101, 111, 124, 135
　　William, 135
　Moffat—
　　Adam, in, (1577) 30
　　Christopher, in, (1819), 44
　　John, in, 44, 321, 327
　　Robert, in, 321
　　Thomas, in, (1582) 41
　　William, in, (1582) 41
　Moffatdaill, Lord, of, 141
　Moling, William, in, 35
　Monaghan, Johnstons in, 329, 333, 336
　Montrose, Johnstons in, 347
　Mossop—
　　Adam, of, (1511) 29
　　Robert, of, 127
　Mungo, 112, 127
　MYLNFIELD—
　　Barbara, 136
　　David, 110, 134
　　Edward, 124, 134, 136
　　　„　in, 112
　　George, 125, 133, 134, 135, 136,
　　　　137, 138
　　　„　in, 96
　　James, 137
　　John, 112, 135, 136
　　　„　in, 116, 133, 134
　　　„　of, 105, 114, 124, (1643)
　　　　125, 135, 136, 137, (1653) 139,
　　　　141
　　Mary, 136
　　William, 135

Nathaniel, 116, 309
Neiss, James, of, 136
Nether Barcaple—
　Robert, in, 330
　　„　of, (1713) 27
Nether Garwald, David, in, (1595) 35,
　69
Netherlaw—
　William, in, 328, 329, 330
　　„　of, 27
Netherplace, Mungo, of, 154
Netherwood, John, Colonel, of, 301,
　303,
New Brunswick, Johnston in, 341
New York—
　John, in, (1804) 27
　Johnstons in, 27, 28, 340, 341
New Zealand, Johnstons in, 341, 342

Johnston, Johnstone, Johnstoun, etc.—
　NEWBIE—
　　Abraham, 68, 77, 84, (1585) 98, 100,
　　　101, 115, (1609) 116
　　Adam, de, (1511) 9
　　　„　of, 9, (1511) 46, (1511) 54
　　Agnes, 105, 106, 107
　　Barbara, 102, 103, 105, 135
　　Christine, 105
　　David, 17, 67, 77, 99, 100, 101, 118,
　　　317
　　Edward, 68, 77, 84, 99, 101, 103,
　　　(1726) 155
　　Elizabeth, 77, 99, 105
　　George, 67, 81
　　Gilbert, 99
　　Helen, 100, 101
　　Herbert, 67
　　James, 100, 101, 125
　　Janet, 100, 101, 105
　　Jeannette, 105, 106, 107, 108
　　John, 67, (1577) 76, 77, (1575) 99,
　　　100, 102, 103, (1618) 118,
　　　126
　　　„　M.P., his Will, 99
　　　„　of, 36, 68, (1542) 70, 72, 74, 75,
　　　　76, (1581) 77, 78, (1588)
　　　　81, 85, (1599) 87, (1602)
　　　　89, 102, (1606) 103, 105,
　　　　120, 125, 135, 309
　　　„　Will of, 76
　　Johnstone of, 79, 80
　　Lady, 100, 104
　　Laird of, 62, 72, 73, 112
　　Margaret, 100
　　Marion, 77, 100, 101
　　Mary, 36, 77, 105
　　Robert, 116
　　　„　LL.D., Will of, 125
　　　„　of, 68, (1577) 76, 77, (1579)
　　　　78, 80, 81, 83, 84, 85,
　　　　86, 88, 98, 99, 102, 103,
　　　　104, 111, 112, 114, 123,
　　　　134, 136
　　　„　Sir, of, 98
　　Thomas, 100, 101
　　William, 75, 77, 99, 103
　　　„　Natural son, 120
　　　„　of, (1524) 53, 57, 62, 63,
　　　　66, (1535) 67, 81, 112
　　　„　of, first of, 184
　　　„　of, made a Baron, (1542)
　　　　56
　Newmilns, William, in, 326
　Newton—
　　Andrew, of, 153, (1704) 155
　　Gavin, of, (1557) 43
　　　„　of, in Kirkcudbright (1707)
　　　　32
　　John, 43
　　Johnstons of, in Midlothian, 312
　　Robert, 43
　　　„　in, 43, 76

INDEX

Johnston, Johnstone, Johnstoun, etc.—
  Newton—
    Robert, of, 41, (1565) 68, 95, (1606) 103, 142
  Newton Grange, James, of, 312
  Nicolas, 108
  Ninian, 99
  Nitove, John, of, 65
  Norman de (1439) 7
  North Carolina, Johnstons in, 337, 339
    „ Cray, Rev. Hugh William, 325

Ochiltree, John, of, 326
Ohio, Johnstons in, 336
Orchardton, Orchardtoun—
  David, in, 27, 328
  William, 27
Orkney, Johnstons in, 342
Outbrieks, Joshua, of, 342
Over Howcleuch—
  Johnstoun of, (1492) 47
  Mungo, of, 137
  Rachel, 137
  Robert, of, 120
Overdryfe, William, of, 46

Paisley—
  George, 26
  Helen, 26
Patrick, 108
Penlaw, Jean, of, 96
Pensak, Adam, of, 47
Persbiehall—
  Christopher, of, 147
  John, of, (1712) 23, (1704) 155
Perth, Johnstons in, 347
Peter, 310
Pettinane—
  Herbert, of, (1517) 19
  John, of, (1503) 19
Pitkeirie, Andrew, of, 324
Pocornwell, James, of, (1528) 69
Poland—
  John, M.D., 41
  Johnstouns in, 41
POLDEAN, POWDENE—
  Ambrose, in, (1650) 43
    „ of, (1650) 44
  Christopher, (1618) 43
  Gilbert, 40, 43
    „ of, (1567) 43, 72
  Helen, 42
  Herbert, 40, 43
    „ of, 18, (1496) 39, (1563, 1576) 40, 42, (1576) 44, 46, (1565) 68
  James, 40
  Janet, 42
  John, 40, 43
    „ of, 79
  Johnstouns of, 26, 39
  Marie, (1724) 43
  Ninian, 42

Johnston, Johnstone, Johnstoun, etc.—
  POLDEAN, POWDENE—
    Ninian, in, 43
    „ of, (1621) 42, 95
    Robert, 43
    Simon, of, (1520) 20
    Symon, 43
    „ . of, (1514) 39, 40, 43
    Thomas, 40
    William, 40
  Polton—
    John, of, (1676) 17
    Magdalen, 17
  Pomfret—
    Henry, of, 162
    Nathaniel, of, 162
  Preston—
    David, in, 312
    Patrick, in, 312
  Priestdykes, Johnstoun of, 24
  Priestwodside, Thomas, in, (1579), 78

RAECLEUCH—
  Archibald, 123
  Barbara, 124
  Dorothie, 123
  Francis, 123
  George, 123
  Grizel, 123
  James, 123
  John, 123, 124
  Johnstoun of, 103, 104
  Johnstouns of, 123
  Mungo, 106, 122, 123, 124
  Rachel, 123
  Robert, 123, 124
    „ of, (1618) 35, 36, 42, 49, (1594) 84, 95, 110, 111, 114, 115, (1609) 116, 117, 119, 122, (1626) 123, 124, 128
  Sara, 122, 123
  Symon, 110, 123
  William, 123
Ragiwhat—
  Francis, 23
  Mungo, in, 23
Rathmines, Joseph G., of, 333
Redgatehead, Johnstoun in, 145
Reidhall—
  David, 31, (1608) 32
  George, (1608) 32
  John, of, (1573) 34
  Johnstoun of, 93
  William, of, (1569) 19, 30, (1608) 32, (1569) 34
Rennyhill, Andrew, of, 324
Revox, Thomas, in, (1606) 103,
Richard Vanden Bempdé, 244
  „   „   „ Captain, 205
Rigfoot—
  John, (1553) 42
  Johnstouns in, 42
  William, (1553) 42

INDEX

Johnston, Johnstone, Johnstoun, etc.—
  Righead, David, of, 326
  Robert, (1464) 5, (1520) 20, 96, 112, 144, 145, 158
  Roberthill, Robert, of, 36, 154
  Rowantrieknow, Ninian in, 35
  RYEHILL, RYHILL, RVELL—
    Arthur, 102
    Christopher, 113
    Edward, 112
    „   of, (1624) 22, 35, 42, 85, 95, 99, 102, 103, 105, 108, 110, 111, 112, 113, 114, 115, 116, 118, 119, 120, 121, 122, 123, 124, 125, 127, 133, 134, 135, 136, 145, 149, 156, 158, 161, 309
    John, (1609) 113, 114
    „   of, 77

Salsit, Saulside, Saulsit—
  Abbot of, 34, 59, 60, 61, 63, 93, 95
  Andrew, 35
  Commendator of, (1599) 83
  Cuthbert, 35
  James, Abbot of, 63, 64
  John, Abbot of, (1613) 34, (1599) 35, 36
  „   Commend o of, (1595) 35, 76   at r
  Symon, 35
  William, 83
Salton, Johnstons of, 311
Sands, James, of, 347
Sanquhar, William, of, 322
Sara, 124
Saughtrees, John, in, 321
Seafield, Edward, of, 68, 112, 120, 122, 123, 135
SHEENS—
  Henrietta, 129
  James, of, 129, 154
  Rachel, 129, 154
  Samuel, of, 33, 98, 127, 129
  William, of, 98, 129
Silesia, Johnstons in, 42
Skare, James, of, 51
Smallgills—
  James, of, (1605) 42
  John, of, (1577, 1581) 40
  Symon, of, (1532) 39, (1581) 40
  Thomas, (1532) 39
Snow Hill, Johnstones of, 333
Sophia, 143
Southdean, Johnston of, 339
Springfield—
  George, 323
  James, 323
  John, 323
  „   William Simpson, 323
Standingstones, John, of, 345
STAPLETON—
  Andrew, in, and his son George, (1504) 12

Johnston, Johnstone, Johnstoun, etc.—
  STAPLETON—
    John, of, 160, 337, 339, 340
    Robert, of, 128, 136
  Stenris Hill, Ambrose, of, (1738) 43
  Stobohill, John, in, 37
  Stonehouse, James, Rev., of, 324
  Straiton, James, of, 324
  Sutton—
    Alexander, 128
    Cudworth, 130
    Henry, 128, 131
    „   Rev., 130
    John, Vicar of, 128
    Nathaniel, 128, 130, 131
    Pelham, 130
    Samuel, Dr, 131
    Thomas, 131
    William, 131, 132
    „   Henry, 132
    „   „   Rev., 132
  Sweden—
    David, 94
    John, 94
    Matthew, 94
  Symon, (1572) 34, 79, 99, 140
    „   Natural son, (1595) 35
    „   Parson, 144

Tasmania, Johnston in, 342
Templand—
  Adam, of, (1636) 32
  Wilkin, in, 95
  William, of, 32
Texas, Johnston in, 341
The Wood, Gavin, of, (1485) 29
Thomas, (1479) 24, (1404) 49, 127, 310
  „   C., Rev., 257, 260, 261
Toddelmuir, William, in, (1574) 30
Torbeck Hill, John, of, Rev., (1749) 23
Tremont, James, of, 332
Tundergarth—
  Andrew, of, (1604) 24
  John, of, (1483) 23, (1613) 24
  Matthew, (1483) 23, 24

United States, America—
  Christopher, (1835, 1891) 44
    „   Professor, 44

Vanden Bempdé Johnstones, 205, 301
Viccarland, Vickerland, John, of, 142, 327
Virginia, Johnstons in, 338, 340

Walter, (1421) 5, 154
WAMFRAY—
  Agnes, 23
  Clement, of, 19
  David, 69, 97
  Edward, 70, 97, 111, 115, 327
  Francis, 111
  George, of, 97

INDEX 381

ohnston, Johnstone, Johnstoun, etc.—
WAMFRAY—
Gilbert, 69, 70, 99, 308
,, of, (1605) 42, 70, 87, (1597) 97, 118
James, 69, 70, 97, 98, 308
,, Captain, 98
,, of, 40, (1545) 43, 60, (1528) 69, 98, 327
Janet, 97, 98, 129
John, 70, 97
,, of, (1514) 39, 45, 51, 69, (1617) 97, 98, 129
Johnstons of, 97
Mariot, 97
Mary, 98
Robert, 70, 98
,, of, 23, 70, 95, 97, 98, 104, (1704) 155, 160
Thomas, 69
William, 69, 70, 97, 308
,, of, (1581) 96, 98, 129
Warden of the Marches, 79, 80
Warrentown, Christopher, of, 196
WARRIESTON, WARRISTON—
Alexander, 129, 161, 162
Archibald, 127
,, Lord, 33, 128, 129
,, ,, Death of, 139
,, of, 34, 128, 129, 130, 141, 142, 143, 315
Beatrix, 127
Elizabeth, 139
Helen, 140
James, 161, 162, 163
,, Major, 163
Janet, 127, 140
Jasper, of, 162, 315
John, 127
Johnston of, 127
Margaret, 127, 140
Rachel, 127, 139
Robert, 127
Tutor of, 100
Wellington, N.Z., Johnstons in, 341
West Pans, John, in, 311
WESTERHALL, WESTERAW, WESTRAW—
Agnes Louisa Barbara Snowflake, 297
Alexander, Lieutenant-Colonel, 182
,, Patrick, 239
Anne Elizabeth, 297
Archibald, 175
Aunt Betty, 183
Barbara, 182
Charles John, 297
Charlotte, 182
,, Margaret, 297
Dorothy Frances Catherine, 297
Elizabeth, 23, 183
Francis, 23, 153, 305

Johnston, Johnstone, Johnstoun, etc.—
WESTERHALL, WESTERAW, ETC.—
Frederick Alan George, 297
,, Sir, Bart. of, 287
,, John William, Sir, Bart. of, 297
Gavin, 20
George, Captain, 238
,, Charles Keppel, Colonel, 297
,, Commodore, 177, 178, 319
,, Frederick, Sir, Bart. of, 274, 297
,, Lindsay, 239
,, Thomas Frederick Tankerville, 297
Gideon, Captain, 182, 198, 199
Governor, 205, 238, 239, 240, 241, 273
,, Death of, 242
Grizel, 154
Henrietta, 183
Herbert, (1555) 20
,, of, (1548) 19, (1535) 20
James, 23, (1619) 28, 135, 175, 198, 199, 200
,, Murray, 272
,, of, (1560) 19, (1569, 1570) 20, (1624, 1629) 22, (1576) 28, 33, 42, (1599) 87, (1599) 94, 95, (1606) 103, (1629) 126, 135, 146, (1687) 150, 305
,, of, slain, (1570) 20, 21
,, Primrose, 239
,, Sir, of, 152, 153, 154, 168, 226, 244, 256
,, ,, Bart. of, 129, 154, 199, 203, 204, 243
,, ,, third Bart. of, 175, 176
,, ,, fourth Bart. of, 176, 177
John, (1560, 1576) 19, 20, 154, 160, 163, 165, 167, 175, 178, 179, 180, 181
,, Colonel, 166, 199, 301, 303
,, of, (1508) 20
,, Sir, Bart. of, 154
,, ,, ,, created Baronet, 165
,, Lowther, Sir, Bart. of, 273, 274, 297
Johnstoun of, 114
Johnstouns of, 18
Laura Adeline, 297
Margaret, 153, 154, 182
Matthew, of, 18, (1491) 20, (1450) 45
Patrick, 179
Philadelphia, 154
Robert, 20, (1589) 21
,, of, Mains, 326
Rose Mary Adeline Dagmar Amelia, 297

Johnston, Johnstone, Johnstoun, etc.—
  WESTERHALL, WESTERAW, ETC.—
    Sophia, 239
    Violet Florence Ernestine, 297
    Walter, 165, 175
    William, (1648) 28, 153
    ,,   Sir, of, 158, (1714) 159, 160, 164
    ,,   ,, Bart. of, 129, 154
    ,,   ,, second Bart. of, 175, 301
    ,,   ,, fifth Bart. of, 177, 178
    ,,   Pulteney, Sir, Bart. of, 272
  Westoun—
    Gavin, in, 326
    John, of, 28
    William, (1421) 5, (1484) 10, (1517) 19, (1509) 49, 55, 60, 274, 310
    ,,   Hon., 143
    ,,   Lieutenant-Colonel, 326
    ,,   of, (1479) 24
    ,,   Procurator for the Crown, 39
    ,,   Sir, Major-General, 196
  Woodcoker, Fergus, in, 47
  Woodheid—
    Symon, in, 43
    ,,   of, 95, (1606) 103
  Woodhous, Laurence, of, (1502) 47, 60
  Woodpark—
    George, of, 336
    William, of, 329
  Worcester—
    Edward, in, 188
    James, Dr, in, (1755) 149, 181, 187, 188, 189, 190, 191, 192, 193, 194, 196, 199, 200, 201, 205, 207, 208, 209, 210, 211, 214, 217, 220, 221, 222, 223, 224, 231
  Wormanbie, Laird of, 104
  Wyldcotray, Edward, of, 68
  Wylleis, James, of, (1621) 42

  Ye Pans, John, in, 311

Johnstons, 87, 88
  ,,   in Fifteenth Century, 45
  ,,   Numbers of, 78
  ,,   Respite to, (1594) 83
  ,,   The Earliest, 1
Johnstone Lands, etc.—
  Abbey Mill of Haddington, 17
  Aghadunvane, 334
  Aghamulden, 335
  Alderwood House, 322
  Aldtoun, 69
  Alva, 178, 181, 199, 202, 297, 298
  Annan, 3, 93, 122
  ,,   Castle, 105
  Annandale, 90
  ,,   House, 205

Johnstone Lands, etc.—
  Annandholme, 42, 43
  Arkilton, 53, 66, 68
  Auchen Castle, 323
  Auchinleck, 35
  Auchinsbork, 51
  Auchinskeoch, 35
  Auchinstock, 35
  Auldgirth, 25
  Ayill (Isle), 23

  Ballincrief or Ballincrieff, 13 310, 311
  Ballinderry, 335
  Ballykilbeg, 333
  Ballywillwill, 27, 328, 329, 330
  Balvaig, 306
  Barboy, 100
  Barncleuch, 26
  Barnekirk, 67
  Barony of, (1513) 10
  ,,   of, Taxation of, 114
  Bartycupen, 51
  Bawnboy House, 335
  Beatok, 69, 321
  Beech Hill, 37
  Beirholm or Beirholme 30, 36, 37, 127, 155, 157, 159, 327, 332
  Belriding, 202
  Bignor Park, 299
  Bishopstown, 344, 345
  Blaatwood, 119
  Boginjoss, 345
  Bonshaw, 96
  Brackenside, or Brakinside, or Breckonside, 42, 43, 45
  Brakenhill, 29
  Brakenthwaite, 4
  Briggs, 32
  Brigholme, 78, 84, 85, 86, 106, 111, 112
  Broadholm, 24
  Brocketlea, 23
  Brookhill, 335
  Broomhills, 12
  Brotis, 10, 45, 46, 54, 60
  Brounehills, 134
  Brume, 101, 102, 111, 134
  Brumhill or Brumehill, 30, 42, 43, 99

  Carlaverock, 312, 315
  Carnsalloch, 104, 244, 318, 319, 320
  Carterton, 42
  Caskieben, 326, 335, 342, 343, 344, 345
  Castle Robert, 25
  Castlehill, 23, 24
  Castlemilk, 34, 35, 47, 62, 94, 96, 110, 113, 116, 122, 128, 130, 134
  Cavartholme or Cavertholme, 4, 10, 46, 53, 64, 118, 343
  Chapel Hill or Chapelhill, 39, 40, 41, 103
  Chapelton, 30
  Clackleith, 322
  Clauchrie, or Clochrie, or Clouthrie, 24, 25, 26, 27, 84, 94, 142, 149, 154, 318

INDEX

Johnstone Lands, etc.—
   Closehead, 125, 145, 151, 203, 218
   Cockpool, 119
   Coedfa, 324
   Comlongan Castle, 7
   Conheath, 24, 56, 68
   Cordyce, 344
   Corehead, or Corhead, or Corheid, 30, 40, 41, 42, 76, 97, 99, 139, 142, 147, 153, 155, 175, 244, 321, 323
   Corrie, 8, 9, 31, 48, 53, 54, 56, 57, 60, 66, 67, 73, 74, 81, 84, 85, 95, 96, 99, 114, 119, 127, 137, 157, 309
   Cottis, 63
   Couran, 35, 83
   Cousland, 14, 310, 311
   Cove, 10, 45, 93
   Cowhill, 24, 25, 244
   Craigaburn, 39, 40, 42, 63, 73, 75, 76, 81, 84
   Craighous, 155
   Craigiehall, 164
   Craufurd, 321
   Crawshalt, 323
   Crimond, 344
   Croftheid or Croftheids, 67, 71, 78, 80, 112, 122, 134
   Croy, 325
   Crumhauch, 100
   Cummertrees, 67, 71, 72, 74, 76, 77, 78, 80, 83, 84, 93, 99, 101, 122, 125

   Daldurham, 23
   Dalfibble, 106
   Dargavell, 26
   Daubate, 45
   Denovan, 181, 244
   Dornal, 320
   Dornock, 71, 97, 119
   Drum, 332
   Drumadown, 327
   Drumconnell, 330, 331, 334
   Drumgrey, 10, 35, 69
   Dryfe, Over and Nether, 22
   Dryfesdale, 30, 36
   Dryffehead or Dryfhead, 40, 153
   Duchrae, 25, 26, 27, 328, 341
   Dundoran, 70
   Dunduff, 25
   Dunskellie, 4, 10, 21, 45, 81, 84, 87, 93, 95, 105, 106, 123
   Dunsley Manor, 275, 287, 288, 295
   Dunwoodie, 34

   Eccles, 316
   Edgbaston Hall, 275, 276, 278, 279, 280, 281, 284, 285, 286, 287
   Ellerbeck, 67
   Elphinstone or Elphinstoun, 10, 31, 45, 47, 51, 59, 67, 73, 76, 81, 94, 95, 127, 143, 182, 307, 308, 309, 310, 311, 312, 340
       „   Tower, 15

Johnstone Lands, etc.—
   Elsieschellis or Elsieshields, 10, 26, 29, 30, 31, 32, 33, 34, 36, 37, 46, 56, 63, 69, 72, 76, 78, 83, 84, 85, 94, 95, 97, 125, 128, 144, 147, 309, 317, 339, 340, 343, 346
   Ernemynie, 60
   Erny, 329
   Esbie, 18, 29, 30, 32, 39

   Fairholm, 73
   Fingland, 42, 44, 96, 98
   Flemingraw, 113, 116
   Fort Johnston, 335
   Foulderis or Fouleduris, 30, 51
   Fulford Hall, 111, 255, 257, 287, 288, 295, 298

   Galabank, 78, 111, 112, 114, 115, 116, 125, 133, 134, 135, 136, 137, 140, 144, 145, 147, 148, 149, 150, 151, 152, 156, 157, 158, 161, 164, 167, 168, 169, 170, 171, 172, 184, 191, 193, 197, 202, 203, 208, 209, 210, 211, 213, 214, 215, 217, 218, 219, 220, 224, 225, 226, 228, 255, 258, 264, 267, 268, 274, 275, 285, 286, 296
   Gallowgait, 145
   Galzandleis, 67
   Garwald, 35
   Gavelhill, 41
   Gilford, 327, 328, 329, 330
   Gillespie, 330
   Girthead or Grethead, 39, 96, 155
   Gladsmuir, 203
   Glencore House, 335
   Glendining, 22, 23, 53, 95, 298
   Glenhutton, 41
   Glenquotto, 41
   Glynn, 334
   Gotterbraes, or Gotterby, or Gutterbraes, 37, 125, 145
   Graitney, or Gretna, or Gretno, 3, 8, 9, 10, 11, 12, 19, 30, 45, 47, 48, 51, 52, 53, 54, 55, 56, 57, 62, 63, 64, 65, 66, 67, 68, 69, 71, 73, 74, 75, 78, 79, 80, 81, 82, 83, 84, 85, 87, 89, 90, 91, 93, 94, 95, 97, 99, 100, 103, 104, 110, 111, 115, 116, 117, 118, 119, 120, 133, 143, 156, 170, 173, 175, 219, 317, 339, 340, 343
      „   Hill, 68
      „   Tower, 12
   Granton, 40, 43, 44, 63, 153, 155
   Greskin, 30
   Gulielands, 78, 86, 112
   Gumenbie, 36

   Hackness Hall, 164, 165, 205, 207, 301
   Hailstanemuir, 118
   Halleaths, 24
   Hangingshaw or Hangingshaws, 181, 301
   Hardgray, 106
   Hardrigg, 112
   Harthope, 20, 22, 39, 69
   Hass, 154

INDEX

Johnstone Lands, etc.—
  Hawkhill, 183
  Hayhill, 47, 69
  Hazlebank or Hesilbank, 43, 44, 98, 341
  Hennaland, 42
  Hesilbrae, or Hesliebrae, or Hesliebray, 31, 32, 35, 95, 103
  Hilton, 30, 33, 129, 315, 345
  Hoddam, 47, 48, 74, 119
  Holmains, 119
  Holmends, 76
  Holywood, 34, 36
  Howcleuch, 43, 69, 84
  Howes, 32, 67, 77
  Howgill, 42, 73
  Howmeadow, or Howmedo, or Howmedow, 67, 77, 112, 122, 135
  Hydewood, 67

Johnstoun, 46

Kellobank, 30, 34, 35, 127, 308, 336
Kelton, 26
Killevan, 332
Kilmore, 330, 331, 332
Kilternan, 332
Kincardine Castle, 347
Kinlough, 335
  ,,   House, 334
Kinnellar, 342
Kirk, 30, 33, 133
Kirkhill, 42, 82, 96, 97
Kirkpatrick Fleming, 46, 71, 77, 78, 86
Kirkton, 30, 33, 34, 63, 83, 84, 100, 127, 128
Kirtlebrig, 70
Knockhill, 23, 36, 160, 173
Knowhead, 25

Langhope, 41
Langrigs, 90
Langshaw, 23
Langside, 96
Langwodend, 41
Lathrisk, 100, 324
Leuchie, 12, 14, 15, 310, 312
Lochhouse or Lochous, 35, 42, 76, 81, 91, 97, 99, 104, 111, 113, 114, 118, 122, 124
  ,,   Tower, 8, 79
Lochmaben, 73, 84
  ,,   Castle, 21, 138
Lochwood, 4, 56, 63, 73, 83, 96, 141
  ,,   Tower, 8, 60, 61, 79, 85, 343
Lockerbie, 21, 30, 36, 63, 79, 81, 83, 84, 90, 95, 96, 104, 119, 142, 153, 154, 173, 210, 333
Magheramena Castle, 335
Malinshaw, 30, 68
Marjoribanks, 30, 31, 36, 327
Mid Murthat, 98
Middlebie or Myddilby, 67, 77
Middlegill, 30, 34, 36, 41, 43, 103

Johnstone Lands, etc.—
  Milkymoss, 39, 42, 43
  Millfield, or Milnfield, or Mylfield, or Mylnfield, or Mylneflat, 60, 67, 85, 96, 105, 106, 110, 112, 114, 116, 122, 124, 125, 133, 134, 135, 136, 137, 139, 141, 225,
  Milnbank, 36, 84, 96
  Milnbie or Mylnbie, 101, 111, 124, 135
  Miskares, 106
  Moat, 78, 86
  Moffat, 30, 40, 327
  Moit, 21, 22
  Moling, 35
  Mossop, 29, 127
  Munches, 26
  Mylbie, 77
  Myll, 67

Neiss, 136
Nether Barcaple, 27, 330
Nether Garvald or Nether Garwald, 35, 69
Netherlaw, 27, 328, 329, 330
Netherplace, 154
Newbie, 2, 9, 11, 12, 17, 22, 30, 32, 36, 37, 46, 53, 54, 55, 56, 57, 63, 64, 65, 66, 67, 69, 70, 71, 72, 73, 74, 75, 76, 77, 78, 79, 81, 82, 83, 84, 85, 86, 87, 88, 89, 90, 94, 95, 97, 98, 99, 100, 101, 102, 103, 104, 105, 106, 108, 110, 111, 113, 116, 118, 119, 120, 122, 123, 125, 126, 127, 134, 135, 136, 138, 141, 142, 143, 144, 153, 155, 156, 157, 162, 184, 205, 276, 309, 317, 327
  ,,   Castle, 33, 85, 86, 98, 105, 112, 115, 122, 124, 135, 164, 171, 225
  ,,   ,,   burnt, 143
  ,,   ,,   Dispute about, 102
  ,,   Charter of, 67
  ,,   Destination of, 67
  ,,   sold, 33
  ,,   Taxation of, 114
  ,,   Tower, 42, 68
Newmilns, 326
Newmonkland, 16
Newpark, 321
Newton, 37, 40, 43, 68, 76, 95, 103, 142, 153, 155, 340
  ,,   Grange, 312
  ,,   in Kirkcudbright, 32
Nitove, 65
Northfield, 78, 86, 112, 114, 115, 134

Ochiltree, 326
Outbrieks, 342
Over Howcleuch, 47, 120, 137
Over Wormanbie, 273
Overdryfe, 46

Pashgillfoot, 37
Penlaw, 24, 96
Pensak, 47

INDEX 385

Johnstone Lands, etc.—
  Persbie, 23
  Persbiehall, 147, 155
  Pettinane, 46
  Pitkeirie, 100, 324
  Pocornwell, 69
  Poldean or Powdene, 20, 26, 31, 40, 42, 43, 44, 46, 68, 72, 79, 83, 94, 95, 142, 321, 322, 327, 340
  Polmoody, 48
  Polton, 17
  Portmore, 335
  Pressbutts, 23
  Priestdykes, 24
  Priestwodside or Priestwodsyde, 67, 78

  Raecleuch, 35, 36, 42, 49, 84, 95, 101, 103, 104, 106, 110, 111, 112, 114, 115, 116, 117, 119, 122, 123, 128, 135, 136
  Ragiwhat, 23
  Rahills or Raehills, 10, 188
  Redgatehead, 145
  Redkirk, 119
  Redmyre, 4
  Reidhall, 19, 30, 31, 32, 34, 90, 93
  Rennyhill, 324
  Revox, 103
  Rigfoot, 42
  Righead, 118, 326
  Roberthill, 36, 154
  Robgill, 67, 68, 77, 79
  Rowantriebrae, or Rowantrieknow, or Rowantrieknowe, or Roundstonefute, 35, 43, 321
  Ruthwell, 67, 101, 119
  Ryehill, or Ryell, or Ryhill, 35, 42, 72, 77, 95, 99, 102, 104, 105, 110, 111, 112, 113, 114, 115, 116, 118, 119, 120, 121, 122, 123, 124, 125, 127, 133, 134, 135, 136, 145, 149, 156, 309
    „ Taxation of, 114
    „ Tower, 85
  Ryeholme, 69

  Salsit, 34
  Saltrigs, 112
  Sands, 347
  Sark, 64
  Sarkbrig, 56, 68
  Saughtrees, 321
  Seafield, 68, 112, 120, 122, 123, 135
  Selkirth, 155
  Sheens, 30, 98, 129, 154
  Skare, 51
  Smallgills, 39, 40, 42
  Snow Hill, 333
  Souplebank, 106
  Springfield, 323
  Standingstones, 345
  Stank, 119, 125, 145, 157, 318
  Stapleton, 3, 12, 56, 67, 68, 72, 77, 79, 101, 124, 128, 136, 160, 337, 339, 340

Johnstone Lands, etc.—
  Stenris Hill, 43
  Straiton, 324
  Stramore, 335
  Sunnybrae, 37

  Templand, 32, 95
  The Wood, 29
  Thrieve Castle, 26
  Toddelmuir, 30
  Torbeck Hill, 23
  Tundergarth, 23, 24, 323
  Turriemuir, 154

  Viccarland or Vickerland, 142, 327
  Viewfield, 345

  Wamfray or Wamphray, 8, 9, 10, 19, 23, 31, 39, 40, 42, 43, 45, 51, 57, 60, 63, 66, 69, 70, 73, 77, 78, 79, 82, 83, 84, 87, 90, 94, 95, 96, 97, 98, 102, 104, 110, 114, 116, 118, 119, 122, 124, 127, 129, 142, 155, 160, 173, 308, 327
  Warrieston or Warriston, 30, 33, 34, 127, 128, 129, 130, 139, 141, 142, 154, 161, 162, 315, 343
  Wedderby, 100, 324
  Westerhall or Westraw, 16, 18, 19, 20, 21, 22, 23, 24, 28, 31, 33, 39, 42, 45, 87, 94, 95, 99, 103, 110, 114, 122, 126, 127, 129, 135, 139, 143, 144, 146, 147, 150, 152, 153, 154, 158, 159, 160, 161, 163, 164, 165, 168, 170, 175, 177, 182, 183, 198, 203, 204, 207, 226, 243, 244, 256, 272, 273, 274, 275, 287, 297, 301, 305, 318, 326, 343
  Westerkirk, 242
  Westoun, 28, 326
  Westraw Mains, 326
  Whitriggs, 4
  Whitwynd Hill, 154
  Willies or Wyllels, 42, 120
  Woodcoker, 47
  Woodheid, 43, 95, 103
  Woodhous, 47, 60
  Woodpark, 329, 336, 340
  Wormanbie, 3, 69, 72, 78, 343
  Wyldcotray, 68, 122

Johnstone-Douglas, A. H., 154
Johnstone-Douglases, 36
Johnston-Maxwells, 26
Joinville in Dumfriesshire, 4
Joliffe, Miss, 282
Jones, Caroline Margaret Heywood, 306
  „ E. Madoc, 304
  „ Emily Sophia, 333
  „ Mary Gertrude, 304
  „ Rev. Thomas, 333
Jonson, Ben, 63
Jordan, Mrs, 182
Joseph II., Emperor, 259
  „ „ of Germany, 230
Joyneville, Gulielmo de, 2

INDEX

Kames, Lord, 195
Keate, Dr, 284
Keenan, Thomas, 337
Keene, Colonel, 181
　,, 　Dr, Bishop of Ely, 181
　,, 　Elizabeth Caroline, 181
　,, 　Sir Benjamin, 181
Keir, Captain James, 246
Keith, Archibald, 313
　,, 　Isobel, 313
　,, 　Margaret, 15
　,, 　of Benholme, James, 313
　,, 　Sir John, 344
Kelly, Mr, 235
Kelso Abbey destroyed, 109
Kenmure, Lord, 152, 160
Kennedy, Herbert, 24
　,, 　John, 24
　,, 　of Halleaths, 37, 68
　,, 　　,, 　　George, 24
Kent, Duke of, 281
Ker, Georgiana A., 314
　,, 　Margaret, 111
　,, 　of Cessford, Andrew, 5
　,, 　of Fenton, Andrew, 102
　,, 　of Gateshaw, William, 314
　,, 　Rev. John, 16
Kerr, Lady Isobel, 97
　,, 　Margaret, 336
　,, 　Rev. Joseph, 336
Kers, 100
Kidderminster, (1783) 232
Killiecrankie, Battle of, 153
Kilmarnock, Lord, 171
Kilpatrick, 62
Kincaid, Captain, 323
　,, 　Mr, 217
Kincardine, Lands in, belonged to Johnstouns, 4
King, Sir Henry, Bart., 331
King-Harman, Hon. Lawrence, 301
Kingston, Earl of, 301
Kinmont, Willie, 87, 89
Kinnaird, Lord, 182, 241
Kinnear, Mary, 315
Kintore, Earl of, 344
Kirkconnel, Laird of, 52
Kirkmichel, Laird of, 62
Kirkpatrick, 29, 69, 74, 84
　,, 　Fleming, 116
　,, 　George, 244
　,, 　Ivo, 3
　,, 　Janet, 147, 148, 157
　,, 　John, 66
　,, 　Katherine, 30
　,, 　of Auldgirth, 147
　,, 　of Closeburn, 62, 83, 87, 89, 99, 115, 124
　,, 　　,, 　Sir Thomas, 103, 147, 148, 191, 194
　,, 　of Hoddam, Samuel, 103
　,, 　of Kirkmichael, William, 63
　,, 　of Wod, Roger, 25
　,, 　Roger, 84

Kirkpatrick, Samuel, 105, 125
　,, 　Sir James, 170, 243
　,, 　,, 　Thomas, 138
　,, 　Thomas, 147, 172
Kirkpatricks, 2
Kirkton, Gavin Johnstoun of, 33
Kirwan, Dora, 26
Kitchin, P., 299
Knight, Charles Wyndham, 306
Knok, Laird of, 52, 63
Knowles, Sir Charles, Bart., 305
Knox, John, 94, 108, 109, 126, 307, 308
　,, 　Margaret, 338
Kolpin, Dr, 221
Kroegeborn, Maximilian von, 42
Kyneir, James, 151

L'Estrange, Colonel, 301
　,, 　Sarah Mary, 301
Laidlaw of Mossgrove, 27
Lanark, Earl of, 142
Lancey, Colonel de, 248
Langford, *Modern Birmingham*, 286
Langholm, 78
　,, 　Tower, 59, 60
Langside, Battle of, 19, 72, 73, 75, 76, 84, 155, 309
　,, 　　,, 　Johnstouns at, 16
Larrey, Baron, 288
Latimers, 91
Laud, Archbishop, 344
Lauderdale, Earl of, 315
Laurie, John, 106
　,, 　Marion, 17
　,, 　Robert, 172
　,, 　Sir Robert, 24, 147
Lawley Family, 277
　,, 　Francis, 285
　,, 　Sir Robert, 252
Lawrence, Mr, 238
Lawson, Hugh, 96
　,, 　Mr, 171, 235
Lay Abbots, 93
　,, 　Parsons, 93
Lechmere, Edmund, 233
Lee, Colonel Henry, 338
　,, 　Rev. R. Lauriston, 334
Legge, Heneage, 253
Leicester, Lord, 248, 274
Leigh, Henry, 85, 86
Leighton, Mr, 237
Leith, Baillie of Water of, 81
Lennox, Duke of, 85
　,, 　Earl of, 62, 68
　,, 　Matthew, Earl of, 59, 61, 62
Lent in Scotland, 124
Leslie, Amy, 342
　,, 　Colonel Ludovick, 328
　,, 　Elizabeth, 334
　,, 　Isobel, 17
　,, 　General, 328
　,, 　James, 334
Leveson Gower, Lady Anne, 302

INDEX

Levinge, Archbishop, 254
    „ Robert, 254
    „ Sir Cresswell, 254, 255
    „ „ Walter, 254
Levingston, 74
Liddell, Marion, 47
    „ Sir James, 10
Lidderdaill, James, 106
    „ Marion, 81
Lightfoot, John, 15
Limerick, Countess of, 330
Lincluden College, 79
Lind, Dr, 240, 268
Lindsay, 66
    „ Christian, 14
    „ John, 20, 22
    „ Lord, 72
    „ Margaret, 346
    „ of Covington, John, 48
    „ of Wauchope, John, 54
    „ Patrick, Lord, 13
    „ Rev. Henry, 346
    „ Sir Jerome, 14
Linwood, Mr, 271
Lisbon, Earthquake at, 190
Listowel, Earl of, 303
Liszt, Abbé, 275
Little, Helen, 26
    „ John, 26
    „ William, 309
Littles, 62, 79, 80, 91, 135
Livingston, Captain, 163
    „ of Jerviswood, William, 75
Livingstons, 100
Lloyd, Emma Mary, 294
    „ Francis, 333
    „ J. E., 296
    „ of Bingley, 271
    „ R., 253
    „ Rev. R., 296
    „ Sampson, 295
Lloyd-Davies, Mr, 253
Loch Leven Castle, 72
    „ Mark, 133, 135, 136
    „ Robert, 101, 133
    „ Sir Hugh, 31
Lochar, 74
Lochmaben, 83, 88
    „ Burning of Church of, 21
    „ Castle, 59, 75, 78, 79, 80, 87
    „ „ given into keeping of two Johnstouns, 8
    „ . „ Johnstouns take, 18
Lochmabenstane, 48, 117
    „ Battle of, (1448) 8, 45
Lockerbie, 83
    „ Johnstons of, 36
Lockhart, Charles, 260
    „ Colonel, 142
    „ Count, 230
    „ „ Charles, 265
    „ General, 216, 217, 218, 225, 226, 227, 259, 260

Lockhart, James, 19, 260
    „ John, 51
    „ Macdonald, 260
    „ Mary Anne Matilda, 259
    „ Mrs, 225
    „ of Lee, Allen, 19
    „ „ and Carnwath, Sir James, 21
Lockhart Memoirs, 162
Logie, Captain, 198
Lokert, Oswald, 47
London, Johnstons in, 305
    „ Tower of, Johnstouns in, 5
Londonderry, Siege of, 329, 330
Longfellow, the poet, 288
Lore, Charlotta van, 164
Lothian, Earl of, 97, 114, 122
Loughborough, Lord, 241
Louis IX., King, 2
    „ XIV., King, 139, 185
    „ XV., King, 186
    „ XVI., King, 247
    „ XVIII., King, 283
Louth, Lord, 333
Low, Rev. T., 335
Lowndes, Cressida, 302
    „ W. Selby, 302
Lowry, Hester, 331
    „ Robert William, 331
Lowther, Mr, 88
Lundie, Katherine, 344
    „ William, 344
Lutwyche, T., 253
Lygon, Mr, 235
Lynch, Mrs, 229
Lyndsay, 35
    „ James, 123
Lyon, 62
Lyttelton, Dr, 221
    „ Lady Valentia, 232
    „ Lord, 194, 195, 198, 217, 221, 222, 223, 232, 236, 237, 244, 285
    „ of Hagley, Lord, 188

M'Adam, Susanna, 322
M'Alpine, Lilias, 25
M'Briar, 128
    „ John, 102, 116
    „ of Almagill, Roger, 66
    „ „ William, 118, 119
M'Cara, John, 15
M'Clellan, Margaret, 69, 70, 97, 308
    „ of Bombie, 100, 124
    „ „ Robert, 318
    „ „ Sir Robert, 32, 97
M'Clellans of Bombie, 70
M'Cornoch, Hugh, 26
M'Cready, Janet, 27
M'Cullock of Myrton, Sir Godfrey, 27
    „ of Rusco, Hew, 27
    „ Sir Godfrey, 328
M'Donalds, 172
M'Dowall, James, 328
    „ Johnston, Richard, 330

388

INDEX

M'Dowall Johnstons, 328
„ of Gillespie, 328
M'Farland, Janet, 338
M'Geough, Anne, 332
„ Joshua, 332
M'Guffock, Hew, 330
M'Killop, C. W., 25
„ Eleonora Jane, 25
M Kittrick, Dr, 221
M'Lane, Louisa, 339
M"Math, Elizabeth, 30
M'Millan, Grizel, 321
„ James, Joan, and John, 33
„ Surgeon, 195
M'Murdo, 24
M'Nab, 341
M'Neish, William, 141, 158
Macartney, Lord, 319
Macbriar, Cuthbert, 45
MacGillicuddy of the Reeks, 304
Mackenzie, Clare Millicent, 346
„ Dr, 190, 315
„ John Pitt Muir, 299
„ of Coul, Sir Alexander, 140
„ Roderick, 140
„ Sir John Muir, Bart., 300
Mackie, Margaret, 24
„ of Bargaly, James, 24
„ of Palgowan, John, 244
Mackintosh, Sir James, 251, 252, 256
Maclagan, Archbishop, 316
„ Mrs, 316
Macphersons, 171
Macquair, Mr, 185
Magill, Captain John, 329
„ Susanna, 329
Mahony, Maria, 300
„ Peirce, 300
Maister, Rev. A., 305
Maitland, Chancellor, 91
„ Charles, 324
„ Isabel, 315
„ of Auchencastle, John, 66
Malcolm III., King, 1
Male, George Edward, 272
Maltby, Dr, 286
Manchester in 1778, 246
Manipur, Maharaja of, 293
Mansfield, Captain J., 177
„ Lord, 165, 170, 213, 230, 241
Mansfield Charters, 105
Manson, Helen, 342
Mappin, Isabel Ann, 298
„ Joseph, 298
Mar, Earl of, 89, 114, 120 122, 343
March, Earl of, 7, 116
„ George, Earl of, 10, 12
Margaret, Queen, 1
Maria Theresa, Empress, 227, 259
Marie Antoinette, 230
Marion, General, 338
Marjoribanks, Colonel, 98
„ Joseph, 17

Marjoribanks, Marion and Christian, 17
Marnoch, Isabel, 345
„ John, 345
Marriot, Mrs, 224
Marschal, Mr, 193
Marschall, John, 84
Marsh, Francis, Archbishop of Dublin, 333
Martin, Rev. John, 213
Martyn, Rev. Mr, 251
Mary II., Queen, 150, 152, 153, 333
„ Princess, 56
„ Queen, 13, 19, 31, 58, 64, 69, 71, 72, 73, 91, 109, 111, 308
„ „ and the Johnstouns, 30
„ „ Borderers support, 72
„ „ Execution of, 81
Maryland, Johnstons in, 44
Mason, James, 238
„ Thomas, 238
Masterson, Martha, 305
Maude, Maurice C., 335
„ Rebecca, 335
Maxwell, 8, 24, 29, 51, 96, 107, 159
„ Agnes, 75, 77, 101, 107
„ Alexander, 26, 106
„ Anne, 324
„ attacks the Crichtons, 50
„ Barbara, 26, 107
„ Catherine, 26
„ Charles, 102
„ „ Charteris Wellwood, 244
„ Clementine Herries, 26
„ David, Captain of Lochmaben, 82
„ Death of Lord, 33
„ Earl of Nithsdale, 123
„ Edward, 22, 49, 55, 72, 95, 110
„ Elspeth, 107
„ George, 26
„ Hobe, 74
„ in Cavers, 68
„ J. H., (1843) 26
„ James, 318
„ Janet, 26
„ John, 32, 62, 71, 145, 309
„ Johnston, 26
„ Lord, 9, 10, 11, 14, 30, 39, 46, 47, 48, 49, 50, 53, 54, 55, 56, 57, 58, 59, 60, 64, 70, 71, 72, 75, 78, 79, 80, 81, 82, 83, 84, 85, 89, 95, 99, 104, 105, 116, 117
„ „ Execution of, 115
„ „ John, 21, 22
„ „ killed, 83
„ Marion, 104
„ Nicholas, 321
„ of Barncleuch, 26
„ „ James, 32
„ of Carlaverock, 4
„ of Carnsalloch, 81
„ of Castlehill, Robert, 321
„ of Conheath, 115
„ „ Elspeth, 107
„ of Cowhill, 69, 73

INDEX

Maxwell of Cuil, 328
„ of Dalswinton, William, 318
„ of Dinwiddie, Robert, 97, 115, 125
„ of Gribton, 115, 116, 136
„ „ John, 107, 120
„ „ Sir William, 102, 106, 114
„ „ William, 103
„ of Herries, 65
„ of Hills, Edward, 115
„ of Ile, 68, 83, 84
„ „ John, 75
„ of Kirkconnel, 124
„ of Kirkhous, 117
„ „ Charles, 104, 105
„ „ William, 32
„ of Monreith, Sir William, 324
„ of Munches, 26, 329
„ of Newlaw, 31, 78
„ „ John, Murder of, 31
„ of Orchardtoun, Sir George, 27, 328
„ „ „ Robert, 81, 104
„ of Pook, Sir John, 95, 112
„ of Spots, Sir Robert, 114, 328
„ of Springkell, Sir William, 170, 173, 201, 244
„ Robert, 244
„ Sara, 21, 81
„ Sir George, 144, 163, 329
„ „ Herbert, quoted, 1
„ „ Robert, 22, 95, 100
„ „ William, 106, 218
„ Susanna, 146
„ Thomas, 125
„ W. J. Herries, 26
„ Wellwood, 26
„ „ Johnston, 26
Maxwell's *House of Douglas*, 58
Maxwells, 70, 85, 87, 93, 95, 98, 100, 123
„ in Annandale and Nithsdale, 50
Medicis, Catherine de, 74
Meldrum, Margaret, 343
Melrose Abbey destroyed, 109
Melvill, Janet, 14
„ Katherine, 344
„ Sir James, 14
„ „ Robert, 16
Melville, Janet, 309, 310
Menzies, Sir William, 148
Merchant, Life of a, 94
Merchiston, Lady, 100
Meredith, Mr, 271
Merk, Value of, 100
Merrick, Mrs, 176
Michael, Grand-Duke, 277
Middlemore Family, 247
Middleton, Thomas, 126
Milford, Lord, 303
Millar, Patrick, 24
Miller, Captain, 243
„ of Dalswinton, Patrick, 243
Milligan, George, 321
Mills, Charlotte, 302
„ Sir Charles, 302

Milton, 205
Minto, Lord, 195
Mitchell, Janet, 344
„ Mr, 165, 238
Moffat, Adam, 34
„ Johnstoun Priest at, 93
„ Matthew, 95, 127
„ Murder of Robert, 43
„ of Granton, Robert, 95
„ of Harthope, Gavin, 126
„ of Knok, 42
„ „ Thomas, 66
„ Robert, 41
„ Thomas, 41
Moffats, 83, 84, 91
Moke, C. A., 305
„ Harriet, 305
Molesworth, Imogen I. T., 295
„ Walter Hele, 295
Moncrieff, Rev. W., 225
Monilaws, Rev. J., 225
Monk, General, 139
Monmouth, Duke of, 150, 152
Monro, Dr, 185, 217
Montagu, Lady Charlotte, 163
„ „ Mary Wortley, 171
„ Mrs, 190, 219, 222, 223, 230, 236, 253, 254
„ „ quoted, 198
Montcalm, General, 173
Montgomery, 100
„ Mariot, 97
„ of Longham, Sir Neil, 97
„ Plot, 151
„ Sir R., 164
Montrose, Heart of, 319
„ Marquis of, 141, 142, 145, 153
Monypeny quoted, 93
Monypeny's Chronicle, 56, 85
Moore, Dr John, 176
„ Elean, 336
„ Hugh, 336
„ John G. D., 299
„ Mr, 271
„ Mrs, 218, 323
Moray, Earl of, 308
„ Regent, 19, 73, 74, 109
„ Thomas Randolph, Earl of, 4
Morgan, Elizabeth, 325
Morice, Catherine, 345
„ David, 345
Morison, Helen, 129
Morison's *Johnston of Warrieston*, 162
Morton, Earl of, 72, 79
„ James, Earl of, 13, 34, 40
Morveau, Guyton, 222, 266
Muir, Miss, 328
Mullins, Alice, 314
„ John Beale, 314
Mulready, Mr, 275
Munro, Dr, 169, 170, 190, 288
„ Isabella Margaret, 323
„ Professor, 184

INDEX

Munro, Sir Alexander, Bart., 323
  „   „ Thomas, 319
Murdoch, William, 246
Mure, Marion, 41
Murphy, Fanny, 335
  „   Rev. Henry, 335
Murray, 29, 54, 108, 112, 116, 128, 153, 165
  „   Adam, 265
  ..   Agnes, 201
  „   Ann, 96
  „   Barbara, 175
  „   Blanche, 69
  „   Charles, 45, 101
  „   David, 88, 211, 265
  „   Earl of Annandale, 118, 124, 125, 135, 138, 141
  „   Elizabeth, 148, 157, 211, 265
  „   General, 173, 316
  „   „   James, 203
  „   „   Sir James, 272
  ..   George, 87
  „   Gideon, 100
  „   Homer, 135
  „   Isobelle, 201, 212
  „   James, 117, 149
  „   „   Earl of Annandale, 143
  „   John, 118, 119, 145, 149, 201
  „   Joseph, 157
  „   Lord George, 173
  „   „   Scone, 119
  „   Marianne, 211, 212
  „   Mrs, 206, 207, 208, 211, 214, 215, 217, 218, 219, 260, 265
  „   of Aikett, David, 99
  „   of Belriding, Adam, 184, 193, 197
  „   „   John Adam, 265
  „   of Cockpool, 46, 47, 48, 59, 67, 68, 69, 84, 91, 104, 106, 138, 148, 155
  „   „   Charles, 5, 65, 77
  „   „   Cuthbert, 8, 9, 69
  „   „   David, 99
  „   „   James, 105, 119
  „   „   John, 101, 104, 110, 114
  „   „   Sir James, 118
  „   „   „   John, 52, 97
  „   of Hilhead, Sir James, 17
  „   of Murraythwaite, George, 158
  „   „   John, 244
  „   Richard, 201
  „   Robert, 149
  „   Sir James, 105, 273
  „   Sir John, 10, 122
  „   Viscount Stormont, 119
  „   William, 4
Murrays, 8, 62, 84, 100, 113, 116
  „   of Cockpool, 48
Murthat House, 98
Musgrave, 86
  „   John, 89
  „   Mr, 63
  „   Sir Richard, 65
  „   Thomas, 65

Mynors, Mr, 244, 256
  „   Mrs, 283

Napier, Hester Maria, 318
  „   Lady, 316
  „   Lord, 318, 319
Napoleon, 56
  „   Emperor, 283, 288, 325
Nash, *History of Worcestershire*, 231, 233
  „   Rev. Dr, 235
Natural Sons—their Rights, 120
Neilson, 27
  „   Charles, 25
  „   Mr, 205
  „   Robert, 25
Neilsons, 205
Nelson, Lord, 322
  „   Mr, 203
Nesbit, James, 127
Nesbit's *Heraldry*, 67
New Skares Fishings, 67
  „ York, Johnstons in, 27, 28, 340
Newcastle, Duke of, 201
Newport, Mr, 271
Nicholas, Emperor, 277
Nicholson, Isabella, 346
  „   Jane Clark, 321
  „   Margaret, 347
  „   Rev. Christopher, 347
Nicolson, 21, 88, 89
  „   Bishop, 194
Nimmo, Rev. John, 37
Nithsdale, Earl of, 117, 119, 123, 124, 135, 139, 141, 159, 173
  „   Lord, 107
  „   Lordship of, 7
Noble, John, 312
Norfolk, Duke of, 19
North, Hon. F., 232
Northumberland, Earl of, 53
Norton, Hon. Augusta Anne, 301
  „   Fletcher, 301
Nugent, Admiral, 178
  „   Captain, 342

O'Donnell, Sir Neal, Bart., 330
O'Farrell, 198
O'Mahony, Peirce, 300
Ochiltree, Lord, 85
Ogilvie, a Jesuit, 108
  „   David, Lord, 182
  „   Lady Margaret, 182
  „   Lord, 142
  „   Margaret, 183
Olifants, 100
Oliphant, Eufemia, 22, 23, 94
  „   Sir Laurence, 94
Oliver, John, 211
Onslow, Dean, 258
Orange, Prince of, 91, 162
Orkney, Earl of, 164
Orleans, Duke of, 185
Ormiston, Laird of, 307

INDEX

Ormsby, J. M., 330
Orr, Mrs, 157
Orton, Mr, 232, 237, 238
  „ Rev. Job, 213, 245
Oswald of Auchencrieve, Alexander, 298
Otterburne, Janet, 326

Packer, John, 164
  „ Temperance, 164
Padwick, Edith Arethusa, 325
Paisley, John Johnstoun, Doctor in, (1675) 25
Pakington, Sir John, 232
Palmer, Mr, 209
Pannel, Caroline, 298
  „ Rev. Charles, 298
Papistry, Trial for, 106, 107
Paris in Eighteenth Century, 186
Parke, Sir William, 305
Parkes, John, 271
  „ Mr, 252
Parkes-Belloc, Madam, 252
Parr, Dr, 229, 230, 232, 244, 245, 248, 249, 251, 252, 255, 258, 271, 274
  „ Rev. Dr, 263, 286
Partis of Gallentyre, Matthias, 150
Paterson's *Wamphray*, 43
Patten's *History of Rebellion, 1715*, 57
Paul, Emperor of Russia, 230
  „ Grand-Duchess, 230
Paulet, John, Marquis of Winchester, 331
Payne, Admiral John, 169
  „ Ralph, 169
  „ Sir Peter, 285
Pearson, Anne, 271
  „ Dr, 285
  „ Edward, 271
  „ Elizabeth, 269, 271
  „ Esther, 32
  „ General Hooke, 270
  „ Margaret, 314
  „ Mr, 256, 269, 270, 271
  „ Mrs, 284
  „ Penelope, 271
  „ Thomas, 271
Peddinane or Pettinane, 18, 19
Peel Family, 277
Peile, Rev. W. O., 296
Pelham, Frances Helen, 320
  „ Richard Bury, 320
Pelling, Sarah, 347
Peninsular Campaign, 322
Penman, Francis Garfield, 306
Pennant quoted, 119
Pennell, Eliza, 324
  „ William, 324
Pepys, Sir Lucius, 282
Perceval, Agnes, 336
  „ General J. M., 336
Percival, Dr, 267
Percy, Earl, 8
  „ Henry, 4
Perier, Sir Anthony, 335
Perry, Sir Thomas Erskine, 302

Peterborough, Earl of, 130
Pharmacopœia, Edinburgh, 170
Phayre, Caroline Emily, 300
  „ General R., 300
Philip, King, 2
  „ of Spain, King, 81
  „ Sir John, 5
Philiphaugh, Battle of, 141, 142
Philipps, Sir Richard, 303
Philips, Mr, 233
Phillips, Colonel Molesworth, 331, 332
Pigott, Francis B., 301
Pinchot, Antoinette, 303
  „ J. W., 303
Pinkie, Battle of, 60, 343
Piperdean, Battle of, 307
Pistols, Wearing of, 120, 121
Pitcairn, *Criminal Trials*, 51
Pitman, Eleanor, 334
  „ Mr, 336
  „ Rev. E., 334
Pitt, William, 197, 252
Pixell, Rev. Charles, 257, 278
Plassey, Battle of, 180, 199
Poland, Johnstouns in, 41
Poldean, Johnstouns of, 26, 39
Pool, William, 133
Porson, Professor, 244
Porteous, Christian, 311
  „ Janet, 43
  „ Patrick, 112
Porteus of Hawkshaw, Patrick, 19
  „ Patrick, 95
Portland, Duke of, 251, 253
Portman, Lord, 230
Potatoes in Scotland, 140
Pottinger, Sir Henry, 320
Potts, 71
Poulett, Lord, 163
Pounds, John, 253
Powdene, *see* Poldean, 39
Prendergast, Sir Harry, 292
Preston, Dr, 308
Prestongrange, Lord, 129
Price, Thomas, 253
Priestley, Dr, 187, 229, 244, 247, 248, 249, 25 251, 284
  „ Rev. Dr Joseph, 246
Primrose, Archibald, 99
  „ Family, 15
  „ James, 99, 120, 121
  „ Sir Archibald, 313
Proudfoot, Dorothea, 27
  „ Thomas, 321
Prussia, Princess Louisa of, 259
Prymrois, Gilbert, 34
Pulteney, Henrietta Laura, 272
  „ Miss, 241, 245
  „ Mr, 213, 223, 224, 227
  „ Sir William, 170, 188, 205, 237, 23 239, 240, 242, 243, 244, 245, 256, 260, 26 268, 273, 277, 281, 297, 298
Purcell, Rev. J., 260

Purdon, William, 334
Pyndar, Rev. Reginald, 233

Quebec, Siege of, 203
Queensberry, Duke of, 195, 196, 202, 243, 244
" Earl of, 91, 125
" Marquis of, 97, 154, 170, 196, 210
Quinton, Mr, 292

Rabone, Mr, 271
Rae, Adam, 127
" Andrew, Murder of, 97
" Hector, 111
" Katherine, 111
" " attacked, 115
" Mr, 216
" Thomas, 310
Raes, 71, 112, 135
Ragman Roll, (1296) 3, 4
Raith, Alison, 326
" of Edmistoune, James, 313
Ralston, 66
" Anna, 158, 225
" William, 158
Rampatrick, 116
Ramsay, Dean, quoted, 183
" John, 16
Ramsays, 100
Ramsey, Rev. John, 315
Ratcliffe, Dr, 190
Rathbone, Theodore, 295
Ratisbon, College at, 108
Reformation, The, 58, 84, 109, 123, 146, 307
Reformed Faith, 94
Regent, Prince, 251, 281
Reid, William, 347
Reilly, Captain Edmund George, 299
Renfrew, James, 336
Reston, Lord, 275
Retours, Register of, 145
Richard I., King, 1, 254
Richardson, 157, 205
" Janet, 158
" John, 158
Richardsons, 100, 114, 135
Richmond, Duke of, 332
Riddell, Mr, 24
Ridgeway, Dr, 325
Rig, Gaylies, 125, 135
" " or Egidia, 133
" Marion, 133, 135
" of Carberry, James, 81
" " Mungo, 16
" Robert, 107
" Sir Cuthbert, 93
Rigges, 62
"Right Honourable," applied to Physicians, 93
Riland, Rev. John, 253
Rising of 1715, 160, 172
" 1745, 171, 172, 181
Rizzio, Murder of David, 13, 19, 308
Robert Bruce, King, 155
" I., King, 7

Robert III., King, 7, 10, 45
Robertson, Captain Frederick, 132
" Lieutenant James, 342
" Margaret, 342
" Thomas, 35
Robinson, John, 239
Rogers, Francis, 272
Rollo, Isabel, 98
" Jean, 98
" Lord, 98, 174
Romanists punished, 108
Rome, Scots College in, 108
Romes, 56, 85, 114
Roryson of Bardannoch, Andro, 66
Ros, Laird of, 63, 72
Rosebery, Earl of, 15, 34, 99, 120
Ross, Bernard, 157
" Christina Martha, 345
" John Leith, 345
" Major-General Robert, 331
Rosse, Countess of, 301
Rothes, Earl of, 75
" George, Earl of, 334
Rouelle, M., 185
Routh, Dr, 286
Rowden, A., 296
Roxburgh, Earl of, 124
" Helen, 38
Rubens, Mary Jane, 326
Ruddiman, Jane, 314
" Thomas, 314
Russell, Dr, 232, 233
" William, 251, 252
Russia, Empress of, 230
Rutherford, Dr, 203
" General, 338
" John, 338
Rutherfurd, Dr, 217
Ruthven, 19
" Isabella, 118
" James, Lord, 119
" Lord, 17, 109
" Margaret, 13, 310
" Mary Elizabeth, 119
" Patrick, Lord, 13, 14
" William, Lord, 13, 14
Ruthwell, 74, 116
" Laird of, 45
Rye House Plot, 140
Ryehill Castle, 64
Ryland, Miss, 279

Sadler, 62
Sadler's, Sir Ralph, Memoirs, 58, 60
Salisbury, Gilbert Burnet, Bishop of, 33
Salmon, Close Time for, 75
Salsit, Johnstoun Abbot of, 308
" Monastery of, 3
Salt Works, 138
Salton, Johnstons of, 311
Salwey, Humphrey, 304
Sandie, George, 89
Sandilands, James, 344

INDEX

Sandilands, Jean, 344
Sandys, Lord, 191, 235
   ,,   Miss, 191
Sargent, Lavinia, 299
Sarkbrig, 118
Saxony, Duke of, 237
Scarth, Jonathan, 303
   ,,   Louisa, 303
Schonswar, George, 295
   ,,   Janet, 295
Scoresby, Rev. William, 314
Scotland, Charity in, 161
   ,,   Church in, 167
   ,,   Food in, 189
   ,,   Poverty of, 160
Scotland, New Statistical Account of, 189
Scott, 29, 69, 84
   ,,   Adam and Robert, 69
   ,,   Isabel, 22, 153
   ,,   Jane, 318
   ,,   John, 302
   ,,   Lady Margaret, 99
   ,,   Major, 239
   ,,   Margaret, 81, 302
   ,,   Marion, 46
   ,,   Mariota, 29
   ,,   of Branxholme, Walter, 76
   ,,   of Buccleuch, 73, 79, 80, 81, 84, 87, 90, 91, 142, 309
   ,,   ,,   Marion, 10
   ,,   ,,   Walter, 55
   ,,   of Gala, Hugh, 300
   ,,   of Guildlands, Walter, 75
   ,,   of Harden, Walter, 23
   ,,   of Newburgh, 139
   ,,   of Scotstarvit, David, 119
   ,,   of Thirlestane, Francis, 318
   ,,   ,,   Robert, 34
   ,,   of Tuschelaw, Adam, 51
   ,,   ,,   Walter, 75, 106
   ,,   of Wamfray, 66
   ,,   Robert, 22, 89
   ,,   Sandie, burned, 55
   ,,   Sir Walter, 1, 97, 146, 195, 288, 313
   ,,   ,,   quoted, 151, 189
   ,,   Thomas, 333
   ,,   Thomasina, 333
   ,,   William, 321
   ,,   ,,   Fenton, 302
Scottish Life in 1598, 91
Scotts, 53, 74, 91, 100, 150
   ,,   of Eskdale, 83
Scott's *Fasti* quoted, 167
   ,,   *Guy Mannering*, 323
Scrope, Lord, 65, 73, 74, 79, 80, 83, 86, 87, 88, 89, 111, 309
Scrymgeour, Helen, 339, 340
Seaman, Ann, 131
Sempill, Lord, 85, 86
Serjeant, Rev. Richard, 192
Seton, John, 15
   ,,   Lady, 99
   ,,   Lord, 78, 93

Seton, Lord George, 13
   ,,   ,,   William, 10
   ,,   Sir John, 45
   ,,   ,,   W., 124
Seven Years' War, 201
Seward, Dr, 244
Seymour, Sir John, 331
Shakespear, Colonel, 293, 294
Shakespeare, William, 275
Sharpe of Hoddam, Charles, 170, 243
Shaw, Captain, 320
   ,,   Edith Constance, 320
Shepherd, Rev. Francis, 314
   ,,   ,,   William, 314
Sheppard, Mr, 272
Sherbrooke, Lord, 277
Sheridan, Charles, 233
   ,,   Richard Brinsley, 233
Sheriffmuir, Battle of, 160, 344
Sherrington, 74
Shipley, C. L., 253
Shirley, Walter, 331
Shortt, Dr Thomas, 189
Shrewsbury, Lord, 59
Shuckburgh, Sir George, 249
Sibthorp, Colonel, 299
Siddons, Mrs, 205, 256
Silesia, Johnstons in, 42
Simcox, T., 253
Sime, James, 300
   ,,   Jessie, 300
Simpson, Dr, 322
   ,,   Elizabeth, 323
   ,,   Margaret, 29
   ,,   Sir Matthew, 30
Sinclair, 108
   ,,   Hew, 143
   ,,   John, 47
   ,,   of Roslin, 13
   ,,   of Rysie, David, 15
   ,,   Oliver, 34, 57, 58
Sinclair's *Statistical Account of Scotland*, (1794) 37
"Sir" applied to Professional Men, 93
Skene, Colonel, 292
   ,,   of Curriehill, Sir James, 127, 128
Slavery, Abolition of, 188
Small, David, 346
   ,,   Dr William, 246
   ,,   Mary, 346
Smallpox in Scotland, 171
Smith, Rev. W., 342
   ,,   Sarah L. C., 44
   ,,   Sir James, 279
   ,,   Thomas, 272
Smyth, Dr, 268
   ,,   Dr Carmichael, 222, 266, 267
   ,,   Margaret, 100
Soley, Mrs, 224
Soltray, Monastery of, 3
Solway Moss, Battle of, 57
Somers, Earl, 232
Somerset, Duke of, 60, 61, 62

INDEX

Somerset, Leonora Louisa, 298
„ Sir Henry, 298
Somerville and Westraw quarrel, (1594) 20
„ Florence, 19
„ Laird of, 72
„ Lord, 8, 20
Soutar-Johnstons, 347
Sparkes, Agnes Elizabeth, 345
„ Rev. Richard John, 345
Speed quoted, 93
Spencer, Dr, 247
„ Rev. Dr, 252
Spens, Patrick, 317
Spiers, Mary, 306
Spottiswood, Sir Robert, 142
St. Albans, Duke of, 300
„ Andrews, Murder of Archbishop of, 146
„ Clair, Dr, 184
„ John of Bletsoe, Lord, 325
Stansfeld, Captain Robert J., 298
Stapleton Tower, 52, 54
Stedman, Henry James, 244
„ Rev. Mr, 244
Steill, Rev. John, 342
Stephens, Rev. W. R. W., 296
Steuart, Janet, 155
„ of Castlemilk, 8, 47
Stevenson, James, 314
„ John, 314
Steward, Mr, 271
„ Mrs, 249
„ of Winson Green, 285
„ Walter, 66
Stewart, 29, 115
„ Agnes, 51, 81
„ Ann, 334
„ Dorothy, 14
„ Dugald, 195, 217
„ Earl of Bothwell, 138
„ Elizabeth, 81, 102, 103, 105, 117
„ James, 80
„ Lady Marion, 68
„ Lucinda, 336
„ of Garlies, 70, 83
„ „ Sir Alexander, 51, 81, 102
„ of Physgill, Robert H. J., 324
„ of Sweetheart Abbey, 84
„ Princess Margaret, 5
„ Professor, 217
„ Sir James, 142
„ Victoria, 299
„ William, 145
Stewarts, 84, 100
Stirling, Johnstoun Chaplain at, 93
Stith, Griffin, 44
„ Susanna, 44
Stock, Rev. S., 342
Stodart, Robert Riddell, 339, 340
Stoke, Dr, 246
Stopford, Admiral F., 295
Storer, Dr, 288
Stormont, Lord, 113, 168, 193, 214, 244, 259
„ Viscount, 103

Strathallan, Viscount, 139
Strathearn, Gilbert, Earl of, 13
„ Maria, daughter of Robert, Earl of, 3
Stuart, Lord Dudley, 287
„ of Castlemilk, Andrew, 272
„ of Goodtrees, Sir James, 165
„ of Traquair, 124
„ Prince James, 159
Stutfield, William, 304
Suffrien, Admiral, 319
Sullivan, Henrietta, 299
„ James, 299
Surrey, Earl of, 57
Sutherland, Duke of, 302
„ Earl of, 34
Sutton, Captain Evelyn, 178
„ Case, 241, 242
Swan, Janet, 44
Swann, Robert, 302
Sweden, Gustavus Adolphus, King of, 128
„ Johnstons in, 94
Sweetheart, Abbot of, 32
Swift, Dean, 233
„ Theophilus, 233
Swinton, Sam, 199
Symonds, Mr, 238
Sympson, Jane, 311
Symsoun, Katrena and Helen, 17

Tadman, Sarah, 131
Tailleur, Guillaume de, 2
Talbot, Gwendoline Mary, 303
Tanner, Esther, 326
Tate, Mr, 214, 215, 217
Taxes in 1816, 280
„ sold, 148
Tayleur, John, 271
Taylor, Dr Henry, 342
„ Hugh, 314
„ James, 285, 296
„ Jane, 342
„ Margaret, 27
„ Sarah, 314
„ Sir Herbert, 281
Temple, Archbishop, 316
Tennant, Bryce, 157
Thomason, E., 271
„ Elizabeth, 25
„ J., 25
Thompson, Mr, 212
Thomson, John Anstruther, 300
„ Miss, 316
„ Mr, 251
Thomsons, 62, 85, 91, 100
Thrieve Castle, 59
„ „ Johnstouns take part in Siege of, 9
Thurlow, Chancellor, 255
Thurot, 27
„ M., 198
Tilghman, Madeline Tasker, 44
Tisdall, Rev. A., 296

INDEX

Tissot, Dr, 221
Tobin, Francis James, 314
  „ Rev. John, 314
Todd, Miss, 338
Tolhurst, Jeremiah, 139
Trafalgar, Battle of, 272, 322
Traill, Jane, 329
  „ Rev. Hamilton, 329
Traquair, Lord, 141
Trees, Stealing, 158
Trevelyan, Charlotte A., 324
  „ Rev. G., 324
Trollope, General Sir Charles, 321
  „ W. H., 321
Trotter, 100
  „ Jane, 316
Trumble of Barnhill, Hector, 90
  „ of Bewlie, Mark, 90
  „ of Mynto, Thomas, 90
Trumbles, 52
Tudor, Mary, 304
  „ Queen Margaret, 58
Turing, Janet, 344
Turner, Edith, 296
  „ J., 253
  „ Mrs, 201
Turnour, 84
Tweddell, J., 251
Tye, Mary Ann, 345
  „ William, 345
Tyndings, 135
Tynewald, Laird of, 52

Udward, Barbara, 34, 99, 113, 116, 117
  „ Nathaniel, 113
  „ Nicholas, 309
  „ Nicol, 99, 113, 116
Urwen, John, 34

Vale, Mr, 272
Valentia, Lady, 223
Vans, Margaret, 328
  „ of Barnbarroch, Patrick, 328
Vaughan, Rebecca, 330
  „ Rev. G., 330
Veitch, Hon. James, 244
  „ Mr, 218
Venables, Rowlands, 296
Venice, Johnston in, 28
Vere, John, 51
Verner, Lady, 332
  „ Sir William, Bart., 332
Vernet, Isaac, 185
Vernon, Louisa A. V., 302
Vicary, Mr, 223
Villiers, W., 253

Wade-Dalton, Colonel, 333
Wakefield, Mr, 251
Wakeman, Henry Offley, 306
Wales, Charles, Prince of, 128
  „ Prince of, 251
Walker, Anne, 300

Walker, Edmund, 302
  „ James, 334
  „ Joseph, 300
  „ Mr, 272
  „ Olive Cecil, 321
  „ Sir James, Bart., 321
Wall, Dr, 190, 239
Wallace, Mary, 27
  „ Mr, 216
  „ Sir John, 8
  „ „ William, 3, 4
  „ William, 3, 48, 58
Walpole, Horace, 213
  „ Sir Robert, 247, 302
Walsingham, 21
  „ Sir F., 79, 80
Walter, John, 300
  „ Sarah, 300
Walton, Elijah, 279
Wamfray, Johnstons of, 97
  „ Old Gang of, 43
Warburton, Margaret, 337
Warneford, Rev. Dr, 285
Warner, John, Bishop of Rochester, 190
  „ Miss, 222
  „ Rev. Richard, 271
Warren, Dr, 235
  „ Sir Peter, 196
Warwick, Captain, 179
  „ Miss, 179
Washington, Life of George, 196
Waterloo, Battle of, 272, 283, 322
Watt, James, 246
Wauchope, Amy Octavia, 301
  „ Andrew, 301
  „ Tower, 52
Wearden, Catherine, 254, 255, 257, 258
  „ Letitia, 254, 257
  „ Rev. Thomas, 255
Web, Agnes, 313
  „ Richard, 313
Webb, Mr, 271
Webster Family, 277
  „ Maria Mary Payne, 285
  „ Mr, 276
  „ Mrs, 252, 253, 258
  „ of Penns, Joseph, 285
Wedderburn, 181
  „ Laird of, 310
  „ Sir John, Bart., 183
Weild, George, 134
  „ Sir James, 93
Weir, Barbara, 20
  „ Isabel, 36, 334
  „ James, 335
  „ Ninian, 310
  „ Robert, 46
Welch, Robert, 111
Weld, Rev. Nathaniel, 330
  „ Susanna, 330
Wellesley, Marquis of, 331
Wellington, Duke of, 304, 331
Wells, J., 299

INDEX

Wells, Josephine, 299
Wellwood, Janet, 101
„ Mary, 347
Welsh, 100
„ David, 110
Wemyss, 115
„ David, 100
„ Earl of, 10, 136
„ Sir John, 140
West, Lady Henrietta, 315
Westley, J., 253
Westraw and Somerville quarrel, (1594) 20
„ Johnstouns of, 18
Weyland, Richard, 274
Wharton, 59, 61, 62, 63
„ Lord, 55
„ Mary, 344
„ Sir Thomas, 56, 58, 60, 62, 63
Wheeler, Mr, 261
Wheeley, Mr, 241
Whitaker, Joseph, 314
„ Mary, 314
Whitbread, Mr, 278
Whitehead, Amelia, 314
„ Philip, 314
Whitford, Rev. Walter, 138
Whitmore, Mr, 271
Whittier, Sarah, 332
„ Thomas, 332
Whytt, Dr, 189
Wightman, R., 244
Wigton, Earl of, 108, 125
„ Lady, 101, 122
„ Lord, 100
„ Sarah, Countess of, 125
Wilberforce, Mr, 267
Wilding, Mr, 272
Wilds, 135
Wilkes, John, 271
Wilkin, Bernard, 101
Wilkinson, Emily, 325
William III., King, 27, 131, 146, 147, 150, 151, 152, 153, 161, 162, 190, 329
„ IV., King, 132
Williams, Mr, 272
„ William, 337
Williamson, Bessie, 25
„ Colonel George, 332
„ George, 127
„ Henry, 19
„ James, 312
„ John, 30
„ Lieut.-General Sir Adam, 332
„ Rev. A., *Glimpses of Peebles*, 171
Willoughby, 112

Willshire, Rev. Edward, 151
Wilmot, Sir Eardley, 285
Wilson, Archibald, 313
„ Duncan, 66
„ James, 149
„ Robert, 157
„ Sir C., *History of India*, 181
Wilsons, 100
Wilton, Laura, Countess of, 297
Winchester, John, Marquis of, 331
Windsor, Eliza, 296
Winnington, Sir Edward, 233, 244
Winslow, Mr, 185
Wishart, George, 307
Witchcraft, 312
Witches, Burning of, 145
Withering, Dr, 184, 244, 245, 248, 270, 271, 276
„ „ William, 246
„ L., 256
„ William, 271
Wolfe, General, 131
Wolsey, Cardinal, 55, 58
Wood, George, 14
„ James, 14
„ Janet, 312
„ Mary, 338
„ Mrs, 315
Worcester, (1783) 232
„ Battle of, 142, 328.
Wordsworth, Miss, 212
Worthington, William, 333
Wotton quoted, 137
Wren, Sir Christopher, 288
Wrottesley, Sir John, 268
Wyldcotray, 67
Wylde, Rev. Robert, 296
Wylds, 71, 136
Wyntoun, Andrew, *Chronicle*, 5

Yarmouth, Lord, 244
Yates, Rev. James, 284
„ Samina, 333
„ Samuel, 333
Yester, Lord, 72
York, Archbishop of, 302
„ Duke of, 150, 281, 282
„ Edward, Duke of, 246
Young, Andrew, 313
„ Elizabeth, 96
„ Margaret, 155
„ Patrick, 123
„ Rev. Gavin, 155
„ William, 330
Younger, Amy, 347
„ Henry, 347